# THE RAYS
# AND
# THE INITIATIONS

# BOOKS BY ALICE A. BAILEY

*Initiation, Human and Solar*
*Letters on Occult Meditation*
*The Consciousness of the Atom*
*A Treatise on Cosmic Fire*
*The Light of the Soul*
*The Soul and Its Mechanism*
*From Intellect to Intuition*
*A Treatise on White Magic*
*From Bethlehem to Calvary*
*Discipleship in the New Age — Vol. I*
*Discipleship in the New Age — Vol. II*
*Problems of Humanity*
*The Reappearance of the Christ*
*The Destiny of the Nations*
*Glamour: A World Problem*
*Telepathy and the Etheric Vehicle*
*The Unfinished Autobiography*
*Education in the New Age*
*The Externalisation of the Hierarchy*
*A Treatise on the Seven Rays:*
*Vol. I — Esoteric Psychology*
*Vol. II — Esoteric Psychology*
*Vol. III—Esoteric Astrology*
*Vol. IV — Esoteric Healing*
*Vol. V—The Rays and the Initiations*

# THE RAYS
## AND
# THE INITIATIONS

VOLUME V

A TREATISE ON THE SEVEN RAYS

By

ALICE A. BAILEY

LUCIS PUBLISHING COMPANY

New York

LUCIS PRESS, LTD.

London

*First printing, 1960*
*Fourth Printing 1972 (1st Paperback Edition)*
*Ninth Printing 1993 (5th Paperback Edition)*

*ISBN No. 0-85330-122-0*
*Library of Congress Card Catalog Number: 53-19914*

The publication of this book is financed by the Tibetan Book Fund which is established for the perpetuation of the teachings of the Tibetan and Alice A. Bailey.

This Fund is controlled by the Lucis Trust, a tax-exempt, religious, educational corporation.

The Lucis Publishing Company is a non-profit organization owned by the Lucis Trust. No royalties are paid on this book.

This title is also available in a
clothbound edition.

It has been translated into Spanish,
Dutch, French, German, Greek
and Italian. Translation into other
languages is proceeding.

**LUCIS PUBLISHING COMPANY**
**113 University Place, 11th Fl.**
**PO Box 722, Cooper Station**
**New York, NY 10276**

**LUCIS PRESS, LTD.**
**Suite 54**
**3 Whitehall Court**
**London SW1A 2EF**

MANUFACTURED IN THE UNITED STATES OF AMERICA
By Fort Orange Press, Inc., Albany, N.Y.

# EXTRACT FROM A STATEMENT BY
# THE TIBETAN

Suffice it to say, that I am a Tibetan disciple of a certain degree, and this tells you but little, for all are disciples from the humblest aspirant up to, and beyond, the Christ Himself. I live in a physical body like other men, on the borders of Tibet, and at times (from the exoteric standpoint) preside over a large group of Tibetan lamas, when my other duties permit. It is this fact that has caused it to be reported that I am an abbot of this particular lamasery. Those associated with me in the work of the Hierarchy (and all true disciples are associated in this work) know me by still another name and office. A.A.B. knows who I am and recognises me by two of my names.

I am a brother of yours, who has travelled a little longer upon the Path than has the average student, and has therefore incurred greater responsibilities. I am one who has wrestled and fought his way into a greater measure of light than has the aspirant who will read this article, and I must therefore act as a transmitter of the light, no matter what the cost. I am not an old man, as age counts among the teachers, yet I am not young or inexperienced. My work is to teach and spread the knowledge of the Ageless Wisdom wherever I can find a response, and I have been doing this for many years. I seek also to help the Master M. and the Master K.H. whenever opportunity offers, for I have been long connected with Them and with Their work. In all the above, I have told you much; yet at the same time I have told you nothing which would lead you to offer me that blind obedience and the foolish devotion which the emotional aspirant offers to the Guru and Master Whom he is as yet unable to contact. Nor will he make that desired contact until he has transmuted emotional devotion into unselfish service to humanity, — not to the Master.

The books that I have written are sent out with no claim for their acceptance. They may, or may not, be correct, true and useful. It is for you to ascertain their truth by right practice and by the exercise of the intuition. Neither I nor A.A.B. is the least interested in having them acclaimed as inspired writings, or in having anyone speak of them (with bated breath) as being the work of one of the Masters. If they present truth in such a way that it follows sequentially upon that already offered in the world teachings, if the information given raises the aspiration and the will-to-serve from the plane of the emotions to that of the mind (the plane whereon the Masters *can* be found) then they will have served their purpose. If the teaching conveyed calls forth a response from the illumined mind of the worker in the world, and brings a flashing forth of his intuition, then let that teaching be accepted. But not otherwise. If the statements meet with eventual corroboration, or are deemed true under the test of the Law of Correspondences, then that is well and good. But should this not be so, let not the student accept what is said.

AUGUST 1934.

# THE GREAT INVOCATION

From the point of Light within the Mind of God
    Let light stream forth into the minds of men.
        Let Light descend on Earth.

From the point of Love within the Heart of God
    Let love stream forth into the hearts of men.
        May Christ return to Earth.

From the centre where the Will of God is known
    Let purpose guide the little wills of men —
        The purpose which the Masters know and serve.

From the centre which we call the race of men
    Let the Plan of Love and Light work out
        And may it seal the door where evil dwells.

Let Light and Love and Power restore the Plan on Earth.

"The above Invocation or Prayer does not belong to any person or group but to all Humanity. The beauty and the strength of this Invocation lies in its simplicity, and in its expression of certain central truths which all men, innately and normally, accept—the truth of the existence of a basic Intelligence to Whom we vaguely give the name of God; the truth that behind all outer seeming, the motivating power of the universe is Love; the truth that a great Individuality came to earth, called by Christians, the Christ, and embodied that love so that we could understand; the truth that both love and intelligence are effects of what is called the Will of God; and finally the self-evident truth that only through *humanity* itself can the Divine Plan work out."

ALICE A. BAILEY

# TABLE OF CONTENTS

PART ONE     1

## FOURTEEN RULES FOR GROUP INITIATION

PRELIMINARY REMARKS     3

INTRODUCTORY STATEMENTS     12

Rule One    . . . Group Being and Function     25

Rule Two    . . . Accepted as a Group     47

Rule Three    . . . The Dual Moving Forward     67

Rule Four    . . . Evocation of the Will     88

Rule Five    . . . The Macrocosmic Whole     111

Rule Six    . . . The Group onward moves in Life     124

Rule Seven    . . . The Word of Invocation     132

Rule Eight    . . . The Seven, the Three, and the ONE   147

Rule Nine    . . . The One Initiator     167

Rule Ten    . . . The Creative Sound of O.M.     178

Rule Eleven    . . . The Fourth Great Cycle of Attainment     208

Rule Twelve    . . . Illumined Group Service—Saviourship   225

Rule Thirteen . . . The Hidden Mystery     247

Rule Fourteen . . . The Fivefold Demand     285

PART TWO 321

## THE RAYS AND THE INITIATIONS

INTRODUCTORY REMARKS 323

SECTION ONE. THE ASPIRANT AND THE
MYSTERIES OF INITIATION 347

The Entering of the two Doors of Initiation 347
  The Door of Initiation 347
  The Door to the Way of the Higher Evolution 356

The Entering of the Ashram 366
  The seven Groups of Ashrams within the Hierarchy 373
  The seven Paths confronting the Master 395
    The Path of Earth Service 397
    The Path of Magnetic Work 401
    The Path of Training for Planetary Logoi 405

  Certain Hierarchical Changes 409

    The Path to Sirius 413
    The Ray Path 419
    The Path of the Logos Himself 421
    The Path of Absolute Sonship 422

  An Extract from A Treatise on Cosmic Fire 425
  The World Tension Analysed 428

The Dual Life of the Initiatory Process 431
  The Dual Life of the Disciple 434
  The Dual Existence of the Master 437

The Science of the Antahkarana 441
  Building the Antahkarana 444
  The Nature of the Antahkarana 452
  The Bridge between the three Aspects of the Mind 457

The Bridge as the Agent of Alignment 470
The Technique of Construction 474
  In the Past 477
  In the Present 482
The Six Stages of the Building Process 485
The Immediate Task Ahead 497
The Seven Ray Methods 501


The Meaning of the Initiatory Process 530
  Fusion of the Master's Consciousness with that
    of the Disciple 542
  Impression on the Mind of the Disciple of
    Hierarchical Intent 549


SECTION TWO. THE ASPIRANT AND THE MAJOR INITIATIONS 556

The Relation of the Seven Rays to the Initiations 557
The Rays and the Five Initiations Confronting Humanity 566
  Initiation I    The Birth. Ray VII 567
  Initiation II   The Baptism. Ray VI 575
  Initiation III  The Transfiguration. Ray V 589
  Initiation IV   The Renunciation. Ray IV 602
    The particular Type of Energy involved and
      its initiatory Effect 605
    The Effect of the Energy of Harmony through
      Conflict upon Humanity 611
    The Factor of the Ray of Love-Wisdom as it
      controls Ray IV 614
    The Effect of Ray IV in the modern World of Nations 620
    The Results of Fourth Ray Activity upon the
      individual Disciple 637
    A Summation and Forecast 639


The Rays of Aspect and the Higher Initiations 641
  Initiation V     Revelation. Ray I 643
    The Effect of Ray I on Humanity today 646

Initiation VI      Decision. Ray III                                653
Initiation VII     Resurrection. Ray II                             656
Initiation VIII    Transition. Rays IV, V, VI, VII                  656
        (The four minor Rays)
Initiation IX      The Refusal. Rays I, II, III                     656
        (The three major Rays)

The Seven and the Nine Initiations of our Planetary Life  656

The Significance of the Initiations                        661
    Initiation I      The Birth at Bethlehem                 664
    Initiation II     The Baptism in Jordan                  673
    Initiation III    The Transfiguration                    687
    Initiation IV     The Great Renunciation or Crucifixion  692
    Initiation V      The Revelation                         703

        The Part which Energy plays in inducing Revelation  708
        The Place that the Will plays in the inducing
            of Revelation                                    714

    Initiation VI     The Decision                           718
    Initiation VII    The Resurrection                       729
    Initiation VIII   The Great Transition                   736
    Initiation IX     The Refusal                            736


APPENDIX                                                     739

FIVE GREAT SPIRITUAL EVENTS TODAY                            741
STANZAS FOR DISCIPLES                                        761

INDEX                                                        771

# PART ONE

## THE FOURTEEN RULES
## FOR GROUP INITIATION

# PRELIMINARY REMARKS

It might be here of value, my brothers, if I again laid emphasis upon the fact that the formless world is only entered when the aspirant has acquired somewhat the capacity to center himself on the abstract levels of the mental plane. This involves necessarily certain developments within the aspirant's own nature. The demanded contact would otherwise be impossible. What is needed is self-exertion, the resultant developments of which might be touched upon as follows:

I. *The Repolarisation of the Entire Lower Man* so that his attitude toward the aggregate of forms which make up his field of general contact has changed. He is no longer deluded by the things of the senses but has in his hand that thread or clue which will eventually guide him out of the maze of the lower life perceptions into the field of clear knowledge and the realm where daylight is found; he will then no longer need to walk in the dark. This repolarisation is brought about in four ways, each of which provides the next step forward, and in their totality (and when definitely followed) will eventuate in the total subjugation of the personality. These four ways are:

*A constant and unfailing attempt to center the consciousness within the head.* From this central position the real man, the directing agency will direct and guide all his members, imposing upon the "lunar lords" of the physical body a new rhythm and habit of response. Two factors are of value and helpful in the production of the necessary polarisation:

The reiterated appreciation of the words "I am the Self, the Self am I."

The habit of early morning meditation wherein the Thinker centers himself in the point of control and

starts upon his day's experience and contacts with
the realisation that he is only the Observer, the
Perceiver and Actor.

*A close consideration throughout the day as to the use
and misuse of energy.* Every man should realise that in the
use of energy lies direction and the treading of the Path.
It produces eventually truthful manifestation and the displaying of one's *light* in order that circumstances may be
irradiated and fellow pilgrims helped. Students should familiarise themselves with the "energy concept" and learn to
regard themselves as energy units displaying certain types of
energy. In this connection it should be borne in mind that
when spiritual energy and material energy (the two opposite
poles) are brought into relationship, a third type of energy
is produced, and the work of the fourth or human kingdom
is to demonstrate this peculiar type. It might serve to clarify
thought if students remembered that

Superhuman entities display spiritual energy.
Subhuman entities display the energy of matter.
Human entities display soul energy.

In the perfect manifestation of these three will the plan of
creation be consummated. It should also be borne in mind
that these three are nevertheless a manifestation of duality
—spirit and matter—and that this is the manifestation of a
great Existence and of His appearing. Therefore, what are
called the "three gunas" in Hindu philosophy are but the
qualities He manifests through these types of entities.

Superhuman lives express sattva, the guna of rhythm
and of harmonious response to divine urge, of perfect display of coordinated cooperation with the purpose of manifestation.

Human lives demonstrate the quality of rajas, of mo-
bility, of constant and conscious change in order to ascertain
what is the Real and through the medium of experience
demonstrate the true nature of rhythmic response.

Subhuman lives express the guna of tamas or of inertia.
They work blindly and have no ability to respond con-

sciously to the plan. They are the sumtotal of the "units of inertia" just as the human units are called "the points of light moving within the square." This may have its appeal to Masons.

This subject of the use or misuse of energy is capable of infinite expansion, and in my other books where I give you more upon the centres I have enlarged upon it. I but seek at this time to give you that which can be of immediate use to students and thus lay the foundation for later work.

*A close study of the needed transmutation of astral and emotional energy into love, the energy of love.* This involves the sublimation of personal feeling into group realisation or consciousness, and when carried out successfully produces in time the construction of a higher and subtler body, the buddhic sheath. When this sheath is thus materialised a very high stage of advancement is marked, but the earlier stages can be intelligently approached by any earnest student and probationer. To transmute emotion into love the following realisations will be found necessary:

1. A realisation that all moods, all display of sorrow, of pain, or of happy excitement are due to our identification with the objects of desire, with the form aspect, and with that which is material.

2. An understanding of the emotional or astral body and the place it plays in the student's development. It should be recognised as the shadow of the monad, and a connection should be traced between

> The Astral Sheath  . . . . 6th Plane
> The Buddhic Sheath . . . 4th Plane
> The Monadic Sheath  . . 2nd Plane

and the place the love petals in the egoic lotus play should also be carefully considered.

3. A comprehension of the potency of the astral sheath owing to its undivided nature.

4. A study of the purpose of the solar plexus, and the part it plays as an organ of transference of energy from the three great centres below the diaphragm to the three higher

centres. There is a very close analogy here to the solar lotus, the egoic body, occupying a midway point between the three-fold Monad and the threefold lower man. The more advanced should follow this.

*The development of the faculty of mind control*, so that the Thinker grips and holds steady the mental processes and learns to regard the mind as the interpreter of the states of consciousness, as the transmitter of egoic intent to the physical brain and as the window through which the Ego, the real Man looks out upon vast and (to the majority) unknown fields of knowledge.

II. *An Emergence into Manifestation of the Subjective Aspect in Man.* One of the objects of evolution is that the subjective reality should eventually be brought forward into recognition. This can be expressed in several symbolic ways, all of them dealing with the same one fact in nature:

The bringing to the birth of the Christ within.
The shining forth of the inner radiance or glory.
The demonstration of the 2nd or the Love aspect.
The manifestation of the solar Angel.
The appearing of the Son of God, the Ego or the Soul within.
The full expression of buddhi, as it utilises manas.

This emergence into manifestation is brought about through what is understood by the following terms:

The refining of the bodies which form the casket or sheath hiding the reality.

The process of 'unveiling' so that one by one those bodies which veil the Self are brought to a point where they are simply transparencies, permitting the full shining forth of the divine nature.

An expansion of consciousness, which is brought about through the ability of the self to identify with its real nature as the Onlooker, and no longer regarding itself as the organ of perception.

III. *A Re-alignment of the Lower Sheaths* so that the contact with the Real Man, the Thinker, the Solar Angel, on the higher levels of the mental plane may become complete and continuous. This only becomes possible as the other two points are beginning to be grasped and the theory as to man's constitution and purpose is somewhat understood. As meditation is practiced, as the lower bodies are painstakingly dominated, and as the nature of the Sutratma or Thread is better comprehended it will become increasingly possible to bring into the lower personality on the physical plane that spiritual illumination and that divine energy which is the soul's heritage. Little by little the light will shine forth, year by year the strength of the higher contact will grow, gradually the downpour of divine love and wisdom into the head centres will be increased until eventually the entire lower man will be transformed, his sheaths will be refined, controlled and used, and he will demonstrate upon earth the powers of Director, Teacher or Manipulator according to the major ray upon which his Monad may be found.

IV. *A Series of Tests Leading to Initiation.* When a man is beginning to demonstrate the qualities of his ray and to prove of gradually increasing importance to his group, he will be prepared through tests, through trials, and through temptations for those final stages in development which will put into his power:

The knowledge of certain laws governing matter and form.

The keys of the mysteries connected with energy, with polarity, and with group relation.

Certain Words of Power which will give him control over the elemental forces of nature.

Insight into the planetary plans.

Upon these I need not enlarge, nor need I take up with you here the subject of initiation. *(Discipleship in the New Age,* Volumes I and II). The first work to be done is the stimulat ing of aspirants and the preparing of the few earnest ones to tread the Path of Discipleship. The final point of our theme concerns:

V. *The Basic Essential of Pure Character.* This is something more than just being good. It deals with the matter aspect and has relation to the hold or control that the form has over the man. We might express it this way and therefore give its more occult connotation. If one or other of the three lower elementals (the physical, the astral and the mental) are the controlling factors in the life of the man, he is—by that very fact—put into a position of danger and should take steps to arrest that control prior to an attempt to enter into the formless realm. The reason for this will be apparent. Under the governing law of matter, the law of Economy, the elemental life will attract to itself similar lives and this will result in a dual danger. These dangers are:

One: the gathering into the form, through the dominant note sounded by the form elemental, of matter with a synchronous vibration. This will tend to increase the magnitude of the task before the Ego and sweep into increasing dominance the lower man. The "lunar lords" will become increasingly powerful and the solar Lord correspondingly less august.

Two: the man will find himself surrounded in time with thoughtforms of a lower order (from the standpoint of the soul) and before he can penetrate into the Arcana of Wisdom and find his way into the Master's world he will have to dispel the clouds of thoughtforms which he has attracted to himself.

Unless the disciple learns that aspiration and self-discipline must proceed side by side, he will find that the spiritual energy he may appreciate and contact will only serve to stimulate the latent seeds of evil in his nature and thereby demonstrate the exactitude of the truth that the great Lord taught when He pictured the man who swept his house, cast out seven devils and eventually was in a worse condition than ever. It is essential that aspirants should understand the nature of the lower man and should grasp the fact that every coherent system has its varying types of energy, and that perfection is achieved when the highest type of energy inherently possible dominates.

If the lower energy of the aggregate of the form-atoms is the controlling factor three things will take place:

1. The form itself will grow by accretion and will become ever more potent, until the dominant voice of its 'lunar lords' will stifle all other voices and the man be swept back into

Inertia
Blindness
Bondage

2. Many people are not only under the control of some one or other of their forms but are the captives of all the three. In studying the lower threefold man and the energies or lives that seek to control him it should be remembered that they fall into three categories:

a. The individual tiny lives which we call the atoms or cells of the body. These exist in three groups and compose respectively the four types of bodies: dense physical, etheric, astral and mental.

b. The aggregate of these lives which constitute in themselves four types of elementals or separate coherent, though not self-conscious, existences. These four lunar lords constitute what the Ageless Wisdom teaching calls "the four sides of the square." They are the "lower quaternary," "the imprisoning cubes," or the cross upon which the inner spiritual Man is to be crucified. These four elementals have an intelligence all their own, are upon the involutionary arc, are following the law of their own being when they tend to become powerful, and thereby fully express that which is in them.

c. A dominant controlling lunar lord who is that which we understand by the term the 'lower personality'; he (if the personal pronoun can be used) is the sum-total of the physical, astral and mental elementals, and it is this power which at present forces the 'fiery energies' of the body to feed the lower three centres. The etheric body has a unique and curious position, being simply the vehicle for prana or life and the centre which it uses exists in a category by itself.

3. All subhuman forms in their aggregate prove a powerful deterrent factor in the progress towards emancipation of the Real Man. They form the opposite to what we understand by the world of the Master and the two are in direct opposition to each other from the standpoint of the aspirant.

The adept can enter the world of form, can contact it, work in it and remain unaffected by it because there is nothing in him to respond to it. He sees through the illusion to the reality behind and, knowing where he stands himself, there is naught in the appeal and the demand of these lunar lords to attract him. He stands midway between the pairs of opposites. In the realisation of the nature of this world of form, in a comprehension of the lives which compose it, and in an ability to hear the voice of the "formless One" above the strife of all the lower voices, comes the opportunity for the aspirant to escape from the dominance of matter.

This is the true magical work, my brothers, the understanding of the sounds of all beings, and the ability to speak the language of the soul is the clue to the work. These faculties rightly used impose upon these lesser lives that control which will lead to the final liberation, and which will in due time, lead these lives themselves into the realm of self-consciousness. This aspect of the matter is as yet but little comprehended by the sons of men. If they but realised that by a disposition to fall under lunar control they drive the tiny lives in their little system deeper into the darkness of ignorance, they might more rapidly assume their just responsibilities; if they realised that by the constant attempt to impose the rhythm of the solar Lord upon the aggregate of the lunar lords, they were driving these lives onward to self-conscious unfoldment, they might proceed more earnestly and more intelligently. This is the message that must go forth, for all the varying aspects of the life of God are interdependent and not one proceeds onward into fuller realisation without benefitting the entire group.

A few simple suggestions I will give you. These can be useful to all sincere aspirants.

> In the ordered regulation of the life comes eventual synthesis and the right control of time with all that eventuates therefrom.

> In the right elimination of that which is secondary, and in a sense of rightly adjusted proportion comes that accuracy and one-pointedness which is the hallmark of the occultist.

> In the right aspiration at the appointed time comes the necessary contact and the inspiration for the work that has to be done.

> In the steady adherence to *self-appointed* rules comes the gradual refining of the instrument and the perfecting of the vehicles that will be—to the Master—the medium of help among many little ones.

I commend the above thought to you knowing that you will apprehend the implications and will seriously consider the purport of my remarks.

The world today is in the throes of agony. Just as in the evolving Ego, the moment of greatest development is oft the moment of greatest pain (if apprehension measure up to opportunity) so in the evolving world. To those of you who have the inner sight and intuitive comprehension comes the opportunity to aid that apprehension and to lead a despairing world—deep cast into darkness and distress—one step nearer to the light. The work you have to do is to take the knowledge which is yours and adjust its application to the world's need so that recognition of the truth may be rapid. In the heart of every man lies hid the flower of the intuition. On that you can depend, and no eternal or cosmic fact clothed in a suitable form will fail to receive its meed of recognition and understanding.

# INTRODUCTORY STATEMENT

I have called you from refreshment to labour at this time (October 1942) because the coming few days are exceedingly busy ones for me as they are for all members of the Hierarchy. I seek to give you some further instructions anent the Hierarchy itself.* Students at this time would do well to remember that all basic and fundamental changes taking place upon the physical plane are necessarily the result of inner subjective causes, emanating from some level of the divine consciousness, and therefore from some plane other than the physical. The fact that tremendous and unusual upheavals are taking place in the kingdoms of nature is attributed by men to other men or to certain forces generated by human thinking, frailty and ambition.

Is it not possible that these changes are being brought about as the result of certain profoundly important happenings upon inner planes of such advanced states of consciousness that all the average disciple can know about them is their word symbols and their much deleted effects—if I may use such a phrase to describe the happenings which are rending humanity today. The evil that is being wrought today on earth, by certain evil members of the human family, are effects of their response to the inflowing energies and indicate their basic wickedness and their prompt reaction to that which is counter to the good. Wherever the consciousness is focussed, *there* is the point of major emphasis and importance, and this is true of the individual man and of humanity as a whole. The significance of the present happenings is interpreted (and necessarily so) in terms of human awareness and responsiveness. This world war and its inevitable consequences—good and bad—are looked upon as concerned primarily with humanity, whereas that is not

---

*This teaching is the continuation of that which appears in *Discipleship in the New Age,* Volume I, pp. 671 - 773.

basically so. Humanity suffers and experiences as a result of the inner occurrences and the meeting of subjective forces and inflowing energies.

It is of course not possible for me to give you any true picture of the interior events and happenings in the life of our planetary Being. I can only indicate and point out that the world situation is simply an embodiment of the reaction and the response by mankind to great paralleling and originating happenings which involve the following groups:

1. The emanating Avatar and His relationship to the Lord of the World, our planetary Logos.

2. The Lords of Liberation, focussed in Their high place, as They become conscious of the invocation of humanity and become more closely related to the three Buddhas of Activity.

3. The Great Council at Shamballa and the planetary Hierarchy.

4. The Buddha and His Arhats as They unitedly co-operate with the Christ and His disciples, the Masters of the Wisdom.

5. The Hierarchy, the embodiment of the fifth kingdom in nature, and its magnetic attractive rapport with the human kingdom, the fourth.

6. The effect of all these great groups of Lives upon humanity, and the inherent consequences as they work out in the subhuman kingdoms.

A study of the above in terms of forces and energy will give some idea of the underlying synthesis of relationships and the unity of the whole.

There is therefore a line of descending energy which has its origin outside our planetary life altogether; the inflow of this energy, its inevitable effect under cyclic law and its consequences, as they work out upon the physical plane, has produced and is producing all the changes of which mankind is so terribly aware at this time. This swings into immediate conflict the past and the future, and in this statement I have expressed the deepest esoteric truth which mankind is competent to grasp; it brings into a culminating struggle the Great White Lodge and the Black Lodge and opens the door to great contending energies which we can call spirit and matter, spirituality and materialism, or life and death. These words are, in the last analysis, as meaningless as the terms good and evil, which have significance only in the human consciousness and its inherent limitations.

These descending energies, as they pass through any of the major levels of consciousness which we call planes, produce reactions and responses, dependent upon the state of the conditioning consciousness, and (strange as this may seem to you and well-nigh unintelligible) the effects upon the Hierarchy are even more compelling and transmuting than they are upon humanity. I would add also that the point of lowest descent of the energies has now been reached, and the nature of the present opportunity is therefore changing. These energies have now passed what we might call the turning point and have reached their point of ascension, with all that that phrase implies. As they descend, they produce stimulation; as they ascend, they produce transmutation and abstraction, and the one effect is as unalterable as the other. It is upon this inevitability of the ascending energies, and the effects which they will bring about, that the entire hope of the future depends; nothing can arrest their return or their progress through the planes and back again to their source. Upon this dual process of descent and ascension the whole cyclic panorama of manifestation rests, and upon the inflow and activity of new and higher energies the whole fact of the evolutionary process depends.

It will therefore be apparent to you that the descent of energy brings with it — under the cyclic law — certain new "inspirations," certain new "seeds of hope" for the future, and certain active Agents as well, Who are and will be responsible for the task of preparation, of fertilisation and of all the coming new age enterprises. These descending energies *evoke* also the obstructing forces, and I would here remind you that these obstructing evil forces (so-called) are met with upon the highest spiritual levels because they are — in their turn — evoked by the impelling impact of the coming Avatar Whose "note is heard ahead of Him, and His energy spreads before Him." This is a great mystery and can only be understood (and then merely theoretically) if you bear in mind that all our planes — even the very highest — are the subplanes of the cosmic physical plane. When this fact is somewhat grasped there comes a simplification of thought.

As a consequence of all this, great and fundamental readjustments are going on within the Hierarchy itself and within that intervening area of the divine consciousness to which we give the name (as far as humanity is concerned) of the Spiritual Triad — an area covered by the higher mental planes, the buddhic and the atmic levels of awareness and of divine activity. The downpouring avataric stimulation is enabling certain of the Masters to take some of the major initiations, and to do so far earlier than would otherwise have been possible. Thus a great process of ascension and of spiritual attainment is under way, though as yet only its faint beginnings can be traced, owing to the intensity of the point of conflict. Hence also many probationary disciples are finding their way into the ranks of accepted disciples, and many disciples are taking initiation. To this fact of hierarchical upheaval — paralleling and intensifying the upheaval upon the physical plane — can be traced the process of preparation which I have instituted among some disciples, thus hastening the period and point of attainment, provided I receive due cooperation from them. (*Discipleship in the New Age*, Vols. I and II.)

As regards the Hierarchy itself, speaking esoterically and technically, its Members (many of Them) are "being abstracted from the middle point of holiness and absorbed into the Council of the Lord." In other words, They are passing onward into higher work and are becoming custodians of the energy of the divine will and not simply the custodians of the energy of love. They will work henceforth as power-units, and not just as units of light. Their work becomes dynamic instead of being attractive and magnetic, and is concerned with the life aspect and not just with the soul or consciousness aspect. Their places are being taken — under the Law of Ascension — by Their senior disciples, the initiates in Their Ashrams, and (under the same great process) the place of these initiates, who are thus being "raised" to more important work, is being taken by disciples and probationers. It is this truth, misinterpreted and shockingly travestied, which lies behind the teaching anent the so-called Ascended Masters, put out by the leaders of the "I AM" movement, thus prostituting and bringing down almost into the realm of cheap comedy one of the most notable happenings which has ever taken place upon our planet.

There is therefore, owing to the inflow of energy from extra-planetary sources, a general shifting of the focus of consciousness of embodied and disembodied lives at this time; this shift is one of the prime factors producing the present disruption. Students today are searching for the causes in human motives, in past history and in karmic relationships. To these they add the so-called factor of wickedness. All these factors of course exist, but are of lesser origin and are inherent in the life of the three worlds. They are themselves set in motion by far deeper-seated factors latent in the relationship between spirit and matter and inherent in the dualism of the solar system, and not in its triplicity. This dualism, as far as our planet is concerned, is profoundly affected by the will-purpose of the Lord of the World and by the intensity of His one-pointed thought. He has succeeded in achieving a point of tension, preparatory to bringing about stupendous changes in His life-expression, within His vehicle of manifestation, a planet. This point of invocation will be evocative of great happenings, and will involve every aspect of His nature, including the dense physical; this of necessity involves also all that concerns the human family for "in Him we live and move and have our being." Those three words or phrases express the triplicity of manifestation, for "Being" connotes the Spirit aspect, "moving" the soul or consciousness aspect, and "living" signifies appearance upon the physical plane. Upon that outer plane the basic synthesis of incarnated life is to be found.

It will be apparent to you, therefore, that in this achievement of planetary tension it is not life in the three worlds that is the sphere of this tension, but the realm of hierarchical activity. The shift resulting from this point of tension, the "moving" which is its consequence, is in the realm of soul experience and soul awareness. The secondary effect can be noted in the human consciousness by the awakening which has been going on among men — an awakening to the higher spiritual values, to the trends and ideologies which are everywhere appearing, and to the clear lines of demarcation which have emerged in the realm of human determinations and objectives. These are all the results of great changes in the field of the higher consciousness and are conditioned by the soul of all things, lying largely in the realm of the anima mundi; of this great sumtotal the human soul and the spiritual soul are but aspects or expressions.

It is these changes in the "moving, shifting realities" of the soul consciousness and spiritual awareness of the Members of the Hierarchy which are responsible for the new trends in the life of the Spirit and the new methods in training disciples — in such an experiment, for instance, as externalising the Ashrams of the Masters. It is this new approach to life conditions, as a result of the inflow of new energies, which is producing the universal trend towards *group awareness,* and its highest result in the human family is the taking the first steps towards *group initiation.* Such a thing as group initiation was never heard of prior to the present time, except in connection with the higher initiations emanating from the Shamballa centre. Group initiation is based upon a uniform and united group will, consecrated towards the service of humanity and based upon loyalty, cooperation and interdependence. In the past, the emphasis was upon the individual, his training and approach to initiation, and his solitary admittance to the Temple of Initiation. But this individual concentration will, in the future, give place to a group condition which will enable several disciples unitedly to move forward, unitedly to stand before the Initiator, and unitedly and simultaneously to achieve the great realisation which is the result and the reward of successful discipleship.

In the first thesis which I presented to the public I outlined the Rules for Applicants, *(Initiation, Human and Solar*, pp. 192 - 208), summarising the past propositions and indicating the individual preparation and requirements. These will now apply to the probationary groups of disciples, and not to accepted disciples. They must and will still remain the character and purificatory objectives of the dedicated individual, but are regarded as adequately grasped by humanity; they have been proclaimed by all the great world religions down the centuries and have been recognised as the main conditioning qualities of all disciples.

These same Rules or Formulas of Approach are the lower correspondences of higher rules to which groups of disciples are pledged to conform, and which they must follow and obey together. The Hierarchy into which they will enter when full acceptance and demonstration have been shown will be the same Hierarchy, characterised by the same soul awareness, animated by the same spiritual activity, functioning under the same laws, but conditioned by two progressive and evolutionary developments:

1. A much closer contact — invocative and evocative — with Shamballa, and therefore a fuller responsiveness to the Will aspect of divinity.

2. An invocative attitude on the part of humanity, based on a fundamental decentralisation of the selfish human consciousness and a rapidly awakening group consciousness.

In reality, this means that the Hierarchy will be more closely related to the Great Council at Shamballa, and very much more closely interrelated with humanity, so that a dual fusion will be taking place. This will bring about that integrative process which will be the quality of the New Age and will inaugurate the Aquarian phase of planetary history.

I would now like to bring into a close relation the earlier imparted *Rules for Applicants* and the new *Rules for Disciples,* embodying the new group activity and group discipleship, resulting in group initiation.

These Rules are fourteen in number. Today I will simply give you, first of all the rule for the individual disciple, and then its higher corresponding rule for groups in preparation for group initiation, reminding you that such groups are ever composed of those who have taken the first initiation, and the name of these is legion. They are to be found in every country. There are not, however, so many who are ready for the new era of group initiation.

Rule I.

*For Applicants:* Let the disciple search within the heart's deep cave. If there the fire burns bright, warming his brother yet heating not himself, the hour has come for making application to stand before the door.

*For Disciples and Initiates:* Within the fire of mind, focussed within the head's clear light, let the group stand. The burning ground has done its work. The clear cold light shines forth and cold it is and yet the heat — evoked by the group love — permits the warmth of energetic moving out. Behind the group there stands the Door. Before them opens out the Way. Together let the band of brothers onward move — out of the fire, into the cold, and toward a newer tension.

Rule II.

*For Applicants:* When application has been made in triple form, then let the disciple withdraw that application and forget it has been made.

*For Disciples and Initiates:* The Word has now gone forth from the great point of tension: Accepted as a group. Withdraw not now your application. You could not, if you would; but add to it three great demands and forward move. Let there be no recollection and yet let memory rule. Work from the point of all that is within the content of the group's united life.

## Rule III.

*For Applicants:* Triple the call must be and long it takes to sound it forth. Let the disciple sound the call across the desert, over all the seas and through the fires which separate him from the veiled and hidden door.

*For Disciples and Initiates:* Dual the moving forward. The Door is left behind. That is a happening of the past. Let the cry of invocation issue forth from the deep centre of the group's clear cold light. Let it evoke response from the bright centre, lying far ahead. When the demand and the response are lost in one great SOUND, move outward from the desert, leave the seas behind and know that God is Fire.

## Rule IV.

*For Applicants:* Let the disciple tend the evocation of the fire, nourish the lesser lives and thus keep the wheel revolving.

*For Disciples and Initiates:* Let the group see that all the eighteen fires die down and that the lesser lives return unto the reservoir of life. This they must bring about through the evocation of the Will. The lesser wheels must not for aye revolve in time and space. Only the greater Wheel must onward move and turn.

## Rule V.

*For Applicants:* Let the applicant see to it that the Solar Angel dims the light of the lunar angels, remaining the sole luminary in the microcosmic sky.

*For Disciples and Initiates:* In unison let the group perceive the Triad shining forth, dimming the light of the soul and blotting out the light of form. The macrocosmic Whole is all there is. Let the group perceive that Whole and then no longer use the thought "My soul and thine."

Rule VI.

*For Applicants:* The purificatory fires burn dim and low when the third is sacrificed to the fourth. Therefore let the disciple refrain from taking life and let him nourish that which is lowest with the produce of the second.

*For Disciples and Initiates:* Let the group know that life is one and naught can ever take or touch that life. Let the group know the vivid, flaming, drenching Life that floods the fourth when the fifth is known. The fifth feeds on the fourth. Let then the group — merged in the fifth — be nourished by the sixth and seventh and realise that all the lesser rules are rules in time and space and cannot hold the group. It onward moves in life.

Rule VII.

*For Applicants:* Let the disciple turn his attention to the enunciating of those sounds which echo in the hall where walks the Master. Let him not sound the lesser notes which awaken vibration within the halls of Maya.

*For Disciples and Initiates:* Let the group life emit the Word of invocation and thus evoke response within those distant Ashrams where move the Chohans of the race of men. They are no longer men as are the Masters but having passed beyond that lesser stage, have linked Themselves with the Great Council in the highest Secret Place. Let the group sound a dual chord, reverberating in the halls where move the Masters but finding pause and prolongation within those radiant halls where move the Lights which carry out the Will of God.

Rule VIII.

*For Applicants:* When the disciple nears the Portal, the greater seven must awaken and bring forth response from the lesser seven upon the double circle.

*For Disciples and Initiates:* Let the group find within itself response to the greater seven groups which carry out the hierarchical will with love and understanding. The group contains all seven, the perfect group. The lesser seven, the greater seven and the planetary seven form one great whole, and these the group must know. When this is realised and the Law of the Supplementary Seven is understood let the group understand the Three and then the ONE. This they can do with the united breath and the unified rhythm.

Rule IX.

*For Applicants:* Let the disciple merge himself within the circle of the other selves. Let but one colour blend them and their unity appear. Only when the group is known and sensed can energy be wisely emanated.

*For Disciples and Initiates:* Let the group know there are no other selves. Let the group know there is no colour, only light; and then let darkness take the place of light, hiding all difference, blotting out all form. Then—at the place of tension, and at that darkest point — let the group see a point of clear cold fire, and in the fire (right at its very heart) let the One Initiator appear Whose star shone forth when the Door first was passed.

Rule X.

*For Applicants:* The Army of the Voice, the devas in their serried ranks work ceaselessly. Let the disciple apply himself to a consideration of their methods; let him learn the rules whereby the Army works within the veils of maya.

*For Disciples and Initiates:* The rules for work within the veils of maya are known and have been used. Let the group widen all the rents within those veils and thus let in the light. Let the Army of the Voice be no more heard and let the brothers onward move within the Sound. Then let them know the meaning of the O.M. and let them hear that O.M. as it is sounded forth by Him Who stands and waits at the very centre of the Council Chamber of the Lord.

Rule XI.

*For Applicants:* Let the disciple transfer the fire from the lower triangle to the higher and preserve that which is created through the fire at the midway point.

*For Disciples and Initiates:* Let the group together move the fire within the Jewel in the Lotus into the Triad and let them find the Word which will carry out that task. Let them destroy by their dynamic Will that which has been created at the midway point. When the point of tension is reached by the brothers at the fourth great cycle of attainment, then will this work be done.

## Rule XII.

*For Applicants:* Let the disciple learn to use the hand in service; let him seek the mark of the Messenger in his feet and let him learn to see with the eye which looks out from between the two.

*For Disciples and Initiates:* Let the group serve as Aquarius indicates; let Mercury speed the group upon the upward Way and let Taurus bring illumination and the attainment of the vision; let the mark of the Saviour, as the group toils in Pisces, be seen above the aura of the group.

## Rule XIII.

*For Applicants:* Four things the disciple must learn and comprehend before he can be shown the inmost mystery: first, the laws of that which radiates; the five meanings of magnetisation make the second; the third is transmutation or the secret lost of alchemy; and lastly, the first letter of the Word which has been imparted, or the hidden name egoic.

*For Disciples and Initiates:* Let the group get ready to reveal the hidden mystery. Let the group demonstrate the higher meaning of the lessons learnt, and these are four and yet are one. Let the group understand the Law of Synthesis, of unity and fusion; let the threefold mode of working with that which is dynamic carry the group together towards the Higher Three where the Will of God holds sway; let Transfiguration follow Transformation and may Transmutation disappear. Let the O.M. be heard right at the centre of the group, proclaiming God is All.

## Rule XIV.

*For Applicants:* Listen, touch, see, apply, know.

*For Disciples and Initiates:* Know, express, reveal, destroy and resurrect.

These are the rules for group initiation and I am dealing with them to give you a fuller understanding of the Laws of Group Life with which I dealt in some of my other books.

I will take these rules and expound for you somewhat of their meaning and indicate their significances as far as these can be grasped now. These instructions are written for future disciples towards the end of this century. They form part of the last volume of *A Treatise on the Seven Rays* and will, therefore, go out to the general public who will not understand, but thus the needed teaching will be preserved.

# RULE ONE

We now begin our study of the fourteen rules for those who are seeking initiation, in one or other of its degrees. In *Initiation, Human and Solar* I gave the rules for those proposing to enter the grades of discipleship. I would like for a minute to deal with the significance of the word "Rule" and give you some idea of its occult meaning. There is much difference between a Law, an Order or Command, and a Rule, and these distinctions should be pondered with care. The Laws of the universe are simply the modes of expression, the life impulses and the way of existence or activity of the One in Whom we live and move and have our being. There is no avoiding these laws in the last analysis, and there is no denying them, for we are eternally swept into activity by them and they govern and control (from the angle of the Eternal Now) all that happens in time and space. Orders and commands are the feeble interpretations which men give to what they understand by law. In time and space, and at any given moment and in any given location, these commands are issued by those who are in a position of authority or who seem to dominate or are in a position to enforce their wishes. Laws are occult and basic. Orders are indicative of human frailty and limitation.

Rules are, however, different. They are the result of tried experience and of age-long undertakings and — assuming neither the form of laws nor the limitations of a command — they are recognised by those for whom they exist and hence evoke from them a prompt intuitive response. They need no enforcement but are voluntarily accepted, and are put to trial in the belief that the witness of the past and the testimony of the ages warrant the effort required for the expressed requirements.

This is true of the fourteen Rules which we are now going to study. I would remind you that only the initiate consciousness will truly comprehend their significance, but also that your effort so to do will develop in you the beginning of that initiate consciousness, provided you seek to make practical and voluntary application of these rules in your daily lives. They are susceptible of three forms of application — physical, emotional and mental — and of a fourth application which is best designated by the words "the response of the integrated personality to soul interpretation and understanding."

Another point which I would call to your attention, prior to interpreting this rule, is that your group endeavour must be to seek group application, group meaning and group light. I would emphatically emphasise the words "group light." We are dealing, therefore, with something basically new in the field of occult teaching, and the difficulty of intelligent comprehension is consequently great. The true significances are not the simple ones which appear upon the surface. The words of these rules would seem to be almost tritely familiar. If they meant exactly what they appear to mean, there would be no need for me to be giving hints as to their underlying significances and ideas. But they are not so simple.

To sum up, therefore: these Rules are to be read with the aid of a developing esoteric sense; they are related to group initiation in spite of their having individual application; they are not what they appear to be on the surface — trite truisms and spiritual platitudes; but they are rules for initiation which, if followed, will take the disciple and the group through a major spiritual experience; they embody the techniques of the New Age, which necessitate group activity, group procedure and united action. Earlier I said that these rules are the result of tried experience, and my use of the word "new" in this connotation is related to human knowledge but not to the initiatory procedure. That has always existed and always, at the great crises of initiation, disciples have moved forward in groups, even though they have not been aware of so doing. Now disciples can become so aware, and the various ray ashrams will not only present their groups (large or small) to the Initiator, but the personnel of these groups will now be aware of the fact of group presentation. They will also have to grasp the fact of the *extent of their knowledge being dependent upon their decentralisation.* I would ask you to ponder and reflect upon this last statement.

Let us now proceed to a consideration of Rule I.

## Rule I.

> *Within the fire of mind, focussed within the head's clear light, let the group stand. The burning ground has done its work. The clear cold light shines forth and cold it is and yet the heat — evoked by the group love — permits the warmth of energetic moving out. Behind the group there stands the Door. Before them opens out the Way. Together let the band of brothers onward move — out of the fire, into the cold, and toward a newer tension.*

It will be profitable if we take this Rule I sentence by sentence and try to wrest from each its group significance.

*1. Within the fire of the mind, focussed within the head's clear light, let the group stand.*

In this sentence, you have the idea of intellectual perception and of focussed unity. Intellectual perception is *not* mental understanding, but is in reality the clear cold reason, the buddhic principle in action and the focussed attitude of the Spiritual Triad in relation to the personality. I would call your attention to the following analogies:

| Head | Monad | Atma | Purpose |
|---|---|---|---|
| Heart | Soul | Buddhi | Pure reason |
| Base of spine | Personality | Manas | Spiritual activity |

In these words you have, therefore, the position of the personality indicated as it stands at the penetrating point of the antahkarana as it contacts the manas or lower mind and is thus the agent of the purpose of the Monad, working through the Spiritual Triad which is — as you know — related to the personality by the antahkarana.

The heart as an aspect of pure reason requires careful consideration. It is usually considered the organ of pure love but — from the angle of the esoteric sciences — love and reason are synonymous terms, and I would have you reflect upon why this should be. Love is essentially a word for the underlying motive of creation. Motive, however, presupposes purpose leading to action, and hence in the group-life task of the incarnating Monad there comes a time when motive (heart and soul) becomes spiritually obsolete because purpose has reached a point of fulfillment and the activity set in motion is such that purpose cannot be arrested or stopped. The disciple cannot then be deterred, and no hindrance or difficulty is hard enough to prevent his moving forward. Then we have eventual destruction of what Theosophists call the causal body and the establishing of a direct relation between the Monad and its tangible expression upon the physical plane. The head centre and the centre at the base of the spine will be in direct unimpeded relation; monadic will and personality will likewise will be in a similar unimpeded relation, via the antahkarana. I would have you remember that the will aspect is the final dominating principle.

In the group application of these ideas the same basic and profound development must take place, and a group of disciples must be distinguished by pure reason, which will steadily supersede motive, merging eventually into the will aspect of the Monad — its major aspect. It is, technically speaking, Shamballa in direct relation with humanity.

What, therefore, is the group will in any ashram or Master's group? Is it present in any form vital enough to condition the group relations and to unite its members into a band of brothers — moving forward into the light? Is the spiritual will of the individual personalities of such strength that it negates the personality relation and leads to spiritual recognition, spiritual interplay and spiritual relation? It is only in consideration of these fundamental effects of standing as a group in "the head's clear light" that it is permissible for disciples to bring into the picture personal sensitivities and thought, and this only because of a group temporary limitation.

What is it, therefore, which prevents a disciple — as an individual—from having direct approach and direct contact with the Master without being dependent upon an intermediary? Let me illustrate: In the group I have under training *(Discipleship in the New Age,* Vols. I and II) two or three *have* direct approach; and others have it but know it not; still others are well intentioned and hard driving disciples, but never for a second do they forget themselves; one has had a problem of glamour but now is preoccupied with the problem of spiritual ambition—a spiritual ambition which is working through a very small personality; some could make rapid progress but are too prone to inertia — perhaps I could say that they do not care enough. Each of them (and every other disciple) can place himself. All of them desire to move forward and possess a strong inner spiritual life—hence my finding the time to work with them. But the group antahkarana is still incomplete and the aspect of pure reason and of the heart does *not* control. The evocative power of the Spiritual Triad is not, therefore, adequate to hold the personality steady and the invocative power of the personality is non-existent—speaking from the angle of the group personalities which make up the personality aspect of the ashram. This is a factor with which they oft feel I have not to deal. It can only become a potent factor if certain personality relations are adjusted and inertia is overcome. Then and only then can "the group stand."

2. *The burning ground has done its work.*

Here there is quite apt to be misunderstanding. To most people the burning ground stands for one of two things:

    a. Either the fire of the mind, burning up those things in the lower nature of which it becomes increasingly aware.

    b. Or the burning ground of sorrow, agony, horror and pain which is the characteristic quality of life in the three worlds, particularly at this time.

But the burning ground referred to here is something

very different. When the blazing light of the sun is correctly focussed on or through a glass it can cause ignition. When the blazing light of the Monad is focussed directly upon the personality, via the antahkarana and not specifically through the soul, it produces a blazing fire which burns up all hindrances in a steady, sequential process. Wording it otherwise, when the will aspect streams from the Monad and focusses through the personal will (as the mind can grasp and realise it) it destroys as by fire all elements of self-will. As the energy of Shamballa streams out and makes a direct contact with humanity (omitting the transmission via the Hierarchy, which has hitherto been customary), you have what has been seen in the world today, a destructive conflagration or a world burning ground. When the antahkarana of a group is rightly constructed, then the individualised group-will will disappear in the full consciousness of the monadic purpose or clear directed will. These are points which the disciple preparing for initiation has to consider as he prepares for the higher initiations, and these are the points which any group or ashram in preparation for initiation has also to consider.

The secret of the higher initiations lies in the trained use of the higher will. It does not lie in purification or in self-discipline or in any of the expedients which have acted in the past as interceptors of the truth. This whole problem of the Shamballic will is in process of revelation, and will eventually alter the entire approach of the disciple in the New Age to initiation. The theme of "the Way into Shamballa" requires reflective study and esoteric understanding. In this concept of the new and future section (if I may so call it) of the Way or Path with which the modern disciple is faced lies the secret of the coming revelation and of the spiritual dispensation which will emerge as humanity constructs the new world civilisation and begins to formulate the new culture. The burning, purifying, destructive effects of the monadic will upon its distorted reflection, the individual will, deeply deserve consideration.

For long, aspirants have noted and have been taught the effect of the will upon the astral, or emotional body. It is one of the primary and most elementary of the initial tensions, and is taught upon the Probationary Path. It leads to the purifying and the re-organising of the entire psychic and emotional life, as the result of its destructive action. "If you will only think," "if you will only use a little will," and "if you will only remember that you have a mind," we say to the children of the race and to beginners upon the Path of conscious Return. Little by little, then, the focus and the orientation shift out of the astral life and from the emotional level of consciousness into the mental, and consequently into the reflection of the world of purpose, found in the three worlds. When that stage has been somewhat developed, then there follows, upon the Path of Discipleship and of preparation for initiation, an effort to grasp and understand the higher aspects of this mental process, and the will aspect of the egoic life begins to influence the disciple. The "petals of sacrifice" unfold and the sacred sacrificial aspect of life is revealed in its beauty, purity, simplicity and in its revolutionising quality.

Upon the Path of Initiation, the monadic will (of which the egoic will is the reflection and the individual self-will is the distortion) is gradually transmitted, via the antahkarana, direct to the man upon the physical plane. This produces the higher correspondence of those qualities so glibly spoken of by the well-trained but dense esotericist — transmutation and transformation. The result is the assimilation of the individual will and the egoic will into the purpose of the Monad which is the purpose — undeviating and unalterable — of the One in Whom we live and move and have our being. This is the field of the true burning, for our "God is a consuming Fire." This is the burning bush or the burning tree of life of Biblical symbolism. This highest of all the fires, this deeply spiritual and hitherto seldom recognised burning ground, has its effects summed up for us in the next phrase or sentence of Rule I.

*3. The clear cold light shines forth and cold it is and yet the heat—evoked by the group love—permits the warmth of energetic moving out.*

In these words you have the key to group initiation. The light of the higher initiations can stream in when it is evoked by the group love. That light is clear and cold, but produces the needed "heat," which is a symbolic word used in many of the world Scriptures to express living, spiritual energy. I said "spiritual energy" and not soul force, and herein lies a distinction which you will some day have to grasp.

This group love is based upon the egoic aspect of the will to which we give the name "sacrificial love." This does not connote happy relationships between individual members of the group. It might, presumably, lead to unhappy outer, superficial interplay, but basically it leads to an unalterably staunch loyalty, underlying the surface of the outer life. The Master's influence, as He seeks to aid His disciple, always produces transitory turmoil — transitory from the angle of the soul, but frequently appalling from the angle of the personality. Similarly, the projection of the life and influence of any senior disciple into the periphery or aura of the aspirant or lesser disciple is — in its degree — likewise disturbing and upsetting; this is a point which should be carefully borne in mind, both as regards the disciple's own reactions and training, and as regards any effect which he may call forth in the life of a probationary disciple or lesser disciple in his own sphere of influence. These intrusive influences and their consequent effects which are produced upon an individual or a group by a Master or a senior disciple are usually interpreted in personality terms, and are very little understood. They are nevertheless aspects of the higher will in some higher disciple and are beating upon the personality will and evoking the sacrificial will of the Ego, and hence lead to a period of temporary discomfort. This the aspirant and the inexperienced disciple resent and blame the evoking sources for their discomfort, instead of learning the needed lesson of receiving and handling force.

Where, however, real love exists, it will produce the lessening of the personality will, the evocation of the sacrificial egoic will, and a constantly growing capacity to identify the group with the will or purpose of the Monad. The progress of the group is, therefore, from one burning ground to another — each burning ground being colder and clearer than the preceding one but producing sequentially the burning fire, the clear cold lighted fire, and the consuming divine fire.

Thus in parables the truth goes out, and gradually the initiate grasps the uses of heat, warmth, light and energy; he arrives at an understanding of self-will, sacrificial will and Shamballic purpose, and only Love (self-love, group love, and finally, divine love) can reveal the significance of these symbolic words and the occult paradoxes which confront the true aspirant as he attempts to tread the Way.

As we continue our studies of the rules to be followed by those receiving initiate-training, I would remind you of certain things, some of them already touched upon but requiring re-emphasis. Any usefulness which these Rules may have for you will be dependent upon your grasping a few basic ideas and then proceeding to make them factual as far as in you lies.

First, I would call your attention to what should be the basic attitude of the would-be initiate: *It should be one of purpose, governed by pure reason and working out in spiritual activity.* That is a sentence easily written, but what specifically does it convey to you? Let me enlarge upon it somewhat. The attitude of the initiate-in-training should be one of right spiritual motive—the motive being the intelligent fulfillment of the will aspect of divinity, or of the Monad. This involves the merging of his personality self-will into that of the sacrificial will of the soul; and this, when accomplished, will lead to the revelation of the divine Will. Of this Will, no one who is not an initiate has any conception. It means, secondly, the release of the faculty of spiritual perception and of intuitive understanding, which involves the negation of the activity of the lower or concrete mind, of the lower personal self, and the subordination of the knowledge aspect of the soul to the clear pure light of the divine understanding. When these two factors are beginning to be active, you will have the emergence of true spiritual activity upon the physical plane, motivated from the high source of the Monad, and implemented by the pure reason of the intuition.

It will be apparent to you, therefore, that these higher spiritual faculties can only be brought into play when the bridging antahkarana is beginning to play its part. Hence the teaching which I am giving on the construction of the rainbow bridge.

These Rules are in reality great Formulas of Approach, but they indicate approach to a specific section of the Path and not approach to the Initiator. I would have you reflect upon this distinction. The "Way of the Higher Evolution" lies open to the aspirant to the Greater Mysteries, but he is oft bewildered in the beginning and frequently questions in his mind the difference between the progress or evolution of the personality towards soul consciousness and the nature of the progress which lies ahead and which is essentially different to the unfoldment of pure consciousness. Had you grasped the fact that after the third initiation, the initiate is not concerned with consciousness at all, but with the fusion of his individual will with the divine will? He is not then occupied with increasing his sensitivity to contact, or with his conscious response to environing conditions, but is becoming increasingly aware of the dynamics of the Science of the Service of the Plan. This distinctive realisation can only come when his fused and blended personality and soul expression of will has disappeared in the blazing light of the divine Purpose — a purpose which cannot be frustrated even if at times delayed, as it has been during the past fifty-five years. (Written in February, 1943.)

Much of what I have said above will seem meaningless to you because the finished contact between soul and personality has not been brought about and the will aspect in manifestation is not yet understood in its three phases: Personality, Egoic and Monadic. But, as I have earlier told you, I write for those disciples and initiates who are now coming into incarnation and who will be in the full flower of their consciousness and service at the latter end of this century. But the effort you make to understand will have its effect, even if the brain registers it not.

In the last analysis, these Rules or Formulas of Approach are primarily concerned with the Shamballa or life aspect. They are the only Formulas or embodied techniques at present extant which have in them the quality which will enable the aspirant to understand and eventually express the significance of the words of Christ, "Life more abundantly." These words relate to contact with Shamballa; the result will be the expression of the will aspect. The whole process of invocation and evocation is tied up with the idea. The lesser aspect is ever the invoking factor, and this constitutes an unalterable law lying behind the entire evolutionary process. It is necessarily a reciprocal process, but in time and space it might be broadly said that the lesser ever invokes the higher, and higher factors are then evoked and respond according to the measure of understanding and the dynamic tension displayed by the invoking element. This many fail to realise. You do not work at the evocative process. That word simply connotes the response of that which has been reached. The task of the lesser aspect or group is invocative, and the success of the invocative rite is called evocation.

When, therefore, your life is fundamentally invocative, then there will come the evocation of the will. It is only truly invocative when personality and soul are fused and functioning as a consciously blended and focussed unit.

The next point which I seek to make is that these Formulas of Approach or Rules deal with the unfoldment of group consciousness, because it is only in group formation that, as yet, the Shamballa force of the will can be tapped. They are useless to the individual under the new initiatory dispensation. Only the group, under the proposed new mode of working and of group initiation, is capable of invoking Shamballa. That is why Hitler, the exponent of the reversed reaction to Shamballa (and consequently the evil reaction) had to gather around him a group of like-minded people or personalities. On the upper arc of the evocative cycle (Hitler being the expression of the invocative arc of the Shamballa force) it requires *a group* to bring about evocation.

We now come to my third point in relation to the Rules or Formulas and their objective. They are concerned — above everything else — with group initiation. They have other applications, but for the present here lies their usefulness. What, you may ask, is group initiation? Does it involve the taking of initiation by every member in the group? Can one person have so extensive an influence that he can hold up or delay or even prevent (in time and space) the group initiation? The group need not necessarily contain members who have all taken the same initiation. By this I mean that the necessary initiation of all the members simultaneously into the same group development is *not* required. Basically, what I am endeavouring to say anent these Rules has relation to the third initiation — the initiation of the integrated personality. They necessarily, however, have a correspondence to the second initiation, and are consequently of more general interest, for it is that initiation which faces so many aspirants today — the demonstration of the control of the formidable emotional nature.

I would ask you to think much about this point which I have just made. Group initiation means that the bulk of the members are correctly oriented; that they are proposing to accept the discipline which will prepare them for the next great expansion of consciousness, and that none of them can possibly be deviated from their *purpose* (note that word with its first ray or Shamballic implications), no matter what is happening in their environment or their personal life. You need to reflect on this if you desire to make the needed progress.

In these short instructions, which aim only at a "tentative indication" (note that phrase), it is not necessary to enter into explicit details. In any case, if the Formulas or Rules are not intuitively clear to your minds, anything I could say would only hinder and frustrate my purpose.

Finally, these Formulas or Rules are susceptible of

three forms of application or interpretation and I would have you remember this, because you can thereby discover where your individual focus of attention is and if you are consequently functioning as an integrated personality. Remember always that only an integrated personality can achieve the needed soul focus. This is a fundamental requirement. These three forms of application are physical, emotional and mental in nature. But those words in their simplest connotation have true reference to the task of achieving one or other of the higher initiations. The only way their significance can truly appear is by grasping the following meanings:

1. The *physical* application refers to the usage by the group of the given knowledge and intuitively perceived information in such a way that the needs of the larger group, of which the group itself is a part, are constructively served. The consummation of this ideal is to be found in the activity of the Hierarchy itself which, from progressive point to progressive point, finds itself in the position of intuitive interpreter and force transmitter between the centre of Shamballa and Humanity. The individual initiate, on the way to one or other of the higher initiations, has in his lesser degree to achieve the same dual function and thereby fit himself for the wider cooperation.

2. The *emotional* application has definite reference to the world of meaning, interpreted in a group sense. At present, well-meaning aspirants are satisfied if they are able to interpret their personality conditions, events and happenings in terms of their real meaning. But that still remains an individual reaction. The aspirant who is seeking to comprehend these Rules is more interested in seeing the situations which he contacts in terms of a world whole, and in searching for their meaning in terms of their group significance. This serves to decentralise him and to convey into his consciousness some aspect of that larger whole, and this in its turn contributes to the expansion of the consciousness of humanity as a whole.

*3.* The *mental* application has to be grasped and considered in terms of the "great light." It must be remembered that the mind is the organ of illumination. Therefore it might be asked: Do the united mental processes of the group as a whole tend to throw light on human problems and situations? How much does the light of the individual group member aid in this process? How much light do you, as an individual, register and therefore contribute to the greater light? Is the group light a dim flicker or a blazing sun?

Such are some of the implications lying behind the use of these familiar words, and the careful consideration of their meaning might bring about a definite expansion of consciousness. This expansion normally follows certain clear and definite stages:

1. A recognition of the goal. This goal is often expressed under the word "the door." A door permits entrance into some place larger than the area covered by the standing room of the would-be initiate. This statement refers to the "door of incarnation" through which the incarnating soul enters into life — limited and restricted from the angle of the soul. The door of initiation admits "into a larger room" or sphere of extended expression.

2. The approach, under regulated and imposed and well-tried rules, of the entering one towards a visioned goal. This involves conformity to that which has been tried, known and demonstrated by all previous initiates.

3. The arresting of the steps of the initiate before the door in order that he may "prove himself to be initiate" prior to entry.

4. The passing of certain tests in order to demonstrate fitness.

5. Then comes the stage of entrance — under due and set rules and yet with full freedom of action. You will see, therefore, why ever the need for understanding is emphasised.

Before proceeding to study the final phrases of Rule

One, I would call your attention to the fact that the initiate has faced two major tests, symbolically described as "the burning ground" and the "clear cold light." Only after he has successfully passed these can he — or the group, when considering group initiation — move forward and outward into the wider reaches of the divine consciousness. These tests are applied when the soul grips the personality and the fire of divine love destroys the loves and desires of the integrated personality. Two factors tend to bring this about: the slow moving forward of the innate conscience into greater control, and the steady development of the "fiery aspiration" to which Patanjali* makes reference. These two factors, when brought into living activity, bring the disciple into the centre of the burning ground which separates the Angel of the Presence from the Dweller on the Threshold. The burning ground is found upon the threshold of every new advance, until the third initiation has been taken.

The "clear cold light" is the light of pure reason, of infallible intuitive perception and its unremitting, intensive and revealing light constitutes a major test in its effects. The initiate discovers the depths of evil, and at the same time is enticed forward by the heights of a growing sense of divinity. The clear cold light reveals two things:

A. The *omnipresence of God* throughout nature, and therefore throughout the entire personality life of the initiate or of the initiate group. The scales fall from the eyes, bringing about—paradoxically—the "dark night of the soul" and the sense of being alone and bereft of all help. This led (in the case of the Christ, for instance) to that appalling moment in the Garden of Gethsemane, and which was consummated on the Cross, when the will of personality-soul clashed with the divine will of the Monad. The revelation to the initiate of the ages of severance from the Central Reality, and of all its attendant implications, descends upon the one who is attempting to stand "in isolated Unity," as Patanjali (to quote him a second time) calls the experience.†

---

*The Light of the Soul* (Book II, Sutra 1)  page 119.
†*Ibid.* (Book IV, Sutras 25.34) pages 420, 428.

The omnipresence of divinity within all forms pours in upon the consciousness of the initiate, and the mystery of time, space and electricity stands revealed. The major effect of this revelation (prior to the third initiation) is to bring to the disciple a realisation of the "great heresy of separateness," as it focusses in him, the separated fully conscious individual—aware of his past, conscious now of his ray and its conditioning power, focussed in his own aspiration, and yet part of the great whole of nature. From that moment onward he knows that divinity is all there is, and this he learns through the revelation of the inherent separativeness of the form life, through the processes of "the dark night of the soul" and its culminating lesson of the significance of isolation and the freeing process which brings about the merging into unity through the emission of the sound, the cry, the invocation, such as the cry of the Christ upon the Cross symbolised. His exact words have not been transmitted to us. They vary for each ray, but all bring about the recognition of divine merging, in which all separating veils are "rent from the top to the bottom" (as *The New Testament* expresses it).

B. *The omniscience of the divine Whole* is also brought home to the initiate through the medium of the clear cold light, and the phase of "isolated experience," as it is sometimes occultly called, is forever ended. I would have you realise what this can mean in so far as possible to your present consciousness. Up till the present, the initiate-disciple has been functioning as a duality and as a fusion of soul-energy and personality-force. Now these forms of life stand exposed to him for what they essentially are, and he knows that — as directing agencies and as transitory gods—they no longer have any hold over him. He is being gradually translated into another divine aspect, taking with him all that he has received during the ages of close relation and identification with the third aspect, form, and the second aspect, consciousness. A sense of being bereft, deserted and alone descends upon him as he realises that the control of form and soul must also disappear. Here lies the agony of isolation and the overpowering sense of loneliness. But the truths revealed by the clear cold light of the divine reason leave him no choice. He *must* relinquish all that holds him away from the Central Reality; he must gain life and "life more abundantly." This constitutes the supreme test in the life cycle of the incarnating Monad; and "when the very heart of this experience enters into the heart of the initiate, then he moves outward through that heart into full life expression." Such is the way that the *Old Commentary* expresses this. I know no other way in which to bring the idea before you. The experience undergone is not related to form, nor is it connected with consciousness or with even the higher psychic sensitivity. It consists of pure identification with divine purpose. This is made possible because the self-will of the personality and the enlightened will of the soul have both equally been relinquished.

*4. Behind the group there stands the Door. Before them opens out the Way.*

Note how this passage reverses the usual presentation. Hitherto, in the occult books, the Door of Initiation has been presented as ever moving forward ahead of the initiate. He passes through door after door into a wider experience and expansion of consciousness. But in the initiate consciousness, after the first two initiations, this is not the realisation. It is simply the adhering to an old form of symbolism with the implied limitations of the truth. I would here remind you that the third initiation is regarded by the Hierarchy as the first major initiation, and that the first and second initiations are initiations of the Threshold. For the bulk of humanity, these first two initiations will for a very long time constitute major initiatory experiences, but in the life and realisation of the initiate-soul, they are not. After the two initiations of the threshold have been undergone the attitude of the initiate changes and he sees possibilities and factors and revelations which have hitherto been totally unrealised and unknown, even to his consciousness at his highest moments.

The door of initiation looms large in the consciousness of the neophyte; the higher Way is the determining factor in the life of the initiate of the third degree. It is the Transfiguration; and a new glory pours through the transfigured initiate who has been released from every type of grip by either the personality or the soul. For the first time, the goal of the higher Way and the attainment of Nirvana (as the Oriental calls it) appears before him, and he knows that no forms and no spiritual complexes and no pull by either soul or form, or by both united, can have any effect upon his attaining his final destination.

I would like for a moment to refer here to the door symbology as the initiate begins to grasp the inner meaning of those simple words. For long the teaching, given in the clear cold light, anent the door and the emphasis put upon the presentation of the door lying ahead of the aspirant has been made familiar, but that has been working with the lower aspects of the symbolism, even if aspirants did not realise it; they have been taught the fact of the light in the head, which is the personality correspondence to the clear cold light to which I refer. At the very centre of that light, as many aspirants know theoretically or factually by inconstant experience, is a centre or point of dark indigo blue — midnight blue. Note the significance of this in view of what I have been saying anent the "dark night," the midnight hour, the zero hour in the life of the soul. That centre is in reality an opening, a door leading somewhere, a way of escape, a place through which the soul imprisoned in the body can emerge and pass into higher states of consciousness, untrammelled by form limitations; it has also been called "the funnel or the channel for the sound"; it has been named the "trumpet through which the escaping A.U.M. can pass." The ability to use this door or channel is brought about by *the practice of alignment;* hence the emphasis laid upon this exercise in the attempt to train aspirants and disciples.

Once alignment has been achieved, it will be realised

(remembering the symbolism of the head, the light and the central opening) that many occasions arise in meditation when "behind the group there stands the door; before them opens out the Way." This is the lower correspondence of the higher initiate-experience with which our rule is dealing.

Again, this time in relation to the soul, comes the repetition of the discovery of the Door, its use and its appearance, finally, behind the initiate. This time the door must be found upon the mental plane, and not as earlier upon the etheric level; this is brought about by the aid of the soul and of the lower mind and through the revealing power of the clear cold light of the reason. When discovered, the "revelation of a terrible though beautiful experiment" faces the initiate. He finds that this time alignment is not his need, but the definite undertaking of a creative work — the building of a bridge between the door which lies behind and the door which lies ahead. This involves the construction of what is technically the antahkarana, the rainbow bridge. This is built by the disciple-in-training upon the basis of his past experience; it is anchored in the past and firmly grounded in the highest, rightly oriented aspect of the personality. As the disciple then creatively works, he finds that there is a reciprocal action on the part of the Presence, the Monad — the unity which stands behind the Door. He discovers that one span of the bridge (if I might so call it) is being built or pushed forward from the other side of the gulf separating him from experience in the life of the Spiritual Triad. This Spiritual Triad is essentially, to the initiate, what the threefold personality is to the man in physical incarnation.

I wonder if I have succeeded in giving you at least a general idea of the possibilities lying ahead of the disciple, and incited you to definite conscious response to those possibilities. I cannot do other than speak in terms of consciousness, even though the life of the Triad — leading in its turn to identification with the Monad, as the personality life leads eventually to soul control and expression — has naught to do with consciousness or sensitivity as those terms are

commonly understood. Yet remember how, in all my teachings upon occult unfoldment, I have used the word IDENTI-
FICATION. This is the only word I have found which can in
any way convey the complete unity which is finally achieved
by those who develop a sense of unity, and who refuse to
accept isolation; separateness then fades out entirely. The
isolated unity achieved is unity with the Whole, with Being
in its totality (and this cannot as yet convey much to you).

*5. Together let the band of brothers onward move — out of
the fire, into the cold, and toward a newer tension.*

Here, in very brief form, certain basic instructions are
given. Each of them indicates the new attitudes imposed
upon all who have taken initiation. They cannot be interpreted in terms of the Path of Discipleship or of Probation.
The ordinary and easily-arrived-at significances mean little
to the initiate mind. Let me briefly consider them so that
clarity of concept, though not of detail, may prevail.

    a. *Out of the fire.* This is a symbolic way of indicating
that the personality life is definitely and finally left
behind. It is this phrase which gives the clue to the
initiation which is referred to in this Rule. Each of
these Rules contains within itself the clue to the particular initiation to which reference is being made. The
Rules are not placed in their right order, having sequential reference to the seven initiations. The intuition of the aspirant must be invoked if he is to arrive at
right knowledge. I shall sometimes indicate the initiation involved, but not always, as it would profit not.
The clue to the seventh initiation which lies ahead for
such high Beings as the Christ would be of no service to
you at all. The clue to the initiation of the Transfiguration can be of importance, as it involves the personality,
and many of you in the not so distant future (from the
angle of the aeonial life cycle of the soul) will face that.
The secret of the third initiation is the demonstration
of complete freedom from the claims and demands of
the personality. It does not involve the achievement of

a completely perfect expression of the spiritual life, but it does indicate that the service of the initiate and his life demonstration — regarded in a broad and general way, from the angle of the life-tendency and of entire dedication to humanity — remains untouched by the limitations, still existent, of the personal lower self.

b. *Into the cold.* This means that the focus of the life is now in the realm of clear truth and of pure reason. The life of the initiate is being rapidly transferred out of the egoic centre, the soul vehicle, on to the level of the buddhic life or state of being. Note, I do not say "of consciousness." This is formless, but preserves the fruitage of form experience. It is being oriented towards a realised unity and identification with the life aspect of divinity, and yet preserves its own recognised and achieved identity. On this level of pure impersonality and of right orientation the group stands, obedient to the rule which governs this particular stage of development.

c. *Toward a newer tension.* The interpretation of the phrase presents difficulty. This is owing to the false impression which the word "tension" conveys at this time. It is associated in the minds of the reading public with the thought of nerves, with points of crisis, with courage and with fatigue. Is this not so? But in reality tension, occultly understood, is not associated with these aspects of personality reaction at all. The esoteric significance of tension (as far as I can explain it by limiting words) is "focussed immovable Will." Right tension is the identification of brain and soul with the will aspect, and the preservation of that identification — unchanged and immovable — no matter what the circumstances and the difficulties.

You can see, therefore, how far ahead of present attitudes and goals this teaching is. Identification with the soul and with the Hierarchy is dependent upon the ability of the disciple rightly to love. It is the emergence of the second divine aspect, for love is the expression of group life, and that is rare indeed to find in these days. Right tension indicates the emergence of the first aspect, of the will, and this is seldom to be found as yet, save among the more advanced disciples and initiate members of the Hierarchy.

Love governs the Way into the life of the Hierarchy and is the foundation for all approach to, and appreciation and acceptance of truth.

Will governs the Way into Shamballa and is the foundation for all approach to, appreciation of and identification with, Being.

This developed will expresses itself as tension, esoterically understood. It embodies the ideas of orientation, implacable determination, ability to wait and to preserve intention and orientation unmoved by aught which may occur. It also involves the determination to take the intended action (always of a creative nature and based on loving understanding) at the psychological moment (right timing), or that exact moment which the psyche or soul determines to be correct. Here you have one of the interesting transferences of meaning and of relationship which occur in the Ageless Wisdom. The Son or soul emerges into manifestation with the concurrence and aid of the Mother or of the matter aspect. This is to you a most familiar truth. In the next stage, that of initiate-development, the Son, in its turn, becomes the feminine or negative aspect and, demonstrating as the Psyche, enables the initiate to bring into expression another divine aspect — that of the will. Until the fourth initiation is undergone, it is the soul as a "focal point for descending light and for ascending radiance." This dual activity reveals the nature of the will. Note how this phrase from an ancient writing describes the antahkarana.

It is not possible in these brief instructions to deal adequately with the will aspect of divinity, nor would it profit at this time. Aspirants have to learn the nature of the will by the power of inner illumination and by certain intelligent recognitions. They learn the nature of the self through the aid of the personality, the shadow or distortion of the divine will. They pass from the expression of the will which is purely selfish, self-sufficient and self-focussed, to the grasp of the group will and to the effort to embody that group will. This group will is always concerned with that which is not the will of the separated self.

As this ability to be selflessly decentralised grows and develops, the aspirant reaches a point where the group life and the group good is seen as an integral part of a much greater Whole. This greater Whole is BEING Itself, divorced from form but ever working through form whilst in manifestation, and working with planned purpose. The realisation then grows that intelligence and love are not enough, but that they must be supplemented and implemented by will, which is active intelligent purpose, lovingly applied.

The difficulty of this subject is inherent in the fact that basically (no matter how strange this may seem) love is the line of least resistance for the developed human being. It is the governing principle of the present solar system. Will is the governing principle of the next or coming solar system, which will be brought into manifestation through the agency of those human beings who — in this solar system — arrive at the full expression of the will aspect. Then, in the coming consummating manifestation, love will be to the will aspect what intelligence is, in this solar system, to love.

## RULE TWO

In our study of Rule One on Initiation, we gained (or perhaps fixed more clearly in our minds) three major thoughts:

1. That the Path of Initiation is one on which we develop the Will aspect of divinity.

2. We learn also to use consciousness as a jumping off place for the recognition of a new state of realisation, which is not consciousness at all, as we understand that term.

3. We undergo, prior to each initiation, two major tests — that of the burning ground and that of the clear cold light.

We closed our discussion with the thought of Tension and I defined it as the identification of the brain and soul with the will aspect and the preservation of that identification—unchanged and immovable—in all circumstances and difficulties. I mention this as the "tension" concept or point of attainment underlies the teaching of the rule which we are now going to consider.

Rule II.

> *The* Word *has now gone forth from the great point of tension: Accepted as a group. Withdraw not now your application. You could not, if you would; but add to it three great demands and forward move. Let there be no recollection and yet let memory rule. Work from the point of all that is within the content of the group's united life.*

A close analysis of this rule will convey to the intuition far more than appears upon the surface, and that is rich enough. Each of these rules holds in it the seed of that understanding which must be evoked before the next rule can be mastered. All that is given is ever based on that which has gone before. The "three great demands" of the initiate are based upon the "triple call" found in Rule Two for aspirants and disciples. The triple call was earlier sounded forth. Now its higher significances must be comprehended.

There are only four parts to this rule, which is one of prime importance because it contains the motivating force, the conditioning factors and the place of triumph — all these are indicated. We will, as is our usual custom, study each separate part sequentially and as far as possible in detail bearing in mind that initiation deals with factors in latent manifestation for which our languages have no words, and with ideas which are not yet to be found among the "raincloud of knowable things" (as Patanjali calls it) — that is, knowable to the masses of men. The initiate is, however, dealing with a world of meaning and of affairs which are not yet manifesting in any way. The task of the Master (and of Those higher than He) is to take those steps and precipitate those "waiting events" which will eventually bring them into manifestation. This, I would remind you, is always done by the use of the will and from a point of tension.

*1. The Word has now gone forth from the great point of tension: Accepted as a group.*

I would like here to call your attention to the progressive nature of the esoteric science; it is nowhere better illustrated than in this phrase; nowhere is it more clearly shown and yet, unless the intuition and the sense of correlation are functioning, the idea might escape recognition.

In all the teaching given to the aspirant and to the disciple in the early stages of their training, the emphasis has been upon the "point of light" which must be discovered, brought into full illumination, and then so used that the one in whom the light shines becomes a light-bearer in a dark world. This, the aspirant is taught, becomes possible when contact with the soul has been made and the light is found. This is familiar teaching to many and is the essence of the progress to be made by aspirants and disciples in the first part of their training.

We now, however, pass on to another expression and to the next development in the life of the initiate, which is learning to work from a "point of tension." Here lies the new emphasis, and I am bringing it to the attention of humanity as mankind nears the close, the terrible but liberating finale, of his great test in this modern burning-ground. Now men can pass on into the clear cold light, and from there begin to hold that point of tension which will be evocative of the needed "understanding will-to-move forward" along the line of human will-to-good — the first phase of the development of the will aspect. It is the higher sublimation of the aspirational stage which precedes the attainment of the "point of light" through contact with the soul.

The point of tension is found when the dedicated will

of the personality is brought into touch with the will of the Spiritual Triad. This takes place in three clearly defined stages:

1. The stage wherein the lower will aspect which is focussed in the mental body — the will-to-activity of the personality — is brought into contact with the higher abstract mind; this latter is the interpreting agent for the Monad and the lowest aspect of the Triad. Two things can be noted in this respect:

    a. This contact becomes possible from the moment that the first thin strand of the antahkarana, the rainbow bridge, is completed between the mental unit and the manasic permanent atom.

    b. This demonstrates in an absorbing devotion to the Plan and is an effort, at any cost, to serve that Plan as it is progressively understood and grasped.

This expresses itself in the cultivation of goodwill, as understood by the average intelligent human being and put into action as a way of life.

2. The stage wherein the love aspect of the soul is brought into touch with the corresponding aspect of the Triad, to which we give the inadequate name of the intuition. This is in reality divine insight and comprehension, as expressed through the formulation of ideas. Here you have an instance of the inadequacy of modern language; ideas are formless and are in effect points of energy, outward moving in order eventually to express some "intention" of the divine creating Logos. When the initiate grasps this and identifies himself with it, his goodwill expands into the will-to-good. Plan and quality give place to purpose and method. Plans are fallible and tentative and serve a temporary need. Purpose, as expressed by the initiate is permanent, farsighted, unalterable, and serves the Eternal Idea.

3. The stage wherein — after the fourth initiation — there is direct unbroken relation between the Monad, via the Triad, and the form which the Master is using to do His

work among men. This form may be either His temporary personality, arrived at along the normal lines of incarnation, or the specially created form to which Theosophists give the technical but cumbersome word "mayavirupa." It is the "true mask, hiding the radiant light and the dynamic energy of a revealed Son of God." This is the esoteric definition which I offer you. This stage can be called the attainment of the will-to-be, not Being as an individual expression but Being as an expression of the Whole — all-inclusive, non-separative, motivated by goodness, beauty and truth and intelligently expressed as pure love.

All these stages are achieved by the attainment of one point of tension after another, and the work thus carried forward into the realm of the dynamic steadfast will. This will, as it is progressively developed, works ever from a constant point of tension.

We come now to the consideration of a subject which always proves exceedingly difficult to students: The nature of the WORD, the A.U.M., and its later developments, the O.M. and the Sound. Much confusion exists as to its significance or the necessity for its use. The phase of its recognition through which we are now passing is a purely exoteric one of accustoming the general public to the fact of its existence. This has been brought about in three ways:

1. Through the constant use in all the Christian Churches of the word "Amen," which is a western corruption of the A.U.M. The A.U.M. is here the lowest aspect of the originating Sound.

2. Through the emphasis laid in Masonry upon the Lost Word, thus subtly drawing the attention of humanity to the O.M.; the Sound of the second aspect, the Soul.

3. Through the growing emphasis laid by the many occult groups throughout the world upon the use of the O.M., its frequent use by these groups in public, and by those intent upon meditation.

The soundest approach is that of the Masonic tradition, because it deals primarily with the world of meaning and with a phase of the esoteric teaching. The use of the Amen in the ritual of the Christian Church will eventually be discouraged, because it is basically a materialistic affirmation, being usually regarded by the average churchgoer as setting the seal of divine approval upon his demand to the Almighty for protection, or for the supply of his physical necessities; all this is, therefore, related to the life of desire, of aspiration, of dualism and of request. It involves the attitude of giver and recipient.

The A.U.M. and the Amen are both of them an expression in sound of the principle of active intelligent substance in the divine manifestation, the third aspect, and have served human need in that phase of material and form development. I refer here also to the development of mind or of the mental form. The personality as a whole, when perfected and brought under control of the soul, is the "Word made flesh."

The mass of aspirants and of disciples are today learning the meaning of the O.M., which is not the Word made flesh, but the Word released from form, and expressing itself as soul-spirit and not as body-soul-spirit. It might, therefore, be said that:

1. The A.U.M. (note that I separate each aspect of this triple sound) brings the soul-spirit aspect down on to the physical plane and anchors it there by the force of its outgoing vibration. Using a symbol to make my meaning clear, it is like "a strong wind that pins a man against a wall and makes free effort difficult." It vivifies form; it intensifies the hold of matter upon the soul; it builds around the soul a confining prison — a prison of the senses. It is the "sound of enchantment," the sound that is the source of glamour and of maya; it is the great beguiling and deceptive energy, the note of the involutionary arc. In it are hid the secret of evil or matter, the uses of form, first as a prison, then as a training ground and as a field of experience, and finally as the expression for the manifestation of a Son of God.

2. The O.M. rightly sounded, releases the soul from the realm of glamour and of enchantment. It is the sound of

liberation, the great note of resurrection and of the raising of humanity to the Secret Place of the Most High when all other Words and sounds have failed. It is not a triple sound as is the A.U.M., but a dual sound, significant of the relation of spirit and soul, and of life and consciousness. This lost Word, symbolic of the loss in the three worlds (typified by the degrees of the Blue Lodges in Masonry) must be recovered and is in process of discovery today. The mystics have sought after it; the Masons have preserved the tradition of its existence; the disciples and initiates of the world must demonstrate its possession.

3. The SOUND is the sole expression of the Ineffable Name, the secret appellation of the One in Whom we live and move and have our being, and Who is known to the Great White Lodge through this name. Remember always that name and form are synonymous terms in the occult teaching, and these two words hold the secret of manifestation. The goal of the initiate is identification with all forms of the divine life, so that he can know himself to be an integral part of that Whole and can tune in on all states of divine awareness, knowing for himself (and not just theoretically) that they are also his own states of awareness. He can then penetrate into the divine arcana of knowledge, share in the divine omnipresence and — at will — express the divine omniscience and prepare himself to manifest in full consciousness the divine omnipotence.

I am using words which are futile to convey the underlying meaning of the Word. Understanding can only be arrived at when a man *lives the Word,* hearing its soundless Sound and breathing it forth in a vital life-giving breath to others.

The masses are hearing the sound of the A.U.M. and, in their higher brackets, are finding that A.U.M. the expression of something from which they seek release. The aspirants and disciples of the World are hearing the O.M. and in their personal lives the A.U.M. and the O.M. are in conflict. This may represent a new idea to you, but it conveys an idea of an eternal fact. It may help you to gain an understanding of this phase if I point out for you that for this first group the O.M. can be portrayed in the following symbol as expressing the material $M$ nature whereas the second group can be portrayed by the symbol $m$ expressive of the soul enveloped in matter. You will see, therefore, how the teaching leads man progressively onward and how the occult science brings man in touch with great mental reversals and divine paradoxes. For aeons the Word of the soul and the Sound of spiritual reality are lost. Today, the Word of the soul is being found again, and with that finding the little self is lost in the glory and the radiance of the divine Self.

This discovery is consummated at the time of the third initiation. The initiate and the Master, along with those of higher rank who are approaching identification with Shamballa, are steadily and ever more clearly hearing the Sound emanating from the Central Spiritual Sun and penetrating all forms of divine life upon our planet—via our Planetary Logos Who hears it with clarity and with understanding — the Sound of the lowest syllable of the Ineffable Name of the One in Whom all the Planetary Logoi live and move and have Their Being, for They are centres in the LIFE which is expressing itself through the medium of a solar system.

You can see how little use there is in my enlarging further upon this. Its sole usefulness is to give an expanding impulse to the consciousness of the disciple and to stir his imagination (the seed of the intuition), so that even whilst occupied in expressing the $M$ and then the $m,$ he will be reaching out after the Sound.

Earlier I pointed out that the sound of the A.U.M., the sound of the O.M. and the SOUND itself are all related to vibration and to its differing and varied effects. The secret of the Law of Vibration is progressively revealed as people learn to sound forth the Word in its three aspects. Students would also do well to ponder on the distinction between the breath and the Sound, between the process of breathing and of creating directed vibratory activity. The one is related to Time and the other to Space and they are distinct from each other; and (as the *Old Commentary* puts it) "the Sound, the final and yet initiating Sound, concerns that which is neither Time nor Space; it lies outside the manifested ALL, the Source of all that is and yet is naught." (No *thing*. A.A.B.)

There are, therefore, great points of tension from which the Sacred Word, in its major aspects, goes forth. Let me list them for you:

1. The creative point of tension — a tension achieved by a planetary Logos when He responds to the Sound of the Ineffable Name and breathes it forth in His turn in three great Sounds which make one Sound on His Own plane of expression, thus creating the manifested world, the impulse towards the unfoldment of consciousness, and the influence of life itself. This is the Sound.

2. Seven points of tension on the downward or involutionary arc; these produce the seven planets, the seven states of consciousness, and the expression of the seven ray impulses. This constitutes the sevenfold A.U.M. of which the Ageless Wisdom takes note. It is related to the effect of spirit or life upon substance, thus originating form and creating the prison of the divine life.

3. The A.U.M. itself or the Word made flesh; this creates finally a point of tension in the fourth kingdom in nature, at which point the evolutionary cycle becomes possible and the first dim note of the O.M. can be faintly heard. In the individual man this point is reached when the personality is an integrated and functioning whole and the soul is beginning to control it. It is an accumulative tension arrived at through many lives. This process is expressed in the Masters' Archives as follows:

You must remember that these symbols are an attempt on my part to translate ancient signatures in modern occidental type. The only one which is the same in all languages is, esoterically, the A.U.M.

4. Then comes a point of tension from which the man eventually achieves liberation from the three worlds and stands as a free soul; he is then a point within the circle — the point indicating the point of tension from which he now works, and the circle the sphere of his self-initiated activity.

I need not carry the story further; from tension to tension the initiate passes just as do all human beings, aspirants, disciples and the lower grades of initiates; from one expansion of consciousness to another they go until the third initiation is undergone and points of tension (qualified by intention and purpose) supersede all previous efforts and the will aspect begins to control.

Here, briefly, is a fresh slant upon the familiar theme of the Word — a theme preserved in some form by all the world religions but a theme which, like all else, has been so materialised that it is the task of the Hierarchy to restore the knowledge of its meaning, of its threefold application and its involutionary and evolutionary significances. Students would do well to remember that its sounding forth vocally upon the physical plane means little. The important factors are to sound it silently, inaudibly and within the head; then, having done so, to hear it reverberate there and to recognise that this self-initiated Sound — breathed forth from a point of tension—is a part of the original SOUND as it takes form as a Word. When a man perfectly expresses the A.U.M., he can then sound the O.M. with effectiveness from progressive points of tension, until the third initiation. Then the effect of the O.M. is such that the personality as a separate identity disappears, the soul emerges in all its glory, and the first faint sound of the originating SOUND breaks upon the ear of the transfigured initiate. This is the Voice referred to in the Biblical account of the Transfiguration. This Voice says, "This is my beloved Son." The initiate registers the fact that he has been accepted by Shamballa and has made his first contact with the Planetary Logos, the Hierophant, the Initiator at the third initiation, just as the Christ, the Master of all the Masters, is the Initiator and the Hierophant at the first two initiations.

The Word, however, with which we are now dealing is not the Sacred Word itself, but a signal or sound of acceptance. It is translated in this Rule by the phrase: Accepted as a group. This refers to aggregates and blended combinations through which the Soul in relation to personalities, the Monad in relation to the Spiritual Triad, the Master in relation to His Ashram, and Shamballa in relation to the Hierarchy, can work, expressing *plan* in the initial stages of contact, and *purpose* in the final stages. Bear in mind that the analogy holds true all the way through. A personality is an aggregate of forms and of substantial lives which, when fused and blended, present a unified sumtotal, animated by desire or aspiration, by plan or purpose, and functioning in its place under the inspiration of a self-initiated inner programme. Progress, from the larger angle and from the standpoint of Those Who see life in terms of ever enlarging Wholes, is from group to group.

This pronouncement, issuing from a point of tension, is the Word of the soul as it integrates with the threefold personality when that personality is consciously ready for such a fusion. The hold of the soul upon its instruments of expression, the network of the seven centres and the subsidiary centres, becomes intensified and energy pours in, forcing the acquiescent personality fully to express the ray type of the soul, and therefore subordinating the ray of the personality (and its three subsidiary rays) to the dominating soul energy. This first great integration is *a fusion of force with energy.* Here is a statement of deep import, embodying one of the first lessons an initiate has to master. It is one which can only be properly comprehended through life experience, subject to interpretation in the world of meaning. Some understanding of what this implies will come as the disciple masters the distinction between soul activity and the action of matter, between emotion and love, between the intelligent will and the mind, between plan and purpose. In so doing he acquires the capacity to find his point of tension at any given moment, and this growing capacity eventually brings him consciously to recognise group after group as units with which identification must be sought.

He finds his soul through the fusion of soul and personality; he finds his group through the absorption of this fusing soul-form with a Master's group, and finally he is absorbed into the Master's Ashram; there he, in concert with his group brothers in that Ashram, is fused and blended with the Hierarchy and hears the extension of the Word, spoken originally by his soul: Accepted as a group. Later, much later, he participates at that august recognition which comes when the Voice issues forth — as annually it does — from the centre at Shamballa and the seal is set on the acceptance of the Hierarchy, with all its new associates, by the Lord of the World. This acceptance involves those initiates of the third degree who have been integrated more closely into the hierarchical life than ever before. This is the signal to them (and to their Seniors Who have heard it year after year) that they are part of the instrument whose purpose is to fulfill the plan. Thus the great syntheses are slowly taking place. It has taken many aeons, for evolution (especially in the earlier stages) moves slowly.

In the post-war period and when the new structure of the coming world order is taking shape, the process will be speeded considerably; this will not, however, be for a hundred years, which is but a brief moment in the eternal history of humanity. From synthesis to synthesis the life of God passes. First the synthesis of the atomic lives into ever more perfect forms until the three kingdoms of nature appear; then the synthesis in consciousness, enabling the human being to enter into the larger awareness of the Whole and finally to enter into that mysterious event which is the result of the effect of all preceding developments and to which we give the name of Identification. From the first identification, which is the higher correspondence of the stage of individualisation, progressive absorption into ever larger wholes takes place, and each time the Word goes forth: Accepted as a group.

Have I succeeded in giving you a somewhat wider vision of the significance of initiation in these brief exposi-

tions? Do you see more clearly the growing beauty of the
Whole and the goodness of the Purpose and the wisdom of
the Plan? Do you realise more deeply that beauty, goodness
and wisdom are not qualities, as their inadequate nomenclature would imply, but are great facts in manifestation? Do
you grasp the truth that they are not descriptive of Deity
but are the names of Lives of a potency and activity of
which men can as yet know nothing?

Some understanding of this must slowly seep into the
mind and consciousness of each disciple as that mind becomes
irradiated by soul light in the earlier stages, and later responds to the impact of energy coming from the Spiritual
Triad. Only when this is visioned, even if not understood,
will the realisation come to the struggling disciple that the
words:

2. *Withdraw not now your application. You could not if you
would; but add to it three great demands and forward move*

are a living command conditioning him whether he will or
not. The inability to withdraw from the position taken is
one of the first true results of hearing the Word spoken after
passing the two tests. There is an inevitability in living the
life of the Spirit which is at once its horror and its joy. I
mean just that. The symbol or first expression of this (for
all in the three worlds is but the symbol of an inner reality)
is the driving urge to betterment which is the outstanding
characteristic of the human animal. From discontent to discontent he passes, driven by an inner something which constantly reveals to him an enticing vision of that which is
more desirable than his present state and experience. At
first this is interpreted by him in terms of material welfare;
then this divine discontent drives him into a phase of the
struggle which is emotional in nature; he craves emotional
satisfaction and later intellectual pursuits. All the time this
struggle to attain something ever on ahead creates the instruments of attainment, gradually perfecting them until the
threefold personality is ready for a vision of the soul. From
that point of tension the urge and the struggle become more

acute, until Rule One for Applicants is understood by him and he steps upon the Path.

Once he is an accepted disciple and has definitely undertaken the work in preparation for initiation, there is for him no turning back. He could not if he would, and the Ashram protects him.

In this Rule for accepted disciples and initiates we are faced with a similar condition on a higher turn of the spiral, but with this difference (one which you can hardly grasp unless at the point where the Word goes forth to you): that the initiate stands alone in "isolated unity," aware of his mysterious oneness with all that is. The urge which distinguished his progress in arriving at personality-soul fusion is transmuted into fixity of intention, ability to move forward into the clear cold light of the undimmed reason, free from all glamour and illusion and having now the power to voice the three demands. This he can now do consciously and by the use of the dynamic will instead of making "application in triple form" as was the case before. This distinction is vital and significant of tremendous growth and development.

The initiate has heard the Word which came forth to him when he was irrevocably committed to hierarchical purpose. He has heard the Voice from Shamballa just as he earlier heard the Voice of the Silence and the voice of his Master. Occult obedience gives place to enlightened will. He can now be trusted to walk and work alone because he is unalterably one with his group, with the Hierarchy, and finally with Shamballa.

The key to this whole Rule lies in the injunction to the initiate that he add to his application three demands, and only after they have been voiced and correctly expressed and motivated by the dynamic will, does the further injunction come that he move forward. What are these three demands, and by what right does the initiate make them? Hitherto the note of his expanding consciousness has been vision, effort, attainment and again vision. He has therefore been occupied with becoming aware of the field — an ever-increasing and expanding area — of the divine revelation. In terms of practical occultism, he is recognising an ever widening sphere wherein he can serve with purpose and forward the Plan, once he has succeeded in identifying himself with that revelation. Until this revelation is an integral part of his life it is not possible for the initiate to comprehend the significance of these simple words. Identification is realisation, plus esoteric experience, plus again an absorption into the Whole, and for all of this (as I have earlier pointed out) we have no terminology. Now a master of that which has been seen and appropriated, and being conscious of and sensing that which lies ahead, the disciple "stands on his occult rights and makes his clear demands."

What these demands are can be ascertained by remembering that all that the initiate undergoes and all that he enacts is the higher and esoteric correspondence of the triple manifestation of spirit-energy which distinguished the first and earliest phase of his unfoldment. That is the personality. I would like to call attention to the word "unfoldment," for it is perhaps the most explicit and correct word to use anent the evolutionary process. There is no better in your language. The initiate has ever been. The divine Son of God has ever known himself for what he is. An initiate is not the result of the evolutionary process. He is the cause of the evolutionary process, and by means of it he perfects his vehicles of expression until he becomes initiate in the three worlds of consciousness and the three worlds of identification.

According to ray type this unfoldment proceeds, and each triple stage of the lower unfoldment makes possible later (in time and space) the higher unfoldment in the world of the Spiritual Triad. What I am doing in these instructions is to indicate the relation between the threefold personality and the Spiritual Triad, linked and brought together by the antahkarana. Each of these three lower aspects has its own note and it is these notes which produce the sounding forth of the three demands which evoke response from the Spiritual Triad and thus reach the Monad in its high place of waiting in Shamballa.

In 1922, in my book *Letters on Occult Meditation* I laid the foundation in my first chapter for the more advanced teaching which I am now giving. There I was dealing with the alignment of the ego with the personality, and this was the first time that the entire theme of alignment was brought definitely into focus, for alignment is the first step towards fusion, and later towards the mysteries of identification. Let me quote:

> "As time progresses, and later with the aid of the Master, harmony of colour and tone is produced (a synonymous matter) until eventually you will have the basic note of matter, the major third of the aligned personality, the dominant fifth of the ego, followed by the full chord of the Monad or Spirit. It is the dominant we seek at adeptship, and earlier the perfected third of the personality. During our various incarnations we strike and ring the changes on all the intervening notes, and sometimes our lives are major and sometimes minor, but always they tend to flexibility and greater beauty. In due time each note fits into its chord, the chord of the Spirit; each chord forms part of a phrase, the phrase or group to which the chord belongs; and the phrase goes to the completion of one seventh of the whole. The entire seven sections, then, complete the sonata of this solar system — a part of the threefold master-piece of the Logos or God, the Master-Musician." (Page 4).

We now arrive at a point which it is difficult for disciples to grasp. The initiate or disciple has reached a point in his evolution in which triplicity gives place to duality, prior to the attainment of complete unity. Only two factors are of concern to him as he "stands at the midway point," and these are Spirit and Matter. Their complete identification within his consciousness becomes his major goal, but only in reference to the whole creative process and not now in reference to the separated self. It is this thought which motivates the service of the initiate, and it is this concept of wholeness gradually creeping into the world consciousness which is indicating that humanity is on the verge of initiation. Therefore, it is the material aspect, "the perfected third of the Personality," which makes possible the activity of the initiate as he sounds out his three demands. The "dominant fifth of the ego" makes itself heard at the third initiation, marking the attainment of at-one-ment, and this fades out at the fourth initiation. At that time the egoic vehicle, the causal body, disappears. Then only two divine aspects remain; the perfected, radiant, organised and active substance through which the initiate can work in full control, the matter aspect, and the dynamic life principle, the spirit aspect, with which that "substantial divine Reality" still awaits identification. It is this thought which underlies the initiate's three demands which (according to the Rule earlier given to aspirants and disciples) must sound forth "across the desert, over all the seas and through the fires."

It is not possible for me explicitly to give an understanding of the nature of these demands. I can only give you certain symbolic phrases which, intuitively interpreted, will give you a clue.

The first demand is made possible because "the desert life is passed; it flourished and it flowered, and then the drought arrived and man removed himself. That which had nourished and contained his life became an arid waste and naught was left but bones and dust and a deep thirst which naught in sight could satisfy." Yet to the initiate consciousness it remains clear that the desert land must be made anew to flourish like a rose and that his task is the restoration (by the distribution of the waters of life) of its pristine beauty, and not the beauty of its false flowering. He demands, therefore, upon the note of the lower aspect of the personality (I am talking in symbols), that this flowering forth should take place according to the Plan. This involves upon his part a vision of that plan, identification with the underlying purpose, and the ability — through the medium of the higher mind, which is the lowest aspect of the Spiritual Triad — to work in the world of ideas and to create those forms of thought which will aid in the materialising of the

Plan in conformity with the Purpose. This is the creative work of thoughtform building and that is why, we are told, that the first great demand "sounds forth within the world of God's ideas and towards the desert, a long time left behind. Upon that great demand the initiate who has pledged himself to serve the world returns into that desert, bringing with him the seed and water for which the desert cries."

The second demand is related to the earlier cry of the disciple, which was sounded forth "over the seas." It refers to the world of glamour in which humanity struggles, and to the emotional world in which mankind is sunk as if drowning in the ocean. We are told in the Bible, and the thought is based on information to be found in the Archives of the Masters, that "there shall be no more sea"; I told you that a time comes when the initiate knows that the astral plane no longer exists. For ever it has vanished and has gone. But when the initiate has freed himself from the realm of delusion, of fog, of mist and of glamour, and stands in the "clear cold light" of the buddhic or intuitional plane (the second or middle aspect of the Spiritual Triad), he arrives at a great and basic realisation. He *knows* that he must return (if such a foolish word can suffice) to the "seas" which he has left behind, and there dissipate the glamour. But he works now from "the air above and in the full light of day." No longer does he struggle in the waves or sink immersed in the deep waters. Above the sea he hovers within the ocean of light, and pours that light into the depths. He carries thus the waters to the desert and the light divine into the world of fog.

Yet he never leaves the place of identification, and all that he now does is carried forward from the levels attained at any particular initiation. All that he does "upon the desert, and over the seas" is undertaken through the power of thought, which directs the needed energy and certain destined and chosen forces so that the Plan (let me repeat myself) may go forward according to divine purpose through the power of the dynamic spiritual will. When you can appreciate that the initiate of high degree works with monadic energy and not soul force, you can understand why he finds it necessary ever to work behind the scenes. He works with the soul aspect and through the power of monadic energy, using the antahkarana as a distributing agency. The disciples and initiates of the first two degrees work with soul force and through the medium of the centres. The personality works with forces.

The third great demand has in it a different implication, and sounds forth, we are told, "through the fires." In this solar system there is no evading the fire. It is found at all levels of divine expression as we well know from our study of the three fires — fire by friction, solar fire and electric fire, with their differentiations, the forty-nine fires — of the seven planes. Always, therefore, whether it is the cry of the disciple or the demand of the initiate, the sound goes forth "through the fire, to the fire, and from the fire." Of this technique, underlying the potent demand, there is little that I may say. From the highest plane of the spiritual will, what is technically called "the atmic plane," the demand goes forth and the result of that demand will work out on mental levels, just as the earlier two demands worked out on the physical and astral levels. I would interject here that even though there is no astral plane, from the standpoint of the Master, yet thousands of millions recognise it and labour in its delusive sphere and are there aided by the initiated disciple working from the higher corresponding levels. This is true of all the planetary work, whether accomplished by initiates and Masters, working directly in the three worlds, or from higher levels, as work the Nirmanakayas (the creative Contemplatives of the planet), or from Shamballa from the Council Chamber of the Lord of the World. All the efforts of the Hierarchy or of the "conditioning Lives" (as They are sometimes called) of Shamballa are dedicated to the furthering of the evolutionary plan which will finally embody divine purpose. I keep emphasising this distinction between plan and purpose with deliberation, because it indicates the next phase of the working of the intelligent will in the consciousness of humanity.

More anent these three demands I may not imply. I have told you much, had you the awakened intuition to read the significance of some of my comments. These demands refer not only to the evolution of humanity, but to all forms of life within the consciousness of the planetary Logos. The directing mind of the initiate indicates within the three worlds the goal of attainment.

*3.  Let there be no recollection and yet let memory rule.*

This is not a contradictory statement. Perhaps I can convey to you the right idea as follows: The initiate wastes no time in looking backward towards the lessons learned; he works from the angle of developed habit, instinctively doing the right and needed thing. Instinctual response to environing forms builds, as we well know, patterns of behaviour, of conduct and of reaction. This establishes what might be called unconscious memory, and this memory rules without any effort at recollection.

The *habit* of goodness, or right reaction and of instinctual understanding is distinctive of the trained initiate. He has no need to remember rules, theories, planes or activities. These are as much an established part of his nature as the instinct of self-preservation is an instinctive part of the equipment of a normal human being. Think this out and endeavour to build up the right spiritual habits. In this way the Master wastes no time on soul or personal plans. He has the habit — based on divine instinctual memory — of right activity, right understanding and right purpose. He needs not to recollect.

*4.  Work from the point of all that is within the content of the group's united life.*

This is not, as might appear, the effort to do the work for humanity as it is planned or desired by the group with which the initiate finds himself associated. The mode of working covers an earlier phase and one in which the accepted disciple learns much. First, he finds a group upon the physical plane whose ideals and plans for service conform to his idea of correct activity, and with this group he affiliates himself, works, learns, and in learning, suffers much. Later he finds his way into a Master's Ashram, where his effort is increasingly to learn to use the will in carrying out the Plan and to accommodate himself to the group methods and plans, working under the law of occult obedience for the welfare of humanity.

The initiate, however, works in neither of these ways, though he has acquired the *habit* of right contact with organisations in the three worlds and right cooperation with the Hierarchy. He works now under the inspiration of and identification with the life aspect — the united life aspect of his ray group and of all groups. This means that the significance of the involutionary life and the evolutionary life is fully understood by him. His service is invoked by the group or groups needing his help. His response is an occult evocation given in unison with the group of servers with which he is affiliated on the inner side. This is a very different thing to the mode of service generally understood.

## RULE THREE

The next Rule continues the above theme and gives some instructions in terse phrases and symbols on the Science of Invocation and Evocation and its significant ritual or programme.

This programme is, in reality, an expression or a human formulation of the Science of Sound, just in so far — as yet — as Sound affects humanity and human affairs. Forget not my earlier teaching upon the Word; remember also that the Sound is the sound or note of Life Itself, embodying its dynamic impulse, its creative power, and its responsive sensitivity to all contacts.

Rule III.
   *Dual the moving forward. The Door is left behind. That*
   *is a happening of the past. Let the cry of invocation*

*issue forth from the deep centre of the group's clear cold light. Let it evoke response from the bright centre, lying far ahead. When the demand and the response are lost in one great Sound, move outward from the desert, leave the seas behind, and know that God is Fire.*

This is perhaps one of the two most occult rules which the initiate has to master, whether as an individual or in conjunction with his group. The group recognises and works under the pervasive influence of the purpose; the individual initiate works with the plan. The group expression, as far as in it lies at any given moment in time and space, is in line with the will of the One in Whom we live and move and have our being, the Life of all that is. The individual initiate uses the attractive force (to which we give the oft misleading name of love) of that fundamental Life to gather together that which will give body to form and so manifest the will. The group can be, and frequently is, responsive to the "bright centre," Shamballa, where the initiate by himself and in his own essential identity cannot so respond. The individual must be protected by the group from the terrific potencies which emanate from Shamballa. These must be stepped down for him by the process of distribution, so that their impact is not focussed in any one or all of his centres but is shared by all the group members. Here is the clue to the significance of group work. One of its major functions, esoterically speaking, is to absorb, share, circulate, and then distribute energy.

This process of protection and of distribution is one of the functions of the great meeting of all the Hierarchy, under the aegis of the three Great Lords (the Manu, the Mahachohan and the Christ) in that high and sacred valley in the Himalayas where annually — after due preparation — the Hierarchy makes contact with Shamballa and a relationship is then set up between the "bright and living centre" and the "radiating and magnetic centre," in order that the "acquiescent waiting centre" may be stimulated to move forward upon the ladder of evolution. Even the Hierarchy

itself needs the protection of its full membership in order
rightly to absorb the incoming energies, and later wisely
to distribute the forces of the divine will in the three worlds
where lies Their major responsibility. The focussed will of
God, in its immediate implications and application, constitutes the point of tension from which Shamballa works in
order to bring about the eventual fruition of the divine
Purpose.

There is a definite distinction between Purpose and
Will; it is subtle indeed, but quite definite to the advanced
initiate, and therefore the dualistic nature of our planetary
manifestation and our solar Expression appear even in this.
The Members of the Council at Shamballa recognise this
distinction and therefore divide Themselves into two groups
which are called in the ancient parlance, Registrants of the
Purpose and Custodians of the Will. Will is active. Purpose
is passive, waiting for the results of the activity of the will.
These two groups are reflected in hierarchical circles by the
Nirmanakayas or the Planetary Contemplatives, and the Custodians of the Plan. The function of the Registrants of the
Purpose is to keep the channel open between our Earth, the
planet Venus and the Central Spiritual Sun. The function
of the Custodians of the Will is to relate the Council, the
Hierarchy and Humanity, thus creating a basic triangle of
force between the three major centres of the planetary Life.
This is the higher expression (symbolic, if you like) of the
six-pointed star, formed of two interlaced triangles. A rep-
lica of this fundamental triangle and of this symbol of
energy, with its inflow and distribution, is to be found in the
relation of the three higher centres in the human being —
head, heart and throat — to the three lower centres — solar
plexus, sacral centre and the centre at the base of the spine.
The Science of Invocation and Evocation is also seen to be
symbolically proceeding along evolutionary lines. Worship,
the attitude of the mystic, must give place to Invocation in
the man who knows he is divine. This symbolic revelation
is to be seen in the lifting up of the three lower energies and
their evocative response to the three higher, thus producing

an eventual unity at the point of tension. I realise that this is a hard thing to comprehend because it embodies truths which are difficult for the disciple to grasp. But they will be grasped and mastered by each one as he proceeds along the Path of Discipleship and submits to the needed training for initiation. They will also be mastered, later in this century and in the next, by the rapidly developing humanity, thus demonstrating that the initiation of the moment becomes the past achievement of the masses eventually. This enhanced liberation will later appear as a definite result of the war. The Atlantic Charter and the Four Freedoms, formulated in the tension produced by the world agony and strain, are the reflections of this, and embody all that it is possible for average materially-minded man to grasp of the present will of Shamballa as it conditions the plans of the Hierarchy and is impulsed by the Registrants of the Purpose. This is as far as the two groups of Custodians have been able to convey this revelation to the best human intellects — the first group dealing with the senior members of the Hierarchy and the latter with those initiates and disciples who are closely related to humanity.

Here again we come up against the fact that the Science of Invocation and Evocation, with which this Rule fundamentally deals, is primarily a great and scientific activity of which modern humanity knows practically nothing, but which is related to thought power and to thoughtform building. Only initiates of the highest degree — such as the three Great Lords — have the right to invoke alone and unaccompanied by any protective agency, such as a group, and the reason for that is that They Themselves are members of the Council at Shamballa and are individually Registrants of the Purpose. The annual appearance of the Lord Buddha is the outer demonstration or symbol of the emergence of this Science of Invocation and Evocation in the waking consciousness of humanity. Prayer is the dim, faint and inadequate expression of this; affirmation of divinity in order to gain material well-being is a distortion of this truth. This needs to be remembered. The true significance of this emerging science is that, in the early or first stages, it embodies the seed concept of the new world religion.

In the great invocations which I have given out, the first one* ("Let the Forces of Light bring illumination to mankind . . .") was an effort on my part to put into words the invocative cry of mankind and of all men and women of goodwill throughout the world. Its success was indicative of the strength of that goodwill. The second* ("Let the Lords of Liberation issue forth . . .") can, in reality, only be used with any measure or hope of success by aspirants, disciples and initiates, and hence was not nearly so popular with the general public, though in reality much more powerful and potentially effective. It was essential, however, that a fusion of the two groups should take place before the invocative cry of humanity as a whole could be powerful and effective in evoking response.

Prior to taking up the study, phrase by phrase, of Rule III, I would call your attention to the relation between this Rule and the earlier one given to applicants. The applicant sends out his cry — across the desert, over all the seas and through the fires. His entire personality, integrated and oriented, is focussed at a point of tension; then he utters his cry (symbolic of a voiceless expression) and this cry beats against the door which separates him from the soul, in the first instance, and from the Hierarchy, in the second. The door is only a symbol of separation; it divides one place from another location, one sphere of activity from another, and one state of consciousness from another. It fosters in the aspirant a sense of duality. It is a word descriptive of the mystic attitude. This attitude embraces the concepts of here and there, of soul and body, of God and man, of Hierarchy and humanity. But Rule III, as voiced for initiates, demonstrates that this mystical realisation finally goes; the sense of separation disappears, and the door is left behind.

*1. Dual the moving forward. The Door is left behind. That is a happening of the past.*

---

The first point which should be noted is that we have here the definition of an initiate. He is one who, in his two-fold nature (soul and personality), moves forward. No longer is his point of tension that of the personality. He has fused and blended two divine aspects in himself, and they now constitute one integrated unit. This fusion produces its own point of tension. He has moved forward through the door. A point of tension again ensues in which a Word goes forth in response to the invocative cry of the new initiate. A Word is returned to him: Accepted as a group. Then he, with the group of which he is now a recognised part, moves forward. For the initiate (as I have earlier pointed out) the past is left behind: "Let there be no recollection"; the present embodies a point of tension; the future indicates a moving forward from that point of tension as a result of its effective action. The door closes behind the initiate, who is now an accepted member of his group, and as the *Old Commentary* puts it, "its sound in closing informs the watching world that the initiate has passed into a secret place and that to reach him in the real sense they too must pass that door." This conveys the thought of individual self-initiation, to which all must be subjected, and indicates also the loneliness of the initiate as he moves forward. He does not yet understand all that his group as a whole grasps; he is himself not understood by those on the other side of the door. He has sensed for some time the group with which he is now affiliated, and is becoming increasingly aware of their spiritual impersonality, which seems to him to be almost a form of aloofness and which in no way feeds in him those elements which are of a personality nature; he therefore suffers. Those left behind as a part of his old life in no way comprehend his basic (even if undeveloped) impersonality. This attitude of theirs evokes in him, when sensed, a resentment and a criticism which he realises is not right but which at this stage he seems unable to avoid, whilst those he criticises endeavour to tear him down or (at the least) to make him feel despised and uncomfortable.

In the early stages he takes refuge from those left

behind by withdrawing himself and by much unnecessary and almost obtrusive silence. He learns to penetrate into the consciousness of his new group by strenuously endeavouring to develop their capacity for spiritual impersonality. He knows it is something which he must achieve and — as he achieves it — he discovers that this impersonality is not based on indifference or upon preoccupation, as he had thought, but upon a deep understanding, upon a dynamic focus on world service, upon a sense of proportion and upon a detachment which makes true help possible. Thus the door and the past are left behind. St. Paul attempted to express this idea when he said: "Forgetting the things which are behind, press forward towards the prize of your high calling in Christ." I would ask your attention to the word "calling."

*2. Let the cry of invocation issue forth from the deep centre of the group's clear cold light.*

We are not here dealing with the light in the head or with soul light as it is perceived by the attuned and aligned personality. That too is left behind, and the initiate is aware of the light of the Ashram and the all-including light of the Hierarchy. These are two aspects of soul light which the individual light in the head has revealed. That soul light which the initiate has been aware of from the first moment of soul contact, and at rapidly decreasing intervals, is created by the fusion of the light of the soul with the light of substance itself, and is the inevitable and automatic consequence of the purification of the three vehicles and of creative meditation. We are told in the world Scriptures that "in that light shall we see Light"; and it is to this other Light that I now refer — a light which is only to be perceived when the door is shut behind the initiate. That light is itself composed of the light of buddhi and the light of atma, and these are (to interpret these Sanskrit terms esoterically) the light of the pure reason, which is the sublimation of the intellect, and the light of the spiritual will, which is the revelation of the unfolding purpose. The first is focussed in the Ashram, and the second in the Hierarchy as a whole, and both of them are the expression of the activity of the Spiritual Triad.

Let me make myself clearly understood, if possible. You have, therefore, three great lights, all of them focussed upon the mental plane, for beyond that plane the symbolism of light is not used; divinity is known as life, where the Monad and its expression, the Spiritual Triad, are concerned. All the lights are finally focussed upon the mental plane:

1. The blended light of soul and personality.
2. The light of the egoic group which, when forming a recognised group in the consciousness of the illumined initiate, is called an Ashram, embodying the light of buddhi or pure reason.
3. The light of the Hierarchy as a centre of radiance in the planetary body and embodying the light which understanding of the plan and cooperation with that plan produce, and which comes from identification — upon mental levels — with the spiritual will.

All these three aspects of light can be described as:

1. The light which is thrown upward. This is the lesser light, from the angle of the Monad.
2. The light which the Spiritual Triad reflects upon the mental plane.
3. The focussed light which is produced by the meeting of the two lights, the higher and the lower.

These are the higher correspondence of the blazing forth of the light in the head, when the light of the personality and the light of the soul make contact.

Beyond the mental plane, the initiatory impulse or emphasis is upon the life aspect, upon dynamic energy, and upon the cause of manifestation, and this incentive to progress is not based on revelation, which is ever incident to or related to the significance of light. Light and revelation are cause and effect. The coming revelation for which all men wait, and which will come when world adjustment has reached an already determined point, is concerned with the impartation to the human consciousness of the meaning and purpose of life; this will take place in a gradually unfolding series of spiritual events. I cannot and must not put these truths more clearly, even if the necessary words were available to express what is not as yet even dimly sensed by disciples of the first and second degrees of initiation. What will come through that series of spiritual happenings and their inevitable reaction upon the whole body of humanity is in no way related to consciousness, to revelation or to light. There will come to humanity at some moment still a long way ahead a period of realisation, constituting both a point of crisis and a point of tension. That realisation will summarise, in effective conditioning consciousness, all that the quality of sensitivity has conveyed to mankind throughout the ages. It is the consummation of the activity of the Christ-consciousness, and is the state referred to when it is said of the Christ: "He shall see of the travail of his soul and be satisfied." At the crisis of that revelation, at its highest point of tension, humanity as with one voice will say: "Behold! All things are become new." This is the apotheosis of vision and the prelude to an unfoldment in the general massed human consciousness (from that point in time slowly brought about) of certain powers and capacities of which the race is today totally unaware. The immediate revelation ahead will be only the first step towards this distant related point, and its significance will not be apparent to the present generation, or even to the next; it will, however, be steadily though gradually appreciated as the new world religion with its emphasis upon the invocation of energies and the evocation of "life more abundantly" is developed and has its inevitable effect. Students would do well to bear in mind that the impact of energies upon forms produces results which are dependent upon the quality of the forms receiving the impression. This is a statement of occult law.

One of the purposes lying behind the present holocaust (World War II) has been the necessity for the destruction of inadequate forms. This destruction could have been brought about by an act of God, such as a great natural catastrophe or a universal epidemic, and such had been the original intention. Humanity was, however, swept by forces that carried in themselves the seeds of destruction, and there was that in humanity which responded to those forces. Therefore the Law of destruction was permitted to work through humanity itself, and men are now destroying the forms through which many masses of men are functioning. This is both a good and a bad thing, viewed from the evolutionary angle. It is nevertheless a fact which cannot be gainsaid, and the problem, therefore, confronting the Custodians of the Will, working through the Custodians of the Plan, is to bring good out of the evil which man has wrought, and thus gear events to the larger issues.

That is one of the objectives before the Hierarchy at this time (written April, 1943) as it prepares for participation in the May and June Full Moons. Can the forces be so organised and the energies so distributed that the full measure of good may be evoked from humanity by the invocation sounded forth by Shamballa? Can this evocation of a new cycle of spiritual contact and of liberation be brought about by the invocation of the men and women of goodwill? Can the will-to-good of the spiritual Forces and the goodwill of humanity be brought together and produce those conditions in which the new world order may function? These are the important questions which the Hierarchy is attempting to solve.

It must be remembered that the Science of Invocation and Evocation is a reciprocal effort. Humanity could not be invocative were it not that the Spiritual Hierarchy (and by that term I include both Shamballa and the planetary Hierarchy) is evoking the spirit of man. The invocative cry of humanity is evoked by the invocation or Sound of the spiritual hierarchies. Man's responsibility, however, is to invoke at this time the Lords of Liberation and the Spirit of Peace. These are the Beings which have the power to raise humanity, once the race of men has assumed the right attitude. They correspond to the group, in the third degree of Masonry, who raise the Master. Their response to the cry of mankind is largely, but not wholly, dependent upon the quality of that cry.

I wonder if I could make the problem of invocation clearer to you if I were to suggest that the words, "issue forth from the deep centre of the group's clear cold light," have a meaning both for the individual initiate and for all groups of disciples and all Ashrams? The use of the words, "clear cold light," is deeply symbolical. The clarity of that light indicates the function of the soul, as its great light enables the initiate to see light. The coldness of that light refers to the light of substance, which cannot be warmed into a glow by desire or by the heat of passion, but is now and at last only responsive to the light of the soul. It is therefore cold to all that limits and hinders, and this state of personality consciousness has to be realised at the very centre of man's being; there the clear light of the soul and the cold light of the personality are united in the deepest conscious point of the disciple's nature, at the extreme point of withdrawal (for which all concentration exercises and meditation processes have been a scientific preparation). Then, through the produced tension, the invocative cry can go forth with power and effectiveness. The same is true of the disciple's group or of any group of true and selfless aspirants. There can come a moment in the life of the group when the blended cold light of the contributing personalities and the clear light of their souls can so function that united invocative cry will evoke a response. That cry will ever be concerned with the selfless service of the group — a service which, under the Plan, they are seeking to render to humanity.

As we continue our study of Rule III, I am myself struck with the appositeness of its words in connection with this particular historical cycle and in relation to the truths which are slowly taking form in the consciousness of humanity. New truths (and by that I mean truths which are new to the most advanced thinkers and which are only dimly sensed by the most advanced esotericist) are hovering on the horizon of the human mind. The ground is being prepared for the sowing of this new seed and the stage set for the emergence of new Actors in the great drama of the unfolding revelation of Deity.

Certain great concepts are firmly grasped by man. Certain great hopes are taking form and will become the pattern of man's living. Certain great speculations will become experimental theories and later prove demonstrated facts. Behind all this, two things are happening: Men are being stimulated and brought to that point of necessary tension which (as a result of a crisis) must precede a great moving forward upon the Path of Evolution. Secondly, a process of reorientation is going on which will eventually enable the mass of men to present a united front upon views hitherto regarded as the vague visions of intelligent and optimistic dreamers. A great stirring and moving is going on. The world of men is seething in response to the inflow of spiritual energy. This energy has been evoked by the unrealised and inaudible cry of humanity itself. Humanity has become — for the first time in its history — spiritually invocative.

Let us now consider briefly the nature of that which is being evoked, and thus gain an insight into the interrelation which exists between the three great planetary centres: The human centre, the hierarchical centre, and Shamballa. Each of these is evocative to the one functioning at a slower or lesser speed (if I might use such inappropriate terms) and invocative to the one above it — again using a form of words which is misleading in the extreme; there is no higher or lower and no greater or lesser in our universe of reality. There is only the interpenetration of substances which are all basically expressions of matter, and their vitalisation and organisation into forms of expression of the unknown Real. This essential Reality, we call spirit or life.

As a result of the interplay of these two, humanity eventually appears in time and space. Humanity is the result of all sub-human forms of expression and experience and of the activity of superhuman Beings. These superhuman Beings are the product of past evolutionary systems and are in Themselves the sum total of the great Divine Sacrifice as it focusses itself in our planetary life. Having passed through all previous phases of existence and perfected the consciousness aspect in Themselves through human experiences, They have transcended all that man can know and all states of consciousness with which he is or may be in the future familiar, and are now expressing a phase of divinity of which he can know naught. They LIVE. They are energy itself, and in Their totality They form the "bright centre lying far ahead."

*3. Let it evoke response from the bright centre, lying far ahead.*

To this centre we give the name Shamballa, the component letters of which are numerically: S.H.A.M.B.A.L.L.A. or 1.8.1.4.2.1.3.3.1. This word equals the number 24 which in its turn equals 6. I would call your attention to the fact that the word has in it nine letters, and—as you know—nine is the number of initiation. The goal of all the initiatory process is to admit mankind into realisation of and identification with the will or purpose of Deity. The number 6 is the number of form or of manifestation, which is the agent or medium through which this realisation comes and by which the consciousness is unfolded so that it can become the foundation of the higher process which is instituted at the third initiation. That initiation is closely related to the third major centre, Shamballa; it is the third, from the angle of man's perception and understanding, but the first from the angle of Deity Itself. Again, 6 being the number of the sixth ray, it is therefore the number of idealism and of that driving force which makes mankind move forward upon the path and in response to the vision and press upward towards the light. It is in reality devotion to an unseen goal, ever on ahead, and an unswerving recognition of the objective. Like all other divine qualities, it has its material counterpart, and that is why 666 is regarded as the number of the Beast or of materialism, the number of the dominance of the three worlds prior to the process of reorientation and the expression of developed idealism and purpose. The third aspect expresses itself through pure materialism, and hence the three sixes. In an ancient book on numbers the initiate is defined as "the one who has experienced and expressed 666 and found it naught; who has dropped the 6 and become the 66, and thus has found himself upon the WAY; later, again, he drops the 6 and becomes the perfected 6—form, the instrument and expression of spirit."

The number 24 is of deep interest, expressing as it does the double 12 — the greater and the lesser zodiac. Just as the number 6 expresses *space,* so the number 24 expresses *time,* and is the key to the great cycle of manifestation. It is the clue to all cyclic appearance or incarnation. Its two figures define the method of evolution; 2 equals the quality of love-wisdom, working under the Law of Attraction and drawing man from one point of attainment to another; whilst 4 indicates the technique of conflict and the achieving of harmony through that conflict; 4 is also the number of the human hierarchy, and 2 is the number of the spiritual hierarchy. Technically speaking, until the third initiation, the initiate is "occupied with the relationship of the 2 and the 4; these, when placed side by side, connote relation; and when placed the one above the other, the initiate passes from the 4 into the 2." Needless to say, there is much more to say anent these figures, but the above will suffice to show the satisfactory nature of esoteric numerology — not numerology as understood today.

I would have you note that the sounds which compose the word "Shamballa" are predominantly along the line of will or power or of first ray energy. Of the nine letters, six are on the first ray line of force, 1.1.1.3.3.1. — spirit and matter, will and intelligence. Two of them are along the second line of force, 4 and 2. The number 8 inaugurates ever a new cycle, following after the number 7, which is that of a relative perfection. It is the number of the Christ-consciousness; just as 7 is the number of man, 8 is the number of the Hierarchy, and 9 is the number of initiation or of Shamballa. Forget not that, from the angle of the Hierarchy, the third initiation is regarded as the first major initiation.

These preliminary remarks are intended to convey much esoteric information to those who realise that number gives the clue to the form and purpose of the life which the form veils. At the third major initiation, the third planetary initiation (which is in fact the first solar initiation), the liberated disciple for the first time — alone and unaided — invokes the highest spiritual centre on our planet, Shamballa. This he does because, for the first time, consciously and with understanding, he registers the life aspect (which has brought his soul into action through the medium of form) and vibrates to the Monad. That registration enables him to contact "the bright centre, lying far ahead," to blend his individual will with the divine will, and to cooperate with the purpose aspect of manifestation. He has learnt to function through form; he has become aware, as a soul, of the divine form in its many aspects and differentiations; he now starts off upon the way of the higher unfoldment, of which the first step is contact with Shamballa, involving the fusion of his self-will and his spiritual will with the Will of God.

At the third initiation he stands before the One Initiator, the Lord of the World, and "sees His star shine forth" and hears the sound which — to quote the *Old Commentary.*

". . . pours forth from that central point of power where substance and the outer life have met together, where spirit utters loud the cry which drew the form to meet the highest need; where energy comes forth and blends with force and (in the blending) music had its start within the sphere of blending and of being thus created.

"Man only hears the distant sound and knows it not for what it is. The disciple hears the sound and sees its form. The one who stands for the third time upon the mountain top hears a clear note and knows it as his own, as ours, as yours, and yet the note which none have sounded forth."

*4. When the demand and the response are lost in one great Sound, move outward from the desert, leave the seas behind and know that God is Fire.*

This means more than its obvious significance. Superficially it can mean that when the initiate hears the Sound, he leaves behind the desert life of physical incarnation, the emotional life of the astral plane, seething and unstable as the sea, and functions on the plane of mind, of which the symbol is fire. That is the most elementary and obvious meaning, and as this section of *A Treatise on the Seven Rays* is written for those with initiate understanding, the obvious interpretation will not prove satisfactory. The meaning must be broader and deeper. The words "outward from the desert" have application for the entire life of the incarnated Monad in the three worlds of human endeavour and enterprise. "Leaving the sea behind" has reference to the withdrawal of the initiate from all sensuous experience because, as I have pointed out, the state of consciousness or awareness is superseded when the higher initiations are taken and their place is filled by a state of being for which we have no word but the unsatisfactory one of identification. This state of being is something very different to consciousness as you understand it. The phrase therefore means (if such a misleading form of words can be justifiably used) that the initiate leaves consciousness itself behind and the five worlds of life expression are transcended; at the third initiation the initiate grasps what is meant when the One in Whom we live and move and have our being (note that expression) is referred to as Fire. I elaborated this theme in *A Treatise on Cosmic Fire* — a book which evades understanding by all except those with initiate consciousness. Fire is the sumtotal of that which destroys form, produces complete purity in that which is not itself, generates the warmth which lies behind all growth, and is vitality itself.

This initiate realisation is all brought about by the sudden appreciation or apprehension of sound, by the awakening of the inner ear to the significance of the Voice, just as the disciple in the earlier stage awakened to the significance of vision. That is why, at the third initiation, the initiate sees the star and hears the sound. At the first two initiations, he sees the light and hears the Word; but this is something different and is the higher correspondence to the earlier experience. It will be obvious that I can say no more upon this subject.

It is essential, however, that some knowledge begin to reach the public anent the highest spiritual centre to which (as the Gospel story intimates) Christ Himself was attentive. Frequently we read in the New Testament that "the Father spoke to Him," that "He heard a voice," and that the seal of affirmation (as it is occultly called) was given to Him. Only the Father, the planetary Logos, the Lord of the World, enunciates the final affirmative sound. This has no reference — when it occurs — to the earlier initiations, but only to the final ones. There are five obvious crises of initiation which concern the Master Jesus as step by step He took or re-enacted the five initiations. But lying behind this obvious and practical teaching, lies an undercurrent or thread of higher revelation. This is concerned with the realisations of the overshadowing Christ as He registered the Voice which is heard at the third, fifth, sixth and seventh initiations. The Gospel story gives us the five initiations of the Master Jesus, beginning with the first and ending with the fifth. But it also gives the initiations of the Christ, starting from the second and ending with the seventh. The latter is left incomplete, and the Voice is not recorded, because at the Resurrection and Ascension we are not told of the hearing of the affirmative sound. That will be heard when the Christ completes His work at the time of the Second Coming. Then the great seventh initiation, which is a dual one (love-wisdom in full manifestation motivated by power and will), will be consummated, and the Buddha and the Christ will together pass before the Lord of the

World, together see the glory of the Lord, and together pass to higher service of a nature and calibre unknown to us.

In this connection it is wise to remember that three great energies are focussed in Shamballa, the seat of fire:

1. *The Energy of Purification:* This is the power, innate in the manifested universe, which gradually and steadily adapts the substance aspect to the spiritual by a process which we call purification, where humanity is concerned. It involves the elimination of all that hinders the nature of divinity from full expression, and this again from inherent or latent capacity. This necessitates the leaving behind, stage after stage, cycle after cycle, life after life, and plane after plane, of every tendency in the form nature which veils or hides the glory of God. It is essentially the energy which substitutes good for evil. Human thinking has debased this concept so that purification is related mainly to physical phenomena and physical plane life and to a selfish idealism which is largely based on the thought of the sanitary care of substance. An enforced celibacy and a rigid vegetarianism are familiar instances of this, and these physical disciplines have been put in the place of emotional loveliness, mental clarity, intuitional illumination, and the thoughts of the aspirant become focussed downwards into matter and not outwards and upwards into light.

2. *The Energy of Destruction:* This is a destruction which removes the forms which are imprisoning the inner spiritual life, and hiding the inner soul light. This energy is therefore one of the major aspects of the purificatory nature of the divine Life, and that is the reason why I have put purification ahead of destruction. It is the destroying aspect of life itself, just as there is a destructive agency in matter itself. Two things must be borne in mind in connection with the destroyer aspect of Deity and with those responsible for its appearance:

    a. The destructive activity is set in motion through the will of Those Who constitute the Council at Shamballa and Who are instrumental in bringing the forms in all the subhuman kingdoms into line with the evolving purpose. Under cyclic law, this destructive energy comes into play and destroys the forms of life which prevent divine expression.

b. It is also brought into activity through the determinations of humanity itself which — under the Law of Karma — makes man the master of his own destiny, leading him to initiate those causes which are responsible for the cyclic events and consequences in human affairs.

There is naturally a close connection between the first Ray of Will or Power, the energies concentrated at Shamballa and the Law of Karma, particularly in its planetary potency and in relation to advanced humanity. It will be apparent, therefore, that the more rapidly the individual aspirant approaches the third initiation, the more rapidly and directly will the individual's karma be worked out. Monadic relation, as it becomes established, lets loose the destructive aspect of the basic energy, and all hindrances are destroyed with expedition. This is true also of humanity as a whole. Two factors have, subjectively and spiritually, precipitated this world crisis: The growth and development of the human family and (as you have been told) the inflow of the Shamballa force at this particular time, both as a result of karmic law and the planned decision of the Great Council.

3. *The Energy of Organisation:* This is the energy which set in motion the activity of the great Ray Lives and started the motivation and impulse of that which produced manifestation. Thus were the seven ray qualities brought into expression. The relation of spirit and matter produced this ordered process which again, cyclically and under law, creates the manifested world as a field for soul development and as an area wherein divine purpose is wrought out through the medium of the plan. Again I call your attention to the distinction existing between purpose and plan. This is the aspect, emanating from Shamballa, and inherent also in form (as are the other two), which eventually relates the human will, through the right use of the mind, to the organised planning of his separate and individual life in the

three worlds, and which eventually relates and reorients that will to the Will of God.

These three energies are faintly symbolised for us in the life of Christ when overshadowing the Master Jesus, two thousand years ago.

The purificatory aspect of the monadic force is indicated at the Baptism episode; secondly, the destroyer aspect can be seen expressing itself at the time of the Crucifixion, when it rent the veil of the Temple from the top to the bottom. The episode which indicates the energy of organisation and the relation of the spiritual will of the Christ to the purpose and the will of the Father appears when He said, in the Garden of Gethsemane, "Not my will but Thine be done." This final episode is closely related to the consciously expressed will of the Christ Child when He realised in the Temple that He must be about His Father's business and that His will was to do the will and fulfill the purpose of the Father, the Monad and the One of Whom the Monad is the expression.

It is these three energies which have precipitated the world crisis, and it is helpful for us to recognise the factual nature of the Shamballa forces as they play upon our planetary life and work out human destiny. The great energy of purification is regenerating humanity, and of this the widespread fires which have been such an outstanding characteristic of this war (1914-1945) are the outward and visible sign. Much evil is being burnt out through the revelation of the appalling character of that evil, and through this, unity is being produced. Mankind has looked upon evil in every land and known it to be wrought by men. Men have *seen,* and that sight will never be forgotten, and the horror thus engendered will aid in stiffening the will of humanity to betterment. The energy of destruction has its side of beauty when the spiritual values are grasped. That which has so grossly imprisoned the human spirit is disappearing; the rocky grave of humanity is breaking open and releasing men to a life of resurrection. Forget not that in the interim between the tomb experience and the appearance in living form to His disciples, the Master Jesus went down into hell (figuratively speaking), carrying release for those to be found there. There will be an interim between the darkness of the war with the evil history of the past, and the appearance of a living civilisation and culture based on the spiritual values and intelligently developing the divine purpose. The stage is now being set for this.

The Crucifixion and the tomb experience lead eventually to resurrection and to life. The destruction is appalling, but it is only the destruction of the form side of manifestation in this particular cycle, and (a point which I would beg you not to forget) it is the destruction of much planetary evil, focussed for aeons in humanity as a whole and brought to the surface and precipitated into violent activity by a group of evil men whose destiny it was. This destiny was the result of their own deliberate choice, and of prolonged cycles of purely material selfishness.

I would ask all aspirants and disciples to ponder upon the destructive purpose of God — a purpose which is motivated by love, guided by a balanced judgment as to form, and which cherishes and fosters the life and its resultant spiritual values.

There is an inherent destructive energy in matter itself and an energy of very great potency; it is with this energy that the Axis Powers are working. The destructive energy, emanating from "the bright centre," Shamballa, is something very different, and I would ask you to remember this. The destroying power of spirit is not the same as that of matter. A human being destroys his own form again and again through the evil which he does and by the material focus of his desires; the following of a life of vice will breed disease, as is well known.

The disciple can also destroy his form nature through selfless service and devotion to a cause. In both cases the form is destroyed, but the motivating impulse is different and the energy of destruction comes from different sources. The death of a Master Jesus or of a Father Damien, and the death of a Hitler or of a murderer, are not the result of the same essential energies.

When the din of battle and the smoke and fire of bombing and the cruel effects on human bodies have faded into the past, it will be apparent to the understanding aspirant that much evil has been destroyed in all fields of human activity — in the field of theological religion, in the field of politics, and in the field of selfish economic competition. It will be for humanity then to precipitate and stabilise the appearing good, and this they will learn to do through the utilisation of the third Shamballa energy — the energy of organisation. The new world will be built upon the ruins of the old. The new structure will rise. Men of goodwill everywhere, under the guidance of the New Group of World Servers, will organise themselves into battalions of life, and their first major task must be the development of right human relations, through the education of the masses. This means the paralleling development of an enlightened public opinion, which is (speaking esoterically) right response to the sound which conveys the will of God to the ears of the attentive. Then humanity will indeed move outward from the desert, leave the seas behind, and know that God is Fire.

## RULE FOUR

At the time of the June Full Moon, each year, the love of God, the spiritual essence of solar fire, reaches its highest point of expression. This it achieves through the instrumentality of the Hierarchy, that great group of souls which has ever been the custodian of the principle of light, of enlightened love, and which always — down the ages — focusses its attention upon the race of men when the spiritual influence is at its height. This it does through one of the great Sons of God. The Full Moon of June of 1943 saw this outpouring of divine love reach its highest expression for all time, and at the point of attainment which is, for that particular Son of God, His highest also. Such is the Law. When an embodied Christ in time and space reaches

His goal of achievement, recognition of this comes to Him at the time of the June Full Moon, for in that sign of Gemini the complete victory of life over form, and of spirit over matter, is consummated and celebrated.

The love of God, focussed in the Christ, seeks to express itself in some act of peculiarly useful service to humanity. This service has taken different forms down through the ages, but it has always expressed itself through two episodes: One of them, the first, reveals the Christ in His capacity of the God-Saviour, sacrificing Himself through pure love for His fellowmen. The annals of the Hierarchy contain many such histories of sacrifice and service, dating far back into the very night of time. The saving principle of pure love finds its expression at the hour of humanity's greatest need in the work of a World Saviour and "for the salvation of His people, He comes forth." He thus meets the need, and at the same time strengthens the link which relates the Hierarchy to Humanity. The task of the Christ (as the expression in time and space of the second divine aspect) is *to establish relationships*. Every cyclic Representative of Deity furthers the approach of the Hierarchy to mankind, and seals this service by some final act which becomes the historical nucleus whereby later generations remember Him.

That accomplished, He stays with His people as Head of the Hierarchy until His second opportunity comes, in which as Representative both of Humanity and the Hierarchy, He can relate them both to Shamballa. This He does through a great act of evocation, seeking to bring about a closer relationship between all the three great planetary centres: Shamballa, the Hierarchy, and Humanity. He can do this because the development of the Wisdom aspect in His nature makes it possible. The major linking agent in the universe is the energy of Love-Wisdom. Love relates the Hierarchy to Humanity, and Wisdom relates the Hierarchy to Shamballa. Only when Humanity and the Hierarchy are working together in a practical synthesis, can the Shamballa energy be permitted complete inflow through the medium of the two other centres.

To aid in this process of gradual perfecting and an eventual bringing about of a complete alignment, the help of the Buddha must be invoked and accepted. The work of the Christ as God-Saviour can be carried forward by Him alone and unaided. The work of the Christ as God the Preserver needs the united work, as yet, of the two highest Representatives of the second divine aspect when present together upon the Earth, as is the case today of both the Buddha and the Christ. This is the first cycle in the history of humanity when this has been the case. One or the other has been present down the ages, but not the two simultaneously. The reason for this is that the time has now been reached when Shamballa can be contacted and its energy evoked. Hence we have the activity of the Buddha at the May Full Moon and that of the Christ at the following June Full Moon. Their united activity serves to bring about a much closer approach between the Lord of the World and the Hierarchy, via His four Representatives: the Buddha, the Christ, the Manu, and the Mahachohan — the five points of energy which are creating the five-pointed star of Humanity at this time.

An ancient rule — Rule IV for Applicants gives us in perfect wording the nature of the urge which prompts the present activity of the Christ. He has accomplished His task as God the Saviour. The fourth Rule, as it is given to all applicants and probationary disciples, gives His work the following definition:

> Let the disciple tend the evocation of the fire, nourish
> the lesser lives and thus keep the wheel revolving.

It is given in this short form to all who are approaching the Path, in order to convey to them with the utmost brevity and beauty the nature of the life of the Head of the Hierarchy, the Initiator Whom they must face at the time of the first and second initiations, and upon Whose activities they — as individual aspirants — must learn to model their lives. Only today is it possible to present that work in other terms than those which emphasise the part the Christ plays in the salvaging of man.

It is now possible, however, to present His true and wider task, because man's sense of proportion, his recognition of others, his growing sense of responsibility, his power to suffer for the good, the beautiful and true, his appropriation of the vision, and his point in evolution warrant a truer picture which — if adequately grasped — will enable the disciple to comprehend the requirements of Rule IV as given for disciples and initiates. Only as they grasp the nature of the work of Christ, after His final act of service as God-Saviour, can they understand the nature of group service and begin to pattern their lives and natures so as to meet similar requirements in group formation.

This has become possible because of the point in the evolutionary process which the Hierarchy has attained. The attitude and position of the members of the Hierarchy are not static. All are moving forward. The Christ Who came two thousand years ago embodied in Himself not only the principle of love in the *planetary* sense (a thing which Shri Krishna had achieved), but a cosmic principle of love also, and this for the first time in human history. His achievement was made possible by the fact that the human family had reached a point at which it could produce the perfect Man, Christ, the "eldest in a great family of brothers," a Son of God, the Word made flesh. The future progress of humanity is also aided and hastened because of the attainment and activity of the Christ, and because He remains with us as God the Preserver.

His task today is threefold, and the Rule states in very simple language these three aspects of His divine activity or phases of His work. These are:

1. He *"tends the evocation of the fire."* His major task as Head of the Hierarchy is to evoke the electric fire of Shamballa, the energy of the divine Will, and this in such a form that the Hierarchy can be drawn nearer to the source of Life, and Humanity can consequently profit by this hierarchical Approach and know eventually the meaning of the words "life more abundantly." Christ's evocation of the fire of the will was initiated symbolically in the Garden of

Gethsemane. He has twice symbolically shown His individual response to the Shamballa energy: Once in the Temple of Jerusalem as a child, and again in the Garden as a full grown man at the close of His earthly career. His third and final response (which climaxes His work from our human angle) covers nine years, from the Full Moon of June, 1936, to the Full Moon of June, 1945. This period, in reality, constitutes one event to Him Who lives now free in His Own world and free from the limitations of time and space. Having related Humanity to the Hierarchy (which in the case of individual man means relating the personality to the soul), He now seeks to relate more closely, with the aid of the Buddha, the Hierarchy to Shamballa, love to will, electric fire to solar fire.

2. He *"nourishes the lesser lives."* This refers to the task of the Christ which proceeds day by day, in His capacity of God the Preserver. He "tends the little ones." The work here referred to concerns His activity as Initiator and His responsibility as Head of the Hierarchy. The nourishing of the little lives refers primarily to His task as World Teacher and to His responsibility to lead humanity on into the light, with the aid of all the Masters, working, each of Them through His Own Ashram.

3. He *"keeps the wheel revolving."* This has a specific relation to His work as the Word of God, which manifests as the Word made flesh. This refers specifically to the great Wheel of Rebirth whereby, upon that turning wheel, souls are carried down into incarnation and then up and out of the soul's prison; through the turning of the wheel, human beings learn their needed lessons, create cyclically their vehicles of expression (the response apparatus of the soul in the three worlds) and in this way, under soul guidance, and aided by the Hierarchy and its schools of instruction, they arrive at perfection. This entire process is under the control of the Christ, assisted by the Manu and the Lord of Civilisation. These three Great Lords thus represent the three divine Aspects in the Hierarchy; They, with the four Lords of Karma, form the seven Who control the whole

process of incarnation. The subject is too vast and intricate to be adequately considered here. The above truth does, however, give us a clue as to why the Christ made no specific reference to the work of incarnation in His spoken utterances whilst on Earth. He was then occupied with His task of World Saviour.

His work as Preserver and as Head of the Hierarchy had not then begun. It was at that time dependent upon the experience in the Garden of Gethsemane and upon the Resurrection initiation. Some day the gold and the silver threads of the Gospel story will be disentangled, and men will know the two interpretations which can be put upon the events and episodes in the career of Jesus the Christ. The underlying true events give us great steps and developments in the work of the Christ as He "enveloped humanity in the mantle of love, grasped the rod of initiation on behalf of His brothers, and faced the Lord of Life Himself, unattended, unafraid and in His Own right." The episodes refer to happenings in the life of Jesus.

At the present time, and at the immediate point of tension, Christ has added to His two immediate and constant tasks that of hastening the coming of the Avatar Who waits for the perfected work of the Hierarchy, focussed in the Christ, and the powerful work of Shamballa, focussed in the Lord of the World. When the exact moment has arrived, the work of the Buddha, representing Shamballa, and of the Christ, representing the Hierarchy, plus the sincere demand of Humanity, will bring about an arrangement or an alignment which will release an evocative Sound which will be extra-planetary, and then the Avatar will come.

Ask me not for the date or the hour, brother of mine, for I know it not. It is dependent upon the appeal — the voiceless appeal — of all who stand with massed intent; it is dependent also upon the hour of exact alignment and upon certain aspects of work being done at this time by the senior Members of the Hierarchy, and also upon the steadfastness of the disciples in the world and the initiates — working in their various Ashrams. To this must be added what Christians call the "inscrutable will of God," the un-recognised purpose of the Lord of the World Who "knows His Own Mind, radiates the highest quality of Love, and focusses His Will in His Own high Place outside the Council Chamber of Shamballa."

That the Avatar will come is a predictable certainty. That His forerunner will be the Christ is equally sure. When Christ comes it will be for the advanced units of the human family; they will recognise Him because He has always been with us, whilst His advent will evoke a respon-sive vibration from the masses, but not straight recognition. In connection with the Avatar, it will be a process of hierarchical recognition of an overshadowing Presence within Whose aura the planetary Logos will take His stand as the planetary Representative. Then from Shamballa will descend a stream of spiritual potency, qualified by the will-to-good, and this will reach the attentive Hierarchy. The Members of this Group will, through the medium of the Christ, pour light and healing energy upon the Earth and peculiarly into the consciousness of men. I am not able to express the effect of the outpouring from Shamballa in clearer terms. We are told in the Bible that Christ will come in the air, and that He will bring the "healing of the nations" in His wings. I would call your attention to this thought and to its appositeness to this day and generation. I make no prophetical predictions, I only indicate possibility.

When the Avatar has made His appearance, then will the

> "*Sons of men who are now the Sons of God* with-draw Their faces from the shining light and radiate that light upon the *sons of men who know not yet they are the Sons of God*. Then shall the Coming One appear, His footsteps hastened through the valley of the shadow by the One of awful power Who stands upon the mountain top, breathing out love eternal, light supernal and peaceful silent Will.

> "Then will the sons of men respond. Then will a newer light shine forth into the dismal weary vale of

earth. Then will new life course through the veins of men, and then will their vision compass all the ways of what may be.

"So peace will come again on earth, but a peace unlike aught known before. Then will the will-to-good flower forth as understanding, and understanding blossom as goodwill in men."

So speaks a prophetic passage in the ancient Archives of the Hierarchy which deals with the present cycle of distress (written in June, 1943). For this time men must prepare. You will know when the Avatar links up with the planetary Logos because I will then give you the final Stanza of the Great Invocation (given out in April, 1945). Its use will serve to bring the Coming One to recognition and enable Him to draw upon the resources of the Avatar in the task of world reorganisation and regeneration. He will again come as the World Saviour, but owing to the stupendous nature of the work ahead, He will be fortified and buttressed by the "silent Avatar" Who (occultly speaking) will "keep His eye upon Him, His hand beneath, and His heart in unison with His."

The keynote of Christ's mission will be to evoke from humanity a response to that influence, and an unfoldment on a large scale of intuitive perception. When He came before, He evoked from humanity a gradual response to truth, and mental understanding. That is why at the end of the cycle, which He inaugurated, we have formulated doctrine and mental development.

The work now being done by Shamballa and the Hierarchy on behalf of humanity will tend also to develop group consciousness and the formation of many groups which will be living organisms and not organisations; it will make group initiation possible and will enable certain aspects of the will to flower forth correctly and with safety. The tendency to overlook the distinction between groups and organisations is still very deep-seated; the coming of the Christ will throw much light upon this problem. A study of Rule IV as given to disciples and initiates will also serve to clarify this matter, and with that we shall now concern ourselves.

## Rule IV.

*Let the group see that all the eighteen fires die down and that the lesser lives return unto the reservoir of life. This they must bring about through the evocation of the Will. The lesser wheels must not for aye revolve in time and space. Only the greater Wheel must onward move and turn.*

This is a rule peculiarly related to the fourth Creative Hierarchy, embodying its goal as the Aryan rootrace can sense and approximate it. It is peculiarly related also to the quaternary to which we give the name "personality," composed of a vital or etheric body, a sumtotal of emotional states and a mind, plus that integrated something which we call the whole man. Rightly understood and followed, this rule reveals the nature of the fourth plane or fourth state of consciousness, that of buddhi or the plane of pure reason, the intuition. From the angle of the higher initiate, this rule is related to the activity of Monad, Soul and body within the planetary Life, and covers a great mystery and an entire system of relationships of which man in the three worlds is a dim and uncertain shadow. Some clue to the higher quaternary dealt with in this rule will emerge dimly in your consciousness (more is not yet possible) if you will attempt to realise the following:

1. The Monad relates the initiate to the Will of God, to the Council at Shamballa, to forces active on the planet Pluto, and on another planet which must remain nameless, and also to the Central Spiritual Sun.
2. The Soul relates the initiate to the Love of God, to the consciousness aspect of Deity, to the Hierarchy as a whole, entering it through the Ashram of the Master Who has aided him to take initiation, to the planets Venus and Mercury, to the Sun Sirius, and to the Heart of the Sun.
3. The Personality relates the initiate to the Mind

of God, to the intelligence principle of the planetary Life, to humanity as a whole, to Saturn and Mars, and to the physical Sun through its pranic aspect.

4. The Life aspect of the planet, or that great ocean of forces in which all these three aspects live and move and have their being, relates the initiate to that Life which works out through Shamballa, through the Hierarchy and through Humanity, thus forming part of the great sumtotal of manifestation.

It is to these major quaternaries that Rule IV refers, and their relationships only emerge as the initiate keeps the rules. Let us now take this rule stanza by stanza, and so get some understanding of its basic significances.

*1. Let the group see that all the eighteen fires die down and that the lesser lives return unto the reservoir of life.*

A very casual consideration will show the student that this rule contains four sentences which refer to one or other of the four aspects we have been considering. Bear this in mind as we study significances, interpretations and carry our thoughts into the world of meaning.

A very cursory reading of the Rule leads one to the surmise that one of the most important hints concerns the effect of the group life and radiation upon the individual in the group. "Let the group see that all the eighteen fires die down and that the lesser lives return unto the reservoir of life." These words deal with the group personality, composed of all the personalities of its members. It should be borne in mind that a group is in itself an entity, having form, substance, soul and purpose or objective, and that none of these is better or greater, or more developed than the aggregate of group lives which compose it. Though individuals of varying points in evolution form the group, none of them is below the level of disciples upon the evolutionary ladder. A Master's Ashram has in it disciples and initiates of all degrees, but no probationary disciples at all. No one below the rank of disciples — accepted and dedicated — is admitted. This is one of the first Rules given to an accepted disciple when first admitted into the Ashram, and it is from that angle that we should now consider it.

The three Rules we have earlier considered are general in nature and relate to certain broad themes or demanded hypotheses which must govern the consciousness of the disciple in the future. In this particular Rule we enter the realm of the specific, and are presented with certain "intentional" activities which must govern the disciple's life now that he is an integral part of the Ashram. He is faced with the proposition of making his life of such a nature that it furthers the group purpose, enhances the group strength, eliminates all that might hinder group usefulness, and brings closer the objective for which the group was formed — the carrying out of the Master's plans. It was the disciple's innate, instinctual and individual response to this ray objective, and his effort to subordinate his personality to the dimly sensed soul dedication, which led the Master in the first instance to recognise him and incorporate him into His Ashram. The moment that happened, the disciple came not only under an increased impact of egoic force and egoic impulsive intention (using those words in their occult sense), but the group radiation began its beneficent work upon him. The magnetic "pulling" power which had hitherto led him forward is now superseded by a radiating stimulating potency; this effects great changes in him, and produces both eliminating and substituting results. The effect of the life of the Ashram, as far as the group which forms it is concerned and apart from the Master's Own potency, can be described as follows:

1. The life of the personality is steadily weakened, and its grip upon the soul is definitely loosened. The soul begins to dominate in a very real sense.

2. The necessity of incarnation becomes appreciably less, and finally life in the three worlds of human manifestation becomes needless. All the lessons have been learnt and the soul objective has been attained.

3. The Will of the Monad begins to be sensed; the will aspect blends with the love aspect and makes the

intelligence aspect fruitful and effective for the carrying out of divine purpose, focussed for the disciple through the Ashram.

4. The purposes of time and space, of events and extension, of matter and consciousness have been achieved and are eventually superseded by something for which we have as yet no term and of which we have no conception. It is that which begins to express itself after the third initiation, when the Father aspect "comes into view"— I know not how else to word it.

5. The whole is seen to be of more vital importance than the part, and this not as a dream, a vision, a theory, a process of wishful thinking, an hypothesis or an urge. It is realised as an innate necessity and as inevitable. It connotes death, but death as beauty, as joy, as spirit in action, as the consummation of all good.

It will be obvious, therefore, that the interpretation of these Rules must involve capacity to pass beyond the usual attitudes and what one might call the usual metaphysical and theosophical platitudes, and to see life as the Hierarchy sees it. This means that life is approached from the angle of the Observer and not from that of a participator in actual experiment and experience in the three worlds. This Observer is different to the Observer on the probationary Path. Most of the experiment and experience has been left behind, and a new orientation to a world of values, higher than even the world of meaning, has set in. This attitude might well be described as the mode of approach of all who form a part of an Ashram. Those who form the Ashram are living in the three worlds of experience if they are accepted disciples, but the focus of their attention is not there. If they are initiated disciples, they are increasingly unaware of the activities and reactions of their personalities, because certain aspects of the lower nature are now so controlled and purified that they have dropped below the threshold of consciousness and have entered the world of instinct; therefore there is no more awareness of them than a man asleep is conscious of the rhythmic functioning of his sleeping physical vehicle. This is a deep and largely unrealised truth. It is related to the entire process of death and might be regarded as one of the definitions of death; it holds the clue to the mysterious words "the reservoir of life." Death is in reality unconsciousness of that which may be functioning in some form or another, but in a form of which the spiritual entity is totally unaware. The reservoir of life is the place of death, and this is the first lesson the disciple learns.

The eighteen fires refer to the eighteen states of matter which constitute the personality. They are: seven physical states of matter, seven emotional states, enabling the astral body to function on the seven subplanes of the astral plane, and four states of matter for each of the four conditions of the concrete mind — (7, 7, 4, = 18). These are eighteen grades of substance, eighteen vibratory groups of atoms, and eighteen aggregates of life which form the bodies of the lunar lords (as *The Secret Doctrine* calls them) which in their totality, form the body of the Lunar Lord, the Personality. The above is the very a b c of occultism and a familiar truth to all of you. What is referred to here has, however, no reference to processes of purification, of control or of discipline. These have been much earlier considered and are regarded as the necessary processes instituted upon the probationary path, and should have reached a point prior to the stage of accepted discipleship where — rapid or slow in expression — they are nevertheless automatic in action, sure and inevitable.

The first sentence in this fourth rule refers to Detachment — the detachment of the soul from the body or the institution of those activities which bring about what is called in the Bible "the second death." It is not detachment as the aspirant practices it. It is the scientific breaking of all links and the ending (through completed use) of all contacts which are now regarded as militating against liberation. It is in reality a scientific process of ending karma; it is individual and national karma which brings a man back into a physical vehicle and clothes him with the qualities and aspects of substance. This must end whilst he is a member

THE FOURTEEN RULES FOR GROUP INITIATION

of the Master's Ashram and is preparing himself for the triumph of the fourth initiation. This is brought about by the automatic, ceaseless and unquestioning fulfillment of duty, from the angle of recognised service.

It might be stated that an intelligent understanding of this sentence will lead to those actions which "produce the death and dissipation and final dissolution of the personality through the ending of karma." It must be remembered that a Master has no personality at all. His divine nature is all that He has. The form through which He works (if He is working through and living in a physical vehicle) is a created image, the product of a focussed will and the creative imagination; it is not the product of desire, as in the case of a human being. This is an important distinction and one which warrants careful thinking. The lesser lives (which are governed by the Moon) have been dispersed. They no longer respond to the ancient call of the reincarnating soul, which again and again has gathered to itself the lives which it has touched and coloured by its quality in the past. The soul and the causal body no longer exist by the time the fourth initiation is undergone. What is left is the Monad and the thread, the antahkarana which it has spun out of its own life and consciousness down the ages and which it can *focus at will* upon the physical plane, where it can create a body of pure substance and radiant light for all that the Master may require. This will be a perfect body, utterly adapted to the need, the plan and the purpose of the Master. None of the lesser lives (as we understand the term) form part of it, for they can only be summoned by desire. In the Master there is no desire left, and this is the thought held before the disciple as he begins to master the significance of the fourth Rule.

In this Rule two main ideas are to be found, both of them connected with the first divine aspect: the thought of Death and the nature of the Will. In the coming century, death and the will inevitably will be seen to have new meanings for humanity, and many of the old ideas will vanish. Death, to the average thinking man, is a point of catastrophic crisis. It is the cessation and the ending of all that has been loved, all that is familiar and to be desired; it is a crashing entrance into the unknown, into uncertainty, and the abrupt conclusion of all plans and projects. No matter how much true faith in the spiritual values may be present, no matter how clear the rationalising of the mind may be anent immortality, no matter how conclusive the evidence of persistence and eternity, there still remains a questioning, a recognition of the possibility of complete finality and negation and an end to all activity, of all heart reactions, of all thought, emotion, desire, aspiration, and the intentions which focus around the central core of a man's being. The longing and the determination to persist and the sense of continuity still rest, even to the most determined believer, upon probability, upon an unstable foundation, and upon the testimony of others — who have never in reality returned to tell the truth. The emphasis of all thought on this subject concerns the central "I" or the integrity of Deity.

You will note that in this Rule, the emphasis shifts from the "I" to the constituent parts which form the garment of the Self, and this is a point worth noting. The information given to the disciple is to work for the dissipation of this garment and for the return of the lesser lives to the general reservoir of living substance. The ocean of Being is nowhere referred to. Careful thought will here show that this ordered process of detachment, which the group life makes effective in the case of the individual, is one of the strongest arguments for the fact of continuity and for individual identifiable persistence. Note those words. The focus of activity shifts from the active body to the active entity within that body, the master of his surroundings, the director of his possessions, and the one who is the breath itself, despatching the lives to the reservoir of substance, or recalling them at will to resume their relation to him.

Putting it this way, you will note how the disciple is really enjoined to recognise (with the assistance of his group) that he is essentially the Father aspect himself, the first cause, the creative will and the breath of life within the form. This is a somewhat new attitude which he is asked to take, because hitherto the emphasis upon his focus has been to regard himself as the soul, reincarnating when desire calls and withdrawing when need arises. The group life as a whole is here needed to make possible this shift in realisation away from form and consciousness to the will and life aspect or principle. When this has begun to take place, one of the first recognitions of the initiate-disciple is that form, and his consciousness of form and its contacts (which we call knowledge), have in themselves produced a great thought-form which has summed up in itself his entire relation to form, to existence and experience in the three worlds, to matter, to desire and to all that incarnation has brought him. The whole matter looms, therefore, over-large in his consciousness. The detaching of himself from this ancient thoughtform — the final form which the Dweller on the Threshold takes—is called by him Death. Only at the fourth initiation does he realise that death is nothing but the severing of a thread which links him to the ring-pass-not within which he has chosen to circumscribe himself. He discovers that the "last enemy to be destroyed" is brought to that final destruction by the first aspect in himself, the Father or Monad (which moved originally to create that form), the Life, the Breath, the directing energising Will. It is the will that, in the last analysis, produces orientation, focus, emphasis, *the world of form,* and above all else (because of its relation to *the world of cause), the world of meaning.*

Average man lives and has his being in the world of meaning; the initiate and the Master have their focus in the world of Being. They are then naught but will, illumined by love which links them with the world of meaning, and capable of intelligent activity which links them with the world of form, and is the indication of life. But the desire of the initiate is not now for activity, or even for the expression of love. These qualities are integral parts of his equipment and expression but have dropped below the threshold of consciousness (a higher correspondence of the auto-

matic activities of the physical body which proceed upon
their work without any realised consciousness on the part
of the man). His effort is towards something which means
little as yet to those of you who read these words; it is for
the realisation of Being, immovable, immutable, living and
only to be comprehended in terms which embody the concept of "It is not this; it is not that." It is No-Thing; it is
not thought or desire. It is life, Being, the whole, the One.
It is not expressed by the words "I am" or by the words "I
am not." It is expressed by the words "I am that I am."
Having said that, know you what I mean? *It is the will-to-be
which has found itself through the will-to-good.*

Therefore, the eighteen fires must die down; the lesser
lives (embodying the principle of form, of desire and of
thought, the sum total of creativity, based upon magnetic
love) must return to the reservoir of life and naught be
left but that which caused them to be, the central will which
is known by the effects of its radiation or breath. This dis-
persal, death or dissolution is in reality a great effect
produced by the central Cause, and the injunction is
consequently:

2. *This they must bring about through the evocation of
the Will.*

This type of death is ever brought about by a group, because it is from the earliest moment the one unmistakable
expression of soul activity — as influenced consciously by
the Monad or Father — and this activity is a group activity
which wills the return of the lesser lives to the general reservoir from the very first moment that it has become apparent
that the form experience has served its purpose and that the
form has reached a point of such resilience and capacity
that perfection has been practically achieved. This is definitely consummated at the fourth initiation. Now, at the
end of the great life cycle of the soul, persisting for aeons,
the time is nearing when form-taking and experience in the
three worlds must end. The disciple finds his group in the
Master's Ashram, and consciously and with full understand-

ing, masters death — the long-feared enemy of existence. He discovers that death is simply an effect produced by life and by his conscious will, and is a mode whereby he directs substance and controls matter. This becomes consciously possible because, having developed awareness of two divine aspects — creative activity and love — he is now focussed in the highest aspect and knows himself to be the Will, the Life, the Father, the Monad, the One.

In concluding our study of Rule IV, we are to consider two things:

The method of evoking the Will aspect.
The process of recognising the Life aspect,
the Monad, the Father in Heaven.

The result of these two is given in the two closing phrases of this rule:

*3. The lesser wheels must not for aye revolve in time and space. Only the greater Wheel must onward move and turn.*

There is one point here that I should like to make because it opens the door to new concepts, even if it is not yet possible for these concepts to be defined so that the mass can understand; even the disciples who read these words will fail truly to comprehend. Only those who have taken the third initiation will rightly interpret. Constantly in all esoteric literature reference is made to the factors of time and space as if there were a basic distinction between the worlds in which these two hold sway and in which the aspirants and initiates of all degrees freely move. Constantly the aspirant is reminded that time is cyclic in nature and manifestation, and that "space is an entity." It is necessary that there should be some comprehension of these terms if that which the will controls (when evoked) is to penetrate into the knowing consciousness of the thinker.

Space and substance are synonymous terms; substance is the aggregate of atomic lives out of which all forms are built. With this the *Treatise on Cosmic Fire* largely dealt.

This is both an occult and a scientific truism. Substance is, however, a soul concept, and is only truly known to the soul. Therefore, after the fourth initiation, when the work of the soul is accomplished and the soul body fades out of the picture, only the quality which it has imparted in substance is left as its contribution — individual, group or planetary — to the sumtotal of manifestation. All that remains is a point of light. This point is conscious, immutable and aware of the two extremes of the divine expression: the sense of individual identity and the sense of universality. These are fused and blended in the ONE. Of this ONE the divine Hermaphrodite is the concrete symbol — the union in one of the pairs of opposites, negative and positive, male and female. In the state of being which we call the monadic, no difference is recognised between these two because (if I can bring such ideas down to the level of the intelligence of the aspirant) it is realised that there *is* no identity apart from universality and no appreciation of the universal apart from the individual realisation, and this realisation of iden-tification with both the part and the whole finds its point of tension in the will-to-be, which is qualified by the will-to-good and developed (from the consciousness angle) by the will-to-know. These are in truth three aspects of the divine will which exists in its perfection in the solar Logos and finds a medium of expression through the planetary Logos. This will is therefore working out in seven ways, via the living qualities of the seven planetary Logoi Who express Themselves through the seven sacred planets; They are preoccupied with the endeavour of bringing all the forms of life within the orbit of Their influence up to the same measure of recorded recognition and of registered existence. It will be obvious to you, consequently, that on each of the seven sacred planets one aspect of the divine Will will be dominant.

This is the significance of Space — the field wherein states of Being are brought to the stage of recognition. When that stage has been reached and the Knower, the Soul, is fully aware and fully conscious, then there enters in a new factor which also affects space — though in a different way — but which is related to the monadic Life. That factor is Time. Time is related to the will aspect and is dependent upon the dynamic life, self-directed, which produces persistence and which demonstrates persistence in that dynamic focus of intention by periodic or cyclic appearance.

From the angle of the Will or the Father, these appearances in time and through space are so small a part of the experience of the living Entity Whose life is lived on planes other than the physical, emotional or mental, that they are regarded as no life. To understand this, I would remind you again that we must seek to understand the sum total in the light of the part, the Macrocosm in the light of the Microcosm. That is no easy task and is necessarily most limited.

The disciple knows or is learning to know that he is not this or that, but Life Itself. He is not the physical body or its emotional nature; he is not, in the last analysis (a most occult phrase) the mind or that by which he knows. He is learning that that too must be transcended and superseded by intelligent love (only truly possible after the mind has been developed), and he begins to realise himself as the soul. Then, later, comes the awful "moment in time" when, pendant in space, he discovers that he is not the soul. What then is he? A point of divine dynamic will, focussed in the soul and arriving at awareness of Being through the use of form. He is Will, the ruler of time and the organiser, in time, of space. This he does, but ever with the reservation that time and space are the "divine playthings" and can be used or not at will.

We could paraphrase the last two sentences of this fourth rule as follows: The evocation of the will involves identity with the larger purpose. The little will of the little lives must be merged in the larger will of the whole. Individual purpose must be identified with group purpose, which is as much of the purpose of the Whole or the One Life as the little life can grasp at any given point in time and space. It is in this sense, esoterically understood, that time is an event—which philosophy now points out, groping towards an expression of the initiate consciousness.

In the long run, literally when the path of evolution is trodden to its end, what remains will be the divine purpose and the all-enveloping Life as it materialises the plan in time and space. This is the result of the turning of the greater Wheel of life, causing all the lesser wheels — in time and space — also to turn. In the meantime, the human being is first of all driven by desire, then by aspiration towards some visioned goal, then by his selfish will, which reveals to him the nature of the will: persistent application to some purpose, seen as desirable and to which every power is bent. Having exhausted all tangible goals, the inner life forces the man on towards the intangible, and the quality of his will begins to change. He discovers a larger will than his own and begins slowly to identify himself with it, proceeding stage by stage from one realised purpose to another higher one, each step removing him further from his own so-called will and bringing him nearer to an appreciation of the significance of the divine will or purpose.

It might be stated, in an effort to clarify the method whereby this is done, that by the carrying out of the plan the disciple learns the nature of the purpose, but that the purpose itself can only be grasped by one who is developing monadic consciousness. Monadic consciousness is not consciousness as human beings understand it, but is that state of apprehension which is not consciousness or realisation, as the mystic feels it, or identification, as the occultist terms it, but something that appears when all of these three are appreciated and registered in a moment of time within the orbit of space.

Now, having said this, I would ask you if you are much the wiser, or of what profit it is for me to write these words if you understand them not? For two reasons I write. One of my functions and duties (as a Master of the Wisdom) is to anchor ideas in the mind of man and carry down into the realm of words certain emerging concepts so that they may begin to influence the higher level of thinkers. These latter are responsible for precipitating the ideas deep into the human consciousness. Secondly, I write for the generation which will come into active thought expression at the end of this century; they will inaugurate the framework, structure and fabric of the New Age which will *start* with certain premises which today are the dream of the more exalted dreamers and which will develop the civilisation of the Aquarian Age. This coming age will be as predominantly the age of group interplay, group idealism and group consciousness as the Piscean Age has been one of personality unfoldment and emphasis, personality focus and personality consciousness. Selfishness, as we now understand it, will gradually disappear, for the will of the individual will voluntarily be blended into the group will. It will be obvious to you, therefore, that this could well bring about a still more dangerous situation, because a group would be a combination of focussed energies, and unless these energies are directed towards the fulfillment of the Plan (which coordinates and makes possible the divine purpose) we shall have the gradual consolidation of the forces of evil or of materialism on Earth. I am not speaking lightly, but am endeavouring to show the necessity for the steadfast consecration of the spiritually minded to the task of developing the will-to-good on Earth and the absolute importance of fostering goodwill among the masses. If this is not done after the terrific global housecleaning that has gone on, the last state will be worse than the first. We shall have individual selfishness superseded by group selfishness, which will be consequently still more potent in its evil dedication, focus and results. The little wheels can continue to revolve in time and space, hindering the onward progress of the great Wheel which — again in time and space — is the wheel of humanity. The Heavenly Man and the human being upon that Wheel are developing divine qualities and attributes.

The will aspect of divinity can find expression only through humanity, for the fourth kingdom in nature is intended to be the agent of the will to the three subhuman kingdoms. It was therefore essential that the spirit of inclusiveness and the tendency to spiritual identification should be developed in humanity as a step preparatory to the development of response to divine purpose. It is absolutely essential that the will-to-good be unfolded by the disciples of the world so that goodwill can be expressed by the rank and file of mankind. *The will-to-good of the world knowers is the magnetic seed of the future.* The will-to-good is the Father aspect, whilst goodwill is the Mother aspect, and from the relation of these two the new civilisation, based on sound spiritual (but utterly different) lines, can be founded. I would commend this thought to your consciousness, for it means that two aspects of spiritual work must be nurtured in the immediate future, for on them the more distant hope of happiness and of world peace depends. The New Group of World Servers must be reached and the will-to-good developed in them, and the masses simultaneously must be reached with the message of goodwill. The will-to-good is dynamic, powerful and effective; it is based on realisation of the plan and on reaction to the purpose as sensed by those who are either initiate, and consciously in touch with Shamballa, or disciples who are likewise a part of the Hierarchy but are not yet able to contact the central Purpose or Life. Not yet having taken the third initiation, the monadic vibration is to them largely unknown. It would be just as dangerous for them to be able to reach Shamballa (prior to the third initiation when all personality tendencies are obliterated) as it would be to teach the masses of men today techniques of will which would render their still selfish will effective. The main difficulty would be that the disciples would destroy themselves, whilst the ordinary man would damage himself.

This exegesis of Rule IV is necessarily brief because it is of such deep significance that it requires careful study, sentence by sentence, and even so it is very largely beyond the grasp of the majority of readers. It will, however, be useful for disciples to reflect upon the various meanings (there are several) and upon the esoteric implications.

## RULE FIVE

Rule V, which we are now purposing to consider, is one of great interest and practicality. I would remind you that one of the new things which the coming era of spiritual expansion will see is the inauguration of something entirely new: *Group Initiation*. Hitherto, one by one, units of the human family have found their way through the Door of Initiation. If this system is to persist, and considering the vast numbers of souls in and out of incarnation who must eventually achieve the goal — two-thirds of the total in this world cycle — even the greater cycles which include many world cycles would prove too short a time. The space-time schedule of the planetary Logos Himself would be upset, for He *has* such a schedule for the cycle of His present incarnation. There is a term set for the appearance of His body of manifestation, our planet, just as there is for the human body. He therefore has to work out His plans within a certain time limit, and this factor conditions the experience of all the lives that move within the radius of His expression, including the human kingdom.

It must be remembered also that as humanity develops and more and more people begin to function as souls, the nature of the soul (which is *relationship*) begins to have an effect; men become larger in their outlook and their vision. The outlook of the separated self vanishes, and group relationship and group interest supersede that intense personal and interior relationship and interest which have made evolving man what he is: first of all an integrated personality, and then a disciple — a candidate for initiation. As more and more disciples come into group realisation it will become increasingly possible for the Hierarchy to admit such disciples in group formation. That is one reason necessitating the re-establishing of the Ancient Mysteries on Earth. That group relation has to be demonstrated in the three worlds and expressed by disciples in their group life upon the physical plane. Hence the new experiment being undertaken by the Hierarchy of externalising Their Ashrams. This process involves immense difficulty, owing to the astralism, the ambitions and the growing *personality* influence of so many people. Many groups, under self-seeking leaders, will react to this experiment and will proclaim themselves as Masters with Ashrams and as occupied with training people for initiation. Signs of this can already be seen.

The Hierarchy has been confronted with definite difficulty in this matter, for on the one hand the Masters were faced with the glamour-making tendency and astralism of the majority of people and, secondly, with the rapid advance of the human consciousness into the realm of group relationship, group life, group reactions and group activity. This has brought about the intention of the Hierarchy to train such ready minds and hearts for a united moving forward through the Door of Light onto the Lighted Way. That externalisation has not yet taken place. Tentative experiments are being made with some success and some discouragement.

Two things have therefore been decided upon by the Masters as They face the future of humanity and prepare to take the required steps to meet man's *advancing aspiration*. I have chosen these two words with care. These two requirements have been demanded of the Hierarchy by Shamballa in order to safeguard the Mysteries and prevent a too premature precipitation of the hierarchical life upon the Earth. Both these requirements are expressed in this fifth Rule.

Rule V.

> *In unison let the group perceive the Triad shining forth, dimming the light of the soul and blotting out the light of form. The macrocosmic Whole is all there is. Let the group perceive that Whole and then no longer use the thought, "My soul and thine."*

The first demand made by Shamballa is that the groups being prepared for initiation should consist only of those who are in process of building the antahkarana, the bridge between the Triad and the personality; the second demand is that those being prepared should show some signs of the sense of synthesis.

You will note, therefore, some of the factors that have controlled the presentation of the truth which I have sought to give, down the years. The teaching on the Antahkarana (briefly hinted at by H.P.B.) has been expanded by me in the book, *Education in the New Age* and in this fifth volume of *A Treatise on the Seven Rays (Part II)*, and has already been given to a number of senior aspirants in the hope that they would profit thereby; the need for synthesis has also been emphasised by me, and is closely related to the will-aspect, the first divine aspect. In the past, during the cycle of mysticism through which all aspirants very properly pass, they were taught to "see the vision"— a vision of the goal, of the beauty to be sought, of the loved one to be known, of liberation to be achieved, of spiritual satisfaction and an opened door to greater wonders. In the occult age which has now definitely dawned, the neophyte will be taught to see the picture whole, to think in the larger terms, to emerge out of the normal separative consciousness into the broad state of awareness that "sees no difference." The goal, or rather the result of the mystic and occult way, is the merging of the vertical way of life with the horizontal way of service, and it is this merging which Shamballa demands should condition the attempt now in process of training those who will *together* seek initiation, will *together* pass through the Portal on to the Way, and who can *together* be presented to the One Initiator as a "unit of Light." This sense of synthesis (which must be increasingly demonstrated as each initiation is taken in group formation) is possible only to those who have bridged the gap between the concrete lower mind and the higher mind or — to word it technically and in the language of academic occult science — between the mental unit and the manasic permanent atom.

The goal of the Probationary Path is made beautifully clear in the fifth Rule as given earlier in *Initiation, Human and Solar*. It says:

> Let the applicant see to it that the solar Angel dims the light of the lunar angels, remaining the sole luminary in the microcosmic sky.

The soul must be seen by the probationer as the sun of the life. All lesser lights must be put out by the light of the central luminary; all little fires must be obliterated by solar fire. The solar Angel controls the personality life and its forces. This, in the New Age, is the goal of the probationary path and of the applicant for discipleship. Hitherto it has been the goal of all the teaching given anent the Path of Discipleship, but the higher rate of intelligence of the modern applicant warrants a change, and as time goes on the present requirements for disciples, up to and including the second initiation, will be the requirements for the Probationary Path.

This will necessitate a clearer understanding of the Path of Discipleship. On that path, the major teaching given in the future will concern:

1. The building of the rainbow bridge, the antahkarana.

2. The nature of the intuition and its development, as it supersedes the mind in its two aspects: concrete and abstract, lower and higher.

3. The nature of life as the Monad expresses it.

In these three approaches to truth the new revelation lies hid; it will take the place of the teaching upon the soul for the neophytes and disciples of the world, and the emphasis will be laid — for them — on the life aspect and not so much on the love aspect. The reason for this is that more and more people will be living as souls and therefore expressing love, and for them the nature of life and of monadic experience will constitute the normal next revelation — one that is, however, possible only to those who do attempt to live as souls, who cultivate love or the sense of non-separateness, and who are at least dwelling upon the periphery of the hierarchical world. It would therefore be inevitable that — to those so dwelling or treading the Path of Discipleship — the factors which inspire all hierarchical effort would begin to be dimly apparent and that, slowly, these factors would also assume for them the outlines of a dim and distant goal.

The two parts of this rule are consequently expressive of the new demands for disciples — not applicants. This becomes apparent when you study the two rules: one for applicants and one for disciples. The applicant is referred to the microcosm. The Macrocosm is held before the vision of the disciple.

The two demands are expressed in Rule V as follows:

*1. In unison let the group perceive the Triad shining forth, dimming the light of the soul and blotting out the light of form.*

This is the demand for the building of the antahkarana which relates the disciple in his personality to the Triad.

*2. The macrocosmic Whole is all there is. Let the group perceive that Whole and then no longer use the thought, "My soul and thine."*

This is the demand for a sense of synthesis which is occult vision and not mystic vision. These two demands will be the two basic requirements for the new schools of occultism.

In view of all the instructions given earlier in this volume, and in view also of the clarity of the statement made above, there is little that it will be necessary for me to say anent this first demand. The word "demand" which has been used perhaps requires explanation. In considering this subject it should be remembered that admittance to Shamballa and a divine expression in life and service of the first great divine aspect, the will aspect, is the goal held before the members of the Hierarchy. They too are on the way of evolution, and Their goal is to pass through the "eye of the needle," on Their way to the higher evolution. This higher evolution is that which opens up before a Master of the Wisdom. The use of this esoteric term by Christ in *The New Testament* story gives us a hint as to the nature of the exalted consciousness which He expressed. Faced by the rich young man who possessed so much, Christ indicated that he needed to prepare himself for a great negation and for a step forward. The true significance of this has never been grasped and lies in the fact that the phrase "rich young man" is in reality a technical term which is frequently applied to an initiate of the third degree, just as the words "little ones" or "little child" apply to an initiate of the first or second degree. This rich young man was rich in his range of awareness, rich in his personality equipment, rich in his aspiration and in his recognition; he was rich as the result of age-long experience and evolutionary development. He is told by the Christ that he must now prepare himself for what is called in Rule V "the Triad shining forth"; he must now prepare for the unfoldment of the monadic consciousness and for the fourth initiation. In that initiation, the causal body, the body wherein the soul experiences and reaps the fruit of experience, must be and will be destroyed. This has to take place before the initiate can enter into the Council Chamber of the Most High and express the will-to-good and the will of God in fulfillment of the purposes of God. The will of this particular "rich young man," initiate though he was, was not yet adequate to the requirements, so he went sadly away; he had to prepare himself for the fourth initiation, the Great Renunciation, the Crucifixion, and thus fit himself to pass through the needle's eye.

There is a symbolic utterance in the *Old Commentary* which throws light upon the great opportunities which are found in the critical moments in the life of the soul as it experiences incarnation and becomes enriched thereby:

"Within the womb of time and circumscribed by space and limited by darkness — though sustained always by warmth — the life evolves. It develops faculty. It becomes in miniature that which it is. It takes on form and knows the divinity of separation. Such is its goal. Reflect. Knowledge will come.

"Beyond the door is greater light and life. It knows itself for what it is. It suffices not unto itself and knows that it is That — part of the Whole, divinely one with others. Reflect. Union will come.

"Before the rampart of the place of God Himself, a

Son of God comes forth. He stands before the needle's eye and seeks to pass the hindering wall. He is not circumscribed by time or space, but light and life are his. He realises beauty and he knows that That exists. Instead of time and space and all the rich inducements of the form, he knows himself as rich in love, in knowledge, wisdom, insight, and all the panoply of God (as he can grasp it), except one thing. Reflect. Purpose will reveal itself; the Whole will stand revealed and then the soul — loaded with riches and the fruits of labour long — will vanish as the mist and only God, the living One, be left."

There is still another set of phrases dealing with that through which the perfected Sons of God in Their high place must pass when Their work is done on Earth and a greater glory reveals itself ahead. But this I give not. I give only three symbols, which are:

*The womb* . . . individualisation . . . separation.
    Leading to personality integration and self-realisation.
        Climaxing on the Path of Initiation . . . the birth of the Christ.
            Producing intelligent activity.
            Initiation.

*The two-leaved door* . . . initiation . . . group consciousness.
    Leading to soul expression.
        Climaxing in the third initiation.
            Producing loving living.
            The third initiation.

*The eye of the needle* . . higher evolution . . monadic consciousness.
    Leading to life expression.
        Climaxing in the fifth initiation.
            Producing purposeful life.
            Consummation.

Such are the three points of entrance to the three planetary centres: Humanity, Hierarchy and Shamballa.
    This first demand is, curiously enough, the first expression of recognition — directly accorded — that the Great

Lives at Shamballa are now in direct relation with humanity. Hitherto that contact has not been direct, and They have not been in touch with current developments. Hitherto, all contacts and spiritual impulses from this highest centre have reached humanity via the Hierarchy, and vice versa. This demand concerns the negation, the obliteration, the absorption, the putting out or the synthesis of the lesser lights by the greater. All the words which I have employed are efforts to express the truth and all are entirely inadequate.

The moment the initiate or the disciple sees, even dimly, the light of the Spiritual Triad which veils and hides the Central Spiritual Sun, he realises that all other lights — that of the atom of matter, that of the form and that of the soul itself — must inevitably fade out in the stupendous glory and brilliance which emanate from God Himself and which he senses as in process of revelation. He becomes absorbed — intellectually, intuitively, spiritually and finally factually — in that Light. Here I would remind you that just as the light of the soul revealed to the struggling aspirant a new vision, set for him new goals, enhanced all qualities present in his equipment, and revealed the past, the present and the future of the individual, so this still greater light reveals to the initiate a horizon so vast that it has hitherto escaped his capacity and is yet but possible to vision by an initiate of the third degree, endows him with an occult perception hitherto not realised as existing — a perception which permits him to penetrate increasingly and to cooperate understandingly in the purpose of the Lord of the World. It enables him later to develop the equipment — qualities and gifts of a divine nature — which will eventually enable him to take his place in the Council Chamber at Shamballa and work in full unanimity with the Lords of Karma.

These qualities and gifts concern divine attributes and capacities for which we have as yet no words as they lie beyond the scope of human consciousness, being utterly unknown even to advanced human beings. They only begin to manifest as tendencies between the second and the third initiations, in the same way as the instincts in a small child are, in reality, the germs of later intellectual attitudes and activities. It is needless, therefore, for me to enlarge upon them; unless you are an initiate of the third degree, my words would be meaningless to you and would convey naught. The clue lies for you in understanding the three words — Happiness, Joy, Bliss. Do you, as you speak of bliss, understand wherein it differs from happiness and joy? Bliss is associated with complete Being; it concerns the interior attitude of the Whole.

As the individual disciple builds the rainbow bridge, the antahkarana, and as a group of disciples build the group antahkarana, they make possible the "Triadal perception" referred to above. When the disciple has flung one strand of living light (through the power of magnetic love) across the space separating the Triad and the personality, he discovers that he is a part of a group. This group recognition — faulty and unintelligently expressed at first — is the factor which enables him to pass, along the anchored thread, into the Ashram of a Master.

From the angle of the old teaching, the Ashram of the Master and the focus of the Hierarchy were on the higher levels of the mental plane. Today, that is not so. They are on the plane of spiritual love, of the intuition and of buddhi. The Hierarchy is both retreating towards the higher centre of Shamballa, and at the same time advancing towards the lower centre, Humanity. Both these activities have been made possible by man himself; the growing intuitive perception of humanity, in its higher brackets, enables him to function upon the Path of Discipleship and on higher levels than ever before. This the Hierarchy recognises. The growing aspiration of the masses is also drawing the Masters closer to humanity than ever before. This is an instance of the ability of the initiate consciousness to function on initiate levels and also in the three worlds simultaneously. Of this the dual activity of the mind is a symbol, acting as it does as the common sense and so dealing with all matters in the three worlds, and as the spiritual mind at the same time, dealing with all matters connected with the soul, with light and illumination.

The second demand, that the sense of synthesis should be the goal of the training given to applicants in the New Age, is a direct evidence of the new Shamballa contact, because synthesis is an attribute of the divine will and the outstanding quality of Deity. It was inevitable that intelligence and love should be evolutionary objectives on the planet and the first two divine aspects to be developed, for they are qualities of the will; they make the manifestation of the divine will possible; they guarantee its intelligent application and its magnetic power to draw to itself all that is needed for the expression or the manifestation of the divine envisaged purpose, visualised synthetically, and motivated, implemented, engineered and made possible by the dynamic aspect of the same will.

It is interesting to note that there is every evidence in the world today that the Shamballa energy is directly impinging upon the human consciousness and directly producing results. The destroyer aspect of the first Ray of Will or Power is producing worldwide destruction through the use of the first kingdom in nature, the mineral kingdom. That which is made of metals and chemicals is bringing catastrophe and destruction on earth, primarily in the human kingdom. At the same time the second attribute of the will, synthesis, is evoking an equally widespread response. This sense of synthesis has a mass effect earlier than it has an individual effect, and this is a thing of interest and importance to note at this time. Later, the dynamism inherent in the will, wielded by the New Group of World Servers and by the disciples and initiates of the world, will turn that instinctive mass response into factual experience and produce the "appearance" on earth of the new, developed "quality" which "life" seeks in the New Age to demonstrate. In the first volume of this Treatise, I called attention to the three divine aspects: Life, Quality and Appearance. They are now in process of making their appearance in final form for this particular cycle.

Synthesis dictates the trend of all the evolutionary processes today; all is working towards larger unified blocs,
towards amalgamations, international relationships, global
planning, brotherhood, economic fusion, the free flow of
commodities everywhere, interdependence, fellowship of
faiths, movements based upon the welfare of humanity as a
whole, and ideological concepts which deal with wholes and
which militate against division, separation and isolation.

Little as people realise it, these concepts are relatively
new factors in the human consciousness, and the fact that
they are the result of a new and direct relation between
Those Who implement the will of God and humanity
everywhere is the guarantee of the inevitability of their expression in the future. It is only in the immediate interim —
a period of one hundred fifty years — that delay may seem
the rule. Such, however, will not really be the case. The
*forms* through which these new and impending ideas must
take shape and manifest have yet to be created, and that
takes time, for they are built by the power of thought and
due process of educating the public consciousness until that
consciousness becomes confirmed conviction and demonstrates as an immovable public opinion.

This sense of synthesis is one of the things which the
new esoteric schools will develop in their students and
neophytes, for it will be the people trained interiorly in
these schools who will be the builders of the new world and
the trainers of future public opinion. The labels and the
names whereby these schools may call themselves mean but
little. Many will proclaim themselves as esoteric schools and
will communicate nothing of a truly esoteric nature. They
will but attract to themselves the gullible and the foolish.
There are many such functioning in this manner today.
Others may refrain from all outer indication of esoteric and
occult training, and yet convey the needed teaching. They
will seek to relate the One, the Monad, to the personality,
and to evoke in their students a true sense of synthesis.

It is the sense of synthesis, putting it very simply, which
will be the goal of all the educational movements, once the

New Age idealism is firmly established. Physical coordination, personal integrity (which involves primarily the control
and later the negation of the astral body), and personality
integration will be the essential first steps. To this will succeed processes whereby the fusion of the personality with
the soul, of the lower self with the higher Self, and of form
with the divine Dweller in the form will follow next. Then
the truly esoteric phase of the educational process will be
attempted when the earlier steps or stages have been satisfactorily grasped and there is indication of some measure of
real success. By that time the school of the Mysteries and the
Halls of preparation for initiation will be generally recognised by the thinking people and believed in by the
expectant masses.

In those schools, those who are beginning to function
as souls will be led on to take their next step. Their developed soul nature will be expressing itself through intelligent
love and a sense of group fellowship; these two divine qualities will form a basis or foundation from which the next
unfoldment can emerge and on which a more spiritual
superstructure can be built. The Science of Meditation and
the conscious building of the antahkarana will be the first
two preliminary stages in the esoteric curriculum. Today,
the true teaching of meditation and the construction of the
bridge of light between the Triad and the personality are
the most advanced teaching given anywhere.

Humanity is, however, ready for exceedingly rapid
development and this readiness will demonstrate increasingly
in the postwar period, and for it the disciples of the world
must make ready. Two factors will bring this about: the
first is the tremendous stimulation which the war, its demands and its consequences have given to the human consciousness and, secondly, the coming in of very advanced
souls ever since the year 1925. These souls will be ready to
give the needed training and instruction when the right
time comes, having brought it over with them when they
came into incarnation, and knowing normally and naturally

what the modern esoteric student is struggling to grasp and understand.

A study of what I have here outlined as basic requirements will show that the esoteric schools about which I wrote in *Letters on Occult Meditation* lie far ahead in the distant future. The work of the preparatory schools must come first, and their work will proceed until such time that the work of the Ashrams of the Masters is recognised as forming part of an outer hierarchical activity. This in due time will lead to the giving of the first initiation publicly, as a part of the great service ritual of the then prevalent universal religion. The race of men will then — in its most advanced brackets and groups in every country in the world — be normally clairvoyant, and will therefore see for themselves the light within the candidates; they will know then that the first initiation is justifiably undergone, and they will also see the same light in thousands who in previous incarnations have taken that initiation.

One thing only will I add to the above and to the elucidation of the significance of Rule V. The clue to all this esoteric work demanded by Shamballa is to be found in the development of the Art of Visualisation. Through visualisation, three expressions of the human consciousness will become possible:

1. The antahkarana can be built and the shining of the Triad be definitely *seen*. Such will be the new vision — an outcome of the development of *the sense of vision*.

2. Groups, large wholes and major syntheses will also be visualised, and this will lead to a definite expansion of consciousness. Thus *the sense of synthesis* will be unfolded.

3. All creative art will be fostered by this training, and the new art of the future in all departments of creativity will be rapidly developed as the training proceeds. The unfoldment of the sense of vision and of the sense of synthesis, through visualisation, will lead to *a sense of livingness in form*.

## RULE SIX

A superficial reading of Rule VI would give the impression that it is a simple statement as to the universality of Life, and also that it embodies an enunciation of the basic fact of hylozoism. The Rule runs as follows:

Rule VI.

> Let the group know that life is one and naught can ever take or touch that life. Let the group know the vivid, flaming, drenching life that floods the fourth when the fifth is known. The fifth feeds on the fourth. Let then the group—merged in the fifth—be nourished by the sixth and seventh, and realise that all the lesser rules are rules in time and space and cannot hold the group. It onward moves in life.

I find it extremely difficult to express the significance of this Rule in such a way that it will convey meaning to you, and this for two reasons: First, the idea of the One Life is so prevalent, and so customary and trite an unrealised truth, that it registers on ears with very little effect. Secondly, the whole story of life—which is purpose, divine will, and absolute determination—and the eternal planning of the Lord of the World is so hard of comprehension that we have as yet no words in the language of any nation which can express it.

What I am now writing is a series of instructions for disciples in process of training for initiation. I did not say in training for the higher initiations, for these are given in a different manner and the teaching is imparted in the inner Ashram. Therefore, as you have not taken the third initiation, monadic comprehension lies far beyond you; and only this highest state of understanding suffices for the clear perception of the fundamental divine intent lying behind all world phenomena, all evolutionary development, all unfoldment within the capacity of the four kingdoms in nature, and all preparatory extensions and expansions of consciousness.

All I can therefore do is to touch upon the inner significance of the obvious and seek to express certain ideas which will strain your mental perception, evoke your intuition and institute that process of recognition and registration which leads eventually to the initiate-consciousness.

This sixth Rule is the polar opposite of the rule as it was given to applicants. There, if you will refer to my exegesis upon that rule in *Initiation, Human and Solar*, you will find that the objective of that rule was physical purification with the emphasis upon the need for a vegetarian diet at a certain stage of the preparatory process. The reasons for such a discipline were two in number: purification and the necessity for the applicant (at that stage) to refrain from sharing in the benefits incident to the so-called "taking of life." But, can one take life? I think not. Life IS. Naught in heaven or on earth can touch or affect it. This is a point oft forgotten. The rule as given to applicants consequently concerns their ability to accept and adhere to a self-imposed discipline. Through the means of that discipline, the control of the physical and astral natures are demonstrated by the applicant *to himself*, and the effect of the discipline is to reveal to him certain inevitable and basic weaknesses, such as control of the animal nature, the powerful imposition of desire, a sense of superiority, of pride and separativeness. His ability to sustain the discipline and his appreciation of himself for so doing, plus a sense of superiority to those who are not so disciplined, are all indicative of essential weaknesses. His fanaticism, latent or expressed, emerges in his consciousness with clarity, and — when he is sincere — he is conscious of having brought about a measure of physical purity; but at the same time, he is left with the awareness that he perhaps may be starting with the outer and the obvious when he should be beginning with the inner and with that which is not so easily contacted or expressed. This is a great and most important lesson.

It is also an interesting illustration of the technique of the Masters, whereby They permit a fallacy to remain uncorrected (because it is originated by the disciple himself and must be dissipated by him also) and the use of language which conveys a wrong impression. By so doing, the user of the language discovers eventually his erroneous approach to truth. *Life cannot be taken* in the spiritual sense. This error or mistake in the approach of truth enables men and women upon the Probationary Path to demonstrate the earnestness and sincerity of their aspiration by the discipline of substituting the produce "of the second," and to refrain from sustaining life on the produce "of the third." By sacrificing the life of the second kingdom in nature (to use the applicant's own misstatements) and by nourishing the physical body thereby, the probationary disciple does succeed in ending the grip or potency of the physical nature, and that is always helpful. He as yet does not know that he is adhering to lesser "rules in time and space," and that once he has demonstrated to himself that he can hold them and obey them, he is then freed from them and needs them no more. The disciple and the candidate for initiation knows that life is one, whether it takes form in the second kingdom or in the third or the fourth; he knows that the life in him is one with the life in the first kingdom, the mineral; he learns too that life is impregnable; that it cannot be taken or destroyed but "passes on" from form to form, from experience to experience, until the perfect will of God is expressed through life.

The true disciple does not need vegetarianism or any of the physical disciplines, for the reason that none of the fleshly appetites have any control over him. His problem lies elsewhere, and it is a waste of his time and energy to keep his eye focussed on "doing the right things physically," because he does them automatically and his spiritual *habits* offset all the lower physical tendencies; automatically these developed habits enable him to surmount the appeal of those desires which work out in the fulfillment of lower desire. No one is accepted into the circle of the Ashram (which is the technical name given to the status of those who are on the eve of initiation or who are being prepared for initiation) whose physical appetites are in any danger of controlling him. This is a statement of fact. This applies particularly and specifically to those preparing for the first initiation. Those preparing for the second initiation have to demonstrate their freedom from the slavery of ideas, from a fanatical reaction to any truth or spiritual leader, and from the control of their aspiration which—through the intensity of its application—would sacrifice time, people and life itself to the call of the Initiator—or rather, to be correct, to what they believe to be His call.

I would point out that the third initiation is approached from a level tableland of experience and of consciousness, and not from the heights of aspiration, or from fanatical sacrifice, or from the standpoint of a devotion which handicaps the service of the devotee and of the Master he seeks to serve. He knows, as a candidate for initiation, that:

*1. Life is one and naught can ever take or touch that life.*

His sense of proportion as to form becomes adjusted. He is forward-looking towards the soul, and not backward-looking towards the form nature. Some very sincere devotees and promising applicants are so preoccupied with form and its disciplining that they have no real time to give to soul expansion. They are so interested in their reactions to their self-imposed discipline or to their capacity to conform or their failure to accept the discipline, that the spiritual truths—seeking entrance into their hearts—fail to make such an entrance. Temperance in all things, the wise use of all sustaining forms and self-forgetfulness are the hallmark of the disciple, but not of the beginner. Many disciples today who should be functioning in the Hall of Wisdom are still fanatically working in the Hall of Knowledge and are still so earnest over the physical disciplines that the disciplines of the soul are ignored. I would ask you to reflect on this. Applicants have to learn the significance of the words of Rule VI for disciples, "the lesser rules are rules in time and space and cannot hold the group."

I wonder if you can grasp the type of consciousness which distinguishes the Hierarchy, even if you are only able to do so imaginatively and theoretically. They "onward move in life." They work in the realm of life energy; the form seems to Them something which They have definitely left behind, and the consciousness of appeal or rejection of the form nature and hold is to Them only a memory of a distant battle ground where the victory then won has been forgotten and the gains of victory are so far behind that they lie well below the threshold of consciousness. Broadly and generally speaking, workers in the ranks of the Hierarchy (I did not say "with the Hierarchy") are divided into two main groups: those who are working with the unfoldment of the initiate consciousness in the disciples of the world, and those of a more advanced degree who are working with the life aspect and its expression in the lives of the world initiates. Working disciples (who are working in coopera- tion with the Hierarchy) are also working in two major di- visions: Those who are dealing with applicants and are seeking to see the imposition of the physical disciplines, and with the impartation of certain minor values so that be- ginners may grasp the point that they have reached. There are those also who are working to substitute understanding and service for physical discipline and the earlier, inevitable, selfish ends.

Let me repeat: the physical disciplines are of value in the beginning stage and impart a sense of proportion and an awareness of defects and of limitations. These have their place in time and space, and that is all. Once the world of the soul is entered, the disciple uses all forms wisely, with understanding of their purpose and with freedom from ex- cess; he is not preoccupied with them or fundamentally interested in them. His eyes are off himself and are fixed on the world of true values. He has no sense of self-interest, because a *group* awareness is rapidly superseding his indi- vidual consciousness. The words:

2. *Let the group know the vivid, flaming, drenching life that floods the fourth when the fifth is known*

are of prime importance to those who would and can profit

by what I am seeking to convey, as I interpret — as far as may be — these Rules. The knowing of the fifth kingdom in nature through the medium of the consciousness of the fourth and the sacrifice of the fourth kingdom to the fifth, of the human being to the soul and of humanity to the kingdom of God, is the parallel (on a higher turn of the spiral) of the sacrifice of the third kingdom, the animal kingdom, to the fourth, the human kingdom. Thus it proceeds down the scale — sacrifice always of the lower to the higher.

It therefore behooves the individual disciple to decide whether he is an applicant, and consequently to be controlled by the "rules in time and space," or a candidate for initiation who knows that life is one and that the form is of no material significance, except as a field of experience for the soul.

We now come to the most important part of this particular rule; it conveys the key to the immediate goal for those who have attained a certain measure of understanding. The words of importance are:

3. *Let then the group—merged in the fifth—be nourished by the sixth and seventh.*

In other words: "Then let the group—which is identified with the soul—find its sustenance and vitality by the inflow of the intuition and of the spiritual will, emanating from the Spiritual Triad." There are, of course, other meanings, but this is the most practical for disciples. A larger but similar concept lies in the realisation that the human family, the fourth kingdom in nature, is absorbed by the fifth or by the kingdom of God and (when this is the case) can become increasingly en rapport with the sixth and seventh kingdoms. To these kingdoms no names have as yet been given, because the possibility of their existence is only now just beginning faintly to penetrate into the consciousness of the disciple and the initiate. The sixth kingdom is that of the "overshadowing Triads" — that aggregation of liberated Lives of which the higher initiates in the Hierarchy are a part; They are to that spiritual group what the New Group of World Servers is to Humanity. I know not how else to express this truth to you.

The seventh kingdom in nature is that of the Lives Who participate in full capacity of understanding with the group of Beings Who are the nucleus of the Council at Shamballa. Around the Lord of the World this group pivots; Their consciousness and state of being is only dimly understood by the most advanced Members of the Hierarchy, and the relation of these Lives to the Lord of the World is similar, and yet fundamentally different, to the relation of the Members of the Hierarchy to the three Great Lords — the Christ, the Manu and the Mahachohan. Through these three Lords pours the energy which streams from Shamballa, transmitting the purpose and motivating the plan of Sanat Kumara—His Life Plan. What you call "the Plan" is the response of the Hierarchy to the inflowing purposeful will of the Lord of the World. Through Sanat Kumara, the Ancient of Days (as He is called in the Bible), flows the unknown energy of which the three divine Aspects are the expression. He is the Custodian of the will of the Great White Lodge on Sirius, and the burden of this "cosmic intention" is shared by the Buddhas of Activity and those Members of the Great Council Who are of so elevated a consciousness and vibration that only once a year (through Their emissary, the Buddha) is it safe for Them to contact the Hierarchy.

I am seeking only to point to a wider horizon than that usually registered by disciples and I use these broad analogies to expand your point of view. By so doing I can convey to the enlightened person a sense of synthesis, of purposeful planning and of planetary integrity. This great spiritual structure of Being, of Life and of Direction is something that the disciples and initiates of the world need — at this time — in their effort to stand steady under the pressure of world events, and in their determination to co-operate unwaveringly with the moves and plans made by the world Directors, that "Society of illumined and organ-

ised Minds" which is known under the name of the Hierarchy. It is illumination and consequent organisation which
is needed profoundly at this time.

You will see, therefore, the significance of the teaching
now being given out anent the building of the antahkarana.
It is only through this bridge, this thread, that the disciple
can mount on to that stage of the ladder of evolution which
will lead him out of the three worlds, which will bring the
personality into rapport with the Spiritual Triad, and which
will finally lead the Members of the Hierarchy (when Their
term of service is completed) on to the Path of the Higher
Evolution. The antahkarana is built by aspirants and
disciples and initiates of the seven ray types, and is therefore a sevenfold woven thread; it constitutes the first stage
of the Path of the Higher Evolution. It is to that Path what
experience in the mineral kingdom of the Life of God is to
that same Life when it reaches the fourth or human kingdom. You can see, therefore, how significant is the coming
Science of Comparison; not yet has this science of comparative analysis been turned into a definitely recognised line
of approach to truth. The Law of Analogy is the key which
unlocks the understanding.

Something of the quality and the revelatory power of
the intuition is known by all disciples; it constitutes at
times (from its very rarity) a major "spiritual excitement."
It produces effects and stimulation; it indicates future receptivity to dimly sensed truths and is allied—if you could
but realise it—with the entire phenomena of prevision. A
registration of some aspect of intuitional understanding is
an event of major importance in the life of the disciple who
is beginning to tread the Path to the Hierarchy. It provides
testimony, which he can recognise, of the existence of
knowledges, wisdom and significances of which the intelligentsia of humanity are not yet aware; it guarantees to
him the unfolding possibility of his own higher nature, a
realisation of his divine connections and the possibility of
his ultimate highest spiritual attainment; it steadily supersedes soul knowledge, and the energy pouring in to his con-

sciousness from the Spiritual Triad—particularly the energy of the sixth and seventh spheres of activity—is the specific and particular energy which finally brings about the destruction of the causal body, the annihilation of the Temple of Solomon, and the liberation of the Life.

Then that which in time and space has been termed the soul can "onward move in life." Evolution as we *now* understand it ceases; yet evolutionary unfoldment proceeds along new lines which are based upon the past but which produce very different results to those sensed even by the advanced disciple in his highest moments. A new life-expression appears which moves onward freed from all form yet subject still to limitations "within the circle of influence of the greater Life," but not limited by life within the many forms which progress, surrounded by that circle, that divine ring-pass-not. There is still the broad confining sweep of the purpose and the life-intent of the planetary Logos, but within that periphery and sphere of activity the Triads move with perfect freedom. Their onward push towards the higher states of Being is carried out in conformity with the life urge of the One in Whom they live and move and have their being. You will note, therefore, that these words in reality cover or deal with *life processes* and not with form building or the experience in forms, as usually understood.

A consideration of these at present inaccessible truths may serve to inspire your minds, evoke your intuition and give you vision and increased spiritual perception.

## RULE SEVEN

The Rule which is our theme for consideration at this time is one of deep significance and esoteric interest; it is concerned with the life of Shamballa and with the purposes of the Great Council. This rule is also one of rare beauty and extraordinary implications, and it offers me the opportunity to enlarge upon a subject little known or understood by any esotericist in the average esoteric group. The reason for this is that it is only as the new cycle draws closer — as it is drawing today — that the new and fuller teaching, the greatly extended horizon and the tremendously enhanced perception of the spiritual observer and worker become possible and apparent. Much, very much, has been given out during the past one hundred years anent the Masters, and (as we are considering the subject of initiation and of preparation for that great transitional experience) it is necessary to understand somewhat the nature of Those with Whom the disciple has to associate, and the kind of world and of consciousness in which They live and move and have Their being. The fact of the Hierarchy is to many thinkers an established fact; the hypothesis that there may be a Hierarchy is a widespread recognition. Information concerning its grades, its modes of working and its objectives are now common property; much has been accepted and much proved by those who believe this teaching.

Before proceeding to a discussion of Rule VII, however, I would like to spend a moment studying some of the effects of this steadily growing fund of knowledge. It has become the possession of the many and not only of the rare and discreet esotericist and occult student; this teaching has now seeped down into the consciousness of the masses and is there producing curiosity, relief and hope, speculation and cynical laughter, conscious spiritual effort or sustained ridicule — according to the type of mind, the sensitivity to truth or the crass credulity of the recipient. But the knowledge, belief and hope in the existence of a planetary Hierarchy has today leavened the entire mass of human thinking in a far wider and deeper manner than perhaps the most optimistic suspect; herein lies the hope of the world, and here is to be found also a fertile field for spiritual work during the coming decades. For this all disciples must prepare.

The rules whereby the Hierarchy may be reached are already well known to the aspirants of the world; they must become equally well known to the average person; the objectives of the hierarchical work must be emphasised and the nature of the divine Plan unfolded so that purpose and goal may be presented to humanity; the synthesis of the chain of hierarchical Existences — from the smallest atom of matter up to and including the Lord of Life Himself — must be unfolded; the essential and spiritual interdependence of all and the interrelation of every unit of divine life must be proved. This will eventually lead to that established unity of effort which will express itself in the merging of the fourth and the fifth kingdoms in nature, and to the establishment of that brotherhood which will constitute the germ or the seed of the coming manifestation of *the Hierarchy as the Heart of God* (directly related to the Heart of the Sun) in physical expression. This is necessarily an ambiguous phrase; but is as close an expression, in words, of hierarchical purpose as I find it possible to make.

The entire field of the world—meaning by that phrase all the kingdoms in nature in united inner and outer relationship — will be the medium of recognised spiritual experience and also the field of expression of certain divine qualities and aspects which have hitherto been in quiescent abeyance. What these qualities are, what divine aspects are awaiting precipitation, and which divine purposes are latent in that field of waiting expectancy, I cannot yet reveal or even indicate. The times are not yet ripe.

A great upheaval in all the kingdoms in nature has characterised this day and generation; a stupendous destruction of all forms of divine life and in every kingdom has been the outstanding note of this upheaval. Our modern civilisation has received a death blow from which it will never recover, but which will be recognised some day as the "blow of release" and as the signal for that which is better, new and more suitable for the evolving spirit, to make its appearance. Great and penetrating energies and their evoked forces have met in a conflict which has, figuratively speaking, elevated the mineral kingdom into the skies and which has brought down fire from heaven. I am talking to you factually and not just symbolically. The bodies of men, women and children, as well as of animals, have been destroyed; the forms of the vegetable kingdom and the potencies of the mineral kingdom have been disintegrated, distributed and devastated. The coherent life of all the planetary forms has been temporarily rendered incoherent. As an ancient prophecy has put it: "No true united Sound goes out from form to form, from life to life. Only a cry of pain, a demand for restitution and an invocation for relief from agony, despair and fruitless effort goes out from here to There."

All this upheaval of the "soil" of the world—spiritual, psychological and physical—all this disruption of the forms and of the familiar contours of our planetary life *had* to take place before there could come the emergence of the Hierarchy into the public consciousness; all this had to do its work upon the souls of men before the New Age could come in, bringing with it the Restoration of the Mysteries, and the rehabilitation of the peoples of the earth. The two go together. This is one of the major points which I am seeking to make. The disruption, disintegration and the completely chaotic conditions existing for the past five hundred years within all the kingdoms of nature have at last worked their way out into paralleling physical conditions. This is good and desirable; it marks the prelude to a better building of a better world, the construction of more adequate forms of life and of more correct human attitudes, plus a sounder orientation to reality. The best is yet to be.

Everything is being rapidly brought to the surface — the good and the bad, the desirable and the undesirable, the past and the future (for the two are one); the plough of God has nearly accomplished its work; the sword of the spirit has severed an evil past from the radiant future, and both are seen as contributory in the Eye of God; our material civilisation will be seen as giving place rapidly to a more spiritual culture; our church organisations, with their limiting and confusing theologies, will soon give place to the Hierarchy, with its emerging teaching — clear, factual, intuitive and non-dogmatic.

The Hierarchy has been invoked and its Members are

ready for a great "act of evocation," of response to the in-voking sound of humanity and of a definite (though rela-tively temporary) "act of orientation." This will force the Hierarchy, of its own freewill, to turn towards a new and more intimate type of relation with humanity. That period of orientation will end when a powerful, earthly Hierarchy will factually, externally and in reality hold sway on earth, working in all the kingdoms of nature and thus bringing about (in truth) the expression of the divine Plan. This plan is implemented through the medium of the senior Members of the Hierarchy, Who invoke the "Lights which carry out the Will of God"; They are Themselves invoked by the Light-Bearers, the Masters; They again, in Their turn, are invoked by the aspirants and disciples of the world. Thus is the chain of Hierarchy only a life line, along which travel the love and life of God, from Him to us and from us to Him.

This dual thought of the relationship between human-ity and the Hierarchy, and between the Hierarchy and the highest Centre, Shamballa, is completely covered in Rule VII in its two forms — for applicants, and for disciples and initiates.

Rule VII.

> *For Applicants:* Let the disciple turn his attention to the enunciating of those sounds which echo in the hall where walks the Master. Let him not sound the lesser notes which awaken vibration within the halls of Maya.

> *For Disciples and Initiates: Let the group life emit the Word of invocation and thus evoke response within those distant Ashrams where move the Chohans of the race of men. They are no longer men as are the Masters, but, having passed beyond that lesser stage, have linked Themselves with the Great Council in the highest Secret Place. Let the group sound a dual chord, reverberating in the halls where move the Masters but finding pause and prolongation within those radiant halls where move the "Lights which carry out the Will of God."*

Of real importance, though relatively small, are two contrasts. These emerge with clarity if you compare the instructions given to applicants for discipleship and those given to initiates. The applicant (or young disciple) is addressed as an individual and is told to give forth "those sounds" which will be heard by the Master in His Ashram— for that is the true significance of the words. The initiate functions in a group (always in a group) and has developed or is rapidly developing group consciousness; in unison with his group and as an integral conscious part of it, the Word must be enunciated; this is not a medley of sounds, but is one clear Word of invocation. You need to remember that the disciple is occupied in resolving the many sounds into the Word; when he has done this, his individual approach to reality terminates, and he begins to act with his group where all activity is concerned. This is a point of major importance for the newer type of disciple to grasp. In the past, the emphasis has been on what the individual initiate had to do in order to fit himself to take initiation, and so become a Master of the Wisdom and a member of the planetary Hierarchy. In the coming new cycle the emphasis will be upon *group* work and activity, upon *group* initiation and *group* approach to the Center of Life. The required mode of life and the needed individual eliminations and adjustments are now so well known (theoretically, at least) that they should have dropped below the threshold of consciousness and should consequently be automatic in their effects. This should also provide a steady inducement to thought which will make the initiate what he ought to be, because his conscious mind is free for group functioning. This is a concept which must be increasingly cultivated; "As a man thinketh in his heart, so he is." The lower mind should be the organ of heart expression and be as unconscious in its functioning as is the rhythm of the heart itself—the physical heart. The higher mind is intended to become increasingly the field of the initiate's effort, and hence the constant need for him to build the antahkarana.

In this Rule we are therefore dealing with the work

to be done by a group of pledged disciples and initiates;
they are learning *together* to make an approach to Shamballa (involving the Will element); this is as much a goal
of the Hierarchy as approach to the Hierarchy is the goal of
advanced humanity. It concerns the interrelation of great
centres of force. This is a point which esoteric students
should attempt to grasp for it completes the planetary chain
of Hierarchy and throws a light upon the Way of the
Higher Evolution.

Great movements and progressions have always taken
place upon the subjective side of life; it is these subjective
activities which have made it hard for disciples to grasp the
truth and arrive at some true realisation of the subjective
situation which ever exists between the Hierarchy and
Shamballa. The energies concerned are so subtle, and the
Beings involved are so advanced and so highly developed
(even from the angle of the initiate of the third degree),
that it is well-nigh impossible for the teachings (which I
seek to give) to be worded in such a manner that they become comprehensible. All that I can do is to make certain
statements which (from the standpoint of those I teach) are
*not* verifiable; they have to be accepted on trust and with
the reservation that time and the point of view of the
individual disciple will later prove their truth — or their
non-truth.

The objective of all training given to the disciple is to
shift his conscious awareness from the point where he is to
levels which are higher than those in the three worlds of
definitely human evolution; the intention is to teach him
to function on those planes of conscious contact which are
as yet so subjective that he only accepts them as existent in
theory. The trained initiate knows that they have to become his natural habitat, and that eventually he has to rele
gate the ordinary and normal human experience to the
three worlds of daily expression. These become eventually
the worlds that exist below the threshold of consciousness;
they are relegated to the realm of the subconscious—recoverable consciously, if necessary for right service of humanity,

but as much below the threshold of consciousness as are
the ordinary emotional reactions of the average man. These
are always recoverable (as modern psycho-analysis has demonstrated) and can become capable of expression and of
formulation into conditioning concepts — thus actuating
mental perception if deemed of adequate importance. However, it should be borne in mind that the greater part of
the emotional life of the disciple must become increasingly
subconscious, just as the physical plane life of the normal,
healthy human being is entirely automatic and thus subconscious. When the disciple has striven to expand his consciousness, when he has learnt to stabilise his consciousness
in the Spiritual Triad, then he becomes part of a great and
constant hierarchical effort which strives upwards towards
the "Place of Clear Electric Light," to which the clear cold
light of the reason is the first key to the first door.

There are three doors into Shamballa, speaking figuratively:

1. There is *the door of the reason,* of pure perception
of truth. Christ gave the clue to this teaching when He said
"I am the Way, the Truth and the Life." Of *that Way* we
know much, because upon the Way a vast body of teaching
has been given, and that teaching, if followed, brings a man
into the Hierarchy. He then becomes a factual part of the
hierarchical membership. Of *that Truth,* we know (as aspirants) relatively very little. Truth — as we understand it
during the early treading of the Path of Discipleship — is
concerned with great verities which are (from the insight of
the Enlightened Ones) only the a b c of life. These truths
are:

The manifestation of divinity on the physical plane.
The doctrine of Avatars. This religious history reveals.
The nature of consciousness, through the development
of psychology.
The doctrine of the Trinity, as it expresses itself
through the aspects and the attributes.

These four expressions of truth will be found to convey all
the knowledge with which the initiate must stand equipped

when he climbs the Mount of Transfiguration at the time of the third initiation. They have given him a spiritual perception of the Plan.

Of *that Life,* we know nothing whatsoever. The contemplation of its significance belongs to Those Who can move at will within the "precincts of the Lord of Life" — in Shamballa itself. All we can know about it is its lowest step. This enables us to study the impulse or instinct which enables all forms of life to function, which embodies the principles of responsiveness to contacts and to environment, and which embodies itself in the breath of life; this is also related to the air in some mysterious manner, and also to fire. More anent this subject it would be useless for me to say.

2. There is also *the door of the will.* This is a penetrating power which relates Plan to Purpose and which has in it the faculty of coherent persistence. The reason for this persistence is that it is not dependent upon the content of the form—whether it is the form of an atom, of a man or of a planet—but upon a vital dynamic and immutable purpose, latent in the consciousness of the planetary Being Who, "having pervaded this entire universe with a fragment" of Himself, REMAINS—greater, more inscrutable and "firmer in intent" than any of His creations, even the most advanced and the closest to Him. Only those have clear perception of His divine purpose who do not belong to our earth humanity at all; these are the Lives who came with Him to this planet when He came, and Who remain with Him as "the prisoners of loving intention" until the last "weary pilgrim has found his way home."

This spiritual will is something of which humanity knows nothing; it is hidden and veiled by the self-will of the individual and the group will of the soul. Through both of these experiences the human being moves until his individual will is developed and grounded, focussed and reoriented, and his group will is unfolded so that it includes and swallows up the dedicated, conscious, individual will. When this fusion has taken place (at the third initiation) a

great revelation unfolds itself, and for the first time the
initiate senses and then contacts the universal will; from
that moment the initiate says, "Father, not my will but
Thine be done." Just a little of what that will includes may
emerge as we study this seventh rule and some of the succeeding rules.

3. I can find no words to express the nature of the
third door. Let us, in default of a better term, call it *the
door of the monadic sense of essential duality*. Body and life,
soul and personality, the Spiritual Triad and its expression,
the Christ in incarnation — all these dualities have played
their part. Man has passed from one expansion of consciousness to another. Now he comes to the final duality of
spirit and matter, prior to their resolution into something
to which the terms "isolated unity" and "universal synthesis" give only faint and inadequate clues. To the development of this system of identification the initiate of the
degree of Master of the Wisdom, and also (on a higher turn
of the spiral) of the degree of the Christ, are focussing all
Their efforts. Up to the fourth initiation, the term "system
of expansions" would seem illuminating; after that great
initiation, the term "system of identification" would appear
more appropriate.

When the initiate has passed through the three doors,
symbolically speaking, he then faces all life, all events, all
pre-determinations, all wisdom, all activity and all that the
future may hold of service and progress from the angle of
the pure reason (infallible and immutable), of true spiritual
will (completely identified with the purpose of the planetary
Logos), and of the highest possible focussed relation. The
mystery of relationship becomes revealed to him. Then the
entire scheme of evolution and of the intention of the One
in Whom he lives and moves and has his being becomes
clear to him; he has no more to learn within this planetary
scheme; he has become universal in his attitude to all forms
of life, and is also identified with the "isolated unity" of
Sanat Kumara. Few of the great Lives Who form the inner
group of the Council Chamber at Shamballa are now of

greater advancement than he; the "Supernal Three," the "Radiant Seven," the "Lives embodying the forty-nine Fires," the "Buddhas of Activity," and certain "Eternal Spirits" from such centres of dynamic spiritual life as Sirius, or from the constellation which at any one time forms a triangle with our Sun and Sirius, and a Representative from Venus are of greater — far greater — advancement. Otherwise, all initiates of the sixth degree, and a few of the Masters Who have undergone specialised training because They are upon the first Ray of Will or Power (the ray conditioning Shamballa itself), form part of the Great Council. Many Masters and Chohans, however, after serving upon the planet in various capacities, working with the Law of Evolution, pass out of our planetary life altogether.

All the above information concerning the Lives which are far in advance of the disciples of the world contains little of moment for you, except in so far as it falls into a diagrammatic pattern of our planetary life and purpose, and enabling you, therefore, to get a faint glimpse of a synthetic theme and purpose to which all evolving lives must and will eventually conform.

It must ever be borne in mind that the great theme of LIGHT underlies our entire planetary purpose. The full expression of perfect LIGHT, occultly understood, is the engrossing life-purpose of our planetary Logos. Light is the great and obsessing enterprise in the three worlds of human evolution; everywhere men rate the light of the sun as essential to healthy living; some idea of the human urge to light can be grasped if you consider the brilliance of the physically engendered light in which we live when night arrives, and compare it with the mode of lighting the streets and homes of the world prior to the discovery of gas, and later of electricity. The light of knowledge, as the reward of educational processes, is the incentive behind all our great schools of learning in every country in the world and is the goal of much of our world organisation; the terminology of light controls even our computation of time. The mystery of electricity is unfolding gradually before our rapt eyes and the electrical nature of man is being slowly proven and will later demonstrate that, throughout the human structure and form, man is composed primarily of light atoms, and that the light in the head (so familiar to esotericists) is no fiction or figment of wishful thinking or of a hallucinated imagination, but is definitely brought about by the junction or fusion of the light inherent in substance itself and the light of the soul.

It will be found that this will be capable of scientific proof. It will also be shown that the soul itself is light, and that the entire Hierarchy is a great centre of light, causing the symbology of light to govern our thinking, our approach to God, and enabling us to understand somewhat the meaning of the words of Christ "I am the Light of the world." These words carry meaning to all true disciples and present them with an analogous goal which they define to themselves as that of finding the light, appropriating the light, and themselves becoming light-bearers. The theme of light runs through all the world Scriptures; the idea of enlightenment conditions all the training given to the youth of the world (limited though the application of this idea may be), and the thought of more light governs all the inchoate yearnings of the human spirit.

We have not yet carried the concept up to the Centre of Life where dwells the Ancient of Days, the Eternal Youth, the Lord of the World, Sanat Kumara, Melchizedek—God. Yet from that Centre streams what has been called the Light of Life, the Light Supernal. These are empty words as yet until we know, as trained initiates, that light is a symptom and an expression of Life, and that essentially, occultly and in a most mysterious way the terms, Light and Life, are interchangeable within the limits of the planetary ring-pass-not. Beyond those limits—who knows? Light can be regarded as a symptom, a reaction to the meeting and consequent fusion of spirit and matter.

Therefore, where that great point of fusion and of solar crisis (for that is what it is, even when producing a planetary crisis) appears in time and space, light also immediately appears and of such intensity that only those who know the light of the soul, and who can bear the hierarchical light can be trained to enter into and form part of the light of Shamballa and walk in those "radiant halls where move the Lights which carry out the Will of God."

To carry the concept a little nearer home: only when the will of the personality and the will of the soul come together—evoked by love—does the light of the soul dominate the material light of the personality. This is a statement of importance. Only when the will of the Monad and the will of the Hierarchy of souls meet and blend in the "upper brackets" (if I may use such a modern business phrase) can the radiant light of Life dominate the blended lights of Humanity and of the Hierarchy. Faintly this group fusion and junction can be seen to be taking place.

It is also the first touch of the radiance of Shamballa which is bringing the universal revelation of evil, a radiance which is now producing the world unrest and which has brought about the lining up of good and evil; this touch of radiance is the conditioning factor behind what is called post-war planning and the ideas of reconstruction and of world rebuilding which are dominating the best human thinking at this time.

It should be carefully borne in mind that evil (cosmic evil or the source of planetary evil) is much closer to Shamballa than it is to Humanity. The Great Lives there move entirely free from glamour; Their vision is one of extreme simplicity; They are concerned only with the great and simple duality of spirit and matter, and not with the many forms which the fusion of these two brings into being. *The domination of spirit (and its reflection, soul) by matter is what constitutes evil* and this is true whether the statement is applied to the development of the individual or of the group. The "Lights which carry out the will of God" move free from the spell of evil. The Light in which They move safeguards Them, and Their Own innate and inherent radiance repels evil. But They "move alongside the evil to which all lesser forms are prone"; They are part of a great observing Group which "moves forward in time and space"; its members watch the great war and conflict proceed on Earth between the Forces of Light and the Forces of Evil. They have let loose upon Earth the Forces of Light, whilst the Forces of Evil are inherent in substance itself—cf which all the many forms of life are constructed.

At this time, the work of the Great Council at Shamballa, working until now through the Hierarchy, is with the *life* within the form; They have to proceed with the utmost caution as They thus work, because these Lights know that the danger of *premature direct contact* with humanity, and of consequent overstimulation, is great. One of the causes of the present cataclysm is the fact that humanity was deemed capable of taking and receiving a "touch from Shamballa," without stepping it down via the Hierarchy, as has hitherto been the custom. The determination to apply this touch (which is in the nature of a great experiment) was made in 1825, when the Great Council had its usual centennial meeting. The results you know; they are working out before your eyes. The industrial movement began to take shape one hundred years ago and received a great impetus from this touch. The evil in nations—aggression, greed, intolerance and hate—was aroused as never before, and two world wars occurred, one of which is still raging (written October 1943). Paralleling this was an uprising of good, again in response to the divine "touch," resulting in the growth of understanding, the spread of idealism, the purification of our educational systems and the inauguration of reforms in every department of human life. All has been speeded up and little such growth was seen on a world-wide scale prior to 1825. The knowledge of the Hierarchy is also spreading over the earth; the facts anent discipleship and initiation are becoming common property; humanity has consequently moved onward into a greater measure of light. Good and evil stand out in clearer focus; light and dark are in a more brilliant juxtaposition; issues of right and wrong are appearing with cleared definition, and humanity as a whole sees the great problems of righteousness and love, of sin and separateness upon a worldwide scale.

The old age and the coming new age, old rhythms of thought and new approaches to truth and consequent new and better ways of life are presented with clarity to the minds of men. The guarantee of the success of the experiment started more than a century ago is the fact that (in spite of much that is undesirable) so many nations have ranged themselves upon the side of right, and only two definitely and altogether upon the side of evil. The evil is more concentrated, and therefore more powerful temporarily upon the physical plane; the good is more diffused and not so pure in its concentrated essence being coloured by many undesirable aspects; the good, however, is concentrating rapidly and will triumph. The "Lights that carry out the will of God" now wait to give another touch which will enable the reconstruction work to move forward along right lines, but They wait for the invocative cry of humanity and for the dust of battle and of conflict to die down.

The next two rules will reveal the issues still more clearly and will outline for you when better understood, explained and amplified, the processes and methods of hierarchical work, carried on in conjunction with the Great Council of Shamballa. To this must be added the cooperation— as far as may be—of all enlightened men, working under the Lightbearers, the Masters, and under the inspiration of the Lights which carry out the will of God.

In the foregoing I have endeavoured to give some faint idea of the relation existing between the Hierarchy and Shamballa. I did this in order that you might grasp some measure of the synthesis underlying the entire planetary life; in order also that this rule for initiates could be interpreted as intended, as far as is possible, to the uninitiate consciousness; and finally, in order that the entire concept of Shamballa and its immense reservoir of energy, which we call the will or the life of God, may take its rightful place in the occult presentation of truth. The will of God and the life of God are esoterically synonymous terms, and when the life aspect of an individual and his spiritual, selfless will are completely synchronised, then you have — in a human being — the full expression of divinity or what has been called esoterically, "Shamballa is consummated in him."

This again is, of course, only relative but the expression of this relationship may elucidate the problem somewhat, and the aspirant or disciple needs to remember that it is only through the analogies existing in the microcosm to the Macrocosm that enlightenment can come. And how, I ask you, will he understand the relation existing between the three great planetary centres (Shamballa, the Hierarchy and Humanity) when as yet he scarcely knows himself as a human being? How can he grasp these fundamental and advanced truths when he is only just beginning to learn the nature of the hierarchical quality of love and when his spiritual will (which links him to Shamballa) is as yet totally unawakened? And I mean, totally. But the dim outlines of the general picture must be grasped, and each decade in the future will see the aspirant and the disciple more capable of grasping it.

## RULE EIGHT

Rule VIII now comes up for consideration. The previous seven rules have been of a wide and general connotation. They have been largely postulates, emphasising group life, group planetary relationships, and the fundamental Science of Invocation and Evocation which underlies all world processes, which is the inspiring energy behind all evolutionary unfoldment, and which creates the medium or channel of related communication between the great centres in our planet, through which the life of our Logos flows and His purposes are worked out. I would remind you that the creative process was initiated by Sound, and in that Sound the Logos both invoked and evoked. He issued the call and He engineered and implemented the response and thus the "Army of the Voice" (as *The Secret Doctrine* calls it) came into being.

The Head (the *idea*), the Heart (the *ideal*) and the Throat (the creative agent of the resulting *idol,* the temporary and fleeting expression of the ideal, inspired by the idea) came into being; three great Centres emerged in time and space and—*at this point in the evolutionary cycle*—we call them Shamballa, the Hierarchy and Humanity.

With these fundamental factors the first seven rules have been occupied, and I have tried to help you to see their significance somewhat, from the angle of the initiate-consciousness.

We come now to a close consideration of this Rule VIII, where it might be said that the specific rules for the training of initiates begin. These remaining seven rules must be studied most carefully from that angle. They are not susceptible of casual and superficial analysis. I realise that only those who have taken initiation will be in a position to grasp the esoteric significance of the words I use and of much that I may say, but it is for them I write; their numbers are even today more than are suspected, and their ranks will be steadily increased in the post-war period, both through the strenuous effort of disciples in training to "make the grade," and through the coming into incarnation of initiates of all degrees—some of whom are the children of today.

## Rule VIII.

*For Applicants:* When the disciple nears the Portal, the greater seven must awaken and bring forth response from the lesser seven upon the double circle.

*For Disciples and Initiates: Let the group find within itself response to the greater seven groups which carry out the hierarchical will with love and understanding. The group contains all seven, the perfect group. The lesser seven, the greater seven and the planetary seven form one great whole, and these the group must know. When this is realised and the Law of the Supplementary Seven is understood, let the group understand the Three and then the* ONE. *This they can do with the united breath and the unified rhythm.*

On the surface, this rule appears to be one of surprising complexity and immense difficulty. It deals with so many groups and septenates and this seems to complicate understanding considerably. Yet every person in the world is dealing with the multiplicity of units and combinations of forces which make up his entire daily life and which create his environment and his life circumstances. Life would be simple indeed if the average man had only seven factors to consider, with which to conform, to work with and to use. Advance into the world of spiritual values and into the realm of triadal existence (in which the initiate moves) is definitely an advance into simplicity. It is an advance from the complications of the multiplication table and its resultant arithmetic into the simplicity of the symbolic formulas as used in the higher mathematics; it is a moving out of the world of kaleidoscopic figures in constant movement, into the world of meaning; it is a process of getting behind the world of effects into the world of causes, realising that one simple cause or directed movement of energy can set in motion a myriad of effects. The way of the initiate is not a complicated one, once he has grasped the fact that he must release himself from the world of seeming and of illusion and stand free in the world of light, where all stand clearly revealed. Then he can begin to face the lessons and take the training which will enable him to handle energy—having released himself from the control of forces —and begin to direct energy in conformity with the great Plan. The complexity lies in the thinking of the neophyte. The initiate knows it not.

First let us clearly define the various septenates referred to in this rule. I will first tabulate them in the order of their appearance and define them, and then I will enlarge upon them in order to point out where *the training* enters in, where the rule applies, and how the embodied rule is in the nature of a Law which the initiate may not evade.

I would ask you here to refer to what I earlier said anent rules, laws and orders when starting with you this particular study.

*1. The seven greater groups* . . . The seven groups or Ashrams within the Hierarchy.

### THE HIERARCHY

These carry out the hierarchical will, which is love.

They work through love and understanding.

Each is presided over by a Chohan and a group is called an Ashram.

These major Ashrams have many affiliated Ashrams, presided over by a Master on the same ray as the Chohan, and are capable at any moment of being absorbed into the primary Ashram.

The perfect or complete group is the Hierarchy itself, containing all the seven major Ashrams and their affiliates.

*2. The Planetary seven groups* . . . the seven rays, the central septenate of energy.

### SHAMBALLA

These embody the will of Shamballa, which is divine purpose.

They work as life energy, as quality, and produce appearance.

Each is presided over by one of the seven Spirits before the Throne; by one of the seven Ray Lords.

Each of these rays has its seven subrays which relate it to all the other rays.

These seven rays can, under divine purpose, be re-absorbed into the Three and then into the One.

*3. The lesser seven* . . . the seven types of men and also the seven root races.

### HUMANITY

These embody the intelligence of the Logos as it expresses itself through creativity.

They are learning to work intelligently with matter in order to develop love in response to divine purpose—which is will or life.

Each of the seven types, responsive to one or

other of the seven rays, is conditioned or ruled by its prototype, the soul on its own plane.

These major types or races of men have many subraces and subsidiary types, developed during the evolutionary process; all will eventually demonstrate the seven major types.

The perfect type is the Christ, the Heavenly Man, Who expresses all the major types and Who is the "pattern of things as they *are*."

*4. The supplementary seven* . . . the seven centres of energy in the individual man.

### HUMANITY

These together embody the combined forces of the planetary life as registered by the perfected individual. They will eventually enable the man to achieve perfection.

They enable the individual to respond to material forces, to soul energy and spiritual life, and they constitute a complete response apparatus to the planetary life, purpose, intent and form.

Each of the seven centres is responsive to one or other of the seven rays and their qualities under the conditioning energy of the soul ray and the forces, emanating from the environment.

These centres develop progressively and under the impact of circumstances and the Law of the Supplementary Seven, but all will eventually express in some measure the seven types of ray energy.

The Law of the Supplementary Seven can be worded as follows:

"The Law demands the entrance of that which can effect a change.

The Law demands that right direction should then guide the entering forces.

The Law demands that the changes thus effected remove the form, bring quality to light and lay the emphasis upon life.

The Law demands that this is brought about by the One, working through the Three, energising the Seven and creating the straight line from there to here, and ending in a point which ignores the Three."

When, the rule goes on, this is understood and applied, then four things happen:

1. The group must understand the nature of the Three.
2. The nature of the One must be grasped and comprehended.
3. The group must work through the medium of the united breath.
4. The group must attain a unified rhythm.

Here you have a relatively simple analysis (on the face of it, though not in reality) of a complex rule which the initiate has to apply to himself once he has grasped the significance of the seven basic postulates. The first seven rules provide the framework within which his work has to be done. The last seven rules concern various significant matters which, step by step, are revealed to the initiate as his consciousness is expanded. They relate to:

1. The work which the initiate must accomplish within himself.
2. The group relations of the initiate and his absolute need to work with his group and as an integrated and conscious part of it.
3. The place which invocation and evocation must take as instruments in his pledged intelligent service.
4. The blending of the four lessons which the applicant has to master and the four lessons which the initiate has to complete in order that a complete fusion of personality and Monad can be brought about.
5. The significance of resurrection and ascension, particularly the latter, because little has been given out to date anent ascension.

There are certain major frameworks (if I may continue to use this phrase) within which the initiate has to learn consciously to work, recognising them for what they are; once he has learnt to master that which lies within some particular framework, he finds that it is only a part, a small fraction, of a still greater whole, within which he must also learn to function and play his part.

First he, as a disciple, has to learn to work within *the framework of his blending soul-personality*. This task at first takes the form of character building and disciplining (whilst upon the Probationary Path), of a struggle to see, of an endeavour to make a continuity of his soul contact. Finally, this leads to the beginning of the stage of soul and personality merging and at this point he steps upon the Path of Discipleship, technically understood. From then on his problem is to *know* himself as he truly is, to direct energy to the needed centres which are awaiting scientific attention, to superintend consciously the fitting of himself, as a personality, to act as the instrument of the soul and later of the Hierarchy, to learn to contact energy, to handle and direct it. This entails a comprehension of the mechanism within himself — the seven centres within the vital body — through which the contacted energy must flow under soul direction, and it also means the perfecting of the response apparatus and the newly constructed spiritual mechanism which exoterically enables him to contact the outside world, and esoterically enables him to contact the world of souls. It implies a steady process of interior perfecting until nothing further remains to be done within that individual framework. The bulk of this work has been covered by the time the fourth initiation has been taken, and has been completely covered when the fifth initiation is undergone.

This all takes much time, but when a certain measure of success has been achieved, when the initiate's understanding is somewhat enlightened and his energy-use and his power of direction are becoming intelligently applied, he can then begin to work within *the framework of the greater seven groups,* that is, within the Hierarchy. This he does first upon the periphery of the hierarchical aura and later as a conscious, accepted and pledged worker in some

Ashram — the Ashram being dependent upon his ray type. He then is in a position to discover the close interlocking that exists between the supplementary seven (his own seven centres) and the seven great groups within the Hierarchy; he comes to realise that only when his centres are somewhat awakened and attuned is it possible for him to work within the larger framework of the Hierarchy, and this because the quality of the greater groups and the life expression of the seven planetary groups, the seven rays, are being slowly developed by him under the influence of hierarchical supervision through the medium of his own seven centres — the supplementary seven.

Thus, from a new angle which is practical and not simply theoretical, it begins to dawn on him that he is an inalienable part of a group whole and that this incontrovertible fact involves responsibilities and duties. He discovers that his major responsibility—spiritually speaking— is to permit no hindrance, on the part of the supplementary seven, to the free flow of love from the greater seven, and later the free flow of life (inspired by purpose) from the planetary seven. He knows now that all form a great interlocking directorate through which the will of God is working out. He now knows himself to be a minute part of that great interlocking Whole, a responsible conscious atom within its periphery. Then as he goes on and learns to submit to the Law of the Supplementary Seven, he finds that from the life angle and through his own conscious direction, gradually developed, all the potencies of divinity are his to use, once he can be trusted, as the advanced initiate can ever be trusted. He is then set free for complete cooperation with the purpose lying behind the Plan. He has passed out of the human kingdom into the Hierarchy; later he will pass out of the hierarchical group into Shamballa, or out of our planetary life altogether, and either here or there will begin a greater and more extended service.

Coming down to the immediate practical issues, the initiate is confronted with the problem of work within the individual framework, for I am not here dealing with the requirements for the initiations above or beyond the third. Here the initiate has reached the point where he grasps the significant fact that the way into the innermost *Centre* is most securely guarded; no one can pass onward and take those more advanced steps which admit into the higher worlds of being and of unparalleled potency until he has demonstrated within the framework of his own life a definite control of energy (and this the black adept also possesses), purity of motive (which the black adept can likewise have, if by purity of motive you mean single-hearted and one-pointed intent), deep love of humanity (which the black adept never has), selflessness, willingness to follow the light wherever it may lead, ability to begin work within the larger framework the moment such an attempt becomes possible, clear vision and spiritual insight, a developed intuition, and an undeviating intention and strong faith in the future. When these qualities begin to show themselves, it then becomes possible to admit the initiate to further advancement upon the Way.

It is believed to be safe for him now to move on a few more steps into greater light, and then—having reached his next point of testing—he must there again demonstrate the rightness of his work within the individual framework and his ability to work within the greater framework in group formation. He must appreciate the fact that as he passes upon the upward way he may not safely so do without the safeguards which protect the Way from him until he knows more; he must learn also that the group protects him and that only with the group can he proceed with security; he begins to realise that the group is not only a protection but also his chosen and destined field of service. He begins to learn *with his group* the meaning of the "united breath" referred to in the rule, and also to work with the group in "unified rhythm."

Thus he goes from strength to strength. All the time the Hierarchy is aiding in his development and at the same time protecting the Way from him until such time as glamour cannot reach him. This individual security of his is only reached between the time of taking the second initiation and the third. Prior to that, he is still regarded as a potential hazard and as unstable. After that, he may suffer from illusion, but there is then no fear of his permanently turning back and reaching the left-hand path and so perhaps, in rare cases, finding his way into the Black Lodge. The major liability of the average initiate is sloth or lack of speed. Ponder on that.

I would have you grasp clearly the highly condensed presentation I have given you. Some of it you know already but it is the synthetic presentation which I would have you appreciate and appropriate. We can then take up the work to be done within the individual framework *by the initiate;* I will endeavour to help you to understand somewhat more clearly what the initiate-consciousness would read into the Law of the Supplementary Seven.

Beginning with this eighth rule which we are now studying, we enter upon the consideration of certain major unfoldments, major spiritual happenings and a series of major awakenings in consciousness which are in the nature of events. These involve likewise certain major recognitions and appreciations which will affect the initiate increasingly and bring about his eventual attainment. *These* are the factors which condition the date of his achievement and not the character undertakings and the soul contacts which are so necessary upon the Path of Probation and upon the Path of Discipleship.

We are principally concerned at this point with the interpretation of the Law of the Supplementary Seven. It must be remembered that the *Laws of Nature* are imposed upon the mass of men, and cannot be avoided. If these laws are broken, infringed or evaded, they carry their own penalty within themselves, and this also cannot be avoided. These great protective laws are intended to guard the personalities through which the soul incarnates and eventually to cement and further all the great and possible relationships. The man passes from the stage of antagonism (as an individual) to the control of these natural though divine laws, to a recognition of their inevitability and of their wisdom. They automatically then control him.

When this control by the Laws of Nature has become complete, the man becomes an aspirant and begins to come under the *Laws of the Soul,* which are laws concerned primarily with the establishing of the great Fellowship of the Universe. There has been much confusion among esotericists upon these points. They confuse the discipline to which the personality has to submit when coming under soul influence, with the Laws of the Soul which have naught to do with the petty little affairs of the personality—unimportant and unnoticed by the soul on its own plane—but with the growing recognition of right group relations; these are based upon a growing understanding of the hierarchical mode of work and of inter-hierarchical relationships. The Laws of Nature, therefore, concern the activities of the soul in form and are mandatory and accepted by the form nature. The Laws of the Soul concern the life of the soul upon its own plane, and the relation which the blending soul and personality learn to establish with other souls and with the Hierarchy. These are consciously and voluntarily obeyed, and are not just accepted as mandatory and as forced upon the man by force of circumstances, experience and evolution. They tend to bring about increasing relation between the Hierarchy of Souls and Humanity as a whole, between the great planetary centre which is the custodian of the principle of love and the planetary centre, humanity, which nurtures and distributes the energy of mind.

The Law of the Supplementary Seven is the great synthetic *Law of Life or of Spirit* and is the law with which the initiate works; it is this law he wields. From acceptance of the laws of nature and obedience to the laws of the soul, he passes into the positive phase of understanding and wielding the Law of Life. Because this is a governing law for all initiates, and because we know that the nature of life-energy or of spirit cannot be grasped until after the third initiation, it is exceedingly difficult for me to write in explanation of this law. You have not yet the initiate con-

sciousness. I have therefore had to express this law in terms
of form, whereas the initiate understands it from its formless angle.

This law is concerned with the wielding of energy in
the world of the Spiritual Triad and not with the distribution or the transmission of this energy to the three worlds
in which average humanity habitually dwells. Right wielding of this law (controlling energy in the initiatory world
of causes) automatically brings about activity, movement,
force expression, and right distribution of these forces in
the lower three worlds. These are, under the evolutionary
law, direct reflections of the three higher worlds of the
triadal light and life. Motivation, the use of the eye of
vision (turned this time by the initiate functioning in the
world of causes upon the worlds of human living), and the
correct direction of force in cooperation with the hierarchical Plan condition all the activities of the initiate working
with this law. Clearer than this I cannot be.

This Law of the Supplementary Seven is concerned
with the inflow of energy from the seven planetary centres
to the seven groups or types of men, via the seven groups
within the Hierarchy. In this work of transmission the seven
centres of the initiate are used as agencies; their work, therefore, is not the interrelated work of right transmission of
energy within the septenary constitution of the etheric body
of the individual initiate, implementing his life expression,
but is the task of being responsive to the seven types of
planetary energy which are received in a pure state. It is
then channeled through the seven centres in the initiate's
etheric vehicle and out into the world of men as regenerative and constructive forces. These living spiritual energies
—transmitted by the individual initiate from the planetary
centres—are handled by him under a great uniform plan
and are the means whereby salvation (to use an old familiar
word) can come to the aid of humanity. This is the "saving
force" in its various aspects, of which the Great Invocation
speaks: *"The hour of service of the Saving Force has now
arrived". (The Externalisation of the Hierarchy, page 249.)*

The high Initiates (Those above the rank of Master) work with the energies coming from the seven planets of the solar system at this time active; these feed or implement the seven planetary centres. But the Law of the Supplementary Seven is applied by initiates below the rank of Master, and they are therefore working solely with the seven centres within the Form of the One in Whom we live and move and have our being.

One of their first tasks is to bring about a free flow and right energy relations between the three major centres in our planet which correspond to the head, heart and throat centres in man. They are occupied with the circulation of energy between Shamballa, the Hierarchy and Humanity. This circulation, which for the first time in planetary history includes the highest centre, Shamballa, is not yet completely established. Shamballa has been in touch with the centre called Humanity *by impact* several times in the history of the race. But there has been no reciprocal action and no free flow. Humanity has taken the impact of energy and this impact has wrought changes in the activity of the centre, but there has been no "responsive return," as it is esoterically called, and hence no circulation. The Shamballa force has hitherto been transmitted via the Hierarchy. For the first time, and in this century there has been *direct* impact. The diagram on page 160 may make this clearer.

We shall eventually have a free circulation and a veritable vortex of force set up between the three centres; it will be of such an increasing radiatory activity that—moving in *both* directions around the three centres—it will eventually contact the radiations emanating from the other four centres of the planetary Life, thus completing the interplay and the interrelation between all seven. These four include the three lower kingdoms of nature and a certain basic centre (corresponding to the centre at the base of the spine in man) about which nothing is as yet known nor will be known for ages to come.

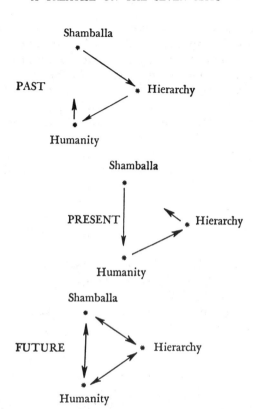

The importance, therefore, of the centre which we call Humanity will be apparent. *The Secret Doctrine* has ever taught that mankind has a special function in saving and regenerating nature. The "saving force"—a circulatory combination of the three major energies—is radiated by humanity as a group-creative impulse, and this gradually sweeps all forms of life into the field of its magnetic potency, thus relating them (or rather the soul of each kingdom) to the Hierarchy and to Shamballa. This involves a great mystery which is closely tied up—little as you may realise it— with the doctrine of Avatars or of World Saviours.

It is in this connection that the words I gave you previously are pertinent:

1. "The group must understand the nature of the Three." This will be seen to refer to the three major centres and the nature of their relationship, and not specifically to the Trinity.
2. "The nature of the One must be grasped and comprehended." This has reference to the fact that our planetary Life is Itself a centre within a still greater Life, and is today one of the three planetary centres (even if not yet one of the seven sacred planets) which are the custodians of the force, in process of transmission, which will be to the greater Life what Shamballa, the Hierarchy and Humanity are to our planetary Logos.
3. "The group must work through the medium of the united breath." This deals with the processes of circulation, for the breath is the life and pours through all the centres.
4. "The group must attain a unified rhythm." This has no reference in reality to the work of a group of disciples, but to a group of centres of life, such as the three major centres or the entire group of seven centres.

A study of these ideas may carry illumination, but I would again remind you that I write for initiates, living at a later period in this century and in the next.

In considering this Law of the Supplementary Seven, I would like to point out that the word "supplementary" is of real significance. It brings in a factor of great interest, from the angle of initiation. You must bear in mind that when the antahkarana is constructed and in use, there is consequently a free play of energy in a direct line between the Spiritual Triad and the personality; i.e., between the Monad and its "earthly anchor." You will also remember that the soul body, the form on the higher levels of the mental plane which has "shrouded" the soul, eventually disappears. This, as you know, takes place at the fourth initiation and is one of the best recognised facts in the occult teaching. In the three worlds, the correspondence to this disappearance of the form of the second divine aspect, the soul, is the dissolution of the astral body—the second aspect of the personality. Then the personality stands free from its control. Sensitivity and reaction to contact in the three worlds has been perfectly developed, but it no longer holds the disciple a prisoner.

Then, at a later stage upon the Path of Initiation, the causal body also disappears and the initiate stands free in the three worlds. The astral body and the causal or soul body are—in the language of esotericism—supplementary to reality. They have had a temporary reality during the evolutionary process, but (having served their purpose and having endowed man with certain required assets — consciousness, feeling, sensitivity, the ability to establish and register contact) they pass away and the initiate remains, possessed of power over form and a fully awakened consciousness. He is a soul and the fusion is complete.

What is true of the individual is true too of the Heavenly Man, the planetary Logos. In the long period of a world cycle there comes a time when the Hierarchy itself, as a body organised and functioning in order to implement certain evolutionary ends, is no longer needed. It is then regarded as "supplementary," and under the Law its life, its potency and its entire consciousness are absorbed into the planetary head centre, Shamballa. A great process of abstraction or of withdrawal takes place, covering necessarily a long period of time, and which is consummated only when evolution—as we know it—comes to an end and the planetary Life (again as we know it) also comes to an end. This process of abstraction is always going on. Men become disciples and then initiates. Some stay as hierarchical workers, choosing to work with the planetary forces of evolution. Others pass on into the great Council Chamber of the Lord of the World, and still others pass out of our planetary ring-pass-not altogether.

Thus the Law of the Supplementary Seven is ever in force. It functions in the processes going on in the seven centres of the individual man, gathering energy from one centre into another until all are centred, controlled and directed in the head. In the stage of what the Hindus call "samadhi" the vital energies from all the centres are concentrated in the highest head centre in the etheric body, in the area just above the physical head. Thus the analogy is complete. The processes of abstraction are (as you may thus see) connected with the life aspect, are set in motion by an act of the spiritual will, and constitute the "resurrection principle which lies hidden in the work of the Destroyer," as an old esoteric saying expresses it. The lowest manifestation of this principle is to be seen in the process of what we call Death—which is in reality a means of abstracting the life principle, informed by consciousness, from the form or the bodies in the three worlds.

Thus, the great synthesis emerges, and destruction, death, and dissolution are in reality naught but life processes. Abstraction is indicative of process, progress and development.

It is this aspect of the Law of Life (or the Law of Synthesis as it is called in certain larger connotations) with which the initiate specifically deals when wielding the Law of the Supplementary Seven. The group angle of the matter can be seen if you remember that the individual initiate, when wielding this law, draws upon the united energy of the Will as the group is expressing it in "unified rhythm." It is by the use of the "united breath" of the entire group (as much of it as his individual will can assimilate, focus, use and direct) that he augments his own will and its directed force. The breath, as we well know, is the life; this Law is the one wielded by the living or risen Christ, in perfect harmony with the will of Shamballa. Herein lies one of the mysteries of the resurrection initiation about which so little has been told, and it is the very heart of the mystery of the ascension initiation. In this latter initiation the living risen Christ withdraws or abstracts Himself and enters consciously and permanently into the great centre, Shamballa. The resurrection and the ascension are the results of the death or destruction of the causal body. It can be seen, therefore, how true the Gospel story is to the purposes of Shamballa.

Let us now briefly interpret or rather paraphrase the

four sentences by means of which I have sought to embody this law, or as much of it as it is possible to put into words, for the enlightenment of the initiates of the future.

*1.　The Law demands the entrance of that which can effect a change.*

Bearing in mind what I have elsewhere given, it is obvious that that which must find entrance is that vital concentrated will which, when set in motion in an individual, in a group, in a nation, in a kingdom of nature (a planetary centre), and in the planet as a whole, i.e., in all the planetary centres simultaneously, will cause a stirring, a changed measure, a new movement and momentum, an uprising and a consequent abstraction. The changes wrought in the centres when the death of the physical body is taking place have never yet been observed or recorded; they are, however, definitely present to the eye of the initiate and prove most interesting and informative. It is the recognition of the condition of the centres which enables the initiate to know — when in process of bestowing healing — whether the physical healing of the body is permissible or not. He can see whether the will principle of abstraction to which I have been referring is actively present or not. The same process can be seen taking place in organisations and in civilisations in which the form aspect is being destroyed in order that the life may be abstracted and later again rebuild for itself a more adequate form. It is the same under the great processes of initiation, which are not only processes of expanding the consciousness but are rooted in the death or the abstraction process, leading to resurrection and ascension.

That which effects a change is *a discharge* (to use a totally inadequate phrase) of directed and focussed will-energy. This is so magnetic in quality that it draws to itself the life of the centres, bringing about the dissolution of the form and the release of the life. Death comes to the individual man, in the ordinary sense of the term, when the will-to-live in a physical body goes and the will-to-abstract takes its place. This we call death. In cases of death in war, for instance, it is not then a case of the individual will-to-withdraw, but an enforced participation in a great group abstraction. From its own place, the soul of the individual man recognises the end of a cycle of incarnation and recalls its life. This it does through a discharge of the will-energy that is strong enough to bring about the change.

2. *The Law demands that right direction should then guide the entering forces.*

The entering forces, working under this law, are directed first of all to the head centre, from thence to the ajna centre and then to that centre which has been the governing and most active centre during the incarnation of the life principle. This varies according to the point reached upon the ladder of evolution, and according to the personality ray, with later the soul ray bringing about a major conditioning and change. In the work of the initiate who is consciously wielding this law, the principle of abstraction (when entering the body) is held focussed in the head and is of such a magnetic potency that the energy of the remaining centres is rapidly gathered up and withdrawn. What is true of the individual process of abstracting the life principle, under the Law of the Supplementary Seven, is equally true of the process in all forms and in all groups of forms. Christ referred to this work of abstraction, as regards the third great planetary centre, Humanity, when He said (and He was speaking as the Representative of the Hierarchy, the second planetary centre into which all human beings achieving initiation are "withdrawn" esoterically), "I, if I be lifted up will draw all men unto me." A different word to this word of His will be spoken at the end of the age when the Lord of the World will speak from Shamballa, will abstract the life principle from the Hierarchy, and all life and consciousness will then be focussed in the planetary head centre — the great Council Chamber at Shamballa.

3. *The Law demands that the changes thus effected remove the form, bring quality to light, and lay the emphasis upon life.*

Here the three great aspects—form, quality and life—are brought into relation and the point of the evolutionary objective is seen in its true light—LIFE. Note this phrasing. Form or appearance, having served its purpose, disappears. Death of the form takes place. Quality, the major divine attribute being developed in this planet, becomes dominant and is "conscious of itself"—as the ancient writings put it. It is identified and individual but has no implementing form, except that of the greater whole in which it finds its place. Neither form nor quality (body nor consciousness) are paramount in the new state of Being, but only the life aspect, the spirit on its own plane, becomes the dominating factor. Some faint dim light on the significance of this may come if you bear in mind that our seven planes are only the seven subplanes of the cosmic physical plane. The process of developing sensitivity in this sevenfold evolution has been undergone in order to enable the initiate to function upon the cosmic astral plane, when withdrawn or abstracted after the higher initiations. He is abstracted from our planetary life altogether. Only one factor could prevent this, and that might be his pledge to serve temporarily within the planetary ring-pass-not. Such Members of the Hierarchy Who pledge Themselves to this work are stated to have the Buddhic consciousness, and the line of Their descent (occultly understood) is from the Eternal Pilgrim, the Lord of the World, then the Buddha, and then the Christ. They remain identified through the free choice with the "quality seen within the light," and for the term of Their freely rendered service They work with the consciousness aspect in order to lay the emphasis later upon the life aspect.

4. *The Law demands that this is brought about by the One, working through the Three, energising the Seven and creating the straight line from there to here, and ending in a point which ignores the Three.*

Let me paraphrase this, for detailed comment is not possible or permissible. The One directed will (of the individual, of humanity, of the Hierarchy) and the great Lords of Shamballa, working through the three major centres (head, heart and throat; Humanity, the Hierarchy and Shamballa), thereby energise all the seven centres (to the point of abstraction), using the straight line of the antahkarana from above downwards (from the centre of power, the head or Shamballa), and gather all upwards into a point which is neither of the Three (Shamballa, the Hierarchy and Humanity) and ignores them, for they must no longer limit the life. This point lies outside manifestation altogether. Abstraction is complete.

Ponder, therefore, upon this doctrine of abstraction. It covers all life processes, and will convey to you the eternally lovely secret of Death, which is entrance into life.

## RULE NINE

As we proceed with the study of these rules the difficulty of interpreting and explaining them becomes increasingly great. We have arrived at a section of the rules which requires initiate-consciousness for right and true comprehension; we are studying ideas for which we have, as yet, no adequate language. Briefly, we have considered certain of the *lower* aspects of the Laws of Life as they appear to the initiate and are interpreted by him within the sphere of his normal consciousness — that of the Spiritual Triad. The presentation which I gave you had to be confined within the area of consciousness which we call "manasic awareness," which is that of the abstract mind. Just in so far as that abstract mind is developed in you and the antahkarana tenuously constructed will be your understanding of my words.

The difficulty becomes still greater as we arrive at the study of Rule IX. It was of real difficulty when presented in its lower form to applicants. That rule, as you may remember, ran as follows:

Let the disciple merge himself within the circle of the other selves. Let but one colour blend them and their unity appear. Only when the group is known and sensed can energy be wisely emanated.

Three major ideas appear in this easier rule:

1. The idea of complete identity with all other selves.
2. The idea of the uniformity of their spiritual presentation to the world when unity is established.
3. The idea that—as a result of the two above achievements—the group force, as a real and focussed energy, can then be used.

Glibly the neophyte talks of identifying himself with others, and eagerly he endeavours to ascertain his group and merge with it; yet in so doing the constant concept of duality is ever present—himself and all other selves, himself and the group, himself and the group energy which he may now wield. Yet this is not so in reality. Where true identity is achieved, there is no sense of this and that; where the merging is complete, there is no recognition of individual activity within the group, because the will of the merged soul is identical with that of the group and automatic in its working; where true unity is present, the individual applicant becomes only a channel for the group will and activity, and this with no effort of his own but simply as a spontaneous reaction.

I have emphasised the above because in the rule for disciples and initiates, this will be found to be still more the case and the results are brought about by a conscious use of the will which is divine synthesis in action; also, the group referred to is not the Ashram of some particular Master, but that of all Ashrams as they in their entirety reflect the purpose of Shamballa and work out the Plan within the active sphere of the hierarchical consciousness.

Ashrams of the Masters are to be found on every level of consciousness in the threefold world of the Spiritual Triad. Some Masters pre-eminently occupy themselves with the mind aspect within all forms, and therefore their Ashrams are conditioned by the manasic consciousness; they are

the Ashrams of those initiates who have taken the fourth
initiation but who are not yet Masters. They are largely
adepts upon the third and fifth rays, and work with the
manas or mind as it is developing in all forms. They do
foundational work of great importance, but are little understood and their lives are consequently lives of great sacrifice
and the term of their service in this particular connection
is relatively short. Certain aspects of their developed consciousness have to be kept in abeyance and must remain
temporarily unexpressed in order to permit them to work
with substance and specifically with the consciousness of
the atoms which constitute the forms in all the subhuman
kingdoms of nature. They do very little work with humanity, except with certain advanced members of humanity
who are on the scientific line, drawing to their Ashrams
only those who are on the third and fifth rays and who can
continue with the work, being trained along peculiar and
special lines.

The Ashrams of the Masters (to be found on all the
rays) Who work in particular with humanity, are mostly to
be found upon the buddhic levels of the triadal consciousness. There the note of "loving understanding" predominates, but even these words must be interpreted esoterically
and not according to their usual and obvious meaning. It is
not a case of "I understand because I love," or that "this,"
with love, understands "that." It is something far deeper,
involving the idea of identification, of participation, and
of synthetic realisation — lovely euphonious words, but
meaning little to the non-initiates.

On atmic levels, the levels of the spiritual will, are
to be found the Ashrams of those Masters Who are interpreting the will of Shamballa and to Whom is committed
the task of transmitting the purpose and organising the
plans whereby that purpose can be fulfilled. As on manasic
levels the Ashrams as a whole are presided over by the
Master R., the Lord of Civilisation, so on buddhic levels
all Ashrams are supervised by the Master K.H., with the
aid of myself (the Master D.K.) and three senior and ini-

tiated disciples; the objective is the unfoldment of group awareness and of loving understanding, in order that the forms prepared and conditioned under the supervision of the Master R. may be sensitised and become increasingly conscious of reality through the development of an inner mechanism of light which—in its turn—will condition and develop the outer mechanism of contact. Ashrams on atmic levels are under the control of the Master M., Who fosters the will aspect within the developed forms and Who (as the *Old Commentary* expresses it) "adds darkness unto light so that the stars appear, for in the light the stars shine not, but in the darkness light diffused is not, but only focussed points of radiance." The symbolism will be obvious to you though not the full significance.

Embracing, fusing and unifying the endeavour of all these groups of Ashrams, stands the living Christ, the Head of all Ashrams and the Master of the Masters, the Mediator between Shamballa and the Hierarchy and between the Hierarchy and Humanity. Will you gain some insight into the all-pervading conditions if I state that His work of mediating between humanity and the Hierarchy was perfected by Him and carried to a conclusion when He was last on Earth, and that He is now achieving facility in the higher mediatorship which will bring about a closer relation of the Hierarchy with Shamballa at this time. This mediatory work, based on the blending of the spiritual will (which He has already developed) with the universal will (which He is developing), marks for Him a goal which will be consummated when He takes the ninth initiation. These are great mysteries and I only indicate them in order to convey to you a sense of the synthesis of the whole scheme and a recognition of the urge-to-good which pervades every aspect of the planetary Life from the smallest atom of substance, through all the intermediate living forms, on and up to the planetary Logos Himself.

The will is too often regarded as a power by means of which things are done, activities are instituted and plans worked out. This general definition is the easiest for men

to formulate because it is understood by them in terms of
their own self-will, the will to individual self-betterment—
selfish and misunderstood at first but tending eventually to
selflessness as evolution carries out its beneficent task.
Then the will is interpreted in terms of the hierarchical
plan, and the effort of the individual man becomes that of
negating his self-will and seeking to merge his will with
that of the group, the group being itself an aspect of the
hierarchical effort. This is a great step onward in orientation and will lead to a change in consciousness eventually.
This last sentence is of importance.

It is at this stage that most aspirants today find themselves. However, the will is in reality something very different to these expressions of it which exist in the human
consciousness as men attempt to interpret the divine will in
terms of their present point in evolution. The clue to understanding (the clue which will be the easiest for you to
understand) is to be found in the words "blotting out all
form." When the lure of substance is overcome and desire
dies, then the attractive power of the soul becomes dominant and the emphasis for so long laid upon individual
form and individual living and activity gives place to group
form and group purpose. Then the attractive power of the
Hierarchy and of the Ashrams of the Masters supersedes the
lower attractions and the lesser focal points of interest.
When these, in their turn, assume their rightful place in
consciousness then the dynamic "pull" of Shamballa can be
felt, entirely unrelated to form or forms, to a group or
groups. Only a group sense of "well-Being," esoterically
understood is realised, for it is comprehended as the will-
to-good. No forms can then hold; no group or Ashram can
then confine the consciousness of the initiate, and all differences of every kind disappear. This preamble is given in an
effort to clarify your minds before we study Rule IX carefully and arrive at its essential meaning.

Rule IX.

*Let the group know there are no other selves. Let the
group know there is no colour, only light; and then let*

> *darkness take the place of light, hiding all difference,*
> *blotting out all form. Then — at the place of tension,*
> *and at that darkest point — let the group see a point*
> *of clear cold fire, and in the fire (right at its very*
> *heart) let the One Initiator appear Whose star shone*
> *forth when first the Door was passed.*

The greatest problem facing aspirants and disciples prior to the third initiation is that of comprehending the nature of identification. This concerns (in the first instance) the relation of the self to the Self and of all selves to the all-inclusive SELF. It involves the mystery of duality with which they are occupied, and the very moment that theory as to essential unity becomes definite realisation, then the realm of synthesis is entered. For that type of realisation, language as we now have it has no words, and it is therefore impossible to formulate concepts to interpret the consequent and resultant state of being. "Identification with" is the phrase which approaches the closest to the initial idea, and until man has grasped his identical at-one-ness with even one human being, it is not possible for him even to think about it in any truly constructive manner. The complete fusion of the negative and the positive aspects in marriage, at the moment that life is transmitted and transferred, is the only tangible though unsatisfactory symbol of this life-sharing process which takes place when an individual or a group knows actually and not simply theoretically that "there are no other selves."

Identification (to use the only word available for our purpose) is connected with dynamic life, with conscious enhancement, with completion and with creative sharing, plus process. It is a process of participation — consciously and constructively undertaken—in the life actions and reactions of the One in Whom we live and move and have our being; it is related to the network of life channels which keep the form aspect of the planetary Logos functioning as a "Divine Representation." Note that wording. It is connected with the circulation of that "life more abundantly" to which the Christ referred when dealing with the true nature of His mission. It might be said that as He uttered this phrase this mission dawned on Him and He made a preliminary effort to serve Shamballa, instead of the Hierarchy of which He was even then the Head. Later, He enunciated as best He could the extent of this realisation, in the words so familiar to Christians, "I and the Father are One." This He also attempted to elucidate in the seventeenth chapter of St. John's Gospel. There is no other passage in the literature of the world which has exactly the same quality. Oneness, unity, synthesis and identification exist today as words related to consciousness and as expressing what is at present unattainable to the mass of men. This manifesto or declaration of the Christ constitutes the first attempt to convey reaction to contact with Shamballa, and can be correctly interpreted only by initiates of some standing and experience. A concept of unity, leading to cooperation, to impersonality, to group work and to realisation, plus a growing absorption in the Plan are some of the terms which can be used to express soul awareness in relation to the Hierarchy. These reactions to the united Ashrams which constitute the Hierarchy are steadily increasing and are beneficently conditioning the consciousness of the leading members of the forefront of the human wave at present in process of evolution.

Beyond this state of awareness there lies a state of being which is as far removed from the consciousness of Members of the Hierarchy as that is, in its turn, removed from the consciousness of the mass of men. Endeavour to grasp this, even if your brain and your power to formulate thought rejects the possibility of this exalted livingness. Be not discouraged at this inability to understand; remember that this state of being embraces the goal towards which the Masters strive, and which the Christ Himself is only now attaining.

It is for this reason that the symbolism of light and darkness is used in the words: *Let the group know there is no colour, only light; and then let darkness take the place of light.*

Just as the individual has to pass through the stage wherein all "colour" goes out of life as he emerges out of the glamour which conditions the astral plane, so groups in preparation for initiation must go through the same devastating process. Glamour disappears, and for the first time the group (as is the case with the individual) walks in the light. As the group thus walks, unitedly its units learn a lesson (one clearly enunciated by modern science) that light and substance are synonymous terms; the true nature of substance as a field and medium of activity becomes clear to the initiate-members of the group. To this H.P.B. referred when he said that the true occultist works entirely in the field of forces and energies.

The next lesson which the group unitedly apprehends is the significance of the words that "darkness is pure spirit." This recognition, realisation, apprehensive, comprehensive (call it what you will) is so overwhelming and all-embracing that distinctions and differences disappear. The disciple realises that they are only the result of the activity of substance in its form-making capacity and are consequently illusion and non-existent, from the angle of the spirit at rest in its own centre. The only realisation left is that of pure Being Itself.

This realisation necessarily comes to the disciple through the means of graded revelation and in balanced sequence; each contact with the Initiator leads the initiate closer to the centre of pure darkness—a darkness which is the very antithesis of darkness as the non-initiate and the unenlightened understand. It is a centre or point of such intense brilliance that everything fades out and *at the place of tension, and at that darkest point, let the group see a point of clear cold fire.*

It is a tension and a point of attainment that is only possible in group formation. Even in the earlier initiations, and when the initiate has proved his right to be initiated, the process is still a group proceeding; it is undergone in the protective presence of initiates of the same standing and unfoldment. It is their united focus that enables the candidate for initiation to see the point of clear cold light and their united will that "brings him upright, standing, unafraid, with open eye before the One Who from the very first has conferred on him the gifts of life and light, and Who now — with lifted rod, surrounded by the fire, reveals to him the significance of life and the purpose of the light." It is that of which the minds of men know naught, and which even the highest intellect is unable to grasp or even sense.

In the familiar words (familiar to all esotericists) which are so often said or chanted at moments of highest spiritual aspiration, the neophyte refers to the time when "we stand where the One Initiator is invoked, when we see His star shine forth." Two ideas then stand forth: the idea of invocation and of the result of that invocation, which is the sudden and unexpected shining forth of the Star. This star is simply a point of vivid light. This invocation, though used as the affirmation of a fixed objective by the aspirant to initiation, is nevertheless a mantram definitely appropriate to the third initiation. It is only effective in its invocative appeal when used in conjunction with a Word of Power. This Word of Power is communicated to the candidate (ever an initiate of the second degree) by the Christ Who has initiated him in the first two initiations but Whose protective aura (in conjunction with the initiate's Master and another Master or an adept of the fourth initiation) is required before the star can shine forth—the focussed light of the One Initiator. For the first time the expanded consciousness of the initiate can contact Shamballa and the One Who rules there, the Lord of the World. For the first time, the focussed purpose which brought Sanat Kumara into incarnation makes an impact upon the enlightened brain of the initiate, bringing something new and different into his equipment, into his nature and his consciousness. I know not how else to express these ideas. It is a blinding conviction of an unalterable will, carrying all before it, oblivious of time and space, aware only of intensity of direction, and carrying with it two major qualifications or basic recognitions to the initiate: a sense of essential being which obliterates all the actions and reactions of time and space, and a focussed will-to-good which is so dynamic in its effect that evil disappears. Evil is after all only an impelling sense of difference, leading inevitably to separative action.

The dualities are then resolved in synthesis and, again for the first time, the initiate comprehends the meaning of the ancient words, so inappropriately translated "isolated unity." To him, in the future, there is no light or dark, no good or evil, no difference or separation. The star that has shone forth, veiling and standing between him and the Lord of the World, the Ancient of Days, is seen as the entrance or doorway and as the admitting agency into something other and larger than simply the planetary life. In the earlier two initiations, the Angel of the Presence stood between the disciple-candidate and the Presence. At the later initiations, the Angel of the Presence is the Christ Himself, one with the soul of the candidate (the individual Angel of the Presence). Through the heart of Christ passes the dynamic power of the One Initiator, as a stream of light, stepped down or toned down by the Christ in order that the candidate can appropriate its potency without risk or danger.

After the third initiation, the candidate must face the One Initiator alone, with no protective Individual standing between him and the eternal source of all-power. The Christ is present, supporting and attentive. He stands directly behind the initiate so as to arrest and distribute the potency passing through the initiate's body and centres; the candidate is also flanked on either side by a Master. Nevertheless, he faces the Initiator alone and unprotected. Even now, at this much later initiation, he cannot see "eye to eye"—as the phrase goes. He becomes aware of a growing point of light which, from a pin-point of intensest brilliance develops before him into a five-pointed star. At the fourth initiation, it is not a star which shines forth before him, but a triangle; and within that triangle he will perceive an eye regarding him, and for the first time he does see the Most High "eye to eye." At the fifth initiation no symbol or light substance separates or protects him, but he stands before the Initiator face to face, and the freedom of the City of God is his. He is not yet a Member of the Great Council, but he has the right of entrance into Shamballa, and from that point he passes on to a more intimate relation, if that is his chosen destiny. He may not even finally become a Member of the Great Council; that is reserved for relatively few and for Those Who can take even still higher initiations within the ring-pass-not of our planet —a task of profound difficulty. There are other and interesting alternatives, as I have elsewhere told you. The initiate may pass out of this planetary life altogether along one or other of the various Paths by means of which a Master can start upon the Path of the Higher Evolution and for which all that has transpired in the past will have prepared Him. Whichever Way He goes, the Master remains a part of the purpose; He knows forever the secret of the darkness which brings light, and the "inscrutable will of God" is no longer a mystery to Him. He comprehends the divine idea and can now cooperate with it; He has reached a point of realisation which enables Him to fathom what lies behind the Plan for which the Hierarchy has worked for aeons.

Just as the disciple enters the *world of meaning* and so can interpret events, just as the Hierarchy works in the *world of mediation,* applying the Plan which the world of meaning has revealed, so the higher initiate works consciously in the *world of purpose* which the Plan implements, the world of meaning interprets, and the *world of events* expresses in sequential order and under the evolutionary Law.

The symbol which expresses the door of evolution is the crescent moon; that of the process of evolution — as it affects the material or substantial life of the man — is the waxing and the waning moon—the symbol of growing desire and of the dying out of desire. The symbol of the world of meaning is Light—the light which shines upon the ways of men, interpreting events and bestowing revelation. The symbol of the world of mediation is the revolving Cross, whilst the symbol of the world of purpose is a twofold one: the five-pointed star and then the radiant heart of the Sun. Remember that when we talk and think in symbols, we are placing something between ourselves and reality — something protective, interpretive and significant, but something nevertheless veiling and hiding. After the fifth initiation all veils are rent and naught stands between the initiate and Essential Being.

## RULE TEN

We now come to one of the most abstruse and difficult of all the rules for initiates; yet at the same time it is one of the most practical in application and of the greatest usefulness. It concerns the etheric levels of activity. I would have you note that I did not say the etheric levels of consciousness, for there is no such thing as consciousness upon the etheric planes. The four planes which constitute the etheric levels of the physical plane are the lowest correspondence to the four planes whereon the Monad and the Spiritual Triad are active, and—as I have oft told you—upon those levels there is no such thing as consciousness as we understand it. There is only a state of being and of activity for which we have no adequate or illustrative words. The four higher planes of our solar system are the four cosmic etheric planes, and one of the lines of development (confronting the initiate) is to function adequately in response to the life of the planetary Logos upon those planes. That, in the last analysis, constitutes the main field of unfoldment and of acquired wisdom for all initiates above the third degree.

In the above paragraph I have presented you with a new concept re initiation — one that has always been implicit in the teaching but one entirely and completely untouched as yet in any discussions on initiate-training.

In the rule as given to applicants, the disciple is cautioned to work within those levels according to the methods of the deva or angel evolution. The rule runs as follows:

The Army of the Voice, the devas in their serried ranks, work ceaselessly. Let the disciple apply himself to a consideration of their methods; let him learn the rules whereby the Army works within the veils of maya.

These particular devas in "their serried ranks" are the directive agents of the divine energy which implements the purposes of Deity upon the physical plane. They work only on etheric levels—either upon our physical plane or on the cosmic etheric levels. They are therefore active in the realm of maya, which is the etheric plane as we usually understand it, or upon the planes of the Spiritual Triad. They are not active on the three gross physical levels or upon the astral or mental planes, nor are they active upon the highest or logoic plane. There they are implicit or latent but not active. They are the great "impulsive factors" in manifestation, organising substance, directing the multiplicity of lives and beings who constitute the forms through which God expresses divinity. In a peculiar sense, they are the embodiment of the divine purpose upon the planes of the Monad and of the Triad, just as the aggregate of energies in man's etheric body is the result of his inner direction and the cause of his outer manifestation. To understand more fully the function of the deva forces, a man must arrive at some understanding of the forces in his etheric body which, in their turn, are the *consequence* of his point of attainment — an attainment demonstrated by his astral (emotional) and mental natures and activities. These indicate his point of development.

The devas are the agents of the divine will because they are a consequence of the point of attainment of our planetary Logos as He exists outside the seven planes of our sphere of existence, the cosmic physical plane. They are conditioned by His cosmic astral and mental vehicles. In a definite sense, they *are* the agents of the Universal Mind, even though they are *not* mental *as we understand that term*. They are sometimes regarded as blind forces, but that is only because they get their inspiration from levels of

divine awareness outside the range of the human consciousness, no matter how high, or when used in its widest
connotation.

Their controlling Agent in manifestation is the Triangle of Energy to which we give the name the "Three
Buddhas of Activity." They are therefore closely connected
with the third aspect of divinity. They are essentially the
"eye within the Triangle"—a most familiar symbol to many
today. They are the expression, in activity, of the "All-Seeing Eye"; through their agency God *sees,* and through them
and the energy directed through them, He directs the creative process. They are under the complete control of the
three Buddhas of Activity, Who are the cosmic Prototypes
of the Lords of the three major rays, but not in the sense
usually understood when the rays are considered in their
relation to man. They are the correspondence of these three
rays and are responsible for the entire manifested universe,
but only within the orbit of the third aspect, the expression
of the Universal Mind.

They come from the cosmic mental plane, just as the
energy — distinctive of the second aspect — comes from the
cosmic astral plane. God is mind. God is intelligent functioning. God is creative activity. *These are the qualities of
the deva evolution.* God is love. God is relationship. God is
consciousness. These are *the three qualities of the Christ
evolution.* This latter evolution is carried on within the
created sphere of influence of the third aspect. God is life.
God is fire. God is pure being. *These are the qualities of
the spirit aspect, the omnipotent aspect of Deity.* All these
three aspects focus themselves and find an outlet for expression upon the levels of the cosmic etheric planes and
upon the levels of the etheric planes known to humanity in
the three worlds. The Law of Correspondences is infallible,
if rightly approached and applied.

This broad and general presentation must be rightly
grasped if the rule, as given to disciples and initiates, is to
be correctly understood.

You have been taught that illusion is the characteristic which must be mastered by the initiate as he "escapes" occultly from the three worlds via the mental plane. *(Glamour: A World Problem.)* Glamour, you are told, is the characteristic of the astral plane, and must be dissipated by the disciple as he "escapes" mystically on to the Path of Initiation, just as the initiate finds himself (after mastering illusion) on the Path of the Higher Evolution. Maya is the conditioning factor on etheric levels, and must be evaded and overcome by the probationary disciple as he "escapes" from the thralldom of the physical plane. Thus he learns to tread the Path of Discipleship. These characteristics are, however, only the reaction of humanity to the activities of the deva evolution, rightly and divinely proceeding with their task of implementing the divine will. When the sphere of their activity comes into contact with the human intelligence, the effect upon humanity (before mastery is gained) is to compel men "to wander in the fields of maya, to drown in the sea of glamour, and to respond to the pull of illusion."

In this teaching, you have presented to you, though in a somewhat different form, the ancient problem of duality, involving as it does the immense potency of the deva evolution. It definitely affects humanity; this is due to the fact that it is an expression of the will aspect of Shamballa. As man develops the will aspect, he learns to break loose from the aura of the deva evolution, and the major task of the Hierarchy (as far as basic essentials are concerned) is to "provide sanctuary" to those who have liberated themselves from the ocean of deva energies in which their vehicles must perforce move and live and have their being, but with which they have otherwise no point of contact, once liberated by their own effort and will "from the angels." Let us now study Rule Ten.

## Rule X.

*The rules for work within the veils of maya are known and have been used. Let the group widen all the rents within those veils and thus let in the light. Let the Army of the Voice be no more heard, and let the brothers onward move within the Sound. Then let them*

*know the meaning of the O.M. and let them hear that*
*O.M. as it is sounded forth by Him Who stands and*
*waits at the very centre of the Council Chamber of*
*the Lord.*

I would here remind you that we are considering work
that the initiate must accomplish, and are not considering
the usual effort of struggling aspirants to deal with and
handle those forces which have worked through into physical expression. These, from the levels of the forty-eight
subplanes are waiting to precipitate themselves into the
dense physical manifested world. The aspirant must ever
work from the outside to the within and must endeavour
to direct his life from above downwards, if these forces are
to be dominated by him and are not to control him. The
initiate, however, works "from within the circle," that is
the circle or field of maya. His activity must therefore be
carried forward from the very heart of the mystery of these
forces; this he can do because he is in a position to *know*
the type of energy with which he has to contend, to understand the nature of the forces with which he can and must
manipulate the "mayavic energies," and thus to dominate
the etheric plane; he is also aware where one veil ends and
another begins, and from what level he can successfully
bring the swirling and living energies into conformity with
the divine pattern.

It should also be noted here that the energies projected
by the initiate into the world of maya are directed by him
from the various centres in his own body and from the
central point of energy in each particular centre employed.
It is the central "jewel in the lotus" from which the initiate
works, and these seven central focal points, these seven
jewels, so-called, are the correspondence of the jewel in the
egoic lotus. This means, therefore, that successful work
"within the veils of maya" involves ever the use of the will
aspect and the conscious employment of that quota of the
Shamballa force which the initiate is able to appropriate
and to use *because* he has begun to work as a focussing
agent of the Spiritual Triad and is no longer working as a

soul or as a personality under soul control. This is an important point to remember.

It is along the antahkarana that the force used by the initiate must pour, and according to the nature of the work to be done will be the particular strand or thread of the rainbow bridge which the initiate employs. There are four veils of maya, constructed necessarily of seven forces, and these produce the factual and phenomenal aspect (in time and space) of the Great Illusion, in its three forms of *illusion, glamour* and *maya*. There are seven points of energy through which different aspects of the force needed to produce the desired effects within the veils of maya can flow, and these correspond to the seven ray types or qualities. But the major type of energy with which the initiate works upon the physical plane is the seventh, the ray or energy of ritual, of ceremony, of order and of law. The work done within the veils is one of rearrangement and the ordination and coordination of the forces, present as existent maya; this must provide, in time and space, the forms through which the plans of the Hierarchy can materialise, the souls of all forms can be subjected to the needed experience, and so progress towards the fulfillment of the will of God.

Maya is not something to be destroyed, dissipated, dissolved or negated. Maya is in reality an aspect of time, and connotes to the initiate the mass of creative forces with which he must work; these are swept into form generation and activity, and embody in the transitional, ephemeral, present moment the phenomenal point in evolution reached by the life of God. The work of the initiate, acting under hierarchical inspiration, is to change the present forms into the more adequate forms demanded by the descending life and its dynamic activity. We are therefore dealing with the precipitated aspect of divine evolutionary process. We are concerned with the relation of the Army of the Voice to the SOUND which conditions evolution, and with the supervisory work of the Hierarchy as it sustains the work of the soul to be found within all forms—built by the Army of the Voice and by the devas in their serried ranks.

The supervisory, directive work of the Hierarchy, carried forward by the Masters and Their groups and by the initiates within those groups, is seldom considered; it is, however, a work of major importance and is one definitely referred to in this rule. Fundamentally, the task set before the Hierarchy is to "let in the light"; but this time not in the sense of revelation, of vision or of illumination. These latter are all aspects of soul light; the work of the initiate is to aid in the construction of the planetary body of light-substance which will finally reveal the nature of Deity and the glory of the Lord. It is the planetary correspondence to the light-body through which Christ and all the Sons of God Who have reached perfection finally manifest. It is a vehicle created by the energy of Will, and it is implemented and "held in being" by the Will. It expresses itself exoterically by the projection of this will energy, via the central point in each of the seven chakras or lotuses.

In studying these rules for the initiate, it must ever be remembered that they concern primarily the use of the will or first aspect. This is the energy of the Monad, utilised via the Spiritual Triad and related to the personality via the antahkarana. Secondary interpretations and tertiary correspondences are always possible, but the main significance of these rules is related to the first divine aspect. You have therefore, as you reflect, think, study and correlate, to bear constantly in mind:

1. The seven ray types.
2. The Monad, the Spiritual Triad and the threefold personality; these constitute another septenate.
3. The seven groups of Masters.
4. The seven centres and their seven central points, or jewels.
5. The four veils of maya.

Various other septenates could also be related, but such relationship is not required by the initiate who has consciously discarded all these lower septenates and works now with the seven major energies, the sevenfold field of their activity and the septenary aspect of the implementing instrument, whether planetary or individual.

Simplification proceeds rapidly as one nears the goal of the spirit. Will ever concerns itself with the essentials and not with the details of manifestation. Love concerns itself with transitional, evolutionary fundamentals, whilst intelligence concerns itself with the detail and its coherent co-ordination in response to the impulse and attractive force of divine love and the dynamic impulse of the spirit.

Let us now proceed, after these few preliminary remarks, to take this tenth rule sentence by sentence. These are five in number, and the first which we will consider is:

*1. The rules for work within the veils of maya are known and have been used.*

Students should remember that the work of the Hierarchy is constantly conditioned by the point in evolution of the human hierarchy. In the early days of human history, thinking and progress had practically no place, and therefore little or no effect upon the forces and energies which were active upon etheric levels. At that period, they were left in a relatively quiescent state or else were swept into activity by definite and planned impression from the Hierarchy; any effect coming from the human kingdom was due solely to mass impulse or impression. This was very little, owing to the lack of coordinated relation between units and groups within the human family. Later, as family units massed together and formed tribes, and then tribe united with tribe to form larger tribes or embryonic nations, this mass effect increased, but there was still but little thinking or direction connected with it; it was largely instinctive and — if I might so express it — the etheric plane was in reality more in the nature of a matrix surrounding a valuable creation, and was essentially protective, separating and slightly energising.

In Atlantean days, the plane whereon humanity received its major direction or unfoldment was such that the emotional, impulsive nature and the field of maturing desire became dominantly active. Then the real difficulty within the realm of maya started. Hitherto only two energies had been felt upon the etheric plane: the energy of life itself, via the sutratma, as it passed through the etheric plane in order to produce exoteric livingness upon the physical plane, and secondly, the energy of the Hierarchy as a whole, producing a slow, broad, though somewhat negative organisation of the prevalent forces. But then a third and most potent force, generated by humanity, was beginning to make an impact upon the etheric forces. Men were beginning, at this early period of human history, to desire, and this desire was not, as hitherto, of a purely animal nature and hence an emanation from dense physical substance (and, therefore, *not* related to a principle), but it embodied a new type of energy and was—in reality—man's first expression of the highest divine aspect. Desire is the lowest reflection within the human consciousness of the will aspect.

This potent vibration of desire was evoked by men who were as yet without any spiritual vision of any kind; they were purely material in their instinctive reactions (and rightly so at that particular time), and these reactions attracted the attention of certain purely evil energies or Beings. These Beings availed themselves of the situation in order to satisfy their desire for power — again a distortion of the will or first aspect. Thus the Black Lodge was founded. It fed upon human desire and resembled a vast overshadowing vampire. It vitiated human living and increased the growth of desire far beyond normal expectancy or hierarchical planning, thus creating false goals and standards, building a barrier between the lowest planetary centre, Humanity, and the "middle point" or centre, the Hierarchy. It will be apparent, therefore, that the following energies were let loose within the realm of maya:

    1. The instinctive force of animal desire. This was not wrong in itself and is subject to negation in time, and normally is controlled.

2. The stream of descending life, and this in two aspects:

    a.  The life aspect, as it bestows being.

    b.  The life aspect, as it preserves form.

3. The steady impact of the attractive power of the soul, implemented by the Hierarchy and increasing in potency as time elapses.

4. The impelling power of material desire, focussed in the Black Lodge, both feeding human desire and drawing a form of life from the massed desire of humanity.

5. Human development along astral lines, expressing itself as certain well-defined energies or force directions:

    a.  Material desire for possessions.

    b.  Desire for that which is owned by others. To this the commandment "Thou shalt not steal" has reference.

    c.  Personality aims and ambitions; these constitute a form of focussed desire of a compelling, life-determining nature.

    d.  Aspiration, leading to vision and to the mystic Way.

    e.  Purification, the conscious handling of desire upon the Probationary Path.

    f.  Initiation. The first two initiations are taken, as you know, upon the astral plane, and bring complete release both from that plane of glamour and from the realm of maya.

All throughout this period, the organisation of the etheric plane has been going on, subject to the impact of energies and forces as listed above, plus certain other energies (latent or potent) with which we have no immediate concern. Both the great White Lodge and its opponent, the Black Lodge, increased steadily in potency. Gradually the forces took organised form and the four "veils of maya" or the seven separating energies became well-defined. When this differentiation was complete, two great planetary events (if I might call them so) were consummated:

1. The seven centres in the human body (five up the spine and two in the head) were esoterically "in shape." The seven lotuses or chakras were functioning, some powerfully, whilst others remained unawakened. These seven were now visible to clairvoyant vision.

2. The seven Ashrams of the Masters in Their seven groups (conditioned by the seven Rays) appeared, motivated from Shamballa, organised at this time upon the higher levels of the mental plane, and gradually supplied with personnel from the ranks of humanity itself, as one by one men achieved initiation.

Paralleling this activity and implemented, fed and sustained by the Black Lodge, was the appearance of glamour upon the astral plane, and to this thickening glamour humanity steadily contributed and responded. Then as evolution progressed and the human intellect began to make itself felt, "the four veils of maya" and the great "curtain of glamour" began to condition the mental plane. Illusion then appeared, and the distinction between truth and falsehood, between good and evil, and between the left hand Path and the Path of Initiation became apparent to the advanced humanity of the time. These distinctions had always been known to the Hierarchy, but now human beings were faced with them and recognised them; the great potency of intellectual choice confronted humanity and the Aryan race (as that name is correctly used to denote modern intelligent humanity) came into being.

As the ages slipped away, men contributed more and more both to the problem and to the solution of maya, of glamour and of illusion. The potency of human thought began to make itself felt; men in increasing numbers sought the Path of Liberation and so passed on into the Hierarchy; they became active and instructed opponents of the Black Lodge and intelligent wielders of energy as it can be projected downwards and used to destroy the four veils, to dissipate glamour and to dispel illusion. Humanity responded more and more sensitively to impacts — both subjective and objective — and their cooperation began to be effective and useful to the Hierarchy, necessitating some changes in hierarchical techniques, releasing some of the hierarchical workers for other and different activities, and greatly complicating the problem and menacing the safety and the status of the Black Lodge.

One of the results of this mental development was the sending of the disciples out into the world of men; they issued forth in large numbers, and whilst preserving their conscious link with the Ashram with which they were affiliated, they could be trusted to live among men as men and to bring their potency to bear upon the problem of maya and glamour, doing so from below upwards. This work had to be done by disciples who could stand under pressure, who would, in spite of all difficulties, live nobly and prepare for and take the initiation which was for them their next step. Several hundred years ago, only a few could be so trusted. Today (1944) there are many in every land, though there are very few in Germany, owing to the concentration in that unhappy land of the power of the Black Lodge and also to the misuse of the Shamballa force. This force has been isolated and its destructive aspect utilised in Germany, and this has been done without the paralleling activity of the love energy of the Hierarchy. It is this fact that has made it impossible (since 1933) for disciples of the White Lodge to enter. Elsewhere, however, the concentration of active disciples is greater than at any other time in human history.

I have emphasised this point because our second phrase, "let the group widen all the rents within those veils," has reference here to disciples and the groups which they have everywhere gathered around themselves. It is these groups, many in number and differing in ray potency, which will lead the world through the post-war period into the New Age. It is their pressure upon the physical plane which has precipitated the crisis between the great White Lodge and the Black Lodge. Their work is to let in the light, and where the light goes the Black Lodge must fade out and disappear. It feeds on glamour and illusion and uses the veils of maya as a protection. Students would do well to avoid naming and differentiating the four veils. The veils themselves are transient and variable. They differ as they come under the impact of the seven rays. It is not possible or practical to distinguish them one from the other, except from the angle of the Hierarchy, and their destruction to-day (though it was not so earlier) has to come from the dense physical plane, and the attack must be made by personalities and individualities dwelling in physical bodies. This is a somewhat new mode of approach, for hitherto only a very few disciples and initiates have been able so to work. Today, hundreds and thousands of disciples are working, and thus learning to use the ancient rules for work within the veils of maya. Let me here give you some of these rules or formulas as they are to be found in *The Masters' Book of Rules* and as I can translate them. Some are untranslatable:

1. Focus the force at the jewel's point and find the veil that it can touch.
2. Carry the force from point to point and then project.
3. Look for the energy in form behind the veil attacked. A rent within the veil exists. Find it and see.
4. A path lies through the veils, giving access to the several courts. Walk on that path, wielding destruction and clearing out the refuse in the court. The court of the money changers is the last.
5. Meet the descending forces and find the current which is yours.
6. Watch for the evil stream of force which seeks to mend the rents. Project upon that stream the energy of which you know. It led you from the Ashram into the veils. Use it and drive the evil back unto the astral plane.
7. Work with the Sound and know it as the source of power. Use first the Voice; then use the O.M., and later use the Sound. All three together will suffice.

There are other rules, but these will give you the

major recognitions needed to do this type of work; these are the rules which the adventuring disciple needs to know. They have been used, and should not be interpreted by the lower mind, but with the aid of the initiate consciousness.

The second phrase runs as follows:

*2. Let the group widen all the rents within those veils and thus let in the light,*

We come now to a definite group injunction or instruction. The aid of the group is invoked almost in the form of an order. The point of this formulated injunction is that in the new era and in the interlude between the past (wherein prominent disciples worked within the veils of maya) and the New Age (wherein humanity itself will consciously function upon the etheric plane), the work of the esoteric groups, under the direction of the New Group of World Servers, is needed. They will have the capacity to recognise the distinction between the various veils. This is the next needed development. The groups must focus the energy at the very centre of the group being; the group must carry the force from point to point and from veil to veil; the group must project the destroying energy and become unitedly aware of what each veil hides; the group must perform the activities (seven in all) of purification; the group must meet, accept and distribute the descending spiritual energy which will finally consummate the work done. The group—through the use of that descending current—will drive the forces of evil back on to the astral plane and will together work with the three aspects of the first ray. These are typified by the Voice, the O.M. and the Sound.

In the above you have in reality a great formula for group activity and also a potent method (once the group can unitedly work together) for the cleansing and the reorganisation of the forces active in the world today. These forces are now raging and running wild; their effect is almost tangible (being in etheric substance) and factually and visibly present under the control of the Black Lodge. This

Lodge uses the *voices* of lying propaganda, the *Word* of death (which I shall not give to you for the O.M., the Word of Life, suffices), and the *Sound* of the densest aspect in manifestation — the sound of power in the mineral kingdom. This constitutes an unparalleled condition and creates a unique concentration of the Forces of Good and the forces of evil upon the etheric plane. The task of all groups which are working under the Masters of the Wisdom is to let in the light, utilising those rents which already exist within the veils of maya.

Three major rents within these veils might here be noted. They are symbolically referred to in *The Bible,* though their essential meaning has not been noted or comprehended.

The first major rent was made by the establishment of the Law of God, and this is portrayed for us symbolically in *The Old Testament* in the story of Moses. He went up into the Mount of God and there received the Ten Commandments. This is the expression of divine law as adapted for humanity and as needed in the projection of those forces which will destroy, purify and reorganise. Moses, the Lawgiver, penetrated to one of the halls within the veils of maya, and there encountered the glory of the Lord. This was of such a radiance that, as the *Old Commentary* puts it:

"He who entered among the first to penetrate within the veils absorbed the light and knew not how to pass it on. Neither he nor they were ready, but the light was there and likewise the two directing eyes. But only one can use, project and send the light upon its mission. The other must be blinded, and of this fact the Lawgiver was aware. He therefore veiled the light, assuming towards this end a fragment of that which he had helped destroy, and so descended from the mountain top, back to the darkness of the earth."

The second, and much the most important rent, was made by the power of the second aspect when the Christ subjected the Master Jesus to the fourth initiation and Their joint influence was triumphant over death. Then we read

that the veil of the Temple was split in twain from the top
to the bottom. The lawgiver assisted at the first rending as
the climax to the third initiation, and there was a somewhat similar process of glorification. A similar event took
place at the Transfiguration of the Christ, overshadowing
or rather working through the Master Jesus. But at the
triumph over death and through the Great Renunciation
or Crucifixion episode, a great and major rending took
place. The Law, when rightly kept and interpreted, defines
man's attitude upon the mental plane and serves to make a
rent in the etheric veil, separating the etheric vehicle in its
fourfold aspect from the dense physical form. The rending
of the second veil at the time of the Crucifixion let in light
on to the second level of the etheric plane, and a new type
of illumination was spread abroad upon the earth. Law and
Love could now penetrate into the consciousness of humanity in a new and direct manner, as the brain of man
became involved through the substance of the etheric counterpart of the physical brain; the instinct to self-preservation (one of the lowest aspects of Law) and the tendency to
sensitivity (feeling or emotion, one of the lowest forms of
Love) could be expressed in a more comprehensive manner.

Another rending of the veil, and one of relatively
minor importance, took place when Saul of Tarsus saw the
glory of the Lord and was changed into Paul the Apostle.
His forward moving and potent directness and sincerity,
pushing along "the road to Damascus," forced him to penetrate through one of the separating veils. The Kingdom of
Heaven suffereth violence and the violent take it by force.
This force, working in Saul, drove him through the veil
which prevented vision, and the rent thereby made brought
him a new revelation. He was, we are told, completely
blinded for three days, and this the esoteric records cor-
roborate. This is a well-known correspondence to the three
days in the tomb and one recognised by esotericists; it corresponds also to the penetration into the third heaven to
which Paul testified later in his life. He realised the nature
of the Law, as his later epistles demonstrate; he was brought

to the feet of the Initiator through the effect of love, and thus he availed himself of the two earlier rents in the veil. Whilst thus reaching out to the light, he wrote that epistle about which so much controversy has raged — The Epistle to the Hebrews. In it the results of the rending of the third veil provide the keynote and express the first and highest aspect, as the two earlier rents lead to the revelation of the third and second divine qualities. This first aspect is seen as synthesis, as the Communion of Saints, and as related to the Lord of the World, Melchizedek. Read that epistle in the light of these remarks, and note how a great initiate endeavoured to reveal some facts, inherent in the will or power aspect. These were, however, far beyond the ken of the disciples and aspirants of the time, but can today form a true part of the realisation of humanity. Law, Love, Union or Synthesis — all these great energies have seeped into the human consciousness and now provide the platform upon which the new civilisation can be founded, the new approach to God be taken, and new human relations be implemented.

Three great rents, therefore, now exist, as well as numerous smaller and less important ones, to which no reference has been or need be made. Three great Sons of God at the moment of initiation made a major contribution to the human consciousness through their determined will-to-law, will-to-love and will-to-synthesis. Mankind was thereby aided to move forward more easily along the "lighted Way," to pass through the halls of maya, aided by the light pouring through the rents made in the separating veils by perfected divine Men at the very moment of Their triumph. A fourth great rent still remains to be made as a result of the energies released and the gained good which the three earlier rents have made possible. This fourth major rent will be made by humanity itself, standing with "massed intent," focussed through the groups which are externalisations of the Ashrams of the Masters. It will therefore be made at the time that the Hierarchy takes physical shape upon the earth again.

Bear ever in mind the symbolical nature of this teaching. The veils are not actually existing veils in the usual sense of that term. They are in the nature of opposing forces and energies which act as inhibitory factors to the aspirant as he seeks to make progress, and to the entire human family as it moves onward upon the Path of Evolution. They are not basically related to consciousness at all, for in the majority of cases these veils "lie on the earthward side of being and not upon the side of light"; they are essentially physical forces, and although they are the result of man's own effort and activity down the ages, they are largely unrealised, unseen obstacles to his progress. They constitute the lowest concentration of forces precipitated from levels of activity other and higher than the physical, as you understand physical substance. If one might use a phrase which, even if true, is misleading, they lie between the subtle inner man, mental and astral, and his *physical brain*. They are that which prevents brain registration of the world of causes and of meaning. This inner world can be emotional or mental in its focus and in its force precipitation on to the etheric plane. It can be the fused result of personality integration and be a combination of energies; or it can be dominated by the effects of soul energy. These, if evoked, can penetrate occultly and drive out or break down and through the separating veiling forces, thus producing coordination eventually between soul and brain.

These veils are as curtains over the windows of vision. They prevent realisation of that which lies beyond the room or area of average or mediocre experience, and they prevent the light from penetrating.

The work of the three Sons of God referred to above is not concerned with the rending of the veils of their own interior life and forces, thus bringing about soul contact unimpeded and clear, or with the illumination of experience upon the physical plane. That had long ago been effected in these special and individual cases. Their service was rendered to humanity and They made rents in the veils which separated mankind as a whole from the higher spiritual experience and from registration of the fact of the existence of the Hierarchy. Theirs was a universal service, and made possible further human progress, for until some greater measure of light had been let in it was not possible for man to see and grasp the necessity to destroy the obstacles to light. The veils remain unperceived by the average aspirant until some light appears through the rents in the "curtain of impediment."

The glory of the Christ and the uniqueness of His accomplishment lies in the fact that He was the first to bring about the rending of the veils from "the top to the bottom." This He could do because He acted as the World Saviour, outside and independent of humanity; He was free from the aura of the human family and — again quoting the *Old Commentary,* as far as it is possible to translate these archaic terms:

"From above He worked and from the further side issued the force which tore its way into the separating forces, driving them in a threefold direction, from the point which is the highest, to the right and to the left, thus letting in that streaming force which resolved itself as light, as love, as lifting energy. Thus worked the One for Whom all men must wait. He is as man, but works not as a man. He works as light divine, as energy supreme and as the Saviour of the world of men."

Let me again quote from the same source and give you the ancient names of the veils:

"Next to the earthly plane is found the Veil of Impulsion and then the Hall of Concentration. To that succeeds the Veil of Distortion, related to the world of glamour as impulsion is to force. Beyond that veil is found the Hall of Choice. And then we find another veil, the Veil of Separation, and beyond it lies the Hall of Blinded Men — blinded by light but facing towards the final veil, the Veil of Aspiration. Four veils, three halls and many men."

I will leave you to make due application of this paragraph of stated truth and of condensed realisation. I would remind you that concentration is one thing to the aspirant, and a very different thing to the initiate, and that the choices made by the initiate resemble not those made by the disciple. The blinding force referred to can range all the way from the deep spiritual darkness in which the average man moves, through the blindness of which Saul of Tarsus was the exponent, up to that condition which overwhelms the highest Initiate as He awaits entrance into the Council Chamber of the Lord.

Blindness is a prelude to initiation of no matter what degree. It is only at the last and highest initiation that the "tendency to blindness" comes to a complete end. In the early stages of evolution, blindness is natural, innate, unavoidable and impenetrable. For ages man walks in the dark. Then comes the stage wherein this normal blindness is a protection, but has also entered a phase wherein it can be overcome. Technically speaking, the blindness to which I have referred is something different. From the moment when a human being catches the first, faint glimpse of the "something other" and sees himself in juxtaposition to that dimly sensed, distant reality, the blindness with which I have dealt is something *imposed by the soul* upon the hastening aspirant, so that the lessons of conscious experience, of discipleship, and later of initiation may be correctly assimilated and expressed; by its means, the hurrying seeker is defended from making too rapid and superficial progress. It is depth and a profound "rootedness" (if I may coin such a word) for which the inner Teacher and later the Master looks, and "occult blindness," its need, its wise handling and its final elimination are part of the curriculum imposed upon the candidate. This truth is recognised, though not truly interpreted, by the Masonic Fraternity. In one of the most important and highest initiations, the candidate enters with unblinded eyes and no hoodwink is applied. Then, halfway through the ceremony, he is blinded, and in that condition passes through the terrific tests, symbolic of a certain high stage upon the Path.

Blindness is therefore, esoterically speaking, the place of learning and is related to the eye, throat and heart doctrine. It is *not* related to the dim vision, the sensing of half truths and the gropings of the aspirant in the process of learning about himself, or as he visions the goal and seeks to walk the Path. That is a familiar condition and one to which all beginners are subjected and which they cannot avoid for it is inherent in their natures. Occult blindness is spiritually induced and "blacks out" the glory and the promised attainment and reward. The disciple is thrown back upon himself. All he can see is his problem, his tiny field of experience, and his — to him — feeble and limited equipment. It is to this stage that the prophet Isaiah refers when he speaks of giving to the struggling aspirant "the treasures of darkness." The beauty of the immediate, the glory of the present opportunity and the need to focus upon the task and service of the moment are the rewards of moving forward into the apparently impenetrable darkness. For the initiate, this blindness is still more esoteric; there remains for him absolutely no light whatsoever — no earth light nor any light within the three worlds at all. There is only blackness. To this the mystic has given the name "the dark night of the soul." The true dark night (of which the mystic's dark night is only a dim reflection, to speak paradoxically) marks a very exalted state of Being and stage of development. It was into the blackness and darkness that Christ penetrated as He overshadowed one of His Masters, the Master Jesus upon the Cross. This will strike a new note for many, and can only now be revealed. It is concerned with the facility with which a Master participates in the experience, subjectively realised, of the disciples whom He has prepared for initiation. It relates also to the still higher identification of the Christ with those initiates who are taking the fourth and fifth initiations, such as the Master Jesus in the experience referred to above. Christ is no longer the Initiator, but stands to the initiate as the Master does to the disciple. It is a curious phase of "identical participation," which evokes no reaction from the Master or the

Master of the Masters, the Christ, except in so far as it enables the divine Participator Himself to face another area of darkness, veiling and hiding a still more supernal glory. The above paragraph is far beyond the comprehension of the average student, but will be comprehended by those whose eyes are open to be blinded.

Students must remember that the four veils upon the etheric plane are only the lower symbolic correspondences to certain great areas of divine expression, and that ever the glory must be approached through the darkness. Such is the Law. These higher veiling factors can be mentioned and enumerated, but more information concerning these mysteries, this separating darkness encountered by the initiate, may not be given:

VEIL I. That which faces the disciple as he wrestles with the Dweller on the Threshold and becomes conscious of the Angel of the Presence, though as yet he sees Him not.

VEIL II. That which the initiate encounters at the fourth initiation and which forces him to cry out in his blindness: "My God, my God, why hast Thou forsaken me." The words uttered by the Christ at that time, and as the Participator, have been forgotten by the orthodox, though preserved by the esotericist. To them H.P.B. refers in *The Secret Doctrine*.

VEIL III. That mysterious blindness which overwhelms the initiate when—as the Embodiment of all the forces of the Spiritual Triad—He faces the Monad and is impelled forward by the "devastating Will" of the first aspect. Of this I may not write. It concerns the sixth and seventh initiations.

VEIL IV. That "unknown impenetrable Void, the utter darkness of negation" which Those Who are in the Council Chamber of the Lord of the World and Who are focussed in Shamballa face when the time comes for Them to "negate" our planetary life-expression and experience altogether. They must then leave behind all the seven planes of spiritual and human experience and pass onward and out into phases of Life and Being for which we have no words, and of which we have no conception. They leave through the fourth veil on the cosmic physical etheric levels (on the highest plane of our seven planes) and pass on to the cosmic astral plane. There They negate its existence as They have earlier negated the existence of the astral plane, so familiar an illusion to all of us. The initiate passes on to the cosmic astral plane and finds—What? Who knows? I do not.

Thus the veils serve their purpose; blindness nurtures and protects, provided it is innate and natural, soul-imposed or spiritually engendered. If it is wilfully self-induced, if it provides an alibi for grasped knowledge, if it is assumed in order to avoid responsibility, then sin enters in and difficulty ensues. From this may all of you be protected.

Step by step, the Brothers of the Light and others who tread consciously the Lighted Way have removed Themselves from the lure of form; the Army of the Voice no longer can succeed in deflecting Their footsteps and the veils of illusion no longer block Their vision and Their moving forward. A relative freedom has been gained and the initiate stands free from much that has hitherto hindered his progress; the world of form, of glamour and of seduction has for him no further appeal. He comprehends the significance of the injunction which is embodied in the third phrase of this tenth rule:

*3. Let the Army of the Voice be no more heard, and let the brothers onward move within the Sound.*

Putting the idea into esoteric terms, the above sentence could be paraphrased as follows: The voices and the Voice fade out. The A.U.M. is replaced by the O.M. and at the centre of that O.M. the brother stands.

The many voices of the world, the flesh and the devil are no longer distinguished; there is nothing within the consciousness of the initiate which can respond to them. The Voice of the Silence dies out also and the Word itself

cannot be heard. Only the SOUND remains. This is the
Sound which reverberates in the formless worlds; it is the
Sound to which the Spiritual Triad responds and of which
the initiate is a part, because the Sound which he makes as
he proceeds upon his creative way is a part of the universal
Sound. It should be pointed out that He Who stands at the
very centre of the Council Chamber of Shamballa sounds
forth all words, the Word, and He also utters the Sound.
This is apt to be forgotten. He it is Who intones the A.U.M.
and all things come to be; He it is Who voices the Word,
the O.M., and God incarnate in humanity appears on earth;
He it is Who utters the SOUND, and upon that outgoing
Breath holds all things in life; and — in the rise and fall
of its cadences — there is found the cyclic rhythm of the
creative process. He it will be Who will withdraw the
Sound and centering the vibration within Himself, will
some day bring to a close this periodic manifestation and
carry the Sound to other localities in space, holding it in
quiescence on the withdrawn breath until a later cycle of
expression dawns. Then it will again be exhaled and sent
forth to provide a new field of experience for the Lives
which, in cyclic rhythm, again seek to manifest. The entire
story of incarnation is hidden in the understanding of the
SOUND and its differentiation into the O.M. and the A.U.M.

When we can identify the Sound and are no longer
"moved" by the O.M., then the initiate becomes a Christ in
expression and makes His appearance, either in physical
form or upon the planes of what to us might be called the
"areas of non-appearance." He can then contain and utilise
the energies of which the Spiritual Triad is the custodian
and which are the expression of the will and purpose of
God. Though the initiate may not be a part of the planetary government, and though he may not be a member of
the Council at Shamballa (for only a limited number of
initiates are so placed), he nevertheless has the right to move
on identical levels and to prepare himself for those higher
evolutionary processes which will give him entrance to the
cosmic astral plane. This will enable him to "see through"

and to recognise "cosmic glamour," and will give him the hidden key to the world of feeling and of sentiency, of which our feeling-response and our emotional and intuitional sensitivity are but the dim and distorted reflections. This is a factor of some importance to have in mind if a right sense of proportion is to be developed. The initiate has learnt on earth that the astral plane is in fact non-existent — at least for those of the higher degrees of initiation. This knowledge constitutes the first step towards the comprehension of the secret of negation, towards a true understanding of the basis of the ever-existent pairs of opposites, and towards the knowledge which lies behind the significance of negation. The above sentence is in all probability of little meaning to you, but it nevertheless contains a truth for which the trials, experiences and initiations of planetary existence prepare the initiate. They endow him with those qualities which will enable him to contact cosmic evil and yet remain untouched, eventually to play his part in bringing the Black Lodge and its Brotherhood to an unholy finish. The roots of the Black Lodge are on the cosmic astral plane, as the roots of the White Lodge and its Brotherhood are on the cosmic mental plane; this is, in reality, only for the time being and in order to see certain organised activities upon the star Sirius perfected and carried to a consummation. This has oft been hinted in my writings.

"The Way of the Higher Evolution" leads to the cosmic astral plane, and the goal which carries a man there is the transcendent vision accorded at some of the higher initiations; the quality which enables him to work as a creative factor in the great White Lodge is the developed buddhic faculty. It is upon the "wings of Sound" that he travels, to use a well-known though little understood metaphor. This can only be when he can

4. *Hear the O.M. as it is sounded forth by Him Who stands and waits at the very centre of the Council Chamber of the Lord.*

These are grave and solemn thoughts, and of small use to the average reader. It is essential, however, that he avoid the concept that the attainment of the highest initiation upon this planet marks the end or the consummation of a great and final stage. It only marks the beginning of significance. This is a statement of esoteric value. Just as the attainment of physical control sets the neophyte free for the learning of higher lessons in preparation for the major initiations, so the surmounting of the conditions presented by the seven planes of our planetary life sets the initiate (such as the Buddha or the Christ) free for still higher and more important conditioning circumstances. Their real work as Members of the White Brotherhood is on the point of beginning, and the true purpose of the existence of the Great White Lodge begins faintly to dawn upon Their entranced and amazed understanding. It is of real value to us, therefore, to endeavour to grasp the continuity of revelation and the vast future or vista of unfolding wonder which, stage by stage, grade by grade and plane by plane, unfolds before the initiate-consciousness.

We enter here into a consideration of realms of advancement of which even advanced humanity has no faintest idea; we are touching upon goals and objectives which confront the advanced Members of the Hierarchy; we are dealing with ideas and concepts for which we have no adequate terminology and which are of such a nature that the human mechanism of thought proves incapable of registering them. What, for instance, do the words or phrases, "Divine purpose, Shamballa, the Lord of the World, states of registration or awareness which have no relation to sentiency as it expresses itself through consciousness, the Lodge on Sirius" and similar concepts convey to you? I would venture to suggest that in reality, they represent nothing, and this because the goal of all who read these words is contact with the soul, recognition of and by the Hierarchy, and initiation. If I say to you that the words "the O.M., as it is sounded forth by Him Who stands within the confines of Shamballa" signify that the one Sound, rounded and full, of O is sounded forth, but that the concluding sound of the M is omitted, does that convey aught to your intelligence? Again I venture to say that it does not. It is therefore of small importance for me to enlarge upon this phase of the Rules. I would be more profitably employed if I elucidated somewhat the meaning of the words "the Council Chamber of the Lord." Three concepts have perchance taken shape in your minds in connection with Shamballa, if you have sought the true esoteric attitude:

1. That Humanity exists as a great centre of intelligent energy in the substance of the planetary Life.

2. That the spiritual centre, where attractive, coherent, magnetic energy is focussed and from whence it flows in two directions

    a. Towards the three worlds and the four kingdoms of nature,

    b. Towards Shamballa and the two higher kingdoms in manifestation

is what we usually call the Hierarchy, the Kingdom of God, the centre of love and of mediating understanding (note these last two words).

3. That there is another centre which is neither spiritual nor human but which is characterised by divinity. Divinity is the expression of the will or purpose of the One in Whom we live and move and have our being. That centre where the will of God is focussed and dynamically sent forth to carry out the purpose is Shamballa.

The time has now come when a distinction must be made by esotericists between the words "spiritual" and "divine." They are *not* the same, nor do they have the same significance. The quality of spirituality is Love. The quality of divinity is Will. There is a definite distinction between the two and the mediating principle (or that which relates or unites the two qualities) is Wisdom. Of that Wisdom the Buddha was the expression *in time and space;* that means that there was only a relative and limited manifestation of that fusing linking principle. His great achievement, unrealised by Him, was an innate and (at that time, not now) unconscious recognition of the distinction between love and will, and an ability to express in Himself a fusing, blending energy which could and did bring together love and will, soul and Monad. At the same time (and later in full expression in Palestine) the Christ demonstrated—for the teaching of humanity—the at-one-ment of love and intelligence, of soul and personality. These are points of real importance to have in mind.

Embodying, therefore, divinity in a sense and form incomprehensible to disciples, and which constitutes the goal of such advanced individuals as the Christ, are a group of Lives or focussed integrated Beings Who stand around Sanat Kumara, the Lord of the World.

As I have earlier said, Sanat Kumara is to the Planetary Logos what the personality, plus soul, is to the disciple. He is also the coherent force within the planet, holding, through His radiatory influence, all forms and all substances in the planetary form so that they constitute one coherent, energised and functioning whole. A parallel to this, though on a much smaller scale, can be seen in the radiatory influence of the Christ as it permeates, energises and holds in coherent expression the Christian Church in all its many aspects in the world; a still smaller analogy can be seen in the influence wielded by a disciple who stands at the centre of a group and holds it also in coherent and useful manifestation. Intermediate between these two symbols of will and love, united in manifestation (the Christ and a disciple), is the work of a world disciple, for the influence is wider and more far-reaching than that of a disciple, yet not as potent or comprehensive as that of the Christ.

Coherency, affecting lives, forms and substances, is an expression of will and purpose, motivated by love and implemented intelligently in carrying forward the plans through which the Purpose seeks expression. When, however, you arrive at the potency of such a Being as Sanat Kumara, you find His individual potency enhanced and

amplified by the fused ability of a group of Lives Who —
though not as far advanced as He is upon the Path of Evolution which stretches before the Planetary Logoi — are yet
greatly in advance of the most developed members of the
spiritual Hierarchy. It is these Lives Who constitute the
innermost circle of the Council Chamber of the Lord of
the World. Their normal contacts are extra-planetary and
are very seldom of a planetary nature. They are in direct
rapport with the Planetary Logos upon His own high plane,
the cosmic mental plane; this great and Unknown Being
uses Sanat Kumara as the soul uses a temporary personality
when that personality is at an advanced stage of initiate
consciousness. This is only a parallel and an analogy, and
must not be unduly elaborated in the detail of relationship.

The major characteristic of these Lives is Will or Purpose. They embody and consciously know and intelligently
appreciate what is the motivating idea which the Planetary
Logos—working consciously on His own high level—seeks
to work out and achieve in His planned incarnation through
a planet. He functions when in incarnation on the cosmic
physical plane, and embodies the seven principles of which
we know, and all is focussed in and through the Individuality of Sanat Kumara, implemented and energised through
the seven planetary centres. The three Buddhas of Activity
(Who are also Members of the Great Council) are expressions of the counterparts on cosmic levels of the energies
latent in the three permanent atoms in the three worlds of
human endeavour. This is again a dangerous parallel to
propose for—as a symbol—it lacks any true analogy.

The Seven Spirits before the Throne of God are also
Members of the Council, and each of Them is in close rapport and contact with one or other of the seven sacred
planets in our solar system, and can thus draw upon the
energies which they embody.

It will therefore be apparent to you inferentially, how
comparatively few of the Members of our Hierarchy have
yet been able to reach the state or condition of development which would warrant Their forming a part of the

great Council, or which would enable them to respond to the O, sounded out at intervals of one hundred years by Sanat Kumara. It is this sound which gathers together the responsive Units into the Council. This Council is held at one hundred year intervals, and as far as our modern humanity is concerned, these Councils have been held—under our arbitrary dates—in 1725, 1825, 1925.

At these Councils, Those Who are responsible for the planetary development, along certain predetermined lines, make Their reports; decision is made as to new unfoldments; certain types of energy, cosmic and solar, are made available for the carrying forward of the Plans which implement the Purpose; the evolution of consciousness in the three worlds receives, necessarily, major attention.

I would have you remember that this refers not only to the human kingdom and its unfoldment, but to the three subhuman kingdoms also which are—from many points of view—of equal importance to the human. This is a hard saying for humanity to accept.

It is these great goals which slowly dawn on the consciousness of the initiate as he advances step by step along the Path of Initiation. They must perforce be noted here, even if dealing with matters incomprehensible to the reader; initiation otherwise would be apt to be regarded as the attainment of a relatively static condition and would land the initiate in an eternal impasse or impassable cul-de-sac. Initiation is in fact the recognition of the goals which are implemented from Shamballa. It is not a process whereby a man becomes solely a Member of the Spiritual Hierarchy. Initiation (as the candidate understands it) is in reality only incidental and preparatory to the Path of the Higher Evolution.

There is little more that I can tell you anent this Rule. The subject is, as you can see, too advanced even for the initiate who, in a few decades, will read and study these instructions. That your vision may expand, and your power to think and reflect abstractly may grow, is my hope and wish for you.

## RULE ELEVEN

I would like to speak, at this point in our discussion of the fourteen rules for initiates, upon the theme of group initiation; these rules are those to which groups that are seeking, in unison, a group expansion of consciousness, must learn to conform. It is for this reason that I have hitherto omitted to go into detail in relating these rules to the seven centres or, specifically, to the great seven solar initiations. Of these seven initiations only five concern average humanity. The remaining two initiations concern only those who are willing to meet certain unusual requirements and to produce that special effort which entitles them to the appellation, "Victors, through the clear pure will."

Group initiation is no easy achievement, particularly as it is practically an untried experiment and constitutes essentially a pioneering effort. That such a development was inevitable, if the evolutionary growth of humanity proved in any way satisfactory, was early realised by the Hierarchy. However, it has taken millenia of years to make it seem — as an hypothetical effort — in any way possible, and only tentative experiments have as yet been attempted. The first objective of these experiments (going on quietly in various places all over the world) is to see if a group of disciples can work together in such a manner that an inner fusion can be seen — by the Masters — to be taking place. The results, hitherto, have not been encouraging. It has, for one thing, been difficult to find disciples who are approximately at the same point in evolution, whose rays are "shining through" adequately, and who can evidence some one quality, or some controlling theme (if I may use such a phrase) which they share in unison and which would suffice to hold them together and prove strong enough to offset personality differences, preferences and barriers. It has not been possible, as yet, to do this. Group after group has been tried and tested out by different Masters in various parts of the world, and hitherto all such attempts have proved failures. When I use the word "failure" I mean failure from the angle of the planned objective. From the angle of the individual growth of any particular disciple there has not necessarily been failure; from the angle of the unwitting, general public, the publication of *Discipleship in the New Age* will prove in years to come an epochal success.

It might be of value to consider briefly what group initiation involves, and to do this factually and not senti-mentally and aspirationally.

One of the problems confronting the Hierarchy in this connection is the elimination of sentiment — that curious, emotional reaction and relationship which links all the members of a group together in the bonds of liking or dis-liking. Where there is liking, then too strong a personality relation is established, as far as the good of the group is concerned. The group equilibrium is disturbed. Where there is disliking, the inner faculty of *rebuff* works con-stantly, and cleavages then occur. Is it not true, my brothers, that your relation to each other is frequently subjected to the impact of approval or of disapproval? When that atti-tude exists, the first steps towards group fusion are absent. This is what we mean by sentiment, and this emotional re-action must disappear as a preliminary stage. I speak not at this time anent impersonality. For some people, imper-sonality is simply an escape mechanism from responsibility; for others, it connotes suppression and entails such hard labour that the entire time of the disciple is given to the achievement of impersonality, thereby guaranteeing non-success. That at which you strenuously strive and which assumes undue place in your thinking, in due time becomes itself a prison and merits later destruction. Such is the oc-cult law. Impersonality is possible only to the disciple who knows truly how to love, and to him who sees life and its phantasmagoria (including all associated persons) in the light of the Spiritual Triad.

It is to this that Rule XI primarily refers, and it will not be possible for you to comprehend the significance of this rule unless there is a measure of clarity in your minds anent true group relationships. Such relationships are not based upon personality or impersonality, or upon liking or disliking, or on criticism or non-criticism, but upon a real comprehension of "divine indifference," spiritual detachment and deep, persistent, unchanging love. To many earnest aspirants the juxtaposition of these phrases will seem paradoxical; but an understanding of the occult paradoxes tends to liberation. In the comprehension of these basic attitudes lies the first lesson of the aspirant to participation in group initiation.

The second point which the group thus striving has to grasp is the necessity for the utilisation of the force of destruction.

A group is brought together under karmic law, ashramic necessity and soul direction. Immediately there is presented to the watching Masters an opportunity for the very definite training of some willing aspirants, but also an equally definite point of tension, indicating real difficulty. There is little, in reality, to link these people except inclination, a joint aspiration and a goal seen and held in unison. The outstanding characteristic of such a group is spiritual selfishness. This statement may surprise you until a close scrutiny of your own heart is undergone, and then I venture to predict that you will discover that it is not divine love of humanity that has enabled you to find your way into the outer group of some Ashram but desire for development, for achievement and for liberation. The first step, therefore, is to recognise this and hence the injunction so oft misunderstood: Kill out desire. This has to be the first destructive activity of the disciple. It is not what the disciple seeks, or wants or desires which should condition him and drive him to what we might call "ashramic acquiescence," but the all-impelling motive of world need. So the disciple begins to rid himself of desire by a process of attrition. He does not positively fight desire with a view to its elimination; he does not seek to transmute it (as should the probationary disciple), but he ceases to give it any recognition; he fails to provide it with the needed stimulation of attention, for as ever, energy follows thought; he is preoccupied with world need and with the service he can render, and—almost inadvertently, as it were—desire dies of attrition.

It will be apparent to you, therefore, that it will take time for all the members of a group to achieve the destruction of individual desire, and that until some measure of this united liberating process is attained, the group cannot go forward together as a unit on the Way of Initiation.

The next step is the destruction of the ties which link the personalities of the group members. These must be severed, and the relation between the group members must be on the basis of soul activity, joint pledge to the Master of the Ashram, and a united service given to humanity. There comes a point of freedom in the group relation which will demonstrate in some definitely planned and united activity, carried forward in the outer world but enriching the life of the Ashram. Until this stage is reached, the activity of the group corresponds to that of the probationary disciple and not to that of the pledged disciple. The spontaneously emerging group work, engendered by the group consciousness and fusing the entire group of disciples at a point of tension in service, is the first indication that the group is ready for further teaching, for an intensification of its group potency and for a closer relation to the Master. This has all been brought about by the group itself, independently of any injunction of the Master, and as a result of the united soul life of the group effectively making its presence felt. These two spiritually destructive processes—the destruction of desire and the severing of all personality ties — are the first two and essential results of true group work.

The third quality which must be utterly rooted out and destroyed is that of all reaction towards recognition, whether that recognition is accorded by the world of men, by other disciples, or by the Master. The ability to work without any token of recognition, to see others claim the reward of action taken, and even to be unaware that the results of the good initiated by the individual disciple or his group are claimed by others, are the hallmarks of the hierarchical worker. The Masters get no recognition for the work done by Their disciples, though They initiated the original impulse and have given both guidance and direction; the disciple carries out the Plan; he shoulders the responsibility; he pays the price, either good or bad, or the karmic results of instituted activity, and he is the one who gains the recognition of the crowd. But—until the disciple seeks *no* recognition, until he fails to think in terms of results and is unaware of the reaction of the world to his work as an individual disciple—he has yet far to go in order to gain the higher initiations. The entire problem becomes increasingly difficult when an entire ashramic group is concerned, for the recognition of the group service seems little to ask from the world which is served; nevertheless, such a demand and such an expectation delay the complete absorption of the group into the inner Ashram.

These are not, however, impossible objectives, or I would not waste your time or mine in their delineation. The group can measure up to the occult necessity if unitedly they recognise the scope of the endeavour and unitedly strive for complete absorption in service — an absorption so deep that it excludes all other recognitions, particularly those of a personal nature. We come back, therefore (as is continually the case), to the fact that when a group can arrive at a suitable point of united tension, non-essential reactions disappear and undesirable qualities are automatically removed.

These three types of work along the lines of destruction merit your careful consideration and — because they are along the line of the destroying aspect — it will be apparent to you that the method employed is that of the utilisation of the group Will. It will be equally apparent that the group Will can only make its appearance under the Law of Occult Continuity when, and if, the group is functioning intelligently and demonstrating love adequately.

We now come to the third factor which group initiation involves. This is diversity in unity, consciously recognised and utilised. A group is not composed of disciples all of whom are being prepared for the same initiation. This is oft a hard saying for group members to accept. The significance of my earlier statement, that a group is composed of men and women all of whom are at the same point in evolution, is a generalisation and simply means that all of them have reached the point where they are pledged and unalterably committed to the work of the Ashram, under some particular Master.

The work, however, requires a diversity of quality and of potencies in order to be effective in manifestation upon the outer plane. It needs those who are in close contact with the Master, and are therefore initiates of a certain standing; it needs also those who have facility of relationship with the inner Ashram and are therefore senior disciples, though not necessarily high initiates; it needs also those not so advanced upon the Path of Discipleship because they have, or can establish, a close connection with ordinary humanity in the life of everyday. A group of disciples such as this is consequently a miniature hierarchy, and a *hierarchy exists in its various degrees in order to permit of a wide range of effective relationships.* Ponder on this statement. You can see now why there is necessity for the elimination of personality reactions, for only thus could the groups function as a coordinated unit with the various members recognising each other's status and yet not moved to jealousy or belittlement thereby; the work is then carried forward on the basis of inspiration, coordination and practical application. The senior members of the group, and those with the most advanced status (whatever that may be), provide the incentive of the Plan as they receive it from the Master; the more experienced among the disciples then coordinate the Plan within the group, relating it to the Ashram and indicating its approach to the world of men; the neophytes—pledged and dedicated though yet without experience — carry out the Plan upon the physical plane. This entails, as you can see, smooth and effective coordination, a proper attention to the general picture, and an application of the detail of work to the immediate necessity. It is a hard task for a group of intensely individualistic disciples (and all disciples are individual) to begin to take the first steps towards these attitudes and the relationships which distinguish the Hierarchy as a whole.

Still another important factor in the group preparation for initiation is the cultivation of silence. How, we ask ourselves at times when the functioning of the Ashram is under discussion, can we train our disciples to realise that, essentially, silence is *not* refraining from speech. So many disciples seem to think that it is, and that they have to learn not to talk if they hope to take initiation. Some would do a great deal better if they talked more than they do—along right lines. The silence imposed in an Ashram is refraining from certain lines of thought, the elimination of reverie and the unwholesome use of the creative imagination. Speech is consequently controlled at its source, because speech is the result of certain inner sources of ideas, of thought and of imagination; it is the precipitation (at a certain point of saturation, if I might so express it) of inner reservoirs which overflow on to the physical plane. The retention of speech and the suppression of words, if they are the result of a realisation that what is to be said is wrong or undesirable, or unwise, or wasteful of energy, will simply increase the inner banking up and will lead eventually to a still more violent display of words at a later date; it may also bring about serious and disastrous conditions within the astral body of the disciple. The silence of thought is to be cultivated and, my brothers, I do not mean silent thinking. I mean that certain lines of thought are refused admission; certain habits of thinking are eradicated and certain approaches to ideas are not developed. This is done by a process of substitution, and not by a violent process of suppression. The initiate learns to keep his thought apparatus in a certain effective condition. His thoughts do not intermingle the one with the other, but are contained (if I may thus pictorially word it) in separate compartments or carefully filed for reference and later use. There are certain layers of thought (again speaking symbolically) which are held within the Ashram itself and are never permitted to enter the mind of the disciple or the initiate when not consciously working in the Ashram; others are related to the group and its work and are given free play within the group ring-pass-not; still others are of a more mundane nature and govern the daily life and relationships of the disciple with personalities and with the affairs of civilised living and physical plane events. These are only indications of what I mean, but will suffice to show (if you duly meditate) a little of what is meant by the silence of the initiate. Within the permitted levels of contact, speech is free and unimpeded; outside those levels, no indication is given that the other spheres of thought activity, with their conditioning speech, even exist. Such is the silence of the initiated disciple.

We have therefore considered briefly but suggestively four qualities which a group preparing for initiation needs to develop, to consider and unitedly to achieve. They are:

1. The achieving of a non-sentimental group interrelation.
2. Learning how to use the forces of destruction constructively.
3. Attaining the power to work as a miniature Hierarchy, and as a group to exemplify unity in diversity.
4. Cultivating the potency of occult silence.

We now come, after these preliminary remarks, to a consideration of the next rule.

## Rule XI.

*Let the group together move the fire within the Jewel in the Lotus into the Triad and let them find the Word which will carry out that task. Let them destroy by their dynamic Will that which has been created at the midway point. When the point of tension is reached by the brothers at the fourth great cycle of attainment, then will this work be done.*

On first reading this rule it is obvious that it concerns the fourth initiation and the consequent destruction of the causal body—the vehicle through the means of which the Monad has created first of all the personality, and then an instrument for the expression of the second divine aspect. We are therefore dealing with one of the major initiations. I would here call to your recollection the fact that (from the angle of the Hierarchy) this initiation is the second major initiation, and not the fourth, as it is regarded from the human angle; the third initiation is technically regarded as the first major initiation. The major initiations are really possible only after the transfiguration of the personality.

What, therefore, brings about the destruction of the soul body? The destroying agent is the second aspect of the Will. The third or lowest aspect of the Will, working through the mind or the manasic principle, was the sustaining factor in the long cycle of personality development; it was the principle of intelligent synthesis, holding the life principle intact and individualised through the long series of successive incarnations. During that cycle the will demonstrated first as the lower man; then it focussed itself in the Son of Mind, the divine Agnishvatta, the soul, and became increasingly a factor of potency. Later, as the disciple builds the antahkarana and thus establishes a direct channel of communication between the Monad and the personality, the lower mind becomes fused with the abstract mind or higher mind (the manasic principle, sublimated and purified), and gradually the soul is — to use a peculiar but sensitively expressing word—*by-passed*. It has by now served its purpose. Love and light are in expression in the physical plane life. Neither the personality vehicle nor the soul body is required, as under the old conditions. Their place can now be taken by the Spiritual Triad and the Monad; the essential life of both the lower aspects (creative in nature and expressive of loving intent as to purpose) can now be withdrawn. Triplicity, from the angle of the three periodical vehicles—Monad, soul and personality—is resolved into duality, and the Monad (reflected in the Triad) can now work upon the lower planes through the medium of a definitely created personality or "point of tension" in the three worlds. It is to this that the rule applies when studied in terms of the individual initiate, whilst the life in which the soul is "by-passed" and its ring-pass-not is destroyed, is of such profound difficulty that it is called the life of crucifixion or of renunciation.

We are, however, concerned with the interpretation of the rule as it affects a group which is preparing for the joint initiation of its members. It is by adhering to the ancient dictum that "as it is with the Macrocosm so will it be with the microcosm," and by the application, therefore, of the Law of Analogy, that we shall eventually arrive at understanding. I cannot hope to do more than indicate significances, but it will now be clear to you why I have dealt with the four qualities which a group must develop in unison prior to initiation. We shall find it useful to relate these qualities to the various phrases or injunctions in this Rule XI. We must consider each of them separately. Let us now look at the first sentence.

*1. Let the group together move the fire within the Jewel in the Lotus into the Triad.*

Let me first remind you that fire always connotes the first aspect and this, as you know, is the life aspect. To this let me add the well-known fact that "Our God is a consuming fire," and call to your recollection that the first aspect is the destroyer aspect. You have immediately established a relation between the first two qualities with which we have been dealing and the work of the crucifixion as a symbolic expression of the fourth initiation. The achieving of a selfless and impersonal group interrelation was the first prerequisite, and the word "together" in this rule deals with the work of the group when—as a closely knit unit—it can move forward. This transference of the life or of the fire has to be the result of united action, taken by the group when full interior unity has been attained. It cannot take place prior to this, any more than an individual initiate can take this particular initiation until such time as complete fusion of the three bodies and the soul has been effectually brought about and divine indifference has been achieved to all lower reactions of the component parts of the fused and interrelated instrument. So must it be with the group.

The group life must express itself upon the physical plane and in group formation. It will possess a sensitive *feeling* apparatus, corresponding to the astral body, and the group mind will be well organised and functioning rhythmically. Thus the group "personality" will be active, but divinely active, by the time this particular stage is reached. The group soul will also be in full flower as an expression of the inner Ashram, and at the very heart of the group life, veiled and hidden by its outer personality expression and by its vibrant loving soul, will be a point of living fire or life which — in due time and under right conditions — must be transferred into the inner Ashram, found on triadal levels. This may or may not mean the destruction of the group causal body and the establishing of a direct line of relationship between the pure Ashram and a group of disciples. It will undoubtedly mean, during the stages preliminary to that desirable attainment, a definite change of focus and the gradual establishing of a point of tension upon slowly realised higher levels, carried on until the transference is completed.

All the time that this is taking place, the fire at the heart of the group life is becoming more and more vital, and consequently more and more *spiritually* destructive. The second quality which we considered, the constructive planned use of the forces of destruction, can now be seen as active. It is these forces which are often responsible for the upheavals, the cleavages, the dispersions and the fatalities which are so frequently the characteristics of the group life in its early stages. The fire is then working under the stimulation of the Spiritual Triad, but is not consciously being manipulated by the group itself. The group becomes esoterically "a burning ground," and much time would be saved and much unnecessary distress and pain and suffering would be eliminated if the group members would realise what was happening to them and would simply stand steady until such time as the "purification so as by fire" has been completed and the life principle in the group heart can shine forth with both brilliance and radiance. It is this quality of patient endurance which is so sorely needed by the members of a group being prepared for initiation. Once, however, the purpose underlying all distressing events and disrupted personnel is grasped, rapid progress can be made—again by the simple practice of divine indifference. This divine indifference was the outstanding quality of the Master upon the Cross at Calvary. The seven words from the Cross were concerned with others, with His mission, with world need, and with relationship with the Father or with the Monad. But disciples and aspirants are so intensely preoccupied with themselves, their effect upon others, their endurances and pain, or with criticism of their brothers or of themselves! The goal and the main objective is not adequately emphasised in their consciousness. The group personality is often functioning with potency, but the fusing love of the soul is absent and the shattering inflow of the life at the heart of the Jewel is not permitted full sway. It is blocked and intercepted by group conditions, and until there is at least some united will to take *together* what is needed in order to shift the life of the group to higher levels of awareness and into the Ashram on buddhic levels, the technique of transference will not be committed to the group by the Master. That is what is meant by the next sentence in the rule:

*2. Let them find the Word which will carry out that task.*

What is this technique of transference? It falls into three stages, each one of which has to be arrived at by the group in unison. The first is the stage of united tension or the attaining of such a focal point of planned and focussed intent that the group is undeviatingly oriented to the immediate task to be done and is functioning from the angle of purpose as one individual. This is perhaps the hardest stage, but it has to be mastered prior to the assistance of the Master in the inner Ashram; He is to the group what the Monad is to the disciple, ever seeking to bring about the esoteric "renunciation" of the causal vehicle. This point of tension has to be held in high vibratory activity all through the process of transference. I would remind you that the outstanding characteristic of Jesus of Nazareth, throughout the period prior to the crucifixion, was one of complete silence; here is where the efficacy of the fourth quality mentioned by me appears. The group, at this stage, is so preoccupied with the task ahead and so conscious of the need for preserving a united and uniform tension, that "the silence of the secret place" settles on it and the work can then proceed apace. When this point has been attained, then the third quality manifests with power to work as a miniature hierarchy, and this becomes increasingly noticeable.

Now comes the result of all these preliminary stages, and it comes spontaneously and automatically. I want to emphasise that the group does not wait in expectancy for a Word to be given to it; it does not search and strive to discover a Word; it does not take some Word as may be suggested by a helpful disciple and then proceed to "empower it." The Word is the result of the point of tension; it emerges from the silence and its first expression is simply the slowly rising tempo of the group "Sound" or note. As you know, every individual and every group of individuals have their own peculiar note or sound which is the creative agent of the focussed group life.

At this point we again touch the fringe of the coming Science of Invocation. This group sound, rising as the tension increases and stabilises, is invocatory in effect and draws forth response eventually from the inner Ashram, owing to its relation to the outer group. When the response of the Master is registered in the group consciousness and His potency is added to the potency of the group, the sound emitted by the group changes in quality, is amplified and diversified, is enriched and then precipitated outside the ring-pass-not of the group life; this precipitation takes the form of a Word. This Word, being the result of group activity, focus and tension, plus the aid of the Master, brings about three results:

1. It produces fusion between the outer group and the inner Ashram.
2. It enables the group life to be transferred along the group antahkarana and focusses it once and for all in the Master's Ashram.
3. The result of this transference is twofold:

a. The outer group *dies,* occultly speaking.
b. The *soul* of the group, being now merged with the life aspect on levels higher than those on which the causal body exists, is no longer of major importance; the Great Renunciation takes place, and the causal body — having served its purpose — dies and is destroyed. So died, according to theological injunction, the Christ upon the Cross. Yet He died not, and still lives, and *by His life* are all souls saved.

It is hard for esoteric students to realise that the emphasis of the coming Schools of Enlightenment will be upon the life aspect, and not upon contact with the soul. The goal will be transference and not union. Aspirants and disciples today are largely the result of the old order of teaching and are the flower of the processes to which humanity has been subjected. This is a vital transition period; disciples and aspirants in the world at this time are, figuratively speaking, at the same stage as the group which we are considering — the stage of the transference of the life from the outer form into the inner being. Hence the difficulty with which you are all faced, and the arduous task it is to comprehend realistically that which I am attempting to convey. The problem of soul contact is something which you can and do grasp, at least theoretically. The problem of life transference from the highest point of present attainment into some vague and mystical spiritual focus is not so easy to understand. Forget not, I am not looking for understanding for I write for those who will come after you, and for those who will be the reincarnated aspects of your present selves.

You will note, therefore, how the four qualities dealt with (page 215) have enabled the group to achieve the sounding of the Word. That Word, now emitted by them as a group under the inspiration of the Master (and I use the word "inspiration" advisedly), has gone forth; it has passed beyond the sphere of the immediate group influence; it has made its initial impact upon the soul of the group and has vitalised to a new potency the life aspect, the Jewel in the Lotus of the soul. Now comes the possibility of fulfilling the third great injunction contained in this rule:

*3. Let them destroy by their dynamic Will that which has been created at the midway point.*

In the fulfillment of the requirement here enjoined, the group enters upon its major test in this work of transference. The group members have unitedly preserved the point of tension; unitedly they have created the antahkarana; unitedly they have invoked by the group sound the attention of the Master and of the Master's Ashram; unitedly that sound has taken the form of a Word, and that Word has made an impact upon the life aspect of the group within the form of the group soul; it has energised it so that the destruction of the causal body is now in order. The tendency of the group would then be to relax, and this quite normally; the irretrievable Word has gone forth and all is well and safely accomplished. But it is not so in verity. By the power of their united love, the group has mastered personnel difficulties and has developed together the four qualities; it has also found the Word which can affect the soul—for the Word is ever related to the second aspect, and because of that it can reach and energise the soul, the second aspect per se.

But now, in the final stages of the great work of transference, the group has to arrive at a new point of tension and of united attainment. It has to use the dynamic will, the energy of the first aspect, and so bring about the final destruction of the causal body. The life within the causal body has been stimulated and vitalised and is now seeking to break out of its confining form. The vehicle of the soul is being subjected to pressure from within but then—both in the case of the individual initiate and of the initiated group—the final blow has to be struck also from without, by an act of the united will; this corresponds to the great cry of the Christ upon the Cross when He exclaimed "It is finished." With these words, we are told, the veil of the Temple was rent from the top to the bottom, and the life of the Christ ascended to the Father. Ponder upon the significances of these phrases. "That which has been created at the midway point" is no longer needed. No mediating principle or intermediary between man and the Father is any longer required; the Monad and the personality are in complete at-one-ment and have achieved perfected relationship; triplicity has given place to duality, and the Way of the Higher Evolution stands open before the initiate.

It will be obvious that this phase of group attainment can as yet be only a hope. It lies far ahead of the present day groups, just as the fourth initiation lies far ahead of the average aspirant or disciple. But groups must have their goals and must strive towards the vision, just as the individual must; I am laying the foundation for the phase of group living and united striving which will be so distinctive an aspect of the coming era. There are three further points which I seek to make:

First, the attainment of the ability to use the group will dynamically can be more easily understood if it is realised that it means the extension of the point of tension into realms which involve the super-consciousness of the disciple; also that the release of the life aspect from the confines of the causal body produces a new cycle of invocation and invocative activity. This brings about an inflow of the destroyer aspect of the divine Will, and consequently the complete destruction of the causal vehicle.

Secondly, it is not to be inferred that all in the group must be disciples who are in process of taking the fourth initiation. A group can be composed of disciples and initiates of all degrees, though there must be among the group personnel at least one disciple who has taken the initiation of crucifixion. This necessity is symbolised for us in the close relation which existed between Jesus as He took this initiation and the Christ Who had taken it in an earlier state of life. The more diversified the group, the richer its life and possibilities. Forget this not. One hint I can give you upon this difficult subject. When the results of the first point of tension, prior to the emergence of the Word, have been reached, initiates of the fourth degree within the Ashram lend their aid and do much to make possible the attainment of the goal by the group.

Thirdly, I would have you note that I have given you much in a brief form and have added much of new information anent the fourth initiation. What I have said is applicable both to the individual aspirant and to a group seeking initiation. Read what I have said with attention, but remember that it is not yet possible for you to differentiate between what is symbolic and what may be factual. The secrets of initiation are thus guarded with care.

One simple rule towards comprehension and attainment ever holds good. The Great Renunciation becomes possible only when the practice of the little renunciations governs the life of a disciple and a group. The renouncing of ambition, of all personality ties, and the renunciation of all that hinders progress as it is revealed to the eye of the soul, lays a sound foundation for the final great transference, based upon the renunciation of that which for aeons has connoted beauty, truth and goodness, and which has seemed the ultimate goal of all aspirational effort. The endeavour to see that which lies ahead and beyond the apparent finality of soul fusion faces disciples, among them some of you, at this time; and that all of you may penetrate beyond the veil of the soul and eventually see that veil "rent from the top to the bottom," and thus be enabled to say with those of like degree "It is finished" is my earnest hope. Then will open for you as for others, the Way of the

Higher Evolution, and the glory of the Lord will be seen in a new light — a light which will dim and throw into the shade all previous goals and visions.


## RULE TWELVE

The Rule which we have now to consider carries us into realms of extra-planetary energy, into a world of a larger consciousness towards which the higher initiates strive and which is related in a peculiar way to both the past and the future. This rule might also be called the formula controlling the work of the New Group of World Servers.

The three remaining rules for initiates and disciples are concerned with the work of the New Age and the coming revelation which will make that work both new and possible. They are therefore of supreme importance to us. Step by step, in the eleven rules already studied, we have seen the initiate or disciple carried from his position as an accepted disciple standing before the Angel of the Presence, to that point of attainment where the spiritual will is released in full service and with full comprehension at the time of the fourth initiation, where atma or pure spirit is in control, where the Spiritual Triad is expressing the nature of the Monad, where identification with the purpose of deity has transcended illumination of the mind, and has also transcended cooperation through pure love with the Plan. These words are all attempts to indicate the path of progress which is—to the initiate consciousness—the necessary preparatory stage to treading the Path of the Higher Evolution, just as the Probationary Path is the necessary preparatory stage to being accepted into an Ashram. Briefly, the eleven rules already dealt with might be regarded as controlling the conscious activity of the initiate in the following stages and relationships.

1. The stage of the burning ground and the establishment of illumined group relation. This is revealed by the mind, functioning as an aspect of the group mind.

2. The stage of ashramic recognition and the establishing of a forward-moving group rhythm; these reciprocal activities produce a needed group tension.

3. The stage of emitting the group sound and the establishing of the power to invoke divinity, followed by a united group realisation that "God is Fire."

4. The stage of extinguishing the lesser fires through the means of the above realisation, and the establishing of a defined group reaction to the divine purpose or will; this results eventually in the negation of the Laws of Karma and Rebirth as they condition life in the three worlds.

5. The stage of triadal perception and the establishing of spiritual contact, thus negating both the life of form and the soul. Duality is no longer recognised.

6. The stage of identification with the life aspect and the establishing of complete divine integration into the greater Whole. The initiate then moves onward in life and not in consciousness—a concept and a truth which it is not possible for you to understand at this time.

7. The stage of a group sounding-forth of the Word and establishing direct relation with Shamballa as an integral part of the Hierarchy. This means the enunciation of a dual chord.

8. The stage of responding to the higher aspects of the seven Ray Lives and establishing contact with the Three and the One. This is done under the Law of the Supplementary Seven.

9. The stage of spiritual negation, as it is called. This establishes a new affirmative attitude and results in a recognition of the true nature of the One Initiator.

10. The stage of the dissipation of all veils and the establishing of the power to work with light energy, thus earning the reward of new utilised ability, i.e., the ability to work with the consciousness aspect in all forms.

11. The stage where the potencies of the death aspect of divine purpose can be used to carry out divine purpose, plus the establishing of complete identification (as a group) with the divine will. This marks the period of the Great

Renunciation and prefaces the complete transition out of the Fourth Creative Hierarchy, the human kingdom.

This is a brief and inadequate summation of the more general and the more easily comprehended results of obedience to these rules. The initiate stands free and becomes consequently a dynamic factor within the working Hierarchy. Rule XII now becomes clear to him, not only through the realisation induced by his illumined mind, but through the higher divine qualities which are related to the expression of the will and purpose of the planetary Logos.

It will of course be obvious to you that only those who have reached the stages of work described in Rules X and XI will truly comprehend my meaning. I would warn you again that the obvious significance of the remaining three rules is not in reality the true spiritual significance because we are in these rules dealing with the planned work of the Hierarchy during the next great cycle, that of the Aquarian Age, we shall therefore be considering those activities and plans which will usher in and mature that new culture and civilisation which will slowly come into being when the world has straightened itself out after the processes of the world war (1914-1945). The rule runs as follows:

Rule XII.

> *Let the group serve as Aquarius indicates; let Mercury speed the group upon the upward Way and let Taurus bring illumination and the attainment of the vision; let the mark of the Saviour, as the group toils in Pisces, be seen above the aura of the group.*

You will remember that the rule as given to applicants emphasised:

1. The use of the hands in service for healing, blessing and for invocation.
2. The mark of the Messenger in the feet; this referred to the use of the intuition, which is governed by Mercury.
3. The use of the "eye." This is not in reality the third eye (which is after all only a symbolic phrase), but the

ability to use developed soul power. This is that intermediate potency found between the power of the mind
and the dynamic electric energy of pure will.

For the initiate, this rule simply carries the same message
but on an infinitely higher scale, and (if I may so express
it) obedience to this rule calls in Aquarian energy, the
reasoning power of Mercury, and the illumination of
Taurus, in order to carry forward hierarchical work upon
a planet and in a planetary cycle which have been conditioned by Pisces for more than two thousand years.

I would have you ponder on this, for in realisation you
will here have the formula for the work of the Hierarchy
as it reconstructs the world after the destruction wrought
since 1900 A.D. You have here also a great triangle of energies, functioning through the medium of Mercury, the
reasonable, reasoning Messenger of the Gods:

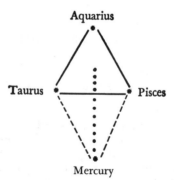

The Hierarchy is, therefore, at this time, conditioned by
three great constellations:

1. Aquarius — The Custodian of that "life more
abundantly" of which the Christ spoke
and which He can draw upon at this
time in a new and dynamic manner in
order to bring about the restoration
needed. This energy is the "implementing force of universality." It concerns the future.

2. Taurus — The Revealer of the vision, the "eye of the Gods," the donor of illumination. It is that which concerns the present.

3. Pisces — The Inspiration of the World Saviour, and also the field of salvation. It is the field of force in which the two other forces must work. It has been produced by the past.

As these three constellations pour their energies into the great Ashram of Sanat Kumara, the Hierarchy, they are there concentrated and retained until released under "the swift design of Mercury" into the field of the human consciousness. The effect of this release is to awaken the intuition (governed as you know by Mercury), and to enlighten advanced humanity. It is through intuitive human beings that knowledge of the Plan is given to humanity and the work of restoration can be carried forward.

At this time and in a peculiar manner, the initiate-consciousness sees the Hierarchy as primarily energised by life, and by the energy of Aquarius, carrying a hitherto unknown aspect of the life energy of deity. This is of course difficult for you to comprehend and will only be understood as it truly is at the close of the Aquarian Age.

The initiate sees the New Group of World Servers brought under the illuminating power of Taurus, with the rest of humanity still under the influence of Pisces. You have, consequently, the "over-shadowing raincloud of knowable things" hovering over humanity, just as the Hierarchy overshadows the New Group and just as the soul overshadows the personality of man; you have all the needed illumination and light upon all the coming problems, waiting to precipitate itself through the New Group of World Servers under the influence of Taurus, the nurturer of all illumination, and you have humanity, at the same time, conditioned and made sensitive by Piscean energy, during the past two thousand years. You have, therefore, a condition of great spiritual promise, and in this combination of

energies you have present those forces which will implement the activities of the Hierarchy, condition its initiates,
affect every Ashram, bring light into the present darkness,
and—as can already be seen—stir into new understanding
the present Piscean consciousness of mankind.

It is in the New Group of World Servers that the training of the needed disciples for the Ashrams of the Masters
takes place at this time in world history. This is a new
hierarchical venture. In this group also accepted disciples
learn to work in the same manner as does the Hierarchy.
The Hierarchy works within the field of the world of
human living; the New Group provides a similar field for
the new disciple. It is towards that group also that initiates
in the various Ashrams converge at times, in order to study
the calibre and quality of the disciples who are engaged in
world salvage, for it is through these disciples that the Hierarchy carries out its plans. Initiates do their main work
upon mental levels and from behind the scenes, and because of this their potency is great; this is particularly so
with those who have taken the third initiation. A certain
percentage of them are, however, active out in the world
of daily living.

You need ever to remember that at this time the *main
technique of the Hierarchy is that of conveying inspiration.* The Masters are not openly lecturing or teaching in
the great cities of the world; They work entirely through
Their disciples and initiates. It will, however, be possible
for Them to appear increasingly among men and evoke
recognition as the influence of Aquarius is more firmly
established. The Masters, in the meantime, must continue
to work "within the silence of the universal Ashram," as it
has been called, and from there They inspire Their workers,
and these latter in their time and way, inspire the New
Group of World Servers.

You will note, therefore, that the effect of Aquarius
upon the Hierarchy (as far as you, at your particular point
in evolution can determine it) is to bring in the energy of
Shamballa which is essentially the energy of life itself, im-

plemented by the will. This necessarily has created (and will increasingly create) major adjustments within the Hierarchy itself. The principal type of energy hitherto used by the Hierarchy is—as you well know—the energy of love. Now, to that must be added the energy of the life-giving will. New methods, new approaches to the human problem and new modes of work will have to be tried; experiment with the incoming forces will necessarily be the order of the day, though they will be experiments based upon vast knowledge and implemented with wisdom and understanding. It is the reaction of modern man to the ancient forces which produces the need for care. Mankind is oft unpredictable, owing to the factor of free will. It is this which lies behind the training given to disciples, upon which I have already given you much instruction. The new techniques and the changed approach from that of individual culture to united group progress will bring about many types of development. It is this different approach to the same basic problems which lies behind the new capacities which are emerging among disciples; it is this which enables disciples of experience to work at high speed and with a life potency that is unusual. I would have all disciples begin to train themselves to respond to the Aquarian energy now pouring into the Hierarchy. Some of you can do so as accepted disciples, and as members of my Ashram. Take advantage, therefore, of the opportunity for re-energising that comes to all those who have established contact, via their souls, with the Hierarchy, or who are members of an Ashram, or who, as probationers, are upon the periphery of the great Ashram of Sanat Kumara, the Hierarchy. This Aquarian influence produces mainly the intensifying of the hierarchical relationship to Shamballa, and therefore affects every member of His Ashram, from the Christ down to the most newly accepted disciple.

It is through the disciples that the New Group of World Servers are brought under the stepped-down Aquarian influence; this has to be an individual matter, largely dependent upon the point of evolution. Some members of the New Group of World Servers will not respond in any way; they cannot. Others will respond as fully as their spiritual status permits. This inflow of Aquarian energy is one of the factors which will enable the Christ to complete His task as World Saviour and World Teacher; it will also enable Him to take the initiation which lies immediately ahead of Him and for which He has been preparing for close upon three thousand years — so exalted and peculiar an initiation it is. It is this influence also which has enabled the Master R. to assume the mantle of the Mahachohan and become the Lord of Civilisation — a civilisation which will be conditioned by the rhythm of the seventh ray.

Incidentally, it is this Aquarian influence which has given the adepts of the Black Lodge the power to bring universal death throughout the world. These evil beings have responded to the will energy of Shamballa and to the life-giving vitality, but have used it in keeping with their own evil intentions and with the power conferred by their standing upon the cosmic ladder of evil. Hence the war. I only mention this as a striking example of the oft misunderstood fact that the same energy or identical force will produce results within the consciousness of a Christ or within the consciousness of anti-Christ. It is the same energy, but the forms upon which it plays differ so vastly that in one case the will-to-good is intensified, and in the others the will-to-evil. Energy per se is entirely impersonal.

The group, therefore, which "serves as Aquarius indicates" is the Hierarchy; the group which is "speeded upon the upward Way" is the New Group of World Servers. This group is ruled by Taurus, and to it that divine Taurian energy brings "illumination and the attainment of the vision." This group is, figuratively speaking, the "bull, rushing forward upon a straight line with its one eye fixed upon the goal and beaming light." But what is that goal? It is not the goal of Self-illumination, for that lies far behind; it is the goal of providing a centre of light within the world of men and of holding up the vision to the sons of men. Let this never be forgotten, and let the New Group of

World Servers realise its mission and recognise the demands of humanity upon it. What are these demands? Let me enumerate them, and then let me ask you to take them in all simplicity and act upon them.

1. To receive and transmit illumination from the kingdom of souls.

2. To receive inspiration from the Hierarchy and go forth, consequently, to inspire.

3. To hold the vision of the Plan before the eyes of men, for "where there is no vision, the people perish."

4. To act as an intermediate group between the Hierarchy and humanity, receiving light and power and then using both of these, under the inspiration of love, to build the new world of tomorrow.

5. To toil in Pisces, illumined by Taurus and responsive in degree to the Aquarian impulse coming from the Hierarchy.

These objectives are not only individual objectives, but the goal for the entire group. All who respond to the life-giving force of Aquarius and to the light-giving force of Taurus can and will work in the New Group of World Servers, even though they have no occult knowledge and have never heard of their co-workers under that name. Forget this not.

Recognition of the successful work of the New Group of World Servers will be accorded by the Hierarchy, and the testimony of the recognition will be the appearing of a symbol in the aura of the group—of the entire group. This will be a symbol projected by the Hierarchy, specifically by the Christ. What that symbol will be it is not for me to say. It is not yet fully earned, and only its dim and uncertain outline can be seen from the level on which the Masters work, and not at all from the level on which the group itself works. It is "the mark of a Saviour" and it will embody the mark or indication (the signature as medieval occultists used to call it) of a new type of salvation or salvage. Up till now the mark of the Saviour has been the Cross, and the quality of the salvation offered has been freedom from substance or the lure of matter and from its hold—a freedom only to be achieved at a great cost. The future holds within its silence other modes of saving humanity. The cup of sorrow and the agony of the Cross are well-nigh finished. Joy and strength will take their place. Instead of sorrow we shall have a joy which will work out in happiness and lead eventually to bliss. We shall have a strength which will know naught but victory and will not recognise disaster. Even the Black Lodge knew of this change in the mode of salvation, and hastily founded its groups of youths, banded together by the motto "joy through strength and strength through joy." It seems to be a law for group development to receive recognition from the side of evil, prior to that recognition coming from the good. But "after weeping cometh joy, and that joy cometh in the morning." Only the dawn is with us as yet—the dawn of the Aquarian Age. The full tide of light is inevitably moving upon its way towards us.

This Rule tells us that "the group toils in Pisces." This simply means that the field wherein the New Group of World Servers works is that of mankind, conditioned and ruled for the past two thousand years by Piscean energy. This is, as you know, the energy which produces mediation and which develops sensitivity in the individual. The work accomplished by and through this energy is so successfully accomplished that it has produced a mediating group of servers; this group acts as an intermediary between the Hierarchy and Humanity, and it has also developed the sensitive response of humanity to contacts, and to such a degree of sensitivity that the response to be accorded to the activities of the New Group of World Servers is very real and cannot be negated.

It should be remembered that the Piscean energy with which the group has to work is opposed to the incoming energies from the Hierarchy and the New Group of World Servers. This is owing to the fact that the energy of this constellation is passing out concurrently with the sixth ray energy, with which it peculiarly "coincided," as it is eso-

terically called. Hence the present difficulties. The passing
out of the influence of Pisces, the slow withdrawal of the
sixth ray force, the incoming Aquarian energy, via the
Hierarchy (affecting at this time mainly the Hierarchy itself
and the mental and astral planes) are conditions to which
we must look for the origin of all our present troubles. In
this involved situation, you have a planetary demonstration
of the significance of inner causes, producing outer effects.
Slowly, however, the Hierarchy is beginning to implement
both the Shamballa energy and that of Aquarius; the Masters Themselves have to learn how to use new incoming
energies in the service of the Plan, just as the individual
has to learn, in any particular incarnation, to work with
and use the available astrological forces which make their
impact upon one or other of his bodies or upon his entire
personality; such energies, as you well know, can be turned
to good uses or to bad. It is not possible for the Masters to
turn energy to evil ends, but They necessarily have to master new techniques and the new methods of work called
for by the new conditions; these can either affect the Hierarchy itself or will produce reactions in the fourth kingdom
and in the other kingdoms, producing rapidly changing
orientation and attitudes.

These forces and energies — from the zodiac or from
one or other of the seven rays — have poured into and
through our planetary Life for countless aeons. Each time
that they cyclically make their appearance, the forms and
substance in the three worlds upon which they impinge and
through which they pass are different in the degree of evolutionary response and of sensitive reaction to impact. The
response and the reactions of the human family as a whole,
or of the individual within that whole, will differ from that
of the previous cycle; with these factors the Hierarchy has
to contend, changing cyclically its technique and altering
its modes of work in order to meet the changing need. Bear
this in mind. This has never been more evident to the
Masters than today. The war might be regarded as a revolt
by the form side of nature against the old conditions, and

against the new incoming conditioning factors on the part of the Black Lodge. Between the two forces—one sensitive, onward moving, ready for that which is new and better, and the other reactionary, static and determined to gain a strangle hold upon the life within the form — the Hierarchy stands at the midway point:

a. Throwing all its weight on the side of that which is new, spiritual and desirable.

b. Adapting itself simultaneously to new conditions and new emerging factors.

c. Standing like a wall of steel, unshatterable and immovable between humanity and the forces of evil.

This has been an epoch of crisis, and the great moment for which the Hierarchy has been preparing ever since it was founded upon the Earth. Slowly down the ages, men have been trained and prepared for initiation; they have been taught to develop the initiate-consciousness; they have taken then their place within the ranks of the Hierarchy and have —later—passed into the higher centre, Shamballa.

Paralleling this line of unfoldment of the individual, there has also been a great though slow expansion of the human consciousness and a gradual steady progress forward into light. It has now become possible to create the New Group of World Servers — men and women sensitive to the inner and newer vision and to the incoming forces and energies. Each group, therefore, whether it is the Hierarchy, the New Group of World Servers, or mankind itself, is wrestling with its own interior problems of response, of recognition and of responsibility; each also is actuated by an outgoing movement in two directions: towards that which is higher and which indicates a better and more spiritual future, with all that that implies, and also towards that which is rooted in and related to the past, which is crystallising, reactionary, blind in its selfishness and materiality, and which is implemented to retain the old things which should pass away and to fight that which is new.

As individual aspirants, you all know that this condition exists in the conflict waged interiorly and expressed exteriorly between the soul and the personality. The same conditioning factors can be seen also working in every group, organisation, world religion, and in every nation, as well as in the planet as a whole. Millions of years ago, the Hierarchy realised that such a time of crisis and of conflict was inevitable. The easiest way to handle it would have been as lesser conflicts were dealt with in the past — by a process of final intervention. Shamballa and the Hierarchy could have unitedly ended this world crisis, but it would then have again arisen and have gone on arising until humanity itself ended it once and for all upon the physical plane.

Of this situation the determination of the United Nations to win and to enforce complete surrender upon the aggressor nations which are the agents of the Black Lodge is symbolic and also symptomatic of the progress of the human spirit. (Written in September 1944.) This time, the Hierarchy refrains from outer action, but simply inspires and transmits the needed energy, leaving mankind to find its own way into freedom, and out of Pisces into the aura and the field of activity of Aquarius, guided by those who are responsive to the illumination which Taurus confers.

See you not the beauty of this plan and its synthesising, culminating usefulness? See you not how the present crisis only indicates the success of the previous evolutionary cycles wherein humanity mastered certain lessons? All the post-war planning, the widespread reaction to ideals (in spite of all the efforts of the evil and reactionary forces), and the seething turmoil reaching throughout all levels of the human consciousness, plus the inspiration of disaster and suffering, are blasting open hitherto sealed areas in the minds of men, letting in illumination, sweeping away the bad old conditions. This is symbolised for us in the destruction of ancient cities and by the intermixture of races through the processes of war; this also signifies progress and is preparatory to great expansions of consciousness. These expansions in the human understanding will, in the next

one hundred and fifty years, completely alter the manner
of man's thinking; they will change the techniques of religion; they will bring about comprehension and fusion.
When this work has been accomplished we shall record an
era of world peace which will be symbolic of the state of
the human spirit. Men will then settle down to the great
task which confronts all of us in the New Age—the task of
dissipating glamour and of bringing about a clearer light
upon the astral plane, in the same way that better physical
conditions will have been brought about upon the physical
plane. All is planned and ordered; the right energies and
forces will be available, for the Hierarchy works ever under
the Law of Cycles and of Cyclic Compensation. The Masters
know exactly that which must be done by right timing and
by what has been called "the crisis of spatial extension."
They call this the interchangeableness of time and space—
a meaningless phrase to you but one which is already being
dimly sensed.

The two Rules which remain for us to study concern
the work of the Hierarchy in the Aquarian Age. Hence
they are specifically for the more advanced disciples and for
initiates. We have seen in many ways that—at this time—
the Hierarchy, because it is the Ashram of Sanat Kumara
Himself, is coming peculiarly and in a new sense under the
influence of His will nature. This means that the Members
of the Hierarchy, familiar as They may be with the Plan
for the immediate cycle with which They and humanity are
confronted, are being brought to a new and more "appropriate" conception of the divine Purpose which lies behind
the Plan and which motivates it. The will of God is becoming plainer to Them. It is taking on more definite lines.
As our planetary Logos nears the climaxing point of the
initiation which He is now undergoing, His Ashram, the
Hierarchy, must and does (as part of a normal development) feel the effect. From the Christ down to the newest
and latest accepted disciple, each in his own place, all are
becoming increasingly responsive to the "will of God." This

does not take place in a blind, acquiescing manner, but with understanding and "fortitude." This receptive attitude on the part of the Hierarchy will bring about great, necessary and unexpected changes. Some of these, I have earlier hinted, may now be taking place; some will follow later. The following ideas may serve to clarify the whole concept in your minds:

1. The entire technique of training disciples for initiation and of absorbing them into the various Ashrams which constitute the great Ashram of the Lord of the World has been altered. The Masters are no longer concerned with an individual, here or there, who endeavours to go forward on the Path, who evidences capacity and who is apparently ready for what has been called "the evocation of the initiate consciousness." It is becoming obvious to the Hierarchy that with the arrival of the Aquarian Age, group preparation, group initiation and group acceptance must and will supersede the older methods. These older methods, built around the direct relationship between a Master and a disciple, reached their highest point of usefulness early in the Piscean Age. For nearly two thousand years these methods have proved so successful that the intensity of humanity's response is such that hundreds are now ready "for absorption." This readiness and success present a difficulty and pose a problem for the Masters, necessitating a reorganisation of Their plans and a readjustment of Their techniques.

2. Not only has the individual approach to the Hierarchy been superseded by a group approach, but it is now found to be possible to make a certain measure of the training objective and exoteric. Hence the establishment of the New Group of World Servers. This is primarily a group which, while working on the outer plane of daily, physical living, yet preserves a close ashramic integration; it thus provides a field of service for accepted disciples who are seeking service-expression, and it also provides a rallying point for all determined aspirants where they can be tried out and where their motives and persistence can be tested, prior to direct acceptance. This is something new, for it

shifts the responsibility of preparing aspirants for accepted discipleship onto the shoulders of the pledged disciple and away from the immediate attention of the accepting Master. He is thus freed for other fields of service. This, in itself, is one of the major indications of the success of the evolutionary process as applied to humanity. This "shift" was initiated by the Christ Himself; he worked with men very frequently through others, reaching humanity through the medium of His twelve Apostles, regarding Paul as substituting for Judas Iscariot. The Buddha tried the same system, but the relation of His group was, in the first instance, to Him and not so much to the world of men. Christ sent His Apostles out into the world to feed the sheep, to seek, to guide and to become "fishers of men." The relation of the disciples of the Christ was only secondarily to their Master, and primarily to a demanding world; that attitude still controls the Hierarchy, yet with no less of devotion to the Christ. What the Buddha had instituted symbolically and in embryo became factual and existent under the demands of the Piscean Age.

3. The third great change has been in the relation of the Hierarchy to Shamballa, and of this you can necessarily know and understand little. I could perhaps express the underlying significance to you in symbolic language. The energy, emanating from Shamballa, has been divided into two direct and distinctive streams. One stream, embodying the dynamic of purpose, is now pouring into the Hierarchy and into its seven major Ashrams; another stream, embodying the dynamic of determination or of enlightened enthusiastic will, is reaching humanity direct, via the New Group of World Servers. Hitherto a blended stream of Shamballa force has poured into the Hierarchy and has streamed, in its undifferentiated type and quality, into all the groups within the Hierarchy. Now the quality of determination, or of what the average person understands by the use of the word "Will," is pouring into the New Group of World Servers, whilst the energy of dynamic purpose, differentiated into seven diverging streams, is pouring into

each of the "seven points of reception," the Masters' Ashrams within the ring-pass-not of the Hierarchy. These seven types of purpose embody the seven energies which will reorganise and redefine the hierarchical undertakings, and thus inaugurate the New Age. These seven purposes might be called:

a. *The unknown, unseen and unheard purpose of Sanat Kumara.* It is the secret of life itself and is known only to Him alone. In its initial phase of this new expression, it works through the Manu and the Master Morya; it is that which veils the central mystery which all esoteric schools—if true to their inaugurating impulse—will eventually reveal. What that is we do not yet know, but it is hinted at in Rule XIII.

b. *The purpose underlying revelation.* This may be a somewhat new idea to you for you are apt to regard revelation as a goal in itself. You seldom consider it as an effect of the inner purpose of Sanat Kumara. The emphasis hitherto has been on the aspect of revelation, making it an effect of what the disciple has done with himself and by means of which he is enabled to be the recipient of revelation. Yet behind all the successive revelations of divinity down the ages is to be found one significant purpose; all of them are and will prove themselves to be aspects of the Great Revelation. It is through the processes of revelation that divinity is slowly dawning upon the human consciousness. It is a sevenfold revelation; each of the seven kingdoms in nature reveals one aspect of it, and each of these seven reaches revelation in seven or fourteen lesser revelations or phases.

Ponder on this and learn to distinguish between *vision* (which is as much of the divine current revelation as a disciple can grasp in time and space) and *revelation* which is the synthesis of the divine expressive purpose. This is related to the will-to-good which is, in its turn, a complete expression of the love nature of Deity.

c. *The (as yet) unrecognised purpose which evoked the creative activity of our Planetary Logos.* This brought the

third aspect of the divine Trinity into play. The usual
reasons brought forward by the finite mind of man to account for what is called by us "manifestation," and to explain the dualism of all existence and the relation of
spirit-matter, are by no means the real explanation of the
divine purpose; they are based on man's own essential dualism; they are the highest explanation of his own divine
nature which he can achieve at this time. This is a point to
be remembered. They are his response to the second Ray
of Mutual Attraction, which the Ray of Love-Wisdom is
sometimes called. They are not an expression of his response
to the Will of God, and only indicate the limitations of his
definition of divine purpose. As you will note, they really
define nothing. Nor can I help you to recognise this third
aspect and the eternal purpose of the Lord of the World.
Just as a soul seeks incarnation in order to carry forward
some fixed design and to take one of the higher initiations,
so Sanat Kumara came into incarnation through the medium of this planet in order to carry forward His fixed de-
signs (known to Him as a cosmic Soul on cosmic mental
levels), and to take one of the higher initiations which mark
the Path of Initiation for these great informing Lives of
planetary spheres. He could take this particular initiation
through the experience to be gained in a vehicle constituted, expressive and at the special state of consciousness of
our entire planetary manifestation. It required an instrument in which the cells and atoms of His body (all lives in
all kingdoms), and the integrated organisms within that
body (the various kingdoms of nature), were at the peculiar
point in evolution at which they are all now to be found.

That is as far as I may go in giving you a hint, and
you can see from this that in order to grasp more and comprehend more of His divine purpose you also will have to
be in preparation for that particular initiation which for
you—on your tiny level of awareness of fixed design—is the
microcosmic parallel of His cosmic intention. Which that
initiation is I may not state. The only service which these
hints can render (as to the sevenfold divine purpose and

the consideration of them) is to develop in you, the disciple, the power to think abstractly—a much needed capacity before you can begin to tread the Way of the Higher Evolution; for this the five initiations open to humanity (as to-day constituted) prepare the human spirit.

d. *The mysterious purpose which has necessitated the calling into activity the Principle of Pain.* Suffering and Pain are essential requirements in order to carry this purpose to completion. The capacity to suffer, which is distinctive of humanity, is the outstanding conscious reaction to environment of the fourth kingdom in nature, the human. It is related to the power to think and consciously to relate cause and effect. It is a process on the way to something undreamt of today. And when I say this, my brother, I mean just exactly that. This same ability to respond through pain is not to be found (in the sense in which the human being comprehends it) in any of the subhuman kingdoms, nor in the superhuman kingdoms, any more than it was found in the previous solar system or will be found in the next. It is related to an aspect of the creative intelligence, an aspect and characteristic peculiar to humanity.

This aspect was not found in the previous solar system, in which the other aspects of the creative intelligence functioned. In this solar system, it has been developed and brought from latency to potency in connection with the substance of the human bodies through which the human soul is gaining experience. It holds the secret of beauty in manifestation, and its first expression can be seen in the creative perfection of certain phases of art for which man, and man alone, is responsible. No other kingdom in nature creates forms, produces colour and sounds in harmonious relation, except the human; all of this type of creative art is the result of aeons of conflict, pain and suffering. The Jews, as a product of the humanity of the previous solar system, and as constituting the incarnating residue from that solar system, have run the gamut of suffering and are in the forefront of the creative arts at this time, particularly in group production such as certain of the great motion pictures and in the field of scientific discovery.

There will be, as you can well see, a close relation between this fourth purpose of Sanat Kumara, the fourth kingdom in nature, the human, and the fourth Ray of Harmony through Conflict. It is the balanced relation of these three, consummated at the fourth initiation, which produces the full beauty of the creative fixed design of the individual soul, or—on a different level of initiatory process—of the fixed design of the universal soul of the Lord of the World. The fourth ray being temporarily out of full incarnation at this time is the reason for the relative interlude in the production of human creative art of a very high order. The cycle of suffering is nearing its close, and we shall later see —when the fourth ray again swings into full objective activity—a recurrence of the arts on a turn of the spiral far more exalted than any lately seen.

e. *The fifth great secret underlying the purpose of Sanat Kumara* is related in a peculiar sense to the cyclic manifestation of all that is found in the three worlds of human evolution. It concerns that which is working slowly into manifestation through the medium of the lower concrete mind as it controls desire and brings substance and matter into conformity with the divine thought along this line. The sumtotal of the highest phases of human thinking along all lines, *materially* affects what appears on the physical plane in all the kingdoms of nature, what precipitates civilisations and cultures, and which expresses the best response *at the moment* of human sensitivity to cosmic impression.

This is all that can be said as we attempt to sum up the fixed desire and the pattern or purpose of divine activity down the ages. We know it to be profoundly inadequate as yet to express or to produce in manifested form the beauty of that design and to create in conformity with God's thought; but—age by age—the thinking capacity of man and his creative imagination have wrought out the slowly unfolding design, and will continue to do so; every great world cycle sees the emergence of greater beauty, and sees the subtle effects of man's thinking upon the subhuman kingdoms in nature steadily bringing the unknown to the surface, altering the nature of the flora and the fauna of the planet, and preparing the way for that time of wonder when the Hierarchy will again be exoterically directing the Plan upon the earth and aiding mankind to work with a fuller understanding of the divine design.

Here again is another reason for the changing plans of the Hierarchy. The Masters have to prepare Themselves for this intended and imminent emergence. They are faced with the necessity of changing Their techniques of work in order to meet adequately the demands upon Them. It is far easier for Them to work, as illumined Minds, upon the mental substance of Their disciples than it will be for Them to work down upon the physical plane, relating the minds and the brains of advanced human beings. People are apt to forget that with each forward advance of humanity, the demands upon the Hierarchy change, new needs must be met, new techniques used, new and experimental methods must be employed. As I write for disciples and initiates, I call this to their attention. Their work of mental training does not end as they attain certain spiritual initiatory goals.

This fifth purpose is therefore closely related to the whole theme of "the garment of God" and to the emergence into manifestation of His "robe of beauty" as it is created and brought into being by humanity, acting as the medium for ideas from the superhuman kingdoms, and then influencing and swinging into creative cooperation the subhuman kingdoms.

f. It is difficult for me to give any idea whatsoever of the purpose with which we are now concerned, because it is expressed in the relation existing between the significance of *Desire, Will, Plan* and *Purpose*. All these words are symbols evolved by man in his attempt to grasp logoic purpose. He recognises the impulses of desire, and in the course of the evolutionary process learns to transmute them into aspiration; he passes on to a vague groping forward in an effort to understand and acquiesce in the "will of God," as he calls it; as long, however, as human approach to that will remains negative, submissive, and acquiescent (as it does under the influence of the theological approach and in the manner inculcated by the Churches), no real light on the nature of that Will will be seen. It is only as human beings enter into relation with the Hierarchy and are gradually absorbed into the hierarchical life and begin to take the higher initiations that the true nature of the divine Will will be grasped and *the purpose* of Sanat Kumara be revealed by an appreciation of the *plan*, followed by a consequent cooperation with that Plan.

All this will be done through the transmutation of desire into aspiration, and then into fixed determination. When, however, the initiate has related these phases of consciousness in his own inner experience, and has permitted those inner realisations to affect his outer experience and daily living, then the underlying Purpose will shine forth and he will no longer be working in the dark. You see, my brother, that all that I can do in these abstruse matters is to indicate what you can do, as an individual, to fit yourself to grasp divine purpose, and thus see the divine design and patterns as they are in reality. Once you have taken the needed steps and complied with the requirements, the mystery disappears.

g. The final phase of the divine purpose is the most difficult of all to indicate, and when I say indicate, I mean exactly that, and nothing more definite and clear. Does it mean anything to you when I say that the ceremonial ritual of the daily life of Sanat Kumara, implemented by music and sound and carried on the waves of colour which break upon the shores of the three worlds of human evolution, reveal — in the clearest notes and tones and shades — the deepest secret behind His purpose? It scarcely makes sense to you and is dismissed as a piece of symbolic writing, used by me in order to convey the unconveyable. Yet I am *not* here writing in symbols, but am making an exact statement of fact. As beauty in any of its greater forms breaks upon the human consciousness, a dim sense is thereby conveyed of the ritual of Sanat Kumara's daily living. More I cannot say.

Here are hints, therefore, as to the divine purpose; each of the seven supplements and completes the other six. Only by attempting to grasp the whole inner synthesis will we arrive at the merest hint of the nature of that exalted consciousness which has brought our planet and all that is within and upon it into being.

## RULE THIRTEEN

Let us now descend to thoughts more practical and within the range of comprehension, and consider the thirteenth rule somewhat in detail. It runs as follows:

Rule XIII.

*Let the group get ready to reveal the hidden mystery. Let the group demonstrate the higher meaning of the lessons learnt, and these are four and yet are one. Let the group understand the Law of Synthesis, of unity and fusion; let the threefold mode of working with that which is dynamic carry the group together towards the Higher Three where the Will of God holds sway; let Transfiguration follow Transformation, and may Transmutation disappear. Let the O.M. be heard right at the center of the group, proclaiming God is All.*

The key to the significance and the clue to the secret of this rule are to be found in the preparatory rule given to applicants in the earlier book *(Initiation, Human and Solar)*. It is included here so that you can refer to it as you study its higher corresponding rule, as given to initiates and to advanced disciples.

*Rule XIII. For Applicants.* Four things the disciple must learn and comprehend before he can be shewn the inmost mystery: first, the laws of that which radiates; the five meanings of magnetisation make the second; the third is transmutation or the secret lost of alchemy; and lastly, the first letter of the Word which has been imparted, or the hidden name egoic.

In this earlier rule, the disciple is told that before he can advance to the mysteries which will be revealed to him sequentially as he advances along the Path of Initiation, there are four things which he must "learn and comprehend." These are:

1. *The laws of that which radiates.* I would call your attention to the fact that this does not refer to the Laws of Radiation. That which radiates comes under its own laws which are different to those which produced radiation. Students need to read with increasing care as they advance upon the occult way which leads to the Way of the Higher Evolution.

2. He must *study the five meanings of magnetisation.* This refers to the five modes in which the Law of Magnetisation works; this is another name for the Law of Attraction.

3. He must *comprehend what transmutation is* and in which consists the secret art (now lost along with the Lost Word) of Alchemy. Esoterically speaking, transmutation is the mode whereby force is transmuted or changed into energy. This means (where a disciple is concerned) the transmutation or changing or stepping up of personality force into egoic energy.

4. He must *know the "hidden name egoic"* or the first letter of the imparted Word. Two things should be noted here. The "Word" here does not refer to the Sacred Word but to the name of the planetary Logos, the hidden name of Sanat Kumara Who is the soul of the world in all its phases, the manifesting Ego of the Logos on the cosmic mental plane. Only the first letter of that "ineffable name" is permitted expression to initiates until the fourth initiation. You will see, therefore, how vast a field this instruction on Rule XIII covers.

The higher correspondences of these four requirements are expressed in the following terms:

1. *Let the group understand the Law of Synthesis.* (This is the law which governs the *thinking* of those great Lives Who form the Council of Sanat Kumara in Shamballa.)

2. *Let the threefold mode of working with that which is dynamic carry the group together towards the Higher Three where the Will of God holds sway.*

3. *Let Transfiguration follow Transformation and may Transmutation disappear.*

4. *Let the O.M. be heard right at the centre of the group, proclaiming God is All.*

You can gather from the above what a tremendous field of esoteric truth is here covered and how abstruse to the average occult student is the theme. Again I would remind you that the real significance will only be perceived by the trained initiate and that what I say here must necessarily be veiled and even meaningless to the non-initiate, even whilst radiantly clear to those who truly know. Again, I would remind you that I write this particular section of *A Treatise on the Seven Rays* entirely for initiates, and that aspirants who have not taken initiation *cannot* understand or duly appreciate the inner meaning of these fourteen rules. In this fact lies no reason for discouragement, nor is there any suggestion that those with initiate consciousness should endeavour to explain, even if — through compassion or from the desire to stimulate approach to the Mysteries—they desired to do so. No true initiate would be so tempted, for he would realise that it would not only be impossible but also that there is a vital necessity for the disciple to work out significances and meanings through the medium of his own life experiment and to arrive at understanding through direct experience. Then no questioning can ever arise and sure knowledge takes its place. There are no questions of any kind in the consciousness of those who form the Hierarchy. The lower analytical concrete mind which questions and separates this from that has been completely controlled and superseded; response to indicated group activity takes place. Students need to realise more concretely that group consciousness, universal awareness, and therefore synthetic effort, synthetic understanding and synthetic activity are possible to a Master or an initiate of the higher degrees. That involves the keynote of this solar system, particularly within this planet, the Earth; it will be succeeded in the next solar system by a type of life activity which is as yet only known in Shamballa.

Here I should like to pause a moment and interpolate some remarks.

There are certain phases of teaching and knowledge which I have given to the world which are relatively new— new to the modern esotericist and occult student though not new to disciples and initiates. It might be useful here if I mentioned one or two of these new aspects of the fundamental Truth which have been given by me to the public. If these new phases of the teaching have been later given to the public by other occult groups, it will have been because the information was gained by those who have read the books put out by A.A.B. for me or who are directly and consciously in touch with my Ashram.

An instance of this is that book by C. W. Leadbeater on "The Masters and the Path" which was published later than my book, *Initiation, Human and Solar*. If the dates of any given teaching are compared with that given by me, it will appear to be of a later date than mine. I say this with no possible interest in any controversy among occult groups or the interested public, but as a simple statement of fact and as a protection to this particular work of the Hierarchy. I would remind you that the instructions given by me as, for instance, those in *A Treatise on White Magic* and *A Treatise on the Seven Rays* were given sequentially over a period of years, antedating the publishing of the books. The same time-factor prevailed in the publishing of the earlier books. All my books were written over a long period of years, prior to publishing. All that appears of the same type of information over other signatures harks back to these books. Even if denied by their writers, a comparison of the dates of publishing with the original dates of issuing the instructions (in the form of monthly sets for reading and study in the Arcane School) or with the books published before the formation in 1925 of the Disciples

Degree of the Arcane School will prove this conclusively. Bear in mind this factor of timing. A.A.B. takes down to my dictation an average of seven to twelve pages of typing (single-spaced) each time she writes for me; but owing to the exigencies of my work I cannot dictate to her every day, though I have found that she would gladly take my dictation daily if I so desired; weeks sometimes elapse between one dictation and another. I write the above paragraphs for the protection of the hierarchical work in years to come and not for the protection of A.A.B. or myself. . . .

What are some of these newer truths for which I am responsible as transmitting agent to the world of occult students? Let me briefly state them in the order of their relative importance:

1. *The Teaching on Shamballa.* Little has ever been given on this subject. Only the name was known. This teaching includes:

   a. Information as to the nature of the will aspect.
   b. Indications as to the underlying purposes of Sanat Kumara.
   c. Directions as to the building of the antahkarana, which is the first step towards achieving monadic consciousness, and thus the first step towards the Way of the Higher Evolution.

2. *The Teaching on the New Discipleship.* This has been revolutionary where the older schools of occultism are concerned. The teaching includes:

   a. A presentation of the new attitude of the Masters to Their disciples, due to the rapid unfoldment of the mind principle and the growth of the principle of "free will." This changed technique negates the old attitudes, such as that portrayed in the Theosophical literature, and it was a recognition of the difficulties of correcting the wrong impression given which prompted H.P.B. in one of her communications to the Esoteric Section of her day, to regret ever having mentioned Their names. That earlier presentation was useful but has now served its purpose. Unless the schools based on the old methods change their techniques and their approach to truth, they will disappear.

b. Information as to the constitution of the Hierarchy and of the various Ashrams of which it is composed. I have presented the Hierarchy as the Ashram of Sanat Kumara in its sevenfold form, thus linking will and love.

c. A presentation of the newer type of meditations, with its emphasis upon visualisation and the use of the creative imagination; I have presented a system of meditation which has eliminated the attention paid hitherto to personal problems and the intense earlier focus on the relation of the disciple and the Master. The keynote of group fusion and of service underlies the newer form of meditation, and not this powerful emphasis upon the personal relation of the disciple to the Master and the achievement of the individual aspirant. This was degenerating into a form of spiritual selfishness and separateness.

3. *The Teaching on the Seven Rays.* The fact of the seven rays was well known to the heads of the Theosophical Society, was mentioned very abstractly and vaguely in *The Secret Doctrine,* and formed in an elementary form some of the teaching given in the Esoteric Section; the names of the rays were given, and some information as to their qualities, and the Masters on the rays, was imparted but not much else. I have given out much information upon the subject and have endeavoured to show the importance of this teaching from the psychological angle, because the new psychology is in the making. If esoteric teaching is eventually to be public in its presentation, it will be given out along the lines of psychology because esoteric teaching in its fullest and deepest sense concerns the consciousness aspect of man and God.

4. *The Teaching on the new Astrology.* This teaching too has gone out to a few hundred students before its publication in book form. This new astrology has been hitherto

ignored by those astrologers who have read it and (with the exception of four astrologers who have deeply appreciated it but who wish I would be more explicit) see little in it. I have given enough, could the open-minded astrologer but realise, to establish the coming astrology on a firm basis; the accuracy of what I have given will in the course of time be ascertained when astrologers who are dealing with the horoscopes of advanced people and disciples will use the esoteric planets as given by me, and not the orthodox planets as usually used. The accuracy of their deductions will necessarily depend upon their own point of development and also upon their ability to recognise an advanced person, a disciple or an initiate when they meet him and undertake to cast his horoscope. If they are themselves advanced disciples, they may have a tendency to set too rigid a standard for those seeking astrological deduction, and thus fail to recognise a disciple; if they are not advanced, they may regard people as advanced who are far from being even true aspirants. In either case then the horoscope may prove inaccurate. It is of no use to use the esoteric planets in relation to the average man.

5. *Information about the New Group of World Servers* and their work. This information includes

    a. The recognition of this group as intermediate between the Hierarchy and Humanity.

    b. The nature of their work as it influences the human soul and as it seeks through the instrumentality of the men and women of goodwill to determine the period in which we live.

    c. The Triangle work which embodies two phases of their work, i.e., the forming of the network of light as the channel of communication between the Hierarchy and Humanity, and the forming simultaneously of the network of goodwill, which is the objective expression of the subjective influence of light. Ponder on this statement.

6. *The attempt to form an exoteric branch of the inner Ashrams.* This is evidenced in the work I have done with a

special group of aspirants and accepted disciples whose instructions, emanating from my Ashram, have been embodied in the book *Discipleship in the New Age* (Vols. I and II).

7. *Teaching upon the new world religion,* with its emphasis upon the three major Full Moon periods (Aries, Taurus, Gemini, falling usually in April, May and June respectively) and the nine (occasionally ten) minor Full Moons each year. This leads to a consequent relation being established between the work of the Christ and of the Buddha in the minds of spiritually inclined people everywhere, with the result of a great broadening of the human aspiration. This work is as yet embryonic, but it should receive increasing attention. Eventually it will demonstrate as the main linking unit between the East and the West, particularly if Shri Krishna is shown to be an earlier incarnation of the Lord of Love, the Christ. Thereby three major world religions — the Christian, the Hindu and the Buddhist — will be intimately related, whilst the Mahommedan faith will be found to be linked to the Christian faith because it embodies the work of the Master Jesus as He overshadowed one of His senior disciples, a very advanced initiate, Mahomet.

A close study of all the above will indicate to you the lines along which I would like to see the work expand in future years. I would ask for a careful study of these words, for I regard this as an important instruction and one which could be regarded as the skeleton outline of the work I wish to see done. It will involve an intensification of the work of the advanced section in the Arcane School, a greater emphasis upon the Full Moon meetings, a careful organisation of the Triangle work and the Goodwill work as an added effort to aid the work of the New Group of World Servers, plus an attempt to recognise the members of the New Group whenever and wherever contacted. This will not be at all an easy task, my brothers, if you look only for those who think and work your way, or who recognise the Hierarchy as you recognise it, or if you exclude those who labour in relation to religious and other fields in a manner different to yours. Forget not, as an instance of this, that the great Labour Movement in the world was initiated by one of the Masters and is implemented from His Ashram at this time.

We come now to a detailed analysis of Rule XIII. In the foregoing pages I gave you certain broad principles and outlined a new aspect of the work which I had undertaken to do for humanity — under instruction from the Hierarchy. The teaching I gave there is very abstruse; little of it can as yet be of real service to the majority of aspirants but a wide and general idea can take form and provide the immovable background for later teaching. I would have you remember that the teaching which I have given out has been intermediate in nature, just as that given by H.P.B., under my instruction, was preparatory. The teaching planned by the Hierarchy to precede and condition the New Age, the Aquarian Age, falls into three categories:

1. Preparatory, given 1875 - 1890 . . . written down by H.P.B.
2. Intermediate, given 1919 - 1949 . . . written down by A.A.B.
3. Revelatory, emerging after 1975 . . . to be given on a worldwide scale via the radio.

In the next century and early in the century an initiate will appear and will carry on this teaching. It will be under the same "impression," for my task is not yet completed and this series of bridging treatises between the material knowledge of man and the science of the initiates has still another phase to run. The remainder of this century, as I told you elsewhere (Destiny of the Nations, page 106), must be dedicated to rebuilding the shrine of man's living, to reconstructing the form of humanity's life, to reconstituting the new civilisation upon the foundations of the old, and to the reorganising of the structures of world thought, world politics, plus the redistribution of the world's resources in conformity to divine purpose. Then and only then will it be possible to carry the revelation further.

It is with the above indicated sequence in mind that I

come to the analysis of the sentences in Rule XIII, beginning with the first:

*1. Let the group get ready to reveal the hidden mystery.*

The readiness here referred to has nothing to do with personal preparedness or with the group unity which I have so often emphasised. It does not refer to individual purity or consecration or to mental development or to group relationships, as they work out in harmony and understanding. I am considering something far different to all these factors which are regarded as automatic and necessarily present. I refer to that which is the result of all of them, just as they in their turn are the result of soul contact. I refer to effects wrought out in the group owing to the present and factual nature of the monadic control which is taking place increasingly.

What does this mean? It signifies the fact that the members of the group are each and all of them upon the Path of Initiation at some one or other of its stages and that the group, as a group, is in process of taking initiation, for *initiation is a process* at this stage, and not an event. It signifies that the group antahkarana is built and is being consciously used, and that therefore divine purpose is being sensed (even if only faintly so) and that the Plan is being obeyed and carried out. It signifies also that the three strands of the "rainbow bridge" are now so strong and so firmly anchored that they not only connect the two aspects of the mental equipment (higher and lower mind), but that they have been carried also through the three levels of the triadal consciousness; it means also that these three strands are firmly anchored in what I have symbolically called the Council Chamber at Shamballa.

This Council Chamber is *not* a location or a place, but a state of consciousness within the all-enveloping Life. These three points of anchorage within the sphere of the planetary Consciousness, or (if you like it better, though remembering ever that we are speaking and thinking in terms of symbols in the planetary brain, find their feeble correspondence in the three points of sensitivity in the head of a disciple or initiate, that is, in the region of the pineal gland, the pituitary body and the carotid gland. These, as you know, are to be found within the areas to which we give the names the head centre, the ajna centre and the alta major centre. These correspondences are very real, even though functioning upon a minute scale; the initiate achieves his desired "perfecting" when the triad within his head is related, and love, will and intelligence are functioning in synthesis. Here we find a relation to the spiritual Triad and the three points in the Council Chamber which are presided over by the three Buddhas of Activity, and within Whose exalted consciousness the three strands of the antahkarana meet and become active in a way incomprehensible to you. Necessarily, this great antahkarana is not constructed correctly except by those whose individual antahkaranas are likewise in process of construction.

See you, therefore, the necessity of eventually organising a group in the world which will be so constituted and so carefully chosen and interiorly related that all its members are initiates, all have created their own "rainbow bridges" with understanding and accuracy, and all can now work in such complete unity that the group antahkarana becomes a channel of unimpeded communication direct from Shamballa to the group *because* every member of the group is a member of the Hierarchy. In this manner the three planetary centres arrive at the needed relationship, and another great triangle reaches true functioning activity. When this takes place, a revelation undreamt of will be manifested upon the Earth; a new divine quality, of which no knowledge at present exists, will make its presence felt, and the work of the Buddha and of the Christ, and the work of the coming Avatar, will be superseded by One for Whom both Shamballa and the Hierarchy have unitedly waited and of Whom the doctrine of the Messiah and the doctrine of Avatars have been and are today only the dim distant symbols. They preserve this concept of the Great Revelation in the consciousness of men, in the expectancy which the Hierarchy evidences, and through the "preparatory work" now being undertaken at Shamballa.

The group, therefore, to whom I address this instruction is not the group or groups who will first receive these papers. The instruction is intended for a group which will come later and which will prepare the way, and of which some of the more advanced aspirants can form part if they "walk humbly with their God." This, my brother, is one of the most advanced injunctions in any of the world Scriptures and is found in *The Bible*. It has no reference to humility as usually interpreted and understood. It signifies the ability to view all life with a sense of divine proportion and from the angle of spiritual mathematics, and (paradoxical as this may sound) with no sense of dualism. The usual meaning is not correct. It involves acceptance and comprehension of purpose, and this in such a manner that the consecrated personality — under control of the Monad, via the antahkarana, and in cooperation with the one known God — walks the ways of Earth as a channel for the three divine qualities (love, will and intelligence), but also as a channel for that which these three qualities will enable him later to sense, know and reveal.

These are solemn and important statements. They have within them the element of prophecy, but it is prophecy which has no relation to the salvation of humanity in any sense at all. It is related to an active Appearance which will, under the Law of Synthesis, indicate *That* which the three great planetary centres of divine life are unitedly intended to reveal. Something lies behind the three divine aspects of so great an importance, beauty and revelatory strength that all the happenings of all time, up to the present emerging Aquarian Age, have been only the initial and the initiatory preparation.

In this rule we find posed two preparatory steps and four major undertakings or demonstrations of fitness, if you like so to call them, for the work to be done. These latter correspond to the "four things the disciple must learn and comprehend before he can be shewn the inmost mystery," as it is said in the Rule for Applicants. There is a definite relation between the two sets of rules and it is one which we shall note as we proceed. The two preparatory injunctions simply summarise the effects in the life of the disciple who has applied and learned the significance of the Rules for Applicants, but they are this time demonstrated by a group of disciples who have passed through certain initiations and are functioning as a unified group. The simplicity of the subject is great and yet it is ever deemed to be complex. The applicant has become soul conscious, and is therefore an initiate; remember always that *the soul on its own plane is an initiate* of all degrees. Initiation is, in the last analysis, the realisation, the recognition in the brain consciousness of various spheres and states of divine awareness, with a consequent life demonstration of this fact, this eternal fact. Because of this, the man thinks only in group terms and does this automatically and without any consciousness that he is so doing; he expresses this group integrity simply as a part of his nature, just as in the personality stage and during the elapsing aeons since individualisation, he has thought only and naturally in terms of the separated self.

As long as a person makes a conscious effort to be group-conscious and has to train and discipline himself to work in group formation and as part of a group, he is still centred in the personality. This personality expression may be of an exceedingly high order and the aspirant or disciple may be the highest kind of selfless person, but true group living is as yet not present. The transition stage is most difficult and oft bewildering; it presents its own problems, based upon a newly presented phase of dualistic consciousness. The disciple reacts to group conditions and group problems; he tunes in with facility on the consciousness of those in the group; he is aware of group reactions and aspirations, but he is still himself; he is still passing through a stage of inner adjustment to a state of being and of awareness for which all past relationships have provided no guiding precedent. The group and the group personnel which are capable of adjustment (and which can carry out and conform to Rule XIII for disciples and initiates) have become so merged with the soul (within themselves and within all other selves) that the situation is reversed. It would now be an effort for such people to think and react as personalities. I word the problem thus, so as to clarify it for you, if possible.

When this stage of centralisation is achieved, then the group can begin to reveal the hidden mystery. All that I can tell you about that mystery is that it concerns the purpose and the reason for which our planetary Logos took incarnation and became the informing Life of our planet, the Earth; it concerns the necessity, inherent in His Own nature, to reach a point upon the cosmic ladder of evolution which would make Him — as a result — the informing Life of a *sacred* planet. Forget not that our planet is not yet a sacred planet, though it is close to that great transformation. The cosmic secret of this transforming process is one that Sanat Kumara is now learning, and when *That* which overshadows Him during this incarnation has wrought the needed changes through a process of transformation and transmutation, then a great Transfiguration will take place and He will take His place among those empowered to work through a sacred planet.

This process is that which implements the evolutionary process. Evolution is an effect of this hidden work, emanating from cosmic levels; only when evolution has run its course through all the multiplicity of forms, of cycles, chains and spheres, of rounds and races and of world periods, will we know something of the true nature of the hidden mystery. In the Council Chamber of Shamballa it is being dimly sensed. The Buddha and the Christ are expressing the qualities which — when more universally demonstrated — will indicate its nature, if I might so express it. They are together mobilising the equipment upon our planet which will make the revelation of the mystery inevitable. This should give you a hint and much food for thought. More I cannot say, and even this you will only vaguely understand. Let us pass now to the second of the preparatory steps.

2. *Let the group demonstrate the higher meaning of the lessons learnt, and these are four and yet are one.*

Aspirants learn, as they proceed upon the Path of Probation, to see the meaning of their physical plane activities in terms of the world of desire, of the astral plane. What they do originates upon that plane and gives their deeds meaning. This is the a.b.c. of elementary occultism and of true psychology. Later, they enter a higher world of meaning and find that "as a man thinketh in his heart, so is he." Thus the lesson of kama-manasic impulse is slowly mastered and (in the process of learning) desire, prompted by the mind and implemented by the personality, loses its hold upon the aspirant. Later again, and as the soul begins to dominate, he learns the meaning of love and slowly, and oft through the mastering of pain, he absorbs the significance or meaning of group activity, group relation, and group initiation. He stands, therefore, at this stage ready (as this Rule expresses it) to learn the higher meaning of four lessons, processes or stages which are in themselves, nevertheless, one lesson. The four lessons which he has learnt up to this point have prepared him for the four lessons which — as an initiate and as one whose consciousness is focussed in the Spiritual Triad — he must now master. To summarise, they constitute the four phases of an activity which will bring him to a point of tension which will indicate the next possible initiatory stage. Four words could be used to express these processes: Radiation. Magnetisation. Transmutation. Impartation. Let me very briefly indicate some of the elementary significances of these words to the initiate-consciousness:

1. *Radiation.* The initiate is a radiating centre of light and love. This radiation has two effects:

   a. It has made him an essential and vital factor for unity in the Master's Ashram.

b. It has enabled him to gather around him his own group and thus begin to form his own ashram.

The personnel of the world group which will reveal the hidden mystery will all of them be "radiant centres" to a greater or lesser degree. They will thus be invocative and evocative. This thought holds the clue to the Law of Synthesis, of unity and of fusion as given in Rule XIII for initiates.

2. *Magnetisation.* The initiate who is radiating light and love is himself being magnetised by the highest of the present known divine aspects — Life. This expresses itself through will and purpose and is therefore dynamic in character. The initiate is charged constantly with life, and consequently can work with the impelling Law of Evolution which (as worded in the rule we are considering) will "carry the group together towards the Higher Three." See you not how the different phases of the teaching lead from one to another and provide a great ladder of approach to reality? I would call to your attention that in the Fourteen Rules for Applicants and in the Fourteen Rules for Disciples and Initiates you have the two great foundational courses of the coming Schools of the Mysteries, for which I have prepared the world in *Letters on Occult Meditation.*

3. *Transmutation.* This indicates here an achievement and not a process; the work of transmuting the lower nature into the higher and desire into love, of transforming personality purpose into group livingness and being, has led to that complete transfiguration which makes the entire process of transmutation no longer needed. But — and this is the point to be emphasised — because of this achievement, the art of transmutation is now the instrument which the initiate can use and transmute that which is not himself, and thus consciously and with clear purpose further the ends of evolution. Transmutation "disappears" out of his own life, but the forces which have been transmuted into spiritual energy begin now to have a dynamic transmutative effect in the world of forms wherein he now chooses to work and serve, according to his ray and ashramic intent.

4. *Impartation.* Reference to this is made in the Book of Revelation, found in *The New Testament*. There we are told that the initiate is given a white stone, and in the stone "a new name" is found written; this is the "hidden name egoic." I am at a loss at this point as to how to express the higher significance of this. This impartation marks a climaxing point in the attainment of the point of tension where the Sound can be heard and not the Word alone. Never forget that the O.M. is simply a symbolically sounded word which is intended to bring into the minds of those upon the Path those two great points of tension wherein

    a. The "hidden name egoic" is conferred upon the disciple. This, as far as he is concerned, is the Word of his soul ray.

    b. The Sound heard of which the O.M. is a symbol. This is the first letter of the sevenfold Name of the planetary Logos. More upon this subject may not be given, nor am I in a position to give it.

These two preparatory injunctions will give you some idea of how abstruse is the teaching conveyed in the rules for initiates. The understanding and the expressing of the four rules for applicants, as demonstrated by the disciple now functioning in a group, can all be summed up in the word: Being. Having said that, what does it mean to you? Being, per se, can only be grasped by those who have "come alive" monadically, who function in the three worlds of the Spiritual Triad with even greater positivity than the highly advanced personality functions in the three worlds of human evolution; and who have grasped somewhat the purpose for which Sanat Kumara has come into being and through directed livingness is working out His intention.

We can now take up the four major injunctions given to the initiated disciple as he prepares to work under the Laws of the Spirit, as a conscious soul, and (for purposes of service) through a personality. There are many initiates working without a body of contact which a personality provides, but we shall not consider them in our studies. We shall only deal with those disciples who can work as a group on the physical plane, fulfilling ashramic intent on the one hand and preparing themselves to tread the Way of the Higher Evolution upon the other. The first major injunction in this Rule XIII reads as follows:

*3. Let the group understand the Law of Synthesis, of unity and fusion.*

The Law of Synthesis, as you know, is the law of spiritual existence, and one of the three major laws of our solar system, as well as of our planet. It is a basic cosmic law, applied from sources of which we know nothing, as are the Laws of Attraction and of Economy. I dealt with these somewhat at length in *A Treatise on Cosmic Fire,* and of these two other laws I have given much and hinted more. Of the Law of Synthesis, I can tell you but little. It is the law governing the activities of the Spiritual Triad, and the conditioning law of monadic living. It works neither through the use of the energy of love nor through the application of the principle of economy. The fulfillment of these laws is necessary and preparatory to an understanding of the Law of Synthesis, and under the Law of Synthesis the worlds of illusion and glamour are mastered and the control of maya is negated; under the Law of Attraction the nature of love is revealed, first of all through desire for form life, and then through attraction to the soul and a consequent resolution of the dualities of soul and personality. This brings about a unity which — in due time — serves to reveal a greater potential dualism — that of soul and spirit; this fundamental duality must also be resolved, leaving the essential, universal planetary duality, spirit-matter, present in time and space. The Law of Synthesis has reference to this relationship and to the factual nature of the tremendous assertion of H. P. Blavatsky that "Matter is spirit at its lowest point of manifestation and spirit is matter at its highest." It is of this synthesis that the group must learn; it is this relation which they must begin to comprehend, and the distinction (for there is a distinction) between synthesis, unity and fusion must in due time be mastered.

To you, it may seem that these three words connote the same thing, but that is not so; *fusion* is ever related to the conscious merging of soul and substance until a point of equilibrium is achieved; at this point, *unity* becomes possible and the point of balance — through the attainment of a point of tension — is disturbed. This takes place in three definitely defined stages when the fusion of personality and soul is brought about through the self-initiated effort of the disciple: first of all upon the Probationary Path, then upon the Path of Discipleship, and finally at the third initiation, upon the Path of Initiation. It is essential that you ever remember that this third initiation, the Transfiguration, is the first major initiation from the standpoint of the Hierarchy, though the third from the limited vision of the aspirant. The initiate then goes on to learn the significance of unity in its true sense; this is only possible when monadic influence can be consciously registered and when the antahkarana is in process of conscious construction. I emphasise the word "conscious" here; much of the work of fusion and of attainment proceeds unconsciously under the fundamental Law of Evolution, which is a Shamballic law, embodying as it does the working out of the inscrutable will of Deity. The work now being done on the three stages of the Path has to be intentional and, therefore, consciously undertaken and intelligently planned; it must be backed, first of all by determination, then by the spiritual will, and finally as an implemented aspect of purpose.

Fusion might therefore be regarded as the individual process of spiritual integration, relating — in full waking consciousness — the three divine aspects in man. Unity might be regarded as the conscious adaptation of the initiated disciple to the greater whole, as his absorption into the group through his obedience to the laws of the soul, and as governing his attitude to that in which he lives and moves and has his being. This goes on until he sees no distinction, registers no differences and is aware of no separative reaction, and all this because the instinct to separation no longer exists in him. It refers to his oneness in the world of energies in which he moves, making him an unimpeded channel for energy and, therefore, an integral and smoothly working part of his total environment and, above all, of the group to which, automatically and under the laws which govern his soul, he has been attracted. He has learnt all that he can learn through the processes of differentiation to which he has been subjected for aeons. The principle of intelligence controls him and the principle of love motivates him, and he has consequently attained unity. But, my brothers, it is the unity of his ray, of his Ashram and of the Plan; it is the unity of the Hierarchy which exists for purposes of service and active work in its seven major groups and its three main departments or divisions. It is indeed attainment and liberation. But more must still be learnt if the Way of the Higher Evolution is to be trodden and a choice between the seven cosmic Paths made — a choice which curiously enough is not dependent upon ray, for all rays are to be found on all these paths.

This can only be done through *synthesis*. This Law of Synthesis

> "works through the Seven which yet are One; which points to the seven ways and yet those upon the seven ways are one; which initiates the universal into the many but preserves its integrity; which originates the plan but preserves intact the purpose; which sees the multiplicity needed under the Law of Sacrifice but subordinates that law unto the Law of Synthesis; which breathes forth the many Breaths and yet is Life Itself."

In this attempt to paraphrase an ancient definition of the Law of Synthesis, I have said all that I can upon the theme. Only as disciples build the antahkarana and function as the Spiritual Triad within the monadic Life will inspiration come, just as they learnt to make contact with the soul and to function as the threefold personality within the soul, and then revelation ensued. Naught is gained by further elucidation. Proceed with the work of building the antahkarana and light will shine upon your way and revelation will attend your steps.

The second major injunction (though the fourth phrase in our rule) is:

*4. Let the threefold mode of working with that which is dynamic carry the group together towards the Higher Three.*

This injunction holds in it information which is some-what new to the modern initiate, functioning in a physical body; it is difficult for him to grasp even a modicum of its significance. To convey any faintest hint of its meaning is incomparably difficult for me where disciples such as you are concerned. All I can do is to fall back upon the Law of Analogy, by means of which the microcosm can arrive at a glimmer of understanding of the more obvious aspects of the Macrocosm.

First, let me make reference to the words "the Higher Three"; let me see if I cannot somewhat clarify the entire complex idea. The words "Higher Three" refer to the three Buddhas of Activity Who still remain actively cooperating with the Lord of the World. They are, as you have been told, close to Sanat Kumara and came with Him when He decided to take incarnation through the medium of our planet, Earth. It is difficult to understand Their mysterious and peculiar functions. They do not belong to this solar system at all; They have passed through the human stage in such far distant and remote world cycles that the experience is no longer a part of Their consciousness; They act as advisors to Sanat Kumara where His initial purpose is concerned, and that is why the words "the will of God holds sway" occur in this rule. It is Their supreme task to see that, in the Council Chamber of Shamballa, that purpose is ever held steadily within the "area of preparation" (I know not how else to word it) of that Council. They function, in a peculiar sense, as linking intermediaries between the Logos of our solar system and the informing Life of the constellation Libra; They relate these two great centres of energy to our plane-tary Logos.

In the last solar system They were the planetary Logoi of three planets in which the mind principle reached its highest stage of development; They embody in Themselves in a most peculiar manner the wisdom aspect of the second ray, as it expresses itself primarily through what has been called in the Bhagavad Gita "skill in action." Hence Their name, the Buddhas of Activity.

Sanat Kumara has now moved one step ahead of Them upon the great cosmic ladder of evolution, for an aspect of the Law of Sacrifice has conditioned Them. However, within the planetary consciousness and among Those Who work out the divine purposes, there are none Who approach the Eternal Youth and these three Buddhas in point of Evolution. They work out Their plans — these four Great Lives — through the medium of the Lords of the Seven Rays. Under the Law of Analogy, They are to Sanat Kumara what the three mind aspects upon the mental plane are to the disciple and the initiate. They represent in action:

The concrete or lower mind of the planetary Logos,
That energy which we call the soul and which the disciple calls "the Son of Mind,"
The higher or abstract mind,

but all this from cosmic levels and with cosmic implications. It was Their activity which (after evolution had run a long course) brought about the act of individualisation and thus brought the human kingdom into existence. In a mysterious sense, therefore, it might be said that the three Buddhas of Activity are responsible for:

1. *The Act of Individualisation.* The work of the particular Buddha responsible at the time for this major activity, has been temporarily quiescent since Lemurian days. He works, when active, through the seventh ray and draws the needed energy from two constellations: Cancer and Gemini.

2. *The Act of Initiation.* I would call your attention to the word *act;* I am not here referring to process. His work only begins at the third initiation when the planetary Logos is the Initiator. At that initiation, the will aspect begins to function. The Buddha behind the initiatory process is extremely active at this time; He works through the Christ

and the Lord of the second ray, drawing the needed energy from the constellations Capricorn and Aquarius.

3. *The Act of Identification.* This involves what has been called a "moment of opening-up," during which the initiate sees that which lies within the cosmic intent and begins to function not only as a planetary unit but as a cosmic focal point. The Buddha of Activity, responsible for this type of planetary activity, works with the Lord of the first ray and functions as an outpost of the consciousness of the informing life of Aries and of Leo. His work is only now beginning to assume importance.

I realise that this information has little meaning to you and lies beyond your understanding, but so was much that I gave you in *A Treatise on Cosmic Fire.* Its sole value for you lies in the revelation of the linking up and the interplay between all parts of our solar system, our universe and the zodiac. Through these three great Buddhas there is a basic relation, established aeons ago and steadfastly held, between our planet, three of the seven sacred planets, and six of the major constellations — the three and the six which most uniquely concern the fourth kingdom in nature. Other planets and other constellations are also related to the human family, but their relation is more aggressively (if I might use that word) related to the three subhuman kingdoms; with these we shall not here deal. Their relation to the human kingdom has been covered by me in the astrological section of this Treatise: *A Treatise on the Seven Rays,* Vol. III *(Esoteric Astrology).*

You will note that I have here indicated the existence of five triangles:

1. That existing in the interplay of the energies of the three Buddhas of Activity Who create a triangle, closely related to the planet Saturn.
2. The triangle of the three rays through whom the three Buddhas work.
3. The three planets which are connected with the three Lords of the three rays and by means of which They express Their impelling energy.

4 - 5. Two interlaced triangles, created by the six constellations from which the three Buddhas of Activity
draw Their needed energy and to which They are
uniquely related through Their individual karma.
These two interlaced triangles are the cause of the six-
pointed star, so familiar among the many occult symbols.

From the Law of Analogy, another exceedingly important
triangle is found in the human body and (esoterically considered) is related to the subject under consideration:

1.   *The ajna centre,* embodying the directing energy of
that body of activity which we call the personality.

2.   *The throat centre,* which is peculiarly active today
in all human beings; this testifies to the success of the
creative work of the Buddhas of Activity. This, in its
turn, has a small symbolic triangle of its own, to which
I would call attention: the thyroid gland and the para-
thyroids.

3.   *The centre at the base of the spine.* This is galvanised
into activity at a certain stage of the evolutionary process, by energy emanating from the Buddhas of Activity
Who are the least active at this particular time. It is
an energy pouring towards the fourth kingdom but *not*
directed towards any individual. These great Lives work
through major groups. Their potency is such that it
would otherwise prove destructive.

The purpose of Deity is necessarily embodied in a
mental proposition; it is through this mental proposition
that the three Buddhas of Activity implement Their work.
I can put it no clearer. There will come a time in the experience of all initiates when — each for himself — a formulation of this mental proposition will be absolutely necessary. By means of this, each initiate will embody his individual understanding of the divine purpose as the Plan has
been revealed to him.

This he can do only through the means of group experience, in cooperation with his group and when the group —
as a whole — has reached a similar point of realisation and

has *together* touched the fringes of this highest of all revelations for humanity. When, for the first time, they succeed in doing this, they will come — as a group — under the direct emanation of the Higher Three and under an aspect of the Council Chamber at Shamballa which has been hitherto unknown and unrealised. This will connote a high stage of initiation of the group and is, in effect, connected with inter-hierarchical activity. It is a working out into the consciousness of the group members of an event which has taken place within the Ashram of Sanat Kumara, the Hierarchy itself; this takes place through the stimulation of all the Ashrams at a certain Full Moon, and concerns the relation of the Ashrams as a whole to Shamballa, and not to Humanity.

Can you grasp something of what I am endeavouring somewhat unsuccessfully to convey? There is an ashramic activity of which disciples know nothing in their brain consciousness until such time as the third initiation has been taken and the results of it are then dimly but increasingly sensed. It is related to the interplay between Shamballa and the Hierarchy, but not between the Hierarchy and Humanity. It concerns the purpose and the plan as the latter is the instrument of the former. The event of realisation takes place via the triad formed by a Master and His two senior disciples, or it is formed by three Masters all upon the same ray, as for instance, the Master K.H. and his Ashram, myself and my Ashram and another affiliated Ashram.

It is for this reason that in all exoteric groups connected with an Ashram, there is always a group leader and two others who are the reflection or the correspondence to the higher triad. This is part of the externalisation of the Hierarchy which is proceeding rapidly at this time.

The importance of understanding the function of triangles is a prime necessity. A hint lies here for students in the political realm, where every country, under differing names, has its chosen ruler, and its ministers responsible for home affairs (or interior relations), and its foreign secretary, responsible for exoteric relationships.

One further point anent the Buddhas of Activity might here be of interest. Each of Them has a special relation to the three races which have been or are strictly human: these are the third, the fourth and the fifth rootraces which we call the Lemurian, the Atlantean and the present Aryan race (I do *not* use the word "Aryan" in the manner of the German race). In some peculiar manner, They represent in Shamballa the soul of each of these three races. One thing complicates this question for you, but it is in reality quite simple. The same souls re-incarnate in each race, and each soul therefore comes in turn under the influence of each of the three Buddhas, each of Whom is of a quality different to that of his two Associates. They represent — in Their lowest aspect — the three aspects of the mind, as I earlier said. There is:

1. *The instinctual nature* as it develops into the mind nature and makes a transition into an automatic, subconscious character and — at the same time — assumes some of its paralleling higher qualities.

2. *The lower concrete mind* in its more developed stage, as it gradually assumes control and supersedes instinct in the consciousness of man. The Buddhas of Activity preside over what might be called (using a technical, occult term) the ahamkara principle — the mind as it serves the selfish interests of man and enables man thereby to achieve a sense of proportion and a finer estimate of values. Forget not that selfishness is a stage of unfoldment, and that it is a necessary stage whereby humanity learns the price of self-interest.

3. *The personality mind.* This assumes control over the man and leads him to prove the nature of power and of success and — above all else — of integration. This too is a necessary phase and precedes a stage of awakening.

These three great Lives Who have associated Themselves with the Lord of the World might be regarded as constituting aspects of His personality, though this is *not* technically so. The name Sanat Kumara is not His true name; it is only the first letter of that name which is known only to the Masters, whilst the second letter is known only to the Chohans. The first syllable of His name is known in the Council Chamber at Shamballa, but the rest of His name remains unknown as yet. The three Buddhas of Activity are to the planetary Logos (to give you another definition) what the Spiritual Triad is to the dedicated personality of the initiated disciple, for such is the spiritual status of the planetary Logos; the one of the three Buddhas now coming into activity is the one Who works through the spiritual will.

Within the body of the planetary Logos humanity is slowly building that which they call the antahkarana; this is, in reality, the linking thread between the head centre of Sanat Kumara and His heart centre. Ponder on these words. There is a mystery involved here and it is little that I can do to make it clearer. As humanity builds or creates the triangles of light and of goodwill, they are in reality invoking a response activity from two of the Buddhas of Activity — the One Who works through the medium of the will aspect, and the One Who works through love in humanity, *intelligently* applied. Forget not that these three great Buddhas summarise in a peculiar sense the transmuted essence of the previous solar system in which intelligent activity was the goal. Today, that essence underlies all the activity of this solar system but is motivated by love, which was not the case in the earlier manifestation. The Buddhas Themselves form a deeply esoteric Triangle.

The two types of triangles now being created by a mere handful of people are related to that basic triangle. A third type of triangle will at some much later date be constructed but only when these two earlier types are well established in the consciousness of humanity. Then the activity of all the three Buddhas will be involved and present, and a major planetary integration will take place. This is symbolised in man when the three centres in the head (the ajna centre, the brahmarandra centre, and the alta major centre) are all functioning and unshakably related, thereby constituting a triangle of light within the head.

From the triangles now being created and those later to be assembled, the Buddhas of Activity will extract that essential quality (at present very rarely to be found) which will go to the building of this aspect of the planetary antahkarana.

The triangles of light and of goodwill are essentially invocative. They constitute the a.b.c. of the coming Science of Invocation. Their strength is dependent upon the depth of feeling in the one case, and the strength of the will in the other, with which they are created. I have here given those disciples who are launching this new project which is so close to my heart a new and useful hint. This work *must* go on. It is because the entire concept is so new and different to anything hitherto projected that it seems so impossible of achievement; the triangles project has its incentive in such highly esoteric sources that some disciples regard the work as exceedingly difficult and thus complicate, by their thinking, its essential simplicity; others regard it as the simplest thing in the world, and by an emphasis upon the exoteric and the organisational angle, they again hinder the true type of triangle being created. Disciples need to be aware of the true proposed plan and find ways to make clear the middle position between the difficulties brought forward and the simplicities which distort.

Perhaps I may help to clarify somewhat the minds responsible for the initial steps in this deeply esoteric enterprise. It is different to the intellectual and practical work which the men and women of goodwill are asked to do and will do; it is not what some earnest people regard as goodwill work or a phase of the goodwill work. The forming of triangles of light and of goodwill concerns the reservoir of energy upon the inner and etheric side of life which will automatically and with full circulatory effect enable the exoteric work of the men and women of goodwill to make progress. It is not goodwill per se, but the creation of triangles of energy within the etheric body of the planet which are deliberately qualified by goodwill. The two phases of the work are necessarily complementary to each other but must not be regarded as one. The triangles of light must be qualified by or become the agents of goodwill, and the two groups are closely interrelated. The men and women of goodwill need know nothing of these triangles unless it is deemed wise and they are individually advanced enough to react correctly, but their work along the lines of goodwill will be successful or non-successful (I speak from the long range view) according to the intensity of purpose and the depth of love demonstrated by the two groups of triangle members.

Those responsible for the creative work upon the outer field must begin with the esoteric work. I am writing here for disciples, some of whom are members of my Ashram, and for the New Group of World Servers; these are responsible for carrying forward the work as planned. The two groups of triangles already formed are in reality building a thoughtform anent this work which will evoke response from the true builders.

It will be apparent to you, therefore, that this creative work, with its intelligent and practical purposes and its ability when rightly functioning to unite the exoteric and the esoteric workers in one spiritual undertaking, originates in reality in Shamballa itself and was grasped—as to intent and purpose — by Masters upon the first and second rays, though primarily the second ray disciple and Master understood it the most easily. Later, when steady and systematic work has been done, and the idea is familiar to the public, this activity will form an important part of the new world religion and be better understood; it will have its own inner group who will work entirely subjectively, building the triangles of light and of goodwill, and then will work objectively, directing the activities of those who are building the organisational aspect of triangles of practical goodwill on Earth with an effective subsidiary activity.

That time is not yet. Today we have the creation of a general thoughtform or the germinating of the seed of an idea. Later, when the true outer work begins, its potency will be objectively demonstrated because the Buddhas of Activity will gradually become aware of the existence of the thoughtform in its nature of light and its quality of goodwill. They will then pour of Their life into it as need arises and emergency decrees. Then gradually "the will of God will hold sway," as our injunction expresses it. Paralleling all this will be the work of the men and women of goodwill throughout the world, but in itself entirely objective — worldwide and amazingly useful.

Disciples need to learn to think in terms of group synthesis. This implies the achieving by them of deepened subjective relationships and increased sensitivity to the higher impression and the inner inspiration. The vertical life of the spirit and the horizontal life of relationship must be expressed simultaneously in some measure, before the significance of these Rules can be somewhat grasped.

We have been considering Shamballa, and I have given you some information (hitherto not communicated in words) re the Council Chamber of Sanat Kumara and of Those Who constitute its membership. I would pause here to remind you of two facts:

1. Shamballa is a state of consciousness or a phase of sensitive awareness wherein there is acute and dynamic response to divine purpose — a response made possible by the synthesis of purpose and of spiritual relationship which exists between Those Who are associated with Sanat Kumara.

2. Brotherhood, as it essentially is, constitutes a major mystery; also it is one which is only in process of solving, and that only on the two higher levels of the cosmic physical plane — those levels which we call the logoic and the monadic.

I am aware that you understand brotherhood in terms of the One Father and His children. That understanding is in itself so limited and inaccurate that it serves mainly to distort the truth; yet all that you can grasp at this time is embodied in this concept. The nearest description of the true relationship might be said to be as follows: Brotherhood is an expression of the relation which the planetary Logos (on the cosmic mental plane) bears to His Personality as it expresses itself through the planet with all its forms of life, upon the cosmic physical plane; this relationship is focussed through Sanat Kumara Who is the individualised Mind of that great Life. Wording it otherwise, the planetary Logos on His Own plane is to Sanat Kumara what the soul is to the human personality upon the physical plane in the three worlds. The sum total of the relation and of the relationships set up is, therefore, inadequately covered by the word "brotherhood." "Fellowship," so frequently used to express a similar idea, is in reality the mode whereby a dimly sensed brotherhood seeks to make its presence felt. The words "the fellowship of Christ" indicate the emergence of this concept subjectively upon the mental plane; this will be followed, as time elapses, by concrete manifestation upon the physical plane. It is this idea which lies behind the glibly used words "idea, ideal and idol," and which is also responsible for the growing sense of responsibility which characterises all human advancement upon the way of life. It is this basic idea which governs the Council Chamber at Shamballa and which constitutes the motivating impulse behind the planetary expression of livingness. It is this also which characterises the ideal for which the Hierarchy stands and which implements the Plan; it is this spiritual planning which results in the growing "forms of relationship" which today seem to be taking definite shape in the concretising of the divine project: Right Human Relations.

I have written these opening remarks because it is this elevated understanding of brotherhood which conditions divine purpose and which leads to the spiritual planning that will give you the clue to the third major injunction, with this we shall now deal. This injunction is worded as follows:

*. Let Transfiguration follow Transformation, and may Transmutation disappear.*

I would here remind you that in these fourteen rules we must approach our theme from the angle of the initiate-consciousness and not from that of the blended soul-personality consciousness. It is the higher approach which is here indicated, the problem of the initiate-group and not that of the individual within the group. Hence the great difficulty in putting any of these teachings into words. To the average aspirant to accepted discipleship, the three words which distinguish this third major injunction (but which symbolically constitute the fifth injunction in the rule) might be defined as follows: The ideas conveyed are those of an aspirant to the Mysteries as he faces initiation. Let us take these words in the order given in Rule XIII.

1. *Transfiguration* — that stage upon the Path of Initiation wherein the third initiation is undergone, wherein the personality is irradiated by the full light of the soul and the three personality vehicles are completely transcended; they have become simply forms through which spiritual love may flow out into the world of men in the salvaging task of creation.

2. *Transformation* — the evolutionary process which is carried on upon the Path of Discipleship, in which the disciple transforms his lower threefold "appearance" or personality and begins to display divine "quality." His physical body becomes obedient to the dictates of his mind, which is becoming responsive to the higher mind through the medium of the soul; his emotional nature becomes the receptacle of buddhi or of the intuition; then, after the third initiation it disappears altogether, and the buddhic vehicle becomes the main instrument of sentiency. The mind, in due course, is equally transformed by impression from the higher mind, as it endeavours to implement the will nature of the Monad.

3. *Transmutation* — the method whereby that which is lower is absorbed by the higher, whereby force is transmuted into energy, whereby the energy of the three lower centres is carried up into the three higher centres (head, heart and throat) and which later enables the initiate to

centralise all the energies in the three directing centres in the head. This transmuting process goes forward under the pressure of daily life experience, under the magnetic effect of soul contact, and as the inevitable result of evolution itself.

All these three spiritualising processes are well known, in theory at least, to all spiritual aspirants; they are expressions of soul-personality intention and effective interplay; they also constitute a paralleling activity to the task of building the antahkarana, as modes of alignment play a large part in the process of transmutation.

It is not, however, with these attitudes, processes and interpretations that the initiate is concerned, but with the significance of these processes in terms of the completed antahkarana and from the point of view of the "angle of intention" of the Monad. In other words: What do Transfiguration and Transformation signify to Members of the Hierarchy as They face the Way of the Higher Evolution? What can these words imply to Those for Whom the soul, the mediating principle, no longer has any factual significance?

Consider for a moment that the initiate who has undergone the first major initiation (the Transfiguration) and the two initiations of the threshold (the Birth and Baptism of the Christian Mysteries) has created the antahkarana in order to establish direct relation between the Monad and the personality, between the centre of universal awareness or identification and the form-expression in the three worlds. The antahkarana is constructed and constitutes an active channel of contact. The soul which has for ages directed the various and varying personalities is no longer in existence; the causal body has disappeared, shattered at the moment when the initiate (at the fourth initiation) cries out and says: "My God, my God, why hast Thou forsaken me?" The Temple of Solomon, the spiritual temple "not made with hands, eternal in the Heavens," is no longer required; it has served its ancient purpose, and that which has been deemed eternal must disappear in the light of

THAT to which eternity is only a phase of that which shall later be revealed. All that now remains for the initiate are the two points of living purpose to which we give the names of spirit-matter or life-appearance. The lesson ahead of the initiate is to realise the inner meaning (not the obvious and easily grasped meaning) that spirit is matter at its highest point, and matter is spirit at its lowest. This involves the free interplay of life-energy, consciously applied as the result of age-long processes, and matter-force, via the antah karana. The "rainbow bridge" becomes a channel for the impact of monadic or life energy upon substance, so that substance, taking form under the cyclic intention of the planetary Logos, may become increasingly coloured or quali- fied by the energy of universality. You can see from the above somewhat involved sentences how inadequate is language to express the understanding and the intention of the Hierarchy.

To the initiate, therefore, the two words, Transfigura- ation and Transformation, mean something quite different than they mean to a disciple, whilst Transmutation is now meaningless to him, for there is nothing within him which requires transmuting. It might consequently be stated that

1. *Transmutation* concerns the expression of the life force upon the three lower planes of human living and evolution.

2. *Transformation* concerns in a most peculiar manner the three aspects of mind upon the mental plane:

    a. The lower mind
    b. The son of mind, the soul
    c. The higher mind.

3. *Transfiguration* concerns the life of the Spiritual Triad upon its own three levels of identification.

To this might be added the fact that:

1. The three lower planes of transmutation are the dense, liquid and gaseous sub-planes of the cosmic physical plane.

2. The mental plane is a unique location (or state of consciousness) whereon or wherein the lower planes are

subjected to impression from the three higher. The higher three and the lower three are subjected to a definitely esoteric and mysterious process, and it is on this plane that the work of transmutation is completed — from the angle of the initiate.

3. The three planes of the Spiritual Triad are the spheres whereon transformation goes forward. This transformation has naught to do with the transforming of the personality, but is uniquely related to the interior work of the Hierarchy and the effect of this living, developing intensity upon the Members of the Hierarchy. Five planes are therefore involved in these two phases of the divine work.

4. The two highest planes (the monadic and the logoic) are the planes of transfiguration, from the point of view of the higher initiate. *By then* the processes of transmutation have dropped below the threshold of consciousness, and though the initiate (working with forms in the three worlds) has his instrument upon the outer physical plane, his own work and hierarchical activity is strictly triadal and monadic, with a steadily growing responsiveness to logoic intent.

Let us now consider the phases of transfiguration and transformation as far as is possible in an exoteric instruction, and "may transmutation disappear" for all disciples as time elapses, and that with speed — owing to the great need today for hierarchical workers.

It might here be asked: What is the work undertaken by the Masters Themselves upon the three planes of the Spiritual Triad? Students are well aware that many of the Masters are occupied with the evolutionary processes of the various kingdoms in nature in the three lower worlds. They forget that the majority are not so occupied. Have you ever wondered what it is that incites a Master to stay working in the three worlds and with His mind focussed upon its evolutionary processes? Have you ever considered what else it might be possible that intrigued and demanded His interest? The self-centred attitude of mankind is inclined to believe that human need, and *incidentally* the need of the

other kingdoms in nature, are all that prompts the Hier
archy to carry on its work of salvaging and stimulation. Bu
that is only a partial estimate of the work which They are
doing. In the processes of carrying forward Their work, the
consciousness of the Master is being steadily expanded, and
this because of the nature of Their work in the three worlds
it necessarily becomes more and more inclusive. That is the
effect upon Him, as He works on behalf of humanity or or
behalf of the other kingdoms in nature. There is a definite
and evolutionary effect. But on the higher three levels o
the Spiritual Triad, another type of evolutionary impulse i
directing His activities. I have told you elsewhere that con
sciousness (as we understand it) is being transcended, and a
new aspect of universal sentiency is taking its place. To thi
development I have given the inadequate name of *Identifica
tion.* This is a word which involves consciousness, which
invokes the will, which is dynamic in nature, inclusive in
contact, and which is also based upon the doctrine of non
separativeness.

    This, however, is only a beginning of an entirely new
phase of development; consciousness eventually drops below
the level of perception. It becomes as automatic and un
registered in its expression as animal instinct is to the hu
man being. It functions, but the man is not consciousl
aware of it. It is a protective mechanism. The will aspec
of the Monad supersedes but does not negate love (which
has become, in its turn, instinctual); a one-pointed, rapier
like assumption of identification takes the place of the in
clusiveness hitherto felt and practised. Perhaps I can conve
to you something of what I mean by pointing out that th
circle with the point at the centre is symbolic of the per
fected man. He is rounded out; he is inclusive both verticall
(soul contact) and horizontally (human relationship), ye
he stands at the centre of his consciousness and of its self
imposed ring-pass-not. From thence he never moves, but i
aware all the time of all that proceeds within his sphere o
influence. Here is the symbol of the Master, from a specifi
point of attainment.

But the Master Himself is *not* static. His field of work is clear; His realm of contacts — human, subhuman and super-human — is also clear. Within the ring-pass-not and in the world of sentiency and in relation to the world of loving understanding, He stands the Master.

It is at this precise point in time and space that the work of Transformation begins for the Master — a trans-formation which is brought about by the unfoldment and the development made possible upon the three levels of the Spiritual Triad. As this transformation takes place, a new activity supervenes which finally enables the Master to break through the planetary ring-pass-not, and thus arrive at the door of the Higher Evolution.

What I have now to say may be made somewhat clearer by means of the following symbol. The Master has now pene-trated into another cosmic level, but He is still within the aura of the One Life. Now the cosmic astral plane is re-vealed to Him. He sees the reason why, first of all, sentiency had to be developed; why it had then to be used and mas-tered and finally had to be completely negated — negated in such a manner that it dropped below the level of con-sciousness. There is no glamour upon the cosmic astral plane, and only those who have dominated sentient reaction upon all levels of the cosmic physical plane and are com-pletely free from it, can then — through the illumined will and through the power of that mysterious quality (if I may so call a factual expression) of identification — direct the lowest aspect of cosmic desire upon the cosmic astral plane. This necessarily has to be tuned in with that to which they are irrevocably related. This identification is therefore the highest expression of divine purpose upon the cosmic physi-cal plane, even whilst it is the lowest aspect of the cosmic astral desire. Therefore, my brothers, the transformation with which this rule deals is the transformation of conscious-ness into identification. More than that I may not say. To express the true meaning I have no words or symbols.

In this line of approach through identification, the Master builds that of which the spiritual correspondence is the manasic antahkarana. The antahkarana which is now emerging is a projection from the Ashram of a Master; there are, therefore, seven ways into the Way of the Higher Evolution. These seven ways correspond to the seven Ashrams upon the seven Rays; they are related also to the seven initiations, to the seven principles of man, and to all the other many septenates. It is the force of Will, generated by the Master, during the process of

1. Attaining the fifth initiation
2. Working in the three worlds of creative salvaging
3. Achieving ashramic purpose and consequent group activity
4. Manifesting ray energy
5. Demonstrating a faculty which is known only to initiates who have passed beyond the third initiation.

This provides the focussed intention which enables the Master to attain what is called transformation, and later, to project the dynamic impulse of His spiritual will in such a manner that He succeeds in piercing the planetary ring-pass-not; He is then given the freedom of the world, and not just the freedom of the worlds.

It will be obvious that I am dealing with the subject of the sixth initiation. When this initiation has been consummated, the Chohan then transcends the three worlds of the Spiritual Triad and is focussed as a "projecting agent of the Lighted Will" as it expresses itself upon the monadic plane. This stage of unfoldment is in reality the Ascension initiation, the true significance of which will be revealed through the medium of the coming world religion.

There then follows, as a result of this, what is called the true Transfiguration. This enables the initiate to function upon the logoic or highest plane of the cosmic physical plane. This — in Christian phraseology — is called the "sitting down upon the right hand of God in Heaven." There the man who has attained this seventh initiation is transfigured. The first contact comes along the line which he has projected as a result of transformation; it is made with

That which has ever overshadowed Sanat Kumara. The Chohan has now taken the seventh initiation.

*5. Let the O.M. be heard right at the centre of the group, proclaiming God is All.*

It is not my intention to interpret this final phrase of Rule XIII. Its meaning lies beyond your most elevated comprehension. It concerns the transmutation of the O.M. into the originating SOUND, bringing certain basic transformation and resulting in a transfiguration which extends to the entire planet and has reference to a certain major planetary initiation. With these matters we are not concerned. With them, only a few of the more advanced Masters are concerned. Therefore we will wait until, through resolution, we have resolved our spiritual problems, transmuted our lower natures and undergone the lower aspects of both transformations, and are consequently ready for the third initiation — that of the Transfiguration.

## RULE FOURTEEN

In this final rule for disciples and initiates, a great summation is embodied. I would here point out again (as I have so frequently in the past) that the obvious meaning — no matter how elevated — is not that with which we shall deal. It is the significance behind the meaning which is ever the concern of the initiate mind. Students would do well to remember the following sequence of words, embodying ideas: Symbol, Meaning, Significance, Light, regarding light as the emanating creative energy — the organiser of the symbol, the revealer of the meaning, the potency of the significance.

We have studied the rules and have penetrated deeply into the world of significances. Most of you have not, however, passed beyond the stage of groping in the world of meaning. The reason for this is that you have not yet taken the third initiation. I would ask you also to bear in mind that the *world of symbols* is that of the personal life, of the phenomenal world as that phrase covers the three worlds of human evolution; the *world of meaning* is the world in which the soul lives and moves with intention and understanding; the *world of significance* is the world of the Spiritual Triad, which only confers its freedom fully after the third initiation.

The words dealt with in this Rule XIV are apparently so simple that they can be easily understood. I will attempt to show you that their real meaning is deep and esoteric to what you call the nth degree.

Rule XIV.

> *For Applicants:* Listen. Touch. See. Apply. Know.
>
> *For Disciples and Initiates: Know. Express. Reveal. Destroy. Resurrect.*

The following relationships should be noted, for the first is the seed of the other.

| APPLICANTS | | INITIATES |
|---|---|---|
| Listen | . . . | Know |
| Touch | . . . | Express |
| See | . . . | Reveal |
| Apply | . . . | Destroy |
| Know | . . . | Resurrect |

You will note that the applicant eventually arrives at knowledge and begins to know; the disciple or the initiate starts with knowing, and through his ability to express esoterically that which he knows is able to reveal the light, and by that light to destroy all illusion, glamour and maya; he brings about resurrection upon the physical plane — a resurrection from the death which physical plane life inevitably confers.

The five words as given to the applicant are indeed relatively simple. Most aspirants understand their meaning to a certain extent. They know that the listening mentioned has naught to do with the sense of physical hearing, and that the touch to be developed has reference to sensitivity and not the sensory perception of the physical vehicle. They know likewise that the sight to be cultivated is the power to see the beauty underlying form, to recognise the subjective divinity and to register also the love conveyed through the medium of symbols. The application of soul energy to the affairs of daily life and the establishing of those conditions which permit of soul knowledge are the elementary lessons of the aspirant. With these I need not deal, except in so far as they give the clue to the significance of the five words as given to the initiated disciple.

Let us take each of these five words and seek to ascertain their significance. But first of all, I would like to point out that here we are concerned with *monadic signatures,* with that which synthesises significances, and with that which contributes vital significance to the initiated life. I would have you, as you read my words, retreat within yourselves and seek to think, feel and perceive at your highest possible level of consciousness. The effort to do this will bear much fruit and bring rich reward to you. You will not grasp the full intention of these words, but your sense of awareness will begin to react to triadal impression. I know not how else to word this, limited as I am by the necessity of language. You may not register anything consciously, for the brain of the average disciple is as yet insensitive to monadic vibration. Even if the disciple is capable of some responsiveness, there are not the needed words in which to express the sensed idea or to clothe the concept. It is therefore impossible to put the divine ideas into their ideal form and then bring them down into the world of meaning, and from thence into the world of symbols. What I say will therefore have more significance towards the close of this century, when men will have recovered from the chaos and cruelty of war, and when the new and higher spiritual influences are being steadily poured out. I write, my brothers, for the future.

## 1. *Know.*

What is the difference between the knowing of the aspirant and the knowledge of the initiated disciple? It is the difference which exists between two differing fields and areas of perception. The aspirant is told first of all to "know thyself"; he is then told to know the relation of form and soul, and the area covered by his knowledge is that of the three worlds, plus the level upon the mental plane on which his soul is focussed. The initiated disciple knows the relation of the periphery to the centre, of the One to the many, and of unity to diversity. The applicant is concerned with triplicity: himself as the knower, his field of knowledge, and that which is the agent of knowing, the mind. The initiated disciple is beyond registering triplicity and is occupied with the duality of manifestation, with life-energy as it affects or is related to matter-force, with spirit and substance. The knowledge of the initiate has naught to do with consciousness as the mind recognises that factor in the evolutionary process; his knowledge is related to the faculty of the intuition and to that divine perception which sees all things as *within itself*. Perhaps the simplest way to express the knowledge of the initiate is to say that it is direct awareness of God, thus putting it into mystical terms; the knowledge of the aspirant is related to that aspect of divinity which we call the soul in form. Putting this in still another way, I might point out that the aspirant is concerned with the knowledge of soul and matter, whilst the initiate is concerned with soul and spirit.

If I say to you, my brothers, that the knowledge of the initiate is concerned with that which is produced by SOUND and not by the A.U.M. or the O.M., I shall have linked up these comments with much else given previously in the analysis of these fourteen rules. The "listening" of the aspirant has now been transformed into the effectual recognition of that which the Sound has created. I refer not here to the creation of the phenomenal world, or to the world of meaning which is essentially the Plan or the pattern underlying that phenomenal world, but to the intention or the Purpose which motivated the creative Sound; I am dealing with the impulsive energy which gives significance to activity and to the life-force which the Sound centralises at Shamballa.

It is not the fault of humanity that it is only now possible for the significance of the divine purpose to emerge more clearly in the consciousness of the initiated disciple. It is a question of timing and of movement in space; it concerns the relation of the Hierarchy, working with the Plan, to Shamballa, the recipient (by means of the Sound) of the creative energy which it is the divine intention to expend in producing a perfect expression of the divine Idea. It is to the knowledge of this relationship and of its effects that the first word of Rule XIV refers.

It was the dawning of this significance upon the consciousness of the Christ — a consciousness enlightened, purified and divinely focussed — that forced Him to cry out: "Father, not my will but Thine be done." He received a vision of the emerging divine intention for humanity and (through humanity) for the planet as a whole. In the hierarchical stage of development which Christ had attained and which made Him the Head of the Hierarchy and the Master of all the Masters, His consciousness was entirely at one with the Plan; its application to life in the three worlds, and its goal of establishing the Kingdom of God on earth and the emergence of the fifth kingdom in nature, were now for Him simply the fulfilling of the law, and to that fulfillment His entire life was and had been geared. The Plan, its goal, its techniques and methods, its laws and their application, its phenomenal effects, the hindrances to be met, the energy (that of love) to be employed, and the close and growing relation and interplay between the Hierarchy and Humanity, between the heart centre of the planetary Logos and the creative centre, were known to Him and fully understood. At the highest point of this consummated knowledge, and at the moment of His complete surrender to the necessary sacrifice of His life to the fulfilling of the Plan, suddenly a great expansion of consciousness took place.

The significance, the intention, the purpose of it all, and the extent of the divine Idea as it existed in the mind of the "Father," dawned on His soul (not on His mind, but on His soul). He saw still further into the significance of divinity than had ever seemed possible; the world of meaning and the world of phenomena faded out and — esoterically speaking — He lost His All. These are words necessarily meaningless to you. For the time being, neither the energy of the creative mind nor the energy of love was left to Him. A new type of energy became available — the energy of life itself, imbued with purpose and actuated by intention. For the first time, the relation of the Will, which had hitherto expressed itself in His life through love and the creative work of inaugurating the new dispensation and the launching for all time of the Kingdom of God, became clear to Him. At that point He passed through the Gethsemane of renunciation.

A hint lies here. This high point of attainment of the Christ — as related in the Gospel story — was reached in Gethsemane, and for a brief moment we are given an insight into an aspect or happening of the Sixth Initiation. It was this event and spiritual crisis in the life of the Christ (taking place as He overshadowed His disciple, Jesus) which enabled Jesus on His own level of spiritual development to take the fourth initiation, that of the Crucifixion or the Great Renunciation. The numbers four and six are closely connected, and the lesser renunciation (great only from the *human* point of view) makes the higher renunciation possible eventually, and vice versa. Running through many parts of the Gospel story are two paralleling histories; the lesser world of discipleship profits by the achievements of those who take the higher initiations, and thus is demonstrated the close unity which forever exists within the Hierarchy and — focussing through the Christ — the synthesis which is beginning to be formed between the Hierarchy and Shamballa. This is taking place in this era for the first time in human history. The recognition of this emerging synthesis between Will and Love produced a definite effect in the consciousness of the Christ and led Him to know much that had hitherto been concealed from Him.

These are deep mysteries. Their value to the disciple in training lies in the recognised and considered relationships.

These rules are — as you know — the rules controlling group life; they constitute the key to the laws under which all planetary groups work. The hierarchical life, through its major aspect of Love, was a familiar area of consciousness and well-known to the Masters and to the Master of Them all, the Christ. But a further "knowing" lay ahead of even this "perfected Son of God"; the nature and the mind of that great Being, embodied in the Lord of the World at Shamballa, was now revealed to Him.

It is this living realisation of Being and of identification with the planetary Logos upon the cosmic mental plane which constituted the unfolding awareness of the Christ upon the Way of the Higher Evolution. Therefore, experience, perception and Being are the keynotes of:

1. The Path of Evolution.
2. The mode of unfoldment upon the Path.
3. The state of divine focus upon the Way.

In other words, you have the states of Individualisation, of Initiation, and of Identification.

The relation between the listening of the aspirant and the knowledge of the initiated disciple has been expressed for us in a certain ancient writing as follows:

"Dimly the one who seeks hears the faint whisper of the life of God; he sees the breathing of that whisper which disturbs the waters of his Spatial life. The whisper penetrates. It then becomes the Sound of many waters and the Word of many voices. Great is the confusion but still the listening must go on.

Listening is the seed of obedience, O Chela on the Path.

More loudly comes the voice; then suddenly the voices dim and listening now gives place to knowing — the knowledge of that which lies behind the outer form, the perception of that which must be done. Order is seen. The pattern clear emerges.

Knowing is the seed of conscious doing, O Chela on the Path.

Listening and knowledge also fade away and that which they produce can then be seen. Being emerges and union with the One. Identity is known — not on this plane but on that higher sphere where move and speak the greater Sons of Life. Being alone is left. The work is done."

## 2. *Express.*

We come now to the second word of the fourteenth rule for disciples and initiates — the word Express. This cannot be correctly understood apart from the earlier word imparted to applicants — the word Touch. I would have you note that all the words given to the neophyte refer basically to something he must do in reference to himself, some task he must undertake which will make him more fit for advancement, or some process of apprehension which will enable him to function in a better and more sensitive instrument. This might be called the "introverted stage" of training because it brings the would-be disciple to a better knowledge of himself; he grasps the fact that he himself, the microcosm, is the key to the Macrocosm; he is the clue to the future, and he holds within himself the revelation which must precede esoteric action. In contradistinction to this, the words for the disciple and the initiate mark the attainment of a capacity to work from a most deeply esoteric centre in a pronouncedly occult way. By this I mean that the initiate, working as we have seen from a standpoint of knowledge, is at the same time no longer self-centred, but is now preoccupied with that in which he lives and moves and has his being. His interests are with the Whole and not with the part; his interests are those which will affect his environment (an aspect of that living vibrant Whole) and not himself; his task is the hierarchical one of the salvaging of others, and not his own salvation.

If you will note your own present attitudes and actions, you will discover that primarily (I might add almost necessarily) they centre around yourselves, your own recognitions, your own grasp of truth, and your own progress upon the Path. But — as you achieve initiate status — self-interest declines until it disappears and, as an ancient Word has it, "only God is left"; only that remains in consciousness which is THAT, which is beauty, goodness and truth; which is not form but quality, which is that which lies behind the form and that which indicates destiny, soul, place, and status. Ponder on these words, for they convey to you where (as evolution goes on) you will later lay the emphasis.

In considering the word Express I can, I believe, make this distinction somewhat clearer. When the beginner on the Path ponders the significance of expression, he is occupied with his ability to express the truth which he theoretically recognises but to which he cannot as yet give form. This is valuable because it feeds his aspiration, centres his attention upon himself and increases his naive self-interest. This, frequently, presents its own problems, such as a sense of failure or an undue registration of success, or it fails to develop a sense of proportion.

When, however, the initiate takes into his consciousness this injunction to express, it signifies to him not his own needs or requirements, but the need of others for those expressions of truth which will guide them on their way. This word, therefore, is to him an injunction to be creative. The initiate creates outside himself that which is his individual contribution to the totality of the creative forms whereby the Hierarchy is attempting to create "a new heaven and a new earth." He is not occupied with what he himself expresses as a soul within a personality; he has developed the habit of right soul expression in the three worlds, and the appearance of his quality (to revert to the use of our original words — life, *quality* and appearance) is automatic and without any planning on his part. He is, however, occupied with the sequence of activities which I will list as follows:

1. The preservation of hierarchical contact, of which direct, conscious soul contact is now an incident because it is now a habit.

2. An awareness, unbroken and consistent, of his ashramic *place;* I refer not to location but to status — a very different matter.

3. Reflective concentration upon the hierarchical Plan as his particular Ashram has assumed responsibility for a measure of it; that responsibility he seeks to share intelligently and effectively.

4. Recognition of the immediate contribution of the Ashram and his immediate contribution as an integral part of it. This does away with visionary mysticism and produces the practicing occultist.

5. A study of the creative methods of his particular Ray and an imaginative visualisation of that which will be expressed when the desired creative work has taken due form.

6. Conscious projection of his contribution onto the outer physical plane. A tangible creative project is undertaken and eventually produced.

7. He thus plays his part in bringing into objectivity the creative undertaking of his Ashram.

The seed of this creative work is that which the Ashram has planned for the exact moment of humanity's presented need, correct as to timing and placement. This may not be what humanity believes it needs; it is essentially what the Hierarchy recognises as the needed factor, leading to the needed progress for the race at any specific moment in time. For instance, humanity believes today that its major need is peace and material comfort and is working vaguely for both; the Hierarchy knows that its major need is the recognition of the folly of past separateness and the cult of goodwill. Towards these ends, workers in the Ashrams are bending every effort. The creative task, therefore, of working disciples and initiates is to produce that presentation (appearance) of the necessitous truths in such a manner that the recognition of humanity may be so sound that right action can duly be taken. Hierarchical workers must therefore *express* the true need in form, appropriate to the registering capacity of humanity at this moment.

The creative work of expression does not consequently concern the development and personal progress of the initiate. He has been taken into the Ashram *because* of his development and *because* of the contribution he should be able to make to the ashramic creative purpose. What, as a neophyte, he "touched" because of what he could gain spiritually for himself (and this with sound motive) has now become that which must be expressed in the field of service of the initiate, exacting from him all that he has and leaving him nothing for the separated self.

A great creative activity involving all Ashrams — major and minor — is now being planned in the hierarchical assembly, and the work of all waiting and attentive disciples is to make that creative plan successful through its full expression upon the physical plane. This they must do through their grouped and blended activities, which will embody the full expression of all that they have achieved and gained in the earlier stages of their individual unfoldment. Thus you will see that from God the Creator of all that IS, down to the humblest disciple in the hierarchical centre, the theme of creativity dominates and is the expression (again occultly understood) of the divine intention. At present, what is called creative work by men is in reality an expression of themselves and of their appreciation of beauty as *they* see it, of truth as *they* grasp it, of psychology as *they* interpret it, of nature as *they* scientifically interpret it. According to their spiritual development and their intelligent perception, so will be the quality and the nature of their expression — but it will be *theirs*.

In the case of hierarchical workers however, the situation is different. They work to express that which the Ashram, through its group of workers, is seeking to express; they seek to express the Plan, or as much of it as they can grasp; they are occupied with the expression of soul as that soul should be known in the culture and the civilisation immediately to be developed. They can work entirely free from self-interest; that which they create is not claimed by them but is regarded as an expression of hierarchical activity; they are free from the spirit to identify themselves with that which they expressed, but — having created that which their ashramic impulse has indicated — they pass on to a fresh expression of the dynamic, ever-moving purpose. They are not occupied with form, but with life, with organism rather than organisation, with ideas rather than ideals, and with essential truth rather than with carefully formulated theologies.

Christ *expressed* in Himself and refrained from putting it into form; He Himself was the truth, yet inevitably (because of its inherent life) that which He expressed took form and has greatly modified and coloured human thinking and planning, and this will be increasingly so. As the essence of Christianity emerges into expression (and in so doing destroys Churchianity) you have again a striking illustration of the truth of what I am seeking to emphasise. In the Christian Church, men have expressed themselves, not the Christ; they have imposed their interpretations of truth on truth itself; they have created a massive organisation in every land but a living organism is non-existent. In the new world religion which is on its way, Christianity will be expressed through the creative activity of the Christ spirit through the medium of the world disciples and initiates; we shall then see the full expression of hierarchical truth — of which the Christ today is the symbol and exponent.

Neophytes and aspirants have "touched" that for which the Christ stood, and have then attempted to impose their comprehension of that which they contacted upon the rest of the world. Knowers, disciples and initiates express that which He represented (love-wisdom). This they do automatically and by force of habit, first in themselves and finally by a definitely planned creative activity in the outer world.

Therefore, my brothers, there lies ahead of all true aspirants an intermediate stage of decentralisation, of automatic spiritual living and of absorption into the Hierarchy through the medium of an Ashram; therein the Plan can be learnt. When this phase of development is completed the disciple can then begin to work creatively in line with hierarchical activity.

As we consider the next word on our list, we must hold in our minds what we have discussed anent the words Touch and Express. It might be said that the words which are given to aspirants and applicants are the seed or germ of the concepts indicated in the words for initiates and disciples. Until the earlier significances are mastered in the earlier phases of discipleship, the later illumined service — based upon the later words — is not possible. Always in the fresh attitude to the developing esoteric understanding of the initiate there is implicit the fact of transition from individual self-interest to a universal state of consciousness; this in time becomes the directing agent for individualised service — as rendered by the individual disciple upon the physical plane. The fusion of the two attitudes — inclusive realisation and specialised service — renders the task of the initiate peculiarly difficult. He has to hold two attitudes simultaneously, whilst at the same time subjecting himself to the training required in order to enable him to take his next step forward upon the Path. It is only whilst this condition persists that the initiate has any sense of triplicity. This is an important point to note. Bear this in mind as we discuss our next two words: See and Reveal.

3. *Reveal.*

The objective of the strictly human evolution in this planetary cycle is *sight,* culminating in that spiritual perception which is the major gift of the soul to the personality when contact is made; this conveys the sense of attractive love, indicates the nature of things, reveals the world of meaning, and gives the great gift of light, knowledge and ultimate illumination. Such are the goals for the mystic, the aspirant and the pledged disciple. The greatest physical gift is that of sight, and it is the same upon a higher turn of the spiral within the world of the soul. When the disciple has achieved *a measure of vision and is "in sight" of his goal, he can then be admitted to an Ashram wherein the nature of revelation can be made known to him.* Men are apt to confuse vision and revelation, and I seek to clarify your minds somewhat on this matter; therefore, the preceding sentence is of major importance. Aspirants are prone to think that the goal towards which they move is that of soul contact, with a secondary goal of hierarchical position, and a third goal of service. This, however, is not correct.

The goal ahead of the aspirant is the consciousness of non-separateness and the recognition of a universal inclusiveness; the secondary goal is the ability to reveal the nature of that reality, Unity; the third goal is the ability to take those measures in the three worlds which will facilitate mankind's apprehension of these fundamentals. You will note how this last definition of the goal removes inevitably the factor of self-interest in its entirety. It might therefore be said that revelation concerns Oneness and nothing else. The practical nature of this truth is only recognised when the disciple attempts to do two things: to realise it individually, and to bring the nature of planetary unity and of non-separateness to the minds and into the lives of men everywhere.

The work of the aspirant is to *see the light;* only when this has become a fact in his consciousness can he begin to grasp the hidden revelation which that contacted and utilised light can reveal. Here is another key sentence for your consideration.

With the theme of light, of vision, and of illumination, I seek not here to deal. I have covered these subjects at length in the books which I have written, and they have also constituted the earnest search of the mystics of all time; and also the Scriptures and the literature of all nations give much information. It is the subject of revelation and the task of the initiate to reveal with which I am concerned. The disciple, who represents the Ashram, must reveal to humanity the essential unity underlying all creation. This he does, first of all, by acting like a clear sheet of glass through which all may see the reality of Oneness as it demonstrates in practicing operation. When he has, through his own life and words, demonstrated his conscious participation in this basic unity, he passes on to practice ashramic methods of making this fundamental truth still more apparent. You can here see why — as a hierarchical technique — we brought to the attention of the general public the fact of the existence of the New Group of World Servers. They offer a practical expression of an existent unity, based upon oneness of motive, of recognition, of orientation (towards the spiritual world and towards the service of humanity), of methods and of ideas; and all this in spite of the fact that the physical plane relationship is usually non-existent and outer organisation and recognition lack. The unity is subjective, and for that reason is impervious to every taint of separateness.

The inner organisation, to which we have given the name of the New Group of World Servers for the sake of recognition and identification, cannot be broken or in any way diminished, for it is constructed around a major principle of evolutionary growth which — when attained — indicates a registered consciousness of unity; this is something which, once recorded and known, cannot be lost or disproved. Once seen and realised, it becomes as much a fact in its possessor's consciousness as the recognition and utilisation of his own physical body. This he knows to be a complex organism which constitutes a functioning unity through the medium of the life principle; it is an incontrovertible fact in the realisation of the intelligent man.

When, therefore, sight has been attained and the light streams forth, revelation of the oneness of all life is a simple and immediate occurrence; it comes first of all to the disciple as a flash of wondrous informative and instinctive realisation and then steadies down, as progress is made, into a constant apprehension and appreciation; it eventually produces the motivating impulse of all action.

What is the immediate revelation which the initiates and the disciples of the world are seeking to bring to humanity? What aspect of this essential unity are they endeavouring to make simple and apparent? One of the easiest things in the world to say (as has, for instance, Krishnamurti) is that life is one; that there is nothing but unity. That is a trite formulation of a very ancient truth, and one which is today an occult platitude. But life is not yet one in consciousness, however true it may be in fact. The reason for this is that *life is loving synthesis in action,* and of that there is little today in demonstration. We have life in activity but love, based on realised unity and leading to expressed synthesis, is still absent. The vision of it is, however, upon the horizon of many, for in these days many are attaining sight and light is pouring in. Revelation will come when the world disciples and initiates have perfected the art of revelation.

The task ahead is simple. The important aspect, at this time, of the basic oneness underlying all forms, and which the workers of today must immediately emphasise, is the *fact* of the kingdom of God, of the planetary Hierarchy. The citizens of that kingdom and the members of that Hierarchy are gathered out of every nation, every political party, every social group, every religious cult or sect, and every organisa- tion — no matter what their expressed objectives — and the universality of the field from which these people emerge, demonstrates their underlying unity. When this unity as- sumes adequate proportions in the eyes of mankind, a real synthesis will follow.

Therefore the call goes out at this time for hierarchical workers to reveal with greater emphasis the *fact* of the Hier- archy. This — if done on a large scale and through proper organisation — will destroy on a large scale the present world structure in the field of religion, of economics, and of politics; it is already doing so. An increase of pressure on the part of all who recognise the factual nature of the inner subjective kingdom of God, will produce amazing results. This kingdom, through its major power (a quality of syn- thesis, could you but realise it), is gathering together into itself men and women out of every nation and out of all parts of the Earth. It is absorbing them into itself not because they are orthodox or religious in the generally accepted sense of the term, but because of *their quality*. Simultaneously, as their numbers increase, a reverse movement is taking place. Men are moving outward on to the physical plane, and doing this as a group in order to prove the factual nature of the world of unity into which they have succeeded in penetrating. They, therefore, are demonstrating oneness and synthesis in such a simple way that men everywhere can grasp it. The New Group of World Servers is the vanguard of the kingdom of God, the living proof of the existence of the world of spiritual Oneness.

To all applicants the call has gone out to *see* the Christ as He is, in order (as *The New Testament* puts it) that "as He is, so should we be in the world." To disciples and initiates the call goes out to reveal to the world the grouped formation of all spiritual workers, the nature of the Christ consciousness which knows no separation, which recognises all men everywhere as Sons of God in process of expression. This is all desired because of the need to emphasise the all-inclusive approach of divinity to humanity. These working disciples and initiates regard all as essentially one and as brothers, which repudiates all man-made theologies (religious, scientific, political or economic) and says to all men everywhere: "We are all the children of God; we are all equally divine; we are all on our way to the revelation of divinity, and this upon the physical plane of existence; it is what we reveal that is of importance; what is revealed to us is of lesser importance, though it has its due place in the process of training and perfecting."

There is an old catechism which seeks to make clear to the neophyte upon the verge of acceptance the distinction and the difference between vision and revelation. It is falling somewhat into disuse, owing to the fact that the applicant today starts on a much higher turn of the spiral than he did at the time the "form of interrogation" was compiled. I would like, however, to quote one or two of the questions and answers for the instruction of present-day aspirants.

## A CATECHISM

*What dost thou see, O disciple on the Path?*

Naught but myself, O Master of my life.

*Look closer at thyself and speak again. What seest thou?*

A point of light which waxes and which wanes and makes the darkness darker.

*Look with intense desire towards the dark and, when the light shines forth grasp opportunity. What now appears?*

A horrid sight, O Master of my life. I like it not. It is not true. I am not this or that. This evil selfish thing, it is not me. I am *not* this.

*Turn on the light with will and power and fierce desire, and then recount the vision that may come. What seest thou?*

Beyond the dark, revealed to me by means of light, I see a radiant form which beckons me. What is this Being, standing gracious in the dark and in the light? Is it and can it be my self?

*What dawns upon thy sight as thou standest on the Way, O worn and tired disciple, yet triumphant in the light?*

A radiant shining form which is my Self, my soul. A dark and sombre figure, yet old and wise, experienced and sad. This is my self, my lower self, my ancient tried appearance upon the ways of earth. These two stand face to face and in between, the burning ground. . . . They move and merge. . . . The Path comes to an end. The Way stretches before. Sight is attained, and in the light reality appears.

*What canst thou now reveal, O Server on the Way?*

Revelation comes through me, O Lord of Life. I see it not.

*Why canst thou see it not? What hinders apprehension?*

Naught hinders me. I seek not sight for I have seen. My task is revelation. I seek naught for myself.

*What comes thy way for revelation? What hast thou to reveal?*

Only that which has for aeons long existed and has for aye been here. The Oneness of the Presence; the area

of love; the living, loving, wise, inclusive One, enfold-
ing all and being all and leaving naught outside.

*To whom must come this revelation, O Server of the world
of living things?*

To all enfolded in the living, loving Presence; to those
who all unknown to them maintain that Presence and
for ever shall endure — as doth that Presence.

*And who are those who live within that Presence but know
it not?*

They are myself and thou, and still they are myself and
still are all I meet. It is the one in every form who
think mayhap that form is all; who living thus in time
and space, see not the light or life within the form,
who hide within, behind the veils, between the four
and five (the four kingdoms in nature and the kingdom
of God. A.A.B.) and see naught else. To them I must
reveal the truth.

*How will you do this hardest of all tasks, O triumphing
disciple?*

By letting it be seen I am myself the truth; by living as
a fragment of that Presence and seeing all its parts. And
thus is revelation brought into the four and by the
fifth.

This is all that I can give you at this time upon the
word and the injunction given to the initiate: Reveal. I
would point out that it is not his task to reveal the world of
symbols. The five senses and the mind principle are adequate to bring that about. It is not his task to reveal the
world of meaning. That, the disciple arrives at and interprets
as he develops soul consciousness. His is the task to reveal
the world of significances, the world of reality and of essential truth. Because of the success of the evolutionary
process, this latter task is growing, and more and more
initiated revealers will be needed during the period immediately ahead. Forget not that the invocative appeal of
the mass of men, and the intelligent voicing of demand by
those prepared intelligently to move forward, will inevitably

call forth the needed response and the needed revealers of
reality.

The next word which we are to consider is one of the
most difficult for me to explain. The reason for my difficulty
is that you are all imbued with the ordinary ideas anent
these familiar words, and therefore it is well-nigh impossible for me to convey their significances to you from the
angle of the initiate-consciousness. Identified as you are with
the form aspect and with life in the three worlds, it is hard
for you to comprehend the state of mind and the type of
awareness which distinguishes those who are free from these
all-compelling forces in the three worlds which condition
human beings, thus bringing about erroneous orientation
and preventing what is really meant by spiritual perception.
The attitude of the average man, and even of the average
disciple, is that of one who looks in from the periphery towards the centre, of one who is preoccupied with the shell
of life and is not conscious of Reality as is a member of the
Hierarchy.

Therefore, when I tell you that these words for initiates
which constitute what I have called Rule XIV have a connotation quite different from that to which you are accustomed, I am propounding for you a most difficult problem. The true understanding is, I realise, not possible for
you but much can be gained by *your effort* to comprehend.
What you mean when you speak of the abstract mind is not
exactly true to the facts; the effort to think abstractly is
really an effort to think as far as possible as an initiate
thinks who has transcended the concrete mind and thinks,
or rather is aware, in terms of life and not of form, of being
and not that which anchors being on the physical plane —
or even in terms of consciousness, as you understand it.
Forget not that I have elsewhere told you that consciousness
(as grasped by the personality and the soul) has little relation to that form of living awareness which distinguishes the
initiate who is essentially an expression of the Monad
through the medium of the three aspects of the Spiritual
Triad. This is peculiarly so in connection with the two

words which remain for us to consider: Destroy and Resurrect.

## 4. *Destroy.*

What is this destruction which the disciple and the initiate (under instruction from this final rule) is asked to bring about? What is he required to destroy? Why is this destruction ordered?

Let me start with a basic statement: Destruction or the power and the wish to destroy which is characteristic of the undeveloped man, of the average man and of the probationary disciple is based upon the following impelling influences:

1. Lack of self-control along some line.
2. Desire to attain one's wishes by the removal of all obstacles.
3. Violent emotional reaction.
4. Revenge, hate, acquisitiveness and similar faults, based on lack of spiritual unfoldment.
5. The effort to remove hindrances within oneself, such as those implied in the rule for probationary disciples: Kill out desire.
6. The deliberate destruction of all that prevents contact with the soul.
7. The destroying of all links which hold the spiritual man in the three worlds.

These motives for destruction are all related to desire, to emotion and also to aspiration, implemented (towards the end of the cycle which leads to the treading of the Probationary Path) by the lower concrete mind. They cover a familiar case history and one which is well known to every sincere aspirant, or one which is realised for what they are at a lower level of life expression by the man who pays the penalties involved by this type of destruction. I feel no necessity to enlarge on this mode of destroying to students such as those who read this Treatise. This type of destruction is concerned mainly with form life in the three worlds, with individual aspiration and enterprise (from the lowest groping physical desire up to the aspiration for conscious soul life), and with experiment and experience upon the three planes of ordinary human living.

But in this word "destroy" given (as an expressed command) for those who are members of the Hierarchy or who have moved or are moving from an affiliated relationship on the periphery of that Hierarchy toward the centre of activity and into close contact with some Ashram, the significance is very different.

The type of destruction here dealt with is never the result of desire; it is an effort of the spiritual will and is essentially an activity of the Spiritual Triad; it involves the carrying out of those measures which will hinder obstruction to God's will; it is the furthering of those conditions which will destroy those who are attempting to prevent divine purpose from materialising as the Plan — for which the Hierarchy is responsible. Therefore, it is connected primarily with the relation of Shamballa to the Hierarchy, and not with the relation of the Hierarchy to Humanity. This is a formidable esoteric statement and its implications must be considered most carefully. This type of destruction has only a secondary relation to the destruction of form life as you know it. When steps are taken to implement divine purpose, the resultant effect may be the destroying of form in the three worlds, but that is an effect and only a secondary destruction; something else has been destroyed on a higher level and outside the three worlds. This, in due time, may produce a form-reaction to which we may give the name of death. But the death of that form was not a primary objective and was not even considered, because it was not within the range of awareness of the destroyer.

The higher destruction which we are considering is related to the destruction of certain *forms of consciousness* which express themselves in great areas or extensive thought-forms; these may have, in turn, conditioned human thinking. Perhaps the simplest illustration I can give you of this type of destruction would be concerned with the major ideologies which down the ages have conditioned or ma condition humanity. These ideologies produce potent effects in the three worlds. This type of destruction affects those civilisations which condition the human family for long periods of time, which concern climatic conditions that predispose the forms in the four kingdoms to certain characteristics in time and space, which produce effects in the great world religions, in world politics and all other "conditioning forms of thinking." Does this convey much or little in connection with the concepts which I am attempting to make clear?

That which is destroyed, therefore, are certain group forms and these upon a large scale; this requires an exercise of the spiritual will to bring about, and does not require simply the withdrawing of the attention of the soul, the decision to vacate the form and the failure of the basic desire to perpetuate, which is what we imply when we speak of death in the three worlds. The lack of the will-to-live of which we so glibly speak has little relation, in reality, to the will itself; it refers only to its faint or distorted reflection in the three worlds; this is much more closely related to desire and aspiration than to pure will, as spiritually comprehended.

The Purpose of God (to use a familiar phrase) is that which implements the Plan. This purpose is the motivating life behind all that emanates from Shamballa and it is that which impulses all the activities of the Hierarchy; the task of the Hierarchy is to formulate the Plan for all forms of life in the three worlds and the four kingdoms in nature. This Plan, in time and space, is not in any way concerned with individual man or with the life of any microcosmic entity in any of the kingdoms of nature, but with the wholes, the cycles of time, with those vast plans of livingness which man calls history, with nations and races, with world religions and great political ideologies and with social organisations which produce permanent changes in types, constitutions, planetary areas and cyclic manifestations. It will therefore be obvious to you that from the standpoint of man's little mind, these plans are well-nigh impossible to grasp. From the standpoint of the vision of the initiate who has developed or is developing the wider grasp and who can see and think and vision (I care not what word you choose) in terms of the Eternal Now, the significance is clear; at times, the initiate creates and then anchors a germ of livingness; at times he builds that which can house his living idea with its conditioning qualities; at times, when these have served their purpose, he definitely and deliberately destroys. The reference is necessarily ever to form; with the initiate it is, however, to the "formless form" which is always the subjective aspect of the tangible world. It must be remembered that from the point of view of esotericism, all forms in the three worlds are tangible, in contradistinction to forms in the two higher worlds of the Spiritual Triad.

The destruction considered is that of the formless structure on which the grosser structure is built. Some understanding of this will come if you consider the relation of the four subplanes of the physical plane, the four etheric levels, and the three subplanes which we call the dense physical planes. These constitute our physical plane in its two aspects. This is only a reflection of the three planes of the three worlds and the four planes from the buddhic plane up to the logoic, which constitute the cosmic physical plane. The destruction considered by the initiate is connected with the subjective worlds of the four higher planes and the three worlds of human living, and of other forms of life such as the three subhuman kingdoms.

In the human family, death supervenes when the soul withdraws its consciousness thread and its life thread; this process of death is contained, however, entirely within the three worlds. The soul has its station on the higher levels of the mental plane, as well you know. In connection with the forms of expression to which I have referred above — cycles, civilisations, cultures, races, kingdoms in nature and so forth — their destruction is brought about from still higher sources than the three worlds in which they manifest. This destruction takes place under the direction of Shamballa as it evokes the will of the Hierarchy or some particular

Ashram or some member of the Hierarchy in order to produce a predetermined result in the three worlds in line with the purpose of God. It might be said (accurately to a certain esoteric extent) that the destruction brought about in obedience to this fourth word in Rule XIV is the destruction of some aspect of the plan as it has been functioning in the three worlds, and this under divine purpose and intent.

This destruction is not outwardly so conclusive as is death — on the physical plane — of a man, though that is not essentially the rapidly consummated process as is usually surmised. The physical form may die and disappear, but an inner process of dying of the subtler bodies supervenes and the death process is not complete until the astral and mental bodies have disintegrated and the man stands free in his causal or soul body. So it is, on a much larger scale, with the death or destruction of phases of the divine Plan, engineered by the Hierarchy in conformity with the divine Purpose. There is an overlapping between the building process and the destroying process. Dying civilisations are present in their final forms whilst new civilisations are emerging; cycles come and go and in the going overlap; the same is also found to be true in the emerging and disappearing of rays and races. Death, in the last analysis and from the standpoint of the average human being, is simply disappearance from the physical plane — the plane of appearances.

The form of destruction we are considering however, is more concerned with the destruction of *quality* than with forms, though the disappearance of these qualities produces the death of the outer form. The withdrawing life of a great expression of the hierarchical plan absorbs the qualities and returns with them, as endowments, later in time and space and manifests anew through the medium of more adequate forms of expression. The soul, however, kills the forms in the three worlds; it is the life aspect (in this higher and more extensive type of destruction) which destroys the innate quality and consequently the form of a civilisation, the type of an ideology and the character of a race or nation, preserving only the essentials but discarding the distortions.

This fourth word is closely related to the fourth initiation in which the causal body or soul vehicle on its own plane is destroyed — that beautiful, intangible, qualitative Identity which has motivated and implemented the man in the three worlds. Does this instance somewhat clarify the difficulty of this subject with which we are concerned? Ponder on this as an illustration of this form of destruction, and seek better understanding.

This higher form of destruction does not manifest under the activity or the non-activity of the Law of Attraction, as does the death which the soul brings about. It is definitely under the Law of Synthesis, a law of the monadic sphere of life, and one therefore most difficult for you to comprehend; it emanates from a point outside *the five worlds* of human and superhuman evolution, just as the destruction of form in the three worlds emanates from the soul functioning outside the three worlds of the lower, concrete mind, the astral world and the physical plane. This statement again may aid you in understanding.

If this is so, it will be apparent to you that only initiates who have taken the fifth initiation and higher initiations can wield effectively this particular form of death — for monadic potency only becomes available after the third initiation, and its first successful use is the destruction of the causal body of the initiate. It is the reward of Transfiguration.

In connection with the use by the initiate of what we might call pure will, it should be remembered that this pure will works into manifestation through one or other of the three aspects of the Spiritual Triad. This activity is determined by the major ray upon which the initiate finds himself, from the angle of his monadic ray. Every spiritual man is upon one or another of the three major rays, for the minor four rays of attribute are all eventually absorbed into the third Ray of Active Intelligence.

If the initiate is upon the first ray, and therefore working in the Department of the Manu, he will use and express the innate will aspect through the atmic nature or through the highest aspect of the Spiritual Triad, to which we give the inadequate name of "divine Will." Students are apt to forget that the Spiritual Triad, related as it is to the Monad in much the same way as the threefold personality is related to the soul, expresses the three major aspects of Shamballic energy, which three are all of them expressions of the will of the planetary Logos and His essential Purpose. If the initiate is on the second ray, and therefore is working in the Department of the Christ, he will use the will through the medium of buddhi, the second aspect of the Spiritual Triad. If he is on the third ray and in the Department of the Mahachohan, the Lord of Civilisation, he will work through the higher mind, the lowest aspect of the Spiritual Triad. Forget not, however, that none of these aspects can be regarded as higher or lower, for all are equally divine. Understanding of these ideas may come if, for instance, you realise that the expression of buddhi, or of the intuition, in the consciousness of the spiritual man will lead to the use of the will in working out the purposes of Shamballa in the field of religions, of education, and of salvaging or saving the life aspect in all forms in the three worlds, but it will have no relation to the individual and personal problems of the man himself. If the expression is that of the higher mind, the use of the will will be in connection with civilisations and cultures for which the third department is responsible, and there will be the carrying out of the will of God in the large and general plans. If it is the will as it expresses itself through the atmic aspect of the Triad, it will function in relation to races, nations, and the kingdoms in nature, and to great planetary arrangements at present unknown to man. The synthesis of this picture will be apparent if carefully studied.

At the same time it must be borne in mind that the destroying aspect of this pure will, expressing through the Monad, implements the purpose of Shamballa and is one of the major manifestations of the Love nature of the One in Whom we live and move and have our being; it is also the guarantee of our ultimate and inevitable attainment, perfection, illumination and divine consummation.

This destruction wrought by the initiate is preparatory to his responsiveness to the fifth word which he receives at the fifth initiation and to which we give the inadequate name: Resurrect.

Prior to considering that word, I would like to point out that these five words have a clear reference to each of the five initiations; they give the initiate the keynote to the work which he must carry forward between the various initiatory processes. The work indicated has nothing whatever to do with the training and the discipline to which he will (needless to say) subject his personality; they are related instead to the work which he has to render. This work concerns what I might call certain essential realities connected with the purpose of Shamballa and with his ability to react or respond to the will of the Monad. As you know, this ability does not become an established fact and functioning realisation until after the third initiation; nevertheless, the preparatory sensitivity (if I may use this word in this connection) is slowly developing and paralleling the two other activities—Destroy and Resurrect—to which he is pledged:

1. The disciplining of his lower nature so that the unfolding initiate-consciousness may find no hindrances and obstacles.
2. Service to the Plan, under hierarchical impression.
3. The development of monadic sensitivity.

It might be of interest at this point if, in view of this third development—responsiveness to pure will—we considered these five words in relation to the five initiations with which you are all so *theoretically* familiar.

The word *Know,* in relation to the initiate-consciousness, concerns the certainty of the initiate, and his profound conviction of the fact of the Christ in the heart; it is at the same time coupled with a reaction which emanates from the sacrifice petals in the egoic lotus—those petals which are composed of the will quality of the Monad and relate the soul to the emanating Monad. The first faint tremor of the impact of monadic "destiny" (I know not how else to express this concept) makes itself felt, but is registered *only* by the soul of the initiate and on the level of soul consciousness; it is never registered by the man on the physical plane who is taking the first initiation; his brain cannot respond to this high vibration. Theoretically, and as a result of the teaching of the Ageless Wisdom, the spiritual man (in incarnation) has known that he is essentially the indwelling Christ, and the attainment of the Christ consciousness has been and will be his goal; the knowledge here referred to concerns something higher still — the Self-identification of the soul on its own plane and the Self-recognition which relates that Self to the enveloping whole, the Monad. If I might word it symbolically, I would say that the soul, the Christ (after the first initiation), *knows* that the inevitable processes of Christ-expression on Earth have been started and that the attainment of "the full-grown man in Christ" cannot be arrested. The centre of interest which has hitherto been directed to bringing this about now shifts and the soul *on its own plane* (not in the reflection of its consciousness on Earth) becomes determined to "go to the Father" or to demonstrate the highest aspect of divinity, the will aspect.

There are in the Gospel story four recorded moments in the life of the Christ wherein this process of development within His consciousness, this monadic centralisation (I know not what other word to use, for we have not yet developed the terminology of the monad, the will aspect) begins to demonstrate and can be traced in a definitely unfolding process. In the past I have incidentally referred to these points, but I would like to gather all four of them together here for your illumination.

1. His statement to His parents in the Temple, "Wist ye not that I must be about My Father's business?" I would have you note that:

    a. He was twelve years old at the time, and therefore the work upon which He had been occupied as a soul was finished, for twelve is the number of completed labour. The symbolism of His twelve years is now replaced by that of the twelve Apostles.

b. He was in the Temple of Solomon, ever a symbol of the causal body of the soul, and He was therefore speaking on soul levels and not as the spiritual man on Earth.

c. He was serving as a member of the Hierarchy, for He was found by His parents teaching the priests, the Pharisees and the Sadducees.

d. He spoke as an expression of the substance aspect (He spoke to His mother) and also as a soul (He spoke to His father), but He was controlled by neither; He now functioned as the monad, above and beyond yet inclusive of both.

2. His statement to His disciples, "I must go up to Jerusalem," after which we read that He steadfastly set His face to go there. This was an intimation that He had now a new objective. The only place of complete "peace" (the meaning of the word Jerusalem) is Shamballa; the Hierarchy is not a centre of peace in the true meaning of the term, which has no relation to emotion but to the cessation of the type of activity with which we are familiar in the world of manifestation; the Hierarchy is a very vortex of activity and of energies coming from Shamballa and from Humanity. From the standpoint of true esotericism, Shamballa is a place of "serene determination and of poised, quiescent will" as the *Old Commentary* expresses it.

3. The exclamation of the Christ, "Father, not my will, but Thine be done," indicated His monadic and realised "destiny." The meaning of these words is not as is so oft stated by Christian theologians and thinkers, a statement of acceptance of pain and of an unpleasant future. It is an exclamation evoked by the realisation of monadic awareness and the focussing of the life aspect within the Whole. The soul, in this statement, is renounced, and the monad, as a point of centralisation, is definitely and finally recognised. Students would do well to bear in mind that the Christ never underwent the Crucifixion subsequent to this episode, but

that it was the Master Jesus Who was crucified. The Crucifixion lay behind Him in the experience of the Christ. The episode of renunciation was a high point in the life of the World Saviour, but was no part of the experience of the Master Jesus.

4. The final words of the Christ to His apostles, gathered together in the upper chamber (in the Hierarchy, symbolically) were, "Lo, I am with you all the days, even unto the end of the age," or cycle. Here He was speaking as Head of the Hierarchy, which constitutes His Ashram, and also speaking as the Monad and expressing His divine Will to pervade or inform the world continuously and endlessly with His overshadowing consciousness; He expressed universality and the ceaseless continuity and contact which is the characteristic of monadic life — of life itself. It was also a tremendous affirmation, sent forth on the energy of the will, and making all things new and all things possible.

If you will carefully study these four statements you will see what is the knowledge referred to in this command given in Rule XIV to the initiate at the first initiation, the command to *Know*. It is the order to reorient the soul to the monad and not an order to reorient the personality to the soul, as is so oft believed.

The word *Express,* in its deepest meaning and when given at the second initiation, does not mean the necessity to express the nature of the soul. It means (behind all other possible meanings) the command to express the will nature of the monad and to "feel after" and embody the Purpose which lies behind the Plan, as a result of the developed sensitivity. Obedience to the Plan brings revelation of the hidden Purpose, and this is a phrasing of the great objective which impulses the Hierarchy itself. As the initiate learns cooperation with the Plan and demonstrates this in his life of service, then within himself and paralleling this activity to which he is dedicated as a personality and soul, there is also an awakening realisation of the Father aspect, of the nature of the will, of the existence and factual nature of

Shamballa and of the universality and the livingness of whatever is meant by the word "Being." He knows and is beginning to express that pure Being as pure will in activity.

When the third initiation is taken the initiate becomes aware, not only of the significance of the command to Know and of his innate ability to Express the will nature of the monad in carrying out the Purpose of Shamballa, but that (through his fused personality-soul) he is now in a position to "make revelation" to the Hierarchy that he is en rapport with the monadic source from which he originally came. He can now obey the command to Reveal, because the Transfiguration is consummated. He is not now revealing the soul only, but all the three aspects now meet in him and he can reveal the life aspect as will and not only the soul aspect as love or the matter aspect as intelligence. This is, as you know the first major initiation from the angle of the greater Lodge on Sirius, because it is the first initiation in which *all* the three aspects meet in the initiate. The first two initiations — oft regarded by humanity as major initiations — are in reality minor initiations from the Sirian point of view, because the relation of the man "under discipline and in training" is only a *tendency;* there is only a developing recognition of the Father and a slowly growing response to the monad, plus an unfolding sensitivity to the impact of the will aspect. But in the third initiation these developments are sufficiently present to merit the phrase, "revelation of the glory," and the Transfiguration initiation takes place.

At the fourth initiation the destroying aspect of the will can begin to make its presence felt; the soul body, the causal body, the Temple of the Lord, is destroyed by an act of the will and because even the soul is recognised as a limitation by that which is neither the body nor the soul, but that which stands greater than either. The awareness of the perfected man is now focussed in that of the monad. The road to Jerusalem has been trodden. This is a symbolical way of saying that the antahkarana has been constructed and the Way to the Higher Evolution — which confronts the higher initiates — has now opened up.

The three aspects of the will, as focussed in the Spiritual Triad, are now in full expression; the initiate is animated by Purpose, but faces still greater evolutionary developments; of these I do not need to speak, as they concern divine aspects as yet unknown and unregistered by man. The reason for this complete ignorance is that the vehicles of any man below the third initiation contain too much "impure matter" to record the impact of these divine qualities. Only the "created body" (the mayavirupa) of an initiate of the fourth initiation can begin to register these divine impacts; it is therefore waste of our time to consider even the possibility of their existence. Even I, a Master, and therefore an initiate of a relatively high degree, am only faintly sensing them, and that because I am learning to obey the fifth word which we will briefly, very briefly, now consider.

## 5. *Resurrect.*

One of the greatest of all distortions, and one of the most misleading of the theological teachings, has been the interpretation put upon the word "resurrection" in the Christian approach. This resurrection has been applied in many cases to the resurrection of the body; it is also applied to the fact (the selfishly motivated wish) of immortality; it is applied also to the physical resurrection of the Christ after he supposedly died upon the Cross. Resurrection teaches essentially the "lifting up" of matter into heaven; it does not teach the eternal persistence of the physical body of a man, as many Fundamentalists today suppose, looking for the reappearance of the discarded physical body; it does teach the "livingness of Life" and the state of "unalterable Being." This unalterable Being constitutes the nature of the Monad, and it is to this condition of awareness that Christ attained when He functioned as a World Saviour and thereby guaranteed, by the force of His achievement as a personality-soul, the same point of attainment for us, for we are equally and essentially sons of the Father or expressions of the Monad, the One. It does not, however, signify the resurrection of some personality in a particular vehicle used in a particular incarnation.

The whole concept of resurrection is the new and most important revelation which is coming to humanity, and which will lay the basis for the new world religion.

In the immediate past, the keynote of the Christian religion has been death, symbolised for us in the death of the Christ, and much distorted for us by St. Paul in his effort to blend the new religion which Christ gave us with the old blood religion of the Jews. In the coming cycle, this distorted teaching on death will assume its rightful place and be known as the disciplining urge to relinquishment and to the ending by death of the hold by matter over the soul; the great goal of all religious teaching will be the resurrection of the spirit in man, and eventually in all forms of life, from the lowest point in evolution to the highest monadic experience. The emphasis in the future will be upon the "livingness of the Christ nature"— the proof of which will be the Risen Christ — and upon the use of the will invoking this "living display." The glory and the radiance of the Transfiguration initiation will eventually be relegated to its destined place, and what is meant by the "display of life" will dimly be sensed in its unimaginable beauty.

The line or the path or the Way of Resurrection is the "Radiant Way" to which we have given the cumbersome name of the Antahkarana; this Way leads straight and directly from one great planetary centre to another — from Humanity to the Hierarchy and from the Hierarchy to Shamballa. This is the Way of Resurrection. It is a Way which is composed of the light of intelligent substance, of the radiant attractive substance of love, and the karmic way which is infused by the essence of inflexible will. Forget not that karma is essentially the conditioned will of the planetary Logos as He orders all things toward the ultimate goal of life itself through the process of livingness, of loving understanding, and of intelligent activity.

Therefore, the order to resurrect, as understood by the

initiate, concerns solely the application of the will nature and the aspect of Shamballa to the impulsing of hierarchical attraction and activity. It does not concern the individual life of the upward-moving aspirant or disciple, no matter what his degree, except incidentally and because major divine macrocosmic impulses must have lesser microcosmic effects. All these stupendous words with which we have been dealing relate to the cooperation of the initiate with the *Will* of Shamballa, and therefore, my brothers, are only dim hints to you.

PART TWO

THE RAYS AND
THE INITIATIONS

# INTRODUCTORY REMARKS

We now come to the final part of *A Treatise on the Seven Rays* and I have in mind three things which it appears to me to be necessary to do; these three will make this Treatise not only the textbook of the new psychology but also a more vital factor in the human consciousness, because the fact of initiation will be emphasised. These three are:

1. I propose to deal with the theme of Initiation in order to prepare the world of men for the restoration of the Mysteries.
2. I will give some definite teaching on the Centres from the planetary angle and also from the angle of the individual aspirant.
3. I will endeavour to relate the seven Ray energies to the five and the seven Initiations and to the three and the seven centres in a new and more arresting manner.

This is a large order and one not easy to fulfill because so much has already been given out anent initiation; the subject is dangerously familiar. By that I mean that certain preconceived ideas are already present in men's minds and many of these are not factual in nature and need to be discarded or, at the best, reinterpreted. I have myself dealt in a broad and general way with the subject of initiation in one of my earliest books: *Initiation, Human and Solar;* also, scattered through all my writings over the years is a mass of information which needs collating and bringing together as a basis for the instruction of disciples in training for an initiation.

In *Discipleship in the New Age,* Volume I, I gave out much more upon this subject and also information of a deeply esoteric nature anent the Ashrams of the Masters. The second volume of the book also contains much that is new and should serve to bring this whole subject much closer to public understanding. In the instructions now to be given, however, I shall endeavour to cover the ground

not already considered, and look at the subject of initiation
from the angle of the seven rays, from the effect upon the
centres, planetary and individual, and from the point of
view of the esoteric training of the accepted aspirant or
disciple. (These instructions were begun in March 1946 and
completed in March 1949.)

This final volume of *A Treatise on the Seven Rays* will
eventually change the attitude of men's minds towards the
Mysteries and towards the activity of *spiritual transference,*
which is one of the names given by the Masters to the basic
mystery of initiation. In due time our educational centres,
particularly those concerned with adult education, will take
into calculation, normally and customarily, the *fact* of future initiation where their students are concerned, and will
study their graduates from this angle in order to give ad-
vice or recommendation. In these institutions the elements
of true esotericism will be taught, though they will not be
then regarded as esoteric.

It will be apparent to you that this long Treatise is in
the nature of a preparatory thesis covering a vast field or
area of information. The first two volumes dealt with the
sevenfold nature of man and with the influence of the seven
basic energies or rays upon his unfoldment and his history,
and (in a briefer manner) upon the world in which he lives
and upon the environment which aids and conditions him.
In the third volume we took into consideration the influences of the constellations and planets upon the man and
upon our planet, the Earth, and gave much time to the
consideration of esoteric astrology; the rays, the signs, the
constellations and the planets are all of them closely interrelated and the human being is the recipient of the energies
and forces which they emanate or distribute. This makes
the man what he essentially is at any one time whilst in
incarnation.

We next considered the subject of healing because of
the necessity of understanding the limitations—psychological
and physical—which restrict man's free expression of divinity. We dealt with a major condition which has to be faced

and comprehended if humanity is ever to step off the ordinary path of evolution on to the path of discipleship and of initiation. Man has to become aware of the ray effects, of the place the centres play in his advance and unfoldment, and of the play of energies and forces which produce the difficulties and the diseases, and can at the same time cure them and bring about the liberation of the man.

From the consideration of limitations we passed on to an entirely new theme and an entirely new concept as regards man's education when he has reached a relatively very advanced stage of unfoldment. I gave you the new teaching anent the antahkarana or the mode and method whereby the initiate could relate in one great fusion or at-one-ment not only the soul and the personality, but monad, soul, and personality. This teaching has carried all that has hitherto been given, down the ages, another step further on and indicated the next stage of development ahead of the disciple. The time has come, as the Hierarchy had foreseen, for further light upon the endless Way.

Teaching anent the five initiations which confront all aspirants has long been given and has become public property; it has meant very little for most people and nothing at all to the mass of men; it has been regarded by the intelligentsia as vague and visionary nonsense; some few have admitted that these initiations may be possible, and others say that they are simply symbolic modes of indicating some final achievement which mankind faces; still others have accepted this teaching and have come to regard the initiations as goals and have then taken the necessary steps to prove the veridical nature of their beliefs; they have proved it, have become initiate, and have attained the status of Master of the Wisdom and taken their place within the Hierarchy. There is, therefore, a certain familiarity about these goals, the service they could entail and the consummation of the hierarchical possibilities; this itself indicates that the time had come when certain faint indications of that which lies behind the Mysteries and of that which is to be seen ahead of those who have achieved initiation should be somewhat clarified; I therefore started to impart three phases of information:

I. I gave out teaching which indicated the mode of bridging the gap between the lower three worlds and the world of the Spiritual Triad. In doing this, it became apparent that there were three groupings or levels of consciousness which had to be recognised:

1. The three worlds of human evolution.
   a. The mental plane.
   b. The astral plane.
   c. The physical plane.
2. The three levels of the mental plane.
   a. The level of the concretising mind, the lower mind.
   b. The level on which the soul is to be found.
   c. The level of the abstract or higher mind.
3. The three worlds of superhuman evolution, the levels of the Spiritual Triad: atma-buddhi-manas.

Between the higher three and the lower three and embracing the mental plane was a definite gap, a break in the continuity of conscious contact or an area where there was no channelling for the inpouring of higher energies. Here the teaching of the conscious building of the antahkarana was required; thus the gap between the mental unit and the manasic permanent atom, between the personality (indwelt by the soul) and the Spiritual Triad could be bridged by the aspirant himself.

II. I found it necessary also to indicate the nature of the Way of the Higher Evolution which had been hinted at but about which absolutely no information had been given. It is the Way which opens out before the Master of the Wisdom, leading to states of identification and levels of awareness which lie outside our planetary sphere altogether. The following of this Way enables the Master to "abstract Himself from the seven planes of our planetary life and divest Himself of all we understand as material existence.

Forget not that our seven planes are only the seven sub-planes of the cosmic physical plane.

III. I therefore opened up the subject of the possibility of the higher initiations which confront the Members of the Hierarchy. In this connection it is useful to remember that:

1. The Council Chamber at Shamballa provides a goal for the Members of the Hierarchy, but *not an abiding place.*

2. The seven Paths which stretch out before a Master are entered by the treading of the Way of the Higher Evolution.

3. The so-called third initiation, the Transfiguration, is only the first major initiation, from the standpoint of the Hierarchy; it marks the moment in time and space when the initiate sees truly and for the first time the door which opens on to this higher Way. Then—if he chooses the Path that the Christ chose (and there is no reason that he should)—he will "set his face to go up to Jerusalem."

These are some of the things which I have hinted at in past writings; they have been touched upon, vaguely and mysteriously, by past teachers and somewhat more explicitly by myself; I propose to be a little more definite in this new section.

Teaching, if true, must be in line with the past and must provide scope for endeavour in the present and must also hold out further enlightenment for those who have succeeded or are succeeding in attaining the indicated goals. There must be a spiritual future indicated. It is that which is required now, for many are attaining the goals proposed by the Hierarchy, and others are working towards them. The taking of initiation is now often to be seen and is far more frequent today than at any other time in the history of the race; for those who have thus succeeded, the next step forward and the new spiritual enticement must be clearly disclosed. Evolution is not a static thing; death cannot be the reward of living effort. To be static, to have attained all that can be attained, and to be at a complete standstill would be utter death and, my brothers, there is no death. There is only progress from glory to glory, a moving forward from point to point on the divine Way, and from revelation to revelation towards those points and revelations which are perhaps part of the Goal of God Himself. What the goals are upon the Higher Way is as yet utterly unknown to you; what divine qualities and objectives may be revealed to the Master and to the Christ as They tread the Way which leads Them off the cosmic physical plane altogether, you cannot know or sense, and if you could, you would not comprehend the meaning. "Eye hath not seen nor ear heard" the things which God will reveal to those who tread the way to the innermost centre, to those who love. This ancient writing can be paraphrased as follows: It is impossible to realise the wonder of the future which the planetary Logos will unfold before those who have unfolded the second divine aspect, *Love,* and who are therefore full Members of the Hierarchy, the centre where the energy of Love is anchored.

It is interesting to realise that the unfoldment of the love nature is that which opens the door which leads to the Way of the Higher Evolution and that nothing else will open it. This Way leads the Master off the cosmic physical plane on to the cosmic astral plane or to a level of cosmic awareness whereon is generated that cosmic impulse which we call Love.

It will be obvious to you that as this Treatise is not written to instruct Members of the Hierarchy, but only for aspirants and disciples and initiates below the grade of the third initiation, much that I will say will be somewhat "blind" or veiled in symbol; much that I could say (if words existed of an adequate nature) will not be said. Those that have eyes to see and ears to hear will read between the lines and correctly interpret my symbols, hints and references. To many what I will say will be as meaningless as *A Treatise on Cosmic Fire* is to the average reader and as the entire theme of initiation is to the ignorant and the undeveloped man. Much, however, should be of practical service to the struggling disciple, and I want in these concluding pages to fire his zeal, deepen his understanding, stimulate his capacity to love, and enlighten his mind. Such is what I seek to do. On his part, let him approach this subject with deep humility, with a meditative and reflective attitude, and with a refusal to materialise the presented concepts, as is so easy a thing to do. Let him refuse to step down the teaching to the level of his physical consciousness. In these words I have conveyed a basic hint.

Love and light are the great revealers, and if the student truly seeks to understand and profit by what I am endeavouring to teach, let him love all men more deeply and let him see to it that his light shines forth in a dark place, for "in that light shall he see Light." It is the lesser light within that reveals the greater light; when the light of the soul combines with the light of the lower man, then that fused and blended light will enable the aspirant to see the Door which opens upon the Way of the Higher Evolution.

In considering our theme I propose to divide what I have to say, according to my usual custom as follows:

The Aspirant and the Mysteries of Initiation
 The entering of the two Doors
 The entering of the Ashrams
 The dual life of the initiatory process
 The science of the Antahkarana

The Aspirant and the Major Initiations
 The relation of the seven Rays to the Initiations
 The significance of the initiations

The Aspirant and the seven Centres

I have given you here and elsewhere in my writings all that it is at this time possible to give anent the planetary centres and the rays, including the rays of nations and of races. You will find a wealth of information hidden in my various books if due search is made and the material is gathered together into a coherent whole. I suggest that you study and compare, read and search *topically* and extract all that I have said about the various nations, their governing constellations and their planetary rulers. This will facilitate research into the relation of the planetary centres to the systemic centres, the sacred planets and the energies pouring through them from the constellations which they "rule" in the esoteric sense. This is one of the paradoxes of occultism but it can be understood if the student remembers that the centres in his etheric body rule *in so far* as they are receptive or non-receptive to the influences emanating from the planet, via the planetary centres. It would not be advisable for me to give out the relation of the planetary centres to the centres of the human being; there is not enough love present as yet to balance such knowledge and to offset any possible misuse with its dire consequences. The reason I include them in the above outline is to show the organic wholeness of our theme, for the life of man encompasses the abstract and subjective as well as the outer physical levels of the manifested world.

I have made two affirmations during the past years anent the Hierarchy. One was that as a result of the cleansing of the Earth through the medium of the world war (1914-1945) and through the suffering to which humanity has been subjected (with a consequent purifying effect which will demonstrate later), it will be possible for the Hierarchy to externalise itself and function openly upon the physical plane. This will indicate a return to the situation which existed in Atlantean days when (using the Biblical symbolism) God Himself walked among men—divinity was present in physical form because the Members of the Hierarchy were guiding and directing the affairs of humanity as far as innate freewill permitted. On a higher turn of the spiral, this again will happen. The Masters will walk openly among men. Secondly, the Hierarchy will then restore the ancient Mysteries, the ancient landmarks so earnestly preserved by the Masonic tradition and which have been securely embalmed in the Masonic ritual, awaiting the day of resurrection.

These ancient Mysteries were originally given to humanity by the Hierarchy, and were—in their turn—received by the Hierarchy from the Great White Lodge on Sirius. They contain the clue to the evolutionary process, hidden in numbers and in words; they veil the secret of man's origin and destiny, picturing for him in rite and ritual the long, long path which he must tread. They provide also, when rightly interpreted and correctly presented, the teaching which humanity needs in order to progress from darkness to Light, from the unreal to the Real and from death to Immortality. Any true Mason who understands, even if only to a slight degree, the implications of that in which he participates will recognise this most ancient of Oriental prayers, giving the key to the three degrees of the Blue Lodge. I mention here the Masonic purpose because it is closely related to the restoration of the Mysteries and has held the clue—down the ages—to that long-awaited restoration, to the platform upon which the restored teaching can be based, and the structure which can express, in powerful ritual and in organised detailed rites, the history of man's moving forward upon the Path of Return.

The Mysteries will be restored in other ways also, for they contain much besides that which the Masonic rites can reveal or that religious rituals and ceremonies can disclose; they contain within their teaching and formulas the key to the science which will unlock the mystery of electricity—that mystery of which H.P.B. spoke; though much progress has already been made by science along this line, it is as yet only embryonic in nature, and only when the Hierarchy is present visibly on earth, and the Mysteries of which the Masters are the Custodians are given openly to man, will the true secret and nature of electrical phenomena be revealed.

The Mysteries are, in reality, the true source of revelation, and it can be only when the mind and the will-to-good are closely blended and conditioning human behaviour that the extent of the coming revelation will be grasped, for only then can humanity be trusted with these secrets. They concern those capacities which enable the Members of the Hierarchy to work consciously with the energies of the planet and of the solar system and to control forces within the planet; they will put the ordinary psychic powers (today so stupidly approached and so little understood) in their rightful place and guide man towards their helpful usage.

The Mysteries will restore colour and music as they essentially are to the world and do it in such a manner that the creative art of today will be to this new creative art what a child's building of wooden blocks is to a great cathedral such as Durham or Milan. The Mysteries, when restored, will make real—in a sense incomprehensible to you at present—the nature of religion, the purpose of science and the goal of education. These are not what you think today.

The ground is being prepared at this time for this great restoration. The Churches and Masonry are today before the judgment seat of humanity's critical mind and the word has gone forth from that mass mind that both of them failed in their divinely assigned tasks. It is realised everywhere that new life must be poured in and great changes wrought in the awareness and in the training of those who work through and in these two media of truth. Those changes have not yet been carried out, for it will take a new vision and a new approach to life experience, and this only the coming generation is capable of giving; they and they alone can bring about the needed alterations and the revitalisation, but it can and will be done:

> "That which is a mystery shall no longer be so, and that which has been veiled will now be revealed; that which has been withdrawn will emerge into the light, and all men shall see and together they shall rejoice. That time will come when desolation has wrought its beneficent work, when all things have been destroyed, and men, through suffering, have sought to be impressed by that which they had discarded in vain pursuit of that which was near at hand and easy of attainment. Possessed, it proved to be an agency of death—yet men sought life, not death."

So runs the *Old Commentary* when referring to the present cycle through which mankind is passing.

The tests for the first initiation, as far as humanity (the world disciple) is concerned, are well-nigh over and the hour of the birth of the Christ as an expression of the fourth kingdom in nature and the consummation of the work of the Fourth Creative Hierarchy is at hand. This there is no gainsaying; the birth hour may be long and the form may be "in labour" for much time, but the Christ will be born and the nature of the Christ and His consciousness will permeate and colour all human affairs. It is this condition—so imminent and so desirable and long foretold and anticipated—which will make possible the return of the Hierarchy and the restoration of the Mysteries.

These occurrences are not only dependent upon the fitness of humanity to provide the right setting and upon the inevitability of evolutionary development itself, but the reappearance of the Hierarchy and that which its Members will accomplish is related also (and primarily) to the interior life and the spiritual impulses within the Hierarchy itself and unrelated to mankind altogether. The Hierarchy pursues its own line of spiritual unfoldment as a paralleling activity to its services on Earth in connection with planetary evolution. Men are so apt to regard their own lives and destiny and the unfoldment of the human consciousness as the factor of only and paramount importance upon Earth and in the evolutionary processes of the planet. These conditions *are* of importance, but they are not the only factors of importance, nor does humanity stand alone and isolated. Humanity occupies a midway point between the subhuman and the superhuman kingdoms, and each of these groups of evolving lives has its own important destiny—important to all contained within the group ring-pass-not. They have their own chosen and differing modes, methods and ways of achievement. Just as individual man has to learn the art or science of relationship to other men and to his environment, so humanity *as a whole* has to learn its relationship to that which lies above and beyond mankind and with that which is below and left behind. This involves a sense of proportion which can be attained only by the mind principle in man and by those who are beginning to be mentally polarised. This sense of proportion will reveal to men their place upon the ladder of evolution and lead them to the recognition of the peculiar destiny and unique goals of other kingdoms in nature, including the fifth kingdom, the Kingdom of God, the spiritual Hierarchy of our planet.

The Hierarchy is itself also at a point of spiritual crisis. Its initiates stand before the Door which leads to the Way of the Higher Evolution and the entire personnel of the Hierarchy waits to make a united move forward, paralleling—on its own level—the move forward which humanity is also destined to make.

But, my brothers, here is the point of interest. Under the great law of synthetic expression (called by us the Law of Synthesis, the law governing the first divine aspect) the Hierarchy must move forward in such a manner that the effort must encompass the physical plane as well as the higher planes. The activity engineered must cover the three worlds of human evolution as well as the three worlds of the Spiritual Triad. Forget not the overlapping of these two worlds which takes place upon the mental plane and warrants the well-known phrase "the five worlds of superhuman evolution." Hence, therefore, the necessity for the externalisation of the Hierarchy and the demonstration of Their united ability to work from the physical plane up to the highest, in order to move unitedly through this Door on to the Way. Speaking symbolically, this externalisation is for the Members of the Hierarchy an act of sacrificial service, but it is also a symbolic gesture. The Hierarchy incarnates on Earth again, and for the first time since its last incarnation in Atlantean days. It is, however, a group incarnation and not the incarnation of individual Members. This is probably a subtle point too difficult for you to grasp.

The externalisation of the Hierarchy, therefore, and the restoration of the Mysteries, are not something done for humanity or simply carried out because men have earned a closer contact, have the right to some reward or are now so spiritual that the Hierarchy can have a good and useful time helping them. The picture is entirely different. What looms with such importance in the consciousness of men is, in reality, quite secondary in relation to the hierarchical crisis which we are considering. This reappearance upon the physical plane and the consequent life of service (involving factors of profound significance to men) are an expression of the inherent spiritual impulse which is impelling hierarchical action in two directions but involving one unified movement, embracing all the five planes of superhuman evolution and necessitating a group recapitulation of incarnated process.

The Hierarchy has its own life and its own goals and objectives, its own evolutionary rhythm and its own spiritual expansions; these are not the same as those of the human kingdom. These goals and rhythms will become more familiar to thinking men as the Hierarchy approaches closer to the physical plane.

This inclusive and planned activity of the Hierarchy is related to spiritual incentives which have their roots in Shamballa. There the life aspect is being almost violently stimulated through the action of the Lords of Liberation Who have swept into planetary activity because of the use of the second Stanza of the great Invocation—which was used potently by Members of the Hierarchy. Again, it was not used by Them solely on behalf of humanity or for the liberation of mankind; it had hierarchical implications also and was in part a demand by the Hierarchy for permission to move along the Way. The releasing of the "saving force" because the hour of service had arrived, permitted (at the same time) the inflow of an aspect of energy which never reached humanity at all and was not intended for strictly human use, but which was retained by the Hierarchy for the vitalising into renewed livingness of the seven major Ashrams, thus enabling the entire Ashram of the Christ to lift itself on to a higher spiritual level and closer to the door which leads to Life.

These statements veil deep hierarchical mysteries and are not in any way related to the Mysteries which will concern humanity when the Hierarchy is externalised. These mysteries will not be revealed to men. Only a general statement of the effects upon the Hierarchy of certain mysterious activities is permissible. They serve to show the steady pulsation of the evolutionary rhythm which permeates every atom, form, group and centre upon our planet, producing effects upon the lowest forms of existence and on and up to the very highest; there is naught anywhere but progress and a steady moving forward into clearer light and greater livingness.

In these instructions I am dealing with the entire theme of initiation from its broad and general angle and from the angle of definition; it is not my intention, therefore, to duplicate here what is given in Volume II of *Discipleship in the New Age*. Our approach will be somewhat different in this final section of our Treatise; we will confine ourselves to the effect of the rays upon the initiate and to the relation existing between the ray energies and various initiations which I have already outlined. In this section also I do not intend to deal with the scientific awakening of the centres or with the technicalities of bringing them into the desired balance and activity. I have already given what is necessary in my various books, where a very great deal of information is given and will be found scattered through all of them. By means of this diffusion and scattering, the teaching is protected and cannot constitute a danger to the general public. Students in the immediate future will have to search out the teaching in all the many volumes and hunt most carefully for the details of the science of the centres and for information anent their nature and processes. The whole subject of the centres is dangerous if misunderstood; the centres constitute a menace when prematurely awakened or unduly energised, and this entire subject can prove most dangerous to the curiosity-impelled man and to the ignorant experimenter. The time is not yet ripe for the presentation of this subject in a fully coordinated manner; students are warned against publishing a clear correlated thesis on the subject as a result of their researches in my books. Neverthe

THE RAYS AND THE INITIATIONS

less, the true aspirant must be given the needed information.

*The Mysteries are revealed,* not primarily by the reception of information anent them and their processes, but *by the action of certain processes, carried out within the etheric body of the disciple;* these enable him to *know* that which is hidden; they put him in possession of a mechanism of revelation and make him aware of certain radiatory and magnetic powers or energies within himself which constitute channels of activity and modes whereby he may acquire that which it is the privilege of the initiate to own and to use.

The disciple upon the Probationary Path starts off on his quest for the door of initiation, and for that which he will contact after passing through that door, with a definite equipment and created mechanism. This has been acquired, and facility in its use has been attained, through many cycles of incarnation. An incarnation is a definitely determined period (from the angle of the soul) wherein *Experiment, Experience* and *Expression* are the keynotes in each incarnation. Each successive incarnation continues the experiment, deepens the experience and relates the expression more closely to the latent unfolding divinity.

The same three words—in greatly enhanced interpretation and with the emphasis upon a much fuller opportunity —can be used to describe the progress of the initiate upon the final stages of the Path; with this we shall be partly engaged in this section. I would ask you, whilst reading and pondering upon all that I say, to have these three words in mind. Every initiation is approached by the disciple or initiate in a spirit of divine experimentation, but with a scientific aspect, because an initiation is a culminating moment of achievement, and success is a graded series of experiments with energy.

Having garnered the fruit of the experiment above indicated, there follows a certain period wherein experience in the use of the related potencies takes place. This occupies the interlude between one initiation and another. This may cover a period of many lives or prove relatively short. The results of the experiment of initiation and of experience with the then endowed energies emerge as the ability of the initiate to express divinity more fully than heretofore; this means that he increasingly can function as a divine creator in relation to the hierarchical Plan, as the manipulator of the attractive energies of love, and as one who determines— under the impelling will of Shamballa—the phase or aspect of the divine purpose with which he must himself be occupied in relation to the manifestation of the planetary Logos. You will note that I do *not* say in relation to humanity. The initiate works in many fields of divine creativity of which the field of mankind is only one.

These three words will therefore indicate the first type of approach to our subject; what I have to say will therefore, in every case, have them in mind.

Secondly, I would have you consider with me the various aspects of our sectional theme from the angle of the seven rays. By this I mean that disciples upon the different rays will all have the same goal, make the same experiments, go through the same experience and arrive equally at divine expression. However, their qualities and their modes of approach, their reactions and their distinctive natures will differ according to their ray type; this constitutes a most interesting and little known phase of our study of initiation. Initiation has been a blanket happening, and no note has been made of the ray implications. This I propose to remedy.

Each of the seven initiations, for instance, is an exemplification or a revealer of one of the seven ray qualities or tendencies; it is governed and conditioned always by a certain ray, and this is one of the factors which disciples have to learn and grasp whilst preparing for an initiation, because it involves success in handling and manipulating certain types of divine energy.

Each of the initiations brings one or other of the seven centres into full functioning activity, not from the angle of awakening or of stimulation, but from the angle of a "wheel turning upon itself." This is an *Old Testament* expression and is wholly inadequate, but I can find none other to substitute. The wording is totally blind and inadequate and will prove to you somewhat meaningless, except to the initiate who has experienced that turning.

As esoteric astrologers know well, there comes a life cycle wherein the disciple reverses himself upon the Wheel of Life (the zodiacal wheel) and from going clockwise around the zodiac, he now begins to go anti-clockwise; he learns that the substance aspect of his nature may still be conditioned by the forces flowing through them sequentially and serially, and according to his horoscope and according to the exoteric mode of the zodiacal revolution; at the same time, the disciple is receiving energy currents from the reversed wheel whereon he, as a soul, finds himself. He is consequently the recipient of two currents of energy, going in reverse directions; hence the increased conflict in his life and circumstances; these constitute the reason for the tests of initiation.

This, on a tiny scale, is true of the centres in the etheric body of the disciple; they too evidence the same dual activity, once the Path of Discipleship is trodden and the Path of Initiation is entered. The zodiacal wheel is itself essentially a cosmic centre; it is a twelve-petalled lotus, but it is a twelve-petalled lotus within the thousand-petalled lotus of an unknown cosmic Entity, the One referred to in my earlier books as the ONE ABOUT WHOM NAUGHT MAY BE SAID.

The multiplicity of zodiacal influences have eventually a dual effect: one upon Shamballa (the planetary head centre) and the other upon the Hierarchy (the planetary heart centre); the effect is also felt in the head centre and the heart centre of every initiate. This final dual activity is registered by the initiate of the highest degrees when he undergoes the eighth and ninth initiations; the other seven initiations are governed by the seven rays.

You have, therefore:

| *Initiation 1.  Birth* | | | |
|---|---|---|---|
| Sacral centre | 7th ray | | Physical plane |
| Beginnings | Relationship | Sex Magic | |

| *Initiation 2.  Baptism* | | | |
|---|---|---|---|
| Solar plexus centre | 6th ray | | Astral plane |
| Dedication | Glamour | Devotion | |

| *Initiation 3.  Transfiguration* | | | |
|---|---|---|---|
| Ajna centre | 5th ray | | Mental plane |
| Integration | Direction | Science | |

| *Initiation 4.  Renunciation* | | | |
|---|---|---|---|
| Heart centre | 4th ray | | Buddhic plane |
| Crucifixion | Sacrifice | Harmony | |

| *Initiation 5.  Revelation* | | | |
|---|---|---|---|
| Base of spine | 1st ray | | Atmic plane |
| Emergence | Will | Purpose | |

| *Initiation 6.  Decision* | | | |
|---|---|---|---|
| Throat centre | 3rd ray | | Monadic plane |
| Fixation | Intelligent cooperation | Creativity | |

| *Initiation 7.  Resurrection* | | | |
|---|---|---|---|
| Head centre | 2nd ray | | Logoic plane |
| The Eternal Pilgrim | Love-Wisdom | Attraction | |

| *Initiation 8.  Transition* | | | |
|---|---|---|---|
| Hierarchy | Four minor rays | | Planetary |
| Choice | Consciousness | Sensitivity | |

| *Initiation 9.  Refusal* | | | |
|---|---|---|---|
| Shamballa | Three major rays | | Systemic |
| Seven Paths | Being | Existence | |

It will not be possible for you to comprehend the synthesis which governs the four final initiations, and for these experiences we have as yet no adequate language. All that is possible is to indicate certain spiritual trends and tendencies and—as this section is written primarily for those who have taken or who are preparing to take one or other of the initiations—I can only hope that some meaning will be conveyed to those persons who are ready.

A careful study of the above tabulation should give you

a somewhat different idea anent the whole subject of initiation. The concept which has to supersede the one at present extant is that of group initiation, and not that of the initiation of an individual aspirant. In the past, and in order to get the idea of initiation into the minds of the people, the Hierarchy chose the mode (now obsolete) of holding out the prospect of initiation before the earnest disciple; upon this they placed an early emphasis of its peculiarity, its rewarding nature, its ritual and ceremonies, and its place in the scale of evolution. Since the fact of initiation had been grasped by many and achieved by some, it has become possible today to reveal what has always been implied, that initiation is a group event. If clear thinking had taken the place of a selfish individual aspiration, the fact of group initiation would have been obvious and for the following reasons, inherent and implied in the whole situation:

1. The soul—in its own nature—is group conscious and has no individual ambitions or individual interests, and is not at all interested in the aims of its personality. It is the soul which is the initiate. Initiation is a process whereby the spiritual man within the personality becomes aware of himself as the soul, with soul powers, soul relationships, and soul purpose. The moment a man realises this, even in a small measure, it is the group of which he is conscious.

2. Only the man whose sense of identity is beginning to expand and become inclusive can "take initiation" (as it is erroneously termed). If initiation were a purely personal achievement, it would throw the man back into the separative consciousness, out of which he is endeavouring to escape. This would not be spiritual progression. Every step upon the Path of Initiation increases group recognition. Initiation is essentially an expanding series of inclusive recognitions.

3. Initiation admits the aspirant into membership in the Hierarchy. This involves, speaking esoterically, the relinquishing of all separative personality reactions in a series of progressive renunciations; these culminate

in the fourth initiation, and are again mysteriously emphasised at the ninth initiation.

It dawns on the initiate, as he proceeds from one initiation to another, that each time he moves forward on the path or penetrates into the heart of the Mysteries in company with those who are as he is, who share with him the same point in evolution, and who are working with him towards the same goal, that he is not alone; that it is a joint effort that is being made. This is in fact the keynote of an Ashram, conditioning its formation. It is composed of disciples and initiates at various stages of initiate-unfoldment who have arrived at their point of ashramic consciousness *together*, and who will proceed *together* until they arrive at that complete liberation which comes when the cosmic physical plane drops below the threshold of consciousness or of sensitive awareness and no longer holds any point of interest for the initiate.

This is one of the new factors in hierarchical methods and techniques which I have had the responsibility of bringing to public attention, and so correcting the erroneous teaching of those trained under orthodox (so called) schools of occultism. The Master K.H., in one of the few (the very few) paragraphs in *The Mahatma Letters* which are genuine and not simply the work of H.P.B., gave a hint to aspirants of that time when He said that so many of them were so "spiritually selfish." This spiritual selfishness has led the average esoteric student to appropriate initiation and to make it personal and individual. Yet one of the prime prerequisites for initiation is a clear and concise recognition of one's own group, not through a process of wishful thinking, but through factual cooperation and work upon the physical plane. I said *group*, my brother, and not organisation, for they are two very different things.

Have carefully in mind, therefore, the fact of group initiation, and forego the process of considered thought anent *your* preparation for initiation. Some groups are being prepared for initiation in which the following factors control—as far as the individual is concerned:

1. A group of men and women whose souls are on some one ray are gathered together subjectively by a Master on the same ray, for group training.

2. Opportunity is given to such people to contact on the physical plane some of those who are thus subjectively linked, and thus mutually convey a sense of group solidarity. The subjective relationship is assured by an objective contact. Recognition is therefore a preliminary test of initiation, and this should be remembered.

3. Such people thus being trained and related are, from the angle of the initiation to be taken, at the same point in evolution. They are taking the same initiation and are being subjected to the same tests and difficulties. These tests and difficulties are due to the fact of the personality ray which may be (and usually is) quite different to the soul ray. It is the personality ray which works to prevent contact, to mislead in recognition, to retard progress and to misinterpret information. As long as a disciple in training is focussed in his personality, group initiation will not be possible for him, his recognition of co-aspirants will be fleeting and rapidly disturbed by the critical lower mind, and a wall of thoughtforms, created by the personality, anent the group members, will be thrown up and prevent a united moving forward through the Door of Initiation.

4. Group initiation cannot be achieved by a group in training until the members, as a group, have developed their particular "spiritual enterprise." It is the law of the spirit that the disciple must appear before the Initiator empty-handed, but that in group formation the group members unitedly contribute something to the enrichment of the Ashram. This may take the form of some considered project in line with the Plan, whereby they testify to their comprehension of that Plan and demonstrate to the initiate-company in which they find themselves, and those senior disciples to whose contact they are to be admitted, that they have already proven their fitness for acceptance and have proven it along the line of service. It has to be a group

enterprise, a group service and a group contribution. The specific contribution of the individual does not appear.

This thought of group initiation must be remembered, for it will colour all that I shall seek to convey to your minds and will hasten the day of your own acceptance.

No one is admitted (through the processes of initiation) into the Ashram of the Christ (the Hierarchy) until such time as he is beginning to think and live in terms of group relationships and group activities. Some well-meaning aspirants interpret the group idea as the instruction to them that they should make an effort to form groups—their own group or groups. This is not the idea as it is presented in the Aquarian Age, so close today; it *was* the mode of approach during the Piscean Age, now passed. Today, the entire approach is totally different. No man today is expected to stand at the centre of his little world and work to become a focal point for a group. His task now is to discover the group of aspirants with which he should affiliate himself and with whom he must travel upon the Path of Initiation—a very different matter and a far more difficult one. He needs to bear in mind the meaning of the following words from the Archives of the Masters, given in question and answer form. The questions are addressed to the neophyte who is getting his first glimpse of group relations leading to group initiation:

"*And dost thou see the Door, O Chela in the light?*
    I see the door and hear a calling voice. What should I do, O Master of my life?

*Go through that Door and waste not time in backward glances at the road just trodden. Go forward into light.*
    The door is far too narrow, O Master of my life. I fear I cannot pass.

*Go closer to the Door and take the hand in thine of another pilgrim on the way of life. Go closer to the Door; seek not to enter it alone.*

I cannot see the door, now that I grasp the hand of the brother on the right and the brother on the left. I seem surrounded by the pilgrims on the way. Alike they seem, their note is one; they seem like unto me, and press around on every side. I cannot see the door.

*Move forward on the Path, O pilgrim in the light, and stand together, hand in hand, before the Door of Light. What seest thou?*

The door again appears, and wide it seems, not narrow as before. What was that I saw before? It was not like the door which now confronts this band of brothers as we stand together on the Path.

*The door you saw before was a figment of your mind; a thoughtform of your separative creation, something that cuts you off from truth—too narrow for your passing yet full of wrong allure. Only the man who holds his brother's hand can see the Door in truth; only the man, surrounded by the many who are one, can enter by that Door which shuts itself upon the man who seeks to enter it alone."*

In Lemurian days, initiates entered alone and one by one, and then only a few managed to attain the goal and one at a time were admitted to the Mysteries. In Atlantean times, when the Door of Initiation stood wide open, the aspirants to the Mysteries were admitted in groups of seven, but had not contacted their fellow group members in physical consciousness; the emphasis was still (during the training period) upon individual attainment and achievement. To-day, so rapidly is man making spiritual progress, the Hierarchy is admitting groups all the time, particularly in connection with those rays which are at present in incarnation. This means that the three major rays (which are always predominantly active though they may have varying cycles of increased or decreased activity) have large groups undergoing their preparatory training for some one initiation. This group admission will develop rapidly as the world settles back into a cycle of peaceful growth and unfoldment after the drastic experience of the world war (1914-1945); it is for this that information such as I am here attempting to give must be made available.

One other point I would seek to make clear. As you know, an Ashram has in it disciples and initiates at all points of evolutionary development and of all grades and degrees; these all work together in perfect unison and yet— *within* their differentiated ranks, for each degree stands alone yet united with all the others—with their own established rapport, their coded telepathic interplay, and a shared occult secrecy and silence which guard the secrets and knowledges of one grade from another and from the unready. Similarly, when an aspirant, seeking upon the physical plane to find those who will share with him the mystery of his next immediate step or demonstrated expansion, discovers his own group, he will find that it has in it those who have not reached his particular point of wisdom and those also who have already left him far behind. He will be drawn into a vortex of force and a field of service simultaneously. Ponder on this statement. He will learn, therefore, the lessons required by one who is to work in an Ashram and will know how to handle himself with those who may not yet share with him the secrets which he already knows, and with those who have penetrated deeper into the Mysteries than he has.

# THE ASPIRANT

## AND THE

## MYSTERIES OF INITIATION

Let us now take up our first point in this section and see what is really meant by the hackneyed words "door of initiation," and what constitutes the difference between the door which faces the disciple and that which confronts the Master.

### THE ENTERING OF THE TWO DOORS OF INITIATION

It is of course obvious to you that the use of the word "door" is purely symbolic; the interpretation given to the word by the ordinary esoteric student and the orthodox Theosophist is that of a point of entry, and the significance of it to him is that it offers an opportunity to pass to new experience and fresh revelation—much of which is regarded by him as due reward for discipline and aspiration. That is largely an interpretation based on wishful thinking and is of quite secondary importance.

### *The Door of Initiation*

The real meaning underlying the phrase "door of initiation" is that of obstruction, of something which bars the way, of that which must be opened, or of that which hides or stands between the aspirant and his objective. This is a much more exact significance and one much more useful for

347

the aspirant to grasp. The picture of a man moving along the Path of Evolution until suddenly one day he stands before an open door through which he may joyously pass has no faintest resemblance to the truth; the idea that a man of a nice disposition and possessing certain character developments such as those portrayed in such books (by Annie Besant) as *The Open Court* and the *Path of Discipleship,* which condition the theosophical aspirants, is exceedingly misleading. These books are very useful and should be carefully studied by the man upon the Path of Probation, but are not so useful to the disciple, for they lead him to put the emphasis in the wrong direction and to focus upon that which should already have been developed. Naturally, the character development must be present and assumed to be stable in the man's equipment; these characteristics have, however, little bearing on initiation and passing through the "door" on the Path. They are indicative of the point reached upon the Path of Evolution, as a result of experiment, experience and continuous expression, and should be common to all aspirants who have reached the point of facing discipleship; they are unavoidable developments and connote simply the reaction of the personality to time and experience. It is eternally true that no one may pass through this door unless these character indications are developed, but that is due to the fact that the aspirant has progressed to a certain stage of unfoldment and automatically now has a measure of self-control, of mental understanding and of purity.

I would point out also that even the black magician possesses these qualities, for they are the *sine qua non* of all magical art, both black and white; the black magician passes through the door of initiation as it opens twice for the first two initiations. He passes through on the strength of his will and his character accomplishments and because the group-conscious aspect of the soul is active in him as in his brother seeking affiliation with the Great White Lodge. The love aspect is, however, lacking in the black magician. Forget not that all is energy and there is nothing else. The energy which is an aspect of the soul and which we call magnetic attraction (the group-building quality) he shares with the spiritual aspirant. He is essentially group conscious, and though his motives are separative, his methods are those of the group, and these he can get only from the soul.

You see again another reason why the first and second initiations are not regarded by the Lodge of Masters as major initiations. Only the third is so regarded, because at that initiation the entire personality life is flooded with energy coming from the Spiritual Triad, via the "sacrifice petals" of the will and purpose aspect of the soul. To this type of energy the black magician is not responsive. He can and does respond to the knowledge — most ancient and hardly won — stored up in the "knowledge petals" of the soul; he can appropriate and utilise the energy of attraction (erroneously called love by some students) stored up in the "love petals" of the soul, but he cannot respond to and use the energy of divine love, working out in the divine Plan which controls all knowledge and converts it into wisdom, and which actuates and clarifies the motive which brings *loving* magnetic attraction into action and which we call true group consciousness and group cohesion. It is at this point that the two ways—of darkness and of light—become widely divergent. Until the third initiation is taken, glamour may condition the attitude of those seeking to understand the life of a man upon the Path, and they may mistake the spurious for the real. The black magician leads a disciplined life, analogous to that of the spiritual aspirant; he practices purity for his own safeguarding and not in order that he may become a channel for the energy of light; he works with power (the power of magnetic attraction) with and in groups, but he does this for his own selfish ends and for the fulfillment of his own ambitious purposes. But at the third initiation there comes to the true spiritual initiate the revelation which is the reward of perseverance and purity rightly motivated—the revelation of the divine purpose, as the soul records it in terms of the hierarchical plan, though not yet in terms of the Monad. To this purpose and to the loving Will of God (to use a trite Christian phrase) the black brother cannot respond; his aims are different. You have here the true meaning of the oft-used and misunderstood phrase, "the parting of the ways."

But both groups of aspirants (the black and the white) stand before the door of initiation and take the needed steps to open it on two similar occasions. Both overcome glamour after the second initiation, and see their way clearly ahead; but their goals emerge as widely different; one treads the broad way which leads ever deeper into matter and materialism, into darkness and "black power"; the other leads to the straight and narrow way, to the razor-edged path which leads into light and life. One group has never freed itself from the principles which governed the first solar system. They were principles entirely related to matter and substance, and were at that time and in that period (so remote that the number of years of distance can be stated only in superastronomical figures) the conditioning factors for the initiation of the time. Certain units of humanity—then existent —were so completely conditioned by these material principles and so *deliberately* unready for moving on to the comprehension of another set of principles (more expressive of the divine nature) that they remained of "fixed and selfish material purpose" and a *planned* distortion of the divine will was intelligently created by them. You have here a hint as to the nature of evil and a clue to a part (though only a part) of the mystery to be noted in the statement that evil and good are reverse aspects of the same one reality, and evil is that good which we should have left behind, passing on to greater and more inclusive good. Forget not that the black magicians of today were the initiates of a previous solar system. When the door of initiation is ready to open for the third time, the parting of the ways takes place. Some follow selfish intention and the fixed determination to remain with the separative condition of matter; and to others, the divine will is clearly impressed upon them and becomes the motivating power in their lives. It was under instructions from the Great White Lodge on Sirius that the door remains closed the third time to the dark brothers. Evil, as we understand it, has absolutely no place on Sirius.

To the black magician, at this third opportunity, the door of initiation presents an insuperable barrier and obstacle; to the true spiritual neophyte, the door connotes "overcoming." We shall not consider further the approach of the black brothers to that door, but shall confine ourselves to a consideration of the initiations of the Great White Lodge.

This door of initiation is connected with the great problem of what H.P.B. calls the "mystery of electricity"; the door is itself an electrical phenomenon essentially. Having said this, even if you do not understand my meaning, you can, however, grasp the possibility that (being electrical in nature) it can easily present an obstructing force, a repelling energy to the approach of the aspirant; this is the correct way to look at it. It is only when the electrical energy of which the door is constituted and that of which the man is constructed at any particular time synchronise and vibrate in unison that the aspirant can pass through to greater light. This gives you a somewhat new and rather abstruse definition of initiation. Nevertheless, as science arrives at a better understanding of the human being as an electrical unit of power and light, and of his triple mechanism as created of three aspects of electricity, a truer comprehension of the significance of initiation will eventuate. The three fires of which all things are made are electrical in nature and—speaking symbolically—it is only when "fire by friction" is dominated by "solar fire" that the first four initiations can be taken, culminating in the fifth initiation in which these two fires are subordinated to "electric fire" emanating from the monad and giving a new revelation. This monadic process begins at the third initiation. It might be added that the third initiation (culminating in the Transfiguration) is taken on the three higher levels of the mental plane, and that it is therefore upon the fourth level of the mental plane that the aspirant first of all stands before the door, seeking initiation. That electrical unit or phenomenon of electricity which we call the fourth kingdom in nature, on this fourth subplane of the mental plane esoterically "ejects" the unit of electricity which is ready to be absorbed by the higher form of electricity. Fire by friction dies out and solar fire takes its place, and the relationship between the two higher forms of electricity becomes established.

It is solar fire which forms and likewise guards the door of initiation for the first four initiations. It is the electrical fire which forms the door of initiation for those initiations which guard the Way to the Higher Evolution.

There are four types of fire by friction which create the "obstructing door" in unison with solar fire, of which it is essentially created. These are as follows:

1. Electrical energy, composed of two forces of electricity: the innate, inert and latent force of the physical plane atoms of the dense physical vehicle, and the force which we call prana which is an aspect of the energy composing the etheric body. These two blend, combine and form the "door" through which the spiritual man must pass when he undergoes the first initiation. This provocative energy tests out every part of his physical equipment and—as he passes the test—the door opens, the opposing energies symbolically "die out," and he can pass on to the Path of Initiation, free from that type of obstruction. The physical body no longer rules him, either through its limitations and faults or through the physical disciplines which have been hitherto needed but are no longer required.

2. The electrical energy of the astral or emotional body next confronts him as he prepares to take the second initiation. You can call this energy, if you so choose, the sum total of all the glamours; a glamour is essentially a bewildering, deceiving and illusory energy-form which seeks to sidetrack and mislead the neophyte and which is attracted to him by ancient habit and old controls. He is therefore responsible for the impact of this energy. This type of energy takes form, and the massed forms of these glamours constitute the opposing door and oppose the passing of the

aspirant on to the next phase of the Path. With this electrical energy he must deal before he takes the second initiation. These particular energies are not thoughtforms; they are drifting, undefined and exceedingly fluid. Of this type of energy water is the symbol, and this is one reason why this second initiation is called the Baptism initiation, or the initiation of "entering the stream."

3. The electrical energy of the mind now creates the door for the third initiation, and the obstruction which confronts the initiate is that of the electrical figments of his own thinking, shining with a light which is all their own (for they are of the highest order and type), but veiling the pure light which shines behind them. They constitute the sumtotal of illusion. This "door" is formed by the coming together of the three types of energy: fire by friction, solar fire (playing in full force at this third initiation), and electrical fire from the Spiritual Triad, making its first impact on the other two fires, for all three are in full activity at this initiatory crisis. All are localised and concentrated in that symbol of progress, the "door of initiation."

It should be becoming increasingly clear to you why the initiate is ever portrayed as one who works with the forces and energies of the planet and the system. To him, there is naught else.

4. The fourth type of "fire by friction" which confronts the initiate as he stands prepared for that initiation which we call the Great Renunciation is the electric energy of the entire integrated personality. That which is the product of every incarnation — the highly developed, powerful and "clear-eyed" personality (as it is called)—is the final event and presents the final great obstruction.

In the Gospel story there are two major episodes in the life of the Master Jesus which throw some light upon this fourth entrance through the door of initiation: the Transfiguration and the Crucifixion. In both of them the three aspects of the personality are symbolised. In the first case, they are symbolised by the three apostles who in bewilderment and profound humility took part in the third initia-

tion, the Transfiguration; in the second case, the three were
depicted by the three Crosses—the two thieves and the central Master. The difference in the fourth initiation is definite; it lies in the fact that the four aspects of the personality
(counting the dense physical body as one aspect and the
etheric vehicle as a second aspect of the physical body) are
involved, for this fourth emanation of fire by friction has a
potent and destructive effect upon the dense physical body.
The Great Renunciation involves the rejection of the physical life at any cost, and that cost frequently involves its
physical death.

The Great Renunciation or fourth initiation has, therefore, two aspects: the outer involvement or objective happening in the eyes of the physical plane onlooker, and the
subjective aspect, portrayed symbolically by the three
Crosses and those who hung upon them.

The implications emerging out of this symbolism are
not easy to see, even when the superficial meaning is apparent, because that superficial meaning hides and veils a universal reality. The Master Jesus passed through the door of
the fourth initiation and overcame the final hindrances offered by His perfected personality. He died upon the Cross.
All the four aspects of His personality participated in the
event, and all four aspects electrically obstructed His passing through this door, even to the point of their complete
destruction—bringing a final liberation. Something universal was also symbolised which had naught to do with the
Initiated Master Jesus.

This symbolism and its meaning are related to the three
Crosses which stood side by side and to the relationship between those who hung upon them. In the three figures
humanity itself is portrayed and also related to the Hierarchy, and this "pictorial event" is a parallel to the one
already considered—the initiation of the Master Jesus. In
the Crucifixion, in this fourth passing through the door of
initiation and in the staging of this event, two great and
different individualities—the Master Jesus and the World
Saviour, the Christ—are implicated; two major happenings

are indicated, and the Christian Church has confused the two and related both of them without discrimination to the Master Jesus. Yet one event was a hierarchical occurrence and the other was a great human crisis; one was the entrance of an initiate into the Mysteries of death, involving in the process all the four aspects of His nature; the other was a dramatic portrayal to mankind of three groups to be found within the human family:

1. Unregenerate man, pictured by the unrepentant thief.

2. The struggling aspirant, moving consciously towards liberation, symbolised for us in the repentant thief.

3. The Hierarchy, composed of all who have passed to liberation through the medium of human experience, and thereby representing to us a guarantee of achievement.

Students would do well to keep this fourfold picture and this threefold symbol clearly distinguished in their minds, for individual attainment and the group possibilities are both involved; each is, however, distinct; in the one case the Master Jesus is the participator, and in the other and the more esoteric occurrence it is the One Who overshadows Him, the Christ. It was the Master Jesus who "died" and entered into the tomb, thus climaxing His long series of incarnations and ending—by destruction—the hold of matter on the spirit; through the tomb He passed into the Hierarchy, and the destiny of the Christian Church was committed to Him; that destiny still lies in His hands. But in the Gospel story, it is the Christ Who is indicated as appearing after the resurrection and not the Master Jesus, except in the one brief episode wherein He appeared to Mary, weeping outside the door of the sepulchre. The other episodes are universal in their implications, as indicated by:

1. Christ walking with the two disciples on the road to Emmaus—a symbol of the essential dualism of spirit and matter, as embodied in a world Saviour.

2. Christ appearing to the disciples in the upper room,

symbolising the zodiac, for Judas Iscariot was there, standing for the sign at the time in power; the other eleven disciples representing the remaining signs through which the sun must pass.

3. Pentecost. This event does *not* portray the triumph of orthodox Christianity (as the theologians believe and teach), but signifies the universal dissemination of the Christ consciousness throughout all time in the heart of every human being; to this the words and promise, "Lo, I am with you all the days, even until the end of the world," bear witness.

It is owing to the deeply esoteric meaning of the Resurrection and the Ascension and their major significance, referring to the consciousness of the Christ, that nothing much is told us about these initiations in *The New Testament*, except the vaguest generalities, in contradistinction to the wealth of detail given anent the other four initiations. Four of these initiations are related to the "door of initiation" as occultly understood and with the interpretation of which we are familiar; these four are related also to the electrical "fire by friction" of which that door is constructed, and which spreads to and creates the burning ground across which the initiate must four times move in order to "enter through that door."

The other two initiations (vaguely called the Resurrection and the Ascension) are related to the second so-called "door." This door is not in the same sense an obstruction as is the first door; it opens on to the Way of the Higher Evolution. The first door symbolically admits the initiate into the "heart of the Sun," whilst the second door—in a most mysterious sense—indicates the route which must be followed by the liberated initiate who seeks to penetrate to the Central Spiritual Sun—to which all the seven Paths eventually lead.

## The Door to the Way of the Higher Evolution

I write now for those initiates who have taken the third initiation, whose personality is soul-dominated and who "walk ever in the light." It will therefore be obvious that there is relatively little that I can say at this point which will be comprehensible, as far as the true meaning goes, to you who have not as yet achieved that state. The key to your understanding lies in the realisation that our seven planes are only the seven subplanes of the cosmic physical plane, and that all that now transpires in the life of the initiate simply releases him from physical experience (technically physical, even on the atmic, monadic and logoic planes), into that vortex of force which we know and understand as LOVE, or onto the cosmic astral plane. The note, the quality and the influence of the cosmic astral plane is love—the higher correspondence of emotion as experienced upon the astral plane of the planetary or solar manifestation. It is therefore to be realised that the Hierarchy is definitely under the impact of energies emanating from the cosmic astral plane, whilst Shamballa reacts to influences coming from the cosmic mental plane. The related stream of energy can therefore be seen to be from:

1. The cosmic astral plane.
2. The solar buddhic plane, reflected in our planetary buddhic plane.
3. The astral plane, the plane of glamour in the three worlds.

In relation to the mind, you have:

1. The cosmic mental plane.
2. The solar atmic plane, reflected in our planetary atmic plane.
3. The mental plane, the plane of illusion.

In connection with the references to glamour and illusion, (see *Glamour: a World Problem*) it must be borne in mind that the reason glamour predominates and illusion functions in the three worlds is due to the fact that men identify themselves with the dense physical brain, and interpret life in terms of experience in the three worlds. There is no true astral plane, from the angle of personality identifications, but only what might be regarded as the figments of the imagination; yet fundamentally and sub-standing what we know as the astral plane is the reflection of the cosmic principle of love. However, being essentially a reflection, it lacks basic reality from the *angle of the true disciple* and must be ignored as an expression of fundamental truth; at the same time, the astral plane exists from the *angle of the Master,* because it is an expression in dense physical cosmic substance of cosmic love. Its potency is, however, so great that it produces glamour in those who are not yet liberated. Students should remember that focussed power produces glamour where wrong identification is involved, but only reality and truth where there is freedom from the factor of form life. Therefore, temporarily, there is no astral plane for the disciple who is withdrawing identification; there is a field of service for the Master Who has no longer the power to identify His consciousness with anything in the three worlds; He can, however, relate cosmic sources with planetary and solar expressions of energy.

As we study the whole subject of initiation and the advanced initiations, it will be found necessary to remember always the relation of our seven planes to the cosmic range of planes. It is necessary also to bear in mind a fact oft forgotten, but which has been known and taught ever since modern occultism began to influence human thinking: the four planes which connote the highest possible spiritual influences, as far as humanity is concerned, are only—in the last analysis—the four etheric subplanes of the cosmic physical plane. These highest planes of our planetary life are, therefore, the source of all energy and all originating activity in our entire planetary expression and experience. These four planes are (as you already know):

1. The highest plane . . . Logoic plane . . . Will
   (Adi) Life                 1st aspect
2. The monadic plane . . . Universal    . . . Love
   Human monads              2nd aspect
3. The atmic plane     . . .    3rd aspect . . . Intelligence
4. The buddhic plane . . . Pure reason  . . . Intuition

This 4th or buddhic is a fusion of 2 and 3, of love and

intelligence, and produces understanding and intuitive perception.

All influences and energies, therefore, which are prevalent in our planetary existence, flow through and create the four above-mentioned planes and thus determine the nature of the evolutionary process at any given time in the three worlds. From the standpoint of a Master, the four planes are composed of forces which are basically responsive to, and finally conditioned by, the energies wielded by the Hierarchy and directed by Shamballa. In a peculiar manner, and under the Law of Correspondences, the three lower planes—mental, emotional and physical—constitute the three *dense* physical subplanes of the cosmic physical plane and are not, consequently, regarded as embodying principles. H.P.B. says, in connection with our physical plane (the lowest subplane of the cosmic physical plane), that it is not a principle, and this holds good also for the greater whole. The dense physical plane is matter conditioned by a previous solar system, and is almost automatic in its response to etheric energies; these constitute the etheric bodies of all forms created out of this "unprincipled substance," as it is occultly called.

The three lower planes of our seven planes are, from the angle of the esotericist, the equally unprincipled dense cosmic substance; the mark or indication of the true initiate is the transfer of his life and his point of identification from unprincipled substance and substantial forms to "principled" substance and etheric forms. The tendency of the occult student to think ever in terms of spiritual abstraction can (and often does) militate against a grasp of the truth and presents a false picture to the intelligence; the facts which I have just emphasised have much to do with the nature of the higher initiations. I would ask you to remember this.

The third initiation, therefore, releases the initiate from the planes of unprincipled substance (the lower subplanes of the cosmic physical plane), whilst the next two initiations make it possible for him to work with intelligence and love on the two lower levels of the cosmic etheric plane—the buddhic and the atmic, the planes of spiritual love and intelligent will. The Way of the Higher Evolution leads through the monadic and logoic planes (the two highest levels of the cosmic physical plane); when the four planes of the cosmic etheric plane are completely mastered and under occult direction, the initiate is faced with the seven Paths and with the choice to tread one or other of them. His choice is naturally dependent upon ray determinations and past activity but is nevertheless a free choice, because all limitation has been removed, all wrong identification with physical forms is now impossible, and the initiate's only limitation is that imposed by entrance into cosmic levels of awareness with which he is still unfamiliar. Bear, therefore, continually in mind that the highest spiritual attainment upon and within the seven planes of our recognised planetary life is entirely conditioned by the fact that they are the seven subplanes of the cosmic physical plane and are composed of the three dense physical planes (our three worlds of human evolution) and the four cosmic etheric planes (the four levels of so-called spiritual development); these are conditioned by three forces and four energies. I have emphasised this by constant repetition on account of the great importance the recognition of these facts will play in any grasp you may achieve anent the Way of the Higher Evolution.

After the Master has taken the fifth initiation, He has —as you know—covered and mastered the ordinary field of evolution for humanity; that means the three worlds of ordinary human experience and the two worlds of superhuman effort, making the five fields of the spiritual activity of man. Love and intelligence are now perfectly developed in Him, though their expression and emphasis may vary according to His rays; He is aware of the fact of the Will or of the first divine aspect, with its two qualities (veiling a third) of destruction and of purpose; He is becoming active on the second plane of our planetary life, the monadic plane, and that great centre of life, Shamballa, is having a definite vibratory effect upon Him; also (and this will be incomprehensible to you) He is becoming sensitive to a range of energies and influences which can now be registered by Him, owing to His increasing monadic polarisation and His contact with Shamballa.

The cosmic astral plane becomes, for the Master, a definite objective; He is beginning to develop a great sensitivity to that level of awareness, but consciousness of that within the planetary life—as He knows it—prevents Him from registering this energy of pure cosmic love as He later will. It is this sense of limitation which is the cause of His recognition of the Door on to the Way of the Higher Evolution, for the fifth and sixth initiations liberate Him into the atmic and monadic states of awareness; these initiations are to the initiate at this stage of development what the first and second initiations are to the disciple who is seeking to tread the earlier stages of the Path of Initiation. They might therefore be regarded as initiations of the threshold—one leading to the awareness of the higher levels of conscious unfoldment which the third initiation (the first major initiation) inaugurates, and the other to those levels of impression, of contact and of future ascension which are the sevenfold goal set before the Master when the sixth initiation (the true ascension) is consummated. It is for this reason that this particular initiation is called the Initiation of Decision. The Master then chooses which of the seven Ways or Paths He will follow, because His aeonial experience has enabled Him to *choose any of them* and know that He has chosen aright. Though these seven Paths, being one of the septenates, are necessarily related to the seven rays, they are *not* ray paths, nor are they governed by the seven rays. Any one of them is open to a Master of the Wisdom, and His choice will not be dependent upon His ray type, though He will take that factor into consideration. They are more definitely related to the seven cosmic planes than to the seven rays; this we will consider in greater detail when dealing with the factor of the seven Ashrams which are "proving" grounds for all the Masters confronted with the Initiation of Decision.

Disciples are more apt to be interested in the Ashrams from the angle of their own development; they are not prone to remember that the life progress and purpose of the Master not only determines the quality of the Ashram but that His own development and His eventual decisions are closely related to the Ashram which He controls. It is not easy for students to shift their attention away from the relation of the Ashram to humanity as a whole, or to realise that this relation is secondary to the Master Whose primary preoccupation is the unfoldment of the purposes of Sanat Kumara and the attainment of that state of Being which is significant of Shamballa. Students need to bear in mind that one phase of preparation for future work is that which will succeed the Initiation of Decision, and that this is dependent upon the type, quality and service rendered by the Master as He conditions and controls His Ashram. This I will attempt to enlarge upon under our next heading. It is useful however, for aspirants to discipleship, and above all for those preparing for initiation and consequently already working in an Ashram, to get this different point of view and begin to unfold within themselves a new sensitivity to impression coming from sources higher than the Hierarchy itself. This involves in them a new and higher type of orientation, and though it remains as yet impossible of attainment there is definite developing value in a grasp of the concept and the effort of the abstract mind and the intuitive perception to seize upon and reflect upon a new and entirely foreign concept. This higher reflective process is to the disciple who is working in an Ashram what aspiration is to the student upon the Probationary Path and the *early* stages of the Path of Discipleship.

In the latter case, the aspirant's emotional body becomes responsive to the principle of buddhi, reaching him via the love petals of the egoic lotus; in the more exalted situation, the disciple becomes aware (for that is all it is) of the *possibility* of an impression reaching him from the cosmic astral plane, via monadic levels of awareness. Note what I say—simply the possibility; for there is at this stage no as-

sured recognition of this goal; it is an impression which is
to the disciple preparing for one of the higher initiations
what an occult theory is to an aspirant on very much lower
levels. The only way in which I can give any faintest idea
of the higher reaches of the initiate consciousness will be
through reference to lower *grasped* capacities and the presentation of undefinable truths in terms of that which has
been defined and which (to these higher states of awareness)
are in the nature of seed thoughts.

Some small grasp of the nature of the consciousness of
Shamballa will emerge as we study this section of the
Treatise, for the higher levels of the cosmic etheric plane
are permeated with energies emanating from the cosmic
astral plane and the cosmic mental plane; these energies,
playing through and directed by the great Lives Who form
a permanent nucleus of the Council Chamber at Shamballa,
do condition and are the impelling, motivating and *relating*
power behind all the evolutionary processes on lower levels.

Yet, the life and consciousness of the Hierarchy are
very different to the life and consciousness of Those Who
constitute the great centre called Shamballa; the developing
sensitivity to increasingly high impression, which is the
result of each stage of the final initiatory process, is the
only way in which the distinction and the goal become apparent. Just as those who read and study these ideas are
occupied with concepts and thoughts totally unrealised and
wholly inexplicable and sometimes even senseless, to the
ordinary everyday businessman in the street, so there are
also ranges of thought and eternal extra-planetary concepts
which are equally unknown and temporarily inexplicable to
the initiate working in an Ashram under some Master.
When the student realises that the great universal Oneness
which he associates with monadic consciousness, is only the
registration of impressions localised (and therefore limited)
and defined within the etheric levels of the cosmic physical
plane, he can perhaps grasp the implications of the wonder
which will be revealed to the initiate who can transcend
the entire cosmic physical plane (our seven planes of the

human, superhuman and the divine worlds) and function upon another cosmic level. This is what the treading of the Way of the Higher Evolution enables a Master eventually to do.

One interesting fact emerges out of all this comparative work and this mode of analogical teaching, and that is that the word "spiritual" refers neither to religious matters (so-called) nor to the Path of Discipleship or the Path of the major or higher initiations, but to the *relationships* on every level of the cosmic physical plane, to every level from the lowest to the highest. The word "spiritual" relates to attitudes, to relationships, to the moving forward from one level of consciousness (no matter how low or gross, from the point of view of a higher level of contact) to the next; it is related to the power to see the vision, even if that vision is materialistic as seen from the angle of a higher registration of possibility; the word "spiritual" refers to every effect of the evolutionary process as it drives man forward from one range of sensitivity and of responsiveness to impression to another; it relates to the expansion of consciousness, so that the unfoldment of the organs of sensory perception in primitive man or in the awakening infant are just as surely spiritual events as participation in an initiatory process; the development of the so-called irreligious man into a sound and effective businessman, with all the necessary perception and equipment for success, is as much a spiritual unfoldment—in that individual's experience—as the taking of an initiation by a disciple in an Ashram.

The assumption by orthodox church people that the word "spiritual" connotes profound and effective interest in orthodox religion is *not* borne out by the facts of the spiritual life. Some day, when the world is increasingly led by its initiates, this erroneous assumption will be discarded, and it will be realised that all activity which drives the human being forward towards some form of development (physical, emotional, intuitional, and so forth) is essentially spiritual in nature and is indicative of the livingness of the inner divine entity.

I have felt it necessary to point this out because it will become apparent as we read and study this section of the Treatise that the Master—moving forward into higher areas of impressionability—may not and frequently will not express this development in terms of what is now regarded as "spiritual" by the religious devotee and by the man used to the wording and the terminology of the churchmen of all faiths. The discoveries of science, my brother, or the production of some great work in literature or in the field of art, are just as much an evidence of "spiritual" unfoldment as the rhapsodies of the mystic or the registration by the so-called occultist of a contact with the Hierarchy.

There will, however, come a point in the experience of all those thus making a spiritual approach along some specialised line, where a meeting place will become apparent, where a joint goal will be unitedly recognised, where essential unity under diversity of forms, of methods and of techniques will be acknowledged, and where pilgrims on all ways of approach will know themselves to be one band of demonstrators of the divine.

One such meeting place is upon the periphery of the Hierarchy during the stage immediately prior to acceptance into an Ashram. It is interesting to note that—on a world-wide scale—the world disciple, Humanity, is today on the verge of this major awakening and joint registration of a unity not hitherto reached; the growth of the spirit of internationalism, the inclusiveness of the scientific attitude, and the spread of a universal humanitarian welfare movement are all indicative of this meeting place.

Another such meeting place is recorded and entered (symbolically speaking) when the third initiation is taken, and still another is realised at the time of the seventh initiation. These all register development in group awareness, as well as in the recognition of the individual initiate, as to what is happening within the consciousness aspect of humanity.

The door into the Way of the Higher Evolution simply permits the entrance of the sensitive initiate into "spheres of intimacy" (as they are sometimes called) which are this time cosmic in their implications, planetary in their effects, and which give to the initiate what has been called the "key to the Sun"—as it conditions the solar system—just as the door to initiation gives to the aspirant the "key to the kingdom of God."

We have dealt in the foregoing pages with deep matters and have touched upon topics too high for the understanding of the average student or probationary disciple; dim recognitions, based on past acceptances are, however, possible to some of you. We have seen, among other things, that the so-called "door of initiation" presents obstacles whose purpose is to block entrance and to draw out the latent will of the applicant; an initiate is one who succeeds in penetrating to the further side of the door, where recognition awaits him. We will now concern ourselves with the basic theme of the Ashram itself.

## THE ENTERING OF THE ASHRAM

This theme necessarily has great interest for all aspirants and would-be disciples, but I am not at first going to deal with the subject from the angle of humanity and its effort to establish contact with the Ashram. I desire first of all to speak of the Ashram as a whole, constituted of many Ashrams and creating an "invoking area" of relationship for the supreme Head of the Ashram, Sanat Kumara, the Lord of the World. I seek to enter into no discussion of this leading Life of our entire planet. HE is to a still greater Being, the One referred to elsewhere as "the One about Whom naught may be said," what the vehicle of a Master in physical incarnation is to Him, and on a less accurate basis, what your personality is to you; it is an expression of the soul or of the Monad when a disciple has attained initiate-consciousness.

All the qualities, the love and the purpose of a supreme Entity, referred to in The New Testament as the "Unknown God," are focussed in Sanat Kumara. Some gauge of the unfoldments which can lie ahead of humanity will enter the human consciousness when:

1. The fact of the Hierarchy,
2. The nature of its relationship to Shamballa,
3. The spiritual nature of Those Who respond in reverent obedience to the slightest wish of the Lord of the World,

are among the accepted truths whereby men live. This will happen after the externalisation of the Hierarchy.

This Lord of the World is the sole repository of the will and purpose of the One of Whom He is an expression; this again can be understood by you as evoking the same relation to the "unknown God" as your personality—when expressing adequately the soul and later the Monad—conditions your perception, knowledge, plans and purpose, and controls the quality of your life and directs the energy which you express.

His vehicle of manifestation is the planet with its seven centres, of which only three are yet recognised by the occult student: Shamballa, His head centre, the Hierarchy, His heart centre, and Humanity, His throat centre. The other four centres are concerned with evolutions which are reached, controlled and related from one or other of these three major centres. The solar plexus is dominated by the Hierarchy, the heart centre of Sanat Kumara, and has a close relation to the deva evolution, hinted at by me in *A Treatise on Cosmic Fire*. The vastness of this subject will be understood by my use of the word "hint" in reference to what I have earlier written on the subject.

The centre which we call Shamballa controls that mysterious centre which is the correspondence to that which we call "the centre at the base of the spine"; this is the inadequate name given to the reservoir of threefold fire, latent and quiescent, which is found at the base of the human spine; it is entirely inactive except in those people who have taken the third initiation. The planetary centre is related to the three fires (electric fire, solar fire, and fire by friction) which are the source of the life, warmth, moisture and growth of all forms upon our planet. It may seem curious and inexplicable to you, but the centre of creativity is affected, and I had almost said guarded, by the "centre which we call the race of men"; the reference in the serious occult books to the future of humanity as the Saviour of all the subhuman kingdoms has relation to this fact.

The ajna centre of the Lord of the World is just beginning to express itself in a recognisable manner through the New Group of World Servers. This intermediate group —between the Hierarchy and Humanity—is a carrier of the energy which makes the Plan possible (the Plan of which the Hierarchy is the custodian). This Plan implements the Purpose, and later, when the New Group of World Servers is organised and is recognised as a living organism, it will definitely receive energy from Shamballa in a direct reception, via the Hierarchy. This information is, I realise, of little immediate importance to you, but—towards the end of the century—it will be found explanatory of much.

Though the Christ is the Head of the Hierarchy, it is Sanat Kumara, the Ancient of Days, Whose Ashram it truly is. The Christ (I am using one of His official names) is indeed the Master of all the Masters and the Coordinator of the entire life of the great Ashram, in conjunction with the two other hierarchical Officials, the Manu and the Mahachohan. The information I gave as to the constitution of the Hierarchy, in *Initiation, Human and Solar,* was along the same line. The Hierarchy is the Ashram of Sanat Kumara, but He has delegated His authority, right down the ages, to the so-called World Saviours successively; Their life expression embodied in every case the goal of the period during which They held office.

In the early days of the Hierarchy, millennia of years ago, neither the official Directors of the Hierarchy nor the Masters were of the calibre which They are today. Had They been so, They would have been too far removed from the factual life of the cycle, and therefore useless for the cycle of divine life which existed. The growth of humanity and its evolutionary status (when compared with primordial and primitive man) can be seen in the quality of the Hierarchy today, *which humanity produced* and towards which it looks for guidance and teaching. This is an interesting point which I offer for your consideration. Never forget, my brothers, that as it is humanity which has furnished the personnel of the Hierarchy—including the Christ, the first of our humanity to achieve divinity—we have, therefore, the guarantee and the assurance of humanity's ultimate success.

The three major Executives of the Hierarchy:

1. The Christ, representing the second Ray of Love-Wisdom,
2. The Manu, representing the first Ray of Will or Power,
3. The Mahachohan, representing the third Ray of Active Intelligence,

are responsible to the Lord of the World for the processing of the life and impulse which condition the evolutionary process. This statement is made without any further definition by me because the whole subject is too abstruse and it would require another Treatise like that on Cosmic Fire to make it even a little clearer.

Humanity can only be the recipient of this type of information after the first Ray of Will or Power has become more active; this will take place when the work of the second Ray of Love-Wisdom has reached its next cyclic crisis point. The crisis points of a ray are ever indicative of success and have in them the quality of joy. Mankind will then be much freer from the spirit of separateness, and a measure of peace, unity and cooperation will be conditioning human relations. There is a constant shifting in the state of the planetary consciousness and this, though implemented from Shamballa, is produced by humanity itself; this unfolding human consciousness leads mankind eventually out of the fourth kingdom in nature into the fifth, the hierarchy of souls, and—at the same time—raises the level of consciousness in all the three subhuman kingdoms. This series of happenings will remain for a long time inexplicable to man, though the results can be seen in the effect which humanity has had on the animal kingdom, through domestication; on the vegetable kingdom, through specialisation and science; and on the mineral kingdom, through the skilled utilisation of metals and the widespread use of the mineral products of the earth.

It must be borne in mind that the Council Chamber of the Lord at Shamballa is a unit, but that the Hierarchy is a differentiation of this basic unity into the seven major Ashrams and the forty-nine Ashrams which are gradually forming. The Hierarchy is, however, a unity within itself, for the entire ashramic life is guarded by a ring-pass-not, created by its radiation; the seven and the forty-nine Ashrams are held together by the magnetic interplay of the whole. It is this radiation which affects by its quality the senior aspirants in the world, and draws them gradually into relationship with itself and finally into its magnetic field. This is aided by the clarity of perception, the intensification of the livingness of the rightly oriented aspirant. I prefer the word "livingness" to that of "vibration," so widely used in modern occultism.

There is therefore a dual inflow into the Ashram of Sanat Kumara, controlled and directed by the three hierarchical Directors:

1. *From Shamballa itself.* This is a flow of energising life or of what we might call "unfettered enlightenment"; this impresses the purpose or the will of the Lord of the World upon the united Hierarchy in a manner incomprehensible to you; it also creates a dynamic magnetic impulse which enables the graded initiates, through the medium of the Ashrams, to organise the Plan and set it in motion, so that the Purpose gradually materialises on earth. Because the senior initiates, from the Christ down to initiates of the fourth degree, are conscious in varying ways (according to ray) of the Eternal Now, and can work free from the compulsion of time, They can see the impressed Purpose as a

more complete whole than can initiates of lesser degree and development. It is this capacity which makes Them responsive to Shamballa, where the living will of the "Unknown God" (for a period of a life cycle) is seen in completeness and is already existent. The Hierarchy is, however, handicapped in its activity by the time sense and the materialistic focus of the "centre which we call the race of men."

2. *From Humanity.* There is a constant (and increasing) flow of reoriented human energy penetrating into and beyond the radiatory periphery. This penetrating energy, implemented by the individual aspirant and disciple, is that of intelligent activity and—little as you may have realised it—it is this constant inflow which aids in the intelligent application of the Plan to human affairs. The Science of Impression, which governs the technique of Shamballa, functions through the three different centres in three different ways:

- a. Shamballa          . . . dynamic impression
- b. The Hierarchy . . . magnetic telepathy
- c. Humanity          . . . radiatory sensitivity

yet these three are only manifestations of the will of God as it works out in the activities of His three major centres.

One point should here be made: the entry of a member of the human family into the ranks of the initiates and his participation in the activity of some one or other of the Ashrams produces a movement out of the Hierarchy of some Master and into the highest centre of all; it has this effect only after the entering initiate has taken the third initiation, and can therefore take his part in the hierarchical life as a monadic expression susceptible to impression from Shamballa. When a Master thus emerges He is immediately confronted with the choice between the seven Paths. With this development and decision we shall later deal. The seven Paths are all concerned *with purpose,* just as the seven Ashrams are all concerned *with the plan.* There is, as you will later see, a direct relation between the seven Paths and the seven Ashrams. Though we shall not deal with the subject at all, there is likewise a correspondence in the third major centre, Humanity. You have, therefore, curiously interrelated:

> The seven Paths
> The seven Rays
> The seven Ashrams
> The seven Races

Students would do well to bear in mind that these relationships are the result of the *involutionary activity* of the life expression of the Lord of the World. The key to the mystery of differentiation is found by the Master when He is faced by the choice of the seven Paths. At that high point of will expression, He discovers the secret of that evolutionary process which proceeds from unity to differentiation, and from differentiation to unity again. Individualisation, Initiation and Identification are the three main stages in the *evolutionary activity* of the life of God and condition the quality of each of the three divine centres. The four related septenates, enumerated above, eventually produce a synthesis which will consummate upon the cosmic mental plane. This is of course beyond my powers to teach or to explain, as I am not yet a liberated Master, though I am a liberated human being.

In the human centre, the man becomes identified with himself; in the Hierarchy, he becomes identified with the group; in Shamballa, He becomes identified with the planetary WHOLE. When that takes place, He is then aware for the first time that other identifications—lying beyond the planetary ring-pass-not—confront Him; His choice of one or other of the Paths is conditioned by the *quality* of His previous identifications, which are in their turn conditioned by His ray type.

Passing from these broad generalisations, which in reality lie far beyond our present grasp but which will have their future usefulness, let us now consider the Hierarchy as it exists (in the consciousness of Sanat Kumara, as His Ashram) and as it constitutes "the noble middle Path" to which the Buddha refers, and fills the intermediate and the mediating place between Shamballa and Humanity. This position of the Hierarchy must never be forgotten.

*The seven Groups of Ashrams within the Hierarchy*

It is because the first Ray of Will or Power, through its Ashram, is related to Shamballa, that the Master Morya is the Head of all truly esoteric schools. In the esoteric enterprise and in the work done by disciples in the Ashrams, the Will is developed so that the Purpose may eventually be understood. He relates the three points of the triangle composed of the Hierarchy, the world of souls on the mental plane, and those human souls who (on all Rays) are ready for contact with the Hierarchy. They have made contact with their souls, and this is registered in the Hierarchy. The triangle is, therefore, as follows:

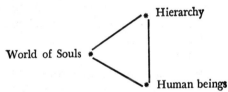

As the externalisation of the Ashram proceeds, those souls upon the physical plane who are ready for enlightenment will find their way into the New Group of World Servers; this group will increasingly assume potent relation between the units of life within its periphery, the Ashram, and humanity. From one point of view, the New Group of World Servers can be regarded not only as a relating group, but also as a great transforming station, dowered later (though not noticeably so at the present time) with two functions in relation to the Ashram:

1. One function is to enable "externalising units of perfection" (the higher initiates and the Masters) to step down Their individual potency to such a degree that They will be able to work in physical objectivity on the earth, with no undesirable effects upon humanity. I refer to average and undeveloped human beings. Students should bear in mind that contact with Those Who are initiates of high degree

and members of an Ashram has the following three effects upon humanity:

    a. On evolved men, aspirants, probationers and disciples, the effect is stimulating and magnetic.

    b. On average human beings, capable of little response yet susceptible to impact and sensitive to impression, the effect is not helpful and is often destructive, because their etheric bodies are not competent to entertain and employ such high vibrations.

    c. On undeveloped humanity, the effect has been called "condensation or concretisation"; all their natural qualities (the qualified substance of their three bodies) are solidified; thus they create an automatic barrier to the entry of the too high impulses and vibrations.

    2. The second function is to enable those who are making definite soul contact, reorienting themselves and nearing the periphery of the Ashram, to absorb with profit the radiation of the Hierarchy.

I would like at this point to refer back to the time sense in relation to the Hierarchy and its work, to which I referred a few pages back. It involves the inability of the average disciple to think in terms of *the* Ashram—the Ashram of the Christ, representing Sanat Kumara. When he turns his thoughts to the Master and the radiatory and magnetic group which He has attracted to Himself, the disciple almost inevitably thinks in terms of "my Master and His Ashram." Yet this is not in any sense a statement of truth. There is one great Ashram, the Hierarchy, radiating (after due absorption of light, understanding and power from Shamballa, and this inflow is adequate to hierarchical need) as it seeks to aid not only the human evolution but all the other evolutions, of which humanity, in several cases, knows nothing. The great Ashram is likewise magnetic in its effect, and through its magnetic potency (brought about by an inflow of first ray power) "units of life and devotion"— human beings—are brought into the Ashram as disciples in preparation for initiation. People are apt to regard magnetic

THE RAYS AND THE INITIATIONS

potency as evidence of love; it is, in reality, evidence of the radiation of love when enhanced and strengthened by first ray energy. *It is the admixture* (if I may use such a peculiar term) *of love and will which produces radiation.* It is the conscious use by the Hierarchy of the power coming from Shamballa which results in the magnetic impact and the spiritual "pull" which draws the soul, incarnated in the body, towards the Ashram. This pull is directed towards the world of souls which is, through its manifesting units, under-going experience in the school of life, yet overshadowed by the soul on its own level. It is this overshadowing soul which absorbs and utilises the magnetic power and which, from soul levels, transfers it to the souls of men.

There is still another point upon which I would like to touch. Owing to the fact that the Law which governs the Hierarchy is the second systemic law, the Law of Attraction, students are apt to think that magnetism is a second ray quality. They are right in so far that all the systemic laws are expressions of the life of God through the medium, at this time, of the second ray, which makes our solar system a second ray system. All other laws and qualities (for a law from the divine angle is the motivating, qualified agent of the divine will, as understood in Shamballa) are related to the second ray as it manifests through our planetary Logos. Nevertheless, magnetic action is more closely allied to first ray functioning than it is to the second ray, and is an aspect or quality of the Law of Synthesis. It was this magnetic power of the first ray to which the Christ referred when He said "I, if I be lifted up (The Ascension Initiation. A.A.B.), will draw all men unto me." He faced then those initiations which would qualify Him to become what is esoterically called "a Shamballa recipient." There is, in magnetic action, more of the element of the will and of an expressing pur-pose. In explanation it might be said that the radiation of the Hierarchy, which is definitely second ray in nature, and which is projected as attractive radiation, is implemented by the magnetic aspect. This—as the *Old Commentary* puts it—is "a point of focussed fire, found in the centre of the jewel.

It stirs to life the quality of love which permeates the Ashram of the Lord. Radiation then can penetrate to other centres and to other lives, and thus the Lord is served." It is this point of focussed dynamic will at the very heart of the Hierarchy which in reality implements the Plan.

To put the matter as simply as possible—too simply to be entirely exact, yet near enough to the truth to be clarifying and helpful—it is this magnetic potency, this dynamic active and energising will, which enables the Hierarchy to move forward upon the eternal Path. Its functions might be listed as follows:

1. It is the connecting energy which comes from Shamballa and "enlivens" (literally and occultly understood) the Ashram of Sanat Kumara. It is, in one sense, the higher correspondence to the prana which "enlivens" the dense physical body of man.

2. It is the stimulating factor which produces cohesion among the various Ashrams, and is one of the sources of hierarchical unity. Putting it in other words, it is the service of the Plan which binds the seven Ashrams, with their subsidiary Ashrams, coherently into the one great Ashram. The Plan is the expression of the Purpose or the Will of God.

3. This Shamballic magnetism not only relates the Ashrams to each other, but it is also the potency which evokes the will or the first ray nature inherent in every man but which is only consciously and definitely unfolded within the periphery of the great Ashram.

4. In a mysterious sense, it is the life of that seed or germ which will come to fruition in the third solar system.

a. In the "centre which we call the race of men" the potency of intelligence (developed in a previous solar system) is brought to fruition and the stirrings of the potency of love are felt.

b. In the "centre which is nearest to the Lord" the potencies of intelligence and love are expressed, and at the third initiation the magnetic pull of the potency of will is felt.

c. In the "centre where the will of God is known" the intelligent loving Master, now responsive to the energy of the will, is faced with the seven Paths whereon that will can come to fruition and the "units of love can be transferred because they also will and know." They can then form part of the third solar system which will be definitely under the influences coming from the cosmic mental plane, just as, in this solar system, the energies coming from the cosmic astral plane have been the major influence.

All this is, of course, an inadequate expression of abstruse truth. The cosmic astral plane is not an illusion, as is the astral plane with which we are all so unhappily acquainted. The reason for this lies in the fact that all our planes constitute the cosmic physical plane and are therefore regarded— as far as three worlds of human evolution are concerned —as illusion, for the dense physical substance is *not* a principle. This you have oft been told. The cosmic astral plane is a reservoir of love energy, pouring into two of our planes which constitute part of the cosmic etheric body—the monadic plane and the buddhic plane.

5. It is that which permeates the radiation from the Hierarchy to which humanity is responsive. No disciple or aspirant can be drawn into the periphery of the Hierarchy, and from thence into an Ashram, without finding that his will nature is being affected. It will only show itself at this stage as persistence and determination. Persistence is a quality of life and related to immortality, whilst determination is the lowest aspect of the will. Their development produces a reorientation which becomes a permanent attitude, and the disciple then becomes responsive not only to the "vitalised radiation" coming from the periphery of the Hierarchy but also, in an increasing measure, to the "magnetic pull" which emanates from the Hierarchy itself, and in particular from the Ashram to which he must eventually find his way.

If you will make a close study of all the above information, you may find some measure of enlightenment. It is the great simplicities which must be ever kept in mind: the three great divine aspects, the septenates of the evolutionary process, the divine qualities or principles, and the relation of energy to force. With these clearly held in mind, the detail is of small moment; the intuition rapidly assimilates and relates the detail, if there be need to do so, to the manifesting whole.

To return to our theme, which is the expression of the great Ashram through the medium of the seven Ashrams, it is this magnetic energy of the first aspect which is found at the heart of the seven Ashrams, energised and enlightened from the reservoir of will energy found at the heart of the great Ashram itself. This reservoir is fed from the "centre where the will of God is known," and the directing agent of this energy, within the Hierarchy itself, is the Christ and His two Associates, the Manu and the Mahachohan. The forty-nine subsidiary Ashrams (not all of which are yet functioning) are energised by the potency of will from the reservoir of energy at the heart of each major Ashram, these in their turn being fed from the central reservoir. The correspondence of this in the human centres is called the "jewel in the lotus."

Let us now study the formation of the great Ashram and then (this will have more meaning for you) the gradual formation of the seven Ashrams under direct ray activity. This process lies in the past history of humanity and I shall only briefly touch upon it. Once formed, it became the task of these seven Ashrams to produce the forty-two Ashrams. These seven Ashrams express ray qualities, and the whole forty-nine are expressive of the forty-nine fires, referred to in *The Secret Doctrine;* through these fires, the God of Fire seeks to make Himself known.

As we study some of the esoteric details connected with the life, the quality and, later, the appearance of the Ashrams of the Masters, I would remind you of certain points I have already made; your minds then will be predisposed to right thinking and interpretation. I am anxious for your approach to the subject to be correct. I have given you a number of definitions of an Ashram in the previous pages and in my other books, and I would have you bear these in mind. The concept of a college group, of a band of workers or of a number of men and women working under the supervision of a Master is too apt to colour your thoughts. The complete freedom from all coercion or from any supervision of daily activity, the instinctive reaction of all *within* the Ashram to the ray influence and to the "breath of the prevailing Will" (as it is called) is something very different. I seek in what I intend to impart to you to give a very different impression. In our next section, on the dual life of the initiatory process, the newer concepts may emerge more clearly. The points I want you to bear in mind are as follows:

1. The great Ashram, the Hierarchy, is composed of many Ashrams, creating an "invoking area" of relationship for Sanat Kumara.

2. The Christ, aided by the Manu and the Mahachohan, is the Coordinator of the entire life of the great Ashram.

3. The personnel of the great Ashram is today entirely provided from the ranks of humanity. This was not so in the earlier cycles.

4. The great Ashram is formed of seven major Ashrams and forty-two secondary Ashrams which are gradually forming.

5. The entire Ashram is a unity, for the ashramic life in its differentiated groups is guarded by a ring-pass-not.

6. This ring-pass-not is provided by radiation.

7. The forty-two lesser Ashrams are held together by the magnetic interplay of the whole.

8. Aspirants are drawn into relation with the Ashram through its radiation and enter finally into its magnetic field.

9. There is a dual flow of energy or force into the great Ashram:

    a. Energising life from Shamballa or what is called "unfettered enlightenment."

    b. The energy of active intelligence from Humanity, thus enabling the Masters to formulate the Plan.

10. The seven Ashrams are all concerned with the Plan.

11. The Master Morya is the Head of all esoteric schools which truly prepare an aspirant for ashramic contact and work. The reason that a first ray Master is thus the Head is because it is the Will aspect which is developed within the Ashram.

12. It is the service of the Plan which binds the seven Ashrams, with their subsidiary Ashrams, into the one great Ashram.

13. It is only within his ray Ashram that the will of the disciple is developed.

14. The magnetic, dynamic energy of the first aspect of divinity is found at the heart of each of the seven Ashrams, fed from a reservoir of will energy which is found at the heart of the great Ashram itself.

15. The forty-two subsidiary Ashrams are energised by the reservoir of will energy found at the heart of each of the major Ashrams.

16. The seven Ashrams express each the quality of their ray, one of the seven ray types.

If you will have these points in mind, the whole hierarchical theme will be recognised and correctly interpreted by you.

There was a time when (in the early history of the planet) there was no Hierarchy; there were only two major centres in the expression of the life of the Lord of the World: Shamballa and His embryonic throat centre, Humanity. Shamballa was the head centre. There was no humanity, such as we now know it, but only something so primitive that it is well-nigh impossible for you to grasp its significance or factual expression. But the life of God was there, plus an inherent "urge" and a dynamic "pull." These two factors rendered the mass of men (if one may call them so) inchoately invocative, thus drawing from high spiritual centres certain developed and informed Lives Who—in increasing numbers—"walked among men" and led them slowly, very slowly, forward into increasing light. The early history of the Hierarchy falls into two historical eras in the process of its becoming a "mediating Centre":

First: The time when the relating, mediating, enlightening correspondences to Those we now call the Masters trod the earth with men and were not withdrawn and apparently invisible, as is now the case. Their task was to bring the primitive intelligence of humanity to the point where there could be the presentation of the Plan, with eventual cooperation. In occult parlance, Their work was the establishing of a rapport between the unrevealed second aspect (to which They were responsive) and Humanity. In this They succeeded, but the matter aspect and quality—that of active intelligence—was so strong that the second historical phase became essential.

Second: The time when the Hierarchy was created as we know it today; the heart centre of Sanat Kumara came into its own life, formed its own magnetic field, possessed its own ring-pass-not, and became a dynamic mediating centre between Shamballa and Humanity.

It has oft been told in occult and theosophical literature that the Hierarchy withdrew as a penalising measure because of the wickedness of mankind. This is only superficially true and is an instance of a man-made interpretation, giving us the first example of the fear-and-punishment psychology which—from that time on—has conditioned all religious teaching. The withdrawing Masters had Their Paul to distort the truth, just as had the Christ, Their august Head today. The truth was far otherwise.

The time came in those distant aeons when a certain percentage of human beings reached, through their own efforts, the stage (at that time demanded) of preparedness for initiation. This attainment brought surprising results:

a. It became possible for certain of the Masters to "return from whence They came."

b. It became necessary to provide conditions where

these men "accepted for unfettered enlightenment" could receive the needed training.

c. The process of creation had reached the evolutionary stage where the centres of the Lord of the World were differentiated; function and radiatory activity were established, and this produced a stronger "pull" and placed the Hierarchy "at the midway point." A station of light and power was formed. All this was made possible because humanity could now produce its own "enlightened ones."

These two historical periods (not events, except in so far that all TIME is a sequence or pattern of events) covered vast cycles; aeon by aeon, the work went on until we have today the three major centres in the planet, demonstrating great activity, much more closely related than ever before, and ready now to enter into a third historical period. In this coming cycle we shall see the first stages of the great spiritual fusion towards which all evolution tends; it will take the form of the externalisation of the Ashram, so that the Hierarchy (or the centre where the *love* of God is known and the purpose of Sanat Kumara is formulated into the Plan) and Humanity will meet on the physical plane and occultly know each other. Two centres then will be "visible in the light"—the Hierarchy and Humanity. When these two centres can work in full cooperation, then Shamballa will take form and will no longer be found existing only in cosmic etheric substance, as is now the case.

What this means, how it will be accomplished, and what the implications are, will be revealed in such a distant future that we need waste no time considering it. We are working and living in the initial stages of the period wherein preparation is being made for the emergence of the Hierarchy into the world of men. This emergence is at present purely on to mental levels, but when the thoughtform of exoteric existence is created by Humanity itself and the invocative cry is intense enough, then the Great Ashram will slowly make its appearance upon the physical plane.

On that plane, the distinction between the two centres

will be preserved, but the inner relationship and the spiritual fusion will steadily proceed until:

> Soul and personality are one,
> Love and intelligence are coordinated,
> Plan and fulfillment are achieved.

All this will be brought about through the invocative spirit in man, plus the initiatory process, carried on in the Ashrams of the great Ashram. What this coming process will entail of change in civilisation, in human nature and in the group expression of the human spirit—religions, society and politics—it is not possible here to say; so much lies hidden in the free will and right timing of mankind. But that future of spiritual cooperation and interplay within and without the great Ashram is assured, and for it all true disciples are working. The world situation today is therefore one of great interest. Humanity, the world disciple, is in process of recovering from a major test, prior to a great step forward towards a conscious approach to more spiritual living; this, factually, means a definite approach to the Hierarchy.

In the meantime the Hierarchy is orienting itself to a much closer rapport with humanity, and to an interior reorganisation which will make it possible to admit disciples in large numbers into the great Ashram. This will lead to the implementation of the lesser Ashrams and also to a preparation for the transmission of more of the Will energy, through the great Ashram, into the throat centre of Sanat Kumara, Humanity.

The seven major Ashrams are each responsive to one of seven types of ray energy and are focal points in the Hierarchy of the seven rays. The central, senior and major Ashram is (at this time) the repository of second ray energy, as this ray governs this second solar system. It is the Ashram of Love-Wisdom—the Ashram in which the Buddha and the Christ received Their initiations and through which each of Them works. It will be obvious that if the process of invocation and evocation governs the interplay of the planetary centres, you have in this fact another reason why the senior Ashram is second ray in quality. Invocation is related to radiation. Evocation is related to magnetism. These are two points worthy of your consideration.

The other six major Ashrams came sequentially into being as the invocation of primitive man reached such a point of intensity of expression that a response was evoked from Shamballa, via its ray Representatives, working with directed energy in the three worlds. A "point of radiatory force" was established, at first in relation to the second ray Ashram, and later to the other Ashrams. One by one, as the rays cycled into activity in the three worlds and eventually on the physical plane, the seven Ashrams were founded, developed and expanded until the time arrived—several aeons ago—when all seven Ashrams were fully organised, and through them passed a steady flow of human beings liberating themselves from the three worlds.

In the earliest times this flow of disciples was exceedingly small. One by one, individual aspirants found their way out of the ranks of humanity and inside the ring-pass-not of the Hierarchy. In the beginning, only the first two initiations were given and only through the instrumentality of the second ray; and at these initiations the World Teacher of the period officiated.

Then at a time when the seventh Ray of Ceremonial Order (the ray which plays so potent and mysterious a part in the phase of discipleship called initiation) was in cyclic activity, a much greater number of disciples appeared, prepared for initiation; the initiatory process was then administered in a seventh ray Ashram; this seventh ray Ashram was the second to be formed, owing to the fact that the seventh ray is the relating factor between life and matter upon the form side. Again, so the ancient Archives tell us, there came a great crisis in the evolution of humanity; this necessitated one of the rare cyclic changes which have distinguished the fluid policy of the Hierarchy. Men began to demonstrate responsiveness to the Law of Integration and *personality* appeared with all its potentiality for good and evil. Man became an integrated unit in the three worlds. A great possibility then emerged; man could, through training and the use of the mind, make contact with the soul. This had not hitherto been done except to a slight degree. This crisis therefore led to the creation, or rather to the appearance, of the initiatory process to which we have given the name of the third initiation.

The Hierarchy for the first time realised the complete success of the vast work, carried on in the human centre for millions of years. Soul and personality could be and were intelligently fused. This is one of the reasons why the Hierarchy regards the third initiation as the first major initiation; it marked a point of complete soul-personality integration. In the earlier initiations, the soul was present but was still only occasionally in control; constant failure in the three worlds was still possible, and the relation between the man in the three worlds and his soul was nebulous and largely potential. You will realise what I mean when I point out that many thousands of people in the world today have taken the first initiation and are oriented towards the spiritual life and the service of their fellowmen; their lives, however, frequently leave much to be desired, and the soul is obviously *not* in constant control; a great struggle is still being waged to achieve purification on all three levels. The lives of these initiates are faulty and their inexperience great, and a major attempt is instituted in this particular cycle to achieve soul fusion. When that is attained, then the third initiation (the first, hierarchically speaking) is taken. Today this triple process of preparation, purification and fusion is the ordinary practice of the disciple and the process has prevailed for untold years; but when this fusion first occurred, it marked a great hierarchical event. It was a crisis of supreme spiritual import.

As you know, the first human being out of that "centre which we call the race of men" to achieve this point was the Christ; in that first great demonstration of His point of attainment (through the medium of what was then a new type of initiation) the Christ was joined by the Buddha. The Buddha had attained this same point prior to the creation of our planetary life, but conditions for taking the third initiation were not then available, and He and the Christ took the initiation together. At this initiation, and since then for all initiates of that degree of attainment, They stood in the Presence of the One Initiator, the Lord of the World, and not in the Presence of the Initiate Who was then Head of the Hierarchy. This third initiation was taken in a fourth ray Ashram, the Ray of Harmony through Conflict. This Ashram had taken form and attained functioning activity some time earlier. You can see, under the Law of Correspondences, why this was so. The first human being in the fourth kingdom in nature to take this initiation did so in a fourth ray Ashram and then, esoterically speaking, "the Way lay open toward the Cross"; the initiate faced the process of extension on the Cross, and from that vantage point could view the three worlds. The fourth initiation then became a possibility; the crucifixion faced the disciple of the third degree with its promise of complete liberation and final resurrection.

You can see, therefore, what a tremendous crisis took place in the relation between Humanity and the Hierarchy —a crisis of such importance that Shamballa became involved and the Lord of the World Himself admitted the initiate to the higher contacts. Between that time and the crucifixion of the Master Jesus, the sixth ray Ashram, the fifth and the third, have all been formed around the nucleus of light, started by the ray Lords much earlier. The point of light and of will energy at the centre of each Ashram has existed for untold millennia of years, but the Ashrams themselves were only slowly formed around the nucleus as the various types of energy swept into manifestation and brought with them human types responsive to the ray energy.

When the Master Jesus took the Crucifixion Initiation, another crisis arose of equally great import, if not greater. The crisis was brought about because simultaneously with the crucifixion of the Master, the Head of the Hierarchy, the Christ, took two initiations in one: the Resurrection Initiation and that of the Ascension. These are the fifth and sixth initiations, according to the Christian terminology.

This was possible because the first ray Ashram was now active, making entry into the Council Chamber at Shamballa possible. When the Christ achieved this, He was deemed worthy of embodying in Himself a new principle in evolution and of revealing to the world the nature of the second ray aspect—the divine principle of love (as humanity calls it) or of pure reason (as the Hierarchy calls it).

Since that time, all the seven major Ashrams have been fully organised and are steadily increasing in radiatory activity. As you will have noted, the order of their appearance —under ray activity—was 2, 7, 4, 6, 5, 3, 1. In giving this item of ashramic information I am giving you more hints than you will immediately realise.

Each Ashram, as you know, expresses ray quality in its purest and most essential form. During the process of creating the seven Ashrams, they have shifted their focus (or location) from the lowest of the three levels of the abstract mental plane at each major crisis, until today the Ashrams are to be found on the buddhic plane and not on the mental plane at all. This marks the triumph of the hierarchical work, because pure reason—through the second ray—is now the dominant quality in all the Ashrams. Forget not in this connection that all the rays are subrays of the second Ray of Love-Wisdom, but that in the early days of hierarchical activity, it was the particular quality of the ray which dominated an Ashram that first demonstrated, and not the quality of the great major ray of which they were all a part.

Today this is all changing, though the process is not yet perfected, and pure reason or true love is beginning to manifest itself through the quality of all the rays, functioning through their respective Ashrams. The secondary ray quality will not die out or in any way be lessened, but each ray quality will serve to implement the expression of pure love, which is the essential and—at this time—the primary quality of the Lord of the World, Sanat Kumara.

As the centuries have slipped away and the potency of the rays has increased on Earth, humanity has become more and more invocative; this has necessitated the expansion of

the Hierarchy itself, and each Ashram has become the creator of six other Ashrams (few of them as yet complete, and
some entirely embryonic), so that, in fact, all the forty-nine
Ashrams are in the making. The second ray, for instance,
has five affiliated Ashrams and one of which only the nucleus
exists, and all these are working under its inspiration and
through the effect of the second ray central fire. All have at
their centre a second ray disciple. The third ray has already
two subsidiary Ashrams; the sixth has four, and so on. The
first ray is the only one at this time with no subsidiary fully
functioning Ashram, and this because the will aspect is as
yet very little understood and few initiates can meet the
requirements of the first ray initiation. This is no reflection
upon humanity. It is a question of divine timing and expediency, and Shamballa is not yet prepared for an influx
of first ray initiates. Ages must pass before this Will aspect
will have reached the stage of unfoldment and expression on
the physical plane and through the medium of mankind
which will warrant the fusing of six first ray fires—the purest
fires there are.

If you will add all the above information as a background to what you know about ashramic work today, you
will have a more complete picture of evocative and spiritual
reality. You know much (for I have told you much) anent
the Ashrams open today and the requirements for acceptance. It is essential that the *uniqueness* of the initiatory
process be discounted. Down the ages men have achieved,
are achieving and will achieve. The only difference is that—
as the intellect of man develops—the requirements for initiation become more drastic and exacting, and the initiate
therefore becomes of a distinctly higher order. The Master
today is infinitely wiser and more full of love and more
"occultly reasonable" than was the Master in Atlantean
times. This in itself constitutes a reasonable fact, does it
not, my brothers?

In considering the work carried forward in the Ashram
as it affects the Masters Themselves, two ideas automatically
emerge:

1. The Masters are also subject to limitation. The general idea of all aspirants is that They represent Those Who have achieved freedom, have been liberated, and are therefore held by no limiting circumstances whatsoever. This is not true, though—speaking relatively, or so far as humanity is concerned—it is a fact that the limitations by which They were held as human beings are no longer present. But one achieved freedom only opens the door to another and wider freedom on ahead, and the ring-pass-not of our planetary Life in itself constitutes a powerful limitation. Speaking symbolically, somewhere in that great dividing wall of our planetary circumference, the Master must find an exit and discover a door which will permit Him to enter the Way of the Higher Evolution in its more cosmic stages. This Way leads Them in awareness and consciousness and experience into that "life more abundantly" of which Christ spoke; the origin and source of this more abundant life is to be found on cosmic levels, and not on the levels of the cosmic physical plane to which humanity and the Masters have hitherto been confined.

2. I am dealing with states of awareness and with experiences and spiritual undertakings which lie outside my own personal realisation. But in spite of this truth, just as you in the position of aspirants and disciples know much about the Hierarchy, its life, aims and conditioning rules, so do I, a Master of the fifth degree, know much concerning what lies ahead of me; I can therefore endeavour to make some small part of these essential truths clearer to those who can profit by them. Such people will necessarily be initiated disciples.

Years ago (in 1922) when I gave the names of the seven Paths along one of which a Master must go *(Initiation, Human and Solar)*, it was felt by Those for Whom I was working that humanity was not ready for the information which I now propose to give. I would here remind you that I have ever stated that even the Hierarchy does not know exactly how humanity will react or what progress they will make within a given time. Since I gave the earlier exoteric information, the world war took place, the forces of hidden evil emerged for a short period and were then routed, and humanity has awakened to truer values and spiritual perception to a totally unexpected extent. Men have been so aroused by the past agony that never again will they fall asleep; they may move slowly but they are, for the first time on a large scale, really thinking and visioning. For this reason, it is now possible to give out teaching hitherto regarded as too advanced. There are those alive today who *will* understand; there are those coming into incarnation during the next fifty years whose feet are already set upon this Higher Way, and it is for them I write.

There are certain preliminary statements which would be useful here, if there is to be any real and true measure of clear thinking and understanding. Their significance will emerge as we study the Seven Paths and the Nine Initiations. I shall do no more than state them, but you must regard them as basic:

1. Our seven planes—the mastery of which is our idealised spiritual goal—are after all only the lowest cosmic plane, the cosmic physical plane. From the cosmic angle, the Masters are only beginners, and even our deeply desired initiations (from the first to the sixth) are simply preparatory initiations for those to be taken later on upon the Way of the Higher Evolution.

2. This Higher Way is a sevenfold Way. The seven Paths form its seven modes of approach to the One Way and together create it. These seven Paths are not ray-conditioned. By that I mean that entering one or another of them is not in any way dependent upon the ray which conditioned the Master earlier. The Masters and the still higher initiates, such as the Christ, can choose any Path which makes its appeal in such a manner that complete rightness is registered in the initiate's consciousness and He *knows* that He can go no other way.

3. At the sixth initiation, called the Initiation of Decision, the Initiate makes His final choice as to the Way that He will go, and from that decision there is no turning back.

4. Three things will necessarily colour any decision the Initiate may make; His ray, which still determines Him, His past activities as they may fit Him for specialised work, plus a sense of freedom hitherto unrealised. The decision might be regarded as the first gesture of the advancing Master toward liberation from all ray limitations. As He moves forward on the Higher Way, He will find Himself, as a result of the new training and field of experience, able to work on any ray.

5. The fifth initiation is usually called that of the Resurrection by the orthodox Christian, but this is not its real name; it is in reality the Initiation of Revelation, because the Initiate gains His first vision of the Door through which He must pass on to the seven Paths. He glimpses it and that is all, but between that initiation and the next in which He must perforce make His decision, He comes to understand the nature of the energy which each Path expresses and which will eventually evoke from Him a decisive activity.

6. By passing through the second great Door of Initiation, the Initiate begins to learn the significance and the attractive potency of the Central Spiritual Sun, to which all the Paths eventually lead.

7. The fifth and sixth initiations are to the Master what the first and second are to the disciple—simply initiations of the threshold and not true initiations from the cosmic angle. The first true initiation upon the Higher Way is called the Initiation of Resurrection; this has no reference to the fifth initiation.

8. The decision made by the Master enables Him to take the required training to enter His chosen Path, and this training is taken entirely upon cosmic etheric levels—the four highest subplanes of the cosmic physical plane—the buddhic, atmic, monadic and logoic planes.

9. On these planes the spiritual and the divine will is developed and brought into use; these are aspects of that undefinable purpose to which we give the simple name: the Will of God. Intelligence and love have been fully unfolded in the Master, but the will is embryonic still, from the

standpoint of Those responsible for training the Master and the higher Initiate. It is only by means of the divine will that the Master begins to free Himself from ray limitations.

10. I would remind you of an earlier statement that the Hierarchy reacts or responds to the energies and influences coming from the cosmic astral plane; from that level of spiritual life true divine love pours into it. Shamballa reacts to the cosmic mental plane, and therefore to the nature and purposes of the Mind of God; the expression of THAT which overshadows Sanat Kumara is similar to the soul overshadowing the incarnated spiritual man.

If you will bear these facts in mind, some light may break through and, in any case, when the student or disciple returns to incarnation, this imparted knowledge (stored in the soul's content) will then be usefully available.

I would like to enlarge somewhat upon an earlier remark. I stated that the "seven Ashrams are 'proving grounds' for all the Masters confronted with the sixth Initiation of Decision."

This constitutes part of the problem facing the Masters Who are thus to move forward; it is particularly crucial for Those Who have chosen the first Path, the Path of Earth Service, and for all in preparation for the sixth initiation. This process of changing for a final, conditioning decision—in line, consciously realised, with divine Purpose and entailing responsiveness to Shamballa—is a major undertaking; it is related to the development of understanding the Will, and concerns the spirit or life aspect; it involves an increasing revelation of the purpose and the "fixed intention" of the planetary Logos but (even more than that) it has relation to extra-planetary sources and energies and to those cosmic conditions which are responsible for the Presence of Sanat Kumara upon the Earth. It is *will* which has brought Him here, and the unfoldment of the will nature of the Masters and still higher Initiates admits Them into His inner deliberations by means of the highest form of telepathic rapport or impression to be found upon our planet.

This impression is, however, made possible by the development of the intuition, and has no relation to the mind nature.

This training in decision is given by forcing the Master to make basic decisions within His Ashram affecting world work and involving all within the Ashram. It is given by His admission to the conclave of the Masters, meeting every seven years. At that conclave They make decisions which concern all forms of life in all the kingdoms in the three worlds and their evolutionary progress; it is put to the test in group form when the entire Hierarchy meets at Its centennial conference and—at that time—decides what form of crisis, on what level of consciousness, and involving what group of lives, must be implemented and presented to humanity, though the other kingdoms of nature will be necessarily implicated. The reason for this is that the meeting of such a planned crisis will hasten certain realisations. Forget not that humanity grows through the presentation of moments of crisis. These moments of crisis, based on past karma, conditioned by the point in evolution already achieved, and on the presence in the three worlds of certain appropriate ray forces, are brought to the point of precipitation by united decision in the conclave of the Masters.

These decisions do not affect man's free will, for the Hierarchy does nothing to condition man's approach to the crisis and, occultly speaking, Their "attitude is deliberately turned to other things" during the period of man's decision; thus the potency of Their thinking does not affect the human mind. Once the precipitation of the crisis is complete, and humanity has begun to take action of some kind, then the full attention of the Masters, working through Their Ashrams, is committed to the giving of full assistance to all those who are seeking to guide humanity along correct lines —a relative few among the countless millions of the ignorant.

While these centennial conclaves are being held at the close of the first twenty-five years of every century, the Lord of the World with the Members of His Council watch the process of decision in order to see how far *the will* of the

Hierarchy conforms to that aspect of the divine will which should be expressed in the three worlds as the result of Their decision. They watch also Those particular Masters Who should in a short time be ready for the sixth initiation, in order to see how much of that divine will They register and what is the nature and quality of Their use of it. By recording that quality, the Council at Shamballa is able to determine with great accuracy which of the seven Paths a certain Initiate will choose. In this manner They become aware of how many senior disciples will be needed to take over the headship of an Ashram, with a consequent admittance of many disciples to the initiation next in order for them. At the same time, aspirants on the periphery of an Ashram are enabled to move forward into full ashramic participation.

All this should give you some idea of the synthesis which expresses itself through the three planetary centres: Shamballa, the Hierarchy and Humanity. These are responsible for the conditioning of the other planetary centres and the consequent demonstration of divine intention. The basic purpose of Sanat Kumara is to bring about right relations in every field of His manifested life. The encouraging factor is today that the activity of humanity itself is, for the first time, concerned with the entire subject of right human relations and how to bring it about. I would have you reflect on this, for it means that, again for the first time, humanity is consciously responding to the will and intention of Shamballa, even though without realising the esoteric implications. This is of far greater importance than you can imagine, for it signifies a new relationship of a spiritual nature and deeply spiritual results.

The preparation of the Masters for this sixth initiation is exceedingly strenuous. They find it as difficult to achieve Their goal as does the average disciple as he looks ahead at the initiation which immediately confronts him. They have to master the technique of handling the most potent energy and influence in the world, that of the intelligence. They have to penetrate into the mystery of electricity and implement its expression in the creative process under the directive of Shamballa; They have to learn to work with electric fire in the same way as—much earlier—They worked with fire by friction as personalities, and with solar fire as disciples and lesser initiates. In this way, They become familiarised with what is meant by the words the "Central Spiritual Sun," just as They were familiar with the appearance of the physical Sun when members of the human family, and with the "Heart of the Sun" as Members of the Hierarchy. Again you can see the same unfolding synthesis—a synthesis which originates in that focal point of attractive dynamic energy, known to us as the Sun and its planets.

Thus within His Ashram the Master learns "occultly to decide" and to condition the creative centre for which He is responsible. He has to do this with the Ashram, surrounded by all those who are in training and who are the agents of His will. Through them He must act, and they thereby limit necessarily the vision to which He reacts, and step down the rate and quality of the energy of which He is the focal point. This energy constitutes the animating life of the Ashram as well as the force which the disciples and initiates must use in their work in the world, this of course in cooperation with the energy which each disciple within himself "occultly generates" and for which he—in his lesser degree—is responsible.

More anent this subject will be given when we study specifically the nine initiations wherein another synthesis, interlocking with the synthesis of the Will, will appear.

*The seven Paths confronting the Master*

It will be apparent to you now that the Master confronts two crises:

1. The crisis of the will, as it demonstrates in unalterable decision.
2. The crisis of the new step which will probably "cast Him adrift upon the shore of some distant sphere wherein His will must be expressed in love." These ambiguous words of the *Old Commentary* mean that

His decision will (with one exception) take Him away from all that He has hitherto known.

The majority of the Masters then enter into realms wherein They are needed "to impart, strengthen and enlighten that which is already fused, already strong and already full of light, but which needs that which He brings in order to express the all-encompassing whole."

I have to leave you with these words as food for reflection as there is little further that I may say upon this point. In any case and for all *deciding* groups of Masters, the work with the Hierarchy is over, except for the few Who choose Path I. Part of the mistake which the Buddha made was connected with this subject of decision. He loved humanity so much that He felt He could not and did not choose the Path which He was in reality ordained to follow; He chose instead the Path of Earth Service—which was not His Path at all. This He knows and will in due time pass on to His rightful Path. This little incident will demonstrate the complete freedom of choice which distinguishes the sixth initiation.

The seven Paths are, as you know from your study of *Initiation, Human and Solar* the following:

1. The Path of Earth Service.
2. The Path of Magnetic Work.
3. The Path of Training for Planetary Logoi.
4. The Path to Sirius.
5. The Ray Path.
6. The Path on which our Logos is found.
7. The Path of Absolute Sonship.

In that first book which I wrote for the world, I gave a simple definition of the exoteric significance of these Paths—so simple as to convey but little. I wrote then for the general public. I will now endeavour to convey some of the deeper meanings, writing as I do for advanced disciples and for initiates who—reading between the lines and understanding the symbolism involved—will comprehend according to their point in evolution.

As we approach the subject of the seven Paths, I would point out that the only basic point which can be presented to you is that of *relationship*. All these seven Paths lead to some objective which is thereby put in touch with our planetary life; these objectives—with the life and conditions they represent—present to the Master a vision of possibility. This vision is adequate to the task of drawing Him forth from the hierarchical Ashram, except in one case where vacancies in Shamballa need to be filled. The progressive experience of the greater Lives Who work in the Council Chamber of Sanat Kumara form no part of our studies. Many of these supreme Workers, as you have read in *A Treatise on Cosmic Fire,* found Their way to our planet from our sister planet, Venus, thereby in Their turn establishing relationship. Remember also that all the seven rays are the subrays of the great *cosmic* Ray of Love-Wisdom, which is ever expressive of relationship, implemented under the Law of Attraction; it is this form of esoteric attraction which draws the Master forth from His Ashram, conditions His decision and eventually leads to His passing through the door which opens on to other spheres and planes of activity.

Let us now consider—very briefly and necessarily inadequately—these seven Paths, taking them one by one:

## 1. The Path of Earth Service

This is the only Path which the Lord of the World regards as within the field of His spiritual interference. He reserves the right to retain in the service of the Hierarchy, and consequently of Humanity and the subsidiary evolutions, Those Masters Whom He regards at any one time as essential to the work to be done. This He does by asking Them to record Their decision when taking the sixth initiation, but to postpone moving on to one or other of the Paths until He gives the word. This word He has lately given in the case of the Buddha, Who has expiated His most understandable mistake and will now move forward—in His own good time—on to the Path which will lead Him to His rightful field of expression. In due time also, though not for some time, the Christ will move forward "to the place which calls Him," and the Master K.H. will assume the role of World Teacher. All these moves present their unique problems; they produce vacancies in the ranks of the Hierarchy which must be filled; they lead constantly to the inflow of new and powerful energies, for it must be recognised that these energies reach us along Paths leading to our planet as well as away from it. The invocative note of our united evolution at stated times and cycles sounds out and reaches Those Who are waiting for spiritual opportunity and service. They then follow the Path to our planet. From other spheres and planes They emerge along the lines of Their destiny and intention; we then call Them Avatars or Great Enlighteners or Planetary Saviours or Spiritual Regents; They act at the request of Sanat Kumara, given on higher cosmic levels.

It is nevertheless a statement of fact that in due time even Those Who choose the Path of Earth Service and remain in hierarchical work are eventually given the right to follow Their decision and pass to extra-planetary service. The Hierarchy, as we have seen, gives the needed training for that wider service, and the theme of what I might call the educational process to which the Masters submit is the unfoldment of the consciousness of the relationships which lie beyond the aura of our planet; this is, in reality, a higher and most abstruse branch of the Science of Impression, which disciples upon their lower level have to master. This aspect of impression is, however, concerned with the formless worlds, whereas all the impressions to which the disciple has to learn to react emanate from and within the cosmic physical plane, of which all our seven planes are an integral part; our highest spiritual world is a part of the substantial world. The Masters, therefore, are working at a conscious receptivity or sensitivity to the cosmic astral plane, the source of the spirit or energy of love. There is a fundamental connection between the Hierarchy (the source of expression of love on Earth) and the cosmic astral plane, and it is towards this objective that the Masters work Who choose the Path of Earth Service. The major ray of our solar system is that of love-wisdom, and there is no better field on which to master the preliminary stages of that divine unfoldment and receive the needed development and education than on the Earth.

On the Earth, the Masters have overcome glamour and illusion, and for Them no astral plane exists. Now ahead of Them, and owing to Their freedom from these "bewilderments," will come the opportunity to enter into the Heart of God, the centre of pure love, and from that centre to tread the way of love. All these seven Paths lead either to the cosmic astral plane or to the cosmic mental plane, according to the decision made at the sixth initiation. Upon the cosmic astral plane there is no glamour, but instead a great vortex of energy—the energy of pure love—under the domination of the Law of Attraction. It might be stated that:

Path 1. The Path of Earth Service leads to the cosmic astral plane.

Path 2. The Path of Magnetic Work leads to the cosmic astral plane.

Path 3. The Path for Training for Planetary Logoi leads to the higher levels of the cosmic mental plane.

Path 4. The Path to Sirius leads to the cosmic astral plane.

Path 5. The Ray Path leads to the cosmic mental plane.

Path 6. The Path the Logos Himself is on leads to the cosmic buddhic plane.

Path 7. The Path of Absolute Sonship leads to the cosmic mental plane.

Three Paths, therefore, lead to the realm of loving attractive energy; one Path leads to its higher correspondence, the cosmic level of pure reason; three lead to the realm of divine Mind. Four of the Paths relate the advancing Master to the Heart of the Great Life Who functions through this solar system, and three to His Mind nature. All of them lead the initiate eventually to the Central Spiritual Sun.

All Who work in Shamballa find Their way to this supreme centre by the three most arduous ways, whilst the remainder reach the same goal via the way of love.

The unfoldment of the will has much to do with Their decision. It must not be thought that Those Masters Who are on the first, third and fifth rays, for instance, follow the Path numerically the same; such is not the case; nor that Those Who are predominantly on the second line of energy find the cosmic astral plane Their goal. Such again is not the case. Their response and decision is based on a realisation of cosmic need—a need of which you can know nothing, any more than it is possible for you to comprehend the nature of cosmic evil.

As to the detail of the work of Those Who choose—until released—to stay on Earth and work in or with the Hierarchy, is there more that I can tell you? You know much anent this subject for I have given much—far more than has ever been given before. I have not dealt with the work of the Hierarchy in relation to evolutions other than the human, for two reasons:

Your unfoldment is still such that you do not and cannot yet include or register the consciousness or nature of the subhuman kingdoms.

The work done by the Hierarchy in those kingdoms is largely carried forward via humanity and modern scientific development.

There are many Masters Who do not work with the human kingdom at all, but are fully occupied with carrying out the divine Will in other kingdoms. With this work we have, at present, no concern. When any one takes the sixth initiation and makes his decision to follow the Path of Earth Service (either temporarily at the request of Sanat Kumara or until the end of the world cycle), he will find himself faced with a secondary decision as to which of the four kingdoms will profitably provide the field of his sacrifice and service. We will now consider:

## 2. The Path of Magnetic Work

In referring to this Path, I have stated that Those Who find Their way on to this Path work with fohat, or with the essential energy of our solar system which differentiates into seven major types of energy. Our planet with its ruling Lord is an integral part of the life expression of a still greater Entity, the solar Logos, and it is with the astral energy incident to His cosmic nature that the Master has to work. He learns to direct the currents of this essential energy, and because of His past relation to the Earth, He is part of the directing agency for astral energy within the planetary ring-pass-not. I also said that many Masters Who have reached liberation upon the fifth ray find Their way to this Path, thus proving the statement that it is not the ray which determines decision. These fifth ray Masters (among many others, of course) will be working in a great second ray vortex of energy.

It must be pointed out that, in its original state, this pure astral energy, directed under law into our planetary life, is free from all that is at present associated with the astral plane: glamour and delusion, emotional fog and poisonous deceiving phenomena. These well-known aspects of the astral plane are all the creation of humanity down the ages and present, therefore, an increasingly difficult problem to all aspirants. The tormenting turmoil and chaos of the astral plane are due largely to three factors:

The force of the constantly developing glamour as self-centered and undeveloped human beings create it.

The force of those aspirants and disciples who are seeking to combat this in their own lives and in the lives of others.

The inflow of pure solar astral energy, under cyclic law and the direction of the Master working on the second Path.

These three factors create great trouble; during the past crisis of the world war (1914-1945) it reached most serious proportions. The hierarchical crisis to which I have earlier referred was involved, and many Masters from the various Ashrams made a decision to work on this second Path in order to bring order out of chaos by pouring into the planetary astral plane pure astral energy, untainted by glamour and revelatory of pure love. They were experts in timing and in energy manipulation.

You will also note how three types of astral energy are therefore related:

The astral force of our planet, distinctive of the planetary astral plane in the three worlds of human enterprise.

The astral force of the solar Logos, the true God of Love.

The astral energy of the cosmic astral plane.

These forces are symbolised to the manipulating Master by a triangle. In the *Old Commentary* it says:

"The Master throws Himself—under the liberating Law of Sacrifice—into the vortex of the astral life of the One to Whom our Lord relates Himself with humble joy. And as the Master works, there forms before His eyes a triangle of force in shades of varying rose. By His magnetic power, He concentrates the energy required. Then through this triangle of force, as through an open door, He sends the potency of love into our planet, and till His cycle ends He thus must work."

This is but a rough translation of some very ancient phrases, and is perhaps less symbolic than it may appear. It is in connection with this Path that the work of the Triangles which I initiated is related; the function of these Triangles is in reality to facilitate the work of distributing the pure incoming love energy (expressing itself as light and as good-will) into the Hierarchy and Humanity. This deeply esoteric purpose of the Triangles will not be understood by the general public, but some of you who read this will appreciate the opportunity to serve in this manner *consciously*.

The Path of Magnetic Work takes the Master, first of all, to the Heart of the Sun, and from thence to the cosmic mental plane, passing through and pausing temporarily upon the cosmic astral plane. The above statement does not in reality refer to progress from point to point in an ordered sequence. It refers to high states of awareness and to a form of cosmic contact which is registered by the Master from the point at which He stands upon this second Path, for all the planes are interpenetrating. This has been somewhat easy to understand in connection with our seven planes, as the rarer substances could be visualised as interpenetrating the denser. It is not so easy to comprehend, however, when we pass out of the cosmic physical plane (in our imagination, needless to say) and enter those planes of which we know nothing and of whose composition and substance (if they are substantial, as we understand the term) we are totally ignorant; besides that, we are not in a position to ascertain the truth.

The method of the Master's work upon this Path is also not easily understood. It can be summed up in the following words which may bring some light via their united meaning (each phrase contributing an idea), if due reflection is brought to bear upon them:

Isolated Unity . . . . . . . . . . . the position of the Master
A positive Focus . . . . . . . . . . the mental attitude
Sound, under the Law
 of Attraction. . . . . . . . . . . the means employed
Precipitation . . . . . . . . . . . . the intention visioned
Passage through the Triangle . . . the projection ensuing
Directive work under
 the Law of Distribution . . . . . direction towards the goal

These phrases may give some vague idea of a process, based on "reception, then direction, producing rejection and impact where the rejecting agency ordained."

Another aspect of the work done by the Master on the second Path is the drawing off of those phases of glamour which no longer have the power to deceive mankind. They are not allowed to accumulate or to remain upon the astral plane. They are therefore, through the magnetic power of the Master, withdrawn from our planetary life and are "occultly absorbed" by the Master; the substance of the glamour, purified and freed from all that conditioned it on the planetary astral plane, and with only the pure essence retained, sets the law in motion which draws this purified remainder into the cosmic astral plane.

Constantly, therefore, this great circulatory process goes on, demonstrating anew the essential synthesis underlying all life—human, planetary, systemic and cosmic; it reveals also that the Law of Attraction, the Law of Magnetic Work, and the cosmic Law of Synthesis are three aspects of one Law for which, as yet, we have no name.

It might be said that the Masters working on the second Path are working in relation to and in contact with certain great Lives Who work on the periphery of the constellation Libra, the Balances. This is due to the fact that Those Masters Who can work with magnetic energies, and with the three above Laws, have achieved a point of balance which makes Their work possible; it involves also a poised attention and directive power, permitting the inflow of energies from Libra which could not otherwise enter our planetary life at all. These Libran energies enter our solar system via the Heart of the Sun and are peculiarly amenable to magnetic attraction and distribution.

All these Paths gradually came into being when our planetary Logos created the Earth and started the *involutionary* process of creation, leading in due time but much later, to *evolution*. They are therefore, all of Them, Paths of Return. This second Path was one of the first to be used and (again quoting the *Old Commentary*) "the door once opening inward now opens outward and permits the exit of those who hold the key because they entered by that door in aeons long gone by."

All the Masters (and not only Those upon the fifth ray) receive careful training in the manipulation of energies, and hence the statement of the Master K.H. to His disciples that the occultist has to learn to master and control the forces and energies within himself; the disciple and the initiate work with hierarchical energies and with the forces of the kingdoms of nature in the three worlds; the Master receives instruction in the handling of the energies which are extra-planetary but within the solar ring-pass-not. Those Masters Whose decision it is to tread the second Path are taught the control and direction of systemic energies and of certain energies emanating from Libra and from one of the stars in the constellation of the Great Bear. In the more advanced stages of Their work, and when the Master is far more advanced than the word indicates, He works consciously upon the cosmic mental plane; His activities will then be concerned with the relation of the energies of the Great Bear to the Pleiades, and their dual relationship (a higher correspondence to atma-buddhi) to the solar system and only incidentally to our Earth. Great is the interlocking, the interdependence and the interpenetration!

## 3.  The Path of Training for Planetary Logoi

It is obviously impossible to say much about this Path. Those Masters Who tread it find Their way to the various schools for the training of planetary Logoi which are found within certain of the major planetary schemes, as stated in *Initiation, Human and Solar*. They are necessarily few in number, and a small group of Them remains to study in our particular planetary enterprise under Sanat Kumara. This They do after making Their decision and passing through the door on the periphery of our planetary ring-pass-not. Then—out of incarnation and working through the medium of the higher telepathy—They receive instruction of a nature incomprehensible to us, from the Members of the Council Chamber at Shamballa, and primarily from two of the Buddhas of Activity. Having learnt the technique and having passed certain tests, They move into the planetary life of Venus, our Earth's Alter-Ego, and there They complete Their training, as far as our solar system can give it, finding Their way eventually on to the cosmic mental plane.

Two things should be borne in mind in connection with this abstruse subject:

First: These Masters work primarily with the "psyche"

or the soul aspect within the solar system. They are occupied with the subtler expressions of consciousness, with occult impressibility and that acute sensitivity which produces instant and accurate registration of all soul reactions within any particular planetary life. These kingdoms are not necessarily identical with those found on the Earth, but they are, in all cases, vast groups of living forms which are manifestations or expressions of the nature of any particular planetary Logos. The Masters taking this training are not occupied with individual states of consciousness *within* any group. *It is the consciousness of the whole,* and its responsiveness to cosmic impacts, that engages Their attention. They are not (if I might so express it) interested in any individual unit of any kind or in its individual reactions, responsiveness or susceptibility to impression. They are only concerned with those higher processes of identification which indicate an advanced state of evolutionary development. Their work is to further progressive development of identification. They begin with the identification of the Monad within our planetary sphere with the Purpose and the Will of the Lord of the World, and proceed—as Their training produces the desired capabilities—with greater identifications within the solar system. Beyond that we need not proceed.

Their whole training is concerned with the planetary, systemic and cosmic building of the antahkarana, for it is via the antahkarana that spirit works, that life processes are controlled, and the will of all developing aspects of Deity function. Forget not that relating our planet to the planet Venus is a planetary antahkarana, passing from thence to the Heart of the Sun and later to the cosmic mental plane. There are "rainbow bridges" carrying the sevenfold energies of the seven rays from planet to planet, from system to system, and from plane to plane on cosmic levels. It is over these bridges that the will of the related spiritual Identities is projected, producing that synthesis of effort which is distinctive of the cooperative systemic life. The work of the Masters in training from our planet is, among other things, to unfold within Themselves not only sensitivity to systemic purpose, but the ability to transmit that Purpose to the Council Chamber at Shamballa. They have—in an extra-planetary sense—a definite correspondence with and relation to the group of Nirmanakayas within our planet Who work in contemplative activity with the antahkarana which connects the Hierarchy with Shamballa and Humanity with the Hierarchy.

As planetary Logoi when Their Own time comes, these Masters will be concerned with the registration of the Purpose and expressed Will of some solar Logos. They will then, through the planetary and systemic antahkarana, supervise the gradual evolutionary impartation of that Will (which is now Theirs) to all the forms through which They function in any particular planet for which They have assumed responsibility. This definitely involves working with the soul aspect and with the unfoldment of conscious responsiveness and sensitive reaction to all the higher impressions.

Second: These Masters are the directing builders and Creators eventually of all forms of planetary life—forms embodying qualities and intentions as yet undreamed of by us. They have developed in Themselves a perfected synthesis of the two energies of atma-buddhi, or of spiritual will and spiritual love, completely unified and energetically active in a comprehensive condition seldom attained by any other group of Masters in training.

It must be realised that the Buddhas of Activity, of Whom there are only three on our planet, are similarly active. They are active love-wisdom or a complete synthesis of active intelligence, active love and active will. The Masters on this third Path will, therefore, some day complete Their training for planetary Logoi by attaining the status of Buddhas of Activity, and will for a period serve in that capacity in some planetary scheme, before taking the control and guidance of Their Own body of manifestation.

The training of these Masters on the third Path might be described as an intensive study of a most exalted form of the Science of Impression. The supreme task of a planetary

Logos is to impress His sevenfold body of manifestation, via its seven states of consciousness and the seven centres, with His will and intention; these are progressively imparted as the etheric body is brought into an increasing state of receptivity through the awakening of the seven planetary centres, primarily the three major centres. The Masters thus in training gain experience of the methods used by the planetary Logoi of all the seven sacred planets, and the training is therefore an exceedingly lengthy one. It must be remembered however that—except in dense physical incarnation and, therefore, conditioned by the brain and its special limitations—the spiritual man is not conscious of time, once He is separated from the physical body. Time is the sequential registration by the brain of states of awareness and of progressive contacts with phenomena. There is no such thing as time on the inner planes, as humanity understands it. There are only cycles of activity or of non-activity; this non-activity for Masters on the third Path takes the form of cyclic periods of contemplation and mental activity, followed by active periods of energy direction to impress the will of certain planetary Logoi and Their agents upon the Council Chamber of our planet in particular, and upon other planets, as Their training is perfected.

It is the impulsive incentive of these Masters which bridges and links between the Monad on the monadic plane and the three worlds of dense expression on the cosmic physical plane; in this process the antahkarana between the spiritual man in incarnation and the Spiritual Triad is aided and finally constructed, but this is only incidental to the far greater work of relating Shamballa to all kingdoms in nature and to other planets.

The number of Masters deciding on this Path is, as I said, not large; the training is peculiarly arduous and is followed, when opportunity is offered to function as a planetary Logos, by an act of sacrifice which confines Them indefinitely to the limitations of the ring-pass-not of Their body of manifestation, a planet. It is for this reason that Sanat Kumara has ever been called "The Great Sacrifice."

*Certain Hierarchical Changes*

Before proceeding with our consideration of the seven cosmic Paths, I would like to pause here and clarify your mind, A.A.B., and answer certain questions which you are formulating.

Some years ago (in 1925) I gave out to the world through your instrumentality *A Treatise on Cosmic Fire*. In that volume I elaborated upon the very elementary information given upon this subject in *Initiation, Human and Solar*—a book published earlier (in 1922). In both these volumes I touched upon the cosmic Paths. I gave (in very abstruse terms) some information; the terms were so abstruse that few can understand their meaning. The true significance is only for advanced initiates, of which I am not one, from Their point of view, though from yours I may be. In *Initiation, Human and Solar* very little was said, because the book was written for the general public and thus only a few ideas were indicated to point direction. Now, in *A Treatise on the Seven Rays* I have added to that already given; this book is, however, intended for a much larger number than those who read (and claim, erroneously, to understand) *A Treatise on Cosmic Fire*. In what I have to say, the teaching is carefully guarded. Two things should, however, be pointed out here in order to save confusion:

1. It had not been the intention of the Hierarchy to give any further information anent these Paths; it was felt that enough had been said about this naturally incomprehensible subject. Owing, however, to the fundamental changes in the hierarchical plans, this decision was altered. I was permitted to add to that already given. This was due to two causes:

a. The tremendous unfoldment of the human consciousness during the last twenty-five years warrants more information; so many aspirants were being admitted to the Path of Discipleship and were finding their way into the Ashrams, thus forcing the passage of many initiates on to the Way of the Higher Evolution. This in itself is a most joyous happening, but necessitated many ashramic adjustments.

b. Owing to this advancement, owing to the increased sensitivity of the human mechanism, and owing to the decisions humanity is in process of making (as a result of the frightful testing period of the war, 1914-1945), the Hierarchy—far earlier than had been hoped or anticipated—has prepared Itself for physical plane manifestation, or for what is called by Them "the process of externalisation."

This has necessarily produced problems, and among them the strictly hierarchical problem of the passage of the initiate of the sixth degree on to the cosmic Paths. You will find, if you study closely the three presentations of the teaching (in *Initiation, Human and Solar, A Treatise on Cosmic Fire,* and *A Treatise on the Seven Rays*) what may appear to you as contradictions or differences. This is not truly so, but the casual reader may feel them to be present even though the differences are apparent more than real. Two causes account for this:

a. The decision to throw open initiations higher than the fifth to the ready Master, and to familiarise the world of aspirants with their existence. Little has ever been given beyond the fifth initiation. Many initiates are becoming Masters, and many disciples are achieving the first initiation, and this fact confronts the three Great Lords Who rule the Hierarchy with a definite problem.

b. To make the sixth initiation and not the fifth initiation the Initiation of Decision. Here I must state the existence of a hierarchical problem: the use of the will aspect in the unfoldment of the initiate. It must be remembered that this first ray aspect is:

A definite and most potent energy. It is the most potent energy in the planetary life and is carefully held in leash by Those Who are in a position to wield it.

The medium whereby the *purpose of creation* is finally revealed.

The force which enables the Hierarchy to present the Plan in the three worlds.

The needed dynamic whereby the "deciding" Master sets His foot upon the Path of the Higher Evolution.

Owing to the success of the influence of this Shamballa energy upon humanity when the experiment was made to test its impact without stepping it down through the medium of the Hierarchy, the entire course of man's spiritual history was most peculiarly altered. This had not been anticipated, for—as oft I have told you—the Masters know not which way mankind will go, nor may They interfere by action or thinking in humanity's decision. It was therefore necessary to control more definitely the passage of initiates on to the seven Paths; only a certain number are required to fulfill cosmic intention; it was therefore decided to make the rules of entrance more difficult and more rigid.

Forget not, brother of mine, that this is not the first time that this has happened. Changes were made in Atlantean times; the door of entrance for the animal kingdom or for animal man into the human kingdom was stopped. No more units have since then been admitted from the third kingdom into the fourth, except in a few cases and for specific reasons. Here, however, you have a reverse situation. The Hierarchy, owing to its constitution at that time and to the fact that very few, relatively, of our Earth humanity were members of the Hierarchy, could not influence directly the more developed human beings or train more aspirants. They therefore closed the door. That particular condition does not now exist, and the supreme Directors of the seven cosmic Paths are today in the same position as was the Hierarchy then; the word has gone forth to our three Great Lords—the Manu, the Christ and the Mahachohan—via the three Buddhas of Activity, to act in order to tighten up on requirements, to make the sixth initiation and not the fifth, the decisive one, and to present those on the seven rays with a wider range of choices and a greater diversity of choice. Thus the Masters will have nine choices to face when They face Their decision; there will then be no need for Those on certain rays to pass to certain already determined Paths, but They can move forward under Their Own inspiration and with greater freedom. The cosmic mental plane is not barred to Them, as has hitherto been the case.

All these changes have been due to the successful response of our planetary life, expressed through the human kingdom at this time, to the processes of evolution and to the inflow (since 1825) of the will energy from Shamballa. This, in its turn, is due to the progress of Sanat Kumara Himself, within His Own identified life upon the cosmic Path which emerges from the cosmic mental plane. All that we can contact and know is interdependent, and the unfoldment of the Life in Whom we live and move and have our being affects every aspect and department of His manifestation, just as the successful spiritual unfoldment of a human being and his ability to contact his soul produces incredible changes in the personality and affects every aspect and organ of his little manifestation upon the physical plane.

2. The intelligence of humanity now is of such a nature that certain earlier initiations no longer exist, and mankind has shown itself to possess the potentialities which will enable its individual units to tread not only the one or two cosmic Paths hitherto open to them, but all of them, if given the right training. This the premature discovery of the release of atomic energy has well demonstrated to the Hierarchy.

All these factors have forced a reorganisation in the Plans at Shamballa and, in a unique conference, in that far greater Council Chamber over which our Solar Logos presides, greater opportunity was consequently offered to the Members of our planetary Hierarchy. I stress that point: the opportunity was not offered or presented to the fourth kingdom in nature, but to the fifth kingdom.

It is all these facts which have caused what may look to you like discrepancies and limitations in what I have given and in comparison with that given in the earlier volumes of this Treatise, but they are not so in reality. The Master of the fifth initiation, even if now He does not at that time make His decision, faces intelligently and with some understanding of the choices to be made, the sixth initiation and its decisions. He begins to take also the particular training, and to this the teaching in *A Treatise on Cosmic Fire* now applies. He is shewn the newer opportunity, the modes of decision, and the limitations which are no longer legitimate. I would like to point out here that these changes are a cause of deep joy to the Hierarchy and to the Great Lives in the Council Chamber at Shamballa, for they indicate the strength and potency of Sanat Kumara's success and the incredible progress made in the consciousness of humanity as a consequence; this will lead also to future paralleling decisions on the physical plane in human affairs; this deeply spiritual and mysterious success (mysterious because the human mind knows naught about it) was also the reason for the violent attempt of the Forces of Evil to gain control, and their resultant failure.

### 4.  *The Path to Sirius*

I have frequently hinted in my various books that the Sun, Sirius, is closely related to our planetary Life; much is known in the Hierarchy anent this connection, and the particular relationship of this fourth Path to humanity, the fourth kingdom in nature, but little can be communicated to the general public. I may, however, tell you certain things which may make your imaginative rangings (if I may use so strange a phrase) creatively profitable to you.

This great Sun which is to our solar Logos what the Monad is to the spiritual man, has a peculiar part to play where our Earth is concerned. It might be considered by those with a sound sense of occult proportion that our tiny planet with its planetary Logos (one of the "imperfect Gods" of *The Secret Doctrine)* would be too small to enter in the slightest way into the consciousness of that Supreme Illumined Entity Who is greater even than our Solar Logos.

Such, however, is the case. There is a relationship of very
ancient date between our Lord of the World, Sanat Kumara,
and the Lord of Sirius, and this exists in spite of the fact that
our planet is not a sacred planet. It might be added that
our planet is, in the immediate cycle, owing to the factors
I have lately considered with you, rapidly passing out of
this category, and on the inner planes and subjectively considered is a sacred planet; the effects of this transition from
non-sacred to sacred have not fully demonstrated themselves
objectively. The mystery of this relationship *is* partially revealed at one of the higher initiations and it is then realised
by the initiates that there is a good and adequate reason
for the relation and that the following esoteric events, relations and happenings are simply consequences:

1. The majority of liberated humanity, and therefore
a large number of the initiates who have to make decision,
choose this way to the cosmic centre.

2. The relationship as it expresses itself is between the
Hierarchy and Sirius, and not between Shamballa and that
stupendous Sun. The energy evoked in response to this relationship enters the Hierarchy via the Heart of the Sun,
creating as a consequence a triangle of spiritual energy of
enormous potency. You have, therefore:

Sirius<br>*<br>The Hierarchy  *  *  Heart of the Sun

3. As progress is made in the course of taking the
higher initiations, it becomes apparent to the initiate that
two major streams of energy enter our planetary life:

a. A stream of energy coming from the cosmic mental
plane and from that focal point which is to Sanat
Kumara what the egoic lotus, the soul, is to the spiritual
man; it carries the life principle of our planet and centres itself in Shamballa. From there it is dispersed
throughout all forms upon the planet and we call it
LIFE. It must be remembered that this life principle
embodies or is impregnated with the will and purpose

of THAT which overshadows Sanat Kumara as the soul overshadows the personality.

b. A stream of energy coming from the sun, Sirius; this enters directly into the Hierarchy and carries with it the principle of buddhi, of cosmic love. This, in a mysterious way, is the principle found at the heart of every atom.

The life principle follows the line of 1.3.5.7, whilst the buddhic flow follows the line of 2.4.6. Thus atma-buddhi becomes the blended reality which is brought to full unfold-ment as evolution proceeds. The energy of Sirius by-passes (to use a modern word) Shamballa and is focussed in the Hierarchy. Its effect is not felt until after the third initiation, though the Masters use this energy whilst training disciples for the second, the fourth and the sixth initiations.

4. The entire work of the Great White Lodge is con-trolled from Sirius; the Ashrams are subjected to its cyclic inflow; the higher initiations are taken under its stimula-tion, for the principle of buddhi, of pure love (i.e., love-wisdom) must be active in the heart of every initiate prior to the initiation of the great decision; it is therefore only initiates of the fifth, sixth and higher initiations who can work consciously with the potent buddhic "livingness" which permeates all Ashrams, though unrecognised by the average disciple.

5. This Sirian influence was not recognised, and little of it was definitely focussed in the Hierarchy, until Christ came and revealed the love of God to humanity. He is the expression, par excellence, of a Sirian initiation, and it is to that high place He will eventually go—no matter what duties or hierarchical obligations may take Him elsewhere between that time and now. The Buddha was originally to have chosen the fourth Path but other plans confront Him now and will probably claim His choice.

6. Sanat Kumara is not on the Sirian line but—to speak in symbols, not too deeply veiled—Lucifer, Son of the Morn-ing, *is* closely related, and hence the large number of human beings who will become disciples in the Sirian Lodge. This

is the true "Blue Lodge," and to become a candidate in that Lodge, the initiate of the third degree has to become a lowly aspirant, with all the true and full initiations awaiting him "within the sunshine of the major Sun."

7. None of the above facts indicates divergence of view between Shamballa and the Hierarchy, nor do they signify cleavage or differing aims and goals. The whole subject is reflected in such minor relations on Earth as those between:

a. The Spiritual Triad and the Personality.
b. The mental unit and the manasic permanent atom.
c. Atma-Buddhi.
d. The Christ and the Buddha.

The above somewhat uncorrelated items of information will give you a general idea of the significant connection between our unimportant little planet and that vast expression of divinity, the Life which is manifesting through Sirius; it is an expression which is organised and vital beyond anything man can vision and which is free to a completely unlimited extent, again beyond the power of man to comprehend. The principle of freedom is a leavening energy which can permeate substance in a unique manner; this divine principle represents an aspect of the influence which Sirius exerts on our solar system and particularly on our planet. This principle of freedom is one of the attributes of Deity (like will, love and mind) of which humanity knows as yet little. The freedom for which men fight is one of the lowest aspects of this cosmic freedom, which is related to certain great evolutionary developments that enable the life or spirit aspect to free itself from the impact, the contact and the influence of substance.

It is the principle of freedom which enables Sanat Kumara to dwell on the Earth and yet stand free from all contacts, except with Those Who have trodden the Path of Liberation and now stand free upon the cosmic physical plane; it is that which enables the initiate to achieve a state of "isolated unity"; it is that which lies behind the Spirit of Death and forms the motivating power of that great releasing Agency; it is that which provides a "pathway of power" between our Hierarchy and the distant sun, Sirius, and gives the incentive towards the "culture of freedom" or of liberation which motivates the work of the Masters of the Wisdom; it is that which produced the ferment and the vortex of conflict in far distant ages and which has been recognised in the present through the results of the Law of Evolution in every kingdom in nature; this is that which "substands" or lies under or behind all progress. This mysteriously "exerted influence," this "pulling away" from form (as we might simply call it), emanates from Sirius and for it we have no name; it is the law of which the three cosmic laws—the Laws of Synthesis, of Attraction and of Economy—are only aspects. None of these three subsidiary laws imposes any rule or limitation upon the Lord of the World. The Law of Freedom, however, does impose certain restrictions, if one can use such a paradoxical phrase. It is responsible for His being known as the "Great Sacrifice," for (under the control of this law) He created our planetary life and all that is within and upon it, in order to learn to wield this law with full understanding, in full consciousness, and yet at the same time to bring release to the myriad forms of His creation.

The Law of Economy affects humanity as a whole today throughout every phase of its life; the Law of Attraction is beginning to gain some control, particularly in the work which the Hierarchy undertakes to do; and many initiates and senior disciples are becoming aware of the significance of the Law of Synthesis and are reacting to its impact. Later on, when moving to one of the seven Paths, the Master will work with the Law of Freedom. This is not, as you may well surmise, its true name, for in the last analysis, freedom and liberation are *effects* of its activity. This unique and mysterious law governs the Life and the Lives upon Sirius, and it is to that unknown "sphere of functioning and intelligent activity" what the Law of Economy is to our planet—the lowest of the laws controlling existence in planetary form.

This Law of Economy includes, as you know from my earlier writings, many lesser or subsidiary laws; it might therefore be stated that this Law of Freedom also does the same. Until more divine attributes are realised as existing and recognised as aspects, it is not possible for the name of the law which embodies the Law of Freedom to be given, for there is no word in our language adequately available. The above information will, however, link Sirius and our little planet, the Earth, in your minds.

Masonry, as originally instituted far back in the very night of time and long ante-dating the Jewish dispensation, was organised under direct Sirian influence and modelled as far as possible on certain Sirian institutions and bearing a slight resemblance also to our hierarchical life—as seen in the light of the Eternal Now. Its "Blue Lodge" with its three degrees is related to the three major groups of Lives on Sirius, for there are there no kingdoms of nature, such as we possess; these groups receive all Those Who choose the fourth Path, and train Them in the mode of existence and the type of livingness which is found on Sirius. This will make it plain to you that the least developed of the Sirian Lives are—from our standpoint—all of Them initiates of very high degree. Masonry is, therefore, connected in a peculiar way with the fourth Path. Down the ages, the Masonic tradition has been preserved, changing its nomenclature from time to time, reinterpreting its Words of Power, and consequently getting further and further removed from its original beauty and intent.

The time has now come, under cyclic law and in preparation for the New Age, for certain changes to be worked by Masons with spiritual understanding. The present Jewish colouring of Masonry is completely out of date and has been preserved far too long, for it is today either Jewish or Christian and should be neither. The Blue Lodge degrees are entirely Jewish in phrasing and wording, and this should be altered. The Higher Degrees are predominantly Christian, though permeated with Jewish names and words. This too should end. This Jewish colouring is today one of the main hindrances to the full expression of Masonic intention and should be changed, whilst preserving the facts and detail and structure of the Masonic symbolism intact. Whatever form the new nomenclature will take (and this change will inevitably come), that too will pass away after due service rendered. Thus the cyclic transformation will proceed until such time as the bulk of humanity, standing upon the fourth Path, will pass through the initiatory process on Sirius, of which our E.∴ A.∴. degree is a faint reflection.

## 5. The Ray Path

The history of evolution upon the Earth, from the angle of humanity is one of progress, emphatic revolutionary decisions and climaxing crises. Without such a history we should not realise the progress made and the steady though gradual growth of sensitive response to environment, to contact and to impressions—mental and spiritual. The history of evolution is in reality and from the occult point of view the history of the freeing of the spirit by the mode of steadily developing forms which—in orderly unfoldment and at the demand of spirit—meet its requirements in any particular cycle and at every stage of growth, consequent upon the response of substance to spiritual impact and impression.

This impact and this impression relate to the bringing together of substance and spirit, of form and matter, and is also closely connected with the cyclic appearance of the rays, with their varying ray influences, qualities and *intentions*, for they all contribute to the evolutionary process as they cycle in and out of manifested expression. It should be recognised that each ray Lord, whilst following His own path of development, has certain qualities to express and certain aspects of life to unfold and manifest. The effect of these intentions of the ray Lords or Lives upon our planet is, from Their angle, purely incidental and takes place without planning, being due to definite cyclic, circulatory and cosmic activities wherein They are eternally engaged. Their intention and purposes are not, therefore, in any way related to humanity—a fact which men are apt to forget.

It is, however, with these ray intentions that the Initiate of the sixth degree is occupied when He passes on to the fifth or Ray Path. His decision and the intention of the ray

Lord at first, and the united intention of all of Them eventually, are curiously and uniquely connected. The Master on this Path works at the comprehension of the intention and the life purposes of the ray Lords. Many first ray souls find their way on to this Path, for there is a close connection between *the decision* at the sixth initiation and this fifth Path; this might be expected for two reasons: one, that every Master is on one of the three major rays, and secondly, every Master has to develop an understanding of the world of cosmic Purpose. It is a connection based upon the use of the will; it is the will-to-power, the will-to-love and the will-to-know, plus the other four aspects of will* which form the *elementary* basis of the training given on this fifth Path. Souls from other rays reach the same goal and occasionally choose this Path, but it is not the one which constitutes for Them the line of least resistance, as it often is for Masters on the first ray.

Masters from the first ray and the second ray tread it often, and each of Them has a different mode of approach, technique and type of realisation:

1. First ray souls have to negate their "isolated unity" and study the beauty and value of differentiation. This period of training is followed by a mysterious process called "multiple identification." Note how the adjective here conveys the many and the plural whilst the noun gives the concept of unity and the singular. In these two words, apparently contradictory though esoterically significant, there is embodied one aspect of the initiation to be experienced on this ray Path.

2. The second ray Master who decides to go this way has to negate his attractive, magnetic tendencies and learn the meaning of "isolated intention with a multiplicity of goals." I know not how else to translate the archaic phrase which describes the objective of the Master's training on this Path. The exclusive has to become the inclusive in an

---

*A Treatise on the Seven Rays,* Vol. III *(Esoteric Astrology)* Pages 599-601.

entirely newly apprehended world of realisation, whilst the inclusive has to master the technique of exclusiveness and become exclusive in a new realm of realisation; it is an exclusiveness which has in it no slightest element of the great heresy of separateness.

I may not here even indicate the type or quality of the intentions of the ray Lords which the Master of the sixth initiation has to learn to comprehend. The training given Him ends in another tremendous decision which will place Him in a group of Lives on some sacred planet or in some solar system which will be a correspondence to Shamballa on our little planet. Shamballa embodies the will or purpose of our planetary Logos. The goal which these initiates (trained on the ray Path) eventually reach is some sphere of activity wherein sublime purposes and divine intentions are worked out.

## 6. The Path the Logos Himself is on

It should be remembered as this peculiarly abstruse subject is approached that the Solar Logos is as far removed (in the evolutionary sense) from our planetary Logos as the latter is from the point of attainment of an accepted disciple. Yet the two are linked by a subjective unity and similarity of objective. At certain points upon the Way of the Higher Evolution Their two lines of energy meet and blend. Our Solar Logos also plays a peculiarly interesting part in the development of our entire planetary life. For the sake of clarity, yet at the same time speaking symbolically, Sanat Kumara might be regarded as a personal disciple of the Solar Logos, with all that that indicates of cosmic responsibility.

We had much difficulty in considering understandingly the path trodden by Those Masters Who decided to tread the Path of training for planetary Logoi. It is therefore far more difficult and practically impossible to say anything anent this Path which is trodden by Those Great Beings Who are in training for Solar Logoi. Of These, Sanat Kumara is One. Not all the planetary Logoi tread the Path of Solar Logoi, for just as exalted positions await Them elsewhere in the universe. Those Masters, as I have said in *A Treatise on Cosmic Fire,* Who tread this Path are rare indeed, and hitherto have had to enter this Path via the angel or deva evolution and by transference then to the fifth or ray Path. Changes have however been made, and a Master can now pass on to this sixth Path directly and without entering the deva evolution.

This sixth Path is one on which the Masters in training have to work with the devas who are so frequently the mobile agents of the creative process in solar creation. The Masters Who enter upon this Path, eventually and as part of Their training, enter the Council Chamber of some of the sacred planets, before transferring into the group which guides our Solar Logos; this in its turn is only a temporary phase, though in both cases the time embraced may cover vast periods, from the point of view of humanity. They work with principles unknown to us on Earth, though two of these principles will later be revealed; many of them are controlling factors on other spheres and in other planetary schemes which are more advanced than ours; the Master in training then acts as the custodian of these "energetic principles" or as distributing agent; in this way Venus was the custodian of what we call the principle of Mind and brought it as a pure gift to embryonic humanity.

## 7. *The Path of Absolute Sonship*

As I have previously pointed out, not much can be given out concerning this mysterious Path which leads into a triangle (if I may so express it) formed of three lines of energy of differing and greatly varying vibratory effectiveness. This triangle is in the nature of an open door, presenting unique and unprecedented opportunity to Those Who discover this Path. Just as one of the seven Paths produced ultimately relationship to the Pleiades, so this Path relates our solar system to the constellation of the Great Bear. You have, therefore, the following triangle composed of one stream of energy emanating from the Great Bear, another stream of energy issuing from the Heart of the Sun or from our Solar Logos, and the base line constituted of the seven streams of energy which come from our seven sacred planets. The potency and the effectiveness of this triangle is therefore unique and apparent; it produces relation between our system, our planets and the universe. This "open" triangle presents opportunity to Those Lives Who, from the other side of the triangle to that presented to our solar system and its contents, seek to help our solar system and bring the non-sacred planets to the point of liberation which is their particular goal. Through this triangular door all the great Avatars enter our system and "find the Point where They can serve."

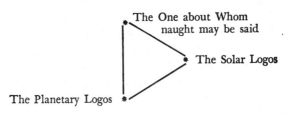

The inflow of extra-solar energy is what produces the seven cosmic Paths. There is no such grouping as the seven solar Paths. In most cases, the Paths lead away from our solar system altogether.

If you will study the more abstruse teaching (more veiled and more symbolic than this) you will find certain statements made which—to the esotericist—will throw much light on the simpler presentations in this *Treatise on the Seven Rays*. It is simpler because only those points are given which carry in them the germ of possible enlightenment to the general public. *A Treatise on Cosmic Fire* is not written for the general public; it is strictly a presentation of truth for the initiated disciple. *Its line is strictly a first ray and third ray presentation, whilst this Treatise is strictly a second ray approach.* This is a statement warranting careful thought, and one that has as yet received no recognition.

Among the changes necessitated by the abnormally rapid development of mankind, with its consequent stepping up of the qualities of disciples, is the fact that no longer does the Master—faced at the sixth initiation with a stupendous decision to make—enter upon the indicated Path entirely blindly, as heretofore. He is now given a revelation of the true united goal of the seven Paths and likewise a vision of their varying intermediate, individual goals. Hence the name of the fifth initiation is that of the "Initiation of Revelation." He can thus make His decision with opened eyes and unblinded by the glory.

One point requires elucidation here. The whole standard of the mental equipment of entering disciples is so much higher than it used to be, owing to the mental and intuitive development of man, that this fact has forced corresponding changes within the Hierarchy itself. The Masters Who are now moving forward on to the Path of the Higher Evolution are equally of much greater unfoldment; the will aspect is present to a great degree (little as you may realise it), and this is a new factor, conditioning much. Love and intelligence distinguished the Masters up to three hundred years ago. Love and intelligence and will distinguish Them today. This again is another reason for the comprehensive changes made and it is interesting to note that the bulk of the changes are due to the response of men to the hierarchical work. It is humanity that has forced these events of so far-reaching a nature; mankind has also forced revelations which it had been believed could not be given to men for thousands of years or until the sixth rootrace had come into being. An instance of the expansion of the information given can be noted in connection with the second Path. Nothing is mentioned in my earlier presentation of the seven Paths in *Initiation, Human and Solar* of a conditioning constellation. In *A Treatise on Cosmic Fire,* I mention that energy enters our system from an unknown source, via Gemini. In this latest contribution on the subject I mention that Libra, the Balances, is involved. Thus there are found on this Path of

Magnetic Work two blended influences, those of **Gemini** and **Libra**. You have, therefore:

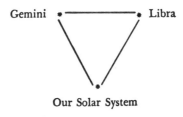

Our Solar System

The dual energy of Gemini is brought to a point of balance by means of the influence of Libra, and this balanced and dual energy is released then into our solar system. This entering stream of balanced energies forms the second Path. I have given you much information in the above statement.

I have asked A.A.B. to incorporate at the close of this instruction a passage from *A Treatise on Cosmic Fire,* for this teaching anent the seven Paths is as a climaxing comment. I shall not enlarge upon it, but if you have spiritual imagination and speculative ability you can comprehend much. I have also asked A.A.B. to add to this instruction the seven tabulations earlier given so as to complete and round out this triple presentation. I do not urge you to study or to give much time to the consideration of the seven paths. The treading of one or other of those Paths lies far ahead of you, and it would be a waste of time. I would however remind you that every effort to live rightly, beautifully and usefully, to control the mind and to achieve loving understanding, lays the foundation for right decision at the sixth initiation; some day you too will stand at this point of unique choice and it is what you do here and now which will determine the way which you will go.

*An Extract from A Treatise on Cosmic Fire*
*Pages 1243 - 1266*

The seven Paths, at a certain stage which may not be defined, become the four Paths, owing to the fact that our solar system is one of the fourth order. This merging is effected in the following way:

The initiates upon Path I "fight their way" on to Path VI.

The initiates upon Path II "alchemise themselves" on to Path VII.

The initiates upon Path III through "piercing the veil" find Themselves upon Path V.

This leaves Path IV to be accounted for. Upon this Path pass all those who, through devotion and activity combined, achieve the goal but who lack as yet the full development of the manasic principle. This being the solar system of love-wisdom or of astral-buddhic development, the fourth Path includes the larger number of the sons of men. In the Hierarchy of our planet the "Lords of Compassion" are numerically greater than the "Masters of the Wisdom." The former must therefore pass to the sun Sirius there to undergo a tremendous manasic stimulation, for Sirius is the emanating source of manas. There the mystic must go and become what is called "a spark of mahatic electricity."

These seven Paths are not concerned with nature or the balancing of the pairs of opposites. They are concerned only with unity, with that which utilises the pairs of opposites as factors in the production of LIGHT.

### PATH I. EARTH SERVICE

| | | |
|---|---|---|
| Attributes | . . . | Wise compassion. |
| Source | . . . | Constellation of the Dragon, via Libra. |
| Method | . . . | Twelve cosmic Identifications. |
| Hierarchy | . . . | The sixth. |
| Symbol | . . . | A green dragon issuing from the centre of a blazing sun. Behind the sun and over-topping it can be seen two pillars on either side of a closed door. |
| Quality gained | . . | Luminosity. |

### PATH II. PATH OF MAGNETIC WORK

| | | |
|---|---|---|
| Attributes | . . . | Responsiveness to heat and knowledge of rhythm. |
| Source | . . . | An unknown constellation, via Gemini. |
| Method | . . . | The entering of the burning-ground. |

Hierarchy . . . The third and fourth.

Symbol . . . A funeral pyre, four torches, and a fivefold star mounting towards the sun.

Quality gained . . Electrical velocity.

### PATH III. PATH OF TRAINING FOR PLANETARY LOGOI

Attributes . . . Cosmic vision, deva hearing and psychic correlation.

Source . . . Betelgeuse, via the sign Sagittarius.

Hierarchy . . . The fifth.

Method . . . Prismatic identification.

Symbol . . . A coloured cross with a star at the centre and backed by a blazing sun, surmounted by a Sensa Word.

Quality gained . . Cosmic etheric vision or septenary clairvoyance.

### PATH IV. THE PATH TO SIRIUS

Attributes . . . Cosmic rapture and rhythmic bliss.

Source . . . Sirius via the Sun which veils a zodiacal sign.

Hierarchy . . . Veiled by the numbers 14 and 17.

Method . . . Duplex rotary motion and rhythmic dancing upon the square.

Symbol . . . Two wheels of electric fire, revolving around an orange Cross, with an emerald at the centre.

Quality gained . . Unrevealed.

### PATH V. THE RAY PATH

Attributes . . . A sense of cosmic direction.

Source . . . The Pole Star via Aquarius.

Hierarchy . . . The first and the second.

Method . . . A process of electrical insulation and the imprisonment of polar magnetism.

Symbol . . . Five balls of fire enclosed within a sphere. Sphere is formed of a serpent inscribed with the mantram of insulation.

Quality gained . . Cosmic stability and magnetic equilibrium.

### PATH VI. THE PATH OF THE SOLAR LOGOS

Not given . . . Not given.

### PATH VII. THE PATH OF ABSOLUTE SONSHIP

Not given . . . Not given.

*The World Tension Analysed*

The tension in the world today,* particularly in the Hierarchy, is such that it will produce another and perhaps ultimate world crisis, or else such a speeding up of the spiritual life of the planet that the coming in of the long-looked-for New Age conditions will be amazingly hastened. I would have you consider carefully what I have said here, remembering what I have told you in the past anent points of tension. This present tension constitutes a major problem for the disciple in training, and therefore our particular theme in this instruction is peculiarly apposite.

There is a great deal of glamour in the world today and a great deal of that glamour is concentrated in Russia, owing to the youth and the basic political inexperience of that people. The United States of America is also young and inexperienced, but not to the same extent as are the Russian people. Today, the Russians are suffering from the glamour of power, the glamour of planning, the glamour of what they consider a great ideal (and such it is), the glamour of prestige and the inevitable—but ephemeral—glamour of totalitarianism. It is this same totalitarianism which also constitutes their weakest point, because it leads inexorably to a revolt of the human spirit. That human spirit is to be found in Russia to exactly the same extent as it is to be found in any other country in the world.

Freedom is an essentially spiritual attribute, underlying the entire evolutionary process; this should always be remembered as a strengthening and conditioning reality by all men everywhere. It has survived aeons of opposition from the principle of enslaving selfishness and is largely responsible, at this time, for the struggle in which we are all participating.

The country which is the most free from selfishness today is Great Britain; she is experienced, old, and therefore mature in her thinking; she has learnt much in a relatively short time and her judgment is sound. The most

---

*Written in April 1947

selfish country in the world today is France, with the United States (though along totally different lines) running her a close second; both are materially selfish and capitalistically engrossed. Russia is also selfish but it is the selfishness of a fanatical ideal, held by an immature, a too young a people. The selfishness of the United States is also due to youth, but it will eventually yield to experience and to suffering; there is—fortunately for the soul of this great people—much suffering in store for the United States. The selfishness of France is less excusable; France too is old and experienced; again and again she has been the victim of the armed forces of Germany and cries aloud to the world about it. France forgets that she frequently over-ran central Europe in the Middle Ages, and the Napoleonic conquests are relatively modern history. Her evil destiny (as she regards it) does, nevertheless, give her the opportunity to become spiritual in her life and attitudes, instead of grossly and intellectually (though brilliantly) material. She has not yet learned her lesson, and as yet shows little inclination to do so. Strain, economic privations and anxiety may teach her; the result will be stability.

In the hands of the United States, Great Britain and Russia, and also in the hands of France, lies the destiny of the world disciple, Humanity. Humanity has been passing through the tests which are preparatory to the first initiation; they have been hard and cruel and are not yet entirely over. The Lords of Karma (four in number) are today working through these four Great Powers; it is, however, a karma which seeks to liberate, as does all karma. In the coming crisis, true vision and a new freedom, plus a wider spiritual horizon may be attained. The crisis, if rightly handled, need not again reach the ultimate horror.

The area of difficulty—as is well known—is the Near East and Palestine. The Jews, by their illegal and terroristic activities, have laid a foundation of great difficulty for those who are seeking to promote world peace. As a Jewish member of my Ashram pointed out (and I commend him on his soul vision), the Jews have partially again opened the door to the Forces of Evil, which worked originally through Hitler and his evil gang. The "sealing" of that door had not been successfully accomplished, and it is the part of wisdom to discover this in time. These Forces of Evil work through a triangle of evil, one point of which is to be found in the Zionist Movement in the United States, another in central Europe, and the third in Palestine. Palestine is no longer a Holy Land and should not be so regarded.

I would have you bear these points in mind while you investigate the world picture. This picture is taking shape and warrants recognition. It involves the Jews (who are not a nation but a religious group) the Near East and Russia. In the maps which are to be found in the Archives of the spiritual Hierarchy, the entire area of the Near East and Europe—Greece, Yugoslavia, Turkey, Palestine, the Arab States, Egypt and Russia—are under a heavy overshadowing cloud. Can that cloud be dissipated by the right thinking and planning of Great Britain, the United States and the majority of the United Nations or—must it break in disaster over the world? Will it present a task too hard for correct handling by that inexperienced disciple—Humanity?

In what I have written above you have the picture of the true situation; it is one which finds Great Britain temporarily weakened and ineffective (except for the clear thinking of her people and her political maturity); it finds the United States, unused to power, somewhat arrogant, with a strong superiority complex, inexperienced and yet at the same time exceedingly well-intentioned and fundamentally sound. It is the mass of the people who are sound in their thinking and not their representatives in Congress.

It is not for me to tell you what will happen, although the Hierarchy knows. Humanity must (as must all disciples) be left entirely free to settle its own destiny. Humanity has not yet learned the difficult lesson which all disciples have to master: the lesson of the dual life of the man whose soul is functioning and whose physical brain is constantly aware of this fact.

## THE DUAL LIFE OF THE INITIATORY PROCESS

In all the many books which I have written, I have said relatively little about the brain and its relation to the personality and the soul. It is not possible to enlarge at any length on that theme here, but I will make certain statements without which this whole process of dual living would be most difficult to explain. I will sum up what I have to say in the form of three basic statements:

1. The brain is a most delicate receiving and transmitting apparatus:

a. It is responsive to information relayed to it, via the senses, from the emotional plane and from the mind.

b. Through its medium the personal lower self becomes aware of its environment, of the nature of its desires, and of its mental peculiarities, as well as of the emotional states and the thoughts of the people contacted in the environment.

2. The brain is largely conditioned by the endocrine system, and this far more than the endocrinologists would care to admit:

a. It is powerfully conditioned by three major glands which are found in close relation to the brain substance. These are the pituitary body, the pineal gland and the carotid gland.

b. These form a triangle, practically unrelated in primitive man, occasionally related in average man, and closely related in the spiritual man.

c. These glands are objective correspondences of the three energy centres, by means of which the soul, or the indwelling spiritual man, controls his physical vehicle.

d. Where the relation is close between the three glands —as is increasingly the case where disciples are concerned — a triangle of circulating energies is always established.

e. This triangle, through the carotid gland in the

medulla oblongata, becomes related to other glands and centres.

3. The brain, as transmitter, becomes a powerful directing agency:

a. As a recipient and transmitter of pure energy or life it uses the carotid gland controlled by the alta major centre, and establishes a close relation with the heart and the heart centre.

b. As a recipient of mental energy or of energy from the soul, the ajna centre becomes the directing agency; this is the centre which controls the pituitary body.

c. These energies are received via the head centre, which controls the pineal gland. Emotional energy enters the personality system via the solar plexus centre, where it either controls or is transmuted and elevated.

It is this triple mechanism in the head—both objective and subjective—which uses the physical brain as a receiving agent and as a transmitting agent. It is this which is brought into creative activity and thus under the control of the disciple in training or in process of being prepared for initiation. I have not hitherto emphasised this, nor do I wish to do so, for it is not desirable for the disciple or aspirant consciously and deliberately to deal with the mechanism in the head. Let him learn to control and consciously employ the mind; let him train his mind to receive communications from three sources:

The three worlds of ordinary living, thus enabling the mind to act as the "common-sense."

The soul, and thus consciously become the disciple, the worker in an Ashram, illumined by the wisdom of the soul, and superseding gradually the knowledge gained in the three worlds. That knowledge, rightly applied, becomes wisdom.

The Spiritual Triad, acting as the intermediary between the Monad and the brain of the personality. This can eventually take place, because the soul and personality are fused and blended into one functioning unit, this superseding again what we mean when we use the erroneous phrase *"the* soul." Duality then takes the place of the original triplicity.

It has been necessary to make these somewhat elementary remarks and to clarify these points, if there is to be true understanding as to what constitutes the dual life of the disciple or the Master, and wherein they differ.

One of the tests of the initiatory process is a hitherto totally unexpected one. Tests which are expected and for which preparation has been made do not constitute true tests in the real sense of the word, esoterically understood. It is a test—imposed with increasing rigidity as initiation after initiation is taken—to see just how far the initiate is capable of retaining or preserving in his brain consciousness the registered facts of several worlds or planes of consciousness; i.e., the three worlds of human endeavour and the world of soul consciousness, or both of these and the world of the Ashram; or again these and the activity of the Hierarchy itself, viewing it as a complete whole; or again, all of these and the world of Triadal experience, until the point is reached where a straight continuity of consciousness can be registered and held which comes directly from the Council Chamber of the Lord of the World to Those Masters Who are functioning in a physical body and must therefore use a physical brain. In every single case the test (in order to be passed correctly) *must* involve the brain consciousness; the facts, registered upon the subtler planes, must be correctly registered, recognised and interpreted simultaneously upon the physical plane.

You can see for yourselves that this is a major and most necessary indication of a developing awareness; a Master has to be aware at any time on any plane and at will. It will also be obvious to you that this will be a growing and an increasing perception for which the intermediate stages, between initiations, prepare the initiate. Gradually, each one of the five senses, plus the common-sense (the mind), has to demonstrate the effectiveness of its higher correspondence and thus of a developing subtle apparatus. Through this apparatus the initiate is put in touch with widening areas of the divine "state of mind" or with the planetary consciousness, until "the mind that is in Christ" becomes truly the mind of the initiate, with all that those words entail of meaning and esoteric significance. Consciousness, Sensitivity, Awareness, Planetary Rapport, Universal Consciousness—these are the words which we must consider, sequentially developed and in their truly esoteric sense.

You have here a wide and general picture, involving the goal, the means or mode, the testing point and the physical brain; these are four factors which have received little or no attention where initiation has been dealt with in the occult writings. They are nevertheless of major importance. I am dealing with them here because of the stage of development now reached by the human mind, because of their increasingly close relation to the physical brain, and because there are now so many aspirants ready to tread the Path of Discipleship, the Path of Initiatory Training. They are now in a position to work consciously at the task of a dual and constant process of spiritual and physical recognitions.

## The Dual Life of the Disciple

I have divided this theme into two parts, owing to the fact that the dualism displayed by a Master and that demonstrated by a disciple are *not* identical or one and the same thing at advancing points of distinction. The subject, when you first approach it, seems of a relative simplicity, but a closer consideration of it will present great and unexpected dissimilarities.

In connection with the dual life of the disciple, the factors involved are the threefold *personality* (with an awakening or onlooking consciousness centred or focussed in the brain), the *soul* which seems at first the ultimate goal of attainment but is later seen as simply a system or collection of fusing spiritual attributes, and the lowest aspect of the Spiritual Triad, the *abstract mind*. The disciple feels that, if he can attain the immediate and fused consciousness of the three, he has attained; he realises also that this involves the construction of the antahkarana. All these factors, for one who has just been admitted to the Path of Discipleship and who is just finding his place within an Ashram, seem an adequately difficult undertaking and one that engrosses every power which he possesses.

This, for the time being, is true and—until the third initiation—these objectives, their conscious fusion, plus a recognition of the divine planes of awareness to which they all admit him, indicate the disciple's task and keep him fully occupied. To the recognitions entailed he has to add a growing capacity to work on the levels of consciousness involved, remembering always that a plane and a state of consciousness are synonymous terms, and that he is making progress, becoming aware, building the antahkarana, training as a hierarchical worker within an Ashram, familiarising himself with new and opening spiritual environments, widening his horizon, stabilising himself upon the Path, and living upon the physical plane the life of an intelligent man within the world of men. He is demonstrating also no freakish peculiarities, but appears as a man of goodwill, of benevolent intelligence, of unalterable goodness, and of stern and unchangeable spiritual purpose. Is that enough of a goal for a disciple? Does it seem well-nigh impossible of accomplishment? Can you undertake such a proposition and make good your undertaking?

Most assuredly you can, for the factor of time enters in and the disciple is free to submit to its conditioning, particularly in the early stages of his discipleship; this he usually does at first, knowing nothing else to do, but the speed or the sattvic or rhythmic nature of the spiritual life eventually changes this attitude; he then works with no true consciousness of time except as it affects other people and his associates upon the physical plane.

At first, his registration of that which is sensed or seen upon the subtler planes or the soul plane is slow; it takes time for contacts and for knowledge gained to penetrate from the higher levels to his physical brain. This fact (when he discovers it) tends to upset his time-awareness, and the first step is therefore taken on the path of timelessness, speaking symbolically. He gains also the capacity to work with greater rapidity and mental coordination than does the average intelligent man; in this way he learns the limitations of time as a brain condition, and learns also how to offset it and to work in such a way that he does more within a set time limit than is possible to the average man, no matter how ardently he may pursue the effort. The overcoming of time and the demonstration of spiritual speed are indications that the dual life of discipleship is superseding the integrated life of the personality, though leading in its turn to a still greater synthesis and higher integration.

The dual life which all disciples lead produces also a rapidity of mental interpretation which is essential to the sane registration of the phenomenal life of the various higher planes and states of consciousness. Forget not that all our planes are subplanes of the cosmic physical plane, and are therefore phenomenal in nature. As they are contacted and recorded and the knowledge is transmitted to the physical brain, via the mind, there must always accompany them a true interpretation and a·correct recognition of "things as they are." It is here that the non-disciple and the psychic go wrong, for their interpretation is almost always fundamentally in error, and it takes time (coming within that cycle of limitation) intelligently to interpret and truly register what the perceiving consciousness has contacted. When the time factor no longer controls, the interpretations registered by the brain are infallibly correct. I have here given you a major piece of information.

You will see, therefore, that in the earlier initiatory process, the factor of time is noted by the initiate and also by the presenting Masters. An instance of a slow permeation of information from the plane of initiation to the physical brain can be seen in the fact that very few aspirants and disciples register *the fact* that they have already taken the first initiation, the birth of the Christ in the cave of the heart. That they have taken it is evidenced by their deliberate treading of the Way, by their love of the Christ—no matter by what name they may call Him—and by their effort to serve and help their fellowmen; they are still, however, surprised when told that the first initiation lies behind them. This is due entirely to the factor of time, leading to their inability to "bring through" past events with accuracy, by a false humility as well (inculcated by the Christian Church, as it attempts to keep people subjugated by the sin idea), and by the intensely forward-looking anticipatory consciousness of the average aspirant. When a true perspective and a balanced point of view have been attained, and some awareness of the Eternal Now is beginning to penetrate into their understanding, then the past, the present and the future will be lost to sight in the consciousness of *the inclusiveness of the moment that IS;* then the limitations of time will be ending and the Law of Karma will be negated; it is at present so closely related to past and future. The dual life of the disciple will then be ended, giving place to the cosmic dualism of the Master. The Master is free from the limitations of time, though not of space, because space is an eternal Entity.

You will see, therefore, the great necessity for a constant emphasis, at this stage in the training of the average aspirant, on the need for *alignment,* or for the creation of a channel of direct relation from the brain to the desired point of contact. To this trained alignment must eventually be added the building of the antahkarana and its subsequent use in a growing system of alignments. The antahkarana must be completed and direct contact must be established with the Spiritual Triad by the time the third initiation has been taken. Then follows the fourth initiation with its destruction of the egoic, causal or soul body, owing to the complete fusion of soul and personality. The dual life of the disciple ends.

## The Dual Existence of the Master

I would have you note here the difference between the two headings. I refer in one place to the *dual life* of the disciple but in another to the *dual existence* of the Master. That distinction is deliberate and intentional. The disciple lives in the three worlds and, until the third initiation, he demonstrates his livingness strictly in relation to the soul and the personality, and therefore strictly to the phenomenal world and to the various levels of the dense cosmic physical plane.

The Master functions on the plane of BEING and demonstrates the fact that He eternally IS, that He *exists* as a divine aspect upon the formless levels of the cosmic etheric planes; this is a very different matter to the life of the disciple and to which little attention has been paid. Existence, Being, Essential Life, Dynamic Energy, Electric Fire are all of them distinctive of the higher initiations; they produce basic distinctions between their constitution and mode of life expression and that of those who live, who are in process of becoming, who express quality, and who fuse and blend solar fire and fire by friction. Being and Existence are not the same as Becoming or of Qualified Appearance. It is largely a question of emphases. A Master has synthesised within Himself all for which the advancing disciple longs to express, all that is possible as Expansion, plus an emphasis upon the dynamic life aspect, plus an ability to stand immovable in pure Being. Here again I find it hard to express that for which no words are to be found.

In the Master, all the divine aspects are proved capable of expression in accordance with this particular time, in this particular round and chain (reverting to the old symbolism of *The Secret Doctrine*) and through any particular racial expression. These divine characteristics—viewed from the angle of time and space—are shewn in a definitely relative form; later cycles and time periods will show these aspects in a still more perfected form. But the relativity of these matters does not really concern us, and the perfection is—from the angle of the human disciple today— exactly what we understand by perfection. The Masters know, however, that a higher, deeper and more intensive manifestation of divinity is potentially possible, but it causes Them no concern or strain, no anxiety or fiery aspiration; They know, as no disciple can know, the workings of the Law of In-evitability. This Law releases the Masters (under the ac-companying Law of Service), at the sixth initiation, into a wider field of experience, with all the divine assets and qual-ities so developed within Them that They know that Their equipment is adequate to the undertaking and that They can, without hesitancy and concern, take the next required steps.

It is hard for the disciple—struggling with glamour and illusion—to realise that the higher initiations are free from all concern and from any emotional or self-centred reactions to the work which lies ahead or to the form side of mani-festation; it is well-nigh impossible for the neophyte to vision a time when he will be free from all reactions engen-dered by life on the dense cosmic physical planes and from all the limitations of life in the three worlds. Today, aspira-tion provides a constant source of anxious questioning, of painful deliberations and of high voltage spiritual ambition, with their consequent limitations and moments of sensed failure and lack of achievement. The Master has left all this behind, knowing that even this so-called "spiritual respon-siveness" is a form of self-centred attitude. Eventually—and disciples should take courage and hope from this statement—all this agonising reaction to the spiritual urge will be left behind. The Master knows the Law and is entirely free from any consideration of the time equation, as far as He Himself is concerned. He only regards time as it may affect the work-ing of the Plan in the three worlds.

The dual existence of the Master involves what we might call the two poles: that of the monadic consciousness, whatever that may be, and that of the self-created form which He may use as a member of the Hierarchy and a worker in the three worlds of human enterprise. I would here remind you that there are many groups and types of Masters, and most of Them are quite unknown to occult students either from Their work or from rumour or from knowledge of the many evolutionary processes of which the human is only one. Not all the Masters work in the three worlds; not all the Masters need or possess physical bodies; not all the Masters "have Their faces turned towards the realm of dark light, but many face for aeons towards the clear cold light of spiritual existence"; not all the Masters make or are required to make the sacrifices which work for the fourth kingdom in nature entails. Not all souls liberated or limited constitute the Kingdom of God in the sense which that phrase conveys to us; that term is limited to the soul which informs units in the human family; not all the Masters work under the great Buddha of Activity Who is responsible to Sanat Kumara for the Plan working out in connection with Humanity. He works through the three Great Lords of the Eternal Ashram of Sanat Kumara, but His two Brothers have Each of Them an equally important work and are responsible—as He is—to the Council Chamber. Each of Them also works through a triangle of energies with grouped subsidiary forces working in seven departments and differentiated also into forty-nine lesser departments, as is the Ashram which we call the Hierarchy. Forget not, there are many Hierarchies and the Human Hierarchy is but one.

This whole theme is one of great complexity and yet at the same time so simple that when the simplicity of the planetary constitution is truly grasped and the analytic disputations of the concrete mind are overcome, the liberated Master enters a world of spiritual endeavour which is free from forms and symbols or the veils which hide the basic truth and the underlying mystery.

Being is simple, free, unlimited and unimpeded and in that world the Master moves and works. Becoming is complex, imprisoning, limited and subjected to hindrances, and in that world the disciple and the lesser initiates live and move and have their being. The Master works simultaneously in two worlds or states of awareness; i.e., that related to pure existence, to the untrammelled life of the planes controlled by the Monad, and also by the Hierarchy. There naught but the Plan engrosses His attention. He deals safely with "the simplicity which is Shamballa" and its sphere or aura of influence and "with the field of relationships which are nurtured from the Ashram of the Christ." I am here quoting one of the Masters Who was endeavouring to explain to a disciple the simplicity of the life which a Master expresses.

## THE SCIENCE OF THE ANTAHKARANA

As we enter on the consideration of "The dual life of the initiatory process" I would call your attention to the wording used, and particularly to its significance in reference to *the initiatory process*. This deals, as we shall see, *not* with the effort of the disciple to live simultaneously the life of the spiritual world and the practical life of physical plane service, but entirely with the preparation of the disciple for initiation, and therefore with his mental life and attitudes.

This statement might be regarded as concerning itself primarily with two major aspects of his mental life and not with the life of relation between soul and personality. It is proper, consequently, to see a duality existing in the consciousness of the disciple, and both of its aspects existing side by side:

1. The life of awareness in which he expresses the soul attitude, soul awareness and soul consciousness, through the medium of the personality *upon the physical plane;* this he learns to register and express *consciously.*

2. The intensely private and purely subjective life in which he—the soul-infused personality—oriented upon the mental plane, brings into increasing rapport:

   a. His lower concrete mind and the higher abstract mind.

   b. Himself and the Master of his ray group, thus developing the ashramic consciousness.

   c. Himself and the Hierarchy as a whole, becoming increasingly aware of the spiritual synthesis underlying the united Ashrams. He thus consciously and steadily approaches the radiant Centre of this solar Ashram, the Christ Himself, the first Initiator.

This inner life with its three slowly revealed objectives concerns essentially the life of preparation for initiation.

There is no initiation for the disciple until he has begun consciously to build the antahkarana, thus bringing the Spiritual Triad and the mind as the highest aspect in the three worlds into a close relationship; later, he brings his physical brain into a position of a recording agent upon the physical plane, thus again demonstrating a clear alignment and a direct channel from the Spiritual Triad straight through to the brain via the antahkarana which has linked the higher mind and the lower.

This involves much work, much interpretive capacity and much power to visualise. I am choosing my words with care. This visualisation is not necessarily concerned with form and with concrete mental presentations; it is concerned with a pictorial and symbolic sensitivity which expresses in-terpretively the spiritual understanding, conveyed by the awakening intuition—the agent of the Spiritual Triad. The meaning of this becomes clearer as the work proceeds. It is difficult for the man who is beginning the work of construct-ing the antahkarana to grasp the meaning of visualisation as it is seen to be related to a growing responsiveness to that which the ashramic group conveys to him, to his emerging vision of the divine Plan as it exists in reality, and to that which is committed to him as the *effect* or the result of each successive initiation. I prefer the word "effect" to the word "result," for the initiate increasingly works consciously with the Law of Cause and Effect on planes other than the physi-cal. We use the word "result" to express the consequences of that great cosmic Law as they demonstrate in the three worlds of human evolution.

It is in connection with this effort that he discovers the value, uses and purpose of the creative imagination. This creative imagination is all that remains to him eventually of the active and intensely powerful astral life which he has lived for so many lives; as evolution proceeds, his astral body becomes a mechanism of transformation, desire being trans-formed into aspiration and aspiration itself being transformed into a growing and expressive intuitive faculty. The reality of this process is demonstrated in the emergence of that basic quality which has always been inherent in desire itself: the imaginative quality of the soul, implementing desire and steadily becoming a higher creative faculty as desire shifts into ever higher states and leads to ever higher realisations. This faculty eventually invokes the energies of the mind, and the mind, plus the imagination, becomes in time a great invocative and creative agent. It is thus that the Spiritual Triad is brought into rapport with the three-fold personality.

I have told you in earlier writings that basically the astral plane is non-existent as a part of the divine Plan; it is fundamentally the product of glamour, of kama-manas—a glamour which humanity itself has created and in which it has lived practically entirely since early Atlantean days. The effect of an increasing soul contact has not simply been to dispel the mists of glamour, but it has also served to con-solidate and to bring into effective use, therefore, the imagi-nation with its overwhelmingly powerful creative faculty. This creative energy, when implemented by an illumined mind (with its thoughtform making ability), is then wielded by the disciple in order to make contacts higher than with the soul, and to bring into symbolic form that of which he becomes aware through the medium of a line of energy— the antahkarana—which he is steadily and scientifically creating.

It might be said (equally symbolically) that at each initiation he tests the connecting bridge and discovers grad-ually the soundness of that which he has created under the inspiration of the Spiritual Triad and with the aid of the three aspects of his mind (the abstract mind, the soul or the Son of Mind, and the lower concrete mind), combined with the intelligent cooperation of his soul-infused personality. In the early stages of his invocative work, the instrument used is the creative imagination. This enables him at the very beginning to act *as if* he were capable of thus creating; then, when the *as if* imaginative consciousness is no longer useful, he becomes consciously aware of that which he has—with hope and spiritual expectancy—sought to create; he discovers this as an existent fact and knows past all controversy that "faith is *the substance* of things hoped for, *the evidence* of things not seen."

## Building the Antahkarana

With the introductory teaching on the science of the Antahkarana we shall not here deal, for the student will find it in the book, *Education in the New Age.* That preliminary presentation should be studied before taking up the more advanced stage which begins here. Let us now consider, step by step this science which is already proving a useful source of experiment and testing.

The human soul (in contradistinction to the soul as it functions in its own kingdom, free from the limitations of human life) is imprisoned and subject to the control of the lower three energies for the major part of its experience. Then, upon the Path of Probation, the dual energy of soul begins to be increasingly active, and the man seeks to use his mind consciously, and to express love-wisdom on the physical plane. This is a simple statement of the objective of all aspirants. When the five energies are beginning to be used, consciously and wisely in service, a rhythm is then set up between the Personality and the Soul. It is as if a magnetic field were then established and these two vibrating and magnetic units, or grouped energies, swung into each other's field of influence. This happens only occasionally and rarely in the early stages; later it occurs more constantly, and thus a path of contact is established which eventually becomes the line of least resistance, "the way of familiar approach," as it is sometimes called. Thus is the first half of the "bridge," the antahkarana, constructed. By the time the third initiation is completed, this Way is completed, and the initiate can "pass to higher worlds at will, leaving the lower worlds far behind; or he can come again and pass upon the way that leads from dark to light, from light to dark, and from the under lower worlds into the realms of light."

Thus the two are one, and the first great union upon the Path of Return is completed. A second stage of the Way has then to be trodden, leading to a second union of still further importance in that it leads to complete liberation from the three worlds. It must be remembered that the soul, in its turn, is a union of three energies of which the lower three are the reflection. It is a synthesis of the energy of Life itself (which demonstrates as the life-principle within the world of forms), of the energy of the intuition or spiritual love-wisdom or understanding (this demonstrates as sensitivity and feeling in the astral body), and spiritual mind, whose reflection in the lower nature is the mind or the principle of intelligence in the form world. In these three we have the atma-buddhi-manas of the theosophical literature—that higher triplicity which is reflected in the lower three, and which focusses through the soul body on the higher levels of the mental plane before being precipitated into incarnation—as it is esoterically called.

Modernising the concept, we might say that the energies which animate the physical body and the intelligent life of the atom, the sensitive emotional states, and the intelligent mind, have eventually to be blended with and transmuted into the energies which animate the soul. These are the spiritual mind, conveying illumination; the intuitive nature, conferring spiritual perception; and divine livingness.

After the third initiation the "Way" is carried forward with great rapidity, and the "bridge" is finished which links perfectly the higher spiritual Triad and the lower material reflection. The three worlds of the Soul and the three worlds of the Personality become one world wherein the initiate works and functions, seeing no distinction, regarding one world as the world of inspiration and the other world as constituting the field of service, yet regarding both together as forming one world of activity. Of these two worlds, the subjective etheric body (or the body of vital inspiration) and the dense physical body are symbols on the external plane.

How is this bridging antahkarana to be built? Where

are the steps which the disciple must follow? I deal not here with the Path of Probation whereon the major faults should be eliminated and whereon the major virtues should be developed. Much of the instruction given in the past has laid down the rules for the cultivation of the virtues and qualifications for discipleship, and also the necessity for self-control, for tolerance and for unselfishness. But these are elementary stages and should be taken for granted by the students. Such students should be occupied not only with the establishment of the character aspect of discipleship, but with the more abstruse and difficult requirements for those whose eventual goal is initiation.

It is with the work of the "bridge-builders" that we are concerned. *First, let me assure you that the real building of the antahkarana takes place only when the disciple is beginning to be definitely focussed upon mental levels,* and when therefore his mind is intelligently and consciously functioning. He must begin at this stage to have some more exact idea than has hitherto been the case as to the distinctions existing between the thinker, the apparatus of thought, and thought itself, beginning with its dual esoteric function which is:

1. The recognition and receptivity to IDEAS.
2. The creative faculty of conscious thoughtform building.

This necessarily involves a strong mental attitude and reorientation of the mind to reality. As the disciple begins to focus himself on the mental plane (and this is the prime intent of the meditation work), he starts working in mental matter and trains himself in the powers and uses of thought. He achieves a measure of mind control; he can turn the searchlight of the mind in two directions, into the world of human endeavour and into the world of soul activity. Just as the soul makes a way for itself by projecting itself in a thread or stream of energy into the three worlds, so the disciple begins consciously to project himself into the higher worlds. His energy goes forth, through the medium of the controlled and directed mind, into the world of the higher spiritual mind and into the realm of the intuition. A reciprocal activity is thus set up. This response between the higher and the lower mind is symbolically spoken of in terms of light, and the "lighted way" comes into being between the personality and the spiritual Triad, via the soul body, just as the soul came into definite contact with the brain via the mind. This "lighted way" is the illumined bridge. *It is built through meditation;* it is constructed through the constant effort to draw forth the intuition, through subservience and obedience to the Plan (which begins to be recognised as soon as the intuition and the mind are en rapport), and through a conscious incorporation into the group in service and for purposes of assimilation into the whole. All these qualities and activities are based upon the foundation of good character and the qualities developed upon the Probationary Path.

The effort to draw forth the intuition requires directed occult (but not aspirational) meditation. It requires a trained intelligence, so that the line of demarcation between intuitive realisation and the forms of the higher psychism may be clearly seen. It requires a constant disciplining of the mind, so that it can "hold itself steady in the light," and the development of a cultured right interpretation, so that the intuitive knowledge achieved may then clothe itself in the right thoughtforms.

It might also be stated here that the construction of the bridge whereby the consciousness can function with facility, both in the higher worlds and in the lower, is *primarily brought about by a definitely directed life-tendency,* which steadily sends the man in the direction of the world of spiritual realities, plus certain movements of planned and carefully timed and directed reorientation or focussing. In this last process the *gain* of the past months or years is closely assessed; the *effect* of that gain upon the daily life and in the bodily mechanism is as carefully studied; and the *will-to-live* as a spiritual being is brought into the consciousness with a definiteness and a determination that makes for immediate progress.

This building of the antahkarana is most assuredly proceeding in the case of every earnest student. When the work is carried on intelligently and with full awareness of the desired purpose, and when the aspirant is not only aware of the process but alert and active in its fulfillment, then the work proceeds apace and the bridge is built.

It is wise to accept the fact that humanity is now in a position to begin the definite process of constructing the link or bridge between the various aspects of man's nature, so that instead of differentiation there will be unity, and instead of a fluid, moving attention, directed here and there into the field of material living and emotional relationships, we shall have learnt to control the mind and to have bridged the divisions, and so can direct at will the lower attention in any desired manner. Thus all aspects of man, spiritual and natural, can be focussed where needed.

This bridging work has in part already been done. Humanity has as a whole already bridged the gap between the emotional-astral nature and the physical man. It should be noted here that the bridging has to be done in the consciousness aspect, and concerns the continuity of man's awareness of life in all its various aspects. The energy which is used in connecting, in consciousness, the physical man and the astral body is focussed in the solar plexus. Many today, speaking in symbolical terms, are carrying that bridge forward and linking the mind with the two aspects already linked. This thread of energy emanates from or is anchored in the head. Some people, fewer of course in number, are steadily linking the soul and the mind, which in its turn is linked with the other two aspects. The soul energy, when linked with the other threads has its anchor in the heart. A very few people, the initiates of the world, having effected all the lower syntheses, are now occupied with bringing about a still higher union, with that triple Reality which uses the soul as its medium of expression, just as the soul in its turn is endeavoring to use its shadow, the threefold lower man.

These distinctions and unifications are matters of form,

symbols in speech, and are used to express events and happenings in the world of energies and forces, in connection with which man is definitely implicated. It is to these unifications that we refer when the subject of initiation is under consideration.

It will be useful if we repeat here a few statements made in an earlier book:

Students should train themselves to *distinguish between the sutratma and the antahkarana,* between the life thread and the thread of consciousness. The one thread is the basis of immortality and the other the basis of continuity. Herein lies a fine distinction for the investigator. One thread (the sutratma) links and vivifies all forms into one functioning whole, and embodies in itself the will and the purpose of the expressing entity, be it man, God or a crystal. The other thread (the antahkarana) embodies the response of the consciousness within the form to a steadily expanding range of contacts within the environing whole. One is the direct stream of life, unbroken and immutable, which can be regarded symbolically as a direct stream of living energy flowing from the centre to the periphery, and from the source to the outer expression, or the phenomenal appearance. It is the *life*. It produces the individual process and the evolutionary unfoldment of all forms.

It is, therefore, the path of life, which reaches from the Monad to the personality, via the soul. This is the thread soul and it is one and indivisible. It conveys the energy of life and finds its final anchor in the centre of the human heart and at some central focal point in all forms of divine expression. Naught is and naught remains but life. The consciousness thread (antahkarana) is the result of the union of life and substance or of the basic energies which constitute the first differentiation in time and space; this produces something different, which only emerges as a third divine manifestation after the union of the basic dualities has taken place.

The life thread, the silver cord or the sutratma is, as far as man is concerned, dual in nature. The life thread proper, which is one of the two threads which constitute the sutratma, is anchored in the heart, whilst the other thread, which embodies the principle of consciousness, is anchored in the head. This you already know, but this I feel the need to constantly reiterate. In the work of the evolutionary cycle, however, man has to repeat what God has already done. He must himself create, both in the world of consciousness and of life. Like a spider, man spins connecting threads, and thus bridges and makes contact with his environment, thereby gaining experience and sustenance. The spider symbol is often used in the ancient occult books and the scriptures of India in connection with this activity of the human being. These threads, which man creates, are triple in number, and with the two basic threads which have been created by the soul, constitute the five types of energy which make man a conscious human being.

The triple threads created by man are anchored in the solar plexus, the head and the heart. When the astral body and the mind nature are beginning to function as a unit, and the soul also is consciously connected (do not forget that it is always unconsciously linked), an extension of this five-fold thread—the basic two and the human three—is carried to the throat centre, and when that occurs man can become a conscious creator on the physical plane. From these major lines of energy lesser lines can radiate at will. It is upon this knowledge that all future intelligent psychic unfoldment must be based.

In the above paragraph and its implications you have a brief and inadequate statement as to the Science of the Antahkarana. I have endeavoured to express this in terms, symbolic if you will, which will convey a general idea to your minds. We can learn much through the use of the pictorial and visual imagination. This bridging must take place:

1. From the physical to the vital or etheric body. This is really an extension of the life thread between the heart and the spleen.
2. From the physical and the vital, regarding them as a

unity, to the astral or emotional vehicle. This thread emanates from, or is anchored in, the solar plexus, and is carried upwards, by means of the aspiration, till it anchors itself in the love petals of the egoic Lotus.

3. From the physical and astral vehicles to the mental body. One terminus is anchored in the head, and the other in the knowledge petals of the egoic Lotus, being carried forward by an act of the will.

Advanced humanity is in process of linking the three lower aspects, which we call the personality, with the soul itself, through meditation, discipline, service and directed attention. When this has been accomplished, a definite relation is established between the sacrifice or will petals of the egoic Lotus and the head and heart centres, thus producing a synthesis between consciousness, the soul and the life principle. The process of establishing this inter-linking and inter-relation, and the strengthening of the bridge thus constructed, goes on until the Third Initiation. The lines of force are then so inter-related that the soul and its mechanism of expression are a unity. A higher blending and fusing can then go on.

I can perhaps indicate the nature of this process in the following manner: I have stated here and elsewhere that the soul anchors itself in the body at two points:

1. There is a thread of energy, which we call the life or spirit aspect, anchored in the heart. It uses the blood stream, as is well known, as its distributing agency, and through the medium of the blood, life energy is carried to every part of the mechanism. This life energy carries the re-generating power and coordinating energy to all the physical organisms and keeps the body "whole."

2. There is a thread of energy, which we call the consciousness aspect or the faculty of soul knowledge, anchored in the centre of the head. It controls that response mechanism which we call the brain, and through its medium it directs activity and induces awareness throughout the body by means of the nervous system.

These two energy factors, which are recognised by the human being as knowledge and life, or as intelligence and living energy, are the two poles of his being. The task ahead of him now is to develop consciously the middle or balancing aspect, which is love or *group relationship*. (See *Education in the New Age,* pages 26-27, 32-33, 92.)

*The Nature of the Antahkarana*

One of the difficulties connected with this study of the antahkarana is the fact that hitherto the work done upon the antahkarana has been entirely unconscious. Therefore, the concept in men's minds relating to this form of creative work and this construction of the bridge meets at first with little response from the mind nature; also, in order to express these ideas, we have practically to create a new terminology, for there are no words suitable to define our meaning. Just as modern sciences have evolved a complete new terminology of their own during the past forty years, so this science must develop its own peculiar vocabulary. In the meantime, we must do the best we can with the words at our disposal.

The second point I would make is to ask those who are studying along these lines to realise that in time they will arrive at understanding, but that at present all that they can do is to depend upon the unalterable tendency of the subconscious nature to penetrate to the surface of consciousness as a reflex activity in the establishing of continuity of consciousness. This reflex activity of the lower nature corresponds to the development of continuity between the superconscious and the consciousness which develops upon the Path of Discipleship. It is all a part—in three stages—of the integrating process, proving to the disciple that all of life is (in terms of consciousness) one of *revelation*. Ponder on this.

Another of the difficulties in considering any of these esoteric sciences that deal with what has been called the "conscious unfoldment of the divine recognitions" (which is true awareness) is the ancient habit of humanity to materialise all knowledge. Everything man learns is applied—as the centuries pass—to the world of natural phenomena and of natural process, and not to the recognition of the Self, the Knower, the Beholder, the Observer. When, therefore, man enters upon the Path, he has to educate himself in the process of using knowledge in reference to the conscious self-aware Identity, or to the self-contained, self-initiating Individual. When he can do this, he is transmuting knowledge into wisdom.

Previously I spoke of "knowledge-wisdom" which are words synonymous with "force-energy." *Knowledge used is force expressing itself; wisdom used is energy in action.* In these words you have the expression of a great spiritual law, one which you would do well to consider carefully. Knowledge-force concerns the personality and the world of material values; wisdom-energy expresses itself through the consciousness thread and the creative thread, as they constitute in themselves a woven dual strand. They are (for the disciple) a fusion of the past (consciousness thread) and the present (the creative thread), and together they form what is usually called, upon the Path of Return, the Antahkarana. This is not entirely accurate. The wisdom-energy thread is the sutratma or life thread, for the *sutratma* (when blended with the consciousness thread) is again also called the *antahkarana*. Perhaps it might clarify the issue somewhat if I pointed out that though these threads eternally exist in time and space, they appear distinct and separate until a man is a probationary disciple, and therefore becoming conscious of himself and not only of the not-self. There is the life thread or sutratma and the consciousness thread—the one anchored in the heart and the other in the head. Throughout all the past centuries, the creative thread, in one or other of its three aspects, has been slowly woven by the man; of this fact in nature his creative activity during the past two hundred years is an indication, so that today the creative thread is a unity, generally speaking, as regards humanity as a whole and specifically of the individual disciple, and forms a strong closely woven thread upon the mental plane.

These three major threads which are in reality six, if the creative thread is differentiated into its component parts, form the antahkarana. They embody past and present experience and are so recognised by the aspirant. It is only upon the Path itself that the phrase "building the antahkarana" becomes accurate and appropriate. It is in this connection that confusion is apt to arise in the mind of the student. He forgets that it is a purely arbitrary distinction of the lower analysing mind to call this stream of energy the sutratma, and another stream of energy the consciousness thread and a third stream of energy the creative thread. They are essentially, all three of them together, the antahkarana in process of forming. It is equally arbitrary to call the bridge which the disciple builds from the lower mental plane—via the egoic, central vortex of force—the antahkarana. But for purposes of comprehending study and practical experience, *we will define the antahkarana as the extension of the threefold thread* (hitherto woven unconsciously, through life experimentation and the response of consciousness to environment) *through the process of projecting consciously the triple blended energies of the personality as they are impulsed by the soul, across a gap in consciousness which has hitherto existed.* Two events can then occur:

1. The magnetic response of the Spiritual Triad (atma-buddhi-manas), which is the expression of the Monad, is evoked. A triple stream of spiritual energy is slowly projected towards the egoic lotus and towards the lower man.

2. The personality then begins to bridge the gap which exists on its side between the manasic permanent atom and the mental unit, between the higher abstract mind and the lower mind.

Technically, and upon the Path of Discipleship, this bridge between the personality in its three aspects and the monad and its three aspects is called the antahkarana.

This antahkarana is the product of the united effort of soul and personality, working *together consciously* to produce this bridge. When it is completed, there is a perfect rapport between the monad and its physical plane expression, the initiate in the outer world. The third initiation marks the consummation of the process, and there is then a straight line of relationship between the monad and the lower personal self. The fourth initiation marks the complete realisation of this relation by the initiate. It enables him to say: "I and my Father are one." It is for this reason that the crucifixion, or the Great Renunciation, takes place. Forget not that it is the soul that is crucified. It is Christ Who "dies." It is not the man; it is not Jesus. The causal body disappears. The man is *monadically* conscious. The soul-body no longer serves any useful purpose; it is no more needed. Nothing is left but the sutratma, qualified by consciousness—a consciousness which still preserves identity whilst merged in the whole. Another qualification is creativity; thus consciousness can be focussed at will on the physical plane in an outer body or form. This body is will-created by the Master.

But in this task of unfoldment, of evolution and of development, the mind of man has to understand, analyse, formulate and distinguish; therefore the temporary differentiations are of profound and useful importance. We might therefore conclude that the task of the disciple is:

1. To become conscious of the following situations (if I may use such a word):

   a. Process in combination with force.

   b. Status upon the path, or recognition of the available qualifying agencies, or energies.

   c. Fusion or integration of the consciousness thread with the creative thread and with the life thread.

   d. Creative activity. This is essential, for it is not only through the development of creative ability in the three worlds that the necessary focal point is created, but this also leads to the building of the antahkarana, its "creation."

2. To construct the antahkarana between the Spiritual Triad and the personality—with the cooperation of the

soul. These three points of divine energy might be symbolised thus:

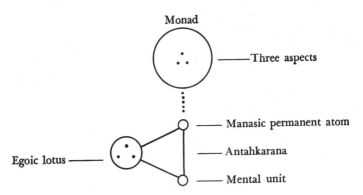

In this simple symbol you have a picture of the disciple's task upon the Path.

Another diagram may serve to clarify:

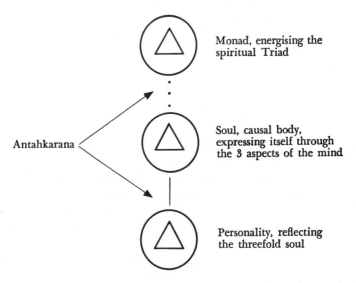

In these you have the "nine of initiation" or the transmuting of nine forces into divine energies:

## The Bridge between the three Aspects of the Mind

There is one point which I would like to clarify if I can, for—on this point—there is much confusion in the minds of aspirants, and this is necessarily so.

Let us for a moment, therefore, consider just where the aspirant stands when he starts consciously to build the antahkarana. Behind him lie a long series of existences, the experience of which has brought him to the point where he is able consciously to assess his condition and arrive at some understanding of his point in evolution. He can consequently undertake—in cooperation with his steadily awakening and focussing consciousness—to take the next step, which is that of accepted discipleship. In the present, he is oriented towards the soul; he, through meditation and the mystical experience, does have occasional contact with the soul, and this happens with increasing frequency; he is becoming somewhat creative upon the physical plane, both in his thinking and in his actions; at times, even if rarely, he has a genuine intuitive experience. This intuitive experience serves to anchor the "first tenuous thread spun by the Weaver in fohatic enterprise," as the *Old Commentary* puts it. It is the first cable, projected from the Spiritual Triad in response to the emanation of the personality, and this is the result of the growing magnetic potency of both these aspects of the Monad in manifestation.

It will be obvious to you that when the personality is becoming adequately magnetised from the spiritual angle, its note or sound will go forth and will evoke response from the soul on its own plane. Later the personality note and the soul note in unison will produce a definitely attractive effect upon the Spiritual Triad. This Spiritual Triad in its turn has been exerting an increasingly magnetic effect upon the personality. This begins at the time of the first *conscious* soul contact. The response of the Triad is transmitted necessarily, in this early stage, via the sutratma and produces inevitably the awakening of the head centre. That is why the heart doctrine begins to supersede the doctrine of the eye.

The heart doctrine governs occult development; the eye doctrine—which is the doctrine of the eye of vision—governs the mystical experience; the heart doctrine is based upon the universal nature of the soul, conditioned by the Monad, the One, and involves reality; the eye doctrine is based on the dual relation between soul and personality. It involves the spiritual relationships, but the attitude of dualism or of the recognition of the polar opposites is implicit in it. These are important points to remember as this new science becomes more widely known.

The aspirant eventually arrives at the point where the three threads—of life, of consciousness and of creativity—are being focussed, recognised as energy streams, and utilised deliberately by the aspiring disciple upon the *lower mental plane*. There—esoterically speaking—"he takes his stand, and looking upward sees a promised land of beauty, love and future vision."

But there exists a *gap in consciousness*, though not in fact. The sutratmic strand of energy bridges the gap, and tenuously relates monad, soul and personality. But the consciousness thread extends only from soul to personality—from the involutionary sense. From the evolutionary angle (using a paradoxical phrase) there is only a very little *conscious awareness* existing between the soul and the personality, from the standpoint of the personality upon the evolutionary arc of the Path of Return. A man's whole effort is to become aware of the soul and to transmute his consciousness into that of the soul, whilst still preserving the consciousness of the personality. As the fusion of soul and personality is strengthened, the creative thread becomes increasingly active, and thus the three threads steadily fuse, blend, become dominant, and the aspirant is then ready to bridge the gap and unite the Spiritual Triad and the personality, through the medium of the soul. This involves a direct effort at divine creative work. The clue to understanding lies perhaps in the thought that hitherto the relation between soul and personality has been steadily carried forward, primarily by the soul, as it stimulated the personality to effort, vision and expansion. Now—at this stage—the integrated, rapidly developing personality becomes consciously active, and (in unison with the soul) starts building the antahkarana—a fusion of the three threads and a projection of them into the "higher wider reaches" of the mental plane, until the abstract mind and the lower concrete mind are related by the triple cable.

It is to this process that our studies are related; earlier experience in relation to the three threads is logically regarded as having occurred normally. The man now stands, holding the mind steady in the light; he has some knowledge of meditation, much devotion, and also recognition of the next step. Knowledge of process gradually becomes clearer; a growing soul contact is established; occasional flashes of intuitive perception from the Triad occur. All these recognitions are not present in the case of every disciple; some are present; some are not. I am seeking to give a general picture. Individual application and future realisation have to be worked out by the disciple in the crucible of experience.

The goal towards which the average disciple has worked in the past has been soul contact, leading eventually to what has been called "hierarchical inclusion." The reward of the disciple's effort has been admittance into the Ashram of some Master, increased opportunity to serve in the world, and also the taking of certain initiations. The goal towards which higher disciples are working involves not only soul contact as its primary objective (for that has to some measure been attained), but the building of the bridge from the personality to the Spiritual Triad, with consequent monadic realisation and the opening up to the initiate of the Way to the Higher Evolution in its various branches and with its differing goals and objectives. The distinction (I said not "difference," and would have you note this) between the two ways can be seen in the following listed comparisons:

| | |
|---|---|
| Desire — Aspiration | Mind — Projection |
| The 1st and 2nd Initiations | The 3rd and 4th Initiations |
| Universal Love and Intuition | Universal Will and Mind |

| | |
|---|---|
| The Path of Light | The Way of the Higher Evolution |
| The Point of Contact | The Antahkarana or Bridge |
| The Plan | The Purpose |
| The Three Layers of the Egoic Petals | The Spiritual Triad |
| The Hierarchy | Shamballa |
| The Master's Ashram | The Council Chamber |
| The Seven Paths | The Seven Paths |

In reality, you have here the two major approaches to God or to the Divine Whole, both merging at the time of the fifth initiation in the one Way, which in itself combines all Ways. Forget not a statement which I have several times made, that the four minor rays must merge eventually into the third ray, and that all five must then finally merge into the second and the first rays; bear also in mind that all these rays or modes of Being are aspects or sub-rays of the second *cosmic* Ray of Love and of Fire.

I would like here also to point out some further relationships. You know well that upon the mental plane the three aspects of mind, or the three focal points of mental perception and activity, are to be found:

1. *The lower concrete mind.* This expresses itself most completely through the fifth Ray of Concrete Science, reflecting the lower phase of the will aspect of divinity and summarising within itself all knowledge as well as the egoic memory. This lower concrete mind is related to the knowledge petals of the egoic lotus and is capable of pronounced soul illumination, proving eventually to be the searchlight of the soul. It can be brought under control through the processes of concentration. It is transient in time and space. Through conscious, creative work, it can be related to the manasic permanent atom or to the abstract mind.

2. *The Son of Mind.* This is the soul itself, governed by the second aspect of all the seven rays—a point I would ask you seriously to register. It reflects the lower phase of the love aspect of divinity and summarises in itself the results of all accumulated knowledge which is wisdom, illumi-

nated by the light of the intuition. Another way of expressing this is to describe it as love, availing itself of experience and knowledge. It expresses itself most fully through the love petals of its innate being. Through dedicated and devoted service it brings the divine Plan into activity in the three worlds of human accomplishment. It is therefore related to the second aspect of the Spiritual Triad and is brought into functioning activity through meditation. It then controls and utilises for its own spiritual ends the consecrated personality, via the illumined mind, referred to above. It is eternal in time and space.

3. *The abstract mind.* This reveals itself most completely under the influence of the first Ray of Will or Power, reflecting the higher aspect of the will of divinity or of the atmic principle; it summarises in itself when fully developed the purpose of Deity, and thus becomes responsible for the emergence of the Plan. It energises the will petals until such time as the eternal life of the soul is absorbed into that which is neither transient nor eternal but which is endless, boundless and unknown. It is brought into conscious functioning through the building of the antahkarana. This "radiant rainbow bridge" unites the illumined personality, focussed in the mind body, motivated by the love of the soul, with the Monad or with the One Life, and thus enables the divine manifesting Son of God to express the significance of the words: God is Love and God is a consuming Fire. This fire, energised by love, has burnt out all personality qualities, leaving only a purified instrument, coloured by the soul ray and no longer necessitating the existence of a soul body. The personality has by this time completely absorbed the soul, or to put it perhaps more accurately, both soul and personality have been fused and blended into one instrument for the use of the One Life.

This is but a picture or a symbolic use of words in order to express the unifying goal of material and spiritual evolution, as it is carried to its conclusion—for this world cycle—through the development of the three aspects of mind upon the mental plane. The cosmic implications will not be lost to you, but it profits us not to dwell upon them. As this process is carried forward, three great aspects of divine manifestation emerge upon the theatre of world life and on the physical plane. These are Humanity, the Hierarchy and Shamballa.

Humanity is already the dominant kingdom in nature; the fact of the Hierarchy and of its imminent approach into physical appearance is becoming well known to hundreds of thousands of people today. Its recognised appearance will later set the stage for the needed preparatory phases which will finally lead to the exoteric rule of the Lord of the World, emerging from His aeonial seclusion in Shamballa, and coming forth into outer expression at the end of this world cycle.

Here is the vast and necessary picture, presented in order to give reason and power to the next stage of human evolution.

The point which I seek to emphasise is that only when the aspirant takes his stand with definiteness upon the mental plane, and keeps his "focus of awareness" increasingly there, does it become possible for him to make real progress in the work of divine bridge building, the work of invocation, and the establishing of a conscious rapport between the Triad, the soul and the personality. The period covered by the conscious building of the antahkarana is that from the final stages of the Path of Probation to the third initiation.

In considering this process it is necessary, in the early stages, to recognise the three aspects of the mind as they express themselves upon the mental plane and produce the varying states of consciousness upon that plane. It is interesting here to note that, having reached the developed human stage (integrated, aspiring, oriented and devoted), the man stands firmly upon the lower levels of that mental plane; he is then faced by the seven subplanes of that plane with their corresponding states of consciousness. He is therefore entering upon a new cycle where—this time equipped with full self-consciousness—he has seven states of mental awareness to develop; these are all innate or inherent in him, and all (when mastered) lead to one or other of the seven major initiations. These seven states of consciousness are—beginning from the first or lowest:

### Mental Plane

1. Lower mental awareness. The development of true mental perception.

2. Soul awareness or soul perception. This is not the perception of the soul by the personality, but the registering of that which the soul perceives by the soul itself. This is later registered by the lower mind. This soul perception is, therefore, the reversal of the usual attitude of mind.

3. Higher abstract awareness. The unfoldment of the intuition and the recognition of intuitive process by the lower mind.

### Buddhic Plane

4. Persistent, conscious, spiritual awareness. This is the full consciousness of the buddhic or intuitional level. This is the perceptive consciousness which is the outstanding characteristic of the Hierarchy. The life focus of the man shifts to the buddhic plane. This is the fourth or middle state of consciousness.

### Atmic Plane

5. The consciousness of the spiritual will as it is expressed and experienced upon atmic levels or upon the third plane of divine manifestation. There is little that I can say about this condition of awareness; its state of nirvanic awareness can mean but little to the average disciple.

### Monadic Plane

6. The inclusive awareness of the Monad upon its own plane, the second plane of our planetary and solar life.

### Logoic Plane

7. Divine consciousness. This is the awareness of the whole on the highest plane of our planetary manifestation. This is also an aspect of solar awareness upon the same plane.

As we strive to arrive at some dim comprehension of the nature of the work to be done in building the antahkarana it might be wise, as a preliminary step, to consider the nature of the substance out of which the "bridge of shining mind stuff" has to be built by the conscious aspirant. The oriental term for this "mind stuff" is *chitta;* it exists in three types of substance, all basically identical but all qualified or conditioned differently. It is a fundamental law in this solar system, and therefore in our planetary life experience, that the substance through which divinity (in time and space) expresses itself is karmically conditioned; it is impregnated by those qualities and aspects which are the product of earlier manifestations of that Being in Whom we live and move and have our being. This is the basic fact lying behind the expression of that Trinity or Triad of Aspects with which all the world religions have made us familiar. This trinity is as follows:

1. *The Father Aspect*    This is the underlying Plan of God.
   The Will Aspect.   The essential Cause of Being.
   Purpose.   Life purpose, motivating evolution.
     The note of synthetic sound.
   *Utilises the sutratma*

2. *The Son Aspect*   The quality of sensitivity.
   The Love Aspect.   The nature of relationship.
   Wisdom. Understanding.   The method of evolution.
   Consciousness. Soul.   The note of attractive sound.
   *Utilises the consciousness thread*

3. *The Mother Aspect*   The intelligence of substance.
   The Intelligence Aspect.   The nature of form.
   The Holy Spirit.   Response to evolution.
     The note of Nature.
   *Develops the creative thread*

The mental plane which must be bridged is like a great stream of consciousness or of conscious substance, and across this stream the antahkarana must be constructed. This is the concept which lies behind this teaching and behind the symbolism of the Path. Before a man can tread the Path, he must become that Path himself. Out of the substance of his own life he must construct this rainbow bridge, this Lighted Way. He spins it and anchors it as a spider spins a thread along which it can travel. Each of his three divine aspects contributes to that bridge, and the time of this building is indicated when his lower nature is:

1. Becoming oriented, regulated and creative.
2. Recognising and reacting to soul contact and control.
3. Sensitive to the first impression of the Monad. This sensitivity is indicated where there is:

   a. Submission to the "will of God" or of the greater Whole.
   b. Unfoldment of the inner spiritual will, overcoming all obstacles.
   c. Cooperation with the purpose of the Hierarchy, the interpreting will of God as expressed in love.

I have enumerated these three responses to the totality of the divine aspects because they are related to the antahkarana and must become defined and conditioned upon the mental plane. They are there to be found expressing themselves in substance:

1. The lower concrete mind.
   The receptive common sense.
   The highest aspect of the form nature.
   The reflection of atma, the spiritual will.
   The throat centre.
   Knowledge.

2. The individualised mind.
   The soul or spiritual ego.
   The middle principle. Buddhi-manas.
   The reflection in mental substance of the Monad.
   Spiritual love-wisdom.
   The heart centre.
   Love.

3. The higher abstract mind.
   The transmitter of buddhi.
   The reflection of the divine nature.
   Intuitive love, understanding, inclusiveness.
   The head centre.
   Sacrifice.

There are necessarily other arrangements of these aspects in manifestation, but the above will serve to indicate the relation of Monad-soul-personality as they express themselves through certain focussed stations or points of power *upon the mental plane*.

In humanity, however, the major realisation to be grasped at the present point in human evolution is the need to relate—consciously and effectively—the spiritual Triad, the soul on its own plane and the personality in its three-fold nature. This is done *through the creative work of the personality, the magnetic power of the Triad, and the conscious activity of the soul, utilising the triple thread.*

You can see, therefore, why so much emphasis is laid by esotericists upon fusion, unity or blending; only when this is intelligently realised can the disciple begin to weave the threads into a bridge of light which eventually becomes the Lighted Way across which he can pass into the higher worlds of being. Thus he liberates himself from the three worlds. It is—in this world cycle—pre-eminently a question of fusion and expressing (in full waking awareness) three major states of consciousness:

1. *The Shamballa Consciousness.*
   Awareness of the unity and purpose of Life.
   Recognition and cooperation with the Plan.
   Will. Direction. Oneness.
   The influence of the Triad.

2. *The Hierarchical Consciousness.*
   Awareness of the Self, the Soul.
   Recognition and cooperation with divinity.
   Love. Attraction. Relation.
   The influence of the Soul.

3. *The Human Consciousness.*
   Awareness of the soul within the form.
   Recognition and cooperation with the soul.
   Intelligence. Action. Expression.
   The influence of the consecrated personality.

The man who finally builds the antahkarana across the mental plane connects or relates these three divine aspects, so that progressively at each initiation they are more closely fused into one divine expression in full and radiant manifestation. Putting it in other words, the disciple treads the path of return, builds the antahkarana, crosses the Lighted Way, and achieves the freedom of the Path of Life.

One of the points which it is essential that students should grasp is the deeply esoteric fact that this antahkarana is built through the medium of a conscious effort *within consciousness itself,* and not just by attempting to be good, or to express goodwill, or to demonstrate the qualities of unselfishness and high aspiration. Many esotericists seem to regard the treading of the Path as the conscious effort to overcome the lower nature and to express life in terms of right living and thinking, love and intelligent understanding. It is all that, but *it is something far more.* Good character and good spiritual aspiration are basic essentials. But these are taken for granted by the Master Who has a disciple under training; their foundation and their recognition and development are the objectives upon the Path of Probation.

But to build the antahkarana is to relate the three divine aspects. This involves intense mental activity; it necessitates the power to imagine and to visualise, plus a dramatic attempt to build the Lighted Way in mental substance. This mental substance is—as we have seen—of three qualities or natures, and the bridge of living light is a composite creation, having in it:

1. Force, focussed and projected from the fused and blended forces of the personality.
2. Energy, drawn from the egoic body by a conscious effort.
3. Energy, abstracted from the Spiritual Triad.

It is essentially, however, an activity of the integrated and dedicated personality. Esotericists must not take the position that all they have to do is to await negatively some activity by the soul which will automatically take place after a certain measure of soul contact has been achieved, and that consequently and in time this activity will evoke response both from the personality and the Triad. This is *not* the case. The work of the building of the antahkarana is primarily an activity of the personality, aided by the soul; this in time evokes a reaction from the Triad. There is far too much inertia demonstrated by aspirants at this time.

One might also look at this matter from another angle. The personality is beginning to transmute knowledge into wisdom, and when this takes place the focus of the personality life is then upon the mental plane, because the transmutation process (with its stages of understanding, analysis, recognition and application) is fundamentally a mental process. The personality is also beginning to comprehend the significance of love and to interpret it in terms of the group well-being, and not in terms of the personal self, of desire or even of aspiration. True love is rightly understood only by the mental type who is spiritually oriented. The personality is also arriving at the realisation that there is in reality no such thing as sacrifice. Sacrifice is usually only the thwarted desire of the lower nature, willingly endured by the aspirant, but—in this phase—a misinterpretation and limitation. Sacrifice is really complete conformity to the will of God because the spiritual will of the man and the divine will (as he recognises it in the Plan) is his will. There is a growing identification in purpose. Therefore, self-will, desire and those intelligent activities which are dually motivated are seen and recognised as only the lower expression of the three divine aspects, and the effort is to express these in terms of the soul and not, as hitherto, in terms of a dedicated and rightly oriented personality. This becomes possible in its true sense only when the focus of the life is in the mental vehicle and the head as well as the heart is becoming active. In this process, the stages of character building are seen as essential and effective, and are willingly and consciously undertaken. But—when these foundations of good character and intelligent activity are firmly established—something still higher and more subtle must be erected on the sub-structure.

*Knowledge-wisdom* must be superseded by intuitive

understanding; this is, in reality, inclusive participation in the creative activity of divinity. The divine idea must become the possible ideal, and this ideal must become unfolded and manifested in substance upon the physical plane. The creative thread, now somewhat ready, must be brought into conscious functioning and activity.

*Desire-love* must be interpreted in terms of divine attraction, involving the right use or misuse of energies and forces. This process puts the disciple in touch with divinity as a progressively revealed Whole. The part, through the magnetic development of its own nature, comes into touch gradually with all that IS. The disciple becomes aware of this sum total in increasingly vivid expansions of consciousness, leading to initiation, realisation and identification. These are the three stages of initiation.

The consciousness thread, in cooperation with the creative thread and the life thread, awakens to a fully aware process of participation in the divine creative Plan—a Plan which is motivated by love and intelligently carried forward.

*Direction-Will* (which are words describing the orientation produced by the understanding of the two processes of knowledge-wisdom and desire-love) must produce the final orientation of the personality and the soul, fused and blended and at-one, towards the freedom of the Spiritual Triad; then the conscious attempt to use these three energies eventuates in creating the antahkarana upon the mental plane. You will note that at this early stage of the process I am emphasising the words "orientation" and "attempt." They simply indicate the final control of substance by the initiate.

One of the indications that a man is no longer upon the Probationary Path is his emerging from the realm of aspiration and devotion into the world of the *focussed will*. Another indication is that he begins to interpret life in terms of energy and forces, and not in terms of quality and desire. This marks a definite step forward. There is too little use of the spiritual will, as the result of right orientation, in the life of disciples today.

In the future, this Science of the Antahkarana and its lower correspondence, the Science of Social Evolution (which is the joint or united antahkarana of humanity as a whole), will be known as the Science of Invocation and Evocation. It is in reality the Science of Magnetic Rapport, in which right relationship is brought about by mutual invocation, producing a responsive process which is one of evocation. It is this science which lies behind all conscious awakening of the centres and their interrelation; it lies behind the rapport between man and man, group and group, and eventually between nation and nation. It is this invocation, and the consequent evocation, which eventually relate soul and personality and soul and monad. It is the outstanding objective of humanity's appeal to God, to the Hierarchy and to the Spiritual Powers of the cosmos, no matter by what name you call them. The appeal goes forth. The invocation of humanity can and will and must evoke response from the spiritual Hierarchy and give the first demonstration upon a large scale of this new esoteric science—esoteric because it is based upon sound. Hence the use of the O.M. Into this science I cannot here go; we must confine our attention to our theme, which is the Science of the Antahkarana.

## The Bridge as the Agent of Alignment

The word "alignment" is used much in modern esoteric training. I would point out that in making his alignment the aspirant is only establishing the first stage of his process of realisation; he is establishing in his own consciousness the fact of his essential *dualism*. I would also point out that the critical aspect of this process is only arrived at when the distinction is sharply defined and recognised between the integrated and potent personality and the soul. It is an occult truism to state that the *aspirant* is to be recognised by ∴ or triplicity; the *disciple* by ⊕ or recognised duality and the *initiate* by ◯ or unity. Note that the symbol of duality for undeveloped humanity is ⊖ in which the separation of the higher nature from the lower is depicted; in the case of the disciple, it is ⊕ showing the "path across" or the narrow razor-edged Path between the pairs of opposites, forming later the antahkarana. These symbols, simple as they are, embody and convey vast truths to the illumined mind.

Relatively speaking, and speaking in terms of the mental consciousness, the realisation of duality is only to be found in the three worlds and on the mental plane. When the third initiation is taken, the power of the lower pair of opposites is no longer felt and exists no more. A liberated consciousness and an unrestricted awareness—unrestricted as regards the initiate, moving within the orbit of the planetary Logos (though not unrestricted as regards that greater Life which moves within still other and greater defined limits)—are both understood and expressed. Within the planetary ring-pass-not the initiate moves with freedom and knows no limitation in consciousness. That is why the higher levels of our planetary and systemic planes are called formless. It is this ⓘ which is the true symbol of alignment, involving as it does the sense of duality but indicating at the same time the way through what are called "the walls of limitation."

Students would do well to consider the building of the antahkarana *as an extension in consciousness*. This extension is the first definite effort made upon the Path to bring in the monadic influence with full awareness, and finally directly. This process constitutes the individual parallel to the present inflow of force from Shamballa, about which I have elsewhere spoken. That highest Centre of energy upon our planet is now having a definite effect upon that centre which we call Humanity. This is brought about by direct alignment, and not via the Hierarchy as has hitherto been the case. When the individual antahkarana has been successfully started, and there is even a tenuous thread of living energy connecting the threefold personality and the Spiritual Triad, then the inflow of the will-energy becomes possible. This, in the early stages, can be most dangerous when not offset by the love energy of the soul. Only one thread of the threefold antahkarana passes through the egoic lotus.

The other two threads relate themselves directly with the Triad, and hence eventually with the Monad, the source of the triadal life. This is true of the individual and of humanity as a whole, and the effects of this alignment can be seen demonstrating in the world at this time.

This rather unexpected responsive activity has necessitated much increased activity on the part of the Hierarchy, in order to offset the consequences of any premature inflow of the will force. After the third initiation, when the soul body, the causal body, starts to dissipate, the line of relation or of connection can be and is direct. The initiate then "stands in the ocean of love, and through him pours that love; his will is love and he can safely work, for love divine will colour all his will, and he can wisely serve." Love and intelligence then become the servants of the will. Soul energy and personality force contribute to the experience of the Monad in the three worlds of life service, and then the age-long task of the incarnating spiritual man is finally accomplished. He is ready for Nirvana, which is but the Way into new fields of spiritual experience and of divine development —incomprehensible as yet, even to the initiate of the third degree. This Way is revealed only when the antahkarana is built and completed and the man becomes focussed in the Triad as consciously as he is now focussed in the threefold lower nature.

Then, and then only, is the *true dualism* of the divine nature apparent and the illusory duality disappears. Then you have Spirit-matter, Life-form. For this the triple experience of the unfolding consciousness is only preparatory. Through the unfolding consciousness, the initiate knows the significance of life and the uses of form, but stands completely unidentified with either, though blending these dualities in himself into a conscious synthesis. The attempt to convey his state of mind, in words that but limit and confuse, leads to apparent contradictions, and this is one of the peculiar paradoxes of the occult science. Do the above imparted facts make sense to you? Have they meaning for your mind? I think not. You have not yet the needed equip ment through which the type of implied awareness can work, or the realisation of that true *Self*-consciousness which would produce in you an understanding reaction. I simply make the esoteric assertion; later will come apprehension of the truth and that consequent energising which always comes when any abstract truth is truly appreciated and assimilated. But the time has not yet come for the comprehension of the above information. Disciples and aspirants grow through the means of a presented vision—unattainable as yet but definitely an extension of the known and previously grasped. Such is the mode of evolution, for it is ever a pressing forward towards the sensed.

Today, through human effort and hierarchical endeavour, a great alignment and linking up is taking place, and Monad-Soul-Personality are being more directly related than has hitherto been possible. One reason for this is that there are present in incarnation upon the planet many more initiates of the third degree than ever before; there are many more disciples being prepared for the third initiation; and in this third strictly human race, the Aryan (using this term in its generic sense and not in its prostituted German connotation), the three aspects of the personality are now so potent that their magnetic influence and their creative effect are making the building of the antahkarana an outstanding achievement, thus linking and aligning the three aspects in man. The same is true of the three divine centres in the planet which embody these divine qualities: Shamballa, Hierarchy, and Humanity. These are now closely aligned, thus producing a fusion of energies which is causing an inflow of the spiritual will, as well as a demonstration of the Destroyer aspect.

I have here indicated much of interest; I have pointed out a goal and indicated a Way. I have related (in consciousness) the Hierarchy and Shamballa. This signifies a great and critical moment in human affairs and an opportunity hitherto unparalleled in history. The need for a due appreciation of this will be evident, and should incite all who read to renewed effort and to fresh endeavour. Students must seek to meet all the planetary changes and opportunities with corresponding changes in their own lives. They must seek those new attitudes and those new creative approaches which will result not alone in the building of the individual antahkarana, but also in the fusion of the many "radiant strands" which will produce those "connecting cables," speaking symbolically, which will relate the planetary centres and present the medium along which can pass the fiery will and the predetermined purpose of Deity. This will bring about the reconstruction of the manifested worlds, and in this task each and every one of you can have his share.

Let us now take up our next point in this section and indicate the technique for the constructing of the antahkarana. This will constitute an intensely practical teaching for which all that I have hitherto given should prove a firm foundation.

### The Technique of Construction

It is my intention to be very practical. The building of the antahkarana (which is consciously undertaken upon the Path of Discipleship) is a process which is followed under certain ancient and proven rules. When these rules are correctly followed, the sequence of events and the appearance of the desired results are inevitable and unavoidable. There is much that I could say which would be of small use to the average aspirant, as it would be concerned with subjective realities which—though existent and occult facts in a natural process—are as yet unrealisable. My problem is to present the process in such a manner that—towards the end of this century—educators will be thinking, speaking and teaching *in terms of bridging,* and thus approaching basic statements which have a definite bearing upon this point which we are considering. I would like here very succinctly to recall a few of them to your attention:

1. Knowledge-force expresses itself through the consciousness thread and the creative thread.
2. These two threads are, for the disciple, a fusion of

past knowledge (the consciousness thread) and the present (the creative thread).

3. The life thread or sutratma proper is closely blended with these two. You then have atma-buddhi-manas (the latter being the agent of creation) functioning to a certain degree consciously in the aspirant.

4. The fusion of personality and soul is in process, but when it has reached a certain point it becomes apparent that a creativity or a creative activity of the Will is needed to bridge between the Spiritual Triad and the personality, via the soul.

5. The bridge which must be constructed is called, technically, the antahkarana.

6. This bridge has to be built by the aspirant who is focussed upon the mental plane, because it is mental substance (in three grades) which must be used, and the three aspects of the mind—the manasic permanent atom, the Son of Mind or Ego, and the mental unit —are all involved in the process.

Students would do well to learn that this process of building the antahkarana is one of the means whereby man, the trinity, becomes a duality. When the task is completed and the antahkarana is definitely built—thus producing perfect alignment between the Monad and its expression upon the physical plane—the body of the soul (the causal body) is completely and finally destroyed by the fire of the Monad, pouring down the antahkarana. There is then complete reciprocity between the Monad and the fully conscious soul on the physical plane. The "divine intermediary" is no longer required. The "Son of God Who is the Son of Mind" dies; the "veil of the temple is rent in twain from the top to the bottom"; the fourth initiation is passed, and there then comes the revelation of the Father.

This is the final and far-reaching result of the building of the bridge which is, in reality, the establishing of a line of light between Monad and personality as a full expression of the soul—between spirit and matter, between Father and Mother. It is evidence that "spirit has mounted on the shoulders of matter" to that high place from whence it originally came, plus the gain of experience and of full knowledge, and of all that life in material form could give and all that conscious experience could confer. The Son has done His work. The task of the Saviour or of the Mediator has been completed. The unity of all things is known to be a fact in consciousness, and a human spirit can say with intention and with understanding: "I and my Father are one."

The above is a brief and probably meaningless statement except theoretically, but it summarises the task which lies ahead and the work of the disciple who is in process of constructing the antahkarana. There is a close connection between the fourth initiation, the quaternary in its evolved condition—vital body, emotional vehicle, mind and soul—and this fourth technical stage of building consciously the "rainbow bridge." You have therefore:

1. The Quaternary, the creative factor on Earth.
2. The fourth initiation, that of the Crucifixion.
3. The fourth technical stage of building the Antahkarana:
    a. Sutratma, the life thread.
    b. The consciousness thread.
    c. The creative thread, itself threefold.
    d. The technical antahkarana, bridging between the threefold personality and the Spiritual Triad.
4. The four stages of the Path of Return:
    a. The stage of evolution itself.
    b. The stage of the Probationary Path.
    c. The stage of the Path of Discipleship.
    d. The stage of the Path of Initiation.

Yet it is one and the same entity which participates in and is responsible for all the differentiated aspects, steps and stages—experimenting, experiencing and expressing consciously in every one of these stages or modes of life, until the fourth initiation. Then consciousness itself gives place to life, and yet remains itself. To the above statement, add the fact that it is the fourth kingdom in nature which undergoes all that is indicated above and is conditioned by the four aspects of the one sutratma. Once this is grasped, the beauty of the symbolism and the numerological relationships emerge significantly.

*The Construction of the Antahkarana ... Past*

In connection with this there is no need for elaboration, as it must be obvious that only the man who is the product of a very long and fruitful past experience is equipped to undertake the task of bridge building. The process involves much scientific experience in the art of living, and only the highly trained human enquirer can soundly and safely build the bridge between the highest and the lowest. Each of the major human races has been responsible for the expression and the employment of the threads which together form the antahkarana:

1. In *ancient Lemuria,* the life thread, the sutratma per se, was the dominant factor in the life expression; the physical body, the animal form nature, and the dense outer factor was the focus of life exuberant, productive and vital.

2. In *old Atlantis,* the consciousness thread began to function in a way unrealised in Lemuria. Sensitivity, awareness and—as a result—desire and reaction were the keynotes. Active sensitivity as a prelude to full consciousness distinguished the human being. The astral vehicle was a controlling factor. The mind was relatively quiescent, except where the foremost members of the human race were concerned. The humanity of that world cycle were, however, all of them extremely psychic and mediumistic; they were "sensitives," in the modern use of the term. The state of awareness was astral, and human beings were—as a race—clairaudient and clairvoyant, though in no way able to interpret that which they contacted; they were not able to distinguish astral phenomena from ordinary physical life (particularly in the middle period of their racial history), and the interpreting mind revealed nothing to them. They

simply lived and felt. Such was their life history. Two of
the threads were functioning; one was not functioning at
all. The bridge was *not* built.

3. In our *modern Aryan race*—modern as far as racial
histories are concerned—the third thread, the creative
thread, comes into active expression and use. I would remind you that all these threads exist from the beginning
of human existence, and that all these three streams of
energy have been indissolubly present from the beginning
of human consciousness. But for the greater part of human
history, up to the present, men remained unaware of them,
and quite unconsciously made use of and continued to make
use of their presence. The process of recognising creative
ability and of opportunity falls into two phases or stages:

> a. The stage wherein the mind principle is de-
> veloped and unfolded and man becomes a mental
> creature. This produces the full activity of the
> mental unit, the integration of the three aspects
> of the personality, and the consequent awareness
> of the Son of Mind or soul.
>
> b. The stage of creative activity wherein the
> creative thread is brought into full use. This per-
> sonality use of the thread—as distinguished from
> racial use—is characteristic of the Aryan race. It
> is only during the past five thousand years that it
> has gradually become the outstanding quality of
> mankind. In the other two races, and in the early
> stages of the Aryan race, although great creative
> monuments appeared everywhere upon the planet,
> they were not the product of the minds of the
> men of the time, but were the imposition of the
> creative will of the planetary Hierarchy upon
> those who were sensitive to the higher impression.
> The responsive sensitivity to creative impression
> was the outstanding quality of the later Atlantean
> consciousness and of the early Aryan period. It is
> today giving place to individual creativity, and
> consequently to the conscious creation of the bridg-

ing antahkarana, which is the outcome of the fused and blended threefold thread.

This brief summation of the past process is intended simply to give a synthetic background to all the work now to be done, and to convey to you an almost visual concept of the method whereby man has reached the stage of conscious life, of full self-awareness and creative expression. All of these were the expression of divine energy as it poured into his mechanism, via the silver thread of divine potency. This might be regarded as a threefold demonstration of the vertical life which becomes the horizontal life through the expression of creativity. Man then indeed becomes the Cross. When, however, he succeeds in constructing the rainbow bridge (which can only be done when man is upon the Fixed Cross), then finally the Cross gives place to the line. This takes place after the fourth initiation—that of the Crucifixion. There remains then only the vertical line "reaching from Heaven to Hell." The goal of the initiate (between the fourth and the seventh initiations) is to resolve the line into the circle, and thus fulfill the law and the "rounding out" of the evolutionary process.

Another summation of the entire process may be found in the lines from *Stanzas for Disciples* which I gave out some time ago (June 1930) and which will also be found elsewhere in this volume.

"In the Cross is hidden Light. The vertical and horizontal in mutual friction create; a vibrant Cross scintillates, and motion originates. When the vertical assumes the horizontal, pralaya supervenes. Evolution is the movement of the horizontal to upright positiveness. In the secret of direction lies the hidden wisdom; in the doctrine of absorption lies the healing faculty; in the point becoming the line, and the line becoming the cross is evolution. In the cross swinging to the horizontal lies salvation and pralayic peace."

It might be said that few, very few, people are today at the Lemurian stage of consciousness wherein the life thread, with its physical implications, is the dominant factor. Many, very many, people are at the Atlantean stage of development of "auric sensitivity." A few—a very few in comparison with the untold masses of human beings—are utilising the results of the triple construction of energy within their own aura of awareness and their area of influence, in order to build, construct and utilise the bridge which links the various aspects of the mental plane. These three aspects they *must* employ simultaneously, and then later supersede them in such a manner that personality and ego disappear and only the Monad and its form upon the physical plane remain. In this connection, my earlier statement on the nature of form may be useful and lead to increased insight and understanding:

The physical plane is a complete reflection of the mental; the lowest three subplanes reflect the abstract subplanes, and the four etheric subplanes reflect the four mental concrete planes. The manifestation of the Ego on the mental plane (or the causal body) is not the result of energy emanating from the permanent atoms as a nucleus of force, but is the result of different forces, and primarily of group force. It is predominantly marked by an act of an exterior force, and is lost in the mysteries of planetary karma. This is equally true of man's lowest manifestations. It is the result of reflex action, and is based on the force of the group of etheric centres through which man (as an aggregate of lives) is functioning. The activity of these centres sets up an answering vibration in the three lowest subplanes of the physical plane, and the interaction between the two causes an adherence to, or aggregation around, the etheric body of particles of what we erroneously term 'dense substance.' This type of energised substance is swept up in the vortex of force currents issuing from the centres and cannot escape. These units of force, therefore, pile up according to the energy direction around and within the etheric sheath till it is hidden and concealed, yet interpenetrating. An inexorable law, the law of matter itself, brings this about, and only those can escape the effect of the vitality of their own centres who are definitely 'Lords of Yoga' and can—through the conscious will of their own being—escape the compelling force of the Law of Attraction working on the lowest cosmic physical subplane.

*A Treatise on Cosmic Fire,* page 789

I have earlier told you that the astral body is an illusion. It is eventually discovered to be nonexistent by the man who has achieved the consciousness of the initiate. When buddhi reigns, the lower psychic nature fades out.

When the antahkarana is built, and the mental unit is superseded by the manasic permanent atom, and the causal body disappears, then the adept knows that the lower mind, the mental body, is also an illusion and is, for him, nonexistent. There are then—as far as his individual consciousness is concerned—only three focal points or anchorages (both of these expressions are inadequate to express the full meaning):

1. *Humanity,* in which he can focus himself at will through the medium of what is called technically the "mayavirupa"—a bodily form which he creates for the fulfillment of monadic purpose.

   He then fully expresses all the energies of the Mutable Cross.*

2. *The Hierarchy.* Here, as a focussed unit of all-inclusive buddhic awareness, he finds his place and mode of service, conditioned by his monadic ray.

   He then expresses the values of the Fixed Cross.*

3. *Shamballa.* This is his highest point of focus, the goal of the exertions of all initiates of the higher degrees and the source of the sutratma, through which (and its differentiations) he can now consciously work.

   Here he finds himself still crucified, but on the Cardinal Cross.*

The task with which the human being in all his stages

---

*A Treatise on the Seven Rays,* Vol. III (Esoteric Astrology), Chapter VI.

of unfoldment has been occupied might therefore be stated
to be the bridging of the gap between:

1. The Mutable Cross and the Fixed Cross.
2. Humanity and the Hierarchy.
3. The lower triplicity, the personality, and
the Spiritual Triad.
4. The Monad on its own plane and the outer
objective world.

This he does through a process of Intention, Visualisation,
Projection, Invocation and Evocation, Stabilisation and
Resurrection. With these various stages, we will now deal.

### The Construction of the Antahkarana in the Aryan Race ... Present

I would like to pause here and make a few remarks
anent this relatively new process of building the antahkarana. It has been known and followed by those who were
training for affiliation with the Hierarchy, but it has not
been given out before to the general public. There are
two things which it is essential that the student should
note: One is that unless it is borne in mind that we are
concerned with *energy,* and with energy which must be
scientifically used, this whole teaching will prove futile.
Secondly, it must be remembered that we are dealing with
a technique and process which are dependent upon the use
of *the creative imagination.* When these two factors are
brought together (consciously and deliberately)—the factor
of energy substance and the factor of planned impulse—
you have started a creative process which will be productive of major results. The human being lives in a world of
varied energies which are sometimes expressing themselves
as dynamic, positive energies, as receptive, negative energies,
or as magnetic, attractive forces. An understanding of this
statement will substantiate that made by H.P.B. that "matter is spirit at its lowest point," and the reverse is equally
true. The whole process is one of establishing constructive
relations between negative and positive energies and the
subsequent production of magnetic force. *This is the crea-*

*tive process.* It is true of the activity of a solar Logos, of a planetary Logos and of a human being—the only conscious creators in the universe. It must prove true of the disciple, who is attempting to bring into a constructive relation the Monad and the human expression in the three worlds of human evolution.

There has been much emphasis upon the life of the soul and its expression upon the physical plane; this has been necessary and a part of the evolutionary development of the human consciousness. The kingdom of souls must eventually give place to the rule of the spirit; the energy of the Hierarchy must become a force, receptive to the energy of Shamballa, just as the force of humanity has to become receptive to the energy of the kingdom of souls. Today all three processes are going on simultaneously, though the receptivity of the Hierarchy to the second aspect of the Shamballa energy is only now beginning to be recognisable. The Hierarchy has for long been receptive to the third or creative aspect of the Shamballa energy, and —at some very distant period—it will be responsive to the first aspect of that same energy. The triple nature of the divine manifestation must also express itself as a duality. This can be understood in a faint way when the disciple realises that (after the third initiation) he too must learn to function as a duality—Monad (spirit) and form (matter) —in direct rapport with the consciousness aspect, the mediating soul being absorbed into both of these two aspects of divine expression, but not functioning itself as a middle factor. When this has been achieved, the true nature of Nirvana will be comprehended, the beginning of that endless Way which leads to the One; this is the Way whereon duality is resolved into unity, the Way that Members of the Hierarchy are seeking to tread and for which They are preparing.

The initial step towards bringing about this dualism is the building of the antahkarana, and this is *consciously* undertaken only when the disciple is preparing for the second initiation. As I have already said, there are literally thousands so preparing, because it can be assumed that all earnest and true aspirants and disciples who work undeviatingly for spiritual advancement (with pure motive), and who are oriented unswervingly towards the soul, have taken the first initiation. This simply connotes the birth of the infant Christ within the heart, speaking symbolically. There should be many who are preparing to begin this task of building the rainbow bridge and who, under the influence of the Ageless Wisdom, are grasping the necessity and the importance of the revelation which this process conveys. What I am here writing has, therefore, a definite and useful purpose. My task has been for a long time the giving out, in book form, information anent the next stage of intelligent and spiritual recognition for humanity. Therefore, again, the understanding of the method of building the antahkarana is essential if humanity is to move forward as planned, and in this moving forward the disciples and aspirants must and do form the vanguard. Humanity will awaken steadily and as a whole to the incoming spiritual urge; an overwhelming impulse towards spiritual light and towards a major orientation will take place. Just as the individual disciple has to reverse himself upon the wheel of life and tread the Way counter-clockwise, so must humanity; and so humanity will. The two-thirds who will make the goal of evolution in this world cycle are already beginning to do so.

In the process, however, the third divine aspect—that of the Creative Actor—comes into activity. It was so in the creative process where the tangible universe was concerned. It must also be when the individual disciple becomes the creating agent. For aeons, he has built and has used his vehicles of manifestation in the three worlds. Then came a time when advanced people began to create upon the mental plane; they dreamed dreams; they saw a vision; they contacted intangible beauty; they touched the Mind of God and returned to earth with an idea. To this idea they gave form and became creators upon the mental plane; they became artists in some form of creative effort. In the task of building the antahkarana the disciple has to work also on mental levels, and that which he there constructs will be of so fine a substance that it may not and cannot appear on physical levels. Because of his fixed orientation, that which he builds will "move upwards toward the centre of life," and not "downwards toward the centre of consciousness or toward light appearance."

Herein lies the difficulty for the beginner. He has, so to speak, to work in the dark, and is not in a position to verify the existence of that which he is attempting to construct. His physical brain is unable to register his creation as an accomplished fact. He has to depend entirely upon the proved technique of the work outlined, and to proceed by faith. The only evidence of success may be slow in coming, for the sensitivity of the brain is involved, and frequently where there is very real success the brain cells are not of the calibre which can register it. The possible evidences at this stage may be a flash of the spiritual intuition or the sudden realisation of the will-to-good in a dynamic and group form; it may also be simply an ability to understand and to make others understand certain spiritual and occult fundamentals; it may be a "facility of revelation," both receptive and conditioning or distributing, and so world effective.

I am attempting to make a very abstruse subject clear, and words prove inadequate. I can but outline to you process and method and a consequent hope for the future; on your side, you can only experiment, obey, have confidence in the experience of those who teach, and then wait patiently for results.

## The Six Stages of the Building Process

I have employed six words to express this process and its resultant condition. It might prove useful to study them from the angle of their occult significance—a significance which is not usually apparent except to the trained disciple who has been taught to penetrate into the world of meaning and to see interpretations not apparent to the neophyte.

Perhaps by the time we have investigated these words, the method of construction and the means whereby the antahkarana is built will appear with greater clarity.

These words cover a building technique or a process of energy manipulation which brings into being a rapport between the Monad and a human being who is aspiring towards full liberation and is treading the Path of Discipleship and Initiation; it can create a channel of light and life between the higher and the lower divine aspects and can produce a bridge between the world of spiritual life and the world of daily physical plane living. It is a technique for producing the highest form of dualism and of eliminating the threefold expression of divinity, thereby intensifying the divine expression and bringing man nearer to his ultimate goal. Disciples must always remember that soul consciousness is an intermediate stage. It is also a process whereby—from the angle of the subhuman kingdoms in nature—humanity itself becomes the divine intermediary and the transmitter of spiritual energy to those lives whose stages of consciousness are below that of self-consciousness. Humanity becomes to these lives—in their totality—what the Hierarchy is to humanity. This service only becomes possible when a sufficient number of the human race are distinguished by the knowledge of the higher duality and are increasingly soul-conscious and not just self-conscious. They can then make this transmission possible, and it is done by means of the antahkarana.

Let us, therefore, take these six aspects of a basic building technique and endeavour to arrive at their occult and creative significance.

1. *Intention.* By this is not meant a mental decision, wish or determination. The idea is more literally the focussing of energy upon the mental plane at the point of greatest possible tension. It signifies the bringing about of a condition in the disciple's consciousness which is analogous to that of the Logos when—on His much vaster scale—He concentrated within a ring-pass-not (defining His desire

sphere of influence) the energy-substance needed to carry out His purpose in manifesting. This the disciple must also do, gathering his forces (to use a common expression) into the highest point of his mental consciousness and holding them there in a state of absolute tension. You can now see the purpose lying behind some of the meditation processes and techniques as embodied in the words so often used in the meditation outlines: "raise the consciousness to the head centre"; "hold the consciousness at the highest possible point"; "endeavour to hold the mind steady in the light"; and many similar phrases. They are all concerned with the task of bringing the disciple to the point where he can achieve the desired point of tension and of energy-focussing. This will enable him to begin the conscious task of constructing the antahkarana. It is this thought which really lies unrecognised behind the word "intention," used so often by Roman Catholics and Anglo-Catholics when preparing candidates for communion. They indicate a different direction, however, for the orientation they desire is not that towards the Monad or spirit, but towards the soul, in an effort to bring about better character equipment in the personality and an intensification of the mystical approach.

In the "intention" of the disciple who is consciously occupied with the rainbow bridge, the first necessary steps are:

a. The achievement of right orientation; and this must take place in two stages: first, towards the soul as one aspect of the building energy, and second, towards the Triad.

b. A mental understanding of the task to be carried out. This involves the use of the mind in two ways: responsiveness to buddhic or intuitional impression and an act of the creative imagination.

c. A process of energy gathering or of force absorption, in order that the needed energies are confined within a mental ring-pass-not, prior to the later process of visualisation and projection.

d. A period of clear thinking anent process and intention, so that the dedicated bridge-builder may clearly perceive what is being done.

e. The steady preservation of tension without undue physical strain upon the brain cells.

When this has been accomplished there will be found to be present a focal point of mental energy which previously had been nonexistent; the mind will be held steady in the light, and there will also be the alignment of a receptive attentive personality and a soul oriented towards the personality and in a state of constant, directed perception. I would remind you that the soul (as it lives its own life on its own level of awareness) is not always constantly aware of its shadow, the personality, in the three worlds. When the antahkarana is being built, this awareness *must* be present alongside the intention of the personality.

2. *Visualisation.* Up to this point the activity has been of a mental nature. The creative imagination has been relatively quiescent; the disciple has been occupied within the mind and upon mental levels, and has "looked neither up nor down." But now the right point of tension has been reached; the reservoir or pool of needed energy has been restrained within the carefully delimited ring-pass-not, and the bridge-builder is ready for the next step. He therefore proceeds at this point to construct the blue print of the work to be done, by drawing upon the imagination and its faculties as they are to be found upon the highest level of his astral or sensitive vehicle. This does not relate to the emotions. Imagination is, as you know, the lowest aspect of the intuition, and this fact must be remembered at all times. Sensitivity, as an expression of the astral body, is the opposite pole to buddhic sensitivity. The disciple has purified and refined his imaginative faculties so that they are now responsive to the impression of the buddhic principle or of the intuitive perception—perception, apart from sight or any recorded possible vision. According to the responsiveness of the astral vehicle to the

buddhic impression, so will be the accuracy of the "plans" laid for the building of the antahkarana and the visualising of the bridge of light in all its beauty and completeness.

The creative imagination has to be stepped up in its vibratory nature so that it can affect the "pool of energy" or the energy-substance which has been gathered for the building of the bridge. The creative activity of the imagination is the first organising influence which works upon and within the ring-pass-not of accumulated energies, held in a state of tension by the "intention" of the disciple. Ponder upon this occult and significant statement.

The creative imagination is in the nature of an active energy, drawn up into relationship with the point of tension; it there and then produces effects in mental substance. The tension is thereby increased, and the more potent and the clearer the visualisation process, the more beautiful and strong will be the bridge. Visualisation is the process whereby the creative imagination is rendered active and becomes responsive to and attracted by the point of tension upon the mental plane.

At this stage the disciple is occupied with two energies: one, quiescent and held within a ring-pass-not, but at a point of extreme tension, and the other active, picture-forming, out-going and responsive to the mind of the bridge-builder. In this connection it should be remembered that the second aspect of the divine Trinity is the form-building aspect, and thus, under the Law of Analogy, it is the second aspect of the personality and the second aspect of the Spiritual Triad which are becoming creatively active. The disciple is now proceeding with the second stage of his building work, and so the numerical significance will become apparent to you. He must work slowly at this point, picturing what he wants to do, why he has to do it, what are the stages of his work, what will be the resultant effects of his planned activity, and what are the materials with which he has to work. He endeavours to visualise the entire process, and by this means sets up a definite rapport (if successful) between the buddhic intuition and the creative imagination of the astral body. Consequently, you will have at this point:

The buddhic activity of impression.

The tension of the mental vehicle, as it holds the needed energy-substance at the point of projection.

The imaginative processes of the astral body.

When the disciple has trained himself to be consciously aware of the simultaneity of this threefold work, then it goes forward successfully and almost automatically. This he does through the power of visualisation. A current of force is set up between these pairs of opposites (astral-buddhic) and—as it passes through the reservoir of force upon the mental plane—it produces an interior activity and an organisation of the substance present. There then supervenes a steadily mounting potency, until the third stage is reached and the work passes out of the phase of subjectivity into that of objective reality—objective from the standpoint of the spiritual man.

3. *Projection.* The task of the disciple has now reached a most critical point. Many aspirants reach this particular stage and—having developed a real capacity to visualise, and having therefore constructed by its means the desired form, and organised the substance which is to be employed in this later phase of the building process— find themselves unable to proceed any further. What then is the matter? Primarily, an inability to use the Will in the process of projection. This process is a combination of will, further and continued visualisation, and the use of the ray Word of Power. Up to the present stage in the process, the method for all the seven rays is identical; but at this point there comes a change. Each disciple, having success-fully organised the bridge substance, having brought into activity the will aspect, and being consciously aware of proc-ess and performance, proceeds now to move the organised substance forward, so that from the centre of force which he has succeeded in accumulating there appears a line of light-substance or projection. This is sent forward upon a

Word of Power, as in the logoic creative process. This is in reality a reversal of the process of the Monad when It sent forth the thread of life which finally anchored itself in the soul. The soul, in reality, came into being through the means of this anchoring; then came the later process, when the soul in its turn sent forth a dual thread which finally found anchorage in the head and the heart of the lower threefold man, the personality. The disciple is focussed in the centre which he has constructed upon the mental plane, and is drawing all his resources (those of the threefold personality and the soul combined) into activity; he now projects a line towards the Monad.

It is along this line that the final withdrawal of the forces takes place, the forces which—upon the downward way or the involutionary path—focussed themselves in the personality and the soul. The antahkarana per se, completed by the bridge built by the disciple, is the final medium of abstraction or of the great withdrawal. It is with the antahkarana that the initiate is concerned in the fourth initiation, called sometimes the Great Renunciation—the renunciation or the withdrawal from form life, both personal and egoic. After this initiation neither of these aspects can hold the Monad any more. The "veil of the Temple" is rent in twain from the top to the bottom—that veil which separated the Outer Court (the personality life) from the Holy Place (the soul) and from the Holy of Holies (the Monad) in the Temple at Jerusalem. The implications and the analogies will necessarily be clear to you.

In order, therefore, to bring about the needed projection of the accumulated energies, organised by the creative imagination and brought to a point of excessive tension by the focussing of the mental impulse (an aspect of the will), the disciple then calls upon the resources of his soul, stored up in what is technically called "the jewel in the lotus." This is the anchorage of the Monad—a point which must not be forgotten. The aspects of the soul which we call knowledge, love and sacrifice, and which are expressions of the causal body, are only effects of this monadic radiation.

Therefore, before the bridge can be truly built and "projected on the upward way, providing safe travelling for the pilgrim's weary feet" (as the *Old Commentary* puts it), the disciple must begin to react in response to the closed lotus bud or jewel at the centre of the opened lotus. This he does when the sacrifice petals of the egoic lotus are assuming control in his life, when his knowledge is being transmuted into wisdom, and his love for the whole is growing; to these is being added the "power to renounce." These three egoic qualities—when functioning with a measure of potency—produce an increased activity at the very centre of soul life, the heart of the lotus. It should be remembered that the correspondences in the egoic lotus to the three planetary centres are as follows:

Shamballa  . . .  The jewel in the lotus.
Hierarchy  . . .  The three groups of petals.
Humanity  . . .  The three permanent atoms within the aura of the lotus.

Students should also bear in mind that they need to rid themselves of the usual idea of sacrifice as a process of giving-up, or renunciation of all that makes life worth living. Sacrifice is, technically speaking, the achievement of a state of bliss and of ecstasy because it is the realisation of another divine aspect, hidden hitherto by both the soul and the personality. It is understanding and recognition of the will-to-good which made creation possible and inevitable, and which was the true cause of manifestation. Ponder on this, for it is very different in its significance to the usual concepts anent sacrifice.

When the disciple has gained the fruit of experience which is knowledge and is learning to transmute it into wisdom, when his objective is to live truly and in reality, and when the will-to-good is the crowning goal of his daily life, then he can begin to evoke the Will. This will make the link between the lower and the higher minds, between spirit and matter and between Monad and personality a definite and existent fact. Duality then supervenes upon triplicity, and the potency of the central nucleus in the egoic vehicle destroys—at the fourth initiation—the three surrounding expressions. They disappear, and then the so-called destruction of the causal body has taken place. This is the true "second death"—death to form altogether.

This is practically all that I can tell you anent the process of projection. It is a living process, growing out of the conscious daily experience and dependent upon the expression of the divine aspects in the life upon the physical plane, as far as is possible. Where there is an attempt to approximate the personality life to the demands of the soul and to use the intellect on behalf of humanity, love is beginning to control; and then the significance of the "divine sacrifice" is increasingly understood and becomes a natural, spontaneous expression of individual intention. Then it becomes possible to project the bridge. The vibration is then set up on lower levels of divine manifestation and becomes strong enough to produce response from the higher. Then, when the Word of Power is known and rightly used, the bridge is rapidly built.

Students need feel in no way discouraged by this picture. Much can happen on the inner planes where there is right intention, as well as occult intention (purpose and tension combined), and the bridge reaches stages of definite outline and structure long before the disciple is aware of it.

*4. Invocation and Evocation.* The three preceding stages mark, in reality, the three stages of personality work. The remaining three are expressions of response from higher levels of the spiritual life; beyond briefly indicating them, there is very little that I can put into words. The task of Invocation, based on Intention, Visualisation and Projection, has been carefully undertaken by the disciple and he has at least some measure of clear perception as to the work he has done by the dual means of spiritual living and scientific, technical, occult work. He is therefore himself invocative. His life effect is registered upon the higher levels of consciousness and he is recognised as "a point of invocative tension." This tension and this reservoir of living energy, which is the disciple himself, is set in motion by projected thought, the use of the will and a sounded Word or Phrase of Power.

The result is that his developed potency and its radius of influence are now sufficiently strong to call out a response from the Spiritual Triad. There is then a going forth towards the aspect of the antahkarana, constructed by the disciple, along which the life of soul and body can travel. The Father (Monad), working through the thread, now goes forth to meet the Son (the soul, enriched by the experience of personality life in the three worlds), and from the higher levels a line of responsive projection of energy is sent forth which will eventually make contact with the lower projection. Thus the antahkarana is built. *The tension of the lower evokes the attention of the higher.*

This is the technical process of invocation and evocation. There is a gradual approach from both the divine aspects. Little by little, the vibration of both becomes stronger reciprocally. There comes then a moment when contact between the two projections is made in meditation. This is not a contact between soul and personality (the goal of the average aspirant), but a contact between the fused soul and personality energy and the energy of the Monad, working through the Spiritual Triad. This does not constitute a moment of crisis, but is in the nature of a Flame of Light, a realisation of liberation, and a recognition of the esoteric fact that a man is himself the Way. There is no longer the sense of personality and soul or of ego and form, but simply the One, functioning on all planes as a point of spiritual energy and arriving at the one sphere of planned activity by means of the path of Light. In considering this process, words prove completely inadequate. At this stage, when very advanced, there is no form attracting the Monad outwards into manifestation. There is no way in which the call of matter or of form can evoke a response from the Monad. There remains only the great pull of the consciousness of humanity *as a whole* and to this, response can be made via the completed antahkarana. Down—or rather across—this bridge, descent can be made at will, in order to serve humanity and to carry out the will of Shamballa.

This is a statement of the final consummation. But before that can take place in its perfected completion, there must be a long period of gradual approach of the two aspects of the bridge—the higher, emanating from the Spiritual Triad, in response to monadic impulse, and the lower, emanating from the personality, aided by the soul —across the chasm of the separating mind. Finally, contact between that which the Monad projects and that which the disciple is projecting is made, and then come the fifth and sixth stages.

5 and 6. *Stabilisation and Resurrection.* The bridge is now built. Thin and tenuous may be its strands at the beginning, but time and active understanding will slowly weave thread after thread until the bridge stands finished, stable and strong and capable of being used. It must perforce be used, because there is now no other medium of intercourse between the initiate and the One Whom he now knows to be himself. He ascends in full consciousness into the sphere of monadic life; he is resurrected from the dark cave of the personality life into the blazing light of divinity; he is no longer only a part of humanity and a member also of the Hierarchy, but he belongs to the great company of Those Whose will is consciously divine and Who are the Custodians of the Plan. They are responsive to impression from Shamballa and are under the direction of the Heads of the Hierarchy.

The "freedom of the three Centres" is Theirs. They can express at will the triple energy of Humanity, the dual energy of the Hierarchy, and the one energy of Shamballa.

Such, my brothers, is the goal of the disciple as he begins to work at the building of the antahkarana. Reflect upon these matters and proceed with the work.

(In some *Talks to Disciples,* the Tibetan makes the following remarks which apply here with peculiar force. A.A.B.)

"Your major need is for an *intensification of your inner spiritual aspiration*. You need to work more definitely from what might be called a point of tension. Study what is said about tension and intensity. It is intensity of purpose which will change you from the plodding fairly satisfactory aspirant into the disciple whose heart and mind are aflame. Perhaps, however, you prefer to go forward steadily, with no group effort, making your work for me and for the group an ordered part of the daily life, which you can adjust pretty much as you like, and in which the life of the spirit receives its reasonable share, in which the service aspect is not neglected, and your life presentation is neatly balanced and carried forward without much real strain. When this is the case, it may be your personality choice or your soul decision for a specific life, but it means that you are *not* the disciple, with everything subordinated to the life of discipleship.

"I would like here to point out two things. First: if you can so change your tension that you are driven by the life of the spirit, it will entail a galvanic upheaval in your inner life. For this, are you prepared? Secondly: it will not produce any outer change in your environing relationships. Your outer obligations and interests must continue to be met, but I am talking in terms of inner orientations, dynamic inner decisions, and an interior organising for service and for sacrifice. Perhaps you prefer the slower and easier way? If that is so, it is entirely your own affair, and you are still on your way. You are still a constructive and useful person. I am simply here facing you with one of the crises which come in the life of all disciples, wherein choices have to be made that are determining for a cycle, *but for a cycle only*. It is pre-eminently a question of speed and of organising for speed. This means eliminating the non-essentials and concentrating on the essentials—the inner essentials, as they concern the soul and its relation to the personality, and the outer ones as they concern you and your environment.

"I would give you three key thoughts for deep reflection

during the next six months; will you ponder on them, one each month for three months, within the head, and during the second three months brood on them in the heart. These key thoughts are:

1. The necessity for speed.
2. The reorganisation of standards of thought and of living.
3. The expression of: Sincerity, Sacrifice, Simplicity."*

In the many strands of light, woven by the aspirants, disciples and initiates of the world, we can see the group antahkarana gradually appearing—that bridge whereby humanity as a whole will be able to abstract itself from matter and form. This building of the antahkarana is the great and ultimate service which all true aspirants can render.

*The immediate Task ahead*

What I have now to say is in the nature of a generalisation. I would like to indicate, as far as possible (asking you to remember that all generalisations are basically sound but erroneous in detail), the point where humanity stands in relation to the antahkarana. It might be said that the whole goal of normal evolution is to bring humanity to the point where a direct line of contact is established between the personality and the Spiritual Triad, via the soul —or rather, through the medium of using the soul consciousness to achieve this awareness. This is consummated at the time of the third initiation. We will now for a minute consider the Monad.

I would remind you that there is an analogy in the relation between personality and soul, to that between the Triad and the Monad. This is an analogy that is essentially complete, from the standpoint of consciousness, but not from the standpoint of form. What finally takes place at the most advanced stage of development is the complete fusion of the unified personality and soul with the unified Monad and Spiritual Triad. Only when this has been truly

---

*Discipleship in the New Age,* Vol. I, page 538.

accomplished is there the complete release of the Lives informing our solar system from all form control. Bear this carefully in mind, realising the significance of the word *Service*, used so frequently in the occult science, and realising also the fact that, for aspirants and disciples, the immediate task ahead is:

1. To bring about the at-one-ment of soul and body, through the medium of alignment.

2. To build the antahkarana, using the six modes or means outlined by me previously, and thus evoke response to the Triad. The thought of Alignment-Invocation-Evocation are the three major ideas for you to hold in mind as we proceed with this study.

The reason that I am giving out what was earlier regarded as some of the preparatory work prior to the third initiation is due to the fact that the race is now at the point of development which warrants complete change in the approach to divinity as taught by the Hierarchy. This does not mean that past teaching is abrogated, but it is shifted back to the earlier stages on the Path of Discipleship, whilst the teaching given in those stages now becomes the work done by the aspirants upon the Probationary Path. Emphasis has been laid upon purification, upon the need for the development of the Christ life, upon the mystical vision and upon philosophy. Occult truths have been given to the race and have evoked much interest, criticism and discussion; they have appealed to all types of mind; they have been distorted and misapplied. Nevertheless, they have been instrumental in aiding advanced aspirants to move forward on to the Path of Discipleship, with a paralleling moving forward of accepted disciples. Once firmly established upon the Path, the truths become self-evident and individual application and verification can be made, leading the disciple inevitably to the Portal of Initiation.

The race *as a whole* stands now at the very entrance to the Path of Discipleship. The racial gaze is forward to the vision, whether it is the vision of the soul, a vision of a better way of life, of an improved economic situation, or of better inter-racial relationship. That this vision is oft distorted, that it is materially oriented or only partially seen is sadly true; but in some form or another there exists today an appreciable grasp of the "new and desirable" by the masses —a thing hitherto unknown. In the past, it was the intelligentsia or the elect who were privileged to have the vision. Today, it is the mass of men. Humanity, therefore, as a whole stands ready for a general alignment process, and that is the *spiritual* reason which lay behind the world war. The "sharp shears of sorrow must separate the real from the unreal; the lash of pain must awaken the sleepy soul to exquisite life; the wrenching away of the roots of life from the soil of selfish desire must be undergone, and then the man stands free." So runs the *Old Commentary* in one of its more mystical stanzas. Thus it points prophetically to the close of the Aryan Race—not a close in the sense of completion, but a closing of a cycle of mental perfecting, preparatory to a cycle wherein the mind will be rightly used as an instrument of alignment, then as the searchlight of the soul, and as the controller of the personality.

For the masses—under the slow processes of evolution —the next step forward is the aligning of the soul and the form, so that there can be a blending in consciousness, following on a mental appreciation of the Christ principle and its deep expression in the life of the race. This is something which can be seen quite clearly emerging, if you have the eyes to see. It is evident in the universal interest in goodwill, leading eventually to peace; this desire for peace may be based on individual or national selfishness, or upon a true desire to see a happier world wherein man can lead a fuller spiritual life and base his efforts on truer values; it can be seen in all the planning which is going on for a new world order, based on human liberty, belief in human rights and right human relations; it is demonstrating also in the work of the great humanitarian movements, the welfare organisations, and the widespread evocation of the human mind through the network of educational institutions throughout the world. The Christ spirit *is* expressively present, and the failure to recognise this fact has been largely due to the prevalent human effort to explain and interpret this phrase solely in terms of religion, whereas the religious interpretation is but one mode of understanding Reality. There are others of equal importance. All the great avenues of approach to Reality are spiritual in nature and interpretive of divine purpose, and whether the religious Christian speaks of the Kingdom of God, or the humanitarian emphasises the brotherhood of man, or the leaders against evil head the fight for the new world order or for the Four Freedoms or the Atlantic Charter, they all express the emergence of the love of God in its form of the spirit of Christ.

Humanity in the mass has therefore reached a point of emergence from darkness; it has itself evoked the reaction of the powers of evil, and hence their attempt to arrest the progress of the human spirit and to stop the onward march of the good, the true and the beautiful.

Aspirants and probationary disciples are occupied with a definite process of focussing their consciousness in the soul. This process falls into two parts:

An intensification of the personality life, so that it is developed to its highest individualistic powers.

A process of moving forward into the light and of conscious soul contact.

This involves the earlier stage of the alignment process, which is a mode of focussed, concentrated effort, according to the ray and life purpose of the soul. This may take the form of a profound application to some scientific endeavour or a deep concentration on the spiritual work of the world, or it may be a complete dedication to humanitarian effort; it matters not. I would call your attention to that statement. In every case the motivating power *must* be betterment; it must be carried forward by extreme effort; but—given right motive and the effort to develop simultaneously a good character and a stable purpose—the aspirant or probationary disciple will eventually find that he has succeeded in establishing a definite soul relation; he will have discovered that the path of contact between soul and brain, via the mind, has been opened, and that he has mastered the first stage in the needed alignment process.

When this has been accomplished, the man passes on to the Path of Discipleship and can undertake the work I am outlining for you in this treatise. Thus you can see how the entire human family has reached a central and most important point upon the evolutionary path. The immediate path ahead for all—each in his own place—is to stand with right orientation, undeterred by circumstances, and then unflinchingly move forward.

I have given you the six methods of building the antahkarana, and as we proceed to take up our next point, I would have you refer to them at frequent intervals. The ray methods with which we shall be concerned are the methods, uniquely possible on the seven major lines of emanatory energy, which differing ray types will bring to bear on these six stages of the building process. All disciples on all these seven rays use the same building technique of Intention, Visualisation, Projection, Invocation and Evocation, Stabilisation and Resurrection. Of these the first two are uniform in technique for all the rays, but when the stage of Projection is reached, then the ray techniques begin to differ, and it is these techniques or methods of ray work, coupled with the seven Words of Power, which we shall now proceed to consider.

## The Seven Ray Methods used in the Construction Process

Until the stage of projection is reached, the methods employed by all disciples on all rays are identical. Their intention is one, and they all have to attain the same measure of tension and of preparation for the construction of the bridge by gathering the needed energy from two sources —the personality and the soul. By this focussing and its resultant tension, by thus evoking the Spiritual Triad and starting the dual process of building from both ends of the bridge (if such a phrase is possible and permissible), the work goes forward uniformly. The use of the creative imagination is now called forth and this forms the second stage. This presents a real difficulty for the first ray and the seventh ray aspirants. Neither type can with facility organise the material energy, orient energy currents, and see their objective clearly in the mind's eye pictorially. It is a process which is profoundly difficult for them. It must, however, in some way be done, because the use of the visual imagination is an essential factor in the building process and one of the major means of focussing, prior to projection.

This process of projection falls into three main activities:

1. After due focussing and after careful, sequential and systematic picturing the "rainbow bridge," the disciple—by a distinct and separate effort—calls in the will aspect of his nature, as far as he can in this incarnation. It is in this connection that the differing ray methods make their appearance, the difference being determined by the quality of the ray life.

2. The disciple has to preserve steadily the triple consciousness, not simply theoretically but also factually, so that three paralleling lines of thought, or three streams of active energy, are used by him simultaneously:

a. He is aware of himself, personality and soul, as occupied with the process of bridge building. He never for one second loses his sense of conscious identity.

b. He is aware of the point of focussed tension which he has succeeded in producing and that three streams of energy have contributed to it—the focussed energy of the personality, poised in the lower concrete mind, the inflowing magnetic energy of the soul, streaming out from the twelve petals of the three tiers plus the innermost tier of the egoic lotus, and the energy of the "jewel in the lotus"—all streaming into the centre of tension on the mental levels of the lower mind.

c. He is aware of as much of the consciousness of his ray energy as can enter into his awareness; this is his egoic ray energy and not personality force. He endeavours to see himself as a point of particular energy coloured by his ray life, and carefully bears in mind that the energy of his egoic ray is the major energy through which the Monad is attempting to express itself, and also that his threefold egoic vehicle is a reflection of and closely related to the three aspects of the Spiritual Triad. It is this relation (and its conscious interplay and effect) which is evoked by the building of the antahkarana, and which eventually (when it is powerful enough) brings into radiant activity the "jewel in the lotus."

3. When these three stages of realisation have been completed as far as the disciple feels he is capable of carrying them, then and only then does he prepare himself for the distinctive use of his ray method in preparing for the "projecting sound" or Word of Power.

You can see from all the above that this constitutes a definitely planned process of a basic scientific nature, and requires as careful following as the procedure of any scientist in search of some advanced chemical formula. The only difference, scientifically speaking, is that the whole process is carried forward upon subjective levels and in the realm of consciousness, thus requiring a consciousness and a concentration not needed when working more tangibly on the outer plane of awareness. At first it seems complicated, as the disciple tries to master the different stages of the process, but it all becomes entirely automatic when once mastered. Here is a summary of process up to the point of definite projection:

    I. Intention, producing focussing and tension.

   II. Visualisation, produced by:
       1. The buddhic activity of "impression."
       2. The tension of the mental body.
       3. The imaginative processes of the astral body.

  III. Projection:
       1. The calling in of the Will aspect.
       2. The preservation of a triple state of awareness in order that:

a. The disciple is aware constantly of his own identity.

b. He is conscious of a fixed point of tension.

c. He is aware actively of his soul ray or his soul energy.

3. He starts in to use that distinctive ray energy correctly.

4. He then, when all the above is completed, uses the Word of Power which is the agent of his Will.

This short tabulation should aid in the process, and you can see how stage grows out of stage and how, once familiarity has been established, it should be possible for the preliminary work to be rapidly carried forward.

When, however, the distinctive methods of the ray energy of the disciple reach the point of definite use, it is not so simple as it sounds. Success in the building process is dependent upon the ability of the disciple to do three things:

1. Hold the mind steady in the light, i.e., preserving the point of tension at its highest possible point at any given time in the disciple's unfoldment and building activity.

2. Register consciousness of soul contact, thus bringing about an increasing fusion between the soul and the personality, so that complete at-one-ment is increasingly attained. Technically, this means that the energy of the soul ray and of the personality ray merge together, with the soul ray dominating always.

3. Hold in mind, specifically and in detail, the method to be employed in building the bridge, according to the particular ray technique, and with the objective in view of relating (in a new and significant manner, factually and not just theoretically) the Spiritual Triad and the personality.

The soul, therefore, as a separate entity, is fading slowly out of the picture because it is being absorbed into and by the personality, which is becoming more and more *the soul in incarnation*. Eventually the relation is established between spirit (Monad) and personality (form or matter), with a tiny point of consciousness eternally present which is aware of both these factors and yet preserves inviolate its own identity. This latter realisation is the result of aeonian work, carried forward by the soul. Paradoxically, we say that the soul fades or drops out, yet in the last analysis it remains, for in this solar system there is naught else but only this consciousness of *being*.

One point I would touch upon here before taking up the seven ray methods of projection. The bridge to be built is called frequently the "rainbow bridge" because it is constituted of all the colours of the seven rays. Speaking specifically and from the angle of the disciple, the bridge which he builds between the personality and the Spiritual Triad is composed of seven strands of energy, or seven streams of force; he uses all the seven rays, having gained facility in so doing because again and again his personality has (in the long cycle of incarnations) been on all the seven rays many times. But his soul ray dominates eventually, and in the rainbow bridge the "colours of his rays are heard vibrating; the note of his ray is seen." The bridge built by humanity as a whole is one bridge composed of the multiplicity of individual bridges, built by the many disciples. It is therefore formed eventually of seven strands or streams of energy coming from the seven egoic groups (one group of each ray type). To this bridge the creative work of all human beings who reach the stage of soul contact contributes. Their dominant strands of light fuse into one whole and their lesser strands are lost to sight in the radiant light of the sevenfold bridge which *humanity* will eventually complete.

Even in this finally completed bridge—at the end of the world cycle—one ray light and colour will predominate, the second ray, with the fourth ray as the subsidiary ray. The fourth ray might be symbolically called "the main cable" for humanity, because it is the dominant note of the Fourth Creative Hierarchy. Now let us take up the seven ray methods, one by one.

As we consider these seven ray techniques with their accompanying Words of Power, you must bear carefully in mind that we are dealing entirely with the Will aspect. This necessitates a higher process of alignment and the evocation of a divine aspect hitherto relatively quiescent, except in so far as the will finds its reflection in the activity of the sacrifice petals of the egoic lotus, plus its distorted shadow in the mind nature. This consequently posits a fairly high stage of spiritual unfoldment upon the part of the builder of the antahkarana; it means that there are indications of it (to say the least) between the mind, the sacrifice petals and the atmic principle. This may be simply the most tenuous thread imaginable, a thousand times finer than a gossamer web, but it must inevitably be present. When, from the angle of the esotericist, this is a tangible fact, you will then have the following direct contact:

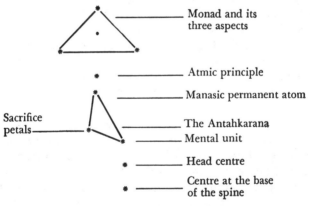

This contact, when completed, marks an entire unit of spiritual work, if I might so word it, bringing the man upon the physical plane into complete alignment; this unity is consummated at the time of the fourth initiation, the Great Renunciation at which time the first aspect begins to dominate the other two.

Then the soul life—as hitherto understood—fades out and the causal body disappears. The sum total of memory, quality and acquirements is then absorbed into the Monad. The words "I and my Father are one" become true. The astral body also vanishes in the same great process of renunciation, and the physical body (as an automatic agent of the vital body) is no longer needed, though it persists and serves a purpose when so required by the Monad. From the form aspect, you then have the Monad, the sphere of the Spiritual Triad and the etheric body upon the physical plane. I would here remind you that the levels of conscious existence which we regard as formless are only relatively so, because our seven planes are the seven subplanes of the cosmic physical plane. The centre of consciousness is now in the Will nature, when this point of attainment is reached, and is no longer in the love nature. Activity and love are still present in full measure, but the focus of the initiate's attention is in the will aspect of divinity.

It has been said in an ancient book belonging to the Masters' Archives that:

> "The preservation of values is the task of the initiate of the first ray; the attainment of positivity is the goal of the initiate of the second ray. He who works upon the third ray must reach the path from here to there.
>
> The initiate of the fourth ray arrives at the will aspect when conflict steps into its rightful place and causes no undue concern. These four attainments mark the goal for men and sway them all upon the lower point of consciousness. The ray of vision and of application indicates the way direct, evokes the will to follow, and welds the love of God, the love of man and all that breathes into the purpose underlying all, and towards that purpose and its earthly consummation the seventh ray gives all it has."

It has not been easy to put these abstruse ideas, expressed in the most archaic language and symbolism, into modern terms and words. I have but conveyed the general idea—the collaboration of all the seven rays in the building processes of Deity and their planned interaction, on a tiny scale, infinitesimal in comparison with the great Whole. Man responds within the circle of humanity, enclosed within the greater circle of the Hierarchy, and becomes conscious of this fusion and uses the potencies of both groups of lives, through the medium of the antahkarana. The moment the disciple approaches that point in consciousness and the antahkarana is firmly anchored (even if as yet but a tenuous structure), he becomes aware of the factor of the greater circle which encloses the other two—Shamballa, the Secret Place where the will of God is formulated for the immediate present and for the long range future.

With this vision and suggested preamble let us now ascertain the seven techniques to be employed at the projection stage of the building process.

Ray One ... Will or Power

To understand the first ray technique, the basic quality of the ray must be grasped. It is *dynamic*. The point at the centre is the First Ray of Power, and its technique is never to move from the centre but from that point to work dynamically. Perhaps the word that would best express its mode of work is *Inspiration*. The Father inspires response from the material aspect, or from the Mother if you like that symbolism, but it accomplishes this by remaining immovably itself. From the point where he is, the Builder (human or divine) works, not by the Law of Attraction, as does the second ray, but by the Law of Synthesis, by a fiat of the will, based on a clearly formulated purpose and programme. You will see, therefore, that the first ray personality has to ascertain (as in fact do all disciples) which aspect he himself is of a particular ray. It is not possible for any disciple who has not taken the third initiation to ascertain his monadic ray, but any disciple building the antahkarana, and who has reached the stage of projection, *should know his soul ray and his personality ray, and should remember that their fused or blended potency must perform the act of projection.* The energy of the Monad can be evoked, but it results in a down-pouring towards its working agent and it is not an act of projection per se. The act of projection is the work of the "shadow and the reflection." The *Old Commentary* says in this connection, when dealing with the Word of Power for each ray:

> "When there is no shadow, for the Sun is clear, and no reflection for the water is no more, then naught remains but the one who stands with eyes directing life and form. The threefold shadow now is one. The three of self exists no more. The higher three descends and all the nine are one. Await the time."

When, therefore, the ray of the soul dominates the ray of the personality, then the self becomes the acting agent, aided by the ray of the lower self. The rays of the three vehicles are no longer active, but only the basic duality of soul and personality remains, and there is no lesser differentiation.

In considering all these seven rays, I seek to do three things in every case:

1. Give the technique of projection. This technique falls into four stages:

a. The preparatory stage in which the consciousness becomes focussed in the soul ray.

b. An interlude in which the projecting agent realises with intensity the existence of the "point of tension" and the finished product of the visualisation process.

c. A focussed activity of the will, according to the ray, in which a line of light or of living substance is imaginatively and creatively sent out or projected from the mental unit, as far as possible towards the Spiritual Triad, using constantly the creative imagination.

d. This line of light (this strand or bridge) is then pictured as coloured by the two ray qualities, and it is held stably aligned in the light of the Spiritual Triad— not the light of the soul. This corresponds to the much earlier stage of development in which the mind was held steady in the light. The mind still is held in this manner, but the mind (as the agent of the soul and the

510 A TREATISE ON THE SEVEN RAYS

personality) is no longer quiescent, but itself becomes an active holding agent.

2. Indicate briefly the effect of the Word of Power. When adequate stability has been acquired, the disciple utters a Word of Power which serves to carry the light still further on and up. *When correctly uttered,* this Word produces three effects:

> a. It keeps the channel for the descending light of the Spiritual Triad clear of all impediments.
> b. It reaches (by means of its vibratory activity) the centre of power which we call the Spiritual Triad, focussed temporarily in the manasic permanent atom, and evokes a response in the form of a thread of descending triadal light.
> c. It causes a vibration throughout the antahkarana which in its turn evokes response from the "rainbow bridge" as built by all other disciples. Thus the work of constructing the *racial* antahkarana is furthered.

I am here doing two things—speaking to you in symbols. There is, literally speaking, no up or down or higher and lower, as you know, nor do any of the separative actions as outlined by the occult sciences exist. Yet the truth has to be thus presented owing to the mind consciousness of the disciple. I have also been giving in human terms the outline of a process which, if adequately followed, will enable you to make real progress in the *preparatory understanding* required by all who hope some day to take initiation.

3. This brings us to the third point, the nature of initiation. Initiation falls really into three major expansions of consciousness.

> a. The expansion of consciousness of the dedicated personality into that of the soul; this is completely consummated at the third initiation.
> b. The expansion of this fused and blended conscious-

ness into that of the Spiritual Triad, completely consummated at the fifth initiation.

c. The expansion of consciousness toward which the Masters are working, which is consummated at the seventh initiation.

Students today have made much progress towards the control of the personality, and the disciples in the world are now so numerous that the hierarchical emphasis is today upon the states of consciousness which follow the third initiation. Hence the giving out to the public of the teaching upon the antahkarana.

You will find below, in tabulated form, the teaching anent the six stages so that you may have a visual picture of the intended process. The following of the process is, of course, another matter and its success is dependent upon more than a theoretical grasp of process. It is dependent upon your ability to live more definitely in the world of meaning than hitherto, upon your knowledge of your soul and personality rays and upon your capacity to focus in your blended consciousness, and from that point—holding the mind steady in the light—utter the Word of Power which will carry your created thread of light forward towards the Spiritual Triad.

### OUTLINE FOR REFLECTIVE CONTEMPLATION

#### ON

### CONSTRUCTING THE ANTAHKARANA

I. *Points to have in mind.*

This work of construction concerns the handling of energy. Students should ponder upon the distinction between energy and force.

It is dependent upon the use of the creative imagination. Students would do well to reflect upon the relationship of the imagination to the intuition and of both to the mind.

The work of building the antahkarana must be done with as much conscious understanding as possible.

II. *The six steps or methods of building the Antahkarana.*

  1. Intention.

    a. The achieving of right orientation

      Towards the soul

      Towards the Spiritual Triad

    b. A mental understanding of the work to be done is necessary.

    c. A ring-pass-not of consciously gathered energies must be created and held in a state of tension.

    d. A period of clear thinking anent this process of Intention must be attempted.

    e. Then follows the preservation of a point of tension.

  2. Visualisation.

    a. The use of the creative imagination or the picture-making faculty.

    b. Response to intuitional or buddhic impression.

    c. Preoccupation with two energies:

      The energy held at a point of tension within the previously created ring-pass-not.

      The active picture-forming energy brought into action by the mind of the builder.

  3. Projection.

    a. The calling in of the will through the method appropriate to the Ray of the disciple, the soul ray.

    b. The simultaneous preservation of three lines of thought:

      Awareness of the blended personality and soul.

      Awareness of the point of focussed tension.

      Awareness of the Ray energy in its will aspect.

    c. The use of one or other of the seven Ray methods of projection, according to the Ray of the disciple.

    d. the use of a Word of Power.

  4. Invocation and Evocation.

    a. The blended soul and personality are now invocative, and their united intention is expressed in the previous three stages.

    b. Then a response comes from the Spiritual Triad, which that intention, propelled by an act of will from a point of tension has evoked.

  5. Stabilisation.

This is brought about by long patient use of the four

previous processes and followed by a conscious use of the antahkarana.

6. Resurrection and Ascension.
   This is the rising up of the consciousness out of soul and personality limitations (from the angle of the Monad) and its passing into that of the Spiritual Triad.

Here I would touch upon one important point connected with all Words of Power. I could give you these words in their ancient Sensa form, but it would not be possible for me to teach, through the medium of writing, their ancient and peculiar pronunciation or the note upon which they should be sounded forth. This used to be regarded of supreme importance. Today, disciples are being taught to work far more upon the *inner planes of meaning* and not to depend, as heretofore, upon the outer activity of sound. Remember that you are not creating now upon the outer plane. The physical sound or sounds are therefore of relatively no importance. What does matter is the ability of the disciple to *feel* the meaning of the Word of Power as he silently utters it. It is *the quality* of his idea which will bring the right effect, and not the way in which he makes a sound with the aid of his vocal cords and his mouth. Students have been taught that the A.U.M. sounded inaudibly and listened for, is of greater potency than when sounded audibly. This was preparatory to the utterance of these Words of Power. They have been learning the significance of the O.M., even if they did not realise it. This was all in preparation for the use of the Ray Words. It is the thought behind the form, the registered feeling anent the words, and the understanding of their significance which are of importance; it is the ability to think, to feel and silently to send out the call of quality to quality, of meaning to meaning, of nature to nature, of form to spirit which matters, remembering ever that that which is found upon the physical plane is *not* a principle. The physical sound is not that which will lead to a successful building of the antahkarana. It is the quality of a particular type of subjective nature (the soul ray as it dominates the personality ray) which makes appeal to that which is still more subjective; that is what in truth accomplishes the work. It should be borne in mind that from the angle of the Spiritual Triad the soul nature is definitely objective. This is a statement of occult fact which will be better understood when the nature of man (as taught in the occult sciences) is admitted by thinkers, scientists and psychologists.

The point I wish to make is that no particular word is going to be given by me, because it would be useless. The O.M. is useless to most people, even though trained students may now be deriving benefit from its use. This general uselessness is caused not only because people do not use the Word correctly, but also because, even when using it they are not holding its significance firmly in their consciousness. So it is with a Word of Power. Of what use would it be if I attempted to give the Word of the first ray, which looks (when presented in its symbolic written form) something like this—UKRTAPKLSTI? Certain sounds in this word-form are omitted because there is no way of depicting them, since they are neither vowels nor consonants. Correctly sounded, the above forms three words. But I can give, as far as possible, the English *equivalent in meaning*, and it is this meaning which I ask you to have in mind as you mentally utter the sound or Word of Power and visually attempt to see it performing the esoteric miracle of bridge building.

The first ray disciple has, therefore, to meet the requirements to the best of his ability and to follow the four stages of the technique of projection (pages 489-493, 509). When he has faithfully followed this outlined routine, personality and soul fusion has to be consciously attempted and to some measure achieved, and then these blended factors are held steady in the triadal light. Another point of focussed intention is now brought about, resulting in a new and still more dynamic tension. In the completed silence which results, the act of projecting the antahkarana is performed, and it is then carried forward on the impetus of a Word of Power. The symbolism connected with this lies behind the Masonic usage of the words, translated into English, "So mote it be," uttered with the right hand stretched forth and signifying the embodied will of the Lodge, itself a symbol of the Will and Purpose of the Most High.

The meaning of the Word of Power to be used at this point of accomplished projection might be summed up in the words: "I ASSERT THE FACT." This is the nearest form I can give you for the word-form earlier mentioned. A little deep reflection on these words will show that if uttered with an understanding of their meaning, they are of terrific potency. The disciple who utters them assumes and then asserts:

1. The Spiritual Triad is a fact.

2. The relation between the fused and blended personality and the soul is a fact.

3. The antahkarana is also a fact.

4. The dual expression of the basic duality of manifestation—personality or form and Monad or Spirit—is a fact.

5. The will of the Monad is the factor to be evoked.

6. The knowing, purposeful One can be depended upon to contact the instrument of its will upon the physical plane.

7. The work is done.

This factual assumption is not faith, but knowledge and conviction, and upon this realised conviction the disciple rests, acts and depends. It becomes an unalterable and unchangeable attitude. The meaning of the above sevenfold statement will become clearer if the disciple will ponder the distinction between faith and conviction. It is this divine assertion which holds the universe in being; it is this divine assertion which is the embodied summation of all knowledge and love, and the first ray disciple must begin to use this technique, resting back upon his divine prerogative of assertion. Ponder on this statement. It is the technique of Shamballa and the established right, prerogative and privilege of all first ray souls.

Ray Two . . . Love-Wisdom

Again the first two stages of Intention and Visualisation have been carefully followed and the four stages of the Projection have been carried through to their highest point. The vivid light of the second ray soul (the most vivid in this second ray solar system) dominates the light of form and radiates out to the triadal light. Then comes a moment of intense concentration and the peculiar Word of Power of the second ray is enunciated. Of this Word, the dual symbol SXPRULXS takes form in the mind of the disciple and signifies the assertion: "I SEE THE GREATEST LIGHT." This statement has relation to the Central Spiritual Sun and not to the Heart of the Sun; it involves, if I might so express it, the most intense effort to see in the light the relation of the whole, and this is one of the most potent experiences to which the disciple can be subjected. It is not vision or even aspiration to see the vision. It is complete sight and of this the Masonic symbol of the "Eye of God," the "All-Seeing Eye," is the expression. It involves realisation of the light of the divine countenance; of this the light of the soul is the dim reflection. The disciple has learnt the significance of solar and lunar light (soul and form light), but this is something other. It is the great obliterating light of reality itself, revealing the fact of the higher Lighted Way which leads to Nirvana. Of this, the projected antahkarana is the stage first consciously realised by the disciple.

I am faced with difficulty in making these Words of Power clear to you, because essentially it is the Word made flesh or the soul in incarnation which at this point *registers power;* it is the symbol (the form aspect) and the power (the Spirit aspect) which acts as a great creative agency and bridges across all barriers and separative states of consciousness, thus establishing complete unity.

I have indicated to you certain vowels and consonants

which are the nearest approach which I can make to making these Words clear, and I have done so in the case of the first and second rays. I shall give you no others, as it is entirely useless. I shall only give you the significances, the concepts involved and the meaning of which these archaic word-forms (which I have attempted to portray in Anglo-Saxon letters) are the embodiment. As the race passes more and more into the world of meaning, these word-forms assume less and less importance, and only the concentrated thought, based on understanding comprehension, can achieve the results. It is into this somewhat new form of work we are now pioneering.

Ray Three . . . Active Intelligence

The processes of Intention and Visualisation have been followed, and again the four stages of the Projection technique have been concluded. At the point of highest tension, the disciple utters the Word of Power for the third ray. It is not easy for the disciple on this ray to achieve the necessary focal point of silence; his intense fluidity leads to many words or to great mental activity, frequently carried forward under the impulse of glamour. This lessens the potency of what he seeks to do. But when he has succeeded in achieving "mental silence" and is simply a point of intelligent concentration, then he can use the Word of Power with great effectiveness. The difficulty is that he has to overcome the tendency to use it with the idea of physical plane results in his consciousness. Always he works from the angle of that divine quality which characterises matter; just as the second ray disciple works always from the angle of quality and the first ray disciple from the positivity of spirit. But once he intuitively comprehends and factually grasps the concept that spirit-matter are one reality, and once he has achieved within himself the sublimation of matter, then he can divorce himself from all that the human being understands in relation to form. He can then utter the Word of Power which will make possible his complete identification with spirit, via the antahkarana. This word is "PURPOSE ITSELF AM I."

A TREATISE ON THE SEVEN RAYS

As regards the other and remaining Words of Power
connected with the four Rays of Attribute, I shall simply
list them, as there is little that I can say about them. They
can be comprehended in the light of what I have said anent
the three Words of Power used upon the Rays of Aspect.

Ray Four  . . . Harmony through Conflict
"TWO MERGE WITH ONE"

Ray Five  . . . Concrete Knowledge or Science
"THREE MINDS UNITE"

(This asserts the fact that the Universal Mind, the
higher mind and the lower concrete mind are blended
through the projected antahkarana.)

Ray Six  . . . Devotion or Idealism
"THE HIGHEST LIGHT CONTROLS"

Ray Seven . . . Ceremonial Law or Order
"THE HIGHEST AND THE LOWEST MEET"

You will note that in all these Words of Power, two
obvious thoughts emerge; first, that the goal of all activity is the complete fusion of the three Aspects, and secondly, that consciousness of this comes through the building
and use of the bridge between the Spiritual Triad and the
Personality. You will note that these are all definite asser-
tions, based on knowledge leading to conviction. The
various schools of affirmation found today throughout the
world are but the distorted efforts of humanity to arrive
at the affirmative position which the blended soul and
personality always necessarily assumes, and demonstrate a
kind of instinctual reaction to a new realisation which is
coming into the consciousness of humanity, via its disciples and initiates.

We have practically concluded our study of the
antahkarana; however, I want to enlarge a little further
upon the three final stages of the building process as dealt
with and outlined earlier. These three stages were most
briefly considered, owing to their abstract nature. They
are part, however, of the six building methods. The first

three were considered in greater detail than the last three, and I have felt that it might serve a useful purpose if I gave more teaching anent Invocation and Evocation in particular, for it will condition—consciously and exoterically —the new world religion, as it has hitherto conditioned it esoterically and unconsciously.

*Invocation and Evocation* (continued from pages 493-495):

These two words are descriptive of that mysterious something—emanation, voiceless appeal, inherent urge towards the light—which is innate in all forms, which produces interplay and relationship, and which is the cause of all progress or pushing forward along the path of an expanding consciousness and a penetration into the light. This is true of a plant pushing its way out of the darkness of earth into the light of the sun, a child extricating itself under the life impulse from the womb of its mother, of the human being pushing himself into realms of greater knowledge and effective physical living, of the aspirant driving forward out of the Hall of Learning into the Hall of Wisdom, of the disciple penetrating into the realm of soul light and life, of the initiate passing from grade to grade in the Hierarchy of Liberation, of the Christ moving on into the Council Chamber of Shamballa, and of the Lord of the World Himself undertaking those processes which will lead Him into realms of divine life—of which even the highest initiate on our planet has no conception. All comes about as part of a great system of invocation and evocation, of appeal and response, and all are distinctive of the "mode of Life" which governs the entire graded hierarchy of Being upon our planet.

This evolutionary pushing forward along the Lighted Way, out of darkness into light, from the unreal to the real, and from death to immortality, is an inherent urge in all forms. It constitutes one of the most subtle and one of the least understood laws of the universe, being related to the Life principle, of which we know as yet naught; it *underlies* the Law of Evolution as well as the Law of Karma and is, in reality, the Law of the Life Purpose of the planetary Logos; it is an expression of His dynamic intention as it forces all substance in manifestation and in time and space to act and react in conformity to His Will. He thus enables His form—the planet which is a compound of all the seven kingdoms in nature—to express logoic intention for the "duration of the Great Breath"; of this breath, time and space are the two aspects. It affects the tiniest atom and the most exalted Being within the sphere of His consciousness and the scope of His livingness; it affects the subhuman kingdoms, unconsciously to them, and is (in relation to them) sometimes spoken of as "the Law of Life of the Sun." The human family, after the stage of personality integration is reached, reacts with increasing consciousness of the divine purpose. Once the antahkarana is constructed and the higher initiations are taken, the initiate then cooperates with that purpose in full understanding and intention. He no longer simply reacts to his own interior urges, which force him ever to invoke the higher aspect of life and of consciousness which he senses on ahead. He now knows. He sees; he participates in the Plan; he relates himself to the divine Intention through an understanding of the doctrine or Science of Tension; he makes the divine Intention his, as far as he can grasp it. This reciprocal interplay produces the mutability of form and the immutability of the divine nature which is distinctive of those liberated Consciousnesses which have freed Themselves from the prison of form.

Elsewhere* I said that "The definition of religion, which will in the future prove of greater accuracy than any yet formulated by the theologians, might be expressed as follows:

> *Religion is the name given to the invocative appeal of humanity and the evocative response of the greater Life to that cry.*

It is, in fact, the recognition by the part of its relationship to the Whole, plus a constantly growing demand for in-

---

*The Reappearance of the Christ, Pages 157-158

creased awareness of that relation; it draws forth the recognition of the Whole that the demand has been made. It
is the impact of the vibration of humanity—oriented specifically to the Great Life of which it feels itself a part—
upon that Life, and the responsive impact of that "All-
surrounding Love" upon the lesser vibration. It is only
now that the impact of the human vibration can dimly
be sensed in Shamballa; hitherto its most potent activity
has only reached the Hierarchy. Religion, the science of
invocation and evocation as far as humanity is concerned,
is the approach (in the coming New Age) of a mentally
polarised humanity. In the past, religion has had an entirely
emotional appeal. It concerned the relation of the individual
to the world of reality, of the seeking aspirant to the sought-
for divinity. Its technique was the process of fitting oneself
for the revelation of that divinity, of achieving a perfection which would warrant that revelation, and of developing a sensitivity and a loving response to the ideal Man,
summarised for present day humanity in the Christ.

Christ came to end the cycle of this emotional approach
which had existed since Atlantean days; He demonstrated in
Himself the visioned perfection and then presented to humanity an example—in full manifestation—of every possibility latent in man *up to that time.* The achieving of
the perfection of the Christ-consciousness became the emphasised goal of humanity."

The activity of all previous Teachers and demonstrating Sons of God became only the presentation of the various
aspects of a divine perfection which the Christ summarised
in Himself. But He did far more than just this. Had this
been all that He accomplished, He would have presented
to humanity a picture of a static achievement, a culmination of perfection such as the evolutionary status of man
at that time demanded; He would have given us, in fact,
a Figure of very great, but at the same time, arrested development. This was of course impossible, but the religion
which He founded has never recognised this fact or considered what lay beyond Christ, what was the nature of *His*

subjective background and what was His point of achievement, and whether He still had other possibilities. This
was perhaps an unavoidable omission owing to the fact that
the idea of evolution was unknown until relatively very
late, in the human consciousness. Orthodox religion has
been preoccupied with an emotional and aspirational approach to this Figure of Perfection; it has not looked beyond the Figure to the Reality which He represents. This
Christ Himself foresaw as a possibility, and sought to obvi-
ate when He pointed out to His disciples that they could
do "greater things" than He had done, because He was
going "to the Father." He, in those words, pointed beyond
Himself to the One Who was responsible for His Being,
and to the Way of the Higher Evolution—a subject with
which the church has never satisfactorily dealt. In the
above words He indicated a state of being which He had
never demonstrated on earth, owing to the unpreparedness
of man, and also to the fact that He Himself was only "on
His Way."

The Way of the Higher Evolution has also its two
phases, as has the Lighted Way. In the early stages of the
unfoldment of the Christ consciousness and in the attainment of the third initiation, the Transfiguration, the aspirant and the initiate-disciple pass along the first part of the
Path of Discipleship. In the treading of the Way of the
Higher Evolution (for which we have as yet only this
somewhat cumbersome name) the initiate-disciple treads the
Way of Antahkarana and the Way of the Higher Initiations
In making this statement I would again remind you that
the third initiation is regarded by the Hierarchy as the first
major initiation, whilst the two previous initiations are
considered as only preparatory in their nature. The training
given in preparation for them, and the consequent expan
sions of consciousness, reveal to the initiate the nature of
the soul, the scope (widespread and universal) of the divine
consciousness, and his relation to the Father, the Monad
They enable him to become the soul in manifestation to
such an extent that his awareness is definitely and unalterabl

that of the soul; at the fourth initiation the soul-body, the causal vehicle, is no longer needed, and it then disappears, dissipates, and is entirely destroyed, thus leaving the initiate free to tread the Way of the Higher Evolution and to follow in the footsteps of the Christ. He was the first of our planetary humanity to blaze the trail (is not that a phrase much used?) to the higher spheres of revelation.

I would here also remind you that, during this stage of human evolution, all these various phases exist simultaneously; this largely accounts for the relative differences and difficulties which characterise all the religions of the world and all relationships. Emotional appeal is needed by the masses, and their goal—some way ahead—is soul consciousness and soul control. It is the mystical way and the way of the early and preparatory stages of the science of Invocation and Evocation. It is the method to be followed by average humanity at this time, because men are largely Atlantean in their approach and their natures; they must learn to tread the Path by becoming the Path Itself, and in this way develop the mechanism and the capacities which are inherent in the divine Mind, which "spins the thread of connecting light and relates all beings within the planetary ring-pass-not into Itself."

By becoming the Path, symbolically speaking, and by a process of reorientation, the aspirant who is seeking to tread the Lighted Way of purification and of discipleship reaches a point where that light and that path have brought him to a specific goal. Then the light which he has generated from within himself, and is learning rapidly to use, reveals to him the Way of the Higher Evolution, the fact of a still greater goal further on ahead—called by the Christ "the Father's House."

At the fourth initiation he becomes aware, for the first time in his experience, that there is a hiatus or gap separating him from his distant goal. This constituted the major part of the agony upon the Cross. There was a fusion of agonies at that supreme moment, if I might attempt to express what occurred. The Master Jesus, crucified there, felt the agony of human need and renounced His own life and gave His all (again symbolically speaking) to meet that need. The Christ, at that time over-shadowing His great Disciple, also passed simultaneously through a great initiatory experience. The agony of His yearning for revelation and increased enlightenment (in order to enhance His equipment as World Saviour) revealed to Him the new possibilities, from which—when confronted with them dimly in the garden of Gethsemane and later upon the Cross—His whole nature shrank.

Great as is this mystery to you, and impossible as it is for you to comprehend that whereof I speak, it is wise to establish the fact in your consciousness that at the Crucifixion initiation, the Master Jesus took the fourth initiation and the Christ took the sixth initiation. The Master Jesus reached the culminating experience of the Lighted Way, whilst the Christ made that final effort which enabled Him entirely to complete and traverse the "rainbow bridge" and to "go to the Father" (as He told His disciples), thus moving forward on to the first stage of the Way of the Higher Evolution.

The practical point for aspirants and disciples to remember is that the Science of Invocation and Evocation entered a new phase when Christ came and presented Himself before humanity; He then gave the teaching which summarised all the past and indicated the new aspects of the future teaching. He opened the door to the Way of the Higher Evolution, hitherto closed, just as the Buddha epitomised in Himself the achievements of the Lighted Way and the attainment of all knowledge and wisdom. Christ, in opening this "greater door beyond the lesser door," anchored—if I may so inadequately express it—the Will of God on Earth, particularly in relation to the consciousness of men. He lifted the entire Science of Invocation and Evocation to the mental plane and made possible a new approach to divinity. It is difficult to give you a symbol which could clarify this matter in your mind. But the one given may carry some enlightenment:

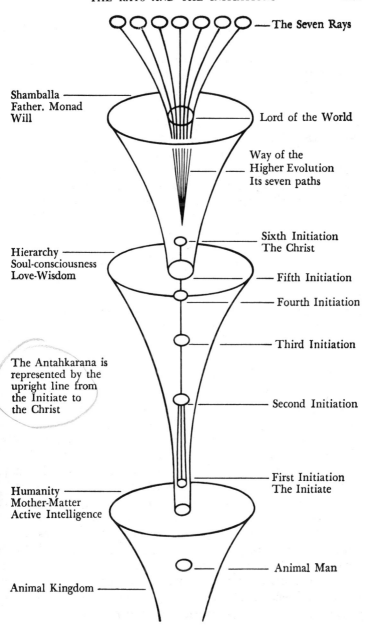

The Seven Rays

Shamballa
Father. Monad
Will

Lord of the World

Way of the
Higher Evolution
Its seven paths

Sixth Initiation
The Christ

Hierarchy
Soul-consciousness
Love-Wisdom

Fifth Initiation

Fourth Initiation

Third Initiation

The Antahkarana is
represented by the
upright line from
the Initiate to
the Christ

Second Initiation

First Initiation
The Initiate

Humanity
Mother-Matter
Active Intelligence

Animal Man

Animal Kingdom

It must be remembered that intelligence and love were present upon Earth, the first in greater degree than the second, and that the task of all the great World Saviours (emerging from the Secret Place, from the illimitable past until the present time) has been to anchor, organise, and implement these divine aspects, energies, attributes, and to further their development within the body of the planetary Logos. They also, from time to time, demonstrated to the humanity of Their period of appearing, the point in that development which had been reached. These Representatives of Deity have been of all grades, degrees and differing points of spiritual unfoldment; They have been chosen for Their aptitude to respond to invocation, to manifest certain divine qualities, and to attract around Themselves those who had latent the same divine qualities, and who could therefore step down the teaching that the World Saviour came to give, and translate into human equivalents as much of the divine inspiration as was possible. Many of Them have been forgotten even if Their work was successful. Others have been resolved into myths by the thoughtform-making faculty of man but Their work is still thereby remembered, and to this, monuments and tradition constantly testify; greater Sons of God possessed a potency and a love of humanity which, even at the close of many centuries, evokes the attention of mankind and conditions even yet the reactions of millions of people.

*Vyasa* — the original Vyasa, Who was the Great Individuality evoked by the invocation of the early animal-men—is still more than just a name, even though He has passed out of our planetary scheme millions of years ago. He opened a door into the human kingdom through His response to the animal kingdom in its higher invocative ranks; His work brought about the process known as individualisation. Down through the ages, these Sons of God have come, evoked by human invocation; in Their turn, They have invoked certain aspects of the divine nature, deeply hidden in mankind—all related hitherto to consciousness and to responsiveness of the part to the Whole.

Eventually *Hercules* came forth and opened the door on to the Path of Discipleship, His work being preserved for us in the Twelve Labours of Hercules. These epitomised the various tests to which all disciples are subjected, prior to the various initiations. *Shri Krishna* came and opened the door through which mankind could pass to the Second Initiation. *The Buddha,* a still greater Figure, the One Who is known as the "Enlightened One," also came and demonstrated to humanity the nature of the Lighted Way, its revelations and its effects in consciousness. He enacted for us the supreme achievements of the mystic way. Then came *the Christ* and performed a triple work:

1. He opened the door to the third initiation.
2. He anchored on Earth "the Will of God in the matrix of love" (as it has been esoterically called).
3. He pointed the way through "the needle's eye" which gives entrance to the passage through the Pyramid (the symbol of the Spiritual Triad in this case. A.A.B.) which leads out on to the Way which terminates in Shamballa.

His work was of a major consummating nature; He demonstrated in Himself two divine aspects, thus giving "shape and substance to love"; this had been sequentially fostered by several preceding lesser World Saviours, of Whom Shri Krishna was the greatest.

The Christ completed the work of the Buddha by manifesting in its fullness the nature of love, thus permitting the full expression of love-wisdom in its dual aspect —the one aspect demonstrated by the Buddha and the other by the Christ. But His greatest work has not yet been emphasised in the worlds of thought and of religion—the revelation of the Way of the Higher Evolution. This entails the bringing through of pure divine will and the relating of the spiritual Hierarchy to the great Council at Shamballa. It will be apparent to you, therefore, that He was the first to carry through—from stage to stage—the complete revelation of humanity to the Hierarchy and of the Hierarchy to Shamballa. This He did by virtue of a

completely finished and constructed antahkarana, and thus
He facilitated the work of all future aspirants and disciples. He made possible their unimpeded progress, as far
as the opening of each stage of the planetary antahkarana
is concerned. He presented the "first thread of living substance, irradiated by love, intelligently woven and energised
by will" which any human being of our Earth humanity
had interwoven with the planetary antahkarana. Here lies
the secret of the sixth initiation, which has not yet received
the attention of the occultist.

Here comes a climaxing note. The whole evolutionary
scheme is based upon *a series of ascensions*. These ascensions are the result of a process, a technique, a method
(choose which word you will) of invocation by the lesser
individual, group or kingdom, and the evocation of that
which is greater, more inclusive and more enlightened.
This is true, whether it concerns a lonely aspirant upon
the Way or an entire kingdom in nature. The greatest of
the incarnating Sons of God are necessarily Those Who
can include whole kingdoms or states of divine Being in
Their consciousness. Here is the key as to why the invocation by a group "standing with massed intent" can bring
forth, and has done so many times in our planetary history, One Who could meet the need which the invocation
voiced, upon "a way of escape," and embody in Himself
the required vision or goal.

You will note here that I have carried the teaching
(earlier given upon the subject) into the realm of the whole.
Previously, I dealt with the process as it applied to the
disciple invoking his soul; later I carried the concept
farther, and we considered the disciple invoking his Father
in Heaven, the Monad. Now, we have briefly touched
upon humanity as a whole, standing at a great point of
invocation wherein the entire human kingdom is involved.
Thus you have the final three of the six great stages in
the process we are considering: Invocation, leading to Evocation, to Revelation (at the Fifth initiation) and to
Decision (at the sixth).

To sum up. We have carried our study of the esoteric aspects of mental unfoldment to a point where we have lifted the entire spiritual man into realms which are neither those of the soul nor of the personality; they are those which make him an integral part of monadic experience. We are therefore dealing definitely with initiate experience. That the personality remains as an instrument or vehicle of expression for the one universal soul in its many aspects upon the physical plane has been duly emphasised; that the soul per se has been lost to consciousness in the sea of universal realisation has also been made clear; that the state of being which the initiate has now reached, as a result of the six stages of conscious building of the antahkarana, has been detailed; but I have pointed out in this connection that what has transpired lies beyond what we call consciousness, and is consequently undefinable by the human intellect. We have dealt with certain high stages of unfoldment which remain impossible to any human comprehension outside that of Those Who can function in the Courts of Shamballa. When these stages have been passed, then the goal of all the evolutionary processes has been reached, as far as humanity is concerned. These concepts cover our presentation of truth and of our theme up to the present point. Further we cannot go, for it would be profitless; nor would the human constitution prove adequate to the imposed task.

I have in these previous sections carried our theme to the point where it climaxes all that has been hitherto given out anent the human mind and its capabilities. I have indicated the method whereby the mind, trained in meditation, and therefore soul-conscious, can—through the construction of the antahkarana—reach heights and stages of inclusiveness which will introduce to it certain aspects of the so-called Universal Mind, the mind of God, as it is familiarly called. What I have really done is to deal very briefly with the mode whereby the disciple or the initiate can, with increasing power, tune in on the mind of the planetary Logos, Sanat Kumara. Just as the disciple can, when soul conscious, tune in on the mind of his Master, so the initiate, upon a higher turn of the spiral, can register the thoughts of the divine Being in Whom we all live and move and have our being.

Through the development of the antahkarana and its conscious, scientific use, the initiate becomes aware of what transpires in the Council Chamber of Shamballa; he can then efficiently begin to work as an exponent of the Will aspect of divinity. Yet all this time we have confined ourselves entirely to the consideration of the mind aspect in its three phases upon the mental plane, and with their extension into states of being unknown to all except trained disciples and initiates. It has been my intention thus to give a theoretical, though not yet practical insight into modes of activity and possible states of being to which you can some day aspire and eventually attain.

## THE MEANING OF THE INITIATORY PROCESS

Before proceeding with our next point concerning the fusion of the Master's consciousness with that of His disciple, I would like to refer to the significance of the words I earlier emphasised, "the initiatory process." I have dealt at length with the theme of initiation in many of my books and have endeavoured to present the subject in such a manner that it becomes apparent that it fits into the evolutionary process as a normal and inevitable procedure. Initiation has been so frequently presented as being a ceremony that I have felt it necessary to offset strenuously that erroneous significance. If, however, you are to comprehend that which I have to say, you will have to call in what measures of enlightened understanding you may possess.

Initiation is only a ceremony in so far that there comes a climaxing point in the initiatory process in which the disciple's consciousness becomes dramatically aware of the personnel of the Hierarchy and of his own position in relation to it. This realisation he symbolises to himself— successively and on an increasingly large scale—as a great rhythmic ceremonial of progressive revelation in which he, as a candidate, is the centre of the hierarchical stage. This is definitely so (from the ceremonial angle) in the first two initiations, and in relation to the Christ as the Initiator. After the third initiation, the ceremonial angle lessens in his consciousness because the higher initiations are not registered by the mind (with its ability to reduce realisation into symbolic form) and thus transmitted to the brain, but they reach the brain and are there registered via the antahkarana; the results of the experience of expansion are now definitely of such a nature that they cannot be reduced to symbols or to symbolic happenings; they are formless and remain in the higher consciousness.

I am not here saying that the teachings given in the past by various occult groups, or in my book *Initiation, Human and Solar,* are not correct or do not recount accurately what the candidate *believes* has taken place. The point I seek to make is that the ceremonial aspect is due to the thoughtform-making capacity of the disciple and (which is of major importance) constitutes his contribution to the future externalisation of the initiatory process in its earlier stages. When an adequate number of disciples will have succeeded in relating the Spiritual Triad to the soul-infused personality and have occultly "precipitated" the energies of the Monad through the medium of the antahkarana, then the first and second initiations can be "ceremoniously" enacted on earth.

The higher initiations cannot be thus presented but will be enacted on the mental plane, through the medium of symbols and not through the details of ceremonious happenings. This symbolic representation will hold good for the third, the fourth and the fifth initiations. After these five great expansions have taken place, the initiations will no longer be registered as factual ceremonials on earth or as symbolic visualisations on the mental plane. It is hard to find a word or a phrase which can express what occurs; the nearest I can approach to the truth is the "existence of illumination through revelation." You will note in this connection that the fifth initiation is given the name of Revelation. You therefore have a sequence of consequences or of the results of spiritual attainment which are as follows:

1. *Factual Ceremonials,* based on externalisation.
   Initiation 1 — The Birth.
   Initiation 2 — The Baptism.
2. *Symbolic Representation,* based on spiritual visualisation.
   Initiation 3 — The Transfiguration.
   Initiation 4 — The Renunciation.
   Initiation 5 — The Revelation.
3. *Illumination through Revelation,* based on living Light.
   Initiation 6 — Decision.
   Initiation 7 — Resurrection.
   Initiation 8 — Transition.
   Initiation 9 — Refusal.

It will be obvious that these three attempts to define the process of initiation present only the outer form aspect; each initiation has three aspects, as has all else in nature, for initiation is a natural process. There is first, its form aspect; then its soul or consciousness aspect; and finally, its life aspect.

The form aspect culminates experience and presents the disciple's comprehension of the initiatory process; the consciousness aspect indicates in a mysterious manner the rate of expansion as the disciple has undergone the process; the life aspect permits of extra-planetary contact, thus indicating the possible future and the eventual processes of identification. It might be added that the *factual ceremonial* admits the disciple into full fellowship with the Hierarchy; that the *symbolic representation* indicates to the disciple the Way into Shamballa, and that *illumined revelation* presents to the initiate the bridge between our cosmic physical plane and the inner subjective and cosmic worlds; this entrance to the bridge (I am speaking in symbols) reveals the existence of the cosmic Antahkarana, created by the Lord of the World and His group of Executives.

This information concerning the initiatory process is coordinating in its nature and is of service to you only in this connection. It demonstrates the underlying solar synthesis which was the fundamental platform I gave out in *A Treatise on Cosmic Fire*. Beyond that implication, the information is of no use to you. It enables you, however, to begin to develop the esoteric sense of synthesis.

These three grades of appreciation or of comprehension of the initiatory process are hinted at in the Masonic Work. The ceremonial aspect can be related to the degrees of Entered Apprentice and of Fellow Craft, plus certain little-practiced degrees, as for instance that of Mark Mason degree and one or two others; these are expansions of the implied teaching. The initiations, covered by the term symbolic representation, find their first hint in the sublime third degree, that of Master Mason, in the Holy Royal Arch and in one or two succeeding degrees; the higher degrees of the Scottish Rite constitute a vague and nebulous attempt to hold before the Masons of the world those expansions of consciousness and of growth into the Light which are experienced in the remaining higher initiations—those subject to the process called illumination through revelation.

The Masonic Work is an ancient and laudable attempt to preserve in some germinal form the spiritual truth anent initiation. In spite of distortion, some loss of the Ancient Landmarks and a deplorable crystallisation, the truth is there and at a later date (in the early part of the next century) a group of enlightened Masons will rearrange the rituals and adapt the present forms and formulas in such a manner that the spiritual possibilities, symbolically indicated, will emerge with greater clarity and a deepened spiritual potency; the coming form of Masonry in the New Age will necessarily rest upon the foundation of a newly interpreted and enlightened Christianity, having no relation to theology and being universal in nature. Its present form, resting as it does on a Jewish foundation which is nearly five thousand years old, must disappear. This must take place, not because it is Jewish, but because it is old and reactionary and has not followed the evolutionary passage of the sun through the zodiac. That passage should and does symbolise human evolution, and just as the sin of the children of Israel in the wilderness was their reverting to a dispensation and religious ritual which had passed and gone (the religion of the people in the time of Taurus, the Bull, symbolised by their falling down and worshipping the golden calf), so today modern Masonry is in line to do the same; and the ancient usages and forms, consistent and right in the Jewish dispensation, are now obsolete and should be abrogated. It is equally true of the Jewish race that in the rejection of the Christ as the Messiah they have remained, metaphorically and practically, in the sign of Aries, the Ram, or of the Scapegoat; they have yet to pass into the sign (again speaking symbolically) of Pisces, the Fishes, and recognise their Messiah when He again comes in the sign Aquarius. Otherwise they are repeating their ancient sin of non-response to the evolutionary process.

Let us now consider what the initiatory process signifies to the disciple as he seeks to lead the dual life which it demands. You will note that I call it a process in contradistinction to the theosophical definition which regards it as a culminating ceremony of a period of training.

The initiatory process is in reality the result of the activity of three energies:

1. The energy generated by the disciple as he seeks to serve humanity.

2. The energy made available to the disciple as he succeeds in building the antahkarana.

3. The energy of the hierarchical Ashram into which he is being "absorbed" or integrated.

It is these three energies, each with its own mode of expression and each producing its own specific results, which implement or engineer the initiatory process; these energies are evoked by the disciple himself, and their increasing strength and revelatory capacity depend largely upon the disciple's determination, purpose and will, his persistence and spiritual integrity. It is through his understanding of the word "process" that the disciple discovers the true meaning of the occult statement that "before a man can tread the Path he must become that Path himself." Increasingly the disciple finds what it is to become a creative agent, using the creative faculties of the mind and conforming increasingly (as he creates) to the Plan of the Creator, the Lord of the World.

The first three initiations are definitely and in a most mysterious way concerned with the creative work, and with the spiritual expression in a human being of the third aspect of divinity, that of intelligent activity. The fourth, fifth and sixth initiations are as definitely related to the second aspect of love-wisdom as it expresses itself through created forms; the seventh, eighth and ninth initiations are occultly "inspired" by the first divine aspect, that of the Will. Only, therefore, at the ninth initiation is the human being a *full* and true expression of divinity; he then realises that in him all the divine aspects meet. Through them he is consciously, creatively and constructively en rapport with the consciousness of the One in Whom we live and move and have our being. All this is *the result* of a process and *the effect* of the inherent livingness which is found in all forms of life from the tiny atom up to Those great Lives Who are little more than names to the disciple.

This initiation process governs the dual life of the disciple in three ways:

1. It is expressed in the results effected in the three worlds and in the tangible and growing proof he gives of definitely defined areas of attainment.

2. It is demonstrated as effects in his consciousness in the form of an increasing fusion of soul and personality as well as growing power to invoke the inflow of the higher light, through the medium of the antahkarana.

3. It is revealed both through the Spiritual Triad and the soul-infused personality as they unitedly prove the *livingness* of the divine Love-Nature. As this revelation takes hold of the disciple's consciousness and conditions his expressive form of service, it initiates him into that mysterious area of the divine consciousness which we call the "Heart of God"; this is our planetary correspondence to the "Heart of the Sun." The heart of God, i.e., of our planetary Logos, and the heart of the Sun, i.e., the solar Logos, are mysteriously related, and it is through this sustained relation that it becomes possible for human beings to enter the Hierarchy. Forget not that the Hierarchy is the expression of the energy of love. The relationship also enables them eventually to pass off the cosmic physical plane on to the cosmic astral plane.

Each divine aspect has three subsidiary aspects, and in our planet and on the cosmic physical plane the lowest aspect of love (that which we call the Will-to-Good) is revealed. For humanity, struggling upon this cosmic physical plane, we subdivide unconsciously this will-to-good into three aspects; these we are only today beginning to grasp as existent possibilities. The lowest aspect we call *goodwill,* little realising the attitude to the universal goal which it sets; the second aspect we vaguely call *love* and hope to demonstrate that we do demonstrate love through our affiliation with the Hierarchy; the highest we call the *will-to-good* and leave it undefined because it is in no way possible, even for initiates of the fifth initiation, truly to comprehend what is the nature and purpose of the will-to-good which conditions divine activity.

The emphasis in the earlier teaching was upon *character* as the determining factor in deciding whether a man could "take initiation" (as it was called), and this was another of the presentations which have greatly misled aspirants. Character *is* of major importance—of such recognised importance that it is not necessary to dwell upon it. It is character, however, which enables a man to become a disciple with the aim in view of eventually entering the Ashram of a Master and passing then through the processes of initiation. It is character which is rightly regarded as the first requirement when a man steps off the Probationary Path on to the Path of Discipleship. But he is still, however, a long way from his goal, and a long way from being accepted by a Master as a disciple. The truth might be expressed this way: When the disciple's eyes are removed from himself and his functioning in the three worlds is becoming spiritually controlled (or is in process of being controlled), then he is faced with becoming a truly mental being, with the focus of his life upon the mental level where it is subject to soul control; it then in turn becomes the directing agent of the man upon the physical plane. This does not mean that he is occupied with making his lower concrete mind active, directing and illumined; that is taking place gradually and automatically through the pressure of the higher influences pouring into and through him. He is occupied with the task of becoming aware of the activities of his higher or abstract mind and of the pure reason which controls and animates the buddhic plane, and which is itself susceptible to impression from the Monad. That plane has to become the one toward which his mental consciousness looks and upon which it focusses its attention. There it must be polarised, in the same sense as the consciousness of average humanity is today polarised on the plane of the emotions and of astral activity but is shifting with rapidity on to the mental plane.

This involves a dual activity; the lower mind becomes a potent factor in directing the service activities of the disciple. These activities become the major motivating potency in the disciple's life and are a consequence of a growing soul fusion with the personality, thus developing and unfolding his sense of inclusiveness. Inclusiveness is the supreme key to the understanding of consciousness. At the same time, the higher mind is impressing the lower mind and drawing it into a higher fusion with itself.

This process of unfoldment creates certain major points of successive fusions, with consequent points of tension; these points of tension (when *consciously* attained) become the actuating energy which enables the disciple to "stand in the light and in that light see greater Light; within that greater Light he knows and sees, grasps and absorbs that which has hitherto been dark and secret and unknown." This is initiation.

Periods of search, periods of pain, periods of detachment, periods of revelation producing points of fusion, points of tension and points of energy projection—such is the story of the Path of Initiation.

Initiation is in truth the name given to the revelation or new vision which ever draws the disciple onward into greater light; it is not something conferred upon him or given to him. It is a process of *light* recognition and of *light* utilisation in order to enter into ever clearer light. Progress from a dimly lighted area in the divine manifestation into one of supernal glory is the story of the Path of Evolution.

In the Masters' Archives there are some *Rules for Disciples* of very ancient origin. Among them is one that is so old and so abstruse that it is only now possible to bring it to the attention of humanity, owing to the increased mental and spiritual perception of the modern aspirant. It can be inadequately translated as follows:

> "The light is seen, a tiny point of piercing light. This light is warm and red. It nearer draws as it reveals the things that are, the things which may be. It pierces the third centre and removes all glamour and desire.

> "A light is seen through the medium of the lower light —a light of warmth and heat. It pierces to the heart and in that light all forms are seen pervaded by a glowing light. The world of lighted forms is now perceived, linked each to each by light. This light is blue, and flaming is its nature. Between the warm and reddish light and this clear light there burns a glow of flame— a flame which must be entered, ere the light of blue is entered and is used.

"Another light is then perceived, the clear cold light which is not light but darkness in its purest purity— the LIGHT of God Himself. It renders dark all else beside Itself; all forms fade out and yet the whole of life is there. It is not light as we know light. It is that pure essential essence of that Light which reveals Itself through light."

It was the second light to which the Buddha and the Christ both referred when They said: "I am the light of the world." It is the Light of God Himself, the Lord of the Worlds, in which the Lives within the Council Chamber of Shamballa live and move and have Their Being.

It is the recognition of the varying "lights" upon the Lighted Way that signifies readiness for initiation. The initiate enters into light in a peculiar sense; it permeates his nature according to his development at any point in time and space; it enables him to contact and see the hitherto unseen, and on the basis of the newly acquired knowledge to direct his steps still further.

I am not here speaking in symbols. Each initiation dims the light already acquired and used, and then immerses the initiate in a higher light. Each initiation enables the disciple to perceive an area of divine consciousness hitherto unknown but which, when the disciple has familiarised himself with it and with its unique phenomena, vibratory quality and interrelations, becomes for him a normal field of experience and activity. Thus (if I may so express it) the "worlds of living forms and formless lives become his own." Again duality enters into his mental perception, for he is now aware of the lighted area from which he comes to the point of tension or of initiation; through the initiatory process he discovers a new and more brilliantly lighted area into which he may now enter. This involves no leaving of the former field of activity in which he has worked and lived; it simply means that new fields of responsibility and of opportunity confront him because he is—through his own effort—able to see more light, to walk in a greater light, to prove more adequately than heretofore his capacities within the greatly increased area of possibility.

Initiation is, therefore, a constant fusion of the lights, progressively entered, thus enabling the initiate to see further, deeper and more inclusively. As one of the Masters has said: "The light must enter vertically and be diffused or radiated horizontally." This creates the cross of service upon which the disciple is pendant until the Cross of Sanat Kumara is revealed to him; he knows then why this planet is—for wise and adequate reasons—the planet of distress, dispassion and detachment. When he knows this, he knows all that our planetary life can tell him and reveal to him. He has transmuted knowledge into wisdom.

It is at the centre of this cross of service that the point of fusion and the point of tension must be found. The point of fusion is created by the focussing of all the power, aims and desires of the disciple dynamically upon the mental plane; the point of tension is created when the invocative power of this focal point becomes capable of evoking response from that which is invoked. For the average aspirant and for the disciple, this is either the soul or the Spiritual Triad. The meeting of the two focussed energies produces a point of tension. Disciples should not focus their attention upon the task of producing a point of tension. They should remember the life of dual activity; i.e., that which he is at any given moment of endeavour, and that with which he can fuse and blend this sum total of his achieved development. The potency of his thinking along these dual lines will automatically produce the point of tension, through the medium of the fusion of the appropriate dualities. It is through the activity of the lower mind that fusion with the soul is brought about, with successive, intensifying points of tension; it is through the activity established between higher and lower mind that fusion with the Spiritual Triad becomes possible, with points of tension arising at many points along the bridge, the antahkarana; it is through the activity of pure reason that fusion with the Hierarchy becomes possible, and it is that which produces those points of tension which we call *Initiations*. There are necessarily still higher points of tension, but it is with those called initiations that we are dealing at this time.

Light may enter your mind in this connection if you will constantly bear in mind the essential duality of manifestation itself; the negative and the positive poles present within the consciousness of every form. The achieved point of fusion (the result of active and positive work and effort) is rendered negative to that which is being invoked, and by this means another and positive point of tension can be achieved. Initiation—a dramatic and a major point of tension—connotes essentially the fusion of the negative and the positive aspects. Owing to this, in all initiatory processes, it is the will of the disciple which is active and which produces, first of all, a fusion and (as a consequence) the appearance of a point of tension.

Let me illustrate. In the work of creating the antahkarana, the disciple first of all and as far as in him lies, through the medium of positive mental labour, focusses himself upon the mental plane. The fusion of the soul and of the personality is then present and is the result of a positive activity. The quality and the vibratory nature of that positive focal point is then rendered negative to that higher vibration or contact which is invoked by *the existent radiance* and potency. The response from the opposite pole is (if the disciple could but realise it) immediate and to the extent possible, determined by the disciple's point of attainment.

This invocative-evocative activity produces a point of tension but not—as yet—a point of fusion with the positive pole. From that point of tension the disciple works at the creation of the antahkarana; this will eventually bring about the desired fusion between the soul-infused personality and the Spiritual Triad. The same general process dictates all the desired fusions and produces those points of tension which are the secret of all growth. These points of fusion and of tension the disciple *consciously* endeavours to bring about.

These are the broad and general lines governing the initiatory process; the work here indicated is followed by all disciple-intiates of all degrees, and even by the Lord of the World Himself. He, in His high Place, holds the manifested world of energies in a state of fusion; points of tension successively occur as a consequence of a growing divine realisation within these forms of intelligent activity, of love-wisdom and of the will-to-good. These points of tension vary according to the divine purpose and the individual initiatory problem of Sanat Kumara Himself, as He submits to a *cosmic* initiatory process. Such a point of tension, of stupendous magnitude, is present in the world today; the intention behind this realised fusion and tension is to enable humanity (as an integral part of the divine body of manifestation) to move forward into greater light and nearer to the "heart of love," which is the Hierarchy. As this takes place—and it is taking place—the Hierarchy Itself moves nearer to a conscious fusion with Humanity. The point of tension thereby achieved—and this has not yet appeared—will produce the Kingdom of God on Earth in exoteric form.

We will now consider one of the lesser, though essential, fusions which must be achieved by the disciple, producing consequently in his life a point or points of tension.

### Fusion of the Master's consciousness with that of the disciple

Earlier I stated that the disciple's private life automatically falls (once he has been accepted by the Master) into three stages:

a. The stage in which the lower concrete mind and the higher mind are related in such a manner that the lower mind is not only soul-illumined but is subject also to impression from the Spiritual Triad.

b. His relation to the Master is the next and sometimes paralleling stage and involves the bringing to-

gether of the Master's consciousness and his own. This
has to be slowly developed and consciously grasped,
with very interesting consequences.

c. Later comes the stage when the disciple's consciousness can be gradually brought into a rapport with
the Hierarchy as a whole. It might be mentioned, in
clarification somewhat of this rather vague statement,
that the disciple is absorbed into the Hierarchy and—
at the same time—he *assimilates* in a new and mysterious manner certain united hierarchical impressions.

The disciple by now has made his approach to the
Ashram and has demonstrated his ability to serve and
thereby utilise any ashramic energy which he may contact
and occultly include. He is slowly becoming aware of three
vibratory impressions which are slightly differing though
coloured by the ray which they express. First of all, he
is aware of the vibration of his own soul; then he registers
that of the Ashram, in the early stages focussed for him
through the mediation of some disciple senior to him;
and finally, he becomes conscious of the vibration of the
Master. Slowly he learns to distinguish them and know
them as constituting three different channels whereby
energy reaches him. They contact his consciousness upon
the mental plane; later, he discovers that contact with them
is facilitated once he can register them consciously upon
their appropriate plane and through the appropriate centre;
it naturally takes time to develop this facility and (until
he passes through the third initiation when major changes
take place) he is expected to "retain the impression" upon
the mental plane.

The development of sensitivity to contact, and the
registering of "that which is other than the Self and yet
which is the Self Itself," are part of the great Science of
Impression. This development—in the early stages of human evolution—is carried forward through the medium
of the five senses and is to be found in the animal kingdom
also. With this well-known and well-studied unfoldment I
shall not deal, beyond saying that these five (in reality

seven) senses constitute avenues of spiritual approach to varying aspects of the divine manifestation in the three or five worlds of human evolution. It might here be pointed out that (in a mysterious manner) the seven centres in the etheric body are correspondences to the seven senses, for they are responsive to vibrations coming from the world soul or the human soul, from the Ashram and from the Master, as well as registering eventually the energies of all the seven rays; these pour into the disciple and through him as part of the great circulatory system of the sevenfold divine energy which is the basis of manifestation. I dealt with these senses and the circulating energies somewhat at length in *A Treatise on Cosmic Fire.*

With the theme of the fusion of the soul and the personality I have dealt adequately in other writings and in the teaching on the antahkarana. I will confine myself here to the fusion of the Master's consciousness *(as it is conditioned to the human kingdom)* with that of the disciple. There is no fusion possible or comprehensible between the Master's higher or Shamballic consciousness and that of any disciple who has not taken the fourth initiation. The completeness of the fusion to which I refer is not possible in the early stages of the disciple's unfoldment; there again, the teaching hitherto presented by occult groups in connection with a Master's relation to His disciple has been erroneous and the result of wishful thinking.

The disciple is only permitted to have contact with the Master's mind when his spiritual life has become habitual to him and when he can, at will, flood his personality with soul energy. Those who make occasional and rare soul contacts (and there are many who do) in their meditation work are not so privileged. It is the disciple who has established a usable contact with his soul, of which he can avail himself at any time he so chooses, who can begin to register impressions coming directly to him from the Master.

Aspirants must not confuse teaching given to them by the Master in the work of the Ashram with this later fusion of consciousness. In group formation, disciples are gathered together at times to receive instruction and are thereby protected within the group aura from the tremendous potency of the Master's presence. It is difficult for the average aspirant to realise the necessity for this, yet even disciples themselves, and in the early stages of their admission to the Ashram and of their training, have a potent effect upon those whom they may contact. The effect is produced without intention and is caused by the higher quality of the disciple's vibration or radiance to that of the person or group he contacts. The impression he makes produces stimulation—a stimulation which the person frequently finds it very difficult to handle, evoking not only good but also bad effects.

The application of this radiant energy is a definite mode of spiritual service and activity, but until a disciple has advanced in knowledge and can control his radiation (permitting only those streams of energy to escape from him which are appropriate to the need) the "passing-by" of a disciple can produce much difficulty, both for the individual and for the group.

It will be obvious to you, therefore, that the presence of a Master will have a potent effect where an individual disciple is concerned. I have employed that separative term "individual disciple" because it indicates the cause of the possible difficulty or even danger. Such difficulty is always possible as long as any separative or self-centered instincts exist in the disciple; it takes a long time for a disciple to attain that disinterestedness and that inclusive spirit which will enable him to stand in the presence of the Master and present no barriers to direct contact with the Master's mind. This contact, leading to the desired fusion, falls into certain clearly defined stages:

1. Occasionally in the disciple's hours of meditation, at a moment of great tension or in a crisis (related to his service activities), there may occur a momentary fusion of the minds of the disciple and the Master. This can only

occur when the mental focus is so steady and so firmly directed in intention that emotional reactions or the intrusion of personality affairs are eliminated.

2. Later on in his training, the Master may attempt to impress his mind unexpectedly, and thus train him to recognise what we might regard as a direct call from the Centre of the Ashram.

3. As the disciple proves his value and demonstrates that he is desiring nothing for the separated self, the inter-relation between the two minds—of the Master of the Ashram and the disciple—finds no impediment; there is consequently no risk of overstimulation, of self-satisfaction or of the emergence of qualities which would disturb the rhythm of the Ashram. There can take place (as the Master wills it) a flow of thought between the two. At first, the impression is carried forward entirely on the side of the Master, and the disciple is simply an agent who can be impressed by ideas and instructed along some particular line which may be of service to humanity; he can, however, produce no current of thought flowing back to the Master. Later on, as a disciple moves forward into light and is simultaneously a server, he can be permitted to reach the Master with his own reaction to the impression.

4. Then comes the final stage wherein the disciple can be trusted to be the initiatory agent of impression and of contact and is allowed to evoke the Master's attention and to penetrate to the Centre of the Ashram. Students would do well to relate these four stages to the Six Stages of Discipleship, dealt with in the latter part of *Discipleship in the New Age, Vol. I;* these four stages correspond to the final four considered in that book.

These contacts are naturally in the field of telepathy, which is an aspect of the Science of Impression, and are entirely in the realm of mental interplay. I have dealt with the basic science itself in the book *Telepathy and the Etheric Vehicle.* The relation considered above is between the instrument of contact used by the Master—that of the higher or abstract mind, for the Masters do not work through the lower mind at all—and the lower or concretising mind of the disciple. The Masters are therefore dependent upon the use of the antahkarana which the disciple is in process of building; this is rapidly becoming a part of the group Antahkarana, built by disciples (working in the three worlds but on mental levels) who have been admitted into the Ashram. You can see why, therefore, the teaching anent the Antahkarana was deemed by us to be timely and wise. Relationship to the Ashram and contact with the Master are dependent upon the existence of the Antahkarana. In the early stages of its creative construction, the Antahkarana is adequate to permit some contact with the Ashram and with certain of the disciples, though not with those of very high degree. Later, as the Antahkarana perfects itself, higher and more durable contacts become possible.

The results of these developed and registered contacts are finally seen in the complete impressibility—at any time and without any effort on either side—of the disciple's mind. It is now so attuned to the Ashram and to the Master's ray quality that his mind is one with that of the Master at the centre. Reciprocal activity becomes possible.

It is needless, surely, for me to point out that the theme of all impressions coming from the Master to the disciple, and from the disciple to the Master, is the service of the Plan, the problems connected with group work in the Aquarian Age, or with the life and relationships within the Ashram. Forget not that the Ashram has its own objectives, intentions and inner techniques which are unconnected with the disciple's life and his service in the three worlds. The work of the disciple in preparation for initiation is not basically concerned with his daily world service, though there would be no initiation for him if that life of service were lacking. His life of service is, in reality, an expression of the particular initiation for which he is being prepared. This is a theme too vast for us to consider here, but it is an idea upon which you could well ponder.

One hint I will give you, based on the life of the Christ. The life history and the experiences of the great Initiates are rarely given, but much has been communicated to us anent the life of the Christ, both in the Gospels and in connection with His earlier incarnations. As you know, He took one of the greatest of the initiations (the sixth initiation, that of Decision). This initiation is related to the throat centre and also to its higher correspondence, the throat centre of the planetary Logos; this is the centre which we call Humanity. Thus "the WORD came forth." He had a dual mission to fulfill in order to prove His fitness (if one may use such a word in connection with an initiate of His exalted standing). He had, first of all, to give a great impetus to human evolution by proclaiming two things:

1. That "the blood is the life."
2. That all men everywhere are sons of God, and therefore divine.

Secondly, He had to bring to an end the Jewish dispensation which should have climaxed and passed away with the movement of the sun out of Aries into Pisces. He therefore presented Himself to them as their Messiah, which was His reason for manifesting through the Jewish race. They not only rejected Him, but have succeeded in perpetuating the Jewish dispensation through the medium of its religious presentation throughout the era of the Christian dispensation. This lies at the root of their trouble and is the cause of their constant emphasis upon the past—a past which is based on their experiences in Aries and not upon their growth in Pisces.

This entire subject of the telepathic interplay between the disciple and the Ashram, and between the Master and the disciple, is one of unique interest. It is part of the dual life which all disciples must lead. It is that which intensifies the life of introspection which is only rightly understood and carried forward when the man is in truth a soul-infused personality. It is the source or origin of the extraverted life which the disciple must also lead, producing an intense activity in the three worlds—an activity which in no way disturbs the calm procedures of the life of ashramic contacts. Rightly followed, it produces the possibility with which our third point deals.

*Impression on the mind of the disciple of hierarchical intent*

This is something far greater and more inclusive than the ability of the mind of the disciple to register the content of the minds within the Ashram with which he is affiliated or even the mind of the Master. The *purpose aspect* of the Plan begins to impress his now highly illumined abstract mind, for the integrated purpose—as far as the Hierarchy is concerned—begins slowly to impress him. Little by little, he begins to register impressions from Shamballa. With this I cannot deal; it concerns the growth which follows the fourth and fifth initiations, and therefore training given to a Master. With it you have no concern.

Your major task, as aspirants, is to cultivate the higher sensitivity; to render yourselves so pure and selfless that your minds remain undisturbed by the happenings in the three worlds; to seek that attentive spiritual sense which will enable you to be impressed, and then to interpret correctly the impressions received.

I have said that initiation is in reality a great experiment with energy. The life of the occult student is *consciously* lived in the world of energies. Those energies have always been present, for the whole of existence in all the kingdoms of nature is manifested energy, but men are not aware of this. They are not conscious, for instance, when they succumb to irritation and find themselves voicing that irritation in loud words or in angry thoughts, that they are taking astral energy and using it. The use of this energy admits them with ease to a level of astral living which is not suitable for them; continual use of this energy brings about what the Master Morya has called "habits of residence which imperil the resident." It is when the aspirant recognises that he himself is composed of energy units—held in coherent expression by a still stronger energy, that of integration—that he begins consciously to work in a world of forces similarly composed; he then begins to use energy of a certain kind, and selectively, and takes one of the initial steps towards becoming a true occultist. This world of energy in which he lives and moves and has his being is the living, organised vehicle of manifestation of the planetary Logos. Through it energies are circulating all the time and are in constant movement, being directed and controlled by the head centre of the planetary Logos; they create great vortices of force or major points of tension throughout His body of manifestation. The Spiritual Hierarchy of our planet is such a vortex; Humanity itself is another, and one which is today in a condition of almost violent activity, owing to its becoming a focus of divine attention.

Certain great readjustments are going on in that centre, for it is beginning to conform at long last to divine intention. I have elsewhere pointed out that for the first time in the long history of human development, energy from Shamballa has made a direct impact upon this third planetary centre. This is not due entirely to the point in evolution attained by mankind; this attainment is only a secondary reason or cause. It is due to the will of Sanat Kumara Himself as He prepares for a certain cosmic initiation. This initiation requires the reorganisation of the energies flowing through and composing that "centre which we call the race of men"; this creates a rearrangement within the centre itself, and thus brings into manifested expression certain aspects and qualities—always inherent in those energies—which have not hitherto been recognised. This creative crisis has been made possible by three major happenings:

1. The conclusion of a twenty-five thousand year cycle or movement around what is called the lesser zodiac. This connotes a major cycle of experience in the life of our planetary Logos. It is related to the interplay between the planetary Logos and the solar Logos as the latter responds to energies emanating from the twelve zodiacal constellations.

2. The end of the Piscean Age. This simply means that the energies coming from Pisces during the last two thousand years are now being rapidly superseded by energies coming from Aquarius. These result in major changes in the life of the planetary Logos and potently affect His body of manifestation through the medium of His three major centres: Shamballa, the Hierarchy and Humanity.

3. The increasingly dominant activity of the seventh Ray of Order or Ceremonial Magic, as it is somewhat erroneously called. This ray is now coming into manifestation and is in close cooperation with the two above factors; it produces also the lessening of the power of the sixth Ray of Idealism. This has had a long cycle and has greatly hastened the evolutionary process; it demonstrates its effective work in the emergence today of the great world ideologies. I am necessarily considering these energies only in relation to the human consciousness.

There are other factors present in our planet today, but these are the ones which will (in a vague sense) mean something to you, as you think and seek to understand.

The great cosmic initiation through which our planetary Logos is passing (forget not my words, "initiatory *process*") produces an entire reorganisation of all the energies of which His body of manifestation is composed; it heightens the quality or the vibration of certain of the ray energies, and lessens the potency of others. Direction also enters in; certain planetary centres become the recipients (in a new and vital manner) of the redirected ray potencies. Among these, at this time, the human family (or the third vital centre) becomes a prime objective. The three major centres in the body of the planetary Logos are:

The head centre    —Shamballa  —1st Ray of Will
The heart centre   —Hierarchy  —2nd Ray of Love-Wisdom
The throat centre  —Humanity   —3rd Ray of Active
                                 Intelligence

The impact of the new incoming energies upon Humanity

will result from a planned redirection. This will bring in an era of greatly enhanced creative activity; it will be an activity such as has never been seen before, and which will express itself in every department of human living.

In this connection I would remind you of the relation existing between the sacral centre (the physical creative centre) and the throat centre, and of the teaching anent the raising of the energies from this lower centre to the throat centre. This can be seen happening in the human being as he progresses along the Path of Evolution, and is equally present in the life and experience of the planetary Logos.

This progressive "creative raising" necessarily produces a cycle of tremendous difficulty in the life of the aspirant to initiation, for the microcosm undergoes—in his minute living process—what the planetary Logos undergoes in a cosmic process. When—as is the case today—Humanity itself is in process of becoming creative in the higher sense, and when this synchronises with a major creative planetary activity, then a cycle of very great disturbance eventuates which necessarily affects every individual within "the race of men." Hence the sexual disturbance to be seen everywhere, with the license present in every country and the apparent breakdown of the marriage relation. This indicates the emergence eventually of a creativity of such wondrous dimensions that the world will stand amazed; nothing like it will have been seen before. A creative planning for human well-being and a political expression, implementing this planning, will demonstrate in every country; a creative thinking will be apparent which will express itself in writing and in poetry; creative imagining will produce the new art, the new colours, the new architecture and the new culture; a creative responsiveness to the "music of the spheres" will bring forth the new music. All this will be in response to the creative reorganisation and the newly directed energies which are engaging the attention of the planetary Logos at this time.

All this reorganisation and redirection of energies is carried forward in the realm of the divine third aspect, that of divine active intelligence. Therefore the human centre registers this major aspect and becomes intensely invocative; this invocative appeal, being unitedly directed towards the second major centre, the Hierarchy, inevitably evokes a response. Invocation, accompanied by the creative imagination, will produce that new creative activity which will bring "the new heavens and the new earth" into being.

Three points I would like to make here; they have a definite bearing upon our subject:

1. This intense creative activity falls into two parts:

a. *A destructive cycle,* wherein the old order passes away and that which has been created—human civilisation with its accompanying institutions—is destroyed. With this destructive action Humanity is today occupying itself—mostly unconsciously. The major creative agents are the intelligentsia of the race.

b. *A cycle of restoration,* with many accompanying difficulties in which the mass of men take part, under the influence and inspiration of a regenerated intelligentsia.

2. This process received its initial impulse as a result of a group decision within the Hierarchy itself. Certain Masters Who were facing the sixth *Initiation of Decision* at the time—a relatively small but powerful group—decided together to tread the Path of Earth Service (technically understood) in order to bring about the changes which They sensed as desirable and as already existing within the consciousness of the One Initiator, the planetary Logos. It was Their decision, taken early in this century, which precipitated—in the centre which we call "the race of men" —those potencies and stimulating energies which produced that major destructive agency, the world war (1914-1945). As these energies occultly "fell into the centre," the effect produced was both good and bad. Human unity and unanimity, human planning for group welfare, and human

creativity (expressed primarily at this time through science) received a tremendous stimulation. Simultaneously, the entering potencies released by this decision produced an up-surging of evil in the hearts of men so inclined, leading to an analogous or paralleling unity, unanimity and creative activity of separative and hateful evil. This, in its turn, "opened the door where evil dwelt" and let loose on earth the full fury of the Black Lodge.

That this would be the result the Masters knew when making Their decision; They consciously struck a blow at the materialism which was binding humanity and imprisoning the human spirit. This evoked a prompt reaction from the Forces of Evil which had created and "held in being" the modern materialistic world, with its emphasis upon forms and money. The Masters had confidence that the human spirit would be able to live through the period of upheaval and emerge eventually into the new era, ready to build the new world and to reorganise all human resources—material, mental and spiritual.

3. The response of humanity, from the angle of a spiritual realisation of the presented opportunity, was the emergence of the New Group of World Servers. They appeared in every country, conscious of their task of crystallising and making effective human goodwill, though generally unconscious of their hierarchical relationship. Their appearance evoked an immediate reaction from the Spiritual Hierarchy, and experienced disciples made their appearance in the ranks of the New Group of World Servers, directing their efforts, voicing their aims and stimulating their understanding. The new group worked in and through every department of human thinking, human welfare and human planning; as a result, and almost immediately, the men of goodwill everywhere in the world took heart of grace (a most appropriate phrase) and became active.

The three points made here will demonstrate to you the factual nature of the circulation of energies. All these happenings are part of a process of planetary initiation;

such an initiation cannot take place without important effects, both in the Hierarchy and in the human family. In old Atlantean days, it was the Masters (facing the same sixth initiation) Who "decided" to bring that ancient civilisation to an end; They therefore sacrificed the form aspect of manifestation and created a situation in which the soul of humanity was liberated from the prison in which it found itself. Today, a material catastrophe, such as the flood, has not been deemed necessary; it is believed that humanity can and will find its own way out of the world difficulties.

## THE ASPIRANT AND THE MAJOR INITIATIONS

We now approach the second part of our theme, dealing with the major initiations; we will do so primarily from the standpoint of the ray energies, considering the subject from the initiate's point of view. I wonder if you realise, my brother, that this has never before been done? The teaching hitherto given out on initiation has been pictorially and symbolically presented; the understanding of the process was dependent upon right interpretation. In this materialistic age, that interpretation has been largely material in nature; emphasis has been laid upon the tangible and *supposed* form aspect of initiation.

I here propose a different approach, and would ask you to keep in mind some words out of the ancient Archives which are as follows:

"Energy is all there is, O Chela in the Light, but is not known. It is the cause of knowledge and its application and its comprehension lead to expanded understanding.

Through energy the worlds were made and through that energy they make progression; through energy the forms unfold and die; through energy the kingdoms manifest and disappear below the threshold of the world which ever is and which will be forever.

Through energy the Cross is mounted and from the vortex of the four uniting forces, the initiate passes through the door and is propelled into the Light—a light which grows from cycle unto cycle and is known as supernal Energy Itself."

I shall not be able to avoid a measure of symbolic approach and I am forced to use words which will fail to express the truth. The extent of your understanding will be based upon your point in evolution, upon your attitude

of mind as you approach this theme, and upon the point
of tension you are able to achieve

Initiation is (in its simplest definition) an understanding of the Way, for understanding is a revealing energy
which permits you to achieve. Initiation is a growth in
experience and the attainment thereby of a point of tension. Holding that point of tension, the initiate sees that
which lies ahead. *Initiation permits a progressive entry into
the mind of the creating Logos.* This last definition is perhaps one of the most important I have ever given. Ponder
on my words.

Initiation is a system or a scientific process whereby
the septenate of energies which compose the sum total of
all the existences within our planetary Life are *realised* and
consciously used for the working out of the divine Plan.
It might also be stated that initiation is a method whereby
the circulation of energies is furthered by the opening or
the awakening of certain planetary and human centres
to the impact of their ray quality, potency and divine
intention. It is this statement which lies at the heart of the
teaching on Laya Yoga or the Science of the Centres.

## The Relation of the Seven Rays to the Initiations

It will be obvious to you that, as energy is the basis
of our entire manifested world, an initiation is a condition of consciousness wherein the fully prepared disciple
utilises the available energies (at the time of initiation) to
bring about changes within consciousness of a momentous
and revelatory nature. Each initiation puts the initiate in
a position to control certain related energies and enables
him to become increasingly a trained manipulator of those
energies; each initiation gives him understanding of the
related energy and of its field of activity; each initiation
reveals to him the quality and the type of stimulation to
be evoked when brought into contact with any particular
ray energy; each initiation establishes relationship between
the initiate and the ray energy involved, so that gradually

(no matter what may be his soul ray or his personality ray) he can work with the quality and the creative aspect of all the rays, though ever retaining a greater facility to work on his own soul ray, and later with the ray of the Monad —one of the three major Rays of Aspect.

I would ask you to remember that all human beings must finally express the quality and livingness of one of the three Rays of Aspect, even if—in time and space—their souls may originally be upon one of the four Rays of Attribute. It might be useful here to enumerate the rays, and thus refresh the memory of the neophyte:

*Rays of Aspect:*
    1. The Ray of Power, Will or Purpose
    2. The Ray of Love-Wisdom
    3. The Ray of Active Creative Intelligence
*Rays of Attribute:*
    4. The Ray of Harmony through Conflict
    5. The Ray of Concrete Science or Knowledge
    6. The Ray of Idealism or Devotion
    7. The Ray of Order or Ceremonial Magic

It is contact with the energy of the third Ray of Active Intelligence or (as it is sometimes called) the "acute energy of divine mental perception" which admits the consciousness of the initiate into the "secrets of the Mind of God." It is the four Rays of Attribute which, in the evolutionary cycle, condition his character (or apparatus of contact) and evoke his essential quality. The three Rays of Aspect enable him to take the four higher initiations—initiations 6, 7, 8, 9—and are connected purely with Shamballa. The four Rays of Attribute, particularly as they are synthesised through the medium of the third Ray of Aspect, are related more definitely to the Hierarchy, and therefore are related to the first five initiations. The Rays of Aspect are essentially related to the life or will aspect of divinity; the Rays of Attribute are related to the consciousness aspect.

Every human being, in the earlier stages of his development (in ancient Lemuria and Atlantis, or possessing

today the Lemurian or Atlantean state of consciousness—
and there are many such), comes into incarnation upon
one of the four Rays of Attribute, because these rays are
peculiarly and uniquely related to the fourth kingdom in
nature, and therefore to the fourth Creative Hierarchy.
During the long, long cycle of the present fifth race, the
so-called Aryan race, there came a period (lying now in
the far distant and forgotten past) when individuals who
had attained a certain state of consciousness transferred on
to one of the three Rays of Aspect, according to the pre-
dominance of the energy or the line of force which was
conditioned by these rays. One of the Rays of Aspect and
two of the Rays of Attribute (rays 3, 5, 7) are conditioned
by the first Ray of Power or Will, whilst rays 4 and 6 are
conditioned by the second Ray of Love-Wisdom. This I
much earlier pointed out. A cycle of lives upon the third
Ray of Creative Intelligence (as I prefer to call it) always
precedes this transference. This ray experience covers a vast
period of time. Except in the occult teaching and the
Archives which remain in the custody of the Masters, history—as we know it and as it expresses the emergence from
primitive and primeval times—does not exist. From the
angle of occultism, history only covers the emergence of
those cultures and civilisations which are called the fifth
rootrace, only a small part of it being recognised as Aryan;
the latter is simply a modern and scientific nomenclature
covering a small period of modern history. The Aryan
cycle covers the period of the relation between groups and
nations though positing (as a necessary hypothesis) previous
but unknown cycles of human living wherein primitive
man roamed the earth; or positing sometimes the existence
of previous civilisations which have completely disappeared,
leaving behind them faint traces of ancient organised
civilisations and cultural remains, plus indications of inter-
world relationships of which there is no positive proof;
these, it is suggested, must have existed owing to the similarity of architecture, language roots, traditions and the
myths of religions.

During these earlier periods all human beings were conditioned by the four Rays of Attribute; both as souls and as incarnated persons they were upon one of these four rays. Towards the middle of the Atlantean cycle (untold millions of years ago) the influence of the third Ray of Active Intelligence became exceedingly potent. Certain of the advanced humanity of the period gradually found their way on to, or rather into, the stream of divine energy which we call the third ray. The possibility, therefore, of their becoming integrated personalities was for the first time recognised, and humanly recognised. Such an integration must ever precede conscious human initiation.

Forget not my earlier statement that all the Rays of Attribute are focussed in and absorbed by the third Ray of Aspect. A study of the charts which I gave and permitted to appear in *A Treatise on Cosmic Fire* will help you to understand this. They will prove helpful, provided that you remember always that they are only symbolic in nature and constitute attempts to indicate visually a truth.

The Atlantean race was predominantly a race wherein its leading exponents (the "flower of the race" or the "crest wave," as it is called) expressed an active intelligence. It was intelligence which its initiates had to demonstrate, and not love-wisdom, as is the case today. This expressed itself in a mental focus, a trained mind capable of illumination, and great creative ability. In the Aryan race, which from the occult point of view can be regarded as encompassing practically the totality of history as we have it, the influence of the second Ray of Love-Wisdom is slowly becoming the dominating factor; men are rapidly finding their way on to that ray, and the number of people found upon that line of energy is already very great, though not yet as great as those upon the third ray, as it today expresses itself through one of the four Rays of Attribute. This latest of the human races (again through its foremost exponents) has to manifest the spirit of love through wisdom; the basis of this expression is an unfolding inclusiveness, a developing understanding, and a heightened spiritual perception which is capable of envisaging that which lies beyond the three worlds of human evolution.

It might here be said that the one-pointed life of the focussed intellectual (that life which the higher initiates demonstrated in the Atlantean initiations) and the extensive inclusive life of the modern or Aryan initiate, is the objective held before the disciple upon the Path of Discipleship and in the Masters' ashrams. The presence in humanity today of an ardent intelligence and a growing inclusiveness is symbolised under the words "the vertical and the horizontal life"; it is therefore visually portrayed under the symbol of the Cross. I have here indicated to you, therefore, that *the Cross is strictly the symbol of Aryan unfoldment*. The symbol of old Atlantis was a line, indicating the vertical line of mental unfoldment and aspiration. The Christian consciousness, or the consciousness of the soul, is the perfecting and control of the mind, plus the demonstration of love in service; these are the outstanding characteristics of the Hierarchy and the essential qualities of those who form the kingdom of God.

In the coming race, which lies still far ahead and of which only initiates of degrees higher than the fifth are the expression, the Ray of Aspect which embodies the Will of God will gradually become dominant. Its symbol cannot yet be revealed. There will then come a blending of divine will energy with the developed and manifesting energies of intelligence and love. In the final race (lying untold ages ahead) there will appear a creative synthesis of all these three Rays of Aspect. Then all souls will be upon one of these three rays, and all personalities on one of the four Rays of Attribute. There will then be a perfect expression—through Humanity, the third divine planetary centre—of the livingness, the quality and the creative potency of all the rays.

These are facts which I would have you bear in mind as we consider the relation of the seven rays to initiation in this particular world period and during the cycle of treading the Paths of Discipleship and Initiation. Great transitions are then made; the power to include and to love in the truly esoteric sense automatically produces changes and a basic refocussing in the life of the accepted disciple and of the initiate; these changes, transitions and reactions are brought about by the action of the ray potencies during the period of initiation; the initiate then enters into relationship with rays which are conditioning him at the time. They affect his soul-infused personality, and also the ashram with which he is affiliated. The quality and potency of an ashram is definitely affected by the admission of an initiate; he brings into it not only his own potency and ray qualities as a soul, but also the energy of the rays which produced the changes and which conditioned him during the initiatory process he has just undergone. He then moves into a new stage of conscious contact *within the Ashram.* This new state of perceptive spirituality permits the initiate to enter into a relation with all those who have undergone a similar initiation. He therefore becomes increasingly a constructive and creative agent in the ashram.

It is this which necessitates his careful preparation, which must be paralleled by a demonstration of his understanding of the initiatory process upon the outer plane of activity in service. He cannot be permitted to enter the life of the ashram and become the recipient of exceedingly active energies until he has proved that these energies will not be "occultly retained" by him but will become the "strength and potency" of his service among men.

We are entering now upon a somewhat close analysis of the energies of the seven rays and their effects upon the initiatory processes which face the disciple. Every initiate enters upon the period of initiatory process possessed of a certain definite energy equipment. His personality is expressing itself within the periphery of the three worlds through clearly defined ray forms and relationships. He is a personality through the integration of his mind, his emotional nature and his physical body—the energy of the latter phenomenal factor being focussed in the physical brain. All of these are composed of and conditioned by the energy units of which they are constituted, and all of them "focus their intention" through the medium of the physical brain, thus enabling the personality to be a self-directed entity upon the physical plane. To this personality a fifth major energy must be added: the energy of the soul. Each of these personality expressions is composed of and governed by one of the seven ray energies, so that a great and dynamic synthesis is present which—at the time when the initiatory process is begun—is in reality a composite of five energies:

1. The energy of the soul, in itself a threefold energy.
2. The energies of the personality which is of such a potency (being a fusion of three ray energies) that it has evoked a ray which dominates the personality and is called the personality ray:

    a. The energy composing the mental vehicle.
    b. The energy which demonstrates as the emotional nature.
    c. The energy of the physical body, focussed on the physical plane and conditioning the brain.

All this information is elementary, but I repeat it for the sake of clarity and in order that we may know what it is that we are considering. In the case of the accepted disciple who is in preparation for initiation, the term applied to this system of integrated energies is "soul-infused personality." The fusion is necessarily not complete, but enough soul energy is present to guarantee that minimum of soul control which will make the initiatory process effective.

It might also be said that this system of integrated energies is (through the initiatory process) confronted with still higher fusions, because initiation is a process whereby successive integrations—attended by consequent expansions of consciousness—become possible. These are—in their broader significance, seven, though entailing many minor points of integration—as follows:

1. Fusion of the energies of the soul-infused personality with the triple energies of the Spiritual Triad.
2. Fusion with the Monad—of which the Spiritual Triad is an expression.
3. Fusion with the world consciousness of the planetary Logos to a degree which makes the planetary life, with all its states of consciousness and phenomena, a major confining and constricting form for the initiate.

In connection with this final fusion, it is worth while to point out that, when this stage of development is attained, it then becomes possible to enter into the "exalted state of mind" which holds the planetary Logos focussed in the consciousness of the sacrifice which He has made by means of the entire process of manifestation. As *The Secret Doctrine* has pointed out, this sacrifice which He has made on behalf of the untold myriad of lives which compose His body of manifestation, holds Him in physical expression until "the last weary pilgrim" has found his way home.

The extent and essential purpose of this divine sacrifice become increasingly clear to the initiate after the fifth initiation and constitute one of the prime factors which are considered by him when he faces the Initiation of Decision (the sixth initiation). At no stage of his unfoldment does he comprehend the basic purpose and (speaking occultly) the "dynamic extent" of this sacrifice, as it is implemented by the will of the planetary Logos. Nevertheless, he does respond to a mental understanding of the lowest *objective* aspect of this sacrifice and to the nature of the periphery, or to the imprisoning form (the sum total) in which the planetary Logos has chosen to imprison Himself. For the first time in his life experience he arrives at a comprehension of *the principle of limitation*. Beyond this exalted state of mental perception the initiate is not yet able to penetrate; he is limited by that sphere of activity which we call the seven planes, and which in their totality constitute the cosmic physical plane.

Many lesser fusions take place within the phase of initiatory development which intervenes between initia tion and initiation—a triple mental fusion between the three aspects of the mind (the lower mental vehicle, the soul or the Son of Mind, and the higher or abstract mind), fusion with the Master's consciousness, fusion with the ashram created by the ray energy which conditions his soul, fusion in consciousness with the sum total of the integrated ashrams which form the Ashram of Sanat Kumara. These successive and subsidiary fusions reveal to him the phenomena and quality of the two higher states of consciousness of the Spiritual Triad: the buddhic or the state of pure reason and the atmic or state of spiritually direct will intention. In giving you some insight into the relationship of the rays and the initiations, I find it essential to discover new and arresting words and word phrases by which to express the familiar hints and indications given by the occult groups who have sought to awaken the modern consciousness to the fact and purposes of initiation.

Initiation is a progressive sequence of directed energy impacts, characterised by points of crisis and of tension and governed—in a sense not hitherto realised—by the Law of Cause and Effect. This Law of Cause and Effect (from the spiritual angle) appears to the progressing initiate to reverse the process which has up till now governed his life. Instead of his being impelled forward on the path of evolution by spiritual energies which from higher spheres invoke and evoke his response and a developing expansion of consciousness, each successive initiation undergone, understood and demonstrated upon the physical plane becomes the cause and influence which propels the initiate forward upon the Path of Initiation. In one case the cause of progression is a streaming downward of the energies, producing effects in that which is thus stimulated; in the other case, the cause is to be found in the soul-infused personality and constitutes an upward movement of the initiatory self-directed activity, of the measure of love energy which his soul can express, and of the energy of will which is in itself the result of all the fusions he has at any given moment been capable of consciously focussing and using. These are points which it will be difficult for you to grasp but which are of major importance.

The human being is influenced upon the path of evolution from above downwards; the initiate is directed from within upwards. It is this which formulates the underlying significance of the energy of free will and is something only truly possible through self-direction; this can be seen struggling for expression today in that great world disciple, Humanity.

These concepts are worthy of your careful consideration. The sevenfold energy which is today agitating mankind marks a turning point in human history and indicates the possibility of the transition of humanity on to the Path of Discipleship; on that Path freedom of expression and conscious self-directed living will become increasingly possible.

## THE RAYS AND THE FIVE INITIATIONS CONFRONTING HUMANITY

Let us now consider our theme of the rays and initiation. This signifies in reality a study of the rays as they actively condition the Path of Initiation. Forget not, we are dealing here with the Path of Initiation and not primarily with the Path of Discipleship, even though the two paths are very closely related; we are not dealing with the disciple's character and actions. We are considering one thing only: the type of ray energy which makes any specific initiation possible, irrespective of the rays of the initiate.

We are in fact considering initiation as a planetary process, and not that process as it affects the individual initiate. That we shall consider under our point "The Significance of the Initiations." Then we shall take each initiation and consider it as outlined on page 340. This you will probably find more interesting, but you will comprehend what I then say with greater facility if you grasp some of the implications—as far as in you lies—of what I have now to impart.

These five initiations are under the energy impulses of Rays 7, 6, 5, 4, plus the dynamic influence of Ray 1 at the time of the fifth initiation. You will note, therefore, that these initiations which confront average humanity are all of them conditioned by a minor ray, yet finally bring in the energy of the highest Ray of Aspect, that of Will or Power. This dynamic electric energy has to act in a new and different sense if the four higher initiations are to become living objectives in the initiate's consciousness. It is for this reason that the fifth initiation is called the Initiation of Revelation. Some understanding of the first or will aspect is "conceded" at this initiation, and for the first time the nature of divine Purpose is revealed to the initiate; hitherto he has been preoccupied with the nature of the Plan, which is after all an effect of the Purpose.

In these five preliminary initiations the true nature of the minor rays, in their creative aspect and as expressions of the quality of the manifested world, begins progressively to dawn upon the initiate. In the higher four initiations he slowly arrives at a dim understanding of the purpose of creation; the true purpose, however, and the nature of the will of the planetary Logos will only be revealed in the next solar system wherein the soul-infused Personality of the planetary Logos will demonstrate living purpose within the ring-pass-not of the three lower cosmic planes.

With these abstruse ideas we need not concern ourselves. Let us study the energy conditions wherein the initiate proceeds from one initiation to another until he stands at the portal of revelation.

*Initiation I.   The Birth at Bethlehem. Ray VII.*
The Energy of Order or Ceremonial Magic.

First of all, let us consider the type of energy which the seventh ray expresses and wherein lies its potency and efficacy, from the angle of the initiation. As we study these initiations and their conditioning rays, we will divide our ideas into three parts:

1. The type of energy and its quality in relation to the processes of the particular initiation with which it is associated.

2. Its effect upon humanity, regarding humanity as a world disciple.

3. The stimulating nature of the energy as it expresses itself:

    a. In the three aspects of the initiate's nature—mental, astral and physical.

    b. Through the soul-infused personality, the initiate "in good standing"—a phrase of the deepest occult implication.

At this particular time in world history, seventh ray energy is of a growing potency because it is the new and incoming ray, superseding the sixth ray which has for so long held sway. When we speak of ray energy we are in reality considering the quality and the will-purpose aspect of a certain great Life to Whom we give the name "Lord of a Ray." You will find much about these Ray Lords in the earlier volumes of *A Treatise on the Seven Rays*. His divine intention, will, purpose, or the determined projection of His mind, creates a radiation or stream of energy which —according to type and quality—plays upon all forms of manifested life within our planetary ring-pass-not. These Lords of the Rays are the creating and sustaining energies which implement the Will of the planetary Logos. They cooperate with Him in the defining and the expression of His supreme purpose. Their radiating emanations are cyclically objectified and are cyclically withdrawn. As they radiate forth into the three worlds, the impacting energies produce changes, disturbances, progress and unfoldment; they create the needed new forms and vitalise and qualify that through which the immediate divine intention is expressing itself; they intensify both the quality and the receptivity of consciousness.

At other times, during the process of being withdrawn "to their own place," they cause the fading out or the dying of form aspects, of institutions, and the "organising organisms" (to use a peculiar phrase); they therefore produce cycles of destruction and of cessation and thus make room for those new forms and life expressions which an incoming ray will produce. It has been the gradual withdrawing of the sixth Ray of Idealism and of one-pointed Devotion which has been responsible for the ferment, crystallisation, destruction, death and cleavages of the past century; old things are passing away as the Lord of the sixth Ray withdraws His attention, and therefore His energy; His radiation is today no longer centred or focussed in the life of the three worlds. Simultaneously, the energy and radiation of the Lord of the seventh Ray are becoming steadily more powerful in the three worlds.

This incoming of a ray always produces an intensified period of initiatory activity, and this is the case today. The major effect, as far as humanity is concerned, is to make possible the presentation of thousands of aspirants and applicants for the first initiation; men on a large scale and in mass formation can today pass through the experience of the Birth Initiation. Thousands of human beings can experience the birth of the Christ within themselves and can realise that the Christ life, the Christ nature and the Christ consciousness are theirs. This "new birth" initiation of the human family will take place in Bethlehem, symbolically understood, for Bethlehem is the "house of bread"—an occult term signifying physical plane experience. These great initiations, implemented by the ray energies, must be registered in the physical brain and recorded by the waking consciousness of the initiate, and this must be the case in this amazing period wherein—for the first time since humanity appeared on Earth—there can take place a mass initiation. The experience need not be expressed in occult terms, and in the majority of cases will not be; the individual initiate who takes this initiation is aware of great changes in his attitude to himself, to his fellowmen, to circumstances and to his interpretation of life events. These are peculiarly the reactions which attend the first initiation; a new orientation to life and a new world of thought are registered by the initiate. This will be equally true on a large scale where modern man, the world initiate of the first degree, is concerned. Men will recognise the evidences in many lives of the emergence of the Christ-consciousness, and the standard of living will increasingly be adjusted to the truth as it exists in the teachings of the Christ.

This developing Christ-consciousness in the masses of men will create necessarily a ferment in the daily life of peoples everywhere; the life of the personality, oriented hitherto to the attaining of material and purely selfish ends, will be at war with the new and inner realisation; the "carnal" man (to use the words of Paul, the initiate) will be battling the spiritual man, each seeking to achieve control. In the early stages, after the "birth" and during the "infancy of the Christ-Child" (again speaking in symbols), the material aspect is triumphant. Later, the Christ life triumphs. This you well know. Each initiation indicates a stage in the growth and the development of this new factor in the human consciousness and expression, and this continues until the third initiation, when there emerges the "full-grown man in Christ." The initiate is then ready, at the fifth initiation, to register, realise and record the long awaited revelation.

In connection with the individual and the first initiation, the seventh ray is always active and the man is enabled consciously to register the fact of initiation because either the brain or the mind (and frequently both) are controlled by the seventh ray. It is this fact which is of importance today in connection with humanity, for it will enable mankind to pass through the door admitting them to the first initiatory process. It will be apparent to you why the present period in which human beings (in large groups) can take the first initiation corresponds to a situation in which bread is the major interest of men everywhere. Humanity will pass through this "birth" initiation and manifest the Christ life on a large scale for the first time during a period of economic adjustment o which the word "bread" is but a symbol. This period started in the year 1825 and will continue until the end of this century. The unfoldment of the Christ life—as a result of the presence and activities of the second divine aspect of love—will result in the ending of economic fear, and the "house of bread" will become the "house of plenty." Bread—as the symbol of material human need—will eventually be controlled by a vast group of initiates of the first initiation—by those whose lives are beginning to be controlled by the Christ-consciousness, which is the consciousness of responsibility and service. These initiates exist in their thousands today; they will be present in their millions by the time the year 2025 arrives. All this re-orientation and unfoldment will be the result of the activity of the seventh ray and of the impact of its radiation upon humanity.

The seventh ray is, par excellence, the medium of relationship. It brings together the two fundamental aspects of spirit and matter. It relates soul and form and, where humanity is concerned, it relates soul and personality. In the first initiation, it makes the initiate aware of that relation; it enables him to take advantage of this "approaching duality" and—by the perfecting of the contact—to produce upon the physical plane the emergence into manifestation of the "new man." At the first initiation, through the stimulation brought about by seventh ray energy, the personality of the initiate and the hovering over-shadowing soul are consciously brought together; the initiate then knows that he is—for the first time—a soul-infused personality. His task is now to grow into the likeness of what he essentially is. This development is demonstrated at the third initiation, that of the Transfiguration.

The major function of this seventh ray is to bring together the negative and positive aspects of the natural processes. It consequently governs the sex relationship of all forms; it is the potency underlying the marriage relation, and hence as this ray comes into manifestation in this world cycle, we have the appearance of fundamental sex problems—license, disturbance in the marriage relation, divorce and the setting in motion of those forces which will eventually produce a new attitude to sex and the establishing of those practices, attitudes and moral perceptions which will govern the relation between the sexes during the coming New Age.

The first initiation is therefore closely related to this problem. The seventh ray governs the sacral centre and the sublimation of its energy into the throat or into the higher creative centre; this ray is therefore setting in motion a period of tremendous creative activity, both on the material plane through the stimulation of the sex life of all peoples and in the three worlds through the stimulation brought about when soul and form are consciously related. The first major proof that humanity (through the medium of the majority of its advanced people) has undergone the first initiation will be the appearance of a cycle of entirely new creative art. This creative urge will take forms which will express the new incoming energies. Just as the period governed by the sixth ray has culminated in a world wherein men work in great workshops and factories to produce the plethora of objects men deem needful for their happiness and well-being, so in the seventh ray cycle we shall see men engaged on an even larger scale in the field of creative art. Devotion to objects will eventually be superseded by the creation of that which will more truly express the Real; ugliness and materiality will give place to beauty and reality. On a large scale, humanity has already been "led from darkness to light" and the light of knowledge fills the land. In the period which lies ahead and under the influencing radiation of the seventh ray, humanity will be "led from the unreal to the Real." This the first initiation makes possible for the individual and will make possible for the mass of men.

Seventh ray energy is the energy needed to bring order out of chaos and rhythm to replace disorder. It is this energy which will bring in the new world order for which all men wait; it will restore the ancient landmarks, indicate the new institutions and forms of civilisation and culture which human progress demands, and nurture the new life and the new states of consciousness which advanced humanity will increasingly register. Nothing can arrest this activity; all that is happening today as men search for the new ways, for organised unity and peaceful security, is being implemented through the incoming Ray of Order or Ceremonial Magic. The white magic of right human relations cannot be stopped; it must inevitably demonstrate effectively, because the energy of this seventh ray is present, and the Lord of the Ray is cooperating with the Lord of the World to bring about the needed "re-forming." Soul-infused personalities, acting under this ray influence, will create the new world, express the new qualities and institute those new regimes and organised modes of creative activity which will demonstrate the new livingness and the new techniques of living. It is the distortion of these seventh ray ideals and the prostitution of this incoming energy to serve the unenlightened and selfish ambitions of greedy men which has produced those totalitarian systems which today so terribly imprison the free spirit of men.

To sum up what I have said:

1. The energy of the seventh ray is the potent agent of initiation when taken on the physical plane, that is, during the process of the first initiation.

2. Its effect upon humanity will be:

> a. To bring about the birth of the Christ-consciousness among the masses of intelligently aspiring human beings.
>
> b. To set in motion certain relatively new evolutionary processes which will transform humanity (the world disciple) into humanity (the world initiate).
>
> c. To establish in a new and intelligible manner the ever-existent sense of relationship and thus bring about upon the physical plane right human relations. The agent of this is goodwill, a reflec-

tion of the will-to-good of the first divine aspect. Of this first Ray of Will or Purpose, goodwill is the reflection.

d. To readjust negative and positive relationships, and—today—this will be carried forward primarily in connection with the sex relation and marriage.

e. To intensify human creativity and thus bring in the new art as a basis for the new culture and as a conditioning factor in the new civilisation.

f. To reorganise world affairs and so initiate the new world order. This is definitely in the realm of ceremonial magic.

3. The stimulation of this seventh ray will, in relation to the individual initiate,

a. Bring into being upon the mental plane a widespread and recognised relation between the soul and the mind.

b. Produce a measure of order in the emotional processes of the initiate, thus aiding the preparatory work of the second initiation.

c. Enable the initiate—upon the physical plane—to establish certain service relationships, to learn the practice of elementary white magic, and to demonstrate the first stage of a truly creative life.

As far as the individual initiate is concerned, the effect of seventh ray energy in his life is potent in the extreme; this is easily realised, owing to the fact that his mind and his brain are conditioned by the seventh ray at the time that the initiatory process is consciously taking place. The effect of this upon the mental plane is similar to that seen—on a much larger scale—in the planet, for it was this ray energy which the planetary Logos utilised when He brought together the major dualities of spirit and matter at the commencement of His creative work. The two aspects of the mind (the lower concrete mind and the soul, the Son of Mind) become more closely related and enter eventually into a conscious, recognised association *on the astral plane;* it is the seventh ray which restores order within the astral consciousness, and (on the mental plane) it is this influence which produces creativity, the organising of the life, and the bringing together "within the head" of the lower and higher energies in such a manner that "the Christ is born." This latter point we shall consider in some detail when we take up the significance of the initiations; we shall then find that the relationship between the pituitary body and the pineal gland is involved.

Finally, it is seventh ray energy which—in the initiatory process between the first and the second initiations — enables the initiate (in his physical plane life) to demonstrate a developing sense of order and of organisation, to express consciously and increasingly a desire to help his fellowmen, and thereby establish relationship with them, and to make his life creative in many ways.

All these factors are embryonic in his nature, but he now begins to *consciously* lay the foundation for the future initiatory work; the physical disciplines are at this time of great importance, though their value is frequently over-emphasised and their effect is not always good; the relationships established and fostered are sometimes of small value, owing to the disciple being usually self-centered and thus lacking—from ignorance and lack of discrimination—complete purity of motive. Nevertheless, the changes brought about by the influence of this ray become increasingly effective from life to life; the disciple's relation to the Hierarchy, the reorganising of his life on the physical plane, and his growing effort to demonstrate the esoteric sense of white magic will become more and more vital, until he is ready for the second initiation.

*Initiation II. The Baptism in Jordan. Ray VI.*
The Energy of Idealism and Devotion.

In the initiatory process between the first initiation of the Birth of the Christ and the beginning of the conscious unfoldment of the Christ life and awareness, the life of the initiate has undergone a pronounced reorientation. He is now capable of an equally pronounced and often fanatical adherence to the programme of aspiration and of devotion to the good (as he sees it at this stage). This is symbolised for us in the story of the twelve year old Jesus Who was so conscious that He "must be about His Father's business" that He defied His parents, caused them distress, and astonished those older than He by His spiritual poise and knowledge. This He offset by going down to Galilee and being "subservient" to His parents. A somewhat similar attitude (without the developed and inclusive understanding manifested by the Christ) can be seen expressing itself in the disciple during the period wherein the new orientation is taking place; the disciple is learning to discipline his lower nature and to achieve a measure of mastery over his physical inclinations; he thus releases physical energy and brings order into his life. This takes a very long time and may cover a cycle of many incarnations. He is constantly fighting against his lower nature, and the requirements of his soul (as he somewhat ignorantly interprets them) are in constant session against the animal nature, and increasingly in relation to the emotional nature.

Above all, he becomes aware of a secondary relation, involving a most difficult problem and one which enhances the fight and intensifies his problem. He discovers that his emotional nature, his lower psychic faculties, his astral development and the potency of glamour are now all arrayed against him.

The reorientation with which he is now faced has to be brought about primarily upon the astral plane, because that has been for untold aeons the level of his major polarisation and the sphere of activity and the state of consciousness which has dominated him. The physical body is not a principle; his etheric body has, since Atlantean days, been the agent of his astral energy, for the mind nature is not yet developed and cannot, therefore, adequately take control. He discovers that he lives in a chaos of emotional reactions and of conditioning glamours. He slowly begins to realise that in order to take the second initiation he *must* demonstrate emotional control; he realises also that he must have some knowledge of those spiritual energies which will dissipate glamour, plus an understanding of the technique whereby illumination from the mind—as the transmitting agent of the light of the soul—can dispel these glamours and thus "clarify the atmosphere," in the technical sense.

I might emphasise that as yet no initiate demonstrates complete control during the intermediate period between any initiation and the next higher initiation; the intermediate period is regarded as "a cycle of perfecting." That which is being left behind and subordinated to the higher realisation is slowly dominated by energies which are to be released into the consciousness of the initiate at the initiation for which he is being prepared. This interim period is always one of great difficulty. The energies being registered, made active and finally used, are steadily increasing in number and potency at each initiation; these impacts upon the rays of the soul and the personality rays of the initiate, and on the subsidiary vehicles through which he works in the three worlds and upon their individual conditioning rays, produce at first tremendous difficulties; these the initiate must master and the problems involved he must solve. He thereby becomes a Master, and the process, as it goes forward from initiation to initiation, becomes (after the third initiation, the Transfiguration) less hard and distressing; the reason for this is that he is increasingly master of his own *individual* situation. He is, however, occultly involved in the difficulties and the problems of the group and of that totality of groups which we call humanity.

The initiatory process between the first and the second initiations is for many the worst time of distress, difficulty, realisation of problems and the constant effort to "clear himself" (as it is occultly called), to which the disciple is at any time subjected. The phrase stating that the objective of the initiate is "to clear himself" is perhaps the most arresting and illuminating of all possible definitions of the task to be undertaken. The storm aroused by his emotional nature, the dark clouds and mists in which he constantly walks and which he has created throughout the entire cycle of incarnated living, have all to be cleared away in order that the initiate can say that—for him—the astral plane no longer exists, and that all that remains of that ancient and potent aspect of his being is aspiration, a sensitive response to all forms of divine life and a form through which the lowest aspect of divine love, goodwill, can flow without impediment.

From the larger point of view, it is this struggle to clear the world atmosphere which will confront humanity after the first initiation, so close at hand today. You will see, therefore, why the Christ must come at this time, for He is the One Who presides at the first and second initiations, and it is His coming which will indicate that humanity has taken the first initiation, which will confirm and consolidate the work done and which will inaugurate the world cycle and period in which the task of reorganising the emotional and psychic life of humanity will take place; this period will release the energy of goodwill and thus automatically bring about right human relations.

As regards humanity as a whole, polarised as it is in the emotional nature, the effect of this sixth ray is potent in the extreme. Its energy has been playing upon men ever since it came into incarnation, and the last one hundred fifty years have seen that potency become extremely effective. Two factors have enhanced this effect:

1. The sixth Ray of Idealism or of Devotion is the ray which normally governs the astral plane, controlling its phenomena and colouring its glamour.

2. The stream of energy, coming into our planetary life from the constellation Pisces, has for two thousand years conditioned human experience and is peculiarly fitted to blend with and complement this sixth ray energy and to produce exactly the situation which is today governing world affairs.

The united activity of these two great streams of cosmic energy, playing upon and through the third planetary centre, Humanity, has created the unique condition in which "the race of men" can stand before the planetary Initiator, the Christ, and under the focussed stimulation of the Hierarchy, pass through the appropriate initiation.

It should here be remembered that the masses of men can and will take the first initiation, but that a very large group of aspirants (far larger than is realised) will pass through the experience of the second initiation, that of the purifying Baptism. These are the people who express the essential qualities of ideological recognition, devoted adherence to truth as sensed, profound reaction to the physical disciplines (imposed since they participated in the first initiation many lives earlier) and a growing responsiveness to the aspirational aspect of the astral body; this aspiration is occupied with reaching out towards contact with and expression of the mental principle. This particular group in the human family are "kama-manasic" initiates, just as those taking the first initiation are "physico-etheric" initiates.

It is the activity of this sixth ray which has brought out into the light of day the growing ideological tendencies of mankind. These world ideologies (of which there are many present in the world today) are created by a triple reaction to the two streams of energy mentioned above:

1. The unfoldment of the mental principle in mankind during this Aryan Age has forced desire into the form of great mass concepts; these unitedly are governing the mass tendency toward mental unfoldment.

2. The steadily growing soul influence, working like a leaven on the astral plane, has lifted kama or desire out of its purely self-centred focus and brought in a new and hitherto unexpressed group emotional consciousness; this leads the fused emotional nature of men into great ideological mass expression, still selfishly expressed and impulsed as yet by emotional excesses, but indicating new and better goals. These goals will assume clearer and more desirable

outlines when the second initiation is undergone by the world aspirant.

3. The influence generated by the Shamballa energy which has, for the first time, made direct contact with Humanity, is producing an emotional vortex in which old ideals and institutions are seen divorced from their hitherto controlling glamours, thus permitting the new and better ideologies to emerge in the consciousness of the race.

All these factors are responsible for the world situation at this time; great ideologies, potent groupings of workers and thinkers dedicated to the changing of the old order, and massed efforts to end separativeness are all present simultaneously. The *essential etheric world unity* (of which the telephone, the radio and the airplane are the tangible expression) is swinging vast groups of men everywhere into united emotional activity, thus creating those preliminary testings which ever precede initiation, and by means of which those capable of taking the second initiation are today passing.

I cannot here enlarge upon the various ideologies which are presenting themselves to the world of men— impulsed by the Hierarchy, precipitated into the human consciousness from the mental plane by the new group of world servers, implemented by the energy of the sixth ray, by the dominant Piscean energy and by the organising energy of the incoming seventh ray, and responded to emotionally by the masses of men focussed on the astral plane. To all intelligent observers, this ideological situation is clear; it is a needed and preliminary stage to the creation of the new world order; it provides a point of crisis and the required point of tension which will enable those aspirants who are ready today, in their thousands, to pass through the experience of the second initiation and to undergo the purification of the fluid emotional nature in the Baptism Initiation. Through this experience the kama-manasic aspirant will be in a positive and spiritual condition to bring about (on the astral plane) those fundamental changes, rearrangements and readjustments which will bring that level of planetary consciousness into line with the immediate divine purpose: the manifestation of the Kingdom of God.

The work of sixth ray energy, the result of the long cycle of Piscean energy, and the impact of the incoming Aquarian energy will bring a potent transformation in the "watery realm" of the astral plane. The symbol of that plane has ever been water—fluid, stormy, reflecting all impressions, the source of mist and fog, and yet ever essential to human living. The Piscean Age, now in process of passing away, is also closely related to this plane and to the symbol of water; it fixed in the human consciousness the realisation that "men are as fishes, immersed in the sea of emotions." Aquarius is also known by the symbol of water, for Aquarius is the "water-carrier." The sixth ray will bring together all these energies in time and space: ray energy, Piscean energy, Aquarian energy and the energy of the astral plane itself; this again produces a vortex of force which is invocative of mental energy; it is a controlling factor, which has plunged humanity into a tumultuous awareness of clashing ideologies, which has precipitated a reflected vortex in the world war, and which is responsible for the present crisis and point of tension. This critical point of tension will enable groups of aspirants who — having passed through the first initiation — can undergo the Baptism experience, again a word identified with water. Simultaneously, large masses of men will take the first initiation and "in the house of bread" stand before the Initiator.

The coming Christ will therefore initiate two groups of aspirants within the near future and in preparation for His coming; it is the closer approach of the Christ and of the Hierarchy of Masters to humanity which is implementing the initiatory energies, which is crystallising the ideologies present today in the human consciousness, and fostering —if I may so express it—the latent ideology of the Kingdom of God.

As regards the individual initiate who is to undergo the initiation of the Baptism, the effect of sixth ray energy upon his nature is easily apparent, owing to the extreme potency of the second aspect of the personality in the three worlds, his astral body or nature. In the early stages of the impact of sixth ray energy upon his emotional nature a perfect vortex of force is generated, his emotional reactions are violent and compelling, his glamours are intensified and controlling, and his aspiration steadily mounts, but is at the same time limited and hindered by the strength of his devotion to some sensed ideology. Later, under the influence of an increasing soul contact (itself the second aspect of his essential divinity), his emotional, kamic and aspirational nature becomes quieter and is more controlled through the agency of the mind; his alignment becomes astral-mental-soul. When this state of consciousness has been achieved and the "waters" of the astral body are quiet and can reflect the beautiful and the true, and when his emotions have been purified by intense self-effort, then the disciple can step into the baptismal waters; he is then subjected to an intense purificatory experience which, occultly speaking, enables him "for ever to step out of the waters and be no longer in danger of drowning or of submergence"; he can now "walk on the surface of the sea and with safety proceed onward towards his goal."

The effect of sixth ray activity upon the mental nature is, as you may imagine, a tendency—first of all—to the crystallising of thought, a reaction to imprisoning ideologies, and a fanatical mental adherence to mass ideals, with no understanding of their relationship to the need of the time or to their intended creative aspects. Later, as the disciple prepares for the second initiation, these tendencies are transformed into spiritual devotion to human welfare and to a one-pointed adherence to the Plan of the Hierarchy; all *emotional* reaction to the Hierarchy of Masters fades out, and the disciple can now work without being hindered by constant astral disturbances.

The effect of sixth ray energy upon the integrated personality of the disciple can only be described as producing a condition wherein he is definitely astral-buddhic in his nature; gradually his one-pointed emotional effort towards orientation to the soul makes him "an aspiring point of tension, oblivious of crisis and firmly anchored in the love which streams forth from the soul."

Let me sum up what I have said anent the effect of sixth ray energy:

1. The energy of the sixth ray produces two major results:

   a. An embryonic realisation of the will nature which determines the life of the initiate.

   b. A pronounced conflict between the lower and the higher self. This reveals to the initiate the ancient conflict between the emotional nature and true realisation.

This brings about a basic reorientation of the life of the initiate and of humanity as a whole.

2. In connection with humanity, the effects of the sixth ray are as follows:

   a. The development of a tendency to clarify the world atmosphere, thus releasing the energy of goodwill.

   b. The production of a condition wherein "the race of men" can take either the first or the second initiation.

   c. The sudden and powerful emergence of the world ideologies.

   d. A basic transformation within the astral plane itself which is producing points of crisis and a point of tension.

3. In relation to the individual initiate, the sixth ray produces:

   a. An acute situation wherein a vortex of force is generated.

   b. In this vortex all the emotional and ideological reactions of the aspirant are intensified.

   c. Later, when this subsides, the initiate's alignment becomes astral-mental-soul.

   d. There takes place, in connection with his mental vehicle, a crystallisation of all thought and a fanatical adherence to mass idealism.

e. These tendencies are later transformed into spiritual devotion to human welfare.

f. The personality becomes definitely astral-buddhic in nature and expression.

You will see, therefore, how immediate and important is the opportunity confronting humanity today. Vast numbers of men will take the first step towards the unfolding of the Christ consciousness and thus pass through the first initiation. This often (I might well say usually) takes place without the conscious realisation of the physical brain. This first initiation is—and always has been—mass initiation, even when individually registered and recorded. Thousands of aspirants in every country (as a result of conscious effort to understand) will stand before the initiator and undergo the Baptism Initiation; bread and water are the symbols of these first two initiations; both are basic essentials for life in the physical sense, and are equally basic in their implications spiritually; this the initiate knows. These two initiations are the only two of significant importance at this time, owing to their *relative* immediacy.

It is the return of the Christ which has brought these subjective spiritual tendencies of mankind to the surface and made these two initiations possible; it is the activity of the seventh Ray of Order and of the sixth Ray of Idealism which has generated the tendency in humanity towards the white magic of right human relations. They have fostered the trend to ideological control of the human consciousness. It is the passing out of the Piscean Age with its type of energy, and the coming into power of the Aquarian Age (with its potent purificatory energies and its quality of synthesis and universality) which will make the new world order possible. It is therefore apparent that the opportunity confronting humanity has never been so promising and that the corporate relation and fusion of all these energies makes the manifestation of the Sons of God and the appearance of the Kingdom of God an inevitable happening in our planetary life.

As we study the other ray energies and their initiatory effect, we shall not be able to indicate a great deal in relation to humanity itself. Only the first two initiations which are implemented by the Christ and which are "under the supervisory probation of the spiritual Hierarchy" are as yet possible to humanity. The initiation of the Transfiguration is not yet for the mass of men. We can, however, study the effects of these rays where the individual disciple is concerned, because the later initiations—from the third initiation onward—are administered by the Lord of the World from His high place in Shamballa; in the present world period, these initiations are individually administered and registered, and are undergone consciously and with an entirely awakened awareness.

It will be apparent to you that I shall necessarily have more to say anent the first three initiations and the ray effects upon the initiate and upon humanity than will be possible when the higher initiations come under consideration. The effects of ray impacts in the first three initiations come via the soul, and the initiate is—during this period—a struggling aspirant, under the inspiration and the stimulation of the Hierarchy of which he is becoming increasingly aware. After the third initiation, which is in reality as you well know, the first major initiation, the ray energy is applied (if I may use such an inadequate word) via the Spiritual Triad, utilising the antahkarana.

After the fourth initiation, the effects are felt predominantly in the initiate's group and in his field of service; there, he constitutes a point of tension and precipitates great points of crisis. His own points of crisis and of tension are existent but, mysteriously, only in relation to his consciousness of the group in which he plays an increasingly potent part.

The groups affected by the progressive initiatory process to which the disciple is being subjected are three in number, and these effects differentiate and condition his group service, according to the initiation being undergone; it is from this angle we must study the initiation, the ray effects, and the results produced within the three groups. These are:

1. The group in which the initiate is working upon the physical plane and which is an externalisation (existing on the mental and astral planes) of some phase of work sponsored by the New Group of World Servers. All disciples and initiates in physical manifestation are at this time members of that group, which is the focal point of the present effort being made by the Hierarchy. Through it spiritual energy from five of the Ashrams is flowing. These five are:

a. The Ashram of the Master K.H., particularly in regard to the work of education.
b. The Ashram of the Master D.K. (myself), particularly in regard to aspirants for initiation.
c. The Ashram of the Master R., particularly in regard to the reorganising and the reconstruction of Europe, from the point of view of economics.
d. The Ashram of the Master Morya, as He seeks to find, influence and direct the activities of workers in the political field throughout the planet.
e. The Ashram of the Master Hilarion, as He supervises the discoveries (and the application of such discoveries) of the scientific movement in the world today.

You will note, therefore, the profound and widespread interest of this field of energy wherein ray energy is now active.

2. The group which may regard itself consciously as the initiate's own group, in the sense that he is slowly influencing those around him, collecting the personnel and forming the nucleus of the Ashram by means of which he may some day serve the world. All those who are taking initiation do not necessarily create their own ashrams, though a large number do so. The work of those initiates who do not form an ashram is mysterious in the extreme, from the point of view of aspiring humanity, and there is little that I may say about the subject. These initiates work

in connection with plans emanating from Shamballa, of which humanity can know nothing; they work with the three subhuman kingdoms in nature, each of which has its own peculiar and specific band of initiate-workers. If they do not do this, they transfer into certain groups of workers who are engaged in activities connected with the deva or angel evolution, or in relation to the manifestation of energies about which I can tell you nothing. We shall deal only with the expansion of consciousness and the experience of those initiates who remain—in their activities and aims —related to humanity and to the Hierarchy. It might here be pointed out that:

a. The work of the deva evolution comes under the ray energy of the third Buddha of Activity.

b. The work with humanity comes under the influence of the ray energy of the second Buddha of Activity, Who embodies in a most peculiar sense the conditioning energy of the Hierarchy.

c. The work with the subhuman kingdoms of nature is under the energy stimulation of the first Buddha of Activity.

Each of these great energising Lives works through certain Masters and Initiates of the sixth initiation; these Masters work in full consciousness upon the atmic plane, the plane of the spiritual will; from that high level, They function as transmitting agents for the energy of one of the three Buddhas of Activity. These three Buddhas are the creative Agents of the planetary Logos and are Wielders of the Law of Evolution.

3. The ashramic group of which the initiate is a part and within which his influence or spiritual radiation is increasingly felt.

The awareness of the initiate and his ability to work consciously within this triplicity of groups becomes the major objective of all his efforts, once the third initiation is left behind. His magnetic radiation and the expression of his controlling energies—prior to this stage of unfoldment—

is that of the soul, working through the personality. After the third initiation this radiation and the energy expressed become increasingly monadic and subject to three stages:

1. The stage wherein the lowest aspect of the Spiritual Triad (that of the abstract mind) becomes potent as the conveyor of ideas; these are transformed by the initiate into ideals for the service of humanity.

2. The stage wherein pure reason, plus the spiritual will, makes him an effective server of the Plan and a transmitter, in a progressive manner, of the Purpose underlying the Plan.

3. The stage wherein pure monadic energy pours through him, focussing the will-to-good, as registered by the Hierarchy, and the sense of universality (not a vague phrase, but a specific potency) upon the physical plane.

A close study of these developing ranges of activity and of expanded consciousness will indicate why and how our planetary life is one immense synthesis of ordered activity.

The ray energies, utilising the created form world and the "world of formless forms" (that is, the cosmic etheric levels of activity), constitute a great and applied process of initiatory activity, governing, controlling and conditioning every expression of divine life in all the kingdoms of nature—subhuman, human and superhuman. It is into this world of active moving energies that the initiate penetrates and within which he must consciously play his part. As you well know, the work of the aspirant today is to become a conscious, self-controlled and spiritual worker in energy within the ring-pass-not of the three worlds and—as I have frequently pointed out—to function, first of all, in control of his physical instrument, demonstrating this at the first initiation and during the succeeding initiatory processes; secondly, to control his emotional, feeling nature, demonstrating that control at the second initiation; at the third initiation, he has to bring into visible activity the mental element, and thus function in the three worlds as a soul-infused personality, utilising the illumined mind as the fusing and synthesising factor. These things accomplished, he can—again in full consciousness—begin to be active as "a radiating point of crisis and a producer of the needed tension."

These three groups are essentially points of planetary tension and are producers of crisis in the lives of the individuals influenced and in the Hierarchy, as well as in the planetary life. Thus the conditions are created which make evolution possible. Some day the story of the evolutionary process will be written by an initiate of the great White Lodge, from the angle of its points of crisis and the subsequent points of tension. This enables the living forms, under this dual impact, to emerge into larger areas of consciousness. Each kingdom in nature can itself be regarded as a point of tension within the sphere of Being of the planetary Logos, and each—in time and space—is in process of generating those points of crisis which will produce a potent (and often sudden) moving forward upon the Path of Evolution. Humanity is today, in its present situation as a point of planetary crisis, generating such a point of tension that it will shortly be enabled to move forward into the new age dispensation, culture and civilisation. The study of the individual aspirant parallels this.

These thoughts and ideas must be borne in mind as we study the remaining three major initiations confronting average humanity.

*Initiation III. The Transfiguration. Ray V.*
The Energy of Concrete Knowledge.

As all disciples have to be focussed on the mental plane and must operate from that level of consciousness, the understanding of this type of consciousness is one of major importance. It is glibly and most easily said that disciples and (necessarily so) initiates must use the mind, and that their polarisation must be mental. But what does this mean? Let me give you some concise definitions of this ray energy, leaving you to make your own individual application, and from your study of these concepts anent the mind, learn to gauge your own mental condition.

1. The energy of what is so peculiarly called "concrete science" is the quality or the conditioning nature of the fifth ray.

2. It is pre-eminently *the substance* of the mental plane. This plane corresponds to the third subplane of the physical plane, and is therefore gaseous in nature—if you care to use its correspondence as a symbol of its nature. It is volatile, easily dispersed, is the receptive agent of illumination, and can be poisonous in its effect, for there are undoubtedly conditions in which "the mind is the slayer of the Real."

3. This energy is characterised by three qualities:

a. The quality which is the result of relationship with the Spiritual Triad. We call this "abstract mind" and the impact which affects it comes from the atmic level of the Spiritual Triad, that of spiritual will.

b. The quality which in this solar system is easily responsive to the major ray of the planet, that of love-wisdom. So responsive is it that—in conjunction with emanations from the three worlds—it has produced the one existent form upon the mental plane. This form (in the planetary sense) is that of the Kingdom of God and, in the individual sense, is that of the ego or soul.

c. The quality which is basically related to the emanations or vibrations arising from the three worlds; these creatively result in the myriads of thoughtforms which are found upon the lower levels of the mental plane. It might therefore be said that these qualities or aspects of the fifth ray of spiritual energy produce:

> Pure thought
> The thinker or the Son of Mind
> Thoughtforms

4. This energy (as far as mankind is concerned) is the thoughtform making energy, and all impressions from the physical, etheric and astral planes force it into activity on the level of concrete knowledge, with a resultant kaleidoscopic presentation of thoughtforms.

5. It is fundamentally the most potent energy at this time in the planet, because it was brought to maturity in the first solar system, that of active intelligence.

6. It is the energy which admits humanity (and particularly the trained disciple or initiate) into the mysteries of the Mind of God Himself. It is the "substantial" key to the Universal Mind.

7. It is profoundly susceptible to the energy of Love-Wisdom, and its fusion with the love aspect is given the name of "wisdom" by us, because all wisdom is knowledge gained by experience and implemented by love.

8. This energy, in its three aspects, is related in a peculiar sense to the three Buddhas of Activity. These great Lives reached Their present state of development in the previous solar system.

9. This energy, in so far as it is considered as the mental energy of a human being—and this is one of its minor limitations though a major one for a human being—is the higher correspondence of the physical brain. It might be said that the brain exists because the mind exists and needs a brain as its focal point upon the physical plane.

10. The quality of this energy of concrete knowledge or science is twofold:

   a. It is extraordinarily responsive to impressions coming from some source or other.
   b. It is rapidly thrown into forms in response to impression.

11. The impressions received come from three sources and are sequentially revealed to man. These three are:

   a. Impressions from the three worlds; these come, first of all, from the individual and then, secondly, from the levels of planetary consciousness.
   b. Impressions from the soul, the Son of Mind, upon the level of mentality itself.
   c. Impressions from the Spiritual Triad, via the antahkarana; these come when the antahkarana is constructed or in process of construction.

12. This energy is essentially a light-bearer. It responds —again sequentially in time and space—to the light of the Logos. It is for this reason that the mind is regarded both as illumined when higher contacts are present and as an illuminator where the lower planes are concerned.

13. This energy is (from the human standpoint) awakened and brought into activity through the action of the five senses which are the conveyors of information from the three worlds to the mental plane. It might be said that

a. Five streams of informative energy, therefore, make their impact upon the concrete mind and emanate from the physico-astral plane.

b. Three streams of energy, coming from the soul, also make an impression upon the concrete mind.

c. One stream of energy—during the initiatory process—contacts the mind. This comes from the Spiritual Triad and utilises the antahkarana.

14. The energy of this fifth ray might be regarded as the *commonsense*, because it receives all these impacts of varying energies, synthesises them, produces order out of the many ceaseless impacts and interprets them, thus creating the multiplicity of forms to which we give the name of "world thought."

15. This energy transforms the divine ideas into human ideals, relating the knowledges and sciences of humanity to these ideals, thus making them workable factors in human evolution, its cultures and civilisations.

There is much more that I could add, but the above gives you a series of simple definitions of value as you study the mental unfoldment of the disciple, as he undergoes the initiatory process which is our theme at this time. It also throws light upon the ray effects upon humanity *as a whole*. This ray energy is indeed sadly concrete in its expression in our Aryan race—a race, however, which will see more people take initiation than ever before in human history, and which will, in a peculiar sense, see *the descent* of the Kingdom of God to Earth as a result of *the ascent* of so many upon the ladder of evolution. Just as the disciple or the initiate is a soul-infused personality, so will humanity—upon the physical plane—be also soul-infused, thus precipitating the Kingdom of God and giving birth to a new kingdom in nature. This great spiritual descent will be prefaced (if I may use such a word) by the appearance of the Christ among the peoples of the world and by a stupendous inflow of love-wisdom. There is a tendency in the minds of esotericists always to refer to the great lines of force: 1-3-5-7 and 2-4-6. I would have you remember with still greater emphasis the relation of rays II and V and of the second plane, the monadic plane, and the fifth plane, the mental plane; it is the relation of these major energies which makes the initiation of the Transfiguration possible.

What is the effect of this ray upon humanity as a whole and at this time? The effect of these influences is very great and of supreme importance in this fifth root race, the Aryan race, in this second solar system. Again you can see the clarity of the correspondences which are emerging. I would have you note them again.

1. Ray II, the Ray of Love-Wisdom; and Ray V, the Ray of Concrete Knowledge or Science.
2. The second plane, the monadic plane; and the fifth plane, the mental plane.
3. The second solar system of love; and the fifth root race, the Aryan race, of active intelligence.

In all these basic relationships, that which is the fifth in order is destined to be the instrument, the vehicle or the implementing factor for the second. The Universal Mind, as it works through all the planes of our conscious planetary life, is the creative agent and the form-building factor which makes the revelation of love possible.

Today in our Aryan age and race, we see the vital expression of this fifth ray energy. When I use the word "race" I deal not with man-made or pseudo-scientific differentiations of nations and races or types. I deal with a state of consciousness which is the Aryan or mental consciousness or state of thinking; this finds its exponents and its "race members" in every nation, without any distinction or omissions. This I would have you carefully remember, for there is no new race in process of appearing, from the territorial angle; there is only a general distribution of those persons who have what have been called the sixth root race characteristics. This state of consciousness will find its expression in people as far apart racially as the Japanese and the American or the Negro and the Russian. It posits an ability to function with clarity upon the mental plane, to collate information, rightly to interpret and relate that information, and to create the needed thoughtforms or concepts for those interpretations.

These thoughtforms fall into three major fields of thought or thoughtform areas of consciousness:

1. *Science.* Under this word I include all that which the educational processes cover or are supposed to cover, and such a useful science as medicine.

2. *Philosophy,* with its presentation of great conditioning ideas.

3. *Psychology,* with its effort to account for humanity and to discover what man is essentially and how he functions.

You will note that I have not included religion in this analysis. The reason for this is that *IF* the world religions were really controlled by concrete knowledge or science, they would not be the vague, speculative, mystical and glamour-controlled systems which they are at present. Some day the minds of men—illumined by the light of the soul —will formulate the one universal religion, recognisable by all. Then the Kingdom of God will be known for what it is, another kingdom in nature. Speculation, wishful thinking and hopeful aspiration will disappear. The science of occultism is the first step upon the way of true religion, and the scientific investigation of human psychology will greatly help toward this end.

Today we find this ray energy expressing itself mainly through science—a science sadly debased and corrupted by materialism and human greed, but a science which (when animated entirely by goodwill) will lift humanity on to higher levels of consciousness, thus laying the foundation for that time when humanity on a large scale can pass through the Transfiguration Initiation. Steps in this direction are already being laid and the existence of the press, the radio and the rapid means of transportation have done much to further the revelation of that unity and that Oneness which is the major characteristic of the Universal Mind.

These developments can be regarded as the initial steps of the initiatory process for the third initiation—far ahead as that initiation may lie for the mass of men. It is unification and a growing sense of oneness which is required in order to take this initiation, and it is the integrated personality which takes it. The major sin of Russia, and that which has prostituted and warped the initial divine impulse underlying the ideology of that country, is the determination she demonstrates at this time to be separative and to shut the Russian people away from world contact, using the implements of deception and the withholding of information. It is not the totalitarian nature of the Russian government which is the prime disaster; it is the refusal to develop the universal consciousness. Many governments today are totalitarian in nature, either openly or subtly, but—at the same time—their peoples have free access to press and radio and are not kept in ignorance of world events. Russia is drifting into a pronounced expression of the great heresy of separateness. There lies her problem—a problem which is refused recognition by her rulers.

The existence of a closed mind on a national scale is dangerous in the extreme, just as the individual is in a dangerous "state of mind" when he closes it to world contact, world news and world understanding, and when he refuses to admit new ideas and new modes of behaviour. Fortunately, the influence of this fifth ray energy—which is always present, whether the ray is in incarnation or not— is steadily leading humanity towards illumination.

This ray energy operates always in connection with the Law of Cleavages. Today, tremendous cleavages between the past and the present are in order. The importance of this statement is to be found in the fact that—for the first time in human history—humanity is aware of cleavage *at the time* it is being brought about. Hitherto cleavages have been noted during an historical retrospect. Today, all men everywhere are conscious of the fact that the old order, the old cultures and civilisations are rapidly passing away, and they are universally clamouring for the new. Everywhere men are laying the foundation for the new order, the coming of which is threatened only by one country, Russia, owing to its separativeness (and not because of its ideology), and by one world group in every country, those guilty of financial greed and consequent aggressiveness.

Before humanity can pass through the Transfiguration Initiation the new world order must be functioning and the coming civilisation must be at its height. It is useless for me to consider with you this third initiation in connection with humanity as a whole, or its preparatory or subsequent initiatory process. All this lies too far ahead for even advanced humanity to consider; there are, however, senior disciples who are preparing for this initiation, just as there are a few who are passing through the initiatory process, prior to taking the fourth initiation.

The outstanding expression of this fifth ray energy can be seen in the rapid formulating of the many ideologies which have taken place since the year 1900. Such words as Fascism, Communism, National Socialism, Socialism as the British accept it, and the names of many schools of psychology and philosophy, were unknown one hundred years ago; today they are the common talk and phrases of the man in the street. The inflow of this mental energy into the world of men, the attainment in consciousness of mental ability by many thousands, and the achievement of mental polarisation by aspirants all the world over, are all due to the activity of this fifth ray energy; this may be regarded as preparatory work for the first and the second initiations. Some of this success is due also to a little-realised function of this fifth ray energy—that of telepathic interplay. Few people realise in the slightest degree how naturally telepathic every human being is or how impressionable are their minds; this again is an effect of fifth ray influence.

The creation (and, I should add, the over-creation) of the millions of material things which men everywhere regard as essential to their well-being is also the result of the creative activity of the fifth ray consciousness. This is, of course, as it demonstrates upon the physical plane. When it demonstrates upon the mental plane, we then talk of ideas, concepts, philosophies and ideologies. When it demonstrates upon the astral plane, we are aware of the religious impulse, of mysticism and of the emotional and conditioning desires. All these aspects are present in the consciousness of men everywhere today. Everything is crystallising in human consciousness, and this takes place in order to make man aware of where he stands upon the ladder of evolution, and of what is wrong and what is right. All this again is due to the influence of fifth ray energy. This will begin to transform human living and human desires and also human affairs and attitudes, and will lead eventually (in the middle of the sixth root race) to the great Transfiguration Initiation in which the reality that lies behind all human phenomena will stand revealed.

Let us now consider the effect of this ray energy upon the life of the individual, as he faces the third initiation. This third initiation is, as earlier said, the first initiation, from the angle of the Hierarchy; it is the one in which the spiritual man demonstrates his complete control of the personality. The physical body has been controlled through the medium of the physical disciplines; the emotional nature has been reorganised and made receptive to spiritual impression coming from the plane of pure reason (the buddhic plane) through the transforming processes of the mind or the fifth principle. In this connection, the mind has acted as an organiser of astral reaction and as a dispeller of glamour. The disciple is now focussed in his every-day consciousness upon the mental plane, and the triangular relation of the three aspects of the mind upon this plane is now dominant. In the next initiation, the Renunciation, this relationship becomes a dual one instead of a triangular one, through the destruction of the soul vehicle which is no longer needed. Soul fusion with the personality is now completed.

During the initiatory process preceding the third initiation, the mind works in a new manner. Its *transmuting work* with the physical body has been accomplished; its *transforming work* with the emotional nature has been successful, and now its *transfiguring work* with the personality as a whole is carried forward, making the initiation of the Transfiguration possible. It is of value to the student to consider these three activities of the mind. The transmuting agent in the first case is the lower or concrete mind; the transforming agent is the soul, whilst the transfiguring agent is the Spiritual Triad, working through the higher or abstract mind. You will here note the wonderful synthesis of the spiritual work. When this work is concluded, you have the initiation of the third degree made possible. This produces impelling and new contacts. It should here be remembered that when I use the word "new" I mean that which is new in *consciousness,* for the basic synthesis and fundamental relationship always exists in factual recognition, but is only progressively realised by the evolving spiritual man.

It is well nigh impossible to differentiate the results of fifth ray energy in the various aspects of the personality, for the reason that the initiate is now functioning as a soul-infused personality, and therefore the three aspects of that personality are nothing more or less than agents of the soul, and thus are progressively responsive to the inflow of triadal energy. It might therefore be said that, as a result of the Transfiguration Initiation—the culminating point of strictly human unfoldment—the three types of energy which are expressed through the Spiritual Triad can begin—only begin—to flow through the reflection of itself in the three worlds. Let me state this as follows:

1. The directing energy of the higher mind is—as a result of the Transfiguration Initiation and via the antahkarana—thrown into the brain; therefore the man upon the physical plane is guided, directed and controlled by group purpose and by the hierarchical plan.

2. The illuminating energy of pure reason, emanating from the buddhic plane, pours down into the clarified and organised body of sensitive response which is all that remains of what has been called the astral body. This produces complete freedom from glamour and the creation of "a limpid pool of such reasonable response to the love of divine relationship" that the initiate becomes a sensitive revealer of that love.

3. The dynamic energy from the atmic plane (the highest aspect of the Spiritual Triad) pours into the mind and begins slowly to reveal the will-to-good, which is essentially the will of God.

Behind these three differentiations which are all of them expressions or aspects of the divine or the universal mind, the initiate dimly senses or becomes consciously aware of what has been called the Monad or Spirit or Life. This is subtly revealed in the Transfiguration Initiation of the Master Jesus Who re-enacted all the five human initiations for the benefit of humanity. In this dramatic picturing of the third initiation, the three disciples (or the three vehicles of the personality) prostrate themselves upon the ground and the Master Himself (the glorified personality) is transfigured before them. At this climaxing point they hear that which is called "the voice of the Father" speaking to the transfigured Jesus.

The personality is now possessed of knowledge, for fifth ray energy has done its needed work; the disciple is also aware that he is in possession of the wisdom which enables him to use knowledge in the furtherance of the Plan, and therefore to work as an illuminating factor in the world of men. He knows clearly what has been accom-

600 A TREATISE ON THE SEVEN RAYS

plished and senses something of what lies ahead. The great principle of cleavage (which the fifth ray governs) is the dominating factor in his *time* sense; he now differentiates sharply between past and present and that which has to be ascertained in the future. Cleavage, in the sense of separateness, is finished for him and he now feels and knows something of the essential unity of all manifested life; therefore, from the angle of *space,* he has dominated and overcome cleavage and division; in the sense of *time* he has not. The great heresy of separateness no longer exists in his consciousness; the consciousness of the initiatory process is not yet over, however for that involves the recognition of time.

During the initiatory process between the second and the third initiations, the initiate has to battle with illusion in exactly the same sense as he earlier had to battle with glamour. Illusion is, in the last analysis, the control of the mental processes by great and massive thoughtforms; this conflict persists from the moment that the disciple has achieved mental polarisation (at a midway point between the second and the third initiations) until he stands before the Initiator at the sixth Initiation of Decision, when the last illusion disappears. You will feel and comment that the Masters are therefore subject to illusion. This They definitely are, and there are great and basic illusions governing life within the Hierarchy. Nevertheless, they are illusions of such a high order that—for advanced humanity—they would signify achievement. I may not give you more than one instance of such illusion, but that should prove clear and sufficient. It is not until the sixth Initiation of Decision that the illusion of the planetary ring-pass-not finally disappears. The Master then knows that such a limitation is non-existent. For Him, the choice between the seven Paths becomes possible. This basic illusion constitutes for mankind a great hierarchical mystery and is based upon the Principle of Privation, by means of which the planetary Logos chooses to circumscribe His freedom and to limit His activities.

This curious freedom from successive limitations is experienced at the third, the sixth and the ninth initiations; these are, all three of them, related in a mysterious manner to each other. Transfiguration leads eventually to Decision, which culminates in due time with a final refusal to accept any planetary limitations whatsoever.

It will be obvious to you that the higher the initiation, the less will any involved energy have a personality control or connection. Progressive and recognised fusions have taken place as one initiation after another is undergone; the effect of the energy involved will be noted in relation to humanity as a whole, to the work of the Ashram within the Hierarchy and to the planetary life. This must ever be borne in mind and must necessarily limit the scope of the teaching which I am able to give you.

Let me now summarise the effects of this fifth ray energy in relation to humanity and to the individual initiate:

1. I gave, first of all, fifteen items of information anent this fifth ray energy, or fifteen definitions of its activity. These will warrant careful study.

2. The effect of this fifth ray energy upon humanity in this fifth root race was considered; it was noted that this Aryan effect was dominant and dynamic in the extreme and that it has greatly hastened human evolution.

3. I pointed out the close relation between love and mind, as follows:

a. Ray II and Ray V
b. Plane II and plane V
c. Solar system II and root race V

In all of these relationships, the fifth in order is the prime agent and the revealer of the second type of spiritual energy.

4. The fifth ray energy produces three major areas of thought, or three prime conditions wherein the thought-form-making energy expresses itself:

a. Science      . . . education . . . medicine
b. Philosophy . . . ideas      . . . ideals
c. Psychology . . . in process of modern development

5. This fifth ray energy operates in connection with the Law of Cleavages.

6. It is also responsible for the rapid formation of great conditioning ideologies.

7. This fifth ray energy is the important factor in making possible the first major initiation, the Transfiguration Initiation.

8. Fifth ray energy works in three ways in connection with the three aspects of the personality:

a. As the transmuting agent . . . the physical body
b. As the transforming agent . . the astral body
c. As the transfiguring agent . . . the mental body

This gives you much food for thought; it indicates the personality goal and the mode whereby it is attained. After the third initiation, we reach out in consciousness to higher expansions of consciousness and will then enter a realm of ideas which are not yet easy for the disciple to appreciate or to understand. Much that I will have to say anent ray energy and the higher initiations will mean little to many, but it will mean much to the initiate-consciousness. The world initiates will be coming into incarnation at this time, and will read my words towards the end of this century with great understanding.

*Initiation IV. The Renunciation. Ray IV.*
The Energy of Harmony through Conflict.

Our study today is of profound interest and has a great bearing on the present world situation. I would like to make clear two important facts:

1. The fact that the world war (1914-1945) was quite unavoidable, though the conflict might have been retained upon mental levels, had humanity decided rightly.

2. The fact of the inevitability of the return of the Christ in this era and in the relatively immediate future. We are here dealing with immutable law, for the energies of the various rays move under law; humanity can therefore do naught but accept, determining only what I might

call the locale, or the sphere of activity, of both these major events. The determination of mankind to fight out the issues involved in the world war upon the physical plane, at the same time automatically determined the sphere of Christ's activity—as I shall attempt to show you. In many ways, this particular instruction is one of the most important I have yet given because of its essential and obvious implications. We will therefore study the fourth initiation and its relation to the fourth Ray of Harmony through Conflict.

This fourth ray, as you have several times been told, is out of incarnation, as far as the reincarnating egos or souls of men are concerned. From another angle, however, it is always active and ever present, because it is the ray which governs the fourth kingdom in nature, the human kingdom in the three worlds of strictly human evolution.

It is the dominant energy, always exerting pressure upon the fourth kingdom; this pressure began to exert itself primarily towards the end of the fourth human race, the Atlantean race of men; at that time men began to give evidence of a growing sense of responsibility, and therefore of the power to demonstrate discriminative choice. This led to the great war in the fourth race which culminated in the Flood, to which all parts of the world testify and to which the majority of the world Scriptures bear evidence. In that era, in which the then known world of men was extensively involved, the Black and the White Lodges of adepts were also implicated, and the first major fight between the demonstrators of evil and the Forces of Light took place; it was inconclusive, with the evidence for defeat to be found on the side of the good more than on the side of evil. Under the symbolism of the Flood, it is apparent to students that the fight was focussed primarily upon the astral plane, though fought out historically upon the physical plane; it resulted in the destruction of the world by water, as it might be symbolically expressed.

In the climaxing war of the immediate past, the mental plane was the focus of the amalgamated forces, for the war was in reality a clash of ideologies and has been far more the result of man's thinking than of man's emotional desires. It therefore automatically involved the three levels of human activity and was fought out upon the physical plane, although it was impulsed from the mental plane. The symbol of fire was this time involved, instead of water, and this fire led to the destruction of men and of cities by fire (literally, "fire from heaven"), by the evocation of the fiery emotions so prevalent in the councils of men at this time, and by the drought of the year 1947 which burnt up the terrain in Europe and in Great Britain, being—curiously enough—preceded by the floods and waters of the earlier spring, thus evidencing the repetition of cycles; this repetition is distinctive of natural process, leaving each stage of man's evolution depicted, but producing a climaxing point which is indicative of the past and of the present, but leaving (as is the case today) the future locked in the determinative processes of man's thinking and planning. As man thinks and decides "in his heart," so will the future of humanity prove to be, for it is the same process for mankind as a whole as it is for the individual.

I would like to cover this theme by dividing my subject into the following parts:

1. The particular type of energy involved and its initiatory effect. This concerns the *Principle of Conflict* as contained in the activity of this fourth ray.

2. The effect upon humanity as a whole. The "Renunciation Initiation" is an expression of the result of the activity of this Principle.

3. The factor of the second Ray of Love-Wisdom as it basically controls Ray IV and implements the return of the Christ, because the potency of the heart centre is involved.

4. The effect of this Ray IV in the modern world of nations and of fundamental organisations.

5. The result of this fourth ray activity upon the individual disciple:

a. In the three aspects of his nature, physical, emotional and mental.

b. Upon the soul-infused personality.

6. Summation of the whole theme and a forecast of future possibilities.

I shall attempt to deal with this as concisely as possible, and will keep the handling of this subject exceedingly brief, or as brief as its historical importance will permit and its definitive angle will allow. The whole of human history has been conditioned by the fourth Ray of Harmony through Conflict, and it is this ray which has determined the ring-pass-not within which humanity must work.

At this time, the effect of this ray is predominantly of a group nature, and there are—except in the ranks of disciples of the Great White Lodge—no fourth ray souls in incarnation. Once humanity has decided upon the goal and the method of reconstruction and of reorganisation which is to take place within the periphery of the fourth ray ring-pass-not, then (if humanity's decision is correct and is not postponed) many fourth ray souls will resume incarnation, and so implement human decision. This will mark a great turning point in human history and will enable seventh ray energy to be turned to the best advantage.

*The Particular Type of Energy involved*
*and its Initiatory Effect*

Here we are confronted with a basic problem, i.e., the nature of the Principle of Conflict which is the outstanding characteristic of this fourth Ray of Harmony through Conflict. This is by no means an easy subject to handle or to make clear, for the correctness of conflict, its naturally separative and eliminative effect and its power to condition not only Humanity but also the Hierarchy, will have to be considered. When we study the fourth initiation, that of the Renunciation, the effects of its activity will emerge more clearly.

Fundamentally, this fourth ray is that which is responsible for the strains and the stresses, and for the initial conflict between the major pair of opposites to which we give the name of spirit-matter. It is this fourth ray energy which makes apparent the distinction (so often misunderstood by man) between good and evil. In Atlantean days, the leaders of men, under the influence of this paramount fourth ray energy, made a decision which laid the emphasis upon the matter aspect, according to their desire and their emotional reaction, which is present in the essential duality of manifestation, and thus inaugurated the Age of Materialism. This age has wrought itself out through its accompanying greeds, hate, separativeness and aggression. During the present century, this materialism led to the world war which was in reality the expression of a shifting orientation, and therefore to a certain extent, of a coming triumph of Good.

The balance is slowly, very slowly, swinging over to the side of the spirit aspect of the duality; it has not yet swung, even in intention, completely over, but the issues are becoming increasingly clearer in men's minds and the indications are that man will eventually decide correctly, will attain a point of balance or equilibrium, and will finally throw the weight of public opinion on the side of spiritual values, thus leading to a collective renunciation of materialism, particularly in its grosser and physical forms. The time is not yet, but a great awakening is in process; men, however, will only see correctly when this Principle of Conflict is properly evaluated as a spiritual necessity and is used by humanity as an instrument to bring about emergence from the wrong controls and principles. Just as the individual disciple uses it to emerge out of the control of matter in the three worlds, beginning with the emergence from the control of the physical body, passing out of the control of the emotional nature, and formulating for himself a spiritual ideology which enables him to pass out of the control of the three worlds of forms, and so begin to function as a soul-infused personality, so mankind also has to do the same in mass formation.

This whole process culminates when the fourth initiation, the Great Renunciation, is taken by man today, and by humanity in some distant future; this "point of emergence" is reached by right decision and as a result of a right use of the Principle of Conflict.

It will be obvious to you that this Principle of Conflict is closely related to death. By death, I mean extraction from form conditions—physical, emotional or mental; I mean cessation of contact (temporarily or permanently) with physical form, with astral glamour and with mental illusion; I mean the rejection of Maya, the name of that all-inclusive effect which overwhelms a man who is immersed in materialism of any kind, and is therefore overcome (from the soul angle) by life in the three worlds. It is the Principle of Conflict, latent in every atom of substance, which produces, first of all, conflict, then renunciation, and finally emancipation; which produces war in some form or another, then rejection, and finally liberation. This principle is, as you can well see, closely linked to the law of Karma; it is to this principle that Mrs. Besant refers when she speaks in one of her books of the fact that the substance whereof all forms are made is already—from the very dawn of the creative process—tinged with karma. There is deep occult significance to the thought, often voiced, that death is the great Liberator; it means that the Principle of Conflict has succeeded in bringing about conditions wherein the spirit aspect is released (temporarily or permanently) from imprisonment in some kind of form life, either individual or group.

You will all, as disciples or aspirants, be able to interpret the working of this principle as you watch the effect, in your own lives, of the action of the strains and stresses, the points of crisis or of tension which the conflict between soul and personality produces. Conflict is always present prior to renunciation, and it is only at this fourth great spiritual crisis that conflict, as we understand it, ends. In the realms of formless living wherein the Hierarchy lives and moves and has its being, conflict, which has developed in man the sense of discriminative choice, is superseded by crises of decision—not decision based upon discriminative perception between right and wrong or between spirituality and materialism, but crises of decision based upon perception of the Plan, participation in the Purpose, and the prevention of evil. I would have you ponder on these three phrases which distinguish the crises of decision which confront the Master after the fourth initiation, and which take the place of the crises of discrimination which precede that stage:

> Perception of the Plan.
> Participation in the Purpose.
> Prevention of evil.

These decisions are based, first of all, on goodwill to all forms in the three worlds, and secondly, upon the will-to-good which impulses and implements the three creative and manifesting aspects of divinity.

These are deep things whereof we speak; it is wise to remember that all crises in the material world—individual crises and those related to humanity as a whole—are governed by the Principle of Conflict, whilst crises in the spiritual world are controlled by the esoteric Principle of Decision.

The Principle of Conflict is the prime factor lying behind the evolution of form as the field of experience for the soul in the four kingdoms in nature: the human and the three subhuman. It is based on the intellectual factor of discrimination which is inherent in the smallest atom of substance, and which reaches its fullest expression in advanced humanity; the indications that it has achieved its purpose, as far as humanity is concerned, are to be found in the passing through the Initiation of Renunciation. The Principle of Decision which controls the Master governs His work within the Hierarchy, in relation to Shamballa and in connection with all the service rendered in the three worlds; it is based on the energy of the second Ray of Love-Wisdom, just as the Principle of Conflict is based on the energy of the third Ray of Active Intelligence.

This Principle of Decision, as a controlling factor, is put to the test at the sixth initiation, the Initiation of Decision; at that time, the will aspect of divinity summarises in a unique manner all past achievements of the two principles and brings in a final cycle of unfoldment to which I can give no truly appropriate name, but which climaxes in the ninth Initiation of *Refusal.* You have, therefore, in relation to these principles (which are all related to the Law of Karma) three great initiations at which the effectiveness of the liberation brought about by their inherent action is finally tested:

1. The Initiation of Renunciation . . . 4th Initiation
    The Principle of Conflict
        Governed by Ray IV
            Active in the Human Kingdom, the 4th
                Leading to right Discrimination

2. The Initiation of Decision . . . 6th Initiation
    The Principle of Decision
        Governed by Ray III
            Active in the Hierarchy
                Leading to right Perception
                and Participation

3. The Initiation of Refusal . . . 9th Initiation
    The Principle of liberated Being (shall we
    call it thus?)
        Governed by all three major Rays
            Active in Shamballa
                Leading to one or other of the 7 Paths

In the above tabulation you have a wide and general picture of three major Principles, leading to three great spiritual events, each of which is an expression of the personality, the soul and the Monad. Where humanity as a whole is involved, the effect is upon the reincarnating soul of the human kingdom, then on the liberated souls of the members of the Hierarchy, and finally on the Being which is distinctive of the Council at Shamballa.

A planned synthesis thus appears, producing immutability, inevitability and correct prevision; it is also the result of the liberation of free will, and in no way infringes the right of the individual man or disciple to make free choice, once the Principle of Conflict has made him aware of the basic dualism of the manifested worlds. This presents him with a battle-ground and a field of experience wherein he makes great experimental choices and comes eventually to correct orientation and to the door of initiation, progressively revealed to him as the result of right choice, right perception and right decision. Thus the nine initiations are covered.

The Principle of Conflict has a close connection with the Path of Discipleship, and here lies the reason for the inclusive and synthetic aspect of the present world conflict; though the physical aspects of the conflict are today greatly lessened (but are still present on a small scale in various parts of the world), the conflict is by no means over or yet resolved. It is still being violently waged by advanced human beings upon the mental plane and by the masses upon the plane of emotional reactions; it will be some time before the war truly is brought to a finish.

There could, however, be no disaster more serious than a too abrupt ending of this clash of the emotional reactions of humanity and of the current ideologies. It is essential that the issues become still clearer in the minds of men, prior to any final choice or decision. This must be remembered, and students would do well to avoid discouragement and train themselves to wait with spiritual optimism for the way of humanity to clear. Too prompt a choice at this time might prove only a make-shift decision and one based on expediency and impatience. The Hierarchy is in no way discouraged, though somewhat concerned that the factor of timing may not prove correct.

This Principle of Conflict is a familiar one to every struggling aspirant and conditions his whole life, producing crises and tensions, sometimes almost past endurance; they indicate nevertheless rapid development and steady progress. The activity of this principle is greatly increased at this time through the medium of the following spiritual events (the full discussion appears on pages 741-760):

1. The crisis of the ideologies.
2. The awakening of humanity to better understanding.
3. The growth of goodwill which leads to the presentation of certain fundamental cleavages which must be bridged by human effort.
4. The partial "sealing of the door where evil dwells."
5. The use of the Great Invocation with its extraordinary and rapid effects, at present unrealised by you.
6. The gradual approach of the Hierarchy to a closer and more intimate relation to Humanity.
7. The imminent return of the Christ.

There are other factors, but these will be adequate to demonstrate to you the increased expression of conflict on all the three levels of strictly human evolution. It is a conflict which has engulfed the masses in every land, which is still producing physical conflict, emotional strain and tremendous mental issues, and which will greatly lessen when the masses of people everywhere are convinced that right human relations are of far greater importance than greed, human pride, territorial grabbing, and material possessions.

*The Effect of the Energy of Harmony through Conflict upon Humanity*

It will be obvious that this ray energy, embodying the Principle of Conflict, has a unique and curious effect upon *relationships*. This is due to the interrelation of this Ray of Harmony through Conflict and the second Ray of Love-Wisdom; this second ray is primarily the ray of right human relations—as far as the fourth kingdom in nature is concerned. The energy of love governs all relations between souls and controls the Hierarchy, the Kingdom of Souls; the energy of wisdom should govern all relations within the fourth kingdom, the human; some day it will inevitably do so, hence the emphasis laid upon the need for soul-infused personalities in the world today, as promulgated by all true esoteric schools.

It might be said that the effect of the Principle of
Conflict, operating under Ray IV and controlled by Ray
II, will be—as far as humanity is concerned—to bring
about right human relations and the growth of the universal spirit of goodwill among men. Only the most be-
nighted and uncouth of thinkers would fail to see that these
two results of the conflict, engendered at this time, are the
two most desirable factors for which all men of goodwill
should work. The inflow of energy into humanity at this
time is all in favour of such efforts, and the Principle of
Conflict has worked so effectively that all men are desiring
*harmony,* peace, equilibrium, right adjustment to life and
circumstances, and right and balanced human relations.

In every country and among all types of men—sincerely
or insincerely—the talk of the newspapers, on the radio
and upon the lecture platforms is on behalf of harmony
and a widespread recognition of the needed adjustments.
Even the evil forces which still remain active hide their
greedy purposes behind a spurious desire for world unity,
world harmony and right human relations. The masses of
the people in all lands have been convinced by the evidence made available by the Principle of Conflict that
basic changes in man's attitude and goals must be brought
about if humanity is to survive; they are, in their own
ways (wisely or unwisely), seeking a solution.

The war has produced much good—in spite of the
destruction of forms. The causes of war are better understood; the issues involved are slowly being clarified; information about all nations—even when incorrectly presented
—has awakened mankind to the fact of the One World;
the community of pain, sorrow, anxiety, starvation and
despair have brought all men closer together, and this
relation is a far greater breeder of harmony than man
realises; the world of men today is more closely knit *subjectively* (in spite of all outer cleavages and conflicts) than
ever before in human history; there is a firmer determination to establish right human relations and a clearer perception of the factors involved; the new *Principle of Sharing*

inherent in the second Ray of Love-Wisdom which is concerned so fundamentally with relationships, is gaining ground, and its potency is being released by the activity of the fourth Ray of Harmony through Conflict. This Principle of Sharing, though still divorced from any *official* sanctions, *is* under consideration and will some day be the governing factor in the economic life of the world, regulated and controlled by those men who are alert to human need upon the physical plane.

This Principle of Conflict is also active in all institutions, groups and organisations in all lands and in every department of human thought. Its results are, first, the awakening of humanity to certain major human developments and possibilities, and secondly, it will lead to certain basic renunciations, once the issues are clearly seen and the cleavage which exists in reality between the desirable spiritual values and the undesirable material values has been made clear. In politics, for instance, the two-party system is based upon a correct premise, but it is not at present a satisfactory system because of human stupidity. It stands in truth for the reactionary groups in any land and also for the progressive party who are alert to the new possibilities; one party aims at the holding back of the life of the spirit, at clarifying by obstruction and at holding back or preventing the too rapid rushing forward of the impatient and the immature; the progressive party should be composed of those who are aware of the unneeded and old issues, and who *pioneer* all the time, even though frequently without much skill in action. Such a clear line of demarcation between the two basic world parties is not yet possible, nor are the spiritual values of either group appreciated by the unthinking masses. Today, party politics are as selfish, and therefore as reactionary, as are the mass of men; the real good of humanity is not the goal of the average politician in either group, for usually only his own selfish ambition and the desire to preserve a certain political ideology which has put him into power are the goal of his efforts.

The Principle of Conflict is working also in the churches, but more slowly, unfortunately, owing to the corruption and soporific effect of theological churchianity; I would have you note my choice of words; I said not "of Christianity," for true Christianity, as Christ taught it, is free from theological abuses and must and will be restored or—perhaps more accurately—reach its first stage of expression.

Everywhere the fourth Ray of Harmony through Conflict is active in the human family and is dominating human affairs; everywhere in the life of the individual, in the lives of groups, organisations and churches, in the life of nations and in the life of mankind as a whole, the issues are being clarified, and humanity is being led from one renunciation to another, until some day the human kingdom will unitedly take the fourth initiation and the Great Renunciation will be accepted; this step, lying far ahead as yet in the future, will affiliate humanity with the Hierarchy and release millions of men from the thralldom of materialism. This moment in human history will inevitably come. The first indication that the distant vision has been glimpsed might perhaps be noted in the prevalent instinct to *share,* motivated at present by the instinct to self-preservation, but definitely developing as a possible mode of action upon the far horizon of man's thinking. True sharing definitely involves many little renunciations, and it is upon these small renunciations that *the capacity* for freedom is slowly being generated and *the habit* of renunciation can eventually be stabilised; this capacity and these habits, these unselfish activities and these spiritual habitual attitudes are the preparatory stages for the Initiation of Renunciation, just as the effort to serve one's fellowmen is preparatory to the taking of the third Initiation, of the Transfiguration.

*The Factor of the Ray of Love-Wisdom as it controls the Ray of Harmony through Conflict and implements the Return of the Christ*

In the first paragraph of this instruction, I ascribed the inevitability of Christ's imminent return to the decision of humanity to precipitate the existent conflict on to the physical plane, thus determining the sphere of Christ's activity. In earlier teachings also I have pointed out that He might come in one of three ways or in all three of them simultaneously. The issues which have emerged as the result of the conflict upon the physical plane, and of its shifting (by man's decision) today on to the mental plane, have made completely evident the fact that the locale of Christ's influence will be, therefore, the entire three worlds of human evolution, which naturally includes the physical levels of experience and demands His physical Presence.

Let me make the facts somewhat clearer and enlarge somewhat upon these three modes of His appearing, of His coming, His advent and of His physical recognition by humanity:

1. *By His overshadowing of all initiates and disciples* who are today, or will be at the time of His arrival, active in the three worlds of human evolution. This involves His influencing their minds telepathically. This overshadowing or influencing will be His primary work upon *the mental plane*. This will constitute one of His most effective methods in His proposed spiritual interference in world affairs. Through the medium of these members or affiliates of the Hierarchy, He will have outposts of His consciousness in every nation. Through them He can work.

2. *By the pouring out of the Christ life or consciousness upon the masses* everywhere and in every nation. This spiritual inflow will bring about the reorienting of human desire and will evoke the emotional reaction to His Presence. This therefore brings *the astral plane* within the active sphere of His influence; this involves the release of the energy of goodwill into the hearts of men, predisposing them towards right human relations. It is this establishing of right relations which is the major objective of His coming triple activity. The masses everywhere will be responsive to the work and the message of the Christ, as it is

implemented from the mental plane by the disciples and initiates, overshadowed by the mind of Christ.

3. *By His physical appearance among men.* Through His Own immediate appearance, He can establish a potent focal point of hierarchical energy upon Earth in a manner not hitherto possible. He has never deserted humanity and has always kept His promise to stay with us all the days, even unto the end of the age. Men in all lands will know where He can be found. The locale of this focal point of His threefold spiritual activity cannot here be disclosed, for it is contingent upon the results of the sequential processes of overshadowing and outpouring.

The first of the methods which will lead to the eventual physical reappearance of the Christ has already been set in motion; disciples and initiates in all lands are starting the work preparatory to the outpouring of the Christ spiritual force, leading to the awakening of the Christ consciousness (as it is usually called) in the hearts of men. This outpouring will come as the result of three activities:

1. The work and the teaching of the trained disciples and initiates, as each of them, in his own way, points out the surety of Christ's coming and thus implements the innate expectancy of the masses.

2. The evocation of a united hierarchical response through the use of the Great Invocation. You will note how this invocation can be interpreted in terms of the three modes of the return of the Christ:

a. "Let Light stream forth into the *minds* of men."
   The influencing of the minds of disciples.
      The enlightening of intelligent humanity.
         The mental plane.
            Stanza I.

b. "Let Love stream forth into the *hearts* of men."
   The influencing of the masses everywhere.
      The outpouring of the Christ spirit.
         The astral plane.
            Stanza II.

**c.** "The Purpose which the Masters know and serve."
The anchoring of hierarchical energy on Earth.
The physical appearance of the Christ.
The physical plane.
Stanza III.

What this divine purpose may be the Christ Himself will reveal upon His arrival; the focal point of His activity will be dependent upon the medium used by Him to implement that purpose—known only to Him and to the senior members of the Hierarchy. Should politics be the medium through which He best can serve, that then will determine the locality of the focal point; if it should be the religious organisations of the world, it may prove to be elsewhere; if the field of economics or of the social sciences, then still another locality may prove appropriate. The determining factor in all cases, and that which will indicate to Him the appropriate place for this focal point, will be the number and the ability and status of the disciples found active in the chosen field. More, I may not suggest.

3. The demand or prayer or outgoing desire of the masses for the appearance of a Liberator and for the establishing of right human relations, plus the work of all the spiritually-minded people in all nations and of all faiths. All these three factors are today present but have not yet the needed potency to prove immediately effective. This triple nucleus of determining factors is, however, already firmly established; in this fact is to be found a sure ground for a sane optimism.

It should be pointed out that the Principle of Conflict is motivated strongly by these same factors. *The overshadowing* of all disciples and initiates, and the consequent stimulation of their natures and of their environment, must inevitably produce conflict; the outpouring of the stimulating love of God into the hearts of men must equally and inevitably produce conflict; the line of cleavage between men of goodwill and the unresponsive natures of those uninfluenced by this quality will be made abundantly, usefully and constructively clear. It will be obvious also that when Christ establishes the "centre or focal point of the divine Purpose" in some definite place on Earth, its radiation and implementary potency will also produce the needed conflict which precedes the clarification and the renunciation of obstructions.

But there will come a point in all these three spheres of Christ's proposed activity when conflict will be superseded by harmony; this is due to the fact that the energy of harmony through conflict is under the control or influence of the energy of the second Ray of Love-Wisdom. As far as humanity as a sum total is concerned, the conflict of ideas and of emotional desire is today so acute that it will finally exhaust itself, and men will turn, with relief and with a longing to escape from further turmoil, towards right human relations; this will constitute the first major human decision leading to the longed-for harmony. The attitude of the masses will then be soundly tending towards harmony, owing to the work of the men and women of goodwill as they implement the "streaming forth of the love of God into the hearts of men."

We have now reached a point where the inevitability of Christ's return is established, scientifically and under law; this constitutes a call which He may not deny and one which He must obey. This fourth Ray of Harmony through Conflict works (where the initiatory process is concerned) through the heart, or through what esotericists call "the heart centre"—the focal point through which the energy of love can flow. When the Christ founds His focal point on Earth, it will be in the nature of a tiny heart centre through which the love energy of the Hierarchy can persistently flow. The harmony (which the Principle of Conflict produces) causes an alignment, so that the love—streaming forth from the Heart of God—enters the hearts of men; so that the Hierarchy (which is the heart centre or the place where love prevails upon our planet) is brought into relationship with humanity; so that the New Group of World Servers (implementing the love of God and enlightened by the Mind of God) are brought also into relation with the men and women of goodwill in all lands whose task it is to make men's hearts responsive to and receptive of the love of God; this is another way of saying receptive to the consciousness of the Christ.

This alignment is now in process of being made; it will be brought about automatically when the effectiveness of the Principle of Conflict in producing liberation is generally recognised. Thus the hearts of men, the heart of the planet, i.e., the Hierarchy, and the heart of the Hierarchy, the Christ, are in a state of positive contact; when this channel is open and unobstructed, then the Christ *will* come. Nothing can stop His appearance and—under law—He may not turn His back upon the presented opportunity.

Thus, eventually, the Lord of Love—in response to the invocative cry of humanity, aroused by the Principle of Conflict—must "proceed again to the high place of sacrifice and walk openly with men on Earth." His heart, embodying as it does the love of God, is drawn forth from the heart of the planet (the Hierarchy) to the hearts of men, and the path of His return to Earth service stands unchallenged and unobstructed. Again, under law, a profound optimism is engendered and may be rightly developed.

The heart centre of humanity is created by the sum total of the hearts (symbolically speaking) of all those men of goodwill (in or out of the churches and irrespective of their political concepts) who are serving their fellowmen, sponsoring human welfare movements, working for the establishing of right human relations, and constantly offsetting the separativeness of the human mind through the inclusiveness of the divine love nature. You have, therefore, as a guarantee of the return of Christ into public recognition, an implementing of a great alignment. This alignment, when effectively concluded, will bring about a clear channel or pathway of return or line of light or magnetic power between:

    1. The centre where the will of God is known. This is Shamballa where the will-to-good originates. This will-to-good is essential love.

2. The Hierarchy, which is the planetary heart centre.

3. The Christ, the very heart of love within the Hierarchy.

4. The initiates, disciples and aspirants who form the New Group of World Servers, seeking to embody the love and light needed in the world today.

5. The hearts of the men of goodwill in all lands who are responsive to love as it can express itself through right human relations.

6. The focal point through which the Lord of Love will work on Earth.

If you will study this sixfold progression of divine love from the highest manifestation of Deity down to its appearance through the medium of some focal point in our known modern world, it will be apparent to you that a very definite "structure of approach" has been created, and that a "Path of Return" is being constructed which will bring the long-awaited Christ into our midst. Nothing can stop or prevent His return today; the evidence of this structure can be seen everywhere.

*The Effect of the Ray of Harmony through Conflict in the modern world of Nations*

As we approach what some may regard as a highly controversial subject, I would remind you that we must attempt to see the picture whole in some such manner as the Agents of the divine Will see it, embracing the past of the nations involved (a past which is seldom good), seeing the effects of that past as they work out in the present and as they are the inevitable result of the Law of Cause and Effect, and attempting also to foresee the future in terms of lessons learnt and new habits of a better nature established (written in 1948). I would remind you also that the governing principle of this ray is conditioning all the nations and has done so with increasing potency since the year 1850. Just in the same manner as this principle of conflict controls the battling life of the aspirant and of the world aspirant, the entire human family, so it must inevitably control the life of nations to a greater or lesser degree, according to their materialistic or their spiritual status, according to the type of energy which may be expressing itself through them, and according to the age of the nation under consideration. From certain angles, the youngest of the nations are Germany and Italy, for they only arrived at nationhood in the nineteenth century; the oldest nation with the clearest unified record is Japan. The United States of America is always regarded as a young nation, but from the angle of a unified central government, the two Axis Powers are still younger, and this has had a definite bearing on their activities.

In the world at this time the two aspects of this fourth ray—the aspect or Principle of Conflict and the aspect or Principle of Harmony—are struggling to bring about the liberation into equilibrium of mankind. Until quite lately, the Principle of Conflict has grown increasingly in power, yet as a result of this conflict a definite trend towards harmony can be seen emerging in human thinking; *the concept* of harmony through the establishing of right human relations is slowly coming into recognition. The activities of mankind, and particularly of governments, have been ignobly selfish and controlled by the concepts of fighting, aggression and competition for untold millennia; the territories of the planet have changed hands many times and the earth has been the playground of a long succession of conquerors; the heroes of the race—perpetuated in history, stone and human thinking—have been the warriors, and conquest has been an ideal. The world war (1914-1945) marked a culminating point in the work of the Principle of Conflict and, as I have shown, the results of this work are today inaugurating a new era of harmony and cooperation because the trend of human thinking is towards the cessation of conflict. This is an event of major importance and should be regarded as indicating a turning point in human affairs. This trend is impulsed by a weariness of fighting, by a changing rating as to the values in human accomplishment, and by a recognition that true greatness is not expressed through such activities as those of Alexander the Great, Julius Caesar, Napoleon or Hitler, but by those who see life, humanity and the world as one united whole, interrelated, cooperative and harmonised. Those who struggle for this world unity, and who educate the race in the Principles of Harmony and of right human relations, will some day be recognised as the true heroes.

The factor that must and will relate the Principle of Conflict to the expression of harmony and bring about the new world order, the new civilisation and culture, is the trend and the voice of public opinion, and the opportunity offered to people everywhere to bring about social security and right human relations. It is not the government of any nation which will bring this about, but *the innate rightness* of the people themselves when they have been educated to see the issues clearly, the relationships which should be established, and the immense subjective unity of mankind. This will not come about without an intensive period of planned education, of a truly free press and radio—both free to speak the exact truth and to present the facts as they occur, without being controlled or influenced by governmental interference, pressure groups, religious organisations, or by any dictating parties or dictators. The sin of the Roman Catholic Church is its effort to dictate to people what they should think—theologically and politically—what they should do, read and wear; this, to a still greater extent, is the crime of Russia. The mass of the people in the strictly Catholic countries are not as free in their thinking as are those living in the Protestant lands; the Russian people know no freedom and have no opportunity to form their own point of view; commercial interests and expediency impose restrictions in other countries. By means of these sources of control, the growth of true understanding is prevented, distorted or stunted. Curiously enough, the intention of the dictating agents, in both the Catholic Church and in Russia, is basically good; they believe that the uneducated masses are not fitted to decide for themselves what they should hear, think or decide; they must therefore be protected—in the one case by decrees and prohibitions from the Vatican (via the organised priesthood) as to right attitude and right action to be followed without questioning; and in the other, by withholding the truth as to events and happenings. But men are awakening everywhere and—given some sound leadership, which at present is not to be found in any country in the world—they can be trusted to swing the tide into a great harmonising and unifying movement.

As we study the effect of the Principle of Conflict as the instigator of eventual harmony in relation to the nations, let us remember that the widespread extent of the conflict is indicative of *climax,* that the "points of crisis" which express the conflict are today well known to all men, that a "point of tension" has now been reached (of which the United Nations is a symbol) which will eventually prove to be the agent that will bring about a "point of emergence." I would ask you to keep these three phrases—descriptive of the working of the Ray of Harmony through Conflict—constantly in mind in relation to developments in your own life, in the life of your nation or of any nation, and in the life of humanity as a whole. They embody the technique whereby the spiritual Hierarchy of our planet brings good out of evil without originating the evil or infringing the free will of mankind.

There are certain nations which are necessarily more responsive to the energy of this fourth ray than some of the others, because it is either the energy which is conditioning their personality activities or that which conditions their soul expression. Forget not that nations are like individuals, expressive of soul and body. The nations responsive to this ray energy are:

India, whose personality or material ray is that of Harmony through Conflict. This could be seen in full expression in that unhappy country during the years 1947-1948. India is old and crystallised in her separativeness, in her myriads of diversified sects and religious groups, in her manifold languages and in her ancient antagonisms;

it will be long before there is any basic synthesis or harmony. There lies her problem, and unfortunately she lacks pure disinterested leadership; as is the case elsewhere in the world, party politics and religious cleavages condition her many peoples. The soul energy of India is that of the Will to Power or government, but that spiritual energy will not come into true activity until she has resolved her many differences and has returned to the old ways of spiritual understanding and of enlightened wisdom which distinguished her many centuries ago. India has nearly lost the light, but when she has passed through the coming points of crisis, and has achieved a point of united tension, then she will find the door or point of emergence into light.

The ray governing the *soul expression* of the German race is that of Harmony through Conflict, but her materialistic personality, focussed in the emotional nature and not yet under control of the soul, is conditioned by the first Ray of Power. Germany *as a nation* is too young, immature, and negative to realise the true uses of power; she lacks the wisdom to use power, and her sense of inferiority (based on youth) leads her to misuse it when she has it. The German *race* is very old, and the German leaders during the past one hundred years have confused *racial* issues and *national* ambitions. Races are basically subjective, and nations are basically objective. Their leaders have permitted the ideal of power (which is a great spiritual responsibility) to lead them to make the Germanic race synchronise with the German nation. It was this immaturity and this misguided and almost childish ambition which set the Principle of Conflict operating violently through the world war (1914-1945) in order to bring to an end the increasing nationalism of Germany and of all the nations. Great Britain is at the point of emergence from the nationalistic thoughtform; the United States and Russia are arriving— the first at the point of tension where the concept is concerned, and the other at the point of crisis. Germany's point of crisis and of tension led to the explosion of the world war; nevertheless, after due process of pain, of re-education and of training in right human relations, the German people will discover their soul, and then the soul-infused personality of the German people will demonstrate in a unique manner the significance of harmony. The basic and subjective synthesis of the Germanic race must not be confused with the separate nation of the German people, and the underlying emotional and sentimental unity (using the word "sentimental" in its correct sense) must not be confounded with territorial unity. There is a racial and subjective unity between the British Commonwealth of Nations and the United States of America, but this in turn must not be confused with the outer national groupings and aims.

Italy also is influenced by the Ray of Harmony through Conflict because her personality or material expression is conditioned by this ray. During the world war, Italy had a king, a dictator, and a pope, and this produced a vortex of conflict in the highly intelligent Italian people. The dictator is no longer there; the monarchy has also disappeared, and only the continuing voice of the Vatican is left, but—curiously enough—receives less attention in Italy than in the other Catholic countries. Conflict during the centuries has done much for the Italian people, and their highly extroverted psychology has produced in them a balance which may prove most promising in the future. The conflict of thought through which they have passed during the past one hundred years has worked *well* for them. Torn as they are by party politics, in revolt against ecclesiasticism, and lacking leadership, they are nevertheless well on the way to the resolution of their problem.

When the fourth Ray of Harmony through Conflict is the energy expressing itself through the soul, the indications are that the country concerned is nearing the Path of Discipleship or the Path of Probation. Austria and Germany are nearing the Path of Discipleship; Brazil is on the Path of Probation and will rapidly move forward; Austria is nearer true discipleship than is Germany and, spiritually, Austria has much eventually to give. Spiritual leadership will not be lacking once a measure of security and better living conditions have been assured. Germany has a bitter price to pay because her immaturity and childish interpretation of world affairs, her lack of thinking capacity and her curious innate cruelty permitted the Forces of Evil (temporarily) to work through Germany and precipitate the world conflict. But Germany will recover, provided she does not again permit herself to become a battleground, owing to her strategic position in central Europe. It is for this recovery that all men of goodwill must work.

It is perhaps appropriate to point out here that the spiritual forces of the planet do not greatly fear a renewed outbreak of war upon the physical plane. There are many chances that it can be averted because the mounting revolt of the masses against physical plane war, the general fatigue of the nations and the use of the United Nations councils for the ventilation of difficulties and problems may prove effective.

Each of the three Great Powers has its own internal conflict, conditioned by its historical tradition, its national emphases, and its developed habits of thought or—as the case may be—of feeling.

The major conflict in Great Britain at this time is between the reactionary thinkers and those unskilled labourers in the political field who favour the socialistic ideology. This conflict goes deep and is undermining and destroying old forms and producing intense national friction in all groups and parties. One group is fighting to preserve the old order; the other group is fighting fiercely to abolish all the old ways in the shortest possible time; other groups are fighting for their various ideologies and complicating the problem. The interesting thing is that the conflict is largely between party leaders and their immediate convinced followers, with the mass of people questioning the wisdom, the capacity and the activities of both groups and slowly deciding that they like and desire neither of them, but (lacking real leadership) they know not what to do. The predisposing characteristic of the British is a sense of justice and it is for this that the people seek. They find, however, that neither party has an effective plan or programme, that both are animated by party politics, and that the interests of the people as a whole which could be served by a wise coalition are not of major importance to the present party leaders. This internal conflict is slowly, however, going to produce a harmony of purpose and of intention within the mind of the population; this will largely be the result of the increasing power of women in the land and their increasing penetration in municipal and national politics. The quality of the British historical retrospect has been predominantly masculine. Today the balancing factor of feminine interpretation and the feminine point of view is needed and will be provided. Great Britain, from the angle of its personality or material problem, is governed by the energy or Ray of Will or Power, whilst the soul of the country is conditioned by the Ray of Love-Wisdom. In this you have the presentation of a positive and a negative energy, and when they are fused and blended you will have a balance and a wisdom which is at present lacking.

In France, where the contributing rays are both along the line of the intellect, you have necessarily and naturally a strong materialistic influence and the conflict there is hard to resolve. It is ever the mind aspect which produces all the separativeness, the cleavages and the differences in the human arena in France, making it the playground of untold numbers of conflicting ideas, a diversity of groups and of clashing personalities, and leading to an intense preoccupation with France and its welfare; there is small interest in anything else, or in any other nations or groups, except as they affect France or the French people. The French are in no way as yet ready to balance conflict with harmony, even interiorly. The qualities of the mind—pride, self-centredness, a separative attitude, a selfish planning and a materialism which penetrates deep into the mass consciousness—are dominating in their activity and are focussed upon the material well-being of France. There is no dominant ideology, so that the conflict is not lifted on to the ideological level, and until a recognised idealism begins to sway the French mind and the mass consciousness, France cannot grow; there is no basic religious or spiritual sense to be found on a large scale, because the mind which can so inspiringly illumine the plane of the spirit is focussed primarily upon the three worlds of material living. This pronounced activity of the intellect, of which the French are so proud, is largely responsible for the situation in the political and economic fields in France, plus the difficulties which they share with all the nations which were implicated in the war. Any prospect of internal harmony is still far away *but it will come.* Forget not what I wrote much earlier in one of my books that it is France which will eventually reveal the true nature of the soul or of the psyche and inaugurate the era of true esoteric psychology. To do this she must inevitably find her own soul, and in finding it—through the medium of the illumined mind —she will bring light to humanity. The conflict now raging in France will eventually be resolved into harmony, and France will awaken to the higher spiritual values. Once her soul ray of pure knowledge is active, it will dominate her personality or material Ray of Active Intelligence, once the most powerful of all the rays. The task of the Ray of Harmony through Conflict is to bring this about, thus releasing France into the light.

In the United States, this fourth energy is peculiarly active, because of the conflict of races, nations, ideas, political theories, immature development, corrupt politics, and childish selfishness; this is more prevalent among the leaders in the municipalities and in politics than it is among the masses of little people in every state, who are basically sound though easily misled by their so-called leaders; the southern states are, however, almost unbelievably degenerated and deluded. Remember always, as we look at these various nations dispassionately, that we are concerned with the same trends and ideas which are to be found in each individual aspirant—the conflict of ingrained personality habits and thoughts and faults, with a steadily increasing soul pressure. The United States, though one of the younger nations, is—owing to the many racial types represented—one of the oldest; this curious balancing must inevitably lead to a rapid development, with a consequent assumption of power, a growing incentive to love and a shouldering of responsibility.

The conflict in the United States is between a love of freedom which amounts almost to irresponsibility and license, and a growing humanitarian ideology which will result in world service and non-separateness. The rays of energy governing the United States are the 6th Ray of Idealism, which is the energy of the country's personality, and the 2nd Ray of Love-Wisdom, which governs the soul of the country. I would here point out to you that it is the soul ray of the United States which relates it to Great Britain. The sixth ray personality energy (at the present stage of unfoldment) produces an idealism which requires transmuting and changing from an idealism intensely pre-occupied with the preservation of a high standard of living and physical comfort to an idealistic appreciation of the real spiritual values; these are at present veiled and hidden in the material philosophy of the country. The youthful interpretation of this idealism can be seen in the complete conviction of the American people that everything in the United States is better than anything anywhere else, in its willingness to tell all the world what should or should not be done, in its revolt from all controls, in its unthinking acceptance of any information which falls in with its preconceived ideas and prejudices; the mature aspect of American idealism leads its people to a prompt response to the good, the beautiful and the true, to the expression of an active humanitarianism and an invocative spiritual approach to reality.

It is interesting to note the unusual alignment of ray energies to be found at this time in the United States:

| The energy of the soul | . . . Ray of Love-Wisdom | . . . Ray II |
| The energy of the personality | . . . Ray of Idealism | . . . Ray VI |
| The energy relating the two | . . . Ray of Harmony | |
| | through conflict | . . . Ray IV |

These Rays—2, 4, 6—are all on the second line of spiritual energy and lack all the stiffening and strengthening qualities of the first line of ray energy—1, 3, 5, 7—which are governed by Will or Power. The American civilisation, with all its clamour of youthful precocity, is in reality the heir of the passing sixth ray civilisation, the Piscean; therefore, you have here the reason for the tendency of the American people to adopt violently conditioning idealisms and ideologies. It is the idealistic tendency in conflict with pronounced materialistic trends of this particular modern era which will finally evoke the harmony which will liberate the spirit of America, which will reveal to its people that it is one world and which will enable the people of this land to harmonise with the rest of the world and draw forth the loving response of other nations. It is for this that the men of goodwill must work.

Russia is, if you could but realise it, a battleground today within her own sealed walls. Her iron curtain is to Russia what the Monroe Doctrine was to the American people. In connection with all the three Great Powers—the U.S.S.R., the U.S.A. and the U.K.—certain major conflicts are being specifically precipitated; these will fundamentally affect the destiny of humanity. These three nations constitute the three points of a most potent world triangle of energy, and once there is a free circulation and a true understanding established between them, then world peace will be assured and the Christ can come. This understanding and this free harmony (if I may use such a term) will come as the result of each of the three Nations arriving at a real measure of internal harmony as a result of its own particular conflict, and then moving forward in an effort to harmonise with each other and the rest of the world.

Russia has the same personality ray as the United

States and her seventh ray soul (conditioned by the Ray of Order) is closely related to the personality ray of Great Britain, the first Ray of Will or Power; the will aspect of divinity works out on the physical plane as the seventh Ray of Order or of conformity to the inner divine will.

The interior problem of the U.S.S.R. is the conflict raging between the imposed, arrogant will of a handful of powerful dictators and the fluid, unstable and ignorant reaction of a people from whom the truth is constantly withheld; they therefore have to fight blindly for their freedom, to fight instinctively and without knowledge of the facts. They are not yet waging a successful fight.

The point, however, which is of major importance to us is the recognition that each of these three nations is distinguished by:

a. A similarity of problem.
b. A battleground which is leading to the formation of a triangle of relationships brought about through the Principle of Conflict.

The similarity of problems consists in the fact that each of these three nations is essentially composite in nature and is formed by an amalgamation of many nations, of many peoples speaking many different languages, and is consequently staging a great experiment in fusion.

1. The U.K. is the nucleus or the living germ of the British Commonwealth of Nations wherein *a great experiment in free government* is being tried out; this gives complete internal freedom and choice to each related Dominion, plus an equally complete and free interrelationship. The Dominions are all of them independent nations, but belong to a united Commonwealth; a pattern is thereby presented for world consideration.

2. The U.S.A. is a fusing centre wherein all nationalities are represented and are being slowly blended into a miniature One Humanity. *A great experiment in right relationships* is being undertaken and is making real progress. A culture and a civilisation will emerge which will be the

result of right human relations and which can provide a world pattern in relationships. I refer here to the presentation of democracy. There is nothing satisfactory yet in the presentation of the dreamed-of democracy. France and Great Britain are equally democratic, and more successful because more mature and experienced, but the "melting pot" of the U.S.A. will provide eventually the outstanding experiment in right relations because of its many races and nationalities—all blended together within the borders of one country.

3. The U.S.S.R. is also seeking to blend and unite into one great national project many diverse nations and races —European and Asiatic—and the effort is still largely embryonic. In Russia a world ideology is being wrought out which (when proven) can be presented to the world as a model system; this, however, will not come as a result of dictatorship, nor can it be presented aggressively to the world. Russia is in reality—whether she realises it or not at present—undertaking *a great experiment in education* and, in spite of evil methods and sinning against the soul of human freedom, eventually this educational process will prove convincing to the world and provide a world model. This can only take place when the present group of dictators and arrogant men have passed away or been forced out of power by an awakening people.

In these three great nations, therefore, the three major divine aspects are being brought into manifestation, thus laying the foundation for the new world order. All three are of equal importance.

| In Great Britain | — right human government | — Will or Power |
| In the U.S.A. | — right human relations | — Love-Wisdom |
| In the U.S.S.R. | — right use of the mind | — Intelligence |

This must be remembered and taught, and men of goodwill everywhere should work for a closer relationship between these three peoples. These three points of a divine triangle of energy should not be isolated points, each holding its own point of tension; they should be related points, each point distributing strengthening energy to the other points and admitting a free circulation between all points around the triangle.

These great world problems are also being worked out in each of these three nations:

1. In Great Britain, the problem of socialism is being resolved and the sound judgment of the people will eventually balance the two conditions of a socialist programme and free enterprise; this needs doing, for the extreme position in either case is untenable. This today presents a conflict which all the world is watching. The transition period between group living (in the true and spiritual sense) and the present and past period of an intense individualism is not easy, and in Great Britain the whole matter is being put to the test. The bridge will be built.

2. In the U.S.A. you have the problem of the relationship between capital and labour awaiting solution; the conflict is fierce but a compromise will eventually be worked out if capital concedes certain arrogant powers, recognises the rights of other human beings and demonstrates less selfish greed, and if labour will work with less selfishness, prove less exacting and evince a more understanding spirit. The bridge between these two great groups must and will be built.

3. In the U.S.S.R. you have the problem of the levelling of the masses in all classes; this levelling has produced a low standard of living and the work to be done is *to raise* more than to bridge. This levelling produces serious conflict and one that is little realised by those who cannot penetrate into the sealed citadel which is Russia. It is really a conflict between the *mounting* human spirit and the force of the totalitarian regime which seeks to hold it down, killing individualism. The innate strength of the human spirit to rise has never yet failed, and this conflict will prove the agent in harmonising many factors.

Within the comity of nations, certain of them have ever been prime agents for producing conflict. This is largely owing to their fiery temperament and their strong emotional bias and condition. The Poles and the Irish are prime "catalysts of conflict" and are constantly instigating difficulties between peoples. Such has ever been their history. French aggression in the Middle Ages has also caused difficulty, and in later days, Germany became the prime agent of conflict. Today the Jewish people are engineering trouble, and it is interesting to note that the main contention in the past of Poland, lately of the Irish, and today of the Jews, is *territory*, thus evidencing a most distorted sense of values. There is in the last analysis but one world and one humanity, and in a shorter time than you may think boundaries and territories will mean but little. World citizenship will be the only factor of importance.

The Jews are governed by the third Ray of Active Intelligence, the energy which permeates and controls matter or substance. They were also, during the years immediately following the war, under the control of a glamour imposed by the Zionist Dictators, who were attempting (somewhat unsuccessfully) to be to the Jewish people what Stalin and his group, and Hitler and his gang, have been to their people. They worked through the same methods —terrorising, withholding information, browbeating their opponents, making false claims and bribing and corrupting. They were and are a minority, but a powerful minority because of their great wealth and their being in positions of power. They are claiming a land to which they have no possible right and which the Jews have ignored for two thousand years. Their attitude is perhaps the culminating aggressive action of the age and marks a climaxing point; it has produced a serious world tension, but out of this good may come and a "point of emergence for mankind" be reached. The issue of aggression can be more clearly seen because of their activities. Very few lands today are in the possession of their original inhabitants, and if restoration is made to all original inhabitants (which is not possible) an impossible situation would be brought about just as legitimate as the Zionist position. If the Zionist claims are to be considered (and they have been) they in their turn should realise that (if *The Old Testament* is to be believed) they originally took the land of Palestine away from its original owners nearly three thousand years ago, at the point of the sword and through an unprovoked aggression.

This conflict which the Zionists have precipitated is basic and useful. It constitutes a test case, being based upon physical plane aggression, being fought with the most violent emotional disturbance and being founded upon completely illogical premises. The Jew has ever been (could he but usefully remember it) the symbol of humanity —evolving, seeking, restless, materialistic, separative and greedy. He is the symbol of the mass consciousness, presenting this consciousness in an exaggerated form; he is ever seeking and searching a home and is the true Prodigal Son of *The New Testament*.

Curiously enough, the Jews have never been a fighting race since the time of the sorry story of the conquest of the early tribes in Palestine; they have been persecuted and repudiated down the centuries, but have retaliated simply by moving on—the wandering Jew seeking a home, wandering humanity, saying always, "I must arise and go to my Father." The motive given to the Prodigal Son in the Gospel story is a strictly material one, and we have here an outstanding instance of the prophetic knowledge of the Christ.

The Jewish people have not only repudiated the Messiah (which their race produced), but they have forgotten their unique relation to humanity; they forget that millions in the world today have suffered as they have suffered and that—for instance—there are eighty per cent of other people in the concentration camps of Europe and only twenty per cent Jews. The Jew, however, fought only for himself, and largely ignored the sufferings of his fellowmen in the concentration camps.

I have enlarged thus upon the Jewish conflict because it is the symbol of all past conflicts in human history, based upon universal selfishness and the greed of undeveloped humanity, and because the crucial test of the nations and of the United Nations Assembly is to be found in the decisions which they made and may make concerning Palestine.

The test, as far as the nations are concerned, lies in their willingness to give refuge to the Jews, and such a refuge would have been offered *if* the partitioning of Palestine had been refused. The unwillingness of the nations to admit the Jews (though many have willingly offered), and particularly the refusal of the United States to admit them, is separative, wrong and based upon political expediency. The test, as far as the United Nations is concerned, was whether they would endorse partition, and thus perpetuate the spirit of aggression and territorial greed, against which the Forces of Light were arrayed in the last war. The United Nations has already made a major mistake by their original admittance of Russia—a totalitarian power, as was Germany—to their councils. Now they have made another. In the first mistake they precipitated into the United Nations the element of conflict and that spirit of "fanatical imposition" which is distinctive of the totalitarian ideology; in this second case, through the endorsement of partition, they perpetuate the ancient technique of taking what is wanted (with force of arms, if necessary) from the rightful owners. It was a test for the United States, for it is the American Jews who have created the situation, with relatively little help or endorsement from the Jews of other nations. The United States, urged by expediency, by the financial weight of the Zionists, and by the strategic position of Palestine, have thrown the weight of their influence into the conflict on the side of aggression and of territorial theft. They could have worked for the Principle of Harmony and permitted time and the non-separativeness of the nations to adjust·and solve the Jewish problem.

More I will not say; the symbolic nature of this basic world problem and its dynamic importance to humanity have led me thus to enlarge. The decision anent the Jews is one of hierarchical importance, owing to the karmic relation of the Christ to the Jewish race, to the fact that they repudiated Him as the Messiah and are still doing so,

THE RAYS AND THE INITIATIONS

and of the interpretive nature of the Jewish problem as far as the whole of humanity is concerned.

*The Results of Fourth Ray Activity upon the individual Disciple*

The disciples of the world today are submerged in an ocean of warring energies; the Principle of Conflict touches every life, is potent in the consciousness of each individual aspirant, and is conditioning the mass consciousness of mankind. Emotionally and physically, the masses in every land are roused by this conflict; the disciples on earth and the thinking people everywhere are aroused mentally, as well as emotionally and physically, and hence the intensity of their problem. The *points of crisis* in the lives of disciples have—during the past few decades—been many; a *point of tension* has now been reached of an extreme nature; how rapidly can this tension bring about the needed *point of emergence?*

It is not my intention to deal at length with the effect of this conflict in the life of disciples. It deals with the most familiar story to all of them; the aspirants and the disciples are, from the angle of evolution, the most strictly human beings to be found in the fourth kingdom in nature, for the reason that mind, emotion and physical activity are integrated or are in process of integration into one functioning whole. The disciple knows, however, that—as a result of conflict—the complete harmonising of his entire nature will be brought about; the fusion of soul and personality will be consummated, and for this he works. The same principle can also be applied by him in his consideration of general human affairs; he needs to see in all world conflict the needed steps towards an eventual harmony—a harmony based upon a true mental perception and a sound idealism. It is this process of developing mental understanding and a sound rational yet spiritual attitude which is now going on; the emergence of the many ideologies are the guarantee that the true idealism will eventually appear and control—the ideal of right human relations; it is the

struggle between emotional control and a steadily developing mind control which is conditioning mankind at this
time. When a mental, an emotional and a physical conflict are raging simultaneously, the results must necessarily
be difficult, but they are surmountable.

Today, the conflicts are numerous, vital and unavoidable; they are present in the individual consciousness and
in the mass consciousness; they present constant points of
crises and are today bringing about a point of world tension which seems well-nigh unbearable. But ahead of the
individual disciple and of humanity lies a point of
emergence.

What must the disciple do whilst the point of tension is dominating him and his fellowmen? The answer is
a simple one. Let each disciple and all groups of disciples
develop the ability to think sanely, with right orientation
and a broad point of view; let them think truly, evading
no issues, but preserving always a calm, dispassionate and
loving understanding; let them demonstrate in their environment the qualities which will establish right human
relations and show on a small scale the behaviour which
will some day characterise enlightened humanity; let them
not be discouraged, but let them hold firmly to the conviction of the inevitable spiritual destiny of humanity; let
them realise *practically* that "the souls of men are one"
and learn to look beyond the immediate outer seeming
to the inner (and sometimes remote) spiritual consciousness;
let them *know* that the present world conflict will be
terminated.

The perfect outcome of the conflict will necessarily be
lacking, for perfection is not yet possible to man; nevertheless, a situation can be brought about which will permit the return of the Christ into objective relation with
mankind, and which will enable Him to set about His
task of resurrecting the human spirit, out of the tomb of
materialism into the clear light of spiritual perception. For
this, all men must work.

*A Summation and Forecast*

Let me now summarise for you some of the points of importance in this instruction:

1. The fourth Ray of Harmony through Conflict is a controlling factor in human affairs at all times, and peculiarly today.

2. The Principle of Conflict is the agent of the Principle of Harmony and produces the strains and the stresses which will lead, finally, to liberation.

3. The great initiation of the Renunciation, plus the many smaller renunciations, is the result of inner conflict and ever precedes liberation into harmony and peace.

4. Conflict produces: War—Renunciation—Liberation.

5. Humanity is subjected to *crises of discrimination,* leading to right choice. That is the problem confronting humanity today, leading to a crisis within the United Nations.

6. The Hierarchy is subjected to *crises of decision,* leading to perception of the Plan, participation in the Purpose, and the prevention of evil.

7. The Principle of Conflict is today active in all nations, in all religions, in all organisations, leading to the emergence of the New Age.

8. Conflict produces *points of crisis,* then a *point of tension,* and eventually a *point of emergence.*

9. This Principle of Conflict is preparing the way for the return of the Christ, Who will inaugurate the new era of harmony.

10. Christ will come in three different ways:

a. Through the overshadowing, on the mental plane, of all disciples and aspirants.

b. Through the pouring out of love or of the Christ consciousness upon the masses on the emotional plane.

c. Through His recognised physical Presence upon Earth.

11. Certain nations are today torn with conflict but are

moving toward harmony. Other nations are focal points of discord and thereby serve the Principle of Conflict.

12. The U.S.S.R., the U.S.A., and the U.K. constitute a governing triangle of energy which, when right relations have been established, can and will create and foster right human relations among men.

13. The Jewish race is a symbol of humanity in its mass sense; in the resolution of its conflict and in the taking of right action, a great step forward in human liberation will take place.

14. As the individual disciple learns to harmonise himself through conflict, he sets an example which is of definite aid to humanity as a whole.

What can I prophesy? What may I foretell in relation to human affairs and of the future ahead of the race?

I would remind you that even the Hierarchy of spiritual and liberated souls, the Church of God invisible, knows not the way that humanity will choose to go. General trends are watched and possibilities are considered; the energies pouring into the human family are directed and manipulated, and conditions can frequently be adjusted, but men decide for themselves direct action; they make their own choices and exert unimpeded the free will with which they may at any time be equipped. I prophecy not, because I do not know. I can, however, say that the issues at stake are now becoming so clear that right decision is more possible than at any other time in human history. Unless, therefore, emotional stresses are too acute, humanity will decide upon right action eventually. Emotions are, however, running high and the spiritual people of the world are not sufficiently aroused as yet to handle them. It is the arousing and the awakening to the critical nature of the time and to the world problems which is immediately needed, and this all men of goodwill should regard as their paramount duty.

As I earlier remarked, if the trends which are today being established are rightly developed, the Hierarchy does not foresee the immediacy of war; war can be averted if the nations are fully occupied with the task of reconstruction and if an educational programme in right human relations is launched and systematically and most carefully carried out. If the subjective relations between the nations are emphasised and the outer frictions and the objective disagreements are ignored, a great fusion of human interests can take place; this will be binding and lasting; if the cleavage between separateness and right relations is clearly to be seen, men will know of themselves what action they should take.

In the war raging today between conflicting ideas, it is essential that this cleavage be made abundantly clear. Only the voice of a trained public opinion and the intelligent demand of the masses for right human relations can save the world from chaos. If this is so, then the duty of each individual disciple, man of goodwill and intelligent thinker is also clear. Let me bring the theme to a close with this thought and this indicated action.

## THE RAYS OF ASPECT AND THE HIGHER INITIATIONS

We completed our consideration of the effect of the *four Rays of Attribute* upon humanity as a whole and upon the individual disciple. If you will study the relationship of these rays to each other, you will discover that the energies which made their impact upon the would-be initiate were, first of all, two rays: the seventh Ray of Ceremonial Order and the fifth Ray of Science which are both along the line of the first Ray of Will or Power, plus two other rays, the sixth Ray of Devotion or Idealism and the fourth Ray of Harmony through Conflict, which are both along the line of the second Ray of Love-Wisdom. All these Rays of Attribute were—in connection with the initiations concerned—functioning *within the realm of knowledge;* it is a knowledge, however, dedicated eventually to spiritual intent and attained through conflict.

We come now to the consideration of the *three Rays of Aspect* and their general and momentous effect upon mankind in this cycle, and upon the disciple preparing for initiation. We are dealing, therefore, with

> Ray 1. Will or Power, active in connection with the 5th Initiation.
>
> Ray 2. Love-Wisdom, active in connection with the 7th Initiation.
>
> Ray 3. Active Intelligence, active in connection with the 6th Initiation.

The united activity of these rays lifts humanity to the higher, spiritual realm and concerns those initiations which lie a long way ahead of mankind. They lie also a considerable distance on the Path from the present point of the average disciple. I am dealing with them, however, as best I can, because the next one hundred years will see a demonstrable orientation of trained disciples towards the higher perception. You must make what you can of this information; it concerns primarily action within the Ashram—action which is, however, concerned with human development and welfare.

The 8th and the 9th initiations, governed by the four Rays of Attribute working in synthesis with the three Rays of Aspect (and working simultaneously), will necessarily be far beyond our comprehension; there is little I shall be able to tell you because I know but little myself.

Does this last remark surprise you? It should not. From the exoteric angle, evolution means growth and development and is largely applied to the form side of nature, and the term "evolution" might thus be confined entirely to the evolution of the form nature. It might also be applied to development within the three worlds and to the third aspect of the divine Life. However, from the esoteric angle, *evolution means a steadily increasing sensitivity to light and illumination.* A Master may not possess all knowledge possible from the exoteric angle; this He does not need because (after evolution, along the line of knowledge, decided for Him by His ray type) He is on the "way of light," and the light which is in Him and in which He lives and moves and functions serves a dual purpose:

1. It can be used to ascertain whatever is needed in the realm of knowledge by the revelation of where the needed information can be found; this is far more literally so than you realise. (It was through the use of this form of light that I, for instance, found A.A.B.; I was searching for a secretary with more than the usual education and perception generally to be found, and the light revealed her from the *personality angle* in the three worlds.)

2. It can be used also to reveal to the Master that which lies ahead for Him, and those further reaches of awareness to which He knows He must eventually attain.

The lower aspects of this light are in reality generated by the soul, whilst the higher are those which emanate from the Monad. When an initiate takes the fifth initiation (with which we are now going to deal) he has to demonstrate his facility in using the "light available" by initiating some new project in line with the hierarchical Plan and in tune with his own ray impulses. This project must have both an exoteric side and esoteric. (To illustrate further: The exoteric side of the work which I—as a newly made Master—had purposed to do can be seen in the activities which I have been enabled to accomplish in the outer world through the books which A.A.B. has taken down for me and by the establishing of the Service Activities, associated with the Arcane School. The esoteric side is of course known to me, but an analysis of it would be of no service to you, as you are not yet of the required initiate-consciousness.)

You can see, however, how the above information can throw light upon our immediate theme:

*Initiation V. Revelation. Ray I.*
The Energy of the Will-to-Good. Power.

This initiation has always been called in the Christian church by the name of the Resurrection, whereas it is the seventh initiation which is the true resurrection. The correct name for the fifth initiation is the Initiation of Revelation; this signifies the power to wield light as the carrier of life to all in the three worlds, and to know likewise the next step to be taken upon the Way of the Higher Evolution. This Way is revealed to the initiate in a new light and with an entirely different significance when the fifth initiation is taken. It is the true time of emergence from the tomb of darkness and constitutes an entrance into a light of an entirely different nature to any hitherto experienced.

Development and revelation or (if you so prefer it) a developing revelation, form essentially the entire theme and objective of all activity upon our planet. This gives us a clue to the goal of the planetary Logos. All life, from the first descent of the soul into incarnation, is only a series of revelations, all of which lead up to the revelation accorded at the fifth initiation. The relation between the fifth and the seventh initiations is exceedingly deep and mysterious. It is the revelation accorded in the fifth initiation which makes the seventh initiation possible. The Master, as He emerges at the fifth initiation into the light of day, realises in that light:

1. The true and hitherto unknown significance of the three worlds which he has viewed almost entirely from the angle of *meaning*. Now its *significance* is apparent, and the revelation is so tremendous that "he withdraws into the world of light and joins his brothers. He gathers all his forces and *seeks new light upon the Plan*. That light shines forth and with the force of its revealing power, new loyalties arise, new goals are seen, and that which shall be and the thing which is, both become lost in the radiant light of revelation."

2. That the first vibration or influencing energy of the cosmic ray of prevailing energy in its highest aspect is the Ray of Love-Wisdom, and this is now contacted; this is made possible by the Master's response to the first Ray of Power or of the Will-to-Good, experienced in its second aspect at the fifth initiation. Forget not that all rays have three aspects, and that all three can be contacted by the human consciousness of the spiritual man, thus

placing at his disposal the energies of the seven rays and of the twenty-one forces. It is this synthesis which is revealed at the fifth initiation and—as I said above—the combination of these forces produces the Ascension; this is an exceeding great mystery and one which cannot as yet be grasped by you. From the height of the Mount of Ascension light is thrown upon the hierarchical Plan in such a manner that the purpose in the mind of the planetary Logos is (for the first time) truly grasped.

3. From that height also, the mystery of the human soul is revealed and a great triangular pattern will be seen, relating the human spirit to the world of forms, to the united Hierarchy and to the Council Chamber of the Lord. Upon this I may not here enlarge, for we must not diverge too far from our study. One thing only can be said: from that high place, atma-buddhi-manas (will, love and intelligent action) can be seen in united activity and the theory of an existing Plan and the belief in the three divine aspects, or in the Trinity of Energies, is factually demonstrated.

The first Ray of Will or Power is distinguished by the highest *known* divine quality (there are others still higher). In the word, GOODWILL, the secret purpose of the planetary Logos is hidden. It is being slowly brought to the attention of humanity by means of the three phrases: God is Love. Goodwill. The Will-to-Good. These three phrases, in reality concern the three aspects of the first ray.

When a Master takes the fifth initiation He already knows the significance of the first two aspects, and must become consciously aware of the highest aspect: the Will-to-Good. He has developed in Himself "the love necessary to salvation, His own and that of those He loves, His fellowmen;" all His actions and His thinking are qualified by goodwill, in its esoteric sense, and the significance of the Will-to-Good lies ahead of Him and will be later revealed.

As this first ray is not in incarnation at this time, and therefore souls who can fully express it are absent, the entire theme anent this type of energy, and its influence and quality when related to the energies and the forces, is most difficult to express. Each great ray, as it comes into incarnation, transforms the speech of the cycle, enriches the existent vocabulary, and brings new knowledge to humanity; the many civilisations—past and present—are the result of this.

I would ask you to consider the relation of the fifth initiation, the fifth Ray of Science and the first Ray of Will, for there lies the key to the revelation accorded to the initiate-Master.

As you can see, we are venturing into realms far beyond your comprehension; but the effort to grasp the unattainable and to exercise the mind along the line of abstract thought is ever of value.

It must be remembered therefore (and I reiterate) that the revelation accorded to the disciple-initiate is along the line of the first Ray of Will or Power, and that is a ray which is as yet a long way from full manifestation. From one angle, it is of course always in manifestation for it is the ray which holds the planet and all that is upon it in one coherent manifesting whole; the reason for this coherent synthesis is the evolutionary effort to work out divine purpose. The first ray ever implements that purpose. From another angle, it is cyclic in its manifestation; here I mean from the angle of *recognised* manifestation—and such is the case at this time.

### The Effect of Ray I on Humanity Today

Owing to extra-planetary stimulation, to the immediate planetary crisis and to the present invocative cry of humanity, energy from Shamballa has been permitted to play upon the "centre which is called the race of men" and has produced two potent results: first, the world war was precipitated and, secondly, the fission of the atom, resulting in the atomic bomb, was brought about. Both these events were made possible by the pouring-in of the energy and power of the third aspect of the first Ray of Power or Will. This is the lowest aspect, and definite material effects were produced. The destroyer aspect was therefore the first aspect to take effect. It split the thought-form of materialistic living (which was governing and controlling humanity everywhere) upon the mental plane and, at the same time, it produced a great agent of destruction upon the physical plane.

Thus was the new era ushered in; thus was the stage set for a better future. This was the intent and the purpose of Those Who compose the Council Chamber of the Lord. It rests with humanity itself to take advantage of the proffered opportunity which this *destructive* manifestation made possible.

Shamballa having acted in this manner, it is nevertheless the Hierarchy which will bring into expression a measure of the second aspect of the first Ray of Will or Power, and it is for this that the Hierarchy is preparing; it is for this event that the Christ is fitting Himself to be the distributing Agent and the directing Factor, with the concentrated assistance of the united Hierarchy; it is this that will begin to manifest when He appears. You have here the true reason for His proclaimed Coming or Reappearance. The distinction between material living and spiritual living will be clearly demonstrated. This is made possible by the cleavage of the ancient materialistic thoughtform on mental levels; the reorientation of human thinking, as this fact is grasped, will have its first results upon emotional levels through the focussed expression of human goodwill; this is the lowest aspect of the second Ray of Love-Wisdom, implemented and strengthened by the second aspect of the first Ray of Will.

On the physical plane, the great scientific discovery, called colloquially the "splitting of the atom," will be turned eventually to the production of those conditions which will enable mankind to follow the good, the beautiful and the true. This men will then be able to do, freed from the dread presence of purely materialistic thinking. This is no idle vision or vague dream. Many scientists to-day (and particularly those who love their fellowmen) are not only visioning the non-destructive aspect of atomic energy but are already engaged in harnessing — for the good of humanity — some of its products and its radioactive properties.

Curiously enough, it is the wise, controlled use of the results of this scientific adventure in connection with the atomic bomb which will eventually bring about a specific revelation of the nature of certain forces in relation to light; this event will transform world thinking and lead to a new type of transmutative process, as far as man is concerned.

It must *not* be inferred from the above that humanity, as a whole, will be taking the fifth initiation, for such is not the case. Many advanced souls (perhaps amounting to many thousands) may and will take this initiation, but the masses of men everywhere, constituting the sum total of the world disciple, will eventually take either the first or the second initiation. The effect however of hierarchical happenings, in conjunction with Shamballa, will lead finally to the great stimulation of the fifth Principle of manas, the intelligence principle in man. A revelation which is not perceived, which remains unrelated and unexpressed, is of no true service to mankind, except from a purely subjective standpoint; nevertheless, through the proposed stimulation, through the efforts of those who have taken or who will take the fifth initiation, and through the new direction of first ray energy from Shamballa, the mental plane will receive such an inflow of energy that the thinking principle, the reasoning factor within humanity, will reach new heights. Thus will the "light stream forth into the minds of men," and the first stanza of the Invocation prove that it can and does receive an answer to its invocative appeal.

It would be good to let your *spiritual* imagination look forward into the future, and then vision—if you can— what is the true significance of the tremendous activity of the Hierarchy. One of the signs of the coming of this new light and energy inflow is a definitely curious one; it is to be found in the instability of the human mental mechanism and the human thinking processes at this time. This is due to their premature response to the new incoming potency. It is a mass reaction, and therefore the statistical returns are somewhat misleading. It is *the unready* who thus react, and this entails no possible reflection upon those thus distressed (and they are to be found today in all classes and nations). The Law of Rebirth will take care of this reaction, and in the next incarnation these same people will enter a physical body with a better equipment. In reality, it is this energy from Shamballa in its third and destructive aspect which is acting upon certain members of the human family and unfortunately evoking a ready response. I tell you this for your encouragement; destruction always evokes questioning in minds attuned to human welfare and in those thinkers who are apprehensive of the suffering to which their fellowmen are subjected.

One of the most difficult things for the average thinking man to understand and to interpret is the destructive processes of what he (for lack of a better name) calls "the will of God." This is one of the results (and only one) of a purely materialistic civilisation which has laid all its emphasis upon the form side of experience and thus regards physical well-being and physical comfort, plus material possessions, as the true goal of all human effort. It is upon this widespread attitude and reaction that the new incoming light will concentrate itself; as the light reveals reality, the world of phenomena and the world of spiritual values will enter into a better, directed relation.

From all the above, you will note that some of the effects upon humanity as a whole and the skeleton structure of the new and beautiful future will take place as a result of the new incoming first ray activity. No details can yet be given, but enough has been written down anent the basic, predisposing cause to enable you who read to ponder upon the possible effect, spiritually speaking. What is coming is a civilisation of a different yet still material nature, but animated by a growing registration by the masses everywhere of an emerging spiritual objective which will transform all life and give new value and purpose to that which is material.

Next we must consider what will be the effect of this first ray energy upon the individual disciple as he prepares for and undergoes the fifth initiation, and keys himself up for the promised revelation, thus laying himself open to an entirely new inflow of force. This he must do *consciously*. It is *conscious* absorption of energy and its *conscious* assimilation, plus its *conscious* use which distinguishes the initiate from the rest of mankind; there are of course many degrees of this desired consciousness. What the initiate will receive as a result of first ray energy will be an inflow of the second aspect of this ray—a blazing forth of the light which will focus clearly for him, and in a flash of time, the significance of that which is slowly being revealed on Earth; he sees this vision in toto for the first time. At the fourth initiation, he responds to the third aspect of this ray, the aspect of destruction; this divested him of everything, and finally and eternally destroyed all that which held him in the three worlds of human endeavour. Thus was harmony produced through conflict, and the success of the individual initiate is the guarantee of the final success of the world disciple.

When it comes to a consideration of the effect of this ray at the time of the fifth initiation, you must bear in mind that the disciple has passed, in a previous incarnation, through the Initiation of Renunciation, and has established within himself a condition of complete harmony as a result of conflict—a conflict which has been raging for millennia of years and whose goal has ever been revelation. Just as a camera has to be correctly focussed in order to register correctly that which is visioned, so this harmony, once finally achieved, can be regarded as a form of focussed orientation. Throughout the many lives the disciple has lived, there have been many such moments, but they were brief and passing, serving only to stir the aspiration into activity. With the disciple of the fourth initiation, submitting himself to the fifth initiation, the orientation and the focus attained *remains a permanent condition.* This prefaces an entirely new cycle of spiritual experience— the experience of the higher evolution—leading to that great moment when the revelation of the seven Paths is accorded to him at the following or sixth Initiation of Decision.

Where the ordinary everyday man is concerned, the propelling aspiration (if I may use such an unusual phrase) is of a material nature and concerns his successful progress in the world of everyday physical plane life. It might be wise to consider ambition as the lower expression of aspiration; this ambition covers all the many phases of the Path of Evolution, from the ambition of the raw savage in primeval times to gain food and shelter for himself and family to the ambition of the modern business man to reach the height of financial gain or power. Having achieved that goal, it frequently happens that, on the way to the higher octave of ambition (aspiration), there may come a cycle of lives where the ambition is directed to the creative arts. Next comes gradually the transmutation of all these ambitions into a steadily growing and consciously spiritual aspiration. The man treads then the Probationary Path and eventually the Path of Discipleship, and as his spiritual ambition grows and is paralleled by an equally steady growth in mental realisation, he passes from initiation to initiation, until there comes the culminating fifth initiation.

All his past realisations — both his material and also his spiritual realisation—have been renounced. He stands entirely free from every aspect of desire. The spiritual will has been substituted for desire. Then, reinforced by the inflow of the first ray Shamballic energy, and offering no obstructions or hindrances from within himself, as a personality, he is in a position to receive the stimulation which will enable him "to see that which is to be revealed and to accept revelation," transmuting it into that definite realisation which will enable him to live by means of its light. You have, therefore, certain words which are con-

cerned with the method whereby the vision is accorded and
revelation given:

    1. Ambition, implemented by determination.

    2. Aspiration, implemented by devotion or one-pointed
attention.

    3. Revelation, implemented by the will in its two
lower aspects.

    4. Realisation, implemented by the will in its highest
aspect.

That, briefly, is the evolutionary story of the "initiate in
good standing" and it is basically the story of the will to
self-betterment, the will to human service, goodwill, and
finally, the will-to-good. You can see, therefore, how the
great first aspect of divinity, through its three aspects, is
the hidden, basic, motivating potency of life and of evolution, from the very dawn of the evolutionary cycle.

    The initiate in good standing looks into the heart
of things; he has forced his way to the very "Heart of the
Sun" (using those words in a "planetary" and not in a
"solar" sense) and—from that vantage point—he becomes
aware of the "Central Spiritual Sun" and the Way of the
Higher Evolution which leads inevitably to that assured
centre of the Most High. The three worlds of material
living and the inner world of meaning which the soul has
revealed to him are now left behind; he is suddenly confronted with the world of significances, with the true world
of causes and of origination, and by the realm of the universal. He discovers that all he had thought anent the Law
of Cause and Effect was so limited that—in the light of
this Higher Evolution—it has practically become meaningless, except as the A B C whereby he can teach the children of men. He realises, through the revelation accorded,
more clearly than has hitherto been possible, the Purpose
of the planetary Logos. From the time of the third initiation, this purpose has been gradually revealing itself; he
sees it expressing itself through Sanat Kumara, Who is
the Personality expression of the planetary Logos. During
the coming interval and cycle of preparation for the sixth

initiation, that purpose will burst upon him in blazing and synthetic glory.

The way to the Central Spiritual Sun is therefore revealed to him, and he knows that he faces a period of intense preparation (not training, as that word is usually understood) for a length of time determined by world need, the nature of his service and certain undefinable ray conditions.

He has to fulfill the magnetic condition which will enable him to form his own Ashram; he has to unfold a new phase of selective spiritual discrimination. The word discrimination is, however, misleading, because the form of it which he can now express carries no quality of rejection or of separation. It is a right knowledge and understanding of those karmically linked to him, a right use of an impelling attractive force which will, occultly speaking, attract the attention of those who should enter his Ashram, plus an esoteric process of blending himself and his Ashram into the full body of the Hierarchy. New Ashrams within the Hierarchy present much the same type of difficulty and problems as the entrance of a new disciple into an Ashram.

It might be said that that which holds the Hierarchy together, and that which produces a coherent Ashram, is the revelation, received in the light *which that revelation produced* and which leads to realisation. Ashramic responsibility, constant service within the planetary Life and the subjection of Himself and of His Ashram to cyclic stimulation from Shamballa, plus certain mysterious processes which have naught to do with form or consciousness, but with the "sensitivity of the universe," occupy the interim between the fifth and the sixth initiations.

*Initiation VI. Decision. Ray III*

We have concluded our study of the rays and the five initiations, and there is little more that I can tell you about the remaining four initiations, except one or two points anent the sixth Initiation of Decision; this initiation is governed by the third Ray of Active Intelligence.

The only reason that I am making a few comments upon the sixth initiation is that at this time a number of the Masters are taking this great step, and it has a most peculiar application to the time of the reappearance of the Christ.

At this Initiation of Decision the Master concerned decides usually which of the seven Paths He intends to tread; some Masters decide to remain until the close of our planetary Life, at which time the "last weary Pilgrim will have found his way home"; the Earth can then be prepared for a new Humanity. When this happens, our planet will no longer be known as the planet of sorrow and of pain, but will be distinguished by a quality of tranquillity and by an aura of calm potency wherein the will of God (to be demonstrated in the next solar system) will be focussed; this—in some mysterious way—will enable the solar Logos (not the planetary Logos) to bring the first great divine aspect, that of Will or Power, into expression throughout the solar system. Instead, therefore, of the statement which explains our present solar system, "God is Love," we shall have a dynamic expression of the will-to-good—an energy which will have been generated to some extent upon our Earth. This is the reward which the present Earth humanity will reap, and this is the consummation of the preordained task of our planetary Logos. He undertook, when He came into incarnation (through the medium of our little planet), to aid the work of the Solar Logos in expressing the will aspect of divinity.

It might be simpler if I said that the experiment of manifesting the first divine aspect, through the medium of form and through a humanity which has behind it the experience of five initiations (and is therefore expressing intelligent love), will be attempted. This statement is necessarily misleading, but it embodies a truth and indicates the unfinished story of *solar* expression.

Today, however, in taking this sixth initiation, all of the Masters so doing and under the suggestion of the Christ, continue to make the decision which will control Their future progress on one of the seven Paths of the Higher Evolution, but—at the same time—*all of Them* are post-poning this proposed progress upon Their chosen Path in order, for a brief time, to implement and aid the work of the Christ and help towards the externalisation of the Hierarchy, through the medium of certain of its Ashrams; They will also form a protecting wall around the Christ, and act as liaison officers between Their great Leader and the Avatar of Synthesis.

Christ Himself took this initiation some time ago and passed through the Resurrection Initiation and the experience of the seventh initiation. These Masters can, in a mysterious fashion, implement the expression of the di-vine will-to-good on Earth. They will work in collaboration with Those Masters Whose Ashrams will be the first to be anchored on Earth in the sense of physical expression be-cause, esoterically speaking, it is "the will of God which holds them there."

For ages, the potency of that which lies behind the fifth initiation—in the planetary sense and not in connection with the individual initiation with its revelation indicat-ing first ray purpose—has held sway on Earth. Knowledge, the revealing  of the Mysteries, the attainment of scientific achievement, producing the activity of the fifth plane of mind, has governed human thinking and advancement; God in nature (i.e., the planetary Logos in concrete and material expression) has been revealed, and this has culminated in that tremendous expression of power—the atomic bomb.

Now, the potency of that which lies behind the sixth initiation will take hold of the evolutionary process and will implement divine purpose. What that potency in truth may be, we cannot yet know; we do know, however, that it is closely related to the will-to-synthesis; this will enable the Christ to break down the barriers and the separating walls which selfish, self-centred and materialistic humanity (largely with the aid of the churches of the world, with their materialistic bias) has built, thereby letting in the light of understanding and clearing the way for a fuller expression of the will of God.

I felt that the practical aspect of what the Masters are doing might prove useful to you. As to the remaining three initiations:

Initiation VII  . . .  The Resurrection      . . . Ray II
Initiation VIII . . .  The Great Transition . . . Rays IV, V, VI, VII
                       (the four minor Rays)
Initiation IX   . . .  The Refusal           . . . Rays I, II, III
                       (the three major Rays)

an analysis of them would prove to you that your comprehension has not yet been developed to the point where understanding is possible; it would therefore be a waste of time further to consider them. If you will re-read the instructions earlier given upon the seven Paths (pp. 395-427) you may glean some ideas about these later initiations; they would still, however, be impossible of application and practical usefulness at your particular stage of evolutionary development.

## THE SEVEN AND THE NINE INITIATIONS
### OF OUR PLANETARY LIFE

Now let us look at these initiations from the angle of the planetary Life, as far as in us lies. We have for long looked at them from the angle of humanity, the world disciple, as well as from the angle of the individual initiate, but it must not be forgotten that these initiations have also a planetary significance. From the standpoint of the Hierarchy and of Shamballa, they constitute the major factors which make possible the initiatory process on Earth among men.

This naturally means in relation to our planetary Logos. It must never be forgotten that it is the progress forward upon His chosen cosmic Path which makes the entire evolutionary process possible. Just as a Master Who has taken the fifth initiation has to project His own specific undertaking, through the medium of His Ashram, thus proving His response to the will aspect of the planetary Logos and making Himself responsible for a phase of the planetary Plan, so a planetary Logos has likewise—under the Law of Synthesis—to carry forward a specific project in line with the will of the Solar Logos. This our planetary Logos, Sanat Kumara, is in process of doing, providing a definite culture wherein the germ of the solar will can be fostered in one of its aspects. Then—in conjunction with a similar project going on in two other planets, thus fostering two other aspects—the nucleus of the third solar system will be brought eventually into expression.

It is hard for the human mind to appreciate this basic synthesis and this relationship which exists throughout the entire solar system, with the planetary Logoi implementing divine purpose; men cannot yet grasp the relations within the personality aspect of our planetary Logos—the Earth and all that is therein. But that synthesis exists and is the relating factor between our Earth and the Sun, between the various planetary Logoi and the Solar Logos. All that we can do is to get a general picture of the planetary initiations, the seven initiations and the nine.

The only manner in which we can grasp even a small measure of planetary intention is through a study of the great civilisations which have been developed by humanity under impression from the highest spiritual sources on our planet; these have hitherto reached us via the Hierarchy. To these civilisations must be added the cultures which have evolved out of them. This obviously we cannot do, for it would require research into all the known and the unknown historical periods and cycles, plus a consideration of all the evidence—anthropological, architectural and sociological. To this approach to the intent and the purpose of the planetary Logos must be added a consideration of certain crises in the life of mankind which are in the nature of minor initiations to which the planetary Logos has subjected Himself, in the sense that He is the Initiator. Humanity, being the most highly developed evolutionary product upon our planet, reacts to these initiations; they produce world events, and those stupendous points of crisis which (up to date) have worked destructively where the form aspect is concerned, but which have developed into those stages of sensitive unfoldment and progression when the work of the Builders (the second divine aspect) is added to and takes advantage of the liberty or release brought about by the Destroyer (the first aspect). There are always these two phases.

Through the past civilisations and their eventual catastrophic destruction, the planetary Logos has gradually prepared the ground or planetary field for the "planting of the germ of Will"—the nurturing of which is a future part of human destiny. The seven major phases of the unfoldment of the human race (of which our modern Aryan race is the fifth) are in the nature of seven planetary initiations or unfoldments; the word "initiation" is not to be understood in the exact sense in which human initiations are understood and interpreted. Men are initiated into phases of the divine consciousness through applied stimulation, whereby their vehicles evidence readiness; in connection with the planetary Logos, it is He Who initiated a new process in seven phases, preparatory to the expected divine planting. It must be borne in mind that the use of the word "planting" is purely symbolic. Each phase brings the original divine purpose or spiritual project nearer to fruition, and it is for this that Sanat Kumara came into manifestation or incarnation.

Each of these phases affects all the four kingdoms in nature, producing a higher stage of sensitivity in each successive one, but it is only in the fourth kingdom, the human, that there exists the possibility of a conscious registering and recognition of divine intent and a faint vibrating response to the will aspect of divinity. It has taken a millennia of years to bring this about. When you remember that it has only been in the present world crisis that the planetary Logos dared subject the forms in all the four kingdoms to the direct stimulation of His impelling will, you will realise the long, long patience which is perhaps

His most distinctive characteristic. Patience is a quality of will; it is of the nature of a strict adherence to a fixed intention. At each transition from one civilisation to another (each being built upon the cultural seed of the preceding one, after a due flowering of the civilisation) we could say of Sanat Kumara what has been said of the Christ, that "He sees of the travail of His soul and is satisfied." So blind are men that when a civilisation comes to an end, when the familiar mode of cultural expression is brought (as is usual) under the hand of the destroyer, humanity regards it as a major disaster and dreads and fears the ruin which usually surrounds such an event. But from the standpoint of the world of significances, progress is seen and the day of fulfillment draws much nearer.

Our modern civilisation today (under the hammer of the destroyer aspect) is being changed; old things are passing away, having served their purpose. The new thing is not yet noted or appreciated, though already present. The work of preparation for the planting of the germ or seed of the divine will on Earth is nearly over; when the Hierarchy is externalised, and men as a whole recognise the position on Earth of the Christ and of His church "invisible" (the union of all souls made perfect, which is a true description of the Hierarchy), then—in a manner unforeseen by humanity—Shamballa will assume control, and from the Council Chamber of Sanat Kumara will issue forth the Sower of the seed; He will sow it *within the ground prepared by humanity,* and thus the future is assured, not for the planetary Logos alone, but for that greater Whole in which our planet plays its little part. That moment lies ahead in the civilisation which shall be, and in the next great race which will emerge out of all our modern races and nations, the sowing will take place. The next race will be a fusion of the whole, and a world-wide recognition of the One Humanity is an essential prerequisite of the sowing. It is the creation of this universal recognition which will be one of the major tasks of the reappearing Christ and His attendant Hierarchy. When the "little wills of men" are beginning to respond on a measurably large scale to the greater Will of the divine Life, then the major task of Shamballa will become possible; nevertheless, prior to that, humanity must respond to the light and the love which are the *preparatory* streams of spiritual energy and which are already pouring forth in response to human invocation.

In comprehending the planetary initiatory processes as instituted by the planetary Logos, men must relate them to the great crises which have occurred in all the races of men. Just as the initiate-disciple passes from one initiation to another through a process of continuously leaving behind those aspects of the form life which have been destroyed by him as useless, so humanity leaves behind civilisation after civilisation under the stimulus of the evolving purpose of Sanat Kumara Who initiates constantly that which is new and that which will better serve His will. Men are apt to think that the whole evolutionary process —including the development of the subhuman kingdoms in nature—is merely a mode whereby men can reach perfection and develop better forms through which to manifest that perfection. But in the last analysis, human progress is purely relative and incidental. The factor of supreme importance is the ability of the planetary Logos to carry out His primary intention and bring His "project" to a sound consummation, thus fulfilling the task given to Him by His great superior, the Solar Logos.

The eighth and the ninth initiations (of which neither you nor I can know practically anything) relate to the initiations of those methods and techniques whereby the "seed of will," which will later flower into the third solar system, can be nurtured and fostered and its growth promoted. This nurturing and fostering will be the task of a group of Masters (to be developed in the next major race) Who, at the Initiation of Decision, the sixth initiation, will dedicate Themselves, *as a group,* to the Path of Earth Service. They will specifically and with full enlightenment pledge Themselves to the promotion of Sanat Kumara's project. With this our present group of Masters are not specifically

concerned; Their task is the application of the evolutionary
process with a view to the preparation of the field of the
world for the future divine sowing.

More I cannot tell you. All I have done is to give
you a hint as to the significance of the initiations, instituted
by the Lord of the World. These are not, may I repeat,
initiations to which the planetary Logos is Himself subjected. The world crises, which ever precede initiation on
a planetary scale, are part of the preparatory work, tests
and trials which make possible some cosmic initiation to
which He has been and will eventually be subjected. With
them we have no concern, nor would you understand if I
were to be in any way explicit. The Law of Analogy and
of Correspondences breaks down at a certain point upon
the path of understanding, and something new and utterly
different enters in. The Law of Analogy holds good when
considering the microcosm *within* the life of the Macrocosm,
but if you ventured outside that limited and manifested
Life (if that were possible, which it is not) you would
contact other Laws and other approaches to truth, existent
on cosmic levels.

There is little more that I can tell you anent the
planetary initiations or—as they might be more correctly
called—the planetary initiatory processes. These affect our
entire planetary life but are not essentially initiations as
we understand the term, or as that word could be applied
to Sanat Kumara. They are a definite part of cosmic process
and particularly of solar evolution, but they are, as we
have seen, only preparatory to that initiation for which
our world was made—the manifestation on Earth of the
highest of the three aspects: the WILL of God, as it is universally called.

## THE SIGNIFICANCE OF THE INITIATIONS

We now start our consideration of the nine initiations, only this time we shall be occupied with the relationship and the detail connected with each initiation,

viewing them when possible from the angle of the Hierarchy and its effort on behalf of the evolutionary progress of the race, and not so much from the angle of the soul-infused personality of the disciple. It must be remembered from the start that no disciple can pass through the initiatory experience unless he *is* a soul-infused individual and is consciously aware on soul levels of the various happenings, possibilities, undertakings and implications.

In all the many books which I have given to the world I have taught much anent initiation; I have sought to bring a saner, more reasonable presentation of these great crises in the life of every disciple. It is wise to note that an initiation is in reality a crisis, a climaxing event, and is only truly brought about when the disciple has learnt patience, endurance and sagacity in emerging from the many preceding and less important crises. An initiation is a culminating episode, made possible because of the self-inspired discipline to which the disciple has forced himself to conform.

Much has been said in the occult books about the preparatory work to be done and the effort which such a task entails, plus the realisation of the consequences initiated and expressing themselves through the individual aspirant. Little has been said anent the more important truth that initiation admits a man into some area or level of the divine consciousness—into a plane or rather a state of being hitherto regarded as sealed and closed.

I shall not touch upon the ray effects, because we have already considered them, and because each level of consciousness, each phase or revealed area of the "lighted Way" is open to souls on all the rays and to every type of initiate.

From the standpoint of the Hierarchy, it is not the individual initiate who is of importance, but *the groups* in every land who face initiation, and who fall into three categories:

1. Those in the group who have caught the vision, who accept the fact of the Hierarchy and of proffered op-

portunity, but who are nevertheless quite unready for their next step and must be taught and prepared to take it. Yet they are "set apart for fulfillment," as it is esoterically called, and in spite of fluctuations and the many vicissitudes of the Path, they will eventually attain their goal.

2. Those in preparation for some specific initiation, particularly the first initiation to the third (inclusive). They have set their hands to the plow—another way of saying symbolically that they are toiling for and serving their fellowmen.

3. Those who have had the needed training and await the hour of initiation. As I have said, the first two initiations—those of the Birth and the Baptism—are not regarded by the Hierarchy as major initiations. They are in the nature of initiations of the threshold and are simply phases of, or preparatory to, the third initiation (as occult students call it), which is in reality the first major initiation. This must be most carefully held in mind, for these initiations indicate the process through which the personality can become soul-infused and the energy of the Spiritual Triad can make its presence felt.

For the sake of clarity, however, and because the Birth and Baptism initiations have been counted in with the true major initiations by the modern teachers of theosophy and similar occult bodies, and because people are therefore accustomed so to consider them, we will preserve the old method of counting them. The thought of soul-infusion must be held in mind—a soul-indwelling which culminates at the third initiation, and of monadic control which increasingly possesses the soul-infused personality. This higher possessiveness steadily increases from the time of the third initiation until the seventh initiation; after the seventh initiation a condition can be seen which is extra-planetary in nature and of which little can be known. This brings in—for the first time—a registration or recognition of cosmic consciousness.

Let us now consider these initiations, one by one.

*Initiation I. The Birth at Bethlehem*

I have preserved the above Christian nomenclature because of its familiarity and because (symbolically speaking) it conveys an aspect of a major truth. Just as the birth of a child is an entrance into light, literally speaking, and the beginning of an entirely new way of life, so each successive initiation is in an exactly similar manner an entrance into light, involving the revelation of a different world to the one hitherto known, and the undergoing of entirely new experiences. If students would keep this symbology and this definition carefully in mind, they would arrive at a keener concept of the processes which lie ahead of them. This is particularly true in connection with this first initiation; the analogy holds good from the very dawn of history, where humanity is considered.

In ancient Lemuria, with the coming in of the mental idea and mechanism, the low grade animal life (which, to a certain extent, looked human but was definitely mindless, unknowing and unseeing) became suddenly aware of that which threw light upon its way. It meant little to the animal men of those days, but it came increasingly to have significance as millennia of years elapsed; civilisations came and went; races developed and disappeared. In *Lemurian days,* the indwelling light of perception (though it was a perception so remote from ours as to be practically inconceivable) revealed the physical world and that found upon it which the human being of that time would deem desirable. Later, in *Atlantean times,* that same indwelling light and unfolding light of the mind served to reveal the world of emotions, and in the later half of that period it revealed the more aesthetic values; the arts began to flourish; colour and beauty were registered. In our more *modern Aryan race,* the light has revealed the world of thought and has brought us to a synthesis of the senses; these senses were developed in earlier cycles of human living. Each of these three races, in a mysterious manner, has a correspondence on a racial scale to the first three initiations.

Today, as we enter the new era, the symbology of the fourth initiation, that of the Renunciation, has application; men face the necessity of renouncing the material values and of substituting the spiritual. The ferment of the initiation process goes on all the time, undermining the materialism of the race of men, revealing more and more of the reality underlying the phenomenal world (the only world recognised by the Lemurians) and—at the same time—providing that cultural field of experience in which those sons of men who are ready to do so can undergo the five initiations, technically understood. This is the factor of importance. This, therefore, is our starting point.

The historical process can (and will) reveal the gradual entrance of mankind into ever-expanding "lighted areas" of consciousness; into these areas the way of evolutionary unfoldment has led the race of men right up to the point where there are many, many thousands (and millions if you consider all of humanity—those in incarnation today and those that are out of incarnation upon the inner planes) who have been enabled to step out of the lighted field of the three worlds into another area where the light of the mind can be blended with the still greater light of the soul. They have (in past lives, even though recollection may be lacking) undergone the birth experience and initiation, and as a result of this, that which can reveal what the mind is unable to illumine is now developing and functioning within them. The "light of life" is now available, in a sense far more literally true than you can at this time perceive, and each successive initiation will see this fact more clearly demonstrated. The Birth Initiation lies behind in the experience of many, and this is factually proved by the lives of those who are consciously and willingly oriented towards the light, who see a wider world than that of their own selfish interests, who are sensitive to the Christ life and to the spiritual consciousness in their fellowmen and who see an horizon and vistas of contact unperceived by the average man; they realise a possible spiritual achievement, unknown and undesired by those whose lives are conditioned entirely by either the emotions or the lower concrete mind. At this stage of unfoldment they have a sense of conscious dualism, knowing the fact of the existence of that "something other" than the phenomenal, emotional and mental self.

The first initiation might be regarded as the goal and the reward of the *mystical experience;* it is fundamentally not an occult experience in the true sense of the term, for it is seldom accurately realised or consciously prepared for, as is the case of the later initiations, and this is why the first two initiations are not considered major initiations. In the mystical realisation there is naturally and normally an emphasis upon dualism, but in the new area of unfoldment —visioned and later to be struggled for and attained, initiation by initiation — unity is achieved and dualism disappears. Students should therefore have in mind the following definite occult concept: *The mystical Way leads to the first initiation. Having achieved its purpose, it is then renounced, and the "lighted Way" of occultism is then followed, leading to the lighted areas of the higher states of consciousness.*

Thus both ways are seen to be essential; the mystical way is for the majority at this time, and an increasingly large number of mystics will emerge out of the modern masses of men; paralleling this, the occult way is attracting more and more of the world intelligentsia. Its experience is not basically religious, as the orthodox churchman understands the word. The way of science is as deeply needed by mankind as is the way of religion, for "God" is found equally on both ways. The scientific way leads the aspirant into the world of energies and forces, which is the true world of occult endeavour, revealing the Universal Mind and the workings of that great Intelligence which created the manifested universe. The "new man" who has come to birth at the first initiation must and will tread the occult or scientific way, which inevitably leads him out of the world of mysticism into the scientific and assured perception of God as life or energy.

The first initiation marks the beginning of a totally new life and mode of living; it marks the commencement of a new manner of thinking and of conscious perception. The life of the personality in the three worlds has for aeons nurtured the germ of this new life and fostered the tiny spark of light within the relative darkness of the lower nature. This process is now being brought to a close, though it is not at this stage entirely discontinued, for the "new man" has to learn to walk, to talk, and to create; the consciousness is now, however, being focussed elsewhere. This leads to much pain and suffering until the definite choice is made, a new dedication to service is vouchsafed, and the initiate is ready to undergo the Baptism Initiation.

Members of the New Group of World Servers should watch with care for all those who show signs of having passed through the "birth" experience and should help them toward a greater maturity. They should assume that all those who truly love their fellowmen, who are interested in the esoteric teaching, and who seek to discipline themselves in order to attain greater beauty of life, are initiate and have undergone the first initiation. When they discover those who are seeking mental polarisation and who evidence a desire and aspiration to think and to know, coupled with the distinguishing marks of those who have taken the first initiation, they can, in all probability, safely assume that such people have taken the second initiation or are on the verge of so doing. Their duty will then be clear. It is by this close observation on the part of the world servers that the ranks of the New Group are filled. Today, the opportunity and the stimulation are so great that all servers must keep alert, developing in themselves the ability to register the quality for which search must be made, and giving the help and guidance which will weld into one cooperative band those disciples and initiates who should prepare the way for the Christ.

The first initiation should be regarded as instituting a new attitude towards relationships. This is not yet the case. The relationships hitherto recognised, speaking generally, have been those karmically, physically and emotionally instituted; they are largely objective and predominantly concern the phenomenal plane with its contacts, duties, responsibilities and obligations. The new relationships however, to be increasingly recognised, are subjective and may have but little phenomenal indication. They embrace the recognition of those who must be served; they involve the expansion of the individual consciousness into a growing group awareness; they lead eventually to an eager response to hierarchical quality and to the magnetic pull of the Ashram. Such a development in the recognition of relationships leads finally to a recognition of the Presence of the Christ and to relationship with Him. With the recognition of and the relationship to the planetary Logos we need not at this point deal. All these relationships begin, in their truest connotation and with a correctly realised objective, at the birth of the "new man." To this the Christ referred when He said: "Except a man be born again, he cannot see the Kingdom of God." I am here using the Christian terminology but prefer to speak of the "new man" rather than the strictly Christian phrase "the birth of the Christ Child in the heart." It is by means of the touchstone of relationships that world servers can contact the initiates and the accepted disciples in the world, and can discover those aspirants who can be helped and trained.

Let me bring another point to your attention. In the phenomenal world of the average human being who has not yet passed through the initiatory experience of the rebirth, the emphasis has ever been and is today upon the dual relationship of the sexes and to this our novels, plays, movies and affairs of all men bear testimony. Creativity expresses itself mainly through the propagation of the race, brought about through the relation of male and female, or of the positive and negative poles in the human family. This is right and good and part of the divine Plan. Even though men have prostituted their capacities and debased their relationships, the basic plan is divine and ideal. After the first initiation, the entire sex relationship shifts gradually and steadily into its proper place as simply a natural phase of existence in the three worlds and as one of the normal and correct appetites, but the emphasis changes. The higher experience and correspondence, that of which physical sex is only the symbol, becomes apparent. Instead of male and female, there emerges the magnetic relationship between the now negative personality and the positive soul, with consequent creativity upon the higher planes. Of this relationship the head centre and the centre between the eyebrows (the ajna centre) are the agents and eventually — through the medium of the pituitary body and the pineal gland — they condition the personality, rendering it soul-infused.

I have given you so much information anent initiation and the rays and centres in my many books that there is no need for me to repeat it here; there is, however, great need for you to collect and tabulate the scattered information so that you can register it as a whole. Many who read these instructions and who study the books I have written are in process of preparation for one or other of the initiations, and the entire theme should therefore be of major interest to you. You should decide (at least tentatively) which initiation lies ahead of you and then discover all you possibly can about it and its prerequisites, endeavouring to make practical application of the imparted information; either that which I give to you is true or it is not; if true, it is vital to your future progress and you should aim at achieving a measure of real understanding.

You have been taught that the activity or the inactivity of the centres conditions the personality, working through the endocrine system; the energies which the centres channel and the forces which they generate can be controlled and directed by the soul, by the spiritual man. You have likewise been told that the energy of the sacral centre (the centre most implicated and active at the time of the first initiation) has to be transmuted and raised to the throat centre, thereby transforming the physical creative act into the creative process of producing the good, the beautiful and the true. This is the A B C of your fundamental knowledge: the transmutation of sex. In that transmutative process men have greatly erred and have approached the subject from two angles:

1. They have sought to stamp out natural desire and have endeavoured to emphasise an enforced celibacy; they have thus frequently warped the nature and subjected the "natural man" to rules and regulations which were not of divine intent.

2. They have tried—at the other extreme—to exhaust normal sexual desire by promiscuity, license and perversions, damaging themselves and laying up the basis for trouble for many incarnations ahead.

True transmutation is in reality the achieving of a correct sense of proportion in relation to any phase of human life, and for the race of men today has particular reference to the sacral centre and the energies which bring it into activity. When a proper recognition of the place the sex life should play in the daily life is paralleled by the concentration of thought anent the throat centre, that centre becomes automatically magnetic and attracts the forces of the sacral centre upward through the spine into "the place of creative building"; the normal sex life is then regulated and not atrophied, and is relegated to its rightful place as one of the usual faculties or appetites with which man is endowed; it is brought under control through the lack of directed interest and is subordinated to the law of the land as regards its relation to its opposite pole—either negative and feminine or masculine and positive. To the aspirant it becomes mainly the agent for the creation of the vehicles needed for reincarnating souls. Thus by force of example, by the avoiding of all extremes, by the dedication of the bodily energies to the higher uses, and by the acceptance of the law of the land in any given country and at any given time, the present disorder and the current misuse of the sex principle will give way to orderly living and to the right use of this major bodily function.

This regulated physical life comes about when the

personality is sufficiently integrated and coordinated and the ajna centre (the centre between the eyebrows) is active and is coming under the control of the soul. This has an immediate effect—automatically induced—upon the gland associated with this centre; it becomes a balanced part of the general endocrine system and past imbalance is avoided. Simultaneously, the head centre becomes active as a result of the aspirant's mental perception, meditation and service; this brings the allied gland, the pineal gland, into action. All this is again only the A B C of occultism.

What is oft omitted from normal consideration is the fact that the increasing activity of these two "points of light within the head" is basically related to what is occurring in the sacral and throat centres, as the transmutative process proceeds and the energies of the sacral centre are gathered up into the throat centre—without, however, withdrawing all the energy from the lower centre; thus its normal activity is properly preserved. The two centres in the head then become correspondingly active; the negative and the positive elements affect each other, and the light in the head shines forth; a line of light, permitting free interplay, is established between the ajna centre and the head centre, and therefore between the pituitary body and the pineal gland. When this line of light is present and there is an unobstructed relation between the two centres and the two glands, then the first initiation becomes possible. When this takes place, it must not be inferred that the task of transmutation going on between the lower and the higher centres and the relationship between the two head centres is fully and finally completed and established. The line of light is still tenuous and unstable, but it is in existence. It is the energy let loose at the first initiation and distributed into the sacral and the throat centres (via the slowly awakening head centre) which brings the transmutation process to a successful conclusion and stabilises the relationship within the head. This process may take several lives of steadily intensifying effort on the part of the initiate-disciple.

Thus the work of magical reformation starts, and it is here that the influence of the seventh ray (which governs the first initiation) enters in; one of the functions of this ray is to bring together soul and body, the higher and the lower, life and form, spirit and matter. This is the creative task confronting the disciple who is engaged in lifting the energies of the sacral centre to the throat centre and of establishing a right relation between the personality and the soul. Just as the antahkarana has to be constructed and established as a bridge of light between the Spiritual Triad and the soul-infused personality, so a similar bridge or correspondence is established between the soul and the personality, and, in connection with the mechanism of the disciple, between the two head centres and the two glands within the head.

When that line of light has related the higher spiritual aspects and the lower, and when the sacral centre and the throat centre are in true related alignment, the initiate-disciple becomes a creative worker under the divine Plan and a "magical exponent" of the divine building work; he is then a constructive force, wielding energy consciously on the physical plane. He creates forms as expressions of reality. This is the true work of magic.

You can see, therefore, that in the creative work three energies are brought into a related activity:

1. The energy concentrated in the ajna centre and which is indicative of the personality life.

2. The energy concentrated in the head centre as a result of soul activity.

3. The energy of the seventh Ray of Ceremonial Order or Magic, making possible true creative activity under the divine Plan.

There is nothing spectacular to be told anent the first initiation; the initiate-disciple still works in the dimly lit "cave of the spiritual birth"; he has to continue his struggle to reveal divinity, primarily on the physical plane—symbolised for us in the word "Bethlehem" which means the "house of bread"; he has to learn the dual function o "lifting up the lower energies into the light" and—at the same time—of "bringing down the higher energies into bodily expression." Thus he becomes a white magician.

At this initiation he sees, for the first time, what are the major energies which he must bring into expression, and this vision is summed up for him in the *Old Commentary* in the following words:

"When the Rod of Initiation descends and touches the lower part of the spine, there is a lifting up; when the eyes are opened in the light, that which must be lowered into form is now perceived. The vision is acknowledged. The burden of the future is assumed. The cave is lighted up and the new man issues forth."

That this may be true of all of you who read these words is the prayer and the wish of your friend and counsellor.

### Initiation II. The Baptism in Jordan

The initiation which we are now to study is perhaps one of the most important, because it concerns that aspect of the personality which gives the most difficulty to everybody: the emotional or astral body. Today the mass of men are swept by the emotions and by a sensitive response to circumstance; they are not swept usually by an intelligent reaction to life *as it is*. The normal and usually violent reaction serves only to increase the confusion and the attending difficulties, producing vortices of uncontrolled energies, glamour and delusion. Even though it may at the same time produce a saving aspect in some cases, the violence of the astral testing and the potency of the astral temptation (as it might well be called) leads to a greatly increased sphere of suffering. To this must be added the materialistic bias of the many presented solutions, bringing in the force of the world maya and thus greatly complicating the problem.

Distressing as all this may be, and significant of the end of this age and the cessation of the Atlantean vibration and quality which has carried over so potently into this Aryan cycle, it is however indicative of the attainment of a definitely racial opportunity. Humanity—on a relatively large scale—faces the second initiation, or the Baptism Initiation.

The concept of baptism is ever associated with that of purification. Water has ever been the symbol of that which purifies; it is also the symbol of the astral plane, with its instability, its storms, its tranquillities, its overwhelming emotional reactions and its pliability, which makes it such a good agent for the deceptive thought-forming faculties of the unregenerate man. It reacts to every impulse, every desire and every possible magnetic "pull" coming from the material or substantial form side of nature. In its cycles of tranquillity it reflects equally the good as well as the bad; it is the agent, therefore, of deception when manipulated by the Black Lodge, or of aspirational reaction when influenced by the great White Lodge, the spiritual Hierarchy of our planet. It is the battleground between the pairs of opposites; the problem is complicated by the fact that men have to learn to recognise these opposites before right choice, leading to spiritual victory, is theirs.

Today, desire for peace at any price, for adequate food, warmth and housing, for the restoration of stability and security and for the cessation of anxiety controls the mass of human reactions and makes the astral plane loom so large in men's affairs and in world decisions. This is so dominantly so that the realisation which the mind could reveal and of which the intelligentsia are the custodians is lost to sight and has small influence.

At the third initiation the control of the soul-illumined mind is finally established, and the soul itself assumes the dominant position and not the phenomenal form. All the limits of the form nature are then transcended. It is the vision of this transcendence which is communicated at the time of the second initiation under the symbolism of a positively applied purification.

I am not here emphasising the Biblical account of that purificatory process. That summarised symbolically the watery nature of the astral plane and the "washing by water" of the initiate. It expressed the purely Atlantean form of the initiatory process, giving us the concept of a descent into water and of ascent out of water in response to a Word of Power from on high. The Aryan approach to this same initiation has not yet been fully understood.

This second initiation—as now undergone—is to some extent one of the most difficult. It involves purification, but it is purification by fire, symbolically understood. The occult "application of fire to water" produces certain most serious and devastating results. The water, under the action of fire, "is resolved into steam and the initiate is immersed in the fogs and miasmas, the glamours and the mists" thus caused. Out of this fog and out of the glamours, the initiate must emerge; out of the present fog of human affairs humanity will also emerge eventually. The success of the individual initiate is the guarantee of the racial destiny. The complications, produced by water in conjunction with fire in these Aryan days, are far greater than those produced entirely by water in Atlantean times; this age is kama-manasic and not simply kamic or strictly astral. Remember therefore as you read these words that I am speaking symbolically. The fire of mind today has to be reckoned with in conjunction with the water of desire, and it is owing to this that much of humanity's problem develops. It is because of this that the second initiation has become one of the most difficult which the modern disciple has to take.

The result, however, of the modern initiatory process is of a much higher order. This statement is related to the emerging fact that the Hierarchy and its personnel in process of assembling will be of a much higher order than that previously responsible for human guidance. A more advanced humanity demands a more advanced Hierarchy and hierarchical supervision; this has ever been the case. The evolutionary process covers all that *is*. Even Sanat Kumara is learning and advancing from a relative imperfection to perfection.

This baptism of fire (to which reference is made in

the Western Scriptures) carries with it inevitably the connotation of *pain,* and this to an extent hitherto unknown. Even a casual glance at world affairs will reveal the truth of this statement.

What, therefore, is really happening, and what are the major facts involved? Much will depend upon my answer and upon your interpretation of it. I would ask you consequently to give careful consideration to my reply to these two questions.

Under the influence of the Piscean cycle which is now in process of termination, the sixth Ray of Idealism or Devotion was predominantly active. This is the ray of one-pointed determination and—from one angle—it is *the ray of blind procedure.* The individual, the group or humanity, sees only one aspect of reality at any one time, and (because of man's present point in the evolutionary process) usually the least desirable aspect. All else is sealed to them; they vision only one picture; their horizon is limited to only one point of the compass (speaking esoterically). To the mass of humanity, the aspect of reality which was visioned and for which men lived and died was *the material world, material comfort, material possessions and material enterprises;* to this the labour movement today and the tendencies already apparent in the United Nations bear incontrovertible testimony. To a much smaller group of human beings the world of the intelligence appears paramount, and the concrete mind is the desired ruler or controlling factor. All, therefore, remains within the area of material control and interest.

The solar plexus centre is consequently the dominant factor, because—even in the case of the intelligentsia—it is desire for material well-being, for territorial possessions and for planned governmental and economic material decisions which control and motivate the individual, the group or the nation. These are not necessarily wrong, but (under the present emotional-desire concept) they are placed in the foremost position and are regarded as causal in their nature; nevertheless they are fundamentally secondary in their nature, and are effectual in their essential nature, placing the emphasis upon the word "effect." Humanity, even in its advanced brackets, is not yet able to think on causal levels.

What is the basic goal of the initiate who has taken the second initiation? I would ask you to transit in consciousness from the concept that the process of initiation is a consummation of effort, to the higher and better concept that it is initiatory in effect and marks a beginning and not a consummation. What, therefore, lies ahead of the initiate who has entered the purificatory water, or rather, fire? To what is he pledged? What is to happen within "the area of livingness" (I want you to familiarise yourselves with that phrase) and what results will take place within the mechanism with which he approaches the place of initiation? These are the factors of importance, and these are the aspects of the life process which should condition him. At the close of the initiatory process certain energies and divine aspects should be recognised by him as now playing a part in his thinking and his purposes—energies which heretofore (even if present) were quiescent and not controlling.

Before him lies the third Initiation of the Transfiguration. Facing him is a great transition from an emotional aspirational focus to an intelligent, thinking focus. He has, theoretically at least, cast off the control of the astral body and nature; much still remains to be done; old desires, ancient astral reactions and habitual emotions are still powerful, but he has developed a new attitude to them and a new perspective to the astral body. Water, fire, steam, glamour, delusion, misinterpretation and emotional continuity still mean something specific and undesirable to him. He is now negative to their appeal and positive to the higher demanding focus. That which he now loves and longs for, desires and plans for, lies in another and higher dimension. He has, through his willingness to pass through the second initiation, struck the first blow at his innate selfishness and has demonstrated his determination to think in wider and more inclusive terms. The group begins to mean more to him than himself.

What has happened, technically speaking? The energies of the solar plexus centre are being transferred from the major clearing house below the diaphragm to the heart centre—one of the three major centres into which all the lower energies must transfer. At the first initiation he was granted a vision of a higher creativity and the energy of the sacral centre began its slow ascent to the throat centre. At the second initiation, he is granted a vision of a higher focus, and his place in the larger whole begins slowly to reveal itself. A new creativity and a new focus become his immediate goals, and for him life can never again be the same. The old physical attitudes and desires may still at times assume control; selfishness may continue to play a potent part in his life expression, but—underlying these and subordinating them—will be found a deep dissatisfaction about things as they are and an agonising realisation of failure. It is at this point that the disciple begins to learn the uses of failure and to know certain fundamental distinctions between that which is natural and objective and that which is supernatural and subjective.

Do these ideas make the concept of initiation more useful to you and more practical? Any initiation which does not find interpretation in daily reactions is of small service and basically unreal. It is the unreality of its presentation which has led to the rejection of the Theosophical Society as an agent of the Hierarchy at this time. Earlier and prior to its ridiculous emphasis upon initiation and initiates, and prior to its recognition of the probationary disciples as full initiates, the Society did good work. It however failed to recognise mediocrity and to realise that no one "takes" initiation and passes through these crises without a previous demonstration of a wide usefulness and of a trained intelligent capacity. This may not be the case where the first initiation is concerned, but where the second initiation is involved there must ever be the background of a useful dedicated life and an expressed determination to enter the field of *world* service. There must also be humility and a voiced realisation of the divinity in all men. To these requirements, the so-called initiate of the Theosophical Society (with the exception of Mrs. Besant) did not conform. I would not call attention to their prideful demonstration, were it not that the same claims are being made and the same delusions presented to the public.

The problem of freedom from the limitations of matter should now be considered and the entire theme be rendered practical.

There is perhaps an ultimate opinion that it is the realm of the emotions and the susceptibility to emotional reactions which constitute the major human limitation—both from the individual angle and also from that of the national angle. It is everywhere realised that the demagogue, for instance, who sways public opinion, is one who also and emphatically plays on human emotions as well as upon human selfishness. As the race progresses towards mental expression, this distorting influence will become increasingly less important, and once the masses (composed of the millions of so-called "men in the street") begin definitely to think, the power of the demagogic approach will have disappeared. The major battle in the world today is that of the freedom of the average citizen to think for himself and to come to his own decisions and conclusions. It is here that the major quarrel between the Great White Lodge and the Black Lodge is to be found. It is a battle in which humanity itself is the decisive factor, and for this reason the Black Lodge is working through the group which is controlling the destiny of Russia and also through the Zionist movement. The leaders of the U.S.S.R. are working intelligently and potently against human freedom and particularly against freedom of thought. Communism per se has no such objective; it is the totalitarian policies of the national rulers which are so disastrous, plus their ambition and their hatred of true freedom. Zionism today stands for aggression and for the use of force, and the keynote is permission to take what you want ir-

respective of other people or of their inalienable rights.
These points of view are against the position of the spiritual
leaders of humanity, and therefore the leaders of the Zionist movement, and the group of men who direct and control
the policies of Russia, are against the policies of the spiritual
Hierarchy and are contrary to the lasting good of mankind.

The freedom of the human spirit, the freedom to
think, govern and worship as innate, instinctual human
desire may dictate, under the influence of the evolutionary process, the liberty to decide on the required form
of government or of religion—these are the rightful pre-
rogatives of mankind. Any group of men or any form of
government which fails to recognise this inherent right
runs counter to the principle which governs the Great
White Lodge. The menace to world freedom today lies in
the known policies of the rulers of the U.S.S.R. and in the
devious and lying machinations of the Zionists. In neither
group is there any true spiritual potency, and both are
doomed to failure even though they may succeed from the
angle of material gain; from the spiritual angle, they are
doomed. The leaders of the Russian enterprise against the
freedom of the individual are doomed, because inherently
man is free and fundamentally divine, and it is assured
(from the long range vision) that masses of men in Russia
and in the communistically inclined "satellite states" will
inevitably react divinely and potently. The true communistic
platform is sound; it is brotherhood in action and it does
not—in its original platform—run counter to the spirit
of Christ. The imposition of intellectual and formal communism by a group of ambitious and sometimes evil men
is *not* sound; it does not adhere to the true communistic
platform, but is based on personal ambitions, love of power
and on interpretations of the writings of Lenin and Marx
which are also personal and run counter to the meaning
of these two men, just as the theologians of the Church
interpret the words of Christ in a fashion which has no
relation to His original intention. The rulers of Russia are
*not* truly working for the good of the people, any more

than academic Zionism is working and carrying out its projects for any humanitarian reasons. But *the people* hold the ultimate triumph in their hands, for the heart of the people in all nations is basically sound, fundamentally good and God-inclined. This the rulers of the communistic regime forget.

The leaders of the Zionist movement of aggression constitute a real danger to world peace and human development and their activities have been endorsed by the expediency policy of the U.S.A. and, in a secondary degree, by Great Britain, under the influence of the U.S.A. It is the Zionists who have defied the United Nations, lowered its prestige and made its position both negative and negligible to the world. It is the Zionists who have perpetrated the major act of aggression since the formation of the United Nations, and who were clever enough to gain the endorsement of the United Nations, turning the original "recommendation" of the United Nations into an order. The rule of force, of aggression and of territorial conquest by force of arms is demonstrated today by the Zionists in Palestine, as well as the demonstration of the power of money to purchase governments. These activities run counter to all the plans of the spiritual Hierarchy and mark a point of triumph of the forces of evil. I am emphasising the activities of these two countries because through the leaders of these groups of aggressive men the forces of evil —dammed back temporarily by the defeat of the evil group which Hitler gathered around him—have again organised their attack on the spiritual development of humanity.

The world today still remains divided into people of evil intention and great power and their victims, plus the negative reactions of the remaining nations. There is no nation in the United Nations which has attempted to swing the tide of evil by ranging itself and other nations on the side of freedom. There are only groups of unillumined men who seek to control national destinies. There is still emotional reaction to situations and the emotional exploitation of individuals and nations by those who are in no way emotional but who are mentally convinced that certain lines of activity must be followed, leading to their own individual good but which—in the long run—are not good for the peoples involved.

We therefore come back to the problems of the astral plane, of the emotional level of consciousness, and to the second initiation; this initiation releases men from emotional control and enables them to shift their consciousness on to mental levels, and from that higher point of focus to control their normal and well developed emotional attitudes.

If you will turn back to page 340, you will find that the three keynotes are given for this second initiation and for its technique. I would like to call your attention to them because they present those keynotes which give us the clue to the world problems and indicate at the same time the solution and the way out of the present impasse. These three words are: Dedication. Glamour. Devotion.

It is the dedication of the aspirant which invokes the fire. You have here a statement of major importance. The aspirant upon the higher levels of the astral plane is swept by the "fire of dedication." This immediately focusses his will as it demonstrates on the mental plane, and this focussing in due time starts the serious undertaking of the shifting of his consciousness on to mental levels. Then immediately the "fire" works, and the first reaction (as I have earlier pointed out) is the "meeting of fire and water," and consequently the production of fog, mist, of glamour and illusion. All of these four words must be understood symbolically. The glamours thus induced are dependent upon the ray and the point of evolution of the individual and the nation. It is essential that you learn to think in the widest possible terms. With these I shall not deal. Individuals are rapidly discovering the nature of their glamours, once their "spiritual intention" is determined; also national glamour is well recognised by onlookers, though seldom yet by the nations involved. The factor which leads to the dissipation of glamour is devotion—devotion to an individual, to a Master (as taught by the Theosophical Society) or to some idealistic project. It is finally an unlimited devotion to the Way, to the treading of the Path at any cost, and to the unswerving attachment to service—as constituting the major technique of the Path.

Dedication, resulting in glamour, which is dissipated by devotion—these are the keynotes of the second initiation. Forget not that nationalism is the result of dedication to a particular national set-up and produces the glamours which lead to world difficulty.

These three aspects of evolutionary unfoldment must be recognised by every aspirant; their existence determines his place upon the Path, the initiation for which he is being prepared and the nature of his service for humanity.

And what will be the result of the combination in one's life of these three factors? Primarily two things:

1. The solar plexus centre will be brought, first of all, into a condition of almost violent and compelling activity. This activity is induced by dedication and produces glamour inevitably.

2. The violent energies of the solar plexus centre will eventually be controlled by the quality of devotion. It is this quality which transforms the solar plexus centre into *the great clearing house* for all emotional reactions and for all glamours, and makes it temporarily a cause of disaster, of conflict, of pain and of distress.

As a result of both of these, a great transforming agency is set in motion by the quality of devotion, and the solar plexus centre becomes not only a clearing house but the main factor in lifting both physical and emotional active energies from below the diaphragm into the heart centre. This constitutes a long process which the aspirant is forced to face in the interim between initiations. We are told (and it is factually true) that the longest period between initiations is that to be found between the first and the second initiations. This is a truth which must be faced, but it should also be remembered that it is by no means the hardest period. The hardest period for the sensitive, feeling aspirant is to be found between the second and the third initiations.

It is a period of intense suffering, of the penalty of applying factors of glamour and illusion, of pronounced involvement in situations which, for a long time, remain unclarified, and of a steady moving forward as best the beleaguered aspirant can—under the influence of right direction and spiritual determination. This he has usually to do in the dark, working under the action of the logical and understanding mind, but seldom under the influence of inspiration. Nevertheless, the good work goes on. The emotions are brought under control, and necessarily the factor of the mind assumes an increasingly right importance. Light—flickering and as yet uncertain and unpredictable—pours occasionally in from the soul, via the mind, adding frequently to the complications but producing eventually the needed control which will lead to and result in freedom.

Ponder on these things. Freedom is the keynote of the individual who is facing the second initiation and its aftermath—preparation for the third initiation. Freedom is the keynote for the world disciple today, and it is freedom to live, freedom to think and freedom to know and plan, which humanity demands at this time.

The initiation (that of the Transfiguration) which we are next to study is one of the most important of them all. From one particular angle, it is peculiarly related to the fifth Initiation of Revelation and to the seventh Initiation of Resurrection. All three are concerned with freedom: freedom from the personality, freedom from blindness, or freedom from all the seven planes of our planetary existence —the planes which are sometimes referred to as the planes of human and superhuman evolution. You will have noted that lately I have been emphasising an aspect of initiation hitherto little emphasised—the aspect of freedom. The Path of Initiation has at times been called the Path of Liberation, and it is to this essential aspect of the initiatory process that I am seeking to call your attention. I have pointed out continuously that initiation is not really the curious mixture of self-satisfied attainment, ceremonial, and hierarchical recognition as portrayed by the major occult groups. It is far more a process of excessively hard work, during which process the initiate becomes what he is. This may entail hierarchical recognition, but not in the form usually pictured. The initiate finds himself in the company of those who have preceded him, and he is not rejected but is seen and noted and then put to work.

It is also a graded series of liberations, resulting in the attainment of increased freedom from that which lies behind in his experience; this carries with it the permission (soul enjoined or given) to proceed further on the WAY. These freedoms are the result of Detachment, Dispassion, and Discrimination. At the same time Discipline enforces and makes possible the hard work required to pass the grade. All these four techniques (for that is what they are) are preceded by a series of disillusionments which, when realised and comprehended, leave the aspirant no choice but to move forward into greater light.

I would like to have you study initiation from the angle of liberation, looking upon it as a process of strenuously attained freedoms. This basic aspect of initiation—when realised by the initiate—ties his experience into a firm relation with that of the whole of humanity, whose fundamental struggle is the attainment of that freedom "whereby the soul and its powers can unfold and all men be free because of an individually attained freedom."

If you will study the nine initiations and look upon them from this angle, you will see how each does most definitely mark a point of attainment, and therefore the entire subject of initiation takes on a new beauty and appears more worthy of the pain and struggle of attainment. Let me give you an indication (no more than that) of what I mean.

> *Initiation I.*    *Birth.* Freedom from the control of the physical body and its appetites.
>
> *Initiation II.*   *Baptism.* Freedom from the control of

the emotional nature and the selfish sensitivity of the lower self.

*Initiation III.*   *Transfiguration.* Freedom from the ancient authority of the threefold personality, marking a climaxing moment in the history of all initiates.

*Initiation IV.*   *Renunciation.* Freedom from all self-interest, and the renouncing of the personal life in the interest of a larger whole. Even soul-consciousness ceases to be of importance and a more universal awareness, and one closer to the divine Mind, takes its place.

*Initiation V.*   *Revelation.* Freedom from blindness —a liberation which enables the initiate to see a new vision. This vision concerns the Reality lying beyond any hitherto sensed or known.

*Initiation VI.*   *Decision.* Freedom of choice. I have dealt with these choices in an earlier part of this book.

*Initiation VII.*   *Resurrection.* Freedom from the hold of the phenomenal life of the seven planes of our planetary Life. It is in reality a "lifting out of or above" the cosmic physical plane.

*Initiation VIII.*   *Transition.* Freedom from the reaction of consciousness (as that word is understood by you) and a liberation into a state of awareness, a form of conscious recognition which has no relation to consciousness, as you understand that term. It might be regarded as complete freedom from sensitivity, yet with a full flowering of that quality to which we give the inadequate name "compassion." More I cannot say.

*Initiation IX.*   *Refusal.* Freedom from all possible forms of enticement, particularly with reference to the *higher* planes. It must constantly be remembered (and hence my constant reiteration) that our seven planes are the seven subplanes of the cosmic physical plane.

This goal of freedom is in reality the main incentive to tread the Path of Return. One of the most spiritually exciting things taking place in the world today is the use, in every country, of the word FREEDOM; it was that great disciple, F. D. Roosevelt, who "anchored" the word in a new and more universal sense. It now has a fuller and deeper meaning to humanity.

## Initiation III. The Transfiguration

There is no need for me to enter into the symbolic details anent this initiation. The whole theme is adequately dealt with in a book written by A.A.B. entitled *From Bethlehem to Calvary*—a book to which I gave my approval and endorsement as presenting the subject of the five initiations in a form suitable for the Christian West. I would like to recall to you the fact that this third initiation is in reality the first of the major initiations and is so regarded by the emanating Source of our planetary Logos, Sanat Kumara, and in the two great planetary centres, Shamballa and the Hierarchy. I refer to that stupendous Source of our entire planetary life, the sun Sirius, and to the Lodge of Divine Beings Who work from this heavenly Centre.

The first two initiations—regarded simply as initiations of the threshold—are experiences which have prepared the body of the initiate for the reception of the terrific voltage of this third initiation. This voltage is passed through the body of the initiate under the direction of the planetary Logos, before Whom the initiate stands for the first time. The Rod of Initiation is used as the transferring agent. The second initiation freed the initiate from the astral level of consciousness, the astral plane—the plane of glamour, of illusion and of distortion. This was an essential experience because the initiate (standing before the One Initiator for the first time at the third initiation) must be freed from any magnetic or attractive "pull" emanating from the personality.

The mechanism of the personality must be so purified and so insensitive to the material attractions of the three worlds that there is henceforth nothing in the initiate which could offset the divine initiatory activity. The physical appetites are subdued and relegated to their rightful place; the desire nature is controlled and purified; the mind is responsive primarily to ideas, intuitions and impulses coming from the soul, and begins its true task as an interpreter of divine truth and a transmitter of ashramic intention.

You will note, therefore, how this third initiation is a climaxing point and also inaugurates a new cycle of activity leading to the seventh Initiation of Resurrection. I would call your attention to the fact that the third, fifth and seventh initiations are under the control of the fifth, first and second rays. These, as you might expect, will constitute the emanating energies transmitted through the application of the Rod of Initiation.

Initiation III. The fifth Ray of Science. This inflowing energy produces its major effects upon the mind, or upon manas, the fifth principle; it enables the initiate to use the mind as its major instrument in the work to be done, prior to passing through the fourth and fifth initiations.

Initiation V. The first Ray of Will or Power. At this initiation the disciple appreciates for the first time the significance of the will and uses it to relate the head centre and the centre at the base of the spine, thus completing the integration started at the third initiation.

Initiation VII. The second Ray of Love-Wisdom is here active, as the major planetary ray. The application of the Rod of Initiation by the Initiator (working this time from the highest plane, the logoic plane) produces in a

mysterious way an effect on the totality of humanity and—
to a lesser extent—upon the allied kingdoms. The effect is
similar to that produced in the individual at the fifth initiation, wherein the head centre and the centre at the base
of the spine became closely en rapport—through the use
of the will.

Aspirants and disciples should remember that after
the third initiation, *the effects* of the initiation which they
may be undergoing are not confined simply to the individual initiate, but that henceforth at all the later initiations he becomes the transmitter of the energy which will
pour through him with increasing potency at each application of the Rod. He acts primarily as an agent for the
transmission, for the stepping down and for the consequent
safe distribution of energy to the masses. Each time a disciple achieves an initiation and stands before the Initiator,
he becomes simply an instrument whereby the planetary
Logos can reach humanity and bring to men fresh life and
energy. The work done prior to and at the third initiation
is purely preparatory to this type of service required from
an "energy transmitter." That is why, at the seventh initiation, the dominating ray of our planet—the second Ray
of Love-Wisdom—is employed. There is no energy upon
our planet of equal potency, and no expression of it has
so pure and constructive a quality as that to which the
initiate is subjected at the seventh initiation. This seventh
initiatory climax marks another culminating point in the
career of the initiate, and indicates his entrance into an
entirely different cycle of experience.

You will have noted, if you are comparing these instructions with the outline given by me on page 340, that
in this third initiation it is the ajna centre (the centre
between the eyebrows) which is stimulated. This is a fact
of great interest, because it is at this initiation that the
disciple begins consciously and creatively to direct the energies being made available to him, doing so via the ajna
centre and directed towards humanity as a whole. These
energies are:

1. *The energy of his own soul.* This has a purely group effect and though working through his personality, is consciously directed outward into the world—after the transforming process brought about as the energy received permeates his threefold mechanism.

2. *The energy of the Ashram* to which he belongs. Both this energy and the one above mentioned are necessarily the energy of his soul ray and of the Ashram which is representative of that ray. The effect produced—according to his capacity of absorption and direction—will further the working out of the divine Plan.

3. *The energy of the Hierarchy Itself.* The Hierarchy is primarily controlled by the energy of the second Ray of Love-Wisdom, though this dominant ray is modified and enriched through blending with the other six rays. His use of this energy will at first be largely an unconscious use and he will register at this point no definite intention. This is due to the magnitude of the great reservoir of energies; he is a recipient of the incoming energy largely because he is an initiated member of the Hierarchy and is also a pure channel for transmission.

4. *The peculiar energy which is transmitted to him by Sanat Kumara* at the time of his initiation. This is a totally different energy to that transmitted to him at the earlier initiations. It comes from Shamballa and is uniquely (in a sense undefinable and hence incomprehensible to you) the energy of the planetary Logos Himself. He directs extra-planetary energy (in the initiations which follow the third initiation) from the ajna centre of which He is possessed, to the head centre of the initiate and from thence immediately to the ajna centre of the initiate. Then this energy is directed outward into its destined field of service. This energy is of so high a quality that there is nothing of a registering mechanism in the initiate's equipment capable of registering its admission and circulation through his three head centres. Nevertheless, this energy does pour through him and out into the world, in spite of the fact that he remains unconscious of its presence.

The ajna centre is the "centre of direction"; it is placed symbolically between the two eyes, signifying the twofold direction of the life energy of the initiate—outward into the world of men and upward towards the divine Life and Source of all Being. Where the direction of the energy is consciously undertaken (and there are certain energies of which the initiate is constantly aware), the ajna centre is controlled and dominated by the indwelling spirit of man; this spiritual man bases all action in relation to these entering energies on the ancient premise that "energy follows thought." His thought life becomes, therefore, the field of his major effort, for he knows that the mind is the agent of direction; he endeavours to concentrate within himself so that eventually he may consciously control and direct all the incoming divine energies. This is, in reality, the major hierarchical endeavour and the work to which the Masters are pledged and for which They are in constant training. As the evolutionary process proceeds, new and higher energies become available. This is particularly the case now, as They prepare for the reappearance of the Christ.

There are three words which are *directive words* for the disciple as he handles his life, his environment and his circumstances. They are: Integration, Direction, Science. His task—as he faces it after the third initiation—is to produce a greater personal integration so that he becomes increasingly a soul-infused personality, and also to integrate himself with his environment for service purposes. To this must be added the subtler task of integrating himself into the Ashram so that he becomes an integral part of the Master's band of workers.

As the work of integration proceeds, he is striving all the time to learn the uses of the ajna centre and consciously and with right understanding to work with, absorb, transmute and distribute energy as his major ashramic service. His keynote is right direction as the result of right reaction to hierarchical intention and the injunctions of his own soul. Both integration and direction, he discovers, require understanding of occult, scientific knowledge. He works then as a scientist, and for this reason all the three key-notes of his life as an initiate—before and immediately after the third initiation—are conditioned by and directed by the mind; the mental plane becomes the field of his major endeavour as a server.

Again you see that I am presenting you with no glamorous picture of the initiatory process but only one of hard work, constant effort and strenuous mental and spiritual living. There is much here for you to consider, and what I have here given warrants sound reflection and much thought. It is my earnest hope and wish that you may realise that the teaching here given can be appropriated by you and that the initiatory process is one that eventually you will understand and in which you will participate.

### Initiation IV. The Great Renunciation or Crucifixion

This initiation of renunciation (called "The Crucifixion" by Christian believers) is so familiar to the majority of people that I am hard put to it to say that which will arrest your attention, and thus offset a familiarity which necessarily lessens the importance of the theme in your consciousness. The idea of crucifixion is associated in your minds with death and torture, whereas neither concept underlies the true meaning. Let us consider some of the significances connected with this fourth initiation.

The sign of the Cross—associated in the Western world with this initiation and with the Christian faith—is in reality a cosmic symbol, long ante-dating the Christian era. It is one of the major signs to be found in the consciousness of Those advanced Beings Who, from the distant sun, Sirius, the seat of the true Great White Lodge, watch over the destinies of our solar system, but Who pay particular attention (why They do so is not yet revealed) to our relatively little and apparently unimportant planet, the Earth.

The word "crucifixion" comes from two Latin words signifying to "fix on a cross" (I have asked A.A.B. to look this word up in the dictionary so that you can have a sense of surety). The cross referred to in reference to this particular initiation is the *Cardinal Cross of the heavens*. It is to this cross that the disciple shifts at the fourth initiation, from the *Fixed Cross of the heavens*. This fixed cross is the one on which he has been crucified from the moment he found himself upon the Path of Probation and passed from thence on to the Path of Discipleship. On that Path—having transcended the world of phenomena and established an unbroken contact with the Monad, via the antahkarana—he renounces the *Mutable Cross of existence in the three worlds* (the world of appearances), and after a period of time he transfers from that cross on to the Fixed Cross, which is set up in the world of meaning where he has steadily learnt to dwell. This covers the period of the first three initiations. Now, being liberated through renunciation, he needs no longer to undergo the tests, trials, and difficulties which crucifixion on the Fixed Cross inevitably entails; he can now take his place upon the Cardinal Cross, with all its cosmic implications and opportunities which are then conferred. This—as far as the individual is concerned—is necessarily symbolic and figurative in its teaching. As far as the Heavenly Man is concerned, however, the application is not symbolic. It is far more factual. From the angle of the supreme Masters on Sirius, our planetary Logos, Sanat Kumara, is still on the Fixed Cross; He mounted the Mutable Cross in the first solar system; the Fixed Cross still holds Him in this solar system "fixed in His place"; in the next solar system, He will transfer Himself to the Cardinal Cross, and from "thence return to that High Place from whence He came." You can see, therefore, why I emphasise the fact that these three crosses are simply symbols of experience in relation to the individual disciple. Let us consider this a little more closely:

1. *The Mutable Cross* governs the three worlds and the astral plane in particular. On this cross the average man is "crucified" until he achieves the needed experience and consciously reorients himself to another phase of unfoldment.

2. *The Fixed Cross* governs the five worlds of human development and conditions the experiences of all disciples. Through the discipline and the experiences thus gained whilst on this cross, the disciple passes from one renunciation to another until complete freedom and liberation has been achieved.

3. *The Cardinal Cross* governs the Master as He passes through the remaining five initiations; the fourth initiation is, curiously enough, governed by neither the Fixed Cross nor the Cardinal Cross. The disciple is descending from the Fixed Cross and seeking to mount the Cardinal Cross, and it is this transition period and experience which practically govern Him. It might therefore be noted that there are three initiations which test the disciple as to knowledge and experience: the first, the second and the third; then there comes an initiation of transition, followed by five initiations which the Master undergoes upon the Cardinal Cross.

It should be remembered that the distinctive nature of the man upon the Mutable Cross is that of self-consciousness; that the disciple upon the Fixed Cross is rapidly becoming group conscious when the experiences undergone have been rightly assimilated; and that the Master on the Cardinal Cross is distinguished by a universal consciousness which passes finally into cosmic consciousness—a state of being unknown to you, even in the wildest flights of your imagination. The first hint of the growth of cosmic consciousness comes when the disciple passes through the sixth Initiation of Decision. He determines then (by means of His enlightened will and not His mind) which of the seven Paths He will decide to follow. From that time on, the consciousness of the greater Life which enfolds our planetary Logos, as He enfolds humanity within His consciousness, increasingly controls the attitude, the awareness and the activities of the Master.

You can see, therefore, how this initiation of crucifixion (which the Christian world has appropriated for itself) is far vaster in its implications than students suspect.

Yet this appropriation was intentional under the divine Plan of the Hierarchy, for always some great Teacher—by His life and teaching—will call attention to some particular initiation. The Buddha, for instance, in His Four Noble Truths, stated in reality the platform upon which the initiate of the third initiation takes his stand. He desires nothing of a personal nature; he is liberated from the three worlds. The Christ pictured for us and emphasised the fourth initiation with its tremendous transition from the Fixed Cross to the Mount of Ascension, symbol of transition, through initiation.

This crucifixion initiation has a major instructive feature. This is preserved for us in the name which is frequently given to this fourth initiation: the Great Renunciation. One tremendous experience is vouchsafed to the initiate at this time; he realises (because he sees and knows) that the antahkarana has been successfully completed and that there is a direct line of energy from the Spiritual Triad, via the antahkarana, to his mind and brain. This brings to the forefront of his consciousness the sudden and appalling recognition that the soul itself, the egoic body on its own level, and that which for ages has been the supposed source of his existence and his guide and mentor, is no longer needed; his relation, as a soul-infused personality, is now directly with the Monad. He feels bereft and is apt to cry out—as did the Master Jesus—"My God, my God, why hast Thou forsaken me?" But he makes the needed renunciation, and the causal body, the soul body, is relinquished and disappears. This is the culminating renunciation and the climaxing gesture of ages of small renunciations; renunciation marks the career of all aspirants and disciples—renunciation, consciously faced, understood and consciously made.

I have hinted earlier to you that this fourth or Renunciation Initiation is closely linked with the sixth initiation and with the ninth. The sixth initiation is only possible when the initiate has definitely made the needed renunciations; the reward is that he is then permitted to make a perfectly free choice and thus demonstrate his essential and gained freedom. The ninth initiation (that of the Refusal) has in it no element of renunciation. It is not a refusal to hold, for the initiate is at the point where he asks and holds nothing for the separated self. At that final planetary initiation the Master is brought face to face with what might be called cosmic evil, with that reservoir of evil which cyclically overflows the world, and also with the massed group of masters of the Black Lodge. He refuses recognition. This I will deal with later when we take up that particular initiation.

In connection with this Initiation of Renunciation there are some most interesting correspondences which throw a bright, illuminating light upon its significance. They are known to you in some measure, because I have dealt with the significance of the fourth Ray of Harmony through Conflict, and the fourth kingdom, the human, in my earlier writings; it might, however, serve some useful purpose if I bring some of them together and show how this Initiation of Renunciation is of supreme importance to humanity and to the individual initiate who is, of course, a member of the fourth kingdom. First of all, this great act of renunciation marks the moment when the disciple has nothing in him which relates him to the three worlds of human evolution. His contact with those worlds in the future will be purely voluntary and for purposes of service. I prefer the word "renunciation" to the word "crucifixion" because the last word simply emphasises the suffering undergone by the initiate as he renounces all that is of a material nature and becomes a permanent and (if I may use such a term) a non-fluctuating and unchanging member of the fifth kingdom in nature, the kingdom of God, called by us the Hierarchy. Forget not that the three worlds of ordinary evolution constitute the dense physical subplanes of the cosmic physical plane.

Crucifixion embodies the concept of extreme physical suffering of a protracted nature, its last "three hours" according to the Bible story, typifying the three planes of our evolution. On all three planes, the disciple renounces; on all three planes he is, therefore, crucified. It connotes the ending of a life and—from the cosmic angle—of the *personality* life of the soul through many incarnations. If it is a statement of fact that *the time sense* is the response of the brain to a succession of states of consciousness or of events, and if it is equally true that (to the soul) there is no such factor in consciousness as time but only the Eternal Now is known, then the three worlds of incarnated being constitute *one unit of experience in the life of the soul*—an experience which ends at the crucifixion, because the soul in incarnation definitely, consciously and by the use of the enduring will, renounces all, and turns his back upon the material world, finally and for ever. He has mastered all the uses of the three worlds of experiment, experience and expression (to use three terms with which I have familiarised you in my other books), and now stands liberated.

Each initiate who makes this renunciation and undergoes the consequent crucifixion is in a position to say with the first of our humanity to do so, "I, if I be lifted up, will draw all men unto Me." So spoke the Christ. The initiate is lifted up by his renunciation—which he makes through the "blood of the heart"—out of the world of material phenomena, because he has freed himself from any desire for them, from any interest in them and from any hold they may ever have had over him. He is completely detached. It is interesting to note that the Master Jesus underwent the renunciation initiation whilst at the same time the Christ was raised up at the seventh or Resurrection Initiation. So the two stories of these two great Disciples are parallel—One so obediently serving the Greater, and the Christ submitting His will to that of His Father in Heaven.

This initiation is therefore, in a unique sense, a culminating experience and a point of entrance into a new life for which all the past has been a preparation. After the ninth initiation, the Refusal Initiation, there comes a cosmic repetition of the Renunciation experience, this time devoid of the crucifixion aspect; the initiate at that great moment renounces or refuses contact with the cosmic physical plane on all its seven levels of awareness, unless he has chosen (at the sixth Initiation of Decision) the Path of World Service.

During the experience of the initiatory process in its first three phases, the initiate rejects control of the energies which are seated in the three centres below the diaphragm; he renounces their use for personality or selfish reasons. The centre at the base of the spine has received and distributed the energy of self-will (the will of the lower self) and is emptied and stands ready for the dynamic reception of the higher will which—using the spinal channel as the pathway or the symbol of the antahkarana—will pour into it from the highest head centre. The sacral centre which has received and distributed the energy which has fed the physical appetites to a far greater extent than is at present realised, is also under control—a control which is related to normal and proper direction from the throat centre and to the preservation of life on the physical plane, if the initiate chooses to incarnate for service ends. The solar plexus centre, which has received and distributed the energy of the astral plane, the energy of desire and of emotion, is likewise cleansed and purified; its energy is transmuted to such an extent that it can pass under the complete control of the heart centre, which henceforth and until the seventh Initiation of the Resurrection is "that whereby the initiate performs his hierarchical obligations." Therefore, at the Great Renunciation, the three lower centres reach a point of utter purification or speaking symbolically —of utter emptiness. No energy of their own (related to the selfish aeonial past) is left; they are simply pure receptacles for the energies of the three higher centres. The three lower centres are related to the three worlds of personality evolution; the three higher centres are related to hierarchical work and living and are under the control of the initiate—a control which becomes increasingly perfect until the seventh Initiation of Resurrection. At that momentous resurrection, they become no longer of service; the Master needs no energy centres, and His consciousness is transcended and transformed into a type of awareness of which those who have not experienced these initiations know nothing. If He chooses to take a physical vehicle (as many will when the Christ reappears and the Hierarchy is externalised on Earth), the Master will "function from the above to the below" and not (as is the case today with all disciples, though naturally not with the Masters) on "the below towards the above." I am here quoting ancient phrases to be found in the archives of the Hierarchy. They will therefore need no centres on the etheric levels of our planetary physical plane.

At this fourth initiation the initiate begins to function entirely and always upon the fourth plane, the buddhic levels of the cosmic physical plane—our intuitional plane. This is the case whether you count from below upwards or from above downwards. You have here again an indication of *the central position of this initiation* and of its importance. It is preceded by three initiations and succeeded by three initiations, leading up to that of the seventh or final planetary initiation, because the remaining two initiations are fundamentally not related in any way to our planetary Life. It is because of this permanent transition of the initiate's "living focus"—lifted out of the three worlds on to the buddhic plane—that the concept of resurrection has crept into the Christian teaching so that the Crucifixion Initiation is portrayed as preceding the Resurrection Initiation; this is in reality not the case, except in a lesser degree and as symbol of future experience.

In the same way, the concept of sacrifice has permeated all the teaching anent the Crucifixion or the Renunciation Initiation, both in the East and in the West. This is a sacrifice idea associated with the concept of pain, agony, suffering, patience, prolongation and death. Yet the true root of the word remains the same and gives the true significance: "Sacer," to make holy; that is what in truth happens to the initiate; he is "made holy"; he is "set apart" for spiritual development and service. He is separated off from that which is natural, material, transmitted and handicapping, trammelling and destructive, and from that which lessens right activity for that which is new. He learns to define the Wholeness which is his divine right and prerogative.

The beauty of the interpretation of this initiation and the reward to those who attempt to penetrate to its true meaning and significance are untold; it requires, however, the teaching of the East and of the West to arrive at the true understanding of the experience. The concept of a clean break with the old life in the three worlds of experience which has characterised the work of the soul for so long is obvious. It is death in its truest and most useful form; every death, as it takes place today and on the physical plane, is therefore symbolic in nature, pointing to the time when the soul finally "dies" to all that is material and physical, just as the human being dies to all contact in the three worlds before resuming incarnated living.

On the buddhic or intuitional plane (the fourth level of the cosmic physical plane) the mind nature—even that of the higher mind or the level of abstract thought—loses its control over the initiate and is henceforth only useful in service. The intuition, the pure reason, complete knowledge illumined by the loving purpose of the divine Mind— to mention some of the names of this fourth level of awareness or of spiritual sensitivity—takes its place and the initiate lives henceforth in the light of correct or straight knowledge, expressing itself as wisdom in all affairs—hence the titles of Master of the Wisdom or Lord of Compassion given to Those Who have taken the fourth and the fifth initiations; these follow very closely upon each other. From the buddhic level of awareness, the Master works; on it, He lives His life, undertakes His service and furthers the Plan in the three worlds and for the four kingdoms in nature. Let this not be forgotten. Also, let it be remembered that this achievement of focus and this attained freedom are *not* the result of a symbolic ceremony, but are the result of lives of suffering, of minor renunciations and of *conscious* experience. This conscious experience, leading to the fourth initiation, is *a definitely planned undertaking,* arrived at as true vision is gradually conferred, the divine Plan is sensed and receives cooperation, and intelligent aspiration takes the place of vague longings and sporadic efforts "to be good," as it is normally expressed by aspirants.

It will be clear to you, therefore, why this fourth initiation is ruled or governed by the fourth Ray of Harmony through Conflict. The harmonising of the lower centres with the higher, the harmonising or establishing of right relations between the three worlds of human evolution and the buddhic plane, the rapport gradually being brought about by each succeeding initiation, between humanity and the Hierarchy, plus the service of establishing right human relations among men—these are some of the results which you even now grasp theoretically; these you will also grasp practically and substantially one day in your own experience. It is with this ray energy that the initiate works as he makes the Great Renunciation and is transferred thereby to the Cardinal Cross of the Heavens. This is the energy which enables him to live in the Eternal Now and to renounce the bindings of time. Through the entire experience he fights against that which is material; under the law of our planet (and, if you only knew, under the law of our solar system) nothing is achieved except by struggle and conflict—struggle and conflict associated on our planet with pain and suffering but which, after this fourth initiation, is devoid of suffering. A hint as to the purpose for which our little planet exists and its unique position in the scheme of things can here be noted.

As I mentioned earlier, the initiate now works from "above downwards." This is only a symbolic mode of speech. Like his great Master, the Christ, when he seeks to serve humanity he "descends into hell" which is the hell of materialism and of physical plane life, and there labours for the furtherance of the Plan. We read in the Christian teaching that "Christ descended into hell and taught the spirits which are in prison" for three days. This means that He worked with humanity in the three worlds (for time and the process of events are regarded by philosophers as synonymous in meaning) for a brief period of time, but was called (on account of His unique task of embodying for the first time in world history the love principle of divinity) to be the Head of the Hierarchy.

The same concept of working in the three worlds of physical plane existence (in the cosmic sense) is embodied for us in the phrase found in the New Testament that *"the veil of the temple was rent in twain from the top to the bottom."* This is the veil which, symbolically speaking, divides or shuts off humanity from participation in the kingdom of God. This was rent by the Christ—an unique service which He rendered both to humanity and to the spiritual Hierarchy; He made it easier for a much quicker communication to be set up between those two great centres of divine life.

I would ask you to ponder this Initiation of Renunciation, remembering ever in your daily life that this process of renunciation, entailing the crucifixion of the lower self, is only made possible by the practice of detachment every day. The word "detachment" is only the Eastern term for our word "renunciation." That is the practical use of such information which I have here given to you. I would ask you also (curious as it may seem) to *get used to crucifixion,* if you care to use that word; to permit yourself to get accustomed to suffering with detachment, knowing that the soul suffers not at all, and that there is no pain or agony for the Master Who has attained liberation. The Masters have each and all renounced that which is material; They have been lifted out of the three worlds by Their Own effort; They have detached Themselves from all hindrances; They have left hell behind and the term "spirits that are in prison" no longer applies to Them. This They have done for no selfish purpose. In the early days of the Probationary Path, selfish aspiration is foremost in the consciousness of the aspirant; however, as he treads the path, and likewise the Path of Discipleship, he leaves all such motives behind (a minor renunciation) and his one aim, in seeking liberation and freedom from the three worlds, is to aid and help humanity. This dedication to service is the mark of the Hierarchy.

You can see, therefore, how the Buddha prepared the way for the Initiation of Renunciation or of Crucifixion by His teaching and His emphasis upon detachment. Think on these things and study the great continuity of effort and cooperation which distinguishes the Members of the spiritual Hierarchy. My prayer and wish is that your goal may be clear to your vision and that the "strength of your heart" may be adequate to the undertaking.

*Initiation V. The Revelation*

As we undertake the consideration of the next initiation, you will find that three factors will emerge in a new light in your consciousness. That they are factors related to past experiences, and yet which have reference to experiences which lie far ahead of you upon the Path, will also be inferred from what I say; these will not necessarily meet with your real understanding. These factors are:

The factor of Blindness, leading to revelation.

The factor of the Will, producing synthesis.

The factor of the Purpose, externalising itself through the Plan.

These are all implicit in this new initiatory experience, but they should be approached by you with as much use of the intuition as you can employ; your effort will have to be that you endeavour to think *as if* you had taken the higher initiations. You have to bear in mind that each initiation enables the initiate to "see ahead" a little further, for revelation is always a constant factor in human experience. The whole of life is revelation; the evolutionary process is, in relation to consciousness, a process of leading the blind out of darkened areas of consciousness into greater light, and therefore into a vaster vision.

As you know, this particular initiation has been called the "Resurrection" by the Christian world, emphasising that aspect in the experience of the initiate which leads to revelation; i.e., his "rising out of the ocean of matter into the clear light of day." The thought of revelation can be seen also in the Christian teaching anent the "Ascension" —an initiation which has no factual existence and should not be called an initiation. You have, therefore, the following sequence, connected with the fourth and fifth initiations:

1. Renunciation, producing crucifixion and leading to
2. Ascension, or a complete "rising out of," or "mounting higher," leading to
3. Revelation, giving vision, the reward of the two above stages.

Christian theologians have made three distinct episodes out of these two initiations, but this has in no way mattered (as the initiate in the West soon learns); he now knows that the whole series of initiations, with their causes, their effects and their resultant intentions are only a sequence of processes, leading from the one to the other. A corresponding sequence can be seen in the unfoldment of the consciousness of the human being from infancy to full maturity; each unfoldment is part of a series of revelations, as his vision of life and his capacity to experience develops. This is true of all men from the most primitive to the advanced initiate, the difference consisting in that which each brings to the experience as the result of past effort, his point in consciousness and the quality of the vehicles through which that consciousness is developing. With the initiate-disciple this is also the case; he enters *consciously* into each experience; they are *integral parts of his intention.*

Having renounced the three worlds, and having returned—back from a contact of great importance and interest—to those three worlds and with all that is familiar in them, the initiate suddenly realises that he has indeed been liberated, that he is indeed free, that he has been raised out of darkness and is now free in a new world of experiences.

He knows that he has climbed to the mountain-top or has "ascended" to the buddhic plane, from which plane he must permanently work and not just occasionally, as has been the method hitherto.

He can work through a physical body (with its subtler sheaths) or not, as he sees fit. He realises that he, as an individual, no longer needs a physical body or an astral consciousness, and that the mind is only a *service instrument*. The body in which he now functions is a body of light which has its own type of substance. The Master, however, can build a body through which He can approach His incoming disciples and those who have not taken the higher initiations; He will normally build this body in semblance of the human form, doing so instantaneously and by an act of the will, when required. The majority of the Masters who are definitely working with humanity either preserve the old body in which They took the fifth initiation or else They build the "mayavirupa" or body of maya, of physical substance. This body will appear in the original form in which They took initiation. This I personally did in reference to the first case; i.e., preserving the body in which I took initiation. This the Master K.H. did in creating a body which was made in the form in which He took the fifth initiation.

It may interest you to know that the Christ has not yet decided what type of physical vehicle He will employ should He take physical form and work definitely upon the physical plane. He waits to see what nation or group of nations do the most work, and the most convincing work, in preparation for His reappearance. He will *not,* however, take a Jewish body as He did before, for the Jews have forfeited that privilege. The Messiah for Whom they wait will be one of Christ's senior disciples, but it will *not* be, as originally intended, the Christ. Symbolically, the Jews represent (from the point of view of the Hierarchy) that from which all Masters of the Wisdom and Lords of Compassion emerge: materialism, cruelty and a spiritual conservatism, so that today they live in *Old Testament* times and are under the domination of the separative, selfish, lower concrete mind.

But their opportunity will come again, and they may change all this when the fires of suffering at last succeed in purifying them and burning away their ancient crystal-lisation, thus liberating them to the extent that they can recognise their Messiah, Who will *not*, however, be the world Messiah. The Jews need humility more than any other nation. By humility they may learn something of value as well as a needed sense of proportion. They are dear to the heart of the Christ for—in the performance of His great-est work—He chose a Jewish body, but their materialism and their repudiation of spiritual opportunity has negated His use of their racial type again. It would provide too great a handicap. The probability is that the Master Jesus will assume (under instruction from the Christ) the part of the Messiah.

The Master, standing symbolically upon the Mount of Ascension, is equipped with a full realisation of the past, with a sound appreciation of what He has to offer to the service of humanity, and with a sense of expectancy. During the preceding cycle of lives of initiatory service to humanity, He has several times heard "the Voice of the Father." This is a symbolical phrase, indicating contact with that aspect of himself which was responsible for the appearance of his soul and for its long, long cycle of incarnation: the Monad, the Spirit, the One, the Life, the Father. Each time that that Voice spoke, it gave him recognition. It is in reality the voice of the Initiator in Whom we live and move and have our being. All of the Master's previous visions have led Him to this high point of expectancy; He knows now where His field of service lies—within the Hierarchy, work-ing on behalf of all living beings. He knows also that He Himself has still to make progress, to move forward, and that there faces Him a great Initiation of Decision (the sixth) for which He must prepare. He knows that this entails for Him *right choice*, but also that right choice depends upon right understanding, right perception, right willingness and right vision or revelation. So He stands again upon the mountain-top, awaiting again the Presence. He realises that something more is needed if He is to serve rightly and, simultaneously, make spiritual progress Himself.

It is not possible for me here to indicate the nature of the revelation which is accorded to the initiate of the fifth initiation. It is too closely related to Shamballa, and I have not myself done more this life than take the fifth initiation and climb the Mount of Ascension. The revelation for me is not completed and—in any case—my lips are sealed. I can, however, take up two points with you which may clarify your vision. I would remind you again that what I am here writing in this last volume of *A Treatise on the Seven Rays* is written for disciples and initiates. Disciples will see some of the significances behind the symbol and will make interpretations according to the point they have attained upon the Path. You need to remember that the world of men today is full of those who have taken one or other of the initiations and that there are great disciples, from all the rays, working on the physical plane as senior workers for humanity under the Hierarchy; there will be many more during the next one hundred years. (Written in 1949.) Some of these do not know their particular hierarchical status in their physical brains, having deliberately relinquished this knowledge in order to do certain work. That which I here write is intended—during the next forty years—to find its way into their hands with the deliberate intent of bringing to the surface of their brain consciousness who and what they are in truth. This is a part of the programme planned by the Hierarchy, prior to the externalisation of the Ashrams. The Masters feel that these senior disciples and initiates (being on the spot) should soon begin to work with more authority. This does not mean that they will assert their spiritual identity and claim initiate status. This they could not do on account of their point on the ladder of spiritual evolution. But—knowing who they are from the angle of the Hierarchy and what is expected of them—they will strengthen their work, bring in more energy, and point the way with greater clarity. Their wisdom will be recognised as well as their compassion, but they themselves will recede into the background; they may even appear to be less active outwardly, and so be misjudged, but their spiritual influence will be growing; they care not what others think about them. They recognise also the mistaken views of all the modern religions anent the Christ; some may even be persecuted in their homes or by those they seek to help. None of this will matter to them. Their way is clear and their term of service is known to them.

The two points with which I shall now deal are as follows:

1. The part which energy plays in inducing revelation.
2. The place the Will plays in the revelatory sequence: Revelation. Interpretation. Intention. Will.

These must be looked at from the angle of discipleship and are not to be considered on their face value or in the ordinary manner. They must be approached from the angle of the world of meaning and, if possible, from the world of significances; otherwise, the teaching will be so exoteric that its occult nature will not appear.

*The Part which Energy plays in inducing Revelation*

You will get a hint as to what I have to say if you will refer back to an earlier statement (page 534). There you will find the inference that three energies are necessary for the initiate to employ if he seeks revelation; no matter what the revelation may be or the status of the disciple or the initiation he faces, these same three energies will be brought into play. They are:

a. The energy generated by the disciple.
b. The energy coming from the Spiritual Triad.
c. The energy of the Ashram with which he is affiliated.

These are the three essential energies and without their synthesis in the disciple's mind or in one of the three higher centres, there can be no true revelation of the higher order or related to the processes of initiation.

In connection with *the energy generated by the disciple,* it will be obvious that this will include the energy of the soul ray, until the fifth initiation when it will be superseded by the energy of the Monad. This will reach him, first of all, as the energy of the Spiritual Triad, and later that (in its turn) will be superseded by the direct energy of the Monad itself; the initiate will then know practically (and not just theoretically) what Christ meant when He said, "I and my Father are one."

In the earlier stages on the Path of Discipleship, the disciple works with that measure of the energy of his soul ray to which he can be receptive, plus as much of the energy of the personality ray as is responsive to that soul energy. In doing this a great measure of discrimination can be developed, and it is one of the first places where the value of the injunction, "Know thyself" can be seen. The nature of the soul ray at this time determines the nature of the revelation; the nature of the personality and its ray is, at the same time, either helpful or a hindrance.

To the energies which he has generated within himself the disciple learns to add that of the group which he has attempted to serve with love and understanding. All disciples of any standing gather around them the few or the many that they have found themselves able to aid; the purity of the energy generated by this group depends upon their selflessness, their freedom from authority or the control of the disciple, and the quality of their spiritual aspiration. As the disciple or the Master has helped them to generate this energy, and as all will necessarily synchronise with his, it becomes available as a pure stream of force, flowing through him at all times. This he can learn to focus and incorporate with his own energy (also focussed) in order to prepare himself for further vision, *provided* always that his motive is likewise selfless.

The second group of energies are those *coming to the disciple from the Spiritual Triad.* These are relatively new

to him and embody divine qualities of which he has
hitherto known nothing; even theoretically he knows little,
and his attitude towards them has hitherto been largely
speculative. Since he first put his foot upon the Path, he
has been trying to build the antahkarana. Even that has
meant for him an act of faith, and he proceeds in the early
stages with the work of building, yet scarcely knowing what
he does. He follows blindly the ancient rules and attempts
to accept as factual that which has not been proven to him
to be a fact but which is testified to by countless thousands
down the ages. The whole process is in the nature of a
culminating triumph of that innate sense of Deity which
has driven man forward from the most primitive experiences
and physical adventures to this great adventure of constructing a pathway for himself from the dense material
world into the spiritual. These higher spiritual energies
have hitherto been recognised by him through their effects;
now he has to learn to handle them, first of all, by letting
them pour into and through him, via the antahkarana, and
then to direct them towards the immediate objective of the
divine plan.

Hitherto he has worked primarily with the thread of
consciousness; this is anchored in the head, and through
that consciousness his personality and his soul are linked
together until he has become a soul-infused personality;
he has then attained unity with his higher self. Through
the building of the antahkarana another thread is added
to the soul-infused personality, and the true spiritual individual is linked with and comes under the direction of the
Spiritual Triad. At the fourth initiation the soul body, the
causal body (so called) disappears, and the thread of consciousness is occultly snapped; neither the soul body nor
the thread are any longer required; they become now only
the symbols of a non-existent duality. The soul is no longer
the repository of the consciousness aspect as hitherto. All
that the soul has stored up of knowledge, science, wisdom
and experience (garnered in the life cycle of many aeons of
incarnation) are now the sole possession of the individual

spiritual man. He transfers them into the higher correspondence of the sensory perceptive apparatus, the instinctual nature, on the three planes of the three worlds.

Nevertheless he still possesses awareness of all past events and knows now why he is what he is; much of the information anent the past he discards; it has served its purpose, leaving him with the residue of experienced wisdom. His life takes on a new colouring, totally unrelated to the three worlds of his past experience. He, the sum total of that past, faces new spiritual adventures, and has now to tread the Path which leads him away from normal human evolution on to the Way of the Higher Evolution. This new experience he is well equipped to face.

Three major energies begin to make an impact upon his lower mind. They are:

1. *The impulsive energy of ideas,* coming to him from the abstract mind and travelling along the antahkarana; these make contact with his now illumined lower mind which, at this point, transforms them into ideals so that the divine ideas—implementing the divine purpose—may become the heritage of the race of men. The better trained and the more controlled the mind, the easier it will be to handle this type of energy. It is by means of this impulsive energy that the Hierarchy (upon the buddhic plane) leads humanity onwards.

2. *The energy of the intuition,* which is the word we use to describe a direct contact with the Mind of God at some relatively high level of experience. The effect of this energy upon the soul-infused personality is to give to the mind (already receptive to the energy of ideas) some faint glimmering and brief revelation of the purpose of the ideas which underlie all hierarchical activity on behalf of humanity. The intuition is entirely concerned with group activity; it is never interested in or directed to the revelation of anything concerned with the personality life. The growth of what we might call the buddhic vehicle (though that is a misnomer) prepares the man for the ninth or the final initiation, which enables the initiate—in a manner incom-

prehensible to us—to "intuit" (in a blazing light) the true nature of the cosmic astral plane. Forget not, the buddhic plane is closely allied with the cosmic astral plane, and that all intuitions when regulated require the use of the creative imagination in their working out or in their presentation to the thoughts of men. Speaking generally, the Masters intuit those phases of the divine intention which are immediate; these constitute the "overshadowing cloud of knowable things." These They transform into the Plan; then Their disciples—with their intuitional capacity developing slowly but steadily—begin themselves to intuit these ideas, to present them as ideals to the masses, and thus precipitate the needed aspects of the Plan on to the physical plane.

3. *The dynamic energy of the will* follows next, and (as the disciple perfects the antahkarana) it sweeps through the medium of contact into the mind of the soul-infused personality, and from thence it finds its way to the brain. I am of course referring here to the disciple in training and not to the Masters Themselves Who work at the centre of these energies; the Hierarchy is a great reception point for these three aspects of the Spiritual Triad—the spiritual will, the intuition or pure reason, and the abstract mind.

It is in the Ashrams of the Masters that the disciple comes into direct relation with these dynamic, revealing and impulsive energies. These three energies focus through and are directed by the three Heads of the Hierarchy: the Manu, the Christ, and the Mahachohan. The Manu is receptive to, and the agent of, the energy of the divine will for humanity; the Christ is the agent for the distribution of the energy which brings intuitive revelation; the Mahachohan is responsible for the inflow of ideas into the consciousness of the disciple, the aspirant and the intelligentsia. I would beg you to remember that the main effort of the spiritual Hierarchy is on behalf of humanity, because the fourth Kingdom in Nature is the Macrocosm of the threefold Microcosm of the three lower kingdoms in nature.

This whole subject is too vast to be entered into here,

but I have given you much along these lines in *A Treatise on Cosmic Fire*. Much more than I can possibly give you is revealed to the initiate at the time of the fifth initiation. The clues, the thoughts, the abstract concepts, the fleeting ideas of which all disciples are aware are at this initiation resolved into certainty, and the Master can now take His place as a distributor of Triadal energy. The major problem confronting Him is not the distribution of ideas or the use of the intuition in grasping the stage of the divine Purpose at any particular time; it consists in the development of the spiritual will, in its comprehension and its use in world service. Just as the disciple has to learn to use the mind in two ways:

> As a commonsense, a resolver of information so that a life pattern and a life service, planned and directed, may eventuate, and a perception of relationships,

> As a searchlight, bringing into the light those ideas and intuitions which are needed,

so the Master has to learn the uses of the will. A natural sequence can be seen closely related to the idea of revelation.

On the mountain-top of Ascension, following the experience of "teaching the spirits which are in prison," the Master receives a revelation; this is His right and due and something for which the long previous cycle of initiation has prepared Him. The revelation must be followed by realisation and recognition:

> 1. He realises that the right interpretation of the revelation is the first essential.
> 2. He then comes to the understanding that the next step is for Him to formulate His *intention,* based upon the revelation and directed towards His world service.
> 3. Having received the revelation, interpreted it and determined within Himself what He intends to do, He next realises that the factor of the will must now be employed if He and those He seeks to help are to profit by the revelation.

This opens up the whole subject of the Will, its nature and relationships and this we must study for a while: the sequence of Revelation. Interpretation. Intention. Will.

*The Place that the Will plays in inducing Revelation*

There are three words connected with this initiation which are of real importance to its correct understanding. They are: Emergence. Will. Purpose. With the emergence aspect we have already dealt under the term "raising up" or the "transition" from the darkness of matter to the light of the Spirit. But of the Will, its uses and its function, as yet we know little. Knowledge as to the nature of the will in any true sense only comes after the third initiation. From that time on the initiate demonstrates increasingly and steadily the first divine aspect, that of the Will and the right use of Power. This first aspect of divinity is necessarily closely associated with the first Ray of Power or Will. I shall, however, only consider the ray angle incidentally, for I want to elucidate for you the nature of the will in some clear measure, though complete understanding is not possible.

The Lord of the World is, we are told, the sole repository of the will and the purpose of His overshadowing, cosmic soul. These two words — will and purpose — are not identical in meaning. Sanat Kumara and His Council at Shamballa are the only Beings upon our planet Who know just what is the nature of the divine purpose. It is Their function and obligation to work that purpose out into manifestation, and this They do by the use of the will. *The will ever implements the purpose.* The repository of the will aspect of man's innate divinity is to be found at the base of the spine; this can only function correctly and be the agent of the divine will after the third initiation. The head centre is the one which is the custodian of the purpose; the centre at the base of the spine indicates the will as it implements the purpose. The purpose is slowly, very slowly, revealed to the initiate during the final five initiations and this only becomes possible after the Initiation of Renunciation. At that time the initiate says, in unison with the great head of the Hierarchy, the Christ: "Father, not my will but Thine be done." Then comes the initiation of emergence out of matter and, from that point on, the initiate begins to glimpse the purpose of the planetary Logos; hitherto he has only seen the plan, and to the service of the plan he has been dedicated. Hitherto also, he has only sought to be an exponent of the love of God; now he must express, with increasing fullness, the will of God.

Earlier in these pages (Page 410) we are told that the problem which confronts the Hierarchy as it seeks to prepare disciples for the successive initiations is the right use of the will, both Their Own use of the will in relation to the initiate, and the initiate's use of the will as he works for the Plan as that Plan implements Purpose. To produce this, a direct, understanding and powerful expression of this first aspect is demanded. There are several reasons why the will presents a problem. Let us list a few of them and thereby get understanding.

1. This energy of the will is the most potent energy in the whole scheme of planetary existence. It is called the "Shamballa Force," and it is that which holds all things together in life. It is, in reality, life itself. This life force or divine will (implementing divine intention) is that by means of which Sanat Kumara arrives at His goal. On a tiny scale, it is the use of one of the lowest aspects of the will (human self-will) which enables a man to carry out his plans and attain his fixed purpose—if he has one. Where the will is lacking, the plan dies out and the purpose is not achieved. Even in relation to self-will, it is veritably the "life of the project." The moment Sanat Kumara has attained His planetary purpose, He will withdraw this potent energy, and (in this withdrawing) destruction will set in. This Shamballa force is steadily held in leash for fear of too great an impact upon the unprepared kingdoms in nature. This has reference to its impact also upon humanity.

You have been told that this force has—during this century—made its first direct impact upon humanity; heretofore, it reached mankind in the three worlds after being stepped down and modified by transit through the great planetary centre to which we give the name of the Hierarchy. This direct impact will again take place in 1975, and also in the year 2000, but the risks will then not be so great as in the first impact, owing to the spiritual growth of mankind. Each time this energy strikes into the human consciousness some fuller aspect of the divine plan appears. It is the energy which brings about synthesis, which holds all things within the circle of the divine love. Since its impact during the past few years, human thinking has been more concerned with the production of unity and the attainment of synthesis in all human relations than ever before, and one result of this energy has been the forming of the United Nations.

2. It will be apparent to you, therefore, that this energy is the agent for the revelation of the divine purpose. It may surprise you that this is regarded as presenting a problem to the Hierarchy, but if this power—impersonal and potent—should fall into the hands of the Black Lodge, the results would be disastrous indeed. Most of the members of this centre of cosmic evil are upon the first ray itself, and some of the divine purpose is known to a few of them, for —in their due place and in the initiatory regime—they too are initiates of high degree, but dedicated to selfishness and separativeness. Their particular form of selfishness is far worse than anything which you can imagine, because they are completely detached and divorced from all contact with the energy to which we give the name of love. They have cut themselves off from the spiritual Hierarchy, through Whom the love of the planetary Logos reaches the forms in the three worlds and all that is contained therein. These evil but powerful beings know well the uses of the will, but only in its destructive aspect.

We have spoken much of the purpose of the planetary Logos. When I use the word "purpose" I am indicating the answer to the question: Why did the planetary Logos create this world and start the evolutionary, creative process? Only one answer has as yet been permitted to be given. Sanat Kumara has created this planet and all that moves and lives therein in order to bring about a planetary synthesis and an integrated system whereby a tremendous solar revelation can be seen. Having said that, we have not really penetrated any distance into the meaning of the divine purpose; we have only indicated the method whereby it is being attained, but the true objective remains still an obscure mystery—guarded rigidly in the Council Chamber of Sanat Kumara. It is this mystery and this divine planetary "secret" which is the goal of all the work being done by the Black Lodge. They are not yet sure of the purpose, and all their efforts are directed to the discovery of the nature of the mystery. Hence the hierarchical problem.

3. It is this energy of the will, rightly focussed, that enables the senior Members of the Hierarchy to implement that purpose. Only initiates of a certain standing can receive this energy, focus it within the Hierarchy, and then direct its potency to certain ends known only to Them. Speaking symbolically, the Hierarchy has within it, under the custody of its most advanced Members, what might be called a "reservoir of divine intention." It is the higher correspondence of that to which Patanjali refers under the words, "the raincloud of knowable things" which hovers over the head of all disciples who can see somewhat in the Light. Just as advanced humanity can precipitate the rain of knowledge from this cloud of knowable things (the divine ideas, working out as intuitions in all the many areas of human thinking), so the lesser initiates and disciples within the Hierarchy can begin to precipitate into their consciousness some of this "divine intention." It is this reservoir of power which embodies some of the Purpose and implements the Plan. One of the problems of the Hierarchy is, therefore, right timing in the revelation of divine intention and in the direction of the thinking and the planning done in Their Ashrams by the recipients: initiates and disciples.

Again we come back to the same necessity for right interpretation of the revelation or of the vision.

4. The problem is also one that each Master has to face in connection with His Own spiritual development, for this energy is the needed dynamic or potency which enables Him to tread the Way of the Higher Evolution. On the way to liberation and in treading the Path of Discipleship and the Path of Initiation, the human being has to use the dynamic or the potency of the Love of God; on the Way of the Higher Evolution, it must be the dynamic and the potency of Will.

I would ask you all, therefore, to ponder on the distinction which exists between:

1. Self-will . . . . . . . . . . . . . 2. Determination
3. Fixity of purpose  . . . . . . . . 4. The will
5. The spiritual will  . . . . . . . 6. The divine will

I shall not attempt to discuss these words with you. They each indicate a certain aspect of the will; you will learn more on this point by doing your own thinking and defining.

All that I can hope and pray is that your individual will can be merged into the divine will, that revelation will be increasingly yours, and that you will with increased steadfastness tread the Path from darkness to light and from death to immortality.

## Initiation VI. The Decision

We have been studying along three lines which, in spite of the unavoidable abstruseness of the subject, have meant much to the earnest individual disciple because the words used to express the initiations concerned have been: Renunciation. Ascension. Revelation. All these convey practical and useful concepts to the mind, and yet—at the same time—their true meaning involves a detachment, a divine indifference and the spiritual perception of which no disciple has had more than a glimpse and a dim sensing of possibility. I then lifted these three ideas on to wider levels and endeavoured to show how the crises through which humanity is today passing and will continue to pass during the next fifty years (though with lessening effects of discomfort, if right attitude is assumed) can also be related to these three words. I do not wish you to infer that mankind is, in fact, undergoing these initiatory experiences. The renunciation is being *imposed* by circumstances and is not a free undertaking; the moving onward is the result of a somewhat inchoate and uncontrolled momentum and is not the effort of a liberated soul. The revelation which is to come will be the result of hierarchical activity, focussed through the Christ, though not presented by His coming; it will come as a result of His work and hierarchical activity.

All these initiations have their lower correspondences, and the one we are to consider at this time is no exception; all of them can appeal to the aspirant as embodying for him some immediate goal, but the concept is only preparatory in its nature; this can be illustrated by pointing out that the Great Renunciation becomes possible because, for many lives, the disciple has learnt to renounce and—when treading the Path of Initiation—to renounce *consciously* and with a formulated purpose. In the same manner, the sixth Initiation of Decision also becomes possible because the initiate has, since his affiliation with the Hierarchy, learnt to make right choice, and his ability to do that emerges out of his effort whilst on the Probationary Path and on the earlier stages of the Path of Discipleship to make correct choices and spiritually motivated decisions. I am pointing this out because, as we now begin to study the final four initiations (which are far beyond the understanding of even the advanced disciple), it will not be waste of time; in spite of a lack of true comprehension, qualities and attributes and certain needed lessons will be indicated to the true aspirant, and these he can *now* begin to develop.

I would like first of all to point out that the sixth initiation is to the Master Who stands before the planetary Logos what the second initiation is to the disciple; the fifth Initiation of Revelation and the sixth Initiation of Decision are the higher correspondences to the first two initiations which are regarded by the Lodge on Sirius as initiations of the

Threshold. Have this carefully in mind. Much earlier in this treatise (page 361) I made the comment that the second initiation with its evidenced control of desire (indicating right choice) was "the threshold . . . to those levels of impression, of contact and of future ascension which are the sevenfold goal set before the Master when the sixth initiation (the true ascension) is consummated. It is for this reason that this initiation is called the Initiation of Decision."

This is a point of real interest and of practical value; it reveals in a new sense and quite definitely that all happenings on our planet are in truth simply preparatory to other much greater events and opportunities. They put the Master or the Chohan (we seem to have no word to express the type of consciousness of the initiate who has taken the five initiations of strictly human evolution) in a position where at each initiation He expresses the sum total of all past attainment. His entire past is involved in what He demonstrates. This is not consciously so. All that He is or knows has dropped below the threshold of consciousness, in the same way that the instinctual nature of man is today automatic and spontaneous and not consciously used. In spite of this subjective activity, men are nevertheless in full possession of a definite part of their equipment. So it is with the Master; all that He has been in the spiritual sense and in wisdom, perception and full comprehension is now instinctual, and the powers, knowledges, attributes involved are instantaneously His without effort or conscious activity. He can depend fully upon what He is and has, and—as a result of initiation—He is free from the questionings, the doubts and the uncertainties which are so distinctive of the disciple.

Earlier (page 396) I pointed out that the Masters, at the sixth Initiation of Decision, face realms of service where They will have to "impart, strengthen and enlighten that which is already fused, already strong, and already full of light but which needs that which They bring in order to express the all-encompassing Whole." This is, of course, a mysterious and rather paradoxical statement, but a certain measure of light can be thrown upon it if it is remembered that this sixth initiation is related, in a peculiar way, to Path VI. This is the Path upon which our planetary Logos is found. This Path is necessarily related to the sixth Ray of Devotion or Idealism, and also to the sixth plane, the astral plane—the plane of glamour and of desire. I would have you bear these relationships in mind, but I would have you also remember that at this Initiation of Decision the Master can move forward on any one of the seven Paths which He may decide is, for Him, the field of His future service. This expression of His choice is, as you know, not dependent upon His ray energy or upon what might be the impelling force of the planetary rays; i.e., that of the planet itself (the personality ray of the planetary Logos) or upon the soul ray of Sanat Kumara. It is not for me to tell you whether this dominating ray is His soul ray or the monadic or universal ray.

It is of interest to have in mind also that at this sixth initiation a great moment of basically historic interest occurs. All the Masters Who are initiates of the sixth degree meet in conclave and together, and before making Their final decision (which will probably remove Them from the Path of Earth Service), decide what measures They propose the Hierarchy should take which will drastically and permanently affect the planet on which They have lived and for which They have worked. You will notice that I have here called Them "initiates of the sixth degree," bringing to your minds the fact that before a man takes an initiation of any degree, He is already an initiate of that degree. They in Their totality—at any given time—are the group which makes final decision anent human affairs. It was a decision made by this group of initiates during the ancient Atlantean civilisation which brought it to an end; the decision which They will make now will produce great changes in our modern civilisation. The Masters, however, do not "take this initiation" whenever They are ready to "make decision." The opportunity comes to the Hierarchy every forty-nine years, and the year 1952 will see a group of these higher initiates choose the Path of Their future livingness and Being, but They will do so only after setting in motion certain energy forces which will creatively change matters on Earth. They thereby prove two things: Their grasp of world need and Their recognition of man's freewill to make decision. The last initiation of this kind was therefore held in 1903. Those prepared to pass through this initiation were faced with the fact of the emerging forces of cosmic evil; They had then to decide in what manner They should bring aid to humanity and what situation They should bring about so that mankind would be forced to recognise conditions and also make free choice and decision. What They decided to do led to the world war, to a demonstrated cleavage between right and wrong, between imprisonment and freedom, and which, in 1952 will lead to a decision—the outcome of which is hidden in the consciousness of Those Who will at that time, make it. (Written in 1949.)

At this sixth initiation the Masters Who participate in it no longer come under the jurisdiction of the Hierarchy. They have moved out from under it. Their long connection with the Hierarchy is translated to a higher centre and is transferred to Shamballa, *unless* (as in the case of the Christ) They choose the Path of Earth Service and return to work with the evolutions upon our planet; there are many such evolutions and several kingdoms in nature besides the human, including the deva or angel evolution.

The sixth Initiation of Decision is preparatory to the true Initiation of the Resurrection, the seventh initiation. This can only be undergone when the will of the Master is completely merged in that of the planetary Logos. Between the sixth and the seventh initiations "an interim of divine fusion" takes place; an elementary and somewhat distorted picture of this critical fusion is given to us in *The New Testament*, where we read of the experience of the Christ in the garden of Gethsemane. There again—as in the fourth Initiation of Renunciation—the human element of suffering is emphasised, whereas in the true symbolical "garden" between the sixth and the seventh initiations there is no aspect of suffering. Suffering and pain enter not into the consciousness of the Master. Where it says in *The New Testament* that, "angels came and ministered unto" the Christ, the correct implication is that Those Who dwell and work in Shamballa use this period to instruct the initiate who has made his decision through an expression of his divine nature and in the significance of the divine purpose; this concerns the relation of our planetary Logos to the solar system, and decision is made through the development of that higher sensitivity which leads inevitably to cosmic perception. We have no adequate word for this quality or type of sensitivity, for it is not something which we can consciously understand, nor is it a form of conscious reaction; neither is it awareness as we use that term. It has been occultly defined as something akin to "immersion in a realised state of Being," because the initiate is a *conscious aspect* of that of which he forms an integral part. By means of this statement you will see how impossible it is for me to explain certain things, to make clear certain unknown types of consciousness or to indicate areas of perception which lie beyond the ken even of a Master.

Revelation is a progressive matter. Disciples are not really able to understand the extensive significances of the third initiation, for instance; in like manner, even high initiates fail to comprehend that which lies plainly before Them. Disciples can, however, dimly sense the nature of the Transfiguration which characterises them, from the hierarchical point of view, and Masters can also dimly sense the nature of the decision with which They are faced. *It is this preparatory sensitivity in the disciple which produces true perception at all the various initiatory stages.* This is a statement of major importance and links sensitivity, its interpretation and control, with the everyday life of the ordinary disciple. It is important because of its inclusiveness and because each stage upon the Path of Initiation has in it the germ of comprehension and an understanding (deeply hidden) of the various steps which have to be taken upon the Way of the Higher Evolution. Upon this Way the Master intelligently embarks when He has made His final decision; earlier stages are simply revelatory of the Way.

Initiation has been defined as "a progressive sequence of directed energy impacts." These impacts are characterised by points of tension, and these lead inevitably to points of crisis; the whole process is governed by the Law of Cause and Effect. It is this latter point which I seek now to emphasise, because it has a definite and mysterious relation to this sixth initiation. The Master, as He makes His decision and chooses one of the seven Paths which unitedly form the planetary antahkarana, is forced thereto by the accumulation of past karma. All *evil* karma has necessarily been worked off, but His accumulated *good* karma makes His final decision inevitable; from that instant of decision He stands entirely free and liberated from all aspects and all forms of planetary karma, which is greater and more vast than his little individual karma, be it good or bad. He is then—in Himself—the summation of all past experience. Unless He deliberately chooses the Path of Earth Service and decides to remain within the field, scope or influence of the planetary Life, He faces a solar or a cosmic future of which He knows relatively little, but for which the Path of Evolution, the Path of Discipleship and the Path of Initiation have fitted Him. Even He does not know the conditions into which His "decision" commits Him, or those into which He will have to penetrate; He does know, however, and "appropriates the fact and the faculties" (as one Master has expressed it) of complete revelation and future opportunity.

You have oft been told that there are four Lords of Karma associated with the Council Chamber at Shamballa. They represent—in Their totality—the three Rays of Aspect, and one of Them represents the four minor Rays of Attribute. It is the Lord of Karma Who implements the destinies of Those Who are conditioned by the third Ray of Active Intelligence (and this is ever the case with Those Who are taking the sixth initiation) and Who—symbolically speaking—"wipes clean the slate" of this particular group of initiates at this particular time. Karma no longer holds Them.

The revelation accorded to the Initiate in the first stage of the initiation gives Him a complete picture "in a flash of endless time" of the processes which have brought Him to this creative moment of decision. Immediately He achieves a point of tension which He will continue to hold until the final or ninth initiation, the Initiation of Refusal, wherein He rejects, refuses or repudiates His entire past and enters upon His chosen path entirely "free of recollected concepts, but exhibiting to Those Great Lives Who welcome Him upon the new and untried path all that He is and the essence of His Being."

In dealing with these higher initiations of which I myself have no experience, there is naught for me to do but clarify your minds, and mine also, through the use of ancient phrases and the oral teaching which is permitted to escape into the minds of men.

The point of crisis which ever follows the attainment of tension is the expressed moment of the final decision. Then follows the revelation of what may be, and the initiate knows that he faces the final resurrection and that from being the eternal pilgrim or the planetary wanderer, he now becomes a fixed point upon another cosmic plane, for the physical is, for him, eternally left behind.

This initiation is therefore governed by the third ray, the Ray of Intelligent Activity. This ray is closely related to the mental plane of our planetary life, to the Law of Fixation and the Law of Cleavages. Much anent this I have written earlier, and a search for the significance of certain passages in *A Treatise on Cosmic Fire* may bring enlightenment. Fixation is not permitted to the eternal pilgrim upon our little planet, the Earth, but when that is left behind entirely at the ninth initiation the initiate becomes a "fixed or stationary point of light within his chosen Place, the Place of the Most High and the point of fire upon the mountain-top. From that point he will no more go out."

The concept of cleavage is latent here also. The Master severs all connection with the past and with the planet, but never with the One Life which permeates all spheres and forms of being, which makes possible all states of consciousness and leads to endless activity.

Creativity was one of the three words which I gave you earlier (see page 340) in connection with this sixth initiation. The final four initiations are all distinguished by a "revelation in the living light." At the sixth initiation the Master is brought to an understanding of the nature of creation, of the reason for the intelligent manifestation of substantial forms and their creation to provide forms for Being and for Life, and of the quality of that which He—in the future—must and will create. At the seventh Initiation of Resurrection, He is accorded a revelation of the quality which must express itself through all created forms: the quality of love-wisdom which has animated our planetary Logos and is the basic quality of our entire solar system. In other spheres and in other solar systems and on other cosmic planes, other qualities, unknown to us, may be demonstrated by the appropriate initiates; but those who attain resurrection and liberation upon our planet will always be spiritually qualified by divine love, and that will also be the underlying quality of all that they may later create when freed from our planet. You can see, therefore, why the phrase "God is Love" is really our planetary keynote.

At the eighth Initiation of Transition the purpose of all our planetary activity is revealed to the Master, and all Masters or initiates of this eighth initiation (working either through the Hierarchy or in Shamballa) are needed at this initiation so as to stimulate the point of tension of the new initiate in order to make the revelation possible.

It might be said that They act like a lens through which the living light flows which makes the revelation possible, and They also fulfill the need of acting as a protecting factor. This protection is needed because at this initiation the initiate is shown not only the eternal good underlying planetary purpose, but he is allowed "to see that which is hidden behind the fast sealed door and be in touch with cosmic evil for it can no longer hurt him." He needs nevertheless the protection of Those with Whom he has fitted himself to associate. What the planetary purpose is I know not; when I say that part of the purpose is to liberate light and love into a wider universe and to free the solar system from the attacks of cosmic evil, I am stating a truth, but a truth which remains as yet meaningless to those who have not been put in touch with the completed purpose; it remains a mystery, for the true nature of light, the mystery of electricity, the constitution of the good, the beautiful and the true, the origin of evil, the nature and purpose of the Black Lodge, the place which that Lodge plays within the divine scheme of being, are all unknown to you in their essential significance. Remember that when a Member of the Hierarchy uses the word *essential,* He does not mean (as you oft do) that which is needed or necessary; He is referring to the inmost essence which is found at the heart of all things—both the good and the evil. Therefore, when I say to you also that at this eighth initiation the nature and the purpose of duality is revealed to the initiate, it is again meaningless.

At these three final initiations, therefore, the significance of creation, of quality and of purpose are successively revealed to the Master, and that which makes the revelation possible is not only the action of the One Initiator and of the initiating group (when such a group is required), but the major factor is the developed sensitivity of the initiate himself—a sensitivity which has developed through many aeons of lives and of vital experience.

The objective of the evolutionary process to which all lives on our planet have to submit has been to develop this sensitivity which will make revelation possible, and it might be said that (from one definite angle) the goal of all experience has been revelation—each revelation "carrying the initiate closer to the Heart of the Sun wherein all things are known and felt, and through which all forms, all beings and all things can be bathed in love." Ponder on these words, for the microcosmic correspondence to the macrocosmic fact is full of teaching value. See to it that "each lesson learned each day, each revelation grasped and understood, makes your heart full of love and enables you to love your fellowmen with ardent, fiery warmth." I am quoting some ancient aphorisms for disciples.

At the ninth Initiation of Refusal, the revelation presented to the Master concerns the nature of Being and of existence. There is naught I can say to you which could be in any way explanatory of Being, for Being is related to THAT which creates, to the universal point of planetary or solar Life which is, and has ever been, responsible for the life of all forms from the greatest manifestation to the smallest. When that revelation is accorded to the initiate, he for the first time receives his initial contact with what is called in the occult and esoteric books "the Central Spiritual Sun." He realises for himself that those words concern a basic fact and are related to the purpose of the solar system, just as "the Heart of the Sun" revealed to him the quality of the solar system. When it is realised that our planetary purpose is mysteriously related to the revelation of love upon our little planet, the Earth, through the process of creation, the concept emerges that there is the probability that our planet has a unique relation to the Heart of the Sun. There are many hints for you in what I have said; they are hints to me also, only I can bring to their expansion into ascertained fact a wider knowledge than is as yet your possession.

There is little more that I can say anent this crucial and decisive sixth initiation. It embodies the Master's recognition of liberation, and in its processes He demonstrates that liberation by making free decision anent His future state of Being and of purpose. The future, for the average person and for the average disciple, is contained within his past and is implemented in his present. This is not so with the initiate of the sixth initiation. He is entirely liberated from his past; the Law of Karma no longer has any hold over Him; He makes free decision, and His future is decided by Him not on the basis of its inevitability or as providing Him with a field in which to work off karma, but on the basis solely of qualification for service. This creates a very different situation. The decision once made is a fixed decision, and there is no turning back or relinquishment of it, nor (so free is the Master from all possible hindrances) is there any desire to turn back or possibility that He could do so.

The remaining three initiations demonstrate these points still more clearly and definitely, and the light in which the initiate walks waxes ever brighter and brighter. Light reveals to him the nature and the purpose of the cosmic etheric physical planes (the four highest planes of our planetary Life); this light brings to his attention the nature of certain extra-planetary conditions, and for the first time these become factual to him and not simply hypothetical; the light reveals to him his future opportunities once his final choice or decision is made, and—as said above—it also reveals to him the nature of divine purpose as our planetary Logos conceives it under the inspiration of the solar Logos.

He can now express himself fully upon the monadic plane, the plane of universal life; the great heresy of separateness has slipped away from him and he knows nothing but love, unity, spiritual identification and a universal awareness. Because of this, he can become a creator, for creation is the expression of life, love and purpose, and all these three he can now understand and fully express.

He is now an intelligent cooperator with the Building Forces of the planet and also of the solar system, and upon his chosen ray he will carry out his creative intentions.

## Initiation VII. The Resurrection

There is no idea more cultivated subjectively by humanity than that of the resurrection; when life seems hard and circumstances carry in them no grounds for happiness, and when nothing calls to one of such a nature that one goes forth happily to the day's enterprises, and when the nights of sleep are haunted nights, the thought of rising up and out of all these circumstances, of leaving all behind and of entering into a new life, carries with it strength and hope. In the West, the Festival of the year which is regarded as of the most importance is that of Easter Day—the Day of Resurrection. Yet two thousand years ago the Christ did not rise out of a rocky sepulchre and re-assume His discarded body. He passed through the great seventh initiation which we will consider today, and knew the secret of life, of which immortality is only one of its many attributes. Humanity lays emphasis so frequently upon attribute, quality and reactions, and not upon that which is the basic underlying reality; men deal with effects and not with causes; for instance, mankind is concerned with war and with horrified preparations for more war, and is not primarily occupied with that which causes war and which, if rightly handled, would prevent war. Let us consider some few aspects of the seventh initiation.

The word "resurrection" has deep significance latent in its derivation and one that is not often emphasised. The usual interpretation has been that the word comes from "re," again, and "surgere," to rise, therefore to rise again. Yet a consultation with the dictionary shows that the prefix means "back to an original state" by rising. This return to an original state is pictured for us in *The New Testament* under the story of the Prodigal Son, who said "I will arise and go to my Father," and by the story of the resurrection in which the Master Jesus arose out of the tomb; the chains of death could not hold Him. At that time of His "rising," a far more important event took place and the Christ passed through the seventh Initiation of Resurrection and returned back to His original state of Being—to remain there throughout all the eternities. This is the true and final resurrection. The Son of God has found His way back to the Father and to His originating Source, that state of Existence to which we have given the name Shamballa. The consciousness of the Universal Life is His; this is far more than simply the consciousness of immortality, because the idea or concept of mortality is not contained within it at all. There have been many deaths within the aeonial life cycle of the initiate:

1. The familiar and constantly recurring death of the physical body, incarnation after incarnation.

2. The deaths of the astral and the mental vehicles, as the undying soul discards them life after life—only to create new ones until mastery is attained.

3. Then—as a result of the incarnating process and its evolutionary effects—there comes the death of desire and its replacing by a growing spiritual aspiration.

4. Then, through right use of the mind, comes the "death" of the personality or, rather, its repudiation and renouncing of all that is material.

5. This is followed by the death or destruction of the causal or soul body at the great Initiation of Renunciation. This process of death and resurrection goes on ceaselessly in all the kingdoms of nature; each death prepares the way for a greater loveliness and livingness, and each death (if you analyse it with care) prefaces resurrection in some form or another until we come to this final resurrection and into the position of final attainment.

I will not here elaborate upon this process of constant death followed by constant resurrection, but it is the evolutionary keynote and the evolutionary technique, and only because men love unduly that which is material and hate to lose contact with the form aspect of nature do they fear death. It is wise to remember that immortality is an aspect of the living spiritual being, and is not an end in itself, as men seek to make it. To the Knowers of Life such a phrase as "I am an immortal Soul" is not even true. To say "I am Life Itself and, therefore, am immortal" approaches closer to the truth, but even that sentence is (from the angle of the initiate) only a part of a larger truth. Symbolically, nature is ever portraying to us the essential facts in the annual progress of the four seasons, in the cycles of light and dark and in the wonder of the emergence of beauty or

colour or useful function out of a seed which has struggled
—because of its inherent life—into the light of the sun.

The fear of death is one of the great abnormalities
or distortions of divine truth for which the Lords of Cosmic
Evil are responsible. When in early Atlantean times they
emerged from the place where they had been confined, and
forced *temporarily* the retirement of the Great White
Lodge to subjective levels, their first great act of distortion
was to implant in human beings fear, beginning with the
fear of death. From that time on, men have laid the emphasis upon death and not life, and have been ridden by
fear all their days.

One of the initial acts of the reappearing Christ and
of the Hierarchy will be to erase this particular fear and
to confirm in peoples' minds the idea that incarnation and
the taking of a form is the true place of darkness to the
divine spirit which is man; it is death to the spirit temporarily, and imprisonment. Evolution, men will be taught,
is in itself an initiatory process leading from one living
experience to another, culminating in the fifth Initiation
of Revelation and in the seventh Initiation of Resurrection.

At the fifth initiation it is revealed to the initiate
that life in form is indeed death, and he then knows this
truth in a manner which my few short words cannot convey. Form dies for him and he knows a new expansion of
life and undergoes (if I may so express it) a new understanding of living. The seventh initiation is divorced from
all considerations of form, and the initiate becomes a concentrated point of living light; he knows in a manner in-
describable that life is all that IS, and that it is this life and
its real fullness which makes him a part of THAT which lies
outside of our planetary Life; he may now share in that
extra-planetary Existence in which our planetary Logos
lives and moves and has His being. This is the "life more
abundantly" of which Christ spoke and which only an
initiate of the seventh degree can understand or convey.

After the fifth initiation, the initiate has slowly been
sensing the nature of this greater Life, the Life of "The

Unknown God," as it has been called, which enfolds all livingness and all forms upon and within our planet and yet *remains*—greater than our planetary Life, more all-encompassing than is our planetary Logos, and Whose greatness, beauty, goodness and knowledge are to our planetary Logos what His life is to the lowest form of life in the third or animal kingdom. It is only by such inadequate comparisons that one can arrive at some faint comprehension of that great WHOLE in which our planet and our planetary Logos are but a part. It is this revelation which is accorded to the initiate at this seventh Initiation of Resurrection. He takes this initiation upon what (for lack of a better phrase) we call the "logoic plane," or on the level of consciousness of the Lord of the World.

At this initiation the Initiator is attended by two groups of Beings; one is a small group of the "Knowers of the Purpose, the Custodians of the Will," and the other is a much larger group, the personnel of which are known as "The Wise Ones and the Attractive Energies of Shamballa." I am of course endeavouring to translate certain brief words and intricate symbols into phrases which you can understand and which only dimly convey the true significance of Those Who function on this highest level of the cosmic physical plane. On this level, dynamic electricity is held as in a great reservoir of potency and is directed by these two groups which embody the will and the quality of the will of Deity, called by us the Will-to-Good. They are the directing Agents and are a correspondence to the ajna centre of mankind, only here it is the ajna centre of the planetary Logos, in the same sense as Shamballa is His head centre, the Hierarchy His heart centre and Humanity His creative throat centre. Motion, planned activity and the seven great creative ray energies are directed into action by Them under the influence of the seven Ray Lords; the Ray Lords are embodied livingness qualified by the seven aspects of Love, but Who are Themselves of so high an order that They cannot function as directing creative Agents but work through Their trained and developed Representatives.

Just as there is a group of Contemplative Initiates, called in the Eastern phraseology "Nirmanakayas," Who function in deep meditation at a point midway between the Hierarchy and Shamballa, so this much higher group of Ray Lords function in the deepest cosmic meditation between our planet, the Earth, and our sister planet, Venus. You would find it useful to read with care *The Secret Doctrine* and *A Treatise on Cosmic Fire* and refresh your minds as to this relationship. A lower correspondence to these two important groups has been forming midway between the Hierarchy and Humanity, and to it we give the name of the New Group of World Servers. All these three groups are fundamentally "transmitters of energy"; the two highest are exceedingly susceptible to cosmic impression and to the vibratory quality of the extra-planetary body of Avatars Who hold Themselves in readiness to function as destroying or building Energies in any part of our solar system and are under the direction of the Solar Logos.

The Avatar of Synthesis, Who is working in cooperation with the Christ, is one of Them. Bear in mind that these extra-planetary Avatars have not arrived at Their high state of spiritual unfoldment on our planet or even in our solar system. Their origin, source and spiritual relationships are a great mystery even to the planetary Logoi— to Whose help They go when the invocative appeal of any planet is adequate. Think not that They come to put wrong right or to arrest evil. A few, a very few, may do so, but They work along the line of the seven ray energies in the solar system and produce certain energy effects desired at any particular time; the constructive work of the Avatar of Synthesis will be apparent to you in the name He is known by; He is coming to the Earth in order to further the manifestation of unity, of oneness and of inter-relation, and He comes, therefore, to wield and apply first ray energy. He will charge or galvanise the three groups—the directing Agents in Shamballa, the Nirmanakayas and the New Group of World Servers—with dynamic energy and, in a mysterious way, relate them to each other so that a new synthesis and alignment will be present upon the Earth. All these Avatars embody energy to the extent that any particular planet is capable of receiving it.

These are interesting items of information but are only of value in so far as they convey to you a sense of planetary integrity and of solar synthesis, and present to you a closer spiritual inter-relation in which you, as individuals, can share *if* you are linking your fate and service to that of the New Group of World Servers. Then you will be in the direct line of spiritual descent, of divine energy; in this thought you have the clue to the doctrine (so travestied and misused) of the Apostolic Succession. The details, the personnel and the techniques of the two higher groups lie beyond your ken; They work in cooperation with the planetary Logos Himself, and Those Who compose these groups are all initiates of degrees higher than the fifth. Most of the Nirmanakayas have taken the sixth and the seventh initiations, whilst the group which functions midway between the Earth and Venus have all taken the eighth and ninth initiations. Some of Them, as I mentioned earlier, aid the initiate of the seventh degree; a still larger group of them participate in the activities of the two final initiations.

This seventh initiation gives the initiate the right to "come and go in the courts of Shamballa" as Their work may dictate and Their service may require. It is there also that he goes for the needed periodic or cyclic re-chargings which enable him to work.

There is one aspect of initiation which is apt to be overlooked. Every initiation is a process of energy transmission from a higher centre of energy to a lower; every initiation charges the initiate with electrical force, and this charging and re-charging is related to what H.P.B. calls "the mystery of electricity." These transmissions of energy enhance the magnetic-attractive force of the initiate, and at the same time are eliminative in their effects. In this fact lies a great planetary truth and the key to the science of planetary redemption. When the spiritual and the electrical charging of the three major centres on the planet—Shamballa, the Hierarchy and Humanity—has reached a high stage of receptive efficiency, a certain cosmic Avatar will "become conscious of the vibratory quality of the little point of light within the solar sphere" and will then "turn His gaze and send His force unto that point of light, and cosmic evil will be driven out and find no more a place on Earth."

Two more initiations remain to be considered, but so high is their potency and so mysterious their working that I find myself unable to deal with them in any way. They are:

*Initiation VIII. The Great Transition*
*Initiation IX. The Refusal*

It will of course be apparent that the Transition referred to is related to the sixth Initiation of Decision, when the Master decides which of the seven Paths He will follow to His destined place. I know not what the Great Refusal involves. One thing only I know: It indicates the Initiate's last contact with what we understand as cosmic evil, manifesting on this planet and in relation to the planet. He is accorded this last contact, but such a contact is not based upon anything analogous to evil within Him, but is based upon the "planetary appeal for liberation." This appeal is so strong that the Initiate—because His heart is on fire with love— is tempted to go back upon His decision and stay upon the planet with Those World Saviours Who have chosen the Path of Earth Service. This He may not do, and in the sight of the assembled Initiates He makes His refusal and "does His whole duty as He journeys to the sacred Feet of the ONE WHO stands at the end of His chosen Path."

Again, we come up against the outstanding planetary characteristic which has been presented to us under many differing words, i.e., the sensitivity which in some form or another distinguishes each initiation. We know it also as attraction, the sensitivity which moves outward until it attracts and draws to itself those forms of being which the initiate can instruct or aid; we know it also as the overall activity conferring that spiritual sensory perception which makes the initiate aware—in a universal sense—of all that concerns the sphere of influence of the Will of God. This demonstrates particularly at the eighth Initiation of Transition. In the ninth Initiation of Refusal, this heightened spiritual perception is presented to us under the word "Existence," for existence is a livingness coupled with awareness which "finds its own place and the spiritual house of its Being which is the true home of all Beings, but of this—our planetary forms know naught." This the initiate has at last learnt to find, after the struggle with evil in himself, after the struggle with materialism and with evil in the human family, and after his struggle to aid in the "closing of the door where evil dwells" and his refusal to make any contact (even with good intention) with cosmic evil.

The planetary Lodge of Masters has absorbed Him and, at the final initiation, the Great Lodge on Sirius has recognised Him, and with the Black Lodge of Adepts He will have nothing to do. He will mitigate its evil effects and will struggle to offset its results, but He knows that the final overcoming of cosmic physical evil must be undertaken by Existences much further advanced than even the Members of the Council Chamber at Shamballa; certain solar Entities and certain great Lives from Sirius are dealing with the problem.

The theme of the living consciousness of the planetary Logos is forever and unchangeably the great Hierarchy of Being, that chain of life in which the smallest link is of importance, and the greatest link is related to the smallest through the electrical interplay of spiritual energy. There is naught—from one important angle of life—but Hierarchy, linking sun with sun, star with star, solar system with solar system, planet with planet and all planetary lives with each other. The major keynote of every single planetary initiation, even to the very highest, is RELATIONSHIP. What other qualities may be revealed to the Initiate on other paths we know not, but the goal of all endeavour upon our planet is right relations between man and man and between man and God, between all expressions of divine life, from the tiniest atom up and on into infinity.

From the standpoint of our planetary evolution, there is naught but love, naught but goodwill and the will-to-good. This exists already, and its true manifestation is nearer today than at any time in planetary history.

From stage to stage, from crisis to crisis, from point to point and from centre to centre, the life of God progresses, leaving greater beauty behind it as it moves through one form after another and from kingdom to kingdom. One attainment leads to another; out of the lower kingdoms man has emerged, and (as a result of human struggle) the kingdom of God will also appear. The bringing in of that kingdom is all that truly concerns humanity today, and all living processes in mankind are bent towards preparing each individual human being to pass into that kingdom. The knowledge that there may be greater manifestations than even the kingdom of God may be inspiring, but that is all. The manifestation of the Kingdom of God on Earth, the preparing of the way for its great Inaugurator, the Christ, the making possible the externalisation of the Hierarchy upon Earth give us each and all a fully adequate task and something for which to live and work, to dream and to aspire.

The five volumes composing *A Treatise on the Seven Rays* are now completed, my brothers. It has been for me a labour of love and for A.A.B. a labour! It will suffice for study for many years to come.

May light and love and power shine upon your ways, and may you in due time and with as little delay as possible stand before the Initiator and join the ranks of Those Who —actively and consciously—love Their fellowmen, work as reconstructive and regenerative Energies and forever — SERVE.

I sign myself, because it has been given out who I am, as the Master *Djwhal Khul.*

THE TIBETAN

# APPENDIX

## FIVE GREAT SPIRITUAL EVENTS

## STANZAS FOR DISCIPLES

# FIVE GREAT SPIRITUAL EVENTS

## (Written February 1949)

You (A.A.B.) have asked me what I considered the most important and significant events from the spiritual angle at this present time. This question highlights a theme which is exceedingly apposite, following as it does upon what I have just given anent the Great Renunciation (see pages 602-614) and its consequent revelation or (as the Christian churches call them) the Crucifixion and the Resurrection. The Christian resurrection is, however—from the angle of the great Lodge on Sirius — only a minor one and a passing resurrection, though the revelation subsequently accorded is lasting and permanent in its effects.

*There are five great spiritual events* in which all humanity is today sharing, and two which will take place later, when the first five have established their lasting effects.

These events are based upon a forced and not upon a spontaneous renunciation (as is the case in the true experience of the Renunciation Initiation); they will lead nevertheless to a revelation which is imminent in its dawning and which will confront humanity before so very long.

The war of 1914—1945 is over; its aftermath of suffering, famine, selfish reactions, suspicion and unseemly struggle for supremacy is equally as bad as the past war; the effects are more lasting, because the war has been largely transferred to the mental plane. The physical effects of war are far more easily obliterated than are the mental effects. The great question with which the Hierarchy is today faced is: Will the race of men succeed in renouncing their present material objectives and so prepare the way for a great revelation? The Coming of the Christ Himself is *not* the revelation which is to be accorded, but He will simplify the thinking of men so that a widespread illumination and recognition of the revelation will be possible. The next few years will indicate the way the tide will turn, and whether the reactionary, material and selfish forces which have controlled for millennia of years will finally control. This reactionary and material spirit taints every department of human life, and the churches are no exception. Humanity can, however, learn its lesson and turn thankfully to the "way of righteousness" and to the hitherto unknown technique of right human relations.

I seek not to deal in detail with the evil which holds the world in thrall. Enough is already known and a small handful (small in comparison to the many millions) of hierarchical workers in all departments of life are struggling to awaken humanity to the risks they are running, and to *the finality of the decision* which the next two generations will be forced to make. More will come to the surface as we study present-day happenings from the angle of renunciation and resurrection.

I would like first of all to point out that:

1. The mass of the people are sound, but ignorant of the higher values; that can be slowly righted. They are negative as yet in action, and prone to words and not deeds. They are easily led and also easily swayed by imparted fears.

2. The evil in the world and that which is primarily guilty of swaying the masses at this time is focussed through a few powerful men or groups of powerful men. No country is free from this control, or from this attempted control. These powerful groups are swayed in their turn by the forces of evil—forces which were not "sealed in their own place," because the plan of love and light and power still lacks positive and worldwide presentation.

3. The aspirants, disciples and spiritual workers of the world are not acting in full concert with the Hierarchy. They are swayed by fear, by a sense of futility and by a too acute understanding of the nature of the forces of evil with which they are confronted. The picture of what must be accomplished looms too large; there is little organised

cooperation among them, and no welding together into a united group for world salvage and service.

The spiritual opportunity is, however, emerging with increasing clarity in the minds of thinking men and women, even if it is not expressed by them in orthodox (so-called) terms or in recognised or spiritual terms. Perhaps a clear statement of that which the active spiritual Forces are seeking to bring about may prove helpful. If the Forces of Evil are active and organised, the Forces of Light are equally active, but *not* so well organised. The basic goal is the freedom and the liberation of mankind, but the spiritual workers are handicapped by the fact that men themselves must make free choice and decision in order to be free; they can only be liberated when they—as individuals and later as groups—liberate themselves from the expressed thought-control of the powerful dominating groups and from the fears which these groups intentionally engender. Freedom can never be conferred through totalitarian methods; liberation cannot come through a dictator or dictating groups. A realisation of the manner in which the hierarchical forces are working and a recognition that all men are today immersed in vital spiritual happenings may serve to encourage the faithful and give a quickening vision to those who are struggling on behalf of human freedom.

What are the five spiritual events in which all are consciously or unconsciously participating? Let me list them:

1.  The crisis of the ideologies.
2.  The steady awakening of men everywhere to better understanding.
3.  The growth of goodwill, as it reveals cleavages.
4.  The partial sealing of the door where evil dwells.
5.  The use of the Great Invocation.

These are the five deepest spiritual events happening in the world today. The two which lie ahead in the not too distant future (but which depend upon humanity availing itself of the present opportunity) are:

6.  The closer Approach of the Hierarchy.
7.  The imminent Return of the Christ.

## 1. The Crisis of the Ideologies

Men are today confronted with conflicting and antag-onistic ideologies or schools of thought, and automatically —according to their background, tradition, training and place of birth—they regard some one of these ideas as true and all the others as false and wrong. They are apt to forget that according to the locale of birth, the national mode of schooling and the nature of the national propa-ganda, so will be the chosen ideology or the imposed ideology. Very few people are free agents, even in the democracies. A man born in Central Russia, for instance, knows nothing but Communism; he cannot imagine another suitable form of government; again, a man born in the United States or in Great Britain boasts and is pleased that he was born in a democracy, but the accident of birth ac-counts largely for his attitude. Men need to remember these things and not blame each other for the place in which they are born! We have, therefore, ideologies and their opponents, great schools of thought and modes of government, confronted by organised opposition. One basic premise can be laid down: The platform of the leading ideologies is not necessarily wrong or wicked; it is the imposition *by force* and by a police state of an ideology, and its use by powerful men or groups for their own benefit, plus the keeping of the people in blind ignorance so that no free choice is theirs—which is fundamentally wicked and evil.

We have, for instance, the great crisis in the world today presented by the conflict between Communism and the democratic point of view. I mention this first because it is the one which is occupying a prominent position in the eyes of all men everywhere. This presents a dominant spiritual opportunity. The democratic attitude, dedicated as it claims to be to human freedom (however little of that freedom is yet truly attained) is—because of that freedom factor—sponsored today by the Hierarchy. Communism being an imposed ideology, forced on the people by totali-tarian authority, is regarded as evil. It is not the communistic theories which are necessarily wrong; it is the technique and the methods, rampant in the totalitarian lands, which are counter to the spiritual plan. Imposed Communism and *all* totalitarian methods imprison the human soul, and breed fear and hatred everywhere. Should the democratic principles therefore be *imposed* upon the world or any part of the world by a totalitarian regime, it would be equally wrong.

These conflicting ideologies are presenting clearly to the human consciousness certain great distinctions; these distinctions are found in techniques and methods far more than in the various tenets. Many of the people most violently fighting Communism could not tell you succinctly what those tenets are, but they are fighting—and rightly fighting —the totalitarian methods of cruelty, spying, murder, suppression and the lack of freedom. What they are doing in truth is fighting the abominable methods of imposing the rule of a few evil and ambitious men upon the ignorant masses, *under the name of Communism*. They are fighting the technique of exploiting the ignorant through misinformation, organised lying and limited education. They are fighting against the sealing up of nations within the confines of their own territory, against the police state, the lack of free enterprise and the reduction of men and women to automatons. This is the true imprisonment of the human spirit. The situation is, however, so pronounced and the evil so obvious (and the human spirit so basically and divinely strong) that it will eventually defeat itself; when the present group of totalitarian rulers (behind what you call the "iron curtain") die out a different state of affairs will gradually supervene and a true Communism (in the spiritual sense of the term) will take the place of the present wickedness.

On the other hand, the much vaunted democracies have much to learn. Men are not truly free, even in democratic countries; the Negroes, for instance, lack their constitutional rights in parts of the United States; and in South Africa, their educational facilities and their opportunity to work and live as free men are not equal to those of the white race; in the southern states, the Constitution of the United States is infringed every day by those who believe in white supremacy—a supremacy which will be put to a crucial test when Africa awakes. This attitude of the United States and their failure to live up to the Constitution where Negroes are concerned, have greatly weakened the faith of other countries in the wonder of America, and the situation in South Africa is not honoured by thinking men. I mention these two situations because there is widespread evil even in the democracies; a true house cleaning is sorely needed.

The imperialism of democratic Britain has badly marred an otherwise fine record on behalf of dependent peoples, but it is rapidly becoming a thing of the past, as Britain gives freedom of choice and democratic liberation to India, Pakistan, Ceylon and Burma. Each of those liberations was in the nature of a spiritual expansion of consciousness to the British people and a spiritual opportunity, of which only Ceylon and Pakistan show signs of being aware. Always, in every department of human living, the spiritual and the material aims are making their presence and their differences clearly felt; the spiritual issue, as I have lately pointed out to you, is the imprisonment of the human spirit or its freedom and liberation.

True Democracy is as yet unknown; it awaits the time when an educated and enlightened public opinion will bring it to power; towards that spiritual event, mankind is hastening. The battle of Democracy will be fought out in the United States. There the people at present vote and organise their government on a personality basis and not from any spiritual or intelligent conviction. There is a material, selfish aspect to Democracy (rampant today), and there is a spiritual aspect, little sought after; there are material and spiritual aspects to Communism, but its adherents know them not, and only a ruthless materialism is conveyed to them.

There is again the ideology of Socialism which is regarded by some as a basic evil. Socialism can degenerate into another form of totalitarianism, or it can be more democratic than the present expressions of Democracy. These issues will emerge clearly in Great Britain, where the socialist point of view is gaining ground among the masses, but which at present is a mixture of nationalisation of the public utilities and of free enterprise—a combination which may have true value, if preserved.

There are other ideologies in the political, social and economic fields but these with which I have dealt constitute a triangle of schemes undergoing national and political experiments in different countries throughout the world. All of them have a religious and spiritual side; all of them are tainted with materialism; one of them is wickedly totalitarian and is finding followers; another is the victim of the stupid lack of interest of its people; another is in the throes of an experiment which may or may not prove successful. Under the impact of these ideologies the spiritual growth of the human family is fostered, because the emerging spiritual factor (under the evolutionary law) is ever present, and always there is to be found a tendency towards God and divine expression. That is why the issue is stressed between Christianity and Communism—a controversy emphasised by the Roman Catholic Church, but one into which the communistic nations are already drawing the Protestant churches.

From the standpoint of the Hierarchy, these three ideologies are three aspects of one great spiritual event; the outcome of the interplay between them can eventuate in an increased spiritual approach to divinity or (if the Forces of Light do not triumph) they can drive mankind deeper into the pit or prison of materialism. The intense political interest of the Catholic Church, plus its gross materialism, acts as a great handicap to the steady gain of the spiritual position; if however, the Catholic hierarchy can renounce or relinquish its material and political aims and present the love of God in its beauty, it can do much to lead humanity out of darkness into light. If the United States can equally renounce its gross materialism, it can give a lead to the world along spiritual lines which will be beyond anything yet demonstrated and, aided by Great Britain, the two great democracies, expressing right human relations and the fellowship of man, can do great things for the race. Great Britain is learning a sense of values, and being drawn away from materialism through great privation; it is hoped that she will *consciously* renounce materialism.

I would like to remind you here that the spiritual Hierarchy of our planet cares not whether a man is a democrat, a socialist or a communist, or whether he is a Catholic, a Buddhist, or an unbeliever of any kind. It cares only that humanity—as a whole—avail itself of spiritual opportunity. It is an opportunity which is present today in a more compelling way than ever before.

## 2.  *Man's steady Awakening to better Understanding*

The general effect of these clashing ideologies and the result of the war among the world religions have started men thinking in every land. Men are emerging out of the mental lethargy which has characterised them for so long. The man in the street is today thinking, pondering, wondering, planning and deciding. In past centuries, it was only those who had benefited by education and those in the "upper brackets" who thought and planned. This tendency to thought indicates the coming into activity of a new and better civilisation, and this is preparatory to spiritual events of major importance. The spirit of man, usually unconsciously, is driving onwards towards a more spiritual civilisation and culture. I did not say towards a more religious expression of truth. A more spiritual inter-relation is on its way and the establishing on a worldwide scale of right human relations indicates this. We shall have eventually a spiritual focussing which will be divorced from the present orthodox religions, but which will be in tune with the hidden, spiritual factor in all religions. Men are not, in reality, looking for the Christ to come as a religious leader; they look for Him to come to them in the field of their greatest need, to point the way to resurrection and the revelation which will inevitably follow man's renunciation of the material values.

The prevalent spirit of expectancy and of a truly divine discontent are the guarantees that this second spiritual event is a real factor in our time. Many factors contribute to this awakening. In most countries, through the radio, through the newspapers, through books, magazines and travel, through lectures and forums and simplified human intercourse (to which the automobile and the airplane have greatly contributed) men everywhere are free to know and to understand. This is, of course, not true of those countries where the freedom of the human spirit is attacked. There are two ways in which that freedom of choice can be infringed: First, as in Russia, by keeping the citizenry in ignorance of world affairs, and secondly, by giving them biassed news and misinformation, or a garbled or distorted slant on world affairs, as is the case in most other countries, particularly in the United States. An instance of this can be seen in the fact that the Arabs never got a true hearing in the American newspapers or on the radio; the American people were "pressured" (I think that that is the word you use) into an acceptance of the Zionist position—the motive being oil and mineral riches.

But the mentality of man is daily developing and his ability to grasp world affairs is growing. That is one of the greatest of spiritual events and is the foundational fact which makes the life of the soul and the growth of intuitive perception possible on a large scale. This is a byproduct of the clash of the ideologies, but is the true and beautiful result of the universal educational system which—faulty though it may be and is—has made it possible for all men to read, to write and to communicate with each other.

### 3. The Growth of Goodwill and the Revelation of Cleavages

The result of the world war, of disease, famine and pain, has developed a spirit of community in suffering and in deprivation; this has led to a consequent understanding participation in human difficulties everywhere which is rapidly changing into a spirit of world goodwill.

This worldwide goodwill, when truly established and correctly organised, is the needed preliminary to revelation, for this coming revelation will be a planetary revelation, shared by all men everywhere. Unitedly all men realise, even today, the need to rise out of the prison of self-interest into the freedom of shared opportunity, and the factor which will bring about this resurrection is goodwill.

One interesting aspect of goodwill is that, as it develops in the human consciousness, it first of all brings a revelation of the existent *cleavages* which distinguish the political, the religious, the social and the economic life of people everywhere. The revelation of a cleavage is ever accompanied (for such is the beauty of the human spirit) by efforts along all possible lines to bridge or heal the cleavage. This is testified to by the thousands of groups and organisations working to end cleavages and to pull down the barriers to right human relationships. That these efforts may be faulty and fruitless is often of less importance than the fact that the attempts to heal, to help and to establish right human relations are everywhere being made. Modern psychology is an evidence of this, dealing as it does with the problem of the integration of the human being and the healing of the cleavages of his nature. One of the first things to be done is to educate the individual in the necessity to have goodwill not only to his fellowmen but also to himself. The emphasis of medieval Christianity upon weakness, wickedness and the innate sinfulness of the human being has today to be offset by a true appreciation of divinity in human form.

It is not possible to list the cleavages which represent men's failure to establish and hold good and decent relationships with their fellowmen; there are today cleavages between man and man, between group and group, and also between religions and between nations. The terminology which will express good relations, instead of these, already exists: Union, United, League, Federation, Commonwealth, Right Understanding, Kindness, Human Welfare and many similar terms; they mean, as yet, but little. Some day, however, they will stand for certain substantial realities, but that day is not immediate. The concept of easier, unified and happy relations is nevertheless existent in the minds of many thousands everywhere, and the factual reality will materialise some day.

The first step is the wholesome recognition that cleavages exist; it is here that goodwill can do its most useful and necessary work. I do not intend here to stress the nature of that work or state how it should be carried forward. *That* I have done already many times. It is the cultivation of a spiritual attitude that is needed and the dedication, at all times, and in every possible way, to the will-to-good. The majority of the existent cleavages are now recognised; the delay comes in the task of bridging them and also in shouldering responsibility. Many nations, and especially the U.S.S.R. and the U.S.A., are prompt to adjudicate blame, to point out errors and to advise other nations what is wrong and how to put it right. They both need to clean house themselves and attend to the righting of the wrongs within their own borders. The same is true of all nations, but the others are not so openly engaged in telling other peoples what they should do. Why, for instance, should the U.S.A. deal with the problem of the Indonesian strife and seek to force the Dutch to do what Americans feel should be done, and (at the same time) give not constitutional aid to the just cause of the Negro minority within the States? Why accuse other nations of constant wrong doing, as does Russia, and of breaking treaties, when Russia fails on all points to keep her word or to cooperate in righting world affairs?

The task which the Hierarchy wishes to see accomplished at this time is the spread of goodwill; each person, community and nation should begin with a diagnosis of their own attitude towards goodwill, and then set an example by eliminating cleavages in the home, the business, or the nation. *Goodwill is contagious;* once a definite start has been made in a pure and disinterested spirit, goodwill will permeate the world and right human relations will be rapidly established. The healing of cleavages is a practical matter. The Spirit of Synthesis, working through the great first ray Avatar (the Avatar of Synthesis) is closer to the Earth than ever before, and the clarity which will emerge in the Light of His Presence is already available; the tendency to integration can therefore be more easily fostered and a new synthesis attained among men. Before, however, integration and synthesis are possible, this first ray energy must work to destroy all that prevents integration and all that is hindering a needed synthesis. Human beings themselves must also destroy the prejudices, the animosities and the fixed ideas which have prevented synthesis, which have created cleavages and hindered right understanding.

### 4. *The partial Sealing of the Door where Evil dwells*

Just what do these words mean? More than I can tell you or put into words, for the problem of evil is too difficult a one for the average man to grasp. The problem of the Hierarchy (if I may put it both accurately and yet symbolically) is to liberate the good, free the beautiful, release the true and "immure in prison under seal" that which is no good, that which breeds ugliness and hate, and that which distorts the truth and lies about the future. I have chosen all these words with care; their meaning is obvious, but there are significances far too deep and dangerous for you to grasp.

It has been humanity—cumulatively and over millions of years—which has released evil into the world. Thoughts of hate, deeds of cruelty, lying words, sadistic action, selfish intentions and the foulest kind of ambitious selfishness have created a pathway to the "door where evil dwells." Evil is in reality of two kinds: There is that innate tendency to selfishness and to separation which is inherent in the substance of our planet; of it all forms are made and our planetary Logos inherited it from the residue left over from a previous solar system. That is something unavoidable and something that provides mankind with a needed opportunity and one which men are well equipped to handle and control. There *is* that in them which can transmute and change it, and it is this that basically constitutes the Science of Redemption.

But humanity has not chosen to exert itself in this redemptive activity, and for thousands of years has been controlled by that which is material; it has thus constructed the "broad and easy way" which leads to the place where another kind of evil dwells—an evil which is *not* indigenous to our planet, an evil with which it was never intended that men should deal. For untold aeons, the Hierarchy has stood like a shield, guarding humanity. But with the coming of a greatly increased mental development, with the repudiation of the Hierarchy by the bulk of humanity, and by the prostitution of religion to material ends and narrow theological and mental tenets, the Hierarchy has been forced (much against its will) to withdraw some measure of its protecting power (though not all of it, fortunately for mankind). The way to the door where evil dwells was unimpeded, and humanity opened wide the door. The entrance for what might be regarded as *cosmic evil* was first opened in the decadent days of the Roman Empire (which was one reason why the Christ chose to manifest in those days), was opened wider under the corrupt regime of the Kings of France and, in our own day, has been opened still wider by evil men in every land.

Remember that the evil to which I refer here is not necessarily the foul and vile things about which people speak with bated breath. These are largely curable and the processes of incarnation eventually purify them. The true nature of cosmic evil finds its major expression in wrong thinking, false values and the supreme evil of materialistic selfishness and the sense of isolated separativeness. These (to speak again in symbols) are the weights which keep the door of evil open and which precipitate upon the world the horrors of war, with all its attendant disasters.

The realisation of what was happening did more *temporarily* to unify the world and heal the cleavages among nations than any other thing. The nations of the world allied themselves with the Forces of Light to a very large extent, and little by little, cosmic evil was forced back and the door which "conceals the place of endless death and hides the countenances of the Lords of wicked pride and hateful lust" was partially closed, but not entirely shut; its final closing and sealing is not yet accomplished.

There are certain areas of evil in the world today through which these forces of darkness can reach humanity. What they are and where they are I do not intend to say. I would point out, however, that Palestine should no longer be called the Holy Land; its sacred places are only the passing relics of three dead and gone religions. The spirit has gone out of the old faiths and the true spiritual light is transferring itself into a new form which will manifest on earth eventually as the new world religion. To this form all that is true and right and good *in the old forms* will contribute, for the forces of right will withdraw that good, and incorporate it in the new form. Judaism is old, obsolete and separative and has no true message for the spiritually-minded which cannot be better given by the newer faiths; the Moslem faith has served its purpose and all true Moslems await the coming of the Imam Mahdi who will lead them to light and to *spiritual* victory; the Christian faith also has served its purpose; its Founder seeks to bring a new Gospel and a new message that will enlighten all men everywhere. Therefore, Jerusalem stands for nothing of importance today, except for that which has passed away and should pass away. The "Holy Land" is no longer holy, but is desecrated by selfish interests, and by a basically separative and conquering nation.

The task ahead of humanity is to close the door upon this worst and yet secondary evil and shut it in its own place. There is enough for humanity to do in transmuting planetary evil without undertaking to battle with that which the Masters Themselves can only keep at bay, but cannot conquer. The handling of this type of evil and its dissipation, and therefore the release of our planet from its danger, is the destined task of Those Who work and live in "the centre where the Will of God is known," at Shamballa; it is *not* the task of the Hierarchy or of humanity. Remember this, but remember also that what man has loosed he can aid to imprison; this he can do by fostering right human relations, by spreading the news of the approach of the spiritual Hierarchy, and by preparing for the reappearance of the Christ. Forget not also, the Christ is a Member of the Great Council at Shamballa and brings the highest spiritual energy with Him. Humanity can also cease treading the path to the "door where evil dwells" and can remove itself and seek the Path which leads to light and to the Door of Initiation.

5. *The Use of the Great Invocation*

Some time ago I gave out to the world—under instruction from the Christ—an Invocation that is destined to become of major usefulness in bringing about certain great events. These are:

1. An outpouring of love and light upon mankind, from Shamballa.
2. An invocatory appeal to the Christ, the Head of the Hierarchy, to reappear.
3. The establishing on earth of the divine Plan, to be accomplished willingly by humanity itself.

Incidentally, these three events are relatively near and will be brought about by a conscious working out of the immediate phase of the plan, which it is the divine intention to bring about to a certain extent, before the reappearance of the Christ. The establishing of right human relations is the immediate task and is that phase of the Plan of Love and Light to which humanity can most easily respond and for which they are already evidencing a sense of responsibility.

Little attention has been paid to the factor of invocation as expressed by the people of the world; yet down the

ages the invocative cry of humanity has risen to the Hierarchy and brought response. Some day a scientific study
will be made of the great world prayers, spiritual statements
and invocative appeals and their relation to world events;
this relationship will become illuminatingly apparent and
the result will be a closer linking of earth and the spiritual
centres of love and life. This has not yet been done. Let me
illustrate: The spiritual statement by Shri Krishna, to be
found in the Lord's Song, the *Bhagavad Gita,* was an an-
nouncement, preparatory to the coming of the Christ. In
that Song He says:

> "Whenever there is a withering of the Law and
> an uprising of lawlessness on all sides, *then* I manifest
> Myself. For the salvation of the righteous and the
> destruction of such as do evil, for the firm establishing
> of the Law, I come to birth in age after age."

In the lawless and wicked period of the Roman Empire,
the Christ came.

Another instance of a notable and most ancient invocation is to be found in the *Gayatri* where the people
invoke the Sun of Righteousness in the words: "Unveil to
us the face of the true spiritual Sun, hidden by a disk of
golden light, that we may know the truth and do our whole
duty, as we journey to Thy sacred Feet."

To this we should also add the Four Noble Truths,
as enunciated by the Buddha and which are so well known
to all of us, summarising as they do the causes and the
sources of all the troubles which concern humanity. There
are many translations of these truths to which I have
referred; they all convey the same longing and appeal and
they are all essentially correct as to meaning. During the
Jewish dispensation, there was given a statement as to
human conduct in the words of the Ten Commandments;
upon these, human law has been based and upon them the
laws governing the relationships of people in the West have
been founded. It has eventuated in a somewhat narrow conception of Deity; these Commandments are didactic and

present the negative angle. Then Christ came and gave to us the fundamental law of the universe, the law of love; He also gave us the Lord's Prayer with its emphasis upon the Fatherhood of God, the coming of the Kingdom and right human relations.

Now the Great Invocation, as used by the Hierarchy itself, has been given out to the world. So reactionary is human thinking that the claim made by me that it is one of the greatest of the world's prayers and is on a par with the other voiced expressions of spiritual desire and intention will evoke criticism. That is of no importance. Only a few—a very few—in the early days of Christianity employed the Lord's Prayer, because it needed recording, expression in understandable terms, and adequate translation before its widespread use became possible. That effort took centuries to accomplish. Today, we have all the facilities for rapid distribution and these have all been employed on behalf of the Great Invocation.

The uniqueness connected with the Invocation consists in the fact that it is, in reality, a great method of integration. It links the Father, the Christ and humanity in one great relationship. Christ emphasised ever the Fatherhood of God and substituted it in place of the cruel, jealous tribal Jehovah of the nation to which He had gone for a physical vehicle. Christ was a Jew. In the 17th chapter of St. John's Gospel (which is another of the major spiritual statements of the world) Christ emphasised the relation of the Christ consciousness to the consciousness of Deity itself. He linked the concept of the Monad to the fully developed soul-infused personality, and the underlying unity existing between all beings in all forms and the Father. The possibility which He there expressed still remains distant, except in connection with the spiritual Hierarchy; it is good, however, to remember that They have achieved a goal towards which all true disciples and initiates are working. The Great Invocation relates the will of the Father (or of Shamballa), the love of the Hierarchy, and the service of Humanity into one great *Triangle of*

*Energies;* this triangle will have two major results: the "sealing of the door where evil dwells," and the working out through the Power of God, let loose on earth through the Invocation, of the Plan of Love and Light.

This is no idle dream. From the angle of the human consciousness, the vehicle of Light is, first of all, the great educational systems of the world, with their capacity for improvement and for the extension of science along the lines of the betterment of mankind, and not for its destruction as is so oft the case today; to this must be coupled the steady changing or conversion of scientific attainment, by the enlightenment which wisdom brings; this has in the past safeguarded human aspiration and human progress into light. In the light which enlightenment brings we shall eventually see Light, and the day will come when thousands of the sons of men and countless groups will be able to say with Hermes and with Christ: "I am (or we are) the light of the world."

We are told by the Christ that men "love darkness rather than light because their deeds are evil." Nevertheless, one of the great emerging beauties of the present time is that light is being thrown into every dark place, and there is nothing hidden which shall not be revealed.

When we invoke the Mind of God and say: "Let light stream forth into the minds of men, let light descend on Earth," we are voicing one of the great needs of humanity and—if invocation and prayer mean anything at all—the answer is certain and sure. When we find present in all people at all times, in every age and in every situation, the urge to voice an appeal to the unseen spiritual Centre, there is a fixed surety that such a Centre exists. Invocation is as old as the hills or as old as humanity itself; therefore no other argument for its usefulness or its potency is required.

The usual invocative appeal has hitherto been selfish in its nature and temporary in its formulation. Men have prayed for themselves; they have invoked divine help for those they love; they have given a material interpretation to their basic needs. The invocation, lately given to us by the Hierarchy, is a *world* prayer; it has no personal appeal or temporal invocative urge; it expresses humanity's need and pierces through all the difficulties, doubts and questionings—straight to the Mind and the Heart of the One in Whom we live and move and have our being—the One Who will stay with us until the end of time itself and "until the last weary pilgrim has found his way home."

But the Invocation is not vague or nebulous. It voices the basic needs of mankind today—the need for light and love, for understanding of the divine will and for the end of evil. It says triumphantly: "Let light descend on earth; may Christ return to earth; let purpose guide the little wills of men; let the Plan seal the door where evil dwells." It then sums it all up in the clarion words: "Let light and love and power restore the Plan on Earth." Always the emphasis is laid upon the place of appearance and of manifestation: the *Earth*.

Already this Invocation is doing much to change world affairs—far more than may appear to your eyes. Much remains to be done. I would ask all students, all men of goodwill and all who are participating in the work of the Triangles and helping to build the network of light and goodwill, to do all that is possible to spread the use of the Invocation. The year 1952 will be a year of spiritual crisis and a year when it should prove possible to close more tightly the door where evil dwells.

The Invocation has been sent out by the combined Ashrams of the Masters and by the entire Hierarchy; it is used by its Members with constancy, exactitude and power. It will serve to integrate the two great centres: the Hierarchy and Humanity, and to relate them both in a new and dynamic manner to the "centre where the Will of God is known."

I ask you, therefore, during the coming years to prepare to use and distribute the Invocation and make it a major endeavour. I would have you call all the people in every country in the world (whom you are in a position to reach) to a united voicing of the Invocation on the same day in every land.* I would ask you to collect all that I have said or written anent the Invocation and then prepare a brief manual as to its use and purpose, putting a copy in the hands of all those who are willing to use it. A comprehension of its origin, meaning and potency will render it far more effective. The year 1952 should see a major turning point in the thinking of humanity, in human goals and human affairs. For implementing this I would ask you to work.

Here you have a short resume of the five most important spiritual results of the present century. The war itself has cleared the way for them. They are a natural and normal outcome of the war and have arisen (with the exception of the Great Invocation) out of the masses of the people and from their thinking; it was also their unvoiced demand and the appeal of their suffering hearts which brought the Invocation to them.

The two other spiritual events which I listed lie, as you know, still in the future. They are the closer approach of the members of the spiritual Hierarchy to our humanity, and the reappearance of the Christ. With these two points I will not deal. I have dealt with the last stupendous event in the book by that name; and in the book, *The Externalisation of the Hierarchy,* I have dealt exhaustively with the emergence of the Hierarchy on to the physical plane.

I am anxious to have you concentrate on the work which is preparatory to these two "emergences"; seek to make the five spiritual events which are already within your working knowledge a definite part of your own spiritual endeavour.

Let humanity constitute your field of service, and may it be said of you that you knew the spiritual facts and were a dynamic part of these spiritual events; may it not be said of you that you knew these things and did nothing about them and failed to exert yourself. Let not time slip by as you *work.*

---

*World Invocation Day was launched in June 1952, and is held annually on the day of the June (Gemini) Full Moon.

# STANZAS FOR DISCIPLES

## The Path

Seek not, O twice-blessed One, to attain the spiritual essence before the mind absorbs. Not thus is wisdom sought. Only he who has the mind in leash, and sees the world as in a mirror can be safely trusted with the inner sense. Only he who knows the five senses to be but illusion, and that naught remains save the two ahead, can be admitted into the secret of the Cruciform transposed.

The path that is trodden by the Server is the path of fire that passes through his heart and leads to the head. It is not on the path of pleasure, nor on the path of pain that liberation may be taken or that wisdom comes. It is by the transcendence of the two, by the blending of pain with pleasure, that the goal is reached, that goal that lies ahead, like a point of light seen in the darkness of a winter's night. That point of light may call to mind the tiny candle in some attic drear, but—as the path that leads to that light is trodden through the blending of the pair of opposites—that pin point cold and flickering grows with steady radiance till the warm light of some blazing lamp comes to the mind of the wanderer by the way.

Pass on, O Pilgrim, with steady perseverance. No candle light is there nor earth lamp fed with oil. Ever the radiance grows till the path ends within a blaze of glory, and the wanderer through the night becomes the child of the sun, and enters within the portals of that radiant orb.

## THE CUP OF KARMA

There is a cup held to the lips of those who drink, by four great Lords of Karma. The draught within that cup must all be drained, down to the nethermost drop, e'er it is possible to fill the cup with a purer, sweeter one. The seven Lords of cosmic Love await the hour of filling.

The cup is naught. The draught within distils forth drop by drop. It will not all be drained until the final hour wherein the Pilgrim takes the cup. He lifts it from the hand of those Who, bending, hold it to his lips. Until that day the cup is held, and in inner blind dismay the Pilgrim drinks. After that hour he lifts his head; he sees the light beyond; he takes the cup and, with a radiant joy, drains to the very dregs.

The contents of the cup are changed; the bitter now becomes the sweet; the fiery essence then is lost in cool, life-giving streams. The fire absorbed within has burned and scarred and seared. The draught now taken soothes the burns; it heals the scars and permeates the whole.

The Four bend down and see the work. They release the cup of Karma. The tender Lords of Cosmic Love then mix another draught, and—when the cup is empty seen (emptied by conscious will)—they pour within that which is needed now for broader, larger living. Until the cup has once been used, filled, drained, and seen as naught, it cannot safely hold within that which is later given.

But when to utter emptiness the Pilgrim drains the cup then to the world in torment now he turns. With cup in hand (drained once, filled again, and refused to selfish need) he tends the need of struggling men who tread the way with him. The draught of love, of sacred fire, of cool, health-giving stream he lifts not towards himself but holds it forth to others. Upon the road of weary man he becomes a Lord of Power—power gained through work accomplished, power reached through conscious will. Through the cup of Karma drained he gains the right to serve.

Look on, O Pilgrim, to the goal. See shining far ahead

the glory that envelops and the light that naught can dim. Seize on the cup and swiftly drain, delay not for the pain. The empty cup, the steady hand, the firm and strong endeavour lead to a moment's agony and thence to radiant life.

### THE LISTENING PILGRIM

Listen, O Pilgrim, to the chanting of the Word by the great Deva Lords. Hush all earth vibration, still the restless strivings of lower mind, and with ear intent hark to the sounds that rise to the throne of the Logos. Only the pure in heart can hear, only the gentle can respond.

The stormy sounds of all earth struggle, the shrill vibration of the watery sphere, the crashing note marking the place of thought, dims the sound and shuts out the tone. He who is silent, quiet and calm within, who sees all by means of light divine and is not led by light reflected within the threefold spheres, is he who will shortly hear. From out the environing ether will strike a note upon his ear unlike the tones that sound within the world terrestrial.

Listen, O Pilgrim, for when that sound strikes in colourful vibration upon the inner sense, know that a point has been achieved marking a great transition.

Watch then, O Pilgrim, for the coming of that hour. With purified endeavour mount nearer to that Sound. Know when its tone steals through the misty dawn, or in the mellow sunlight strikes soft upon the ear, that soon the inner hearing will become expanded feeling and will give place to sight and perfect comprehension.

Know when the music of the spheres comes to you note by note, in misty dawn or sunny noon, at cool of eve, or sounding through the deep of night, that in their rhythmic tone lies secret revelation.

## An Esoteric Fragment

*Where is the gate, O Lanoo, which guards the triple-way?*

Within the sacred heart of Him Who is the threefold Path. I reach the gate and pass within, entering thus the Heart, through the means of wide compassion.

*How many gates are there, O Passer on the Way?*

The gates are seven, each leading to the centre of a great sphere of bliss. By the one who seeks to know, the first gate must be found. That entered, in periodic cycles he will find the other six.

*You speak of wide compassion as the key that opens wide the gates. Explain in words the simplest the need that this involves.*

The need of gentle mercy, which knows and sees yet understands; the need of tears of crystal to wash away a brother's sins; the need of fiery courage that can hold a brother's hand, and lift and elevate him though all the world cry "nay"; the need of comprehension, that has experienced and knows; the occult sense of oneness must guide unto the gate.

*What else will lead a man to the portal of the Path?*

Compassion first and conscious oneness; then death to every form that holds and hides the life; next wisdom linked with learning, and the wise use of the Word; speech of an occult nature and the silence of the Centre, held in the noise of all the world.

*Can you, O Lanoo, blend these thoughts into a threefold charge?*

First Oneness, then the Word, and lastly Growth.

## HEALING

A centre of violet, orbed by yellow, melts into red. Yellow develops and protects. It ensheaths the nucleus. When you attain the significance of violet, the laws of health and magnetic alleviation will be no longer sealed. The seal is being loosed by the devas of the shadows; the yellow approaches the violet and the red progresses. The ranks approach and cooperation is possible. In loosening the seal the gateway opens. These three are the great Helpers and in Their hands lies knowledge for the next generation. Approach.

## THE HIDDEN PORTAL

*An immense cone of fire is seen in the midst of an arid desert. A man stands in front of the scene in an attitude of indecision. The cone stands between the man and a fruitful country.*

Rises the cone from out the arid waste. Naught but its heat is felt, naught but its glare is seen. Its flames have swept the country and left the desert bare. It radiates forth a fire that devours all before it. All green things die and the dwellers on the sphere recede before its flame, scorching and burning, cruel and superb.

White is its inner heart, red the surrounding flame, and yellow the spreading fire. Like a mantle of fierce heat it shuts out the vision and obscures the beyond. Like a pall of rosy red tinged with an orange deep it veils all the distance.

From out the country full and green, across the arid waste had travelled far the Pilgrim. Naught had he held and kept, naught save his strong desire, back on the road he might not go, but onward to the fire.

From out that cone of fire, echoing from its heart, swift to his ears a voice that said: "Behold the place of God."

From out the cone of fire a note fell on his ear that touched a chord within his breast, and awakened quick response.

Press on, O Pilgrim, towards the flame; brave the fierce ardour of the fire; enter within the portal which is hidden by its light.

The door is there, unseen, unknown, watched by the Lords of Flame. Deep in the heart of yellow, close by the outer rim, lies the key that holds hid the secret. The threshold of that inner door, the step unseen that must be reached, will meet the feet within the fringe of flame. Put forth the hand and touch the door, knock thrice with pure intent. A voice will answer to that call. The words will sound: "Who is it seeks the way?"

## The Key

Key the first lies hid under the Threshold, guarded by the Watcher. He who breaks in must stoop and seize after a search of strenuous decision. The hand that grasps the key must have the nail-mark through the centre there located. When this is so, door the first will open.

Key the second lies across the Threshold, over the heap of thorns. From the centres in the feet must pour the blood that dissolves all hindrances. In the bloodstained feet and the nail-marked hands lies hid the secret. Seek you them. Then door the second will open to your touch.

Key the third lies half way up. Just at the level of the heart that key is seen. Before it can be seized and used the spear must pierce and thus the blood pour forth, cleansing and making whole. Only those thus purified can grasp the key and pass through door the third.

## An Occult Message

The key is found; and with the pressure of the hands in service of the Light and with a beating heart of love, that key is turned. The door swings wide open.

With hasty feet the one who hastens towards the light enters that door; then waits. He holds the door ajar for those who follow after and thus—in action—waits.

A Voice sounds forth: My brother, close that door, for

each must turn the key with his own hand and each must enter through that door alone. The blazing light within the Temple of the Lord is not for all at the same moment or the same hour of each day. Each knows his hour. Your hour is *Now*.

So, brother, close that door. Remember, those behind know not the door has opened or the door has closed. They see it not. Rest on that thought, my brother, and passing through the door close it with care, and enter upon another stage upon the upward Way—alone, yet not alone.

## The Crucifixion

In the mystic Heart, with its two lobes, lies the key to the reservoir. In the out-going and the return the cross is made. Midway it stands, with the right hand and the left hand path on either side. There the man is crucified, with the two on either hand—one on the right and one on the left. In the apprehension of the key, in the opening and shutting of doors, lies life eternal. Know you and understand.

## The Cross

In the Cross is hidden Light. The vertical and horizontal in mutual friction create; a vibrant Cross scintillates, and motion originates. When the vertical assumes the horizontal, pralaya supervenes. Evolution is the movement of the horizontal to upright positiveness. In the secret of direction lies the hidden wisdom; in the doctrine of absorption lies the healing faculty; in the point becoming the line, and the line becoming the cross is evolution. In the cross swinging to the horizontal lies salvation and pralayic peace.

## The Chalice

The lower chalice rises like a flower of colour dark or somber. Dull it appears to the outer vision, but within a light will sometime shine and shatter the illusion.

Chalice the second rises from out the lower sheath as does the flower from out the calix green. Of colour rose it is, and many shades thereof; and to the onlooker it seems as if the colour might transcend the inner shining light. But this is but illusion which time itself dispels.

Chalice the third surmounts all and opens wide in time its outspread petals. Blue does it appear and blends with the rose, forming at first a deep impenetrable shade which shuts out the light.

Within the three, deep hidden in the heart, tiny at first yet ever waxing greater, shines the light divine. This light, through radiating heat and innate divine vibration, constructs for itself a sheath of iridescence. It emerges from the threefold chalice as a floating bubble alights on a flower.

Within this iridescent sheath burns the inner Flame, and in its turn it burns out the lower gross material. E'en as the Path is neared, clearer the light shines out. Forth through the chalice gross and dark that forms the foundation shines the light supernal, till all who see the radiation cry out within themselves: "Behold, a God is here."

Forth from the chalice rosy red shines the inner glow, till soon the red of earth desire becomes the glow of heaven's fire, and all is lost save aspiration that shades not the cup with karmic colour.

Forth from the chalice blue shines and glows the inner light divine till all the forms are burnt and gone, and naught is left save one divine abstraction. Naught but the shells remain below, naught but the forms for use, and at the culmination what strange event is seen? Tarry, O Pilgrim, at the strange appearance, with bowed head watch the progress of the fire. Slowly the chalice threefold merges into an altar, and from that triple altar mounts the fire unto its Source. As mounts and spreads the inner flame, the beauty of the central sphere, lit with a radiance white, causes the worlds to stand and cry: "Behold, a God is here."

Ever the flames mount higher, ever the warmth streams forth, till—in the moment of the hour set—the flame destroys all, and all is gone, the work of ages passes, in a moment, into nothingness.

But forth from the fourfold fire, up from the altar of

the ages, springs the Liberated One, the Flame. Back to the fire of Cosmos springs the dual flame. Into the Three is absorbed the essence, and becomes one with its Source. The Spark becomes the Flame, the Flame becomes the Fire, and forms part of the great Cosmic blaze that holds the secret of the Five hidden within the heart.

## A Fire Mantram

The point of light within the glowing arc, O Pilgrim on the Way, waxes and wanes as application hard or not betrays the purpose within the heart.

That point is ever there, unnoticed and unseen. Dark is the night and drear, and sore the heart of the unillumi-nated Pilgrim. Dark is the night but drearness is not felt when within the gloomy portal is seen the bright illusive light, the light that flickers ever on ahead, enticing with its gleam the Pilgrim ever onward.

Six times the light may wax and wane, six times the glow is felt, but at the seventh glowing hour the Flame bursts forth.

Six times the Flame bursts forth, six times the burning starts, but at the seventh hour the altar is lost sight of and only Flame is seen.

Six times the circle of the burning fire, six times the roaring furnace burns and separates, but at the seventh naught is left save the ascending Flame, that mounts to the Triadal Spirit.

Six times the Flame mounts up, six times the cloud recedes, but at the seventh naught is seen save everlasting fire.

Six times the Flame absorbs the water, six times the moisture disappears, but at the seventh great absorption naught is left save iridescent fire.

Three times the fire envelops, three times the sun re-cedes; at time the fourth the work is done, and naught is left save Flame primordial. That Flame absorbs, revolves, receives, and remains. When all that is has traversed the Flame, then Time is not.

Training for new age
discipleship is provided
by the *Arcane School.*
The principles of the
Ageless Wisdom are
presented through esoteric
meditation, study and
service as a *way of life.*

*Write to the publishers
for information.*

# INDEX

## A

Abstraction —
doctrine, 167
principle, entering body, procedure, 165
processes, 162, 163
will principle actively present or not, seeing, 164

Adept —
anchorages, three, 481
powers, 10

Ajna centre of initiate, 257

Alignment —
agency of antahkarana, 470-474
direct, Shamballa and humanity, 471
first stage of process of realisation, 470-471
first step towards fusion, 62
modes in transmutation process, 279
need for, 437
perfect, between monad and physical expression, 475
practice, attainment, 42
process, earlier stage, 500-501
release of evocative sound, 93
step towards mysteries of identification, 62
symbol, 471

Alignment-Invocation-Evocation, thought of, importance, 498

Alta-major centre of initiate, 257, 432

Amen, use, 51, 52

Angel of the Presence, 176

Anima mundi, 17

Antahkarana —
agent in alignment, 470-474
building —
by group, 112

circumstances involved, 464-474
conscious task beginning, 487
consciously undertaken, 483
demand for, 115
effect, final, 475-476
extension in consciousness, 471
from both ends, 494, 495, 501
goal, 495
individual, 474
on mental plane, 466-467, 469
period covered, 462
process, 485-495, 501-519
progress, factors, 462
relationships, 265, 442
service, 497
six methods, 486-495, 501, 512-513
steps, 43, 444, 445-452
technique, 474-477, 486-495
use of creative imagination, 482, 487, 489-490, 511, 512
built by conscious effort, 467
completion, 50, 256, 408, 445, 472, 475, 494-495, 695
component parts, 454
connection with abstract mind, 167
cosmic, 406, 407, 533
definitions, 449, 454
effect in free interplay of life-energy, 280
functions, 61, 161, 216, 266, 442, 449, 475, 491, 591
group, 29, 119, 221, 256, 257
left with Monad at fourth initiation, 101
nature of, 452-456
need for, 137, 437
of disciple, dependence on by Master, 547

**771**

of group, formation, 547
of humanity, 273, 505
planetary, 406, 407, 724
projection by disciple, 490-493, 501-510, 512, 514-519
projection from Ashram of Master, 284
seventh woven thread, 131, 505
stabilisation, 495
systemic, 406, 407
threads weaving within consciousness, 466-468
use, 27, 28, 30, 31, 34, 131, 183, 495, 585, 592
Way of Resurrection, 318
Apostolic Succession, true meaning, 735
Appetites, fleshly, none in control, 126
Aquarian —
  energy —
    effect on astral plane, 581
    enabling Christ to complete His task, 232
    enabling Master R. to become Lord of Civilisation, 232
    influence giving Black Lodge power, 232
    influence, hierarchical relationship to Shamballa, 231
    pouring into Hierarchy, response to, 231
  phase of planetary history, inauguration, 19
Aquarian Age —
  characteristics, 584
  planned work of Hieararchy, 227, 238-319
  See also New Age
Aquarius —
  effect upon Hierarchy, 230
  energies superseding Piscean, 551
  energy used by Buddha of Activity, 268-269
Aries, informing Life, 269
"Army of the Voice", 147, 179, 181, 183-184, 200
Art —
  creative, 123, 243, 572, 574

of revelation perfected by initiates, 300
Aryan —
  cycle, 559
  definition, 593-594
  Race, 188, 478, 499, 560-561, 592, 593, 664
"As a man thinketh in his heart", 137, 261
As if consciousness no longer useful, 443-444
Ascension —
  initiation, 163, 284
  true, 361
Ascensions, series, 528
Ashram —
  admittance, 97-98, 126-127, 297-298
  centre, penetration by disciple, 546
  composition, 97-98, 342, 346, 366
  concerns unconnected with disciple, 547
  creative work, 294-297
  definitions, 74, 126
  effects of admission of initiate, 562
  energy, direction into world, 690, 691
  enrichment, requirement for group initiation, 343-344
  formation by initiate, 653
  freedom from coercion or supervision, 379
  inner, 212, 220, 221
  instinctive, reaction to Ray influence and prevailing Will, 379
  keynote, 342
  magnetic pull, response to, 668
  of love-wisdom, 383-384
  of Master, life, effects, 98-99
  of Sanat Kumara, 229, 238, 366-430
  on intuitional buddhic plane, 119
  perfect unison, 346
  quality, determination, 362
  radiation and magnetic field, 379

relation of Master to, 362
teaching by Master, 544-545

Ashramic —
acquiescence, 210
recognition of group, 226

Ashrams —
cyclic inflow from Sirius, 415
energies, dynamic, revealing, impulsive, 712
externalisation. *See* Externalisation.
formation, 378, 388
forty-nine, 370, 388
inner exoteric branch, formation by D.K., 253-254
of Masters, 168-170, 188, 240-241
on buddhic plane today, 387
one-pointed intellect and inclusive life, 561
seven, 335, 361, 380, 383-388
subsidiary, 388
united, spiritual synthesis, 441

Aspirant —
goals, 298
hardest period, 683-684
symbol, 470
work, 182, 298, 588

Aspirants —
all, objective, 444
self-centered attitude, 439
testing, 239-240
who can be helped and trained, means, 668

Aspiration —
advancing, meeting, 112
of masses, growing, effect on Masters, 119
relation to intuitive faculty, 442-443

Astral —
body, 122, 161-162, 442-443, 481
cosmic, plane, 166, 201, 202, 283, 357, 361, 377, 392, 398
development in humanity, 187
energy, wrong use, 549
life, transformation, 442-443
plane, non-existent, 202, 443, 578

plane, transformation, 581
plane, turmoil and chaos, causes, 401-402

Astrology, new, teaching by Master D.K., 252-253

Atlantean —
civilisation, 555
cycle, 560
initiation, 345
Race, intelligence, 560, 561

Atlanteans, unfoldment, 185-188

Atlantic Charter, 70

Atlantis —
consciousnes, thread, 477-480
old, symbol, 561

Atma-buddhi —
blended, reality, 415
synthesis, 407

Atma-buddhi Manas, 445, 475, 645

Atmic —
nature, expression of will aspect, 311
plane, characteristics, 463
plane, dynamic energy, inflow, 599

Atom —
fission, cause, 646-647
permanent manasic, 50, 475

Atomic energy —
release, demonstration, 412, 655
use for good of mankind, 647-648

Atoms of elementals, 9

Attraction of initiate, 736-737

A.U.M., 50, 52, 53, 55, 56, 200-202, 513

Austria, characteristics, 625-626

Avatar —
coming, 13, 15, 93-95, 257
cosmic, elimination of cosmic evil from Earth, 736
forerunner, the Christ, 94, 95

Avatar of Synthesis, 655, 734-735

Avataric stimulation, downpouring, effects, 15

Avatars —
doctrine, 160
great, door of entrance to our system, 423
origin, 398

under direction of Solar Logos, 734, 735

Awareness —
life in initiatory process, 441-443
of happenings in Council Chamber of Shamballa, 530

### B

Bailey, Alice A. —
dictation to, 251
finding by Master D.K., 643
teaching, 255

Beauty —
goodness, and wisdom, 59
in manifestation, secret, 243
of ritual of daily life of Sanat Kumara, 246-247

Becoming, characteristics, 440

Being —
description, 440
Essential, at fifth initiation, 178
grasped, 263
nature of, 104
plane of Master's functioning, 438
related to That Which Creates, 728

Birth of Christ in humanity, results, 333

Black Lodge —
attitude, 236, 679, 681
concentration in Germany, 189
let loose, 554
masters, group, 696
members, Ray, 716
nature and purpose, 727
origin, 186
potency, increase, 187, 188
production of fear of death, 732
reaction of ninth-degree initiate to, 737
roots, 202
safety and status, menacing factors, 189
vs. Great White Lodge, 14
work, 188, 189-190, 191-192, 717

Black magician, initiation, 348-351

Blavatsky, H. P., teaching, 255, 264

Blindness, occult, 9, 196, 197-200, 703

Bliss, concern, 119

Blood stream, use by Sutratma, 451

Blue Lodge, 416, 418

Body created for Master's use, 51, 101, 455, 705

Bomb, atomic —
caused by Shamballa energy, 646-647
culmination of expression of power, 655

Brain —
apparatus, nature and use, 431-432
channel to desired point of contact, need for, 437
conditioning, 431-432
consciousness, factor in initiation, 259
consciousness involved in tests, 433
consciousness, surface recognition of who and what, 707-708
control by Sutratma, 451
direct line to Triad, 695
factor in integration, 562-563
function, 591
insensitive to monadic vibration, 287
interpretations registered, 436
recording agent, channel from Triad, 442
registration, 485
retention of registered facts, test, 433

Brazil on Path of Probation, 625

Breath —
distinction from Sound, 54
united, 148, 155, 161, 163

Breathing process, nature of, 54

Bridge. See Antahkarana.

British Commonwealth, relation to United States, 625, 631

Brotherhood —
definition, 277
due to synthesis, 121
establishment, 134

mystery in process of solving, 276-277

Buddha, Lord —
achievement, 204-205, 524
and arhats, work, effect, 13
and Christ, work, relation, 254
annual appearance, 70
emissary of Great Council, 130
enunciation of platform of third initiation, 695
group work, 240
help today, 90, 92
initiation, 385-386
mistake, 396, 397
passing with Christ to higher service, 83-84
plans, 415
prepared way for fourth initiation, 703
work, 527

Buddhas of Activity, 130, 180, 206, 257, 267-274, 405, 407, 587, 591

Buddhi —
active in hearts of initiates, 415
expression, full, 6
expression of purpose of Shamballa, 311
from Sirius at heart of every atom, 415
responsiveness of emotional body to, 362
See also Intuition.

Buddhic —
awareness of Hierarchy, 481
consciousness of Hierarchy members who remain, 166
cosmic, plane, Path leading to, 399
life, 45
plane —
allied with cosmic astral plane, 712
ashrams on, 119
characteristics, 463
functioning of fourth-degree initiate on, 699
reception of love energy, 377
relation to pure reason, 537
principle in action, 27
vehicle, main instrument of sentiency, 278

Building Forces of planet and solar system, cooperation with, 729

Burning grounds, 29-31, 33, 39, 47, 225


C

Call —
for hierarchical workers, 300
to reveal groups and nature of Christ consciousness, 301
to see Christ as He is, 301

Cancer, energy from, 268

Capital and labour problem in U.S.A., 633

Capricorn, energy from, 269

Carotid gland —
functions, 431-432
of initiate, 257
relation to brain, 431-432

Catechism, esoteric, 302-303

Causal body —
destruction, 28, 132, 161, 162, 163, 216, 475
esoteric "renunciation", 220
shattered, disappearance, 279
vehicle of Monad, 216
See also Lotus, solar; Soul body.

Celibacy, enforced, 84

Central Spiritual Sun. See Sun, Central Spiritual.

Centres, subject dangerous, 336

Chain of Hierarchy, 138

Character, pure, basic essential, 8-11

Chohan on monadic plane, 284

Christ —
accomplishment as World Saviour, 196
act of evocation, 89
activity, sphere, determination, 603
aid and protection by Masters, 655
and Avatar of Synthesis, 655
and Buddha, work, relation established, 254
and Jesus, joint rent in veil of maya, 192-193
approach to, 441

assistance to Buddha of Activity, 268-269

authority delegated by Sanat Kumara, 368

awareness on Way of Higher Evolution, 291

coming, 578, 593, 604, 639

communication of Word of Power, 175

demonstration, 205

destruction of barriers, 655-656

disciples, 755

enabled, by Aquarian energy, to take initiation, 232

evolution, qualities, 180

expression in Himself, 296

expression of Sirian initiation, 415

fitting Himself to be distributing Agent, 647

forerunner of Avatar, 94, 95

freedom, 92

influence on three planes, 615-616

initiations, 83, 385-387

knowledge of secret of life, 730

love of God, 88-89

mission, dual, 548

mission, keynote, 95

not crucified, 314-315

on Way of Higher Evolution, 524

overshadowing initiates and disciples, 615

overshadowing Jesus, 83, 86, 524, 697

passing with Lord Buddha to higher service, 83-84

physical appearance, 616-618, 705

presence, recognition, 668

presentation of fourth initiation, 695

protection of initiate at third initiation, 176

relation to Christian Church, 205

renunciation, 315

resurrection of human spirit out of tomb, 638

resurrection, true, 730

return, implementation, 614-620, 638

return, inevitability, 602

preparation for by Himself, 581

seventh initiation, 83, 655, 697, 730

sixth initiation, 524, 655

spirit present today, 499-500

task, 89, 91-93, 638, 659

vacation of position as World Saviour, 398

veil of temple rent, 702

vision and expansion of consciousness, 289-290, 291

within, birthing, 6

work, 170, 240, 379, 521-522, 527-528

Christ-consciousness —
  attainment, 313-315, 521
  definition, 571
  pouring upon masses, 615-616

Christian Church, perversions, 296

Christianity in New World Religion, 296

Churches, revitalisation, 332

Churchianity, theological, 614

Civilisation —
  modern, death blow, 134
  new, platform, 194, 255, 574

Civilisations, destruction, 306-307

Clear cold light —
  cry of invocation, 73-79
  of reason, 43, 60, 139
  personality correspondence, 42-43
  point of tension, 49
  point, seeing, 174-175
  revelations, 39-41
  standing in, 64
  test, 47

Clearing house for all emotional reactions and glamours, 683

Colour —
  none, only light, 171, 173-174
  restoration by Mysteries, 332

Commonsense, source and action, 592

Conclave of Masters every seven years, 393

Conference of Hierarchy, centennial, 393-394

Conflict —
   harmony through, energy, 602-641
   nature of, 606
   termination, 607
Consciousness —
   centering in head, attempt, 3-4
   connection of physical and astral body, energy used, 448
   continuity. *See* Continuity of consciousness.
   expansions, 6, 237, 469
   extension, 471
   focussed in Spiritual Triad, 261
   forms, destruction, 306-307
   group. *See* Group consciousness.
   higher, changes, results, 17
   human, awakening today, 17
   initiate, 25-26, 119
   left behind, 82
   none on etheric levels, 178
   normal, of initiate, 167
   of disciple in rapport with Hierarchy, 543
      embodied and disembodied lives, shift, 16
      Hierarchy, 127-128
      Master and disciple, bringing together, 542-543
      Shamballa, nature of, grasp, 363
      whole, work with by Masters on third Path, 405-406
   Sensitivity, Awareness, Planetary Rapport, Universal Consciousness, 434
   seven states, 462-463
   stabilised in Spiritual Triad, 139
   thread, 453-455, 458, 464, 469, 474-478
   three states, expression, 466
   transcended, 282, 283
   types concerned with three Crosses, 693-694
   unfoldment, 55
   within form, response to expanding range of contacts, 449
Contact with —
   Master, direct, 29
   Real Man, 7, 11

   Shamballa and Lord of World, first time, 175
Continuity —
   basis, 449
   of consciousness, 433, 452
Control of vehicles at fourth initiation, 698
Cosmic —
   astral plane. *See* Astral, cosmic.
   consciousness, 663, 694
   impacts, responsiveness to, work with, 406
   level, higher, functioning on, benefits, 363-364
   mental plane. *See* Mental cosmic.
*Cosmic Fire, Treatise on* —
   date, 409
   purpose, 423
Council —
   at Shamballa, 13, 18, 70, 84, 132, 145-146, 714
   Chamber, definition, 256
   Chamber, Lives constituting, 141-142, 206, 363, 405
   Great, 177, 207, 248
Creation —
   definition, 729
   nature of, understanding, 726
Creative —
   activity involving all Ashrams, 295-296
   activity, seventh Ray period, 572
   art of very high order, interlude, 244
   imagination. *See* Imagination, creative.
   process in man and Logos, 482-483
   thread, 453, 455, 458, 464, 469, 474-476, 478-479
   undertaking of Ashram, initiate's part, 294
   work, three energies active, 672
Creativity —
   production, 575
   upon higher planes after first initiation, 669-670
Creator —
   conscious, on physical plane, becoming, 450

divine, in relation to hierarchical
  Plan, 338
Crises of decision, 608, 639
Crisis —
  point, of Germany, 624
  point, of Russia, 624
  points, from points of tension,
    724, 725
  points, relation to developments,
    589, 623, 638
  production, 589
Cross —
  Cardinal, 481, 693, 701
  cup of sorrow nearly finished,
    234
  Fixed, 479, 481, 482, 693
  Mutable, 481, 482, 693
  of Sanat Kumara, revelation to
    initiate, 540
  of service, creation, 540
  symbol of Aryan unfoldment,
    561
Crucifixion —
  episode, rending of veil of maya,
    193
  erroneous concept, 692
  initiation, 692-703
  life of, 217
  of soul, 455
  on three Crosses, 693-694
  work symbolic, 217
Culture, new, 574
Custodians —
  of the Plan, 69, 76, 495
  of the Will, work, 69, 70, 76


                    D


D.K., Master —
  aid to Master K.H., 169
  Ashram, work, 586
  My Work, V-VI
  preservation of body in which
    He took initiation, 705
  purpose, 34-35, 249
  statement about writing of books,
    250-251
  teaching, preparatory, inter-
    mediate, and revelatory, 255
  work with disciples, 15, 108-109

Dark night of the soul, 39, 40, 42
Darkness, pure, definition, 174
Death —
  aspect of divine purpose, poten-
    cies, use, 226-227
  definitions, 100, 105, 163
  distorted teaching, 318
  effect on centres, 165
  fear of, causes, 731, 732
  nature of, 103
  process, 164-165, 309
  symbolic nature, 700
  true nature, discovery, 105
  types, 731, 732
Decentralisation —
  development, 47
  necessity for, 27, 29
Decision —
  initiation, 361, 609, 653-656
  making, nine choices instead of
    seven, 412
Dedication, resulting in glamour,
  683
Demand and response lost in one
  great Sound, 82-88
Demands, three, made by initiate,
  59, 60-61, 63-66
Desire —
  death by attrition, 210-211
  individual, in group, destruction,
    211
  none in Master, 101
  origin and nature, 186
  transformation, 442-443
  weakening, 261
Desire-love, interpretation by initiate, 469
Destroy, injunction to initiates,
  286-287, 305-317
Destroyer aspect —
  demonstration today (1948), 473
  effects on mental and physical
    planes, 647
Destruction —
  by dynamic Will, 222-225
  due to effort of Spiritual Will,
    306-317
  energy, purificatory, 84-85
  force, utilisation, necessity, 210-
    212

Detachment —
  emphasis on by Lord Buddha, 703
  of soul from body, 100
  suffering with, 702
  value, 73, 718
Deva —
  energies, liberation from, 181
  evolution —
    aura, breaking loose from, 181
    connection with Fifth and Sixth Path, 422
    expression of Will Aspect of Shamballa, 181
    qualities, 180
    work of initiate with, 587
Devas —
  origin, 180
  relation to Buddhas of Activity, 180
  relation to planetary Logos, 179
  task, 181
  work, 178-180, 184
Devotion, factor leading to dissipation of glamour, 682-683
Differentiation processes, learning under, 266
Direction, centre of, use, 691-692
Direction-Will, definition, 469
Directive, words for disciple, 691-692
Disciple —
  accepted, private life, stages, 542-543
  definition, 107
  duty, 298-299
  hallmark, 127
  individual. *See* Individual disciple.
  knowledge that he is Life Itself, 107
  potential hazard, 156
  recognition of being Father aspect, 102-103
  revelation of essential unity, 298-299
  symbol, 470, 471
  task, 303
  vibration, stimulation of lesser person or group, 545

Disciples —
  active in 1944, 189
  initiation, 15
  new demands for, 115
  probationary, many, acceptance, 15
  probationary, groups, rules, 18
  Rules, for. *See* Rules.
  senior, advancement, 16
  training, *See* Training.
  working, two major divisions, 128
Discipleship, new, teaching on, 251-252
*Discipleship in the New Age* —
  Volume I, success, 209
  Volumes I and II, instructions, 254
Discipline, self-imposed, 125
Disciplines —
  of the soul, 127
  physical, value, 128
Diversity in unity, required by group, 212-214
Divine —
  aspects, three, related by antahkarana, 467
  intention, reservoir, 717
  nature, dualism, true and illusory, 472
Divinity —
  approach to humanity, emphasis, need for, 301
  definition, 74
  first aspect, association with first Ray, 714
  quality, definition, 204
  revelation, 469
Djwhal Khul. *See* D.K., Master.
Door —
  left behind, 71-73
  of evolution, symbol, 177
  of initiation, 41-43, 347-348, 351, 366
  symbolism, 42-43, 71
  to —
    fifth initiation, 356
    first initiation, 352
    fourth initiation, 352, 353-356
    group initiation, entrance, quotation, 344-345

second initiation, 352-353
sixth initiation, 356
third initiation, 117, 352, 353
Way of Higher Evolution, 352,
    356-366
Dual life of disciple, 434-437, 535-
536
Dualities resolved, 264
Dweller on Threshold, final form,
103

### E

Earth —
    planetary purpose related to
        revelation of love, 728
    preparation for new humanity,
        654
East and West, linking unit, 254
Economics of reconstruction of
    Europe, 586
Education —
    aid by Ashram of K.H., 586
    effect of Mysteries, 332
    in New Age, 121-122
*Education in the New Age,* intro-
    ductory book, 444
Educational movements, goal in
    New Age, 121-122
Educators at end of century, use
    of terms of bridging, 474
"Effect" and "result", distinction
    between, 442
Ego, definitions, 475
Eight, numerical value, 80-81
1875-1890, teaching preparing for
    New Age, 255
Eighth initiation, Transition, 531-
    532, 535, 656, 660, 699, 736-
    737
Electrical —
    energy of aspirant and door, syn-
        chronisation, 351
    interplay of spiritual energy,
        effects, 737
Electricity —
    dynamic, direction at seventh in-
        itiation, 733
    mystery, 331, 351, 394-395, 735
Elementals, nature of, 9
Emergence, point, 623, 634

Emotional —
    control, demonstration, 577
    nature, receptacle of intuition,
        278
Endocrine system, centres, control
    and direction, 669-671
Energies —
    animating soul, 445
    descending, ascension, effects,
        14-18
    fusion causing inflow of spiritual
        will today, 473
    impact upon forms, results, 75
    let loose within realm of Maya,
        186-187
    lower, transfer to heart, 678
    manipulation by Masters and
        initiates, 404-405
Energy —
    astral, of solar system, work
        with, 401-405
    between Shamballa, Hierarchy,
        and Humanity, circulation,
        159
    buddhic, from Sirius, at heart of
        every atom, 415
    channels to accepted disciple,
        543
    direction in conformity with
        Plan, 149
    five types making man conscious
        human being, 450
    fusion with force, 57
    generated by disciple inducing
        revelation, 708-709
    handling by initiate, 149
    human, reoriented, flow in ap-
        plication of Plan, 371
    inflowing into planet, effects,
        13-14, 15, 16, 17
    monadic, work with by initiates,
        65, 184
    most potent, 591
    of —
        concrete knowledge, functions,
            589-592
        divine love, working in group
            consciousness, 349
        harmony through conflict,
            602-641
        intuition, 445, 711

life implemented by will from Aquarius, 230-231
seventh Ray, use by initiate, 183
Shamballa. *See* Shamballa.
Sirius, use in training initiates, 415
soul, impressions on concrete mind, 592
will. *See* Will energy.
part played in inducing revelation, 708-714
projection into realm of intuition, 446-447
radiant, effects and use, 545
relation to force, 378
source in four planes, 358
spiritual, electrical interplay, 737
supernal in manifestation, 556
thoughtform making, 590
transference, organ 5-6
transmission process, 735
transmitters, 689
transmutation, 5-6
type expressed by seventh Ray, 567-575
use and misuse, consideration, 4-5
use, selective, results, 550
Errors in interpretation, 436
Esoteric sense, use, 26
Eternal Now, 308, 437, 697, 701
Etheric —
  body, 10, 339
  levels of activity, 178
  plane, work, 182, 187, 191
  planes, cosmic and physical, 178, 180, 360, 391
Evil —
  cosmic, 202, 696, 722, 727, 736, 737
  forces in Israel, 429
  Forces, violent attempt and failure, cause, 413
  nature of, hint and clue, 350
  relation of Shamballa to, 144-145
Evocation —
  definition, 35

mutual, production, 470
of —
  fire, 91-92
  Hierarchy, 135-136
  magnetic response of Triad, 454
  response from bright centre ahead, 79-82
  will aspect, 105
Evocative centres, human, hierarchical, Shamballa, 79
Evolution —
  definition, 642
  goal, two-thirds of humanity, 484
  history on Earth, 419
  human, 6, 297, 466-468, 548
  nature of, 732
  normal, goal, 497
  of form, 608
  of will, 652
  *See also* Higher Evolution.
Evolutionary —
  activity, three stages, 372
  development, divine intent, perception of, 124
  process, 6-7, 14, 177, 359, 363, 372, 589, 655, 703
  progress, 236-237, 240, 244-245, 363
  pushing forward along Lighted Way, 519-520
  rhythm permeating every atom, 336
Existence —
  Being, Essential Life, Dynamic Energy, Electric Fire, 438
  definition, 737
Experiments —
  in externalising Ashrams, 17
  with incoming forces, 112, 231
Express, injunction to initiate, 286-287, 292-297, 315-316
Externalisation of Hierarchy, 111, 112, 136, 271, 334, 367, 382, 410, 655
Extraverted life of disciple, 548-549
Eye doctrine, 457-458
"Eye of God", 516
"Eye of the needle", 115-116, 117

**F**

Failure, uses, learning, 678

"Faith is the substance . . .", 444

Fanaticism, freedom from, requirement, 127

Father —
aspect, description, 464
revelation, 475
symbolism, 86

Fear, economic, ending, 571

Fellowship, definition, 277

Fifth —
and second, numerical aspects, 593, 601
initiation —
all veils rent, 178
attainments, 81
door to Way of Higher Evolution, 356
facility in using light, 643
five-pointed star, 176
higher correspondence to first, 719-720
interior perfecting, 153
liberation into atmic awareness, 361
Ray energy, 643-653, 688
real name, meaning, 391, 424
relationships, 535, 593, 601
revelation of nature of life in form, 732
symbols, 531
use of will, 689
word received, 312

Fifth-degree initiate —
177, 310, 359-360, 549, 564, 644-645, 650-653
*See also* Master.

Fire —
at all levels of divine expression, 65
baptism, 675-676
by friction creating obstructing door, types, 352
clear cold, point, 174
connotation of first aspect, 217
of dedication, invocation, 682

of group life, transference into Triad, technique, 219-220
significance, 82
solar, guardian of door for first four initiations, 352
solar, relation to electricity, 352

Fires —
eighteen, injunction to group, 96-104
three, electrical nature, 351

First initiation —
ceremony, 531
concern, 535
demonstration, 588
energies, 352, 671, 678
given publicity in future, 123
goal and reward of mystical experience, 666
indications, 663
of humanity, 333, 584
preparation for, requirements, 126-127
preparatory to third initiation, 663, 687
reactions attending, 569-570
requirements, 126-127
seeing light, 83
significance, 667-669

First-degree initiate, appelation, 116, 313, 567-575

Flood, culmination of Atlantean war, 603

Fohat, work with, 401

Force —
changed into energy, mode, 248
fusion with energy, 57
receiving from Master or disciple, temporary, harmful, 32
vortices, 550

Forces —
active today, cleansing and reorganisation, formula, 191
control by, release from, 149
nine, transmutation into divine energies, 456
obstructing, evocation, 14-15
ocean, Life aspect of planet Earth, relates initiate, 97
of Evil, attempt and failure, cause, 413

responsive to and conditioned by energies from Hierarchy and Shamballa, 359
twenty-one, 645

Form —
blotting out, 112, 171
death, 493
field of experience for soul, 129
origin, 55
self-created, of Master, 439
uses known by initiate, 472

Formless planes, 471

Forms —
all, linking and vivifying into one whole, 449
control by, 9, 10
in three worlds and Spiritual Triad, 308
inadequate, destruction, 76, 306-307
sustaining, all, wise use, 127

Forty-nine years, every, event, 721-722

Four, numerical relationship, 178, 476-477

Four Freedoms, 70

Four Noble Truths, 695

Fourth initiation —
agency of antahkarana, 491
and death, 103, 104-105
Atma or pure Spirit in control, 225
central position, 699
complete realisation of relation, 455
consummation at, 244
Cross concerned, 692-703
culmination of series of renunciations, 341-342
destruction of causal body, 310, 437, 493
disappearance of causal body, 279
energy, 353-356
first aspect dominating, 506
fusion with personality, 598
governed by fourth Ray, 701
importance, 696
interior perfection, 153

knowledge conveyed, 248
liberation, 132, 697, 700-701
of Jesus, 192-193
passing, effect, 475
point of light developing into five-pointed star, 176
preparation for, 101
process, purity of vehicles, 698
relations, 535, 603
Renunciation, Ray fourth, 602-641
response to third aspect of first Ray, 650
Rule XI, 215-217
significances, 692-703
soul and causal body gone, 101, 106
symbology, 176, 665
training for, use of Sirian energy, 415

Fourth-degree initiate —
attainments, 225
awareness focussed in Monad, 316
discovery of true nature of death, 105
effects of Ray energy, 585
focussed orientation, 650-651
functioning on buddhic plane, 699
impressions from Shamballa, 549
knowledge of himself, 105
revelation of purpose, 714-715
work on buddhic levels, 359-360

Frameworks, work within, 152-156

France, characteristics, 428-429, 627-628

Free will —
energy, underlying significance, 566
liberation, 610
man's, recognition, 722
principle, growth, 251
unimpeded, exertion, 640

Freedom —
capacity for, 614
from limitations of matter, problem, 679-687
keynote, 684
of the world, 284

principle, manifestations, 416-417

violation and ultimate victory, 679-682

Freedoms —
of nine initiations, 685-687
result of Detachment, Dispassion, Discrimination, 685

*From Bethlehem to Calvary*, book, 687

"From the point of Light . . .", VII

Full Moon —
June, every year, 88-89
periods, teaching, 254

Full Moons, May and June, 1943, preparation for by Hierarchy, 76

Fusion —
definition, 265
essential, producing points of tension, 542-555
means of liberation, 216, 466-467
of manifested world, 542
of Master's consciousness with that of disciple, 542-549

Fusions —
of energies, 563-565
points, creation, 537, 541, 542
points, successive, 537, 538
progressive and recognised, 601

### G

Gemini —
energy from, 268, 424-425
victory, 89

Gethsemane experience, 93, 722-723

Germany, characteristics, 189, 621 624-625, 626

Glamour —
appearance on astral plane, 188
disappearance, 174
dissipation, 64, 181, 577, 682-683
freedom from, complete, production, 599
in Russia, 428
mastered, 264

none on cosmic astral plane, 283
product, 443
work with by Master on Second Path, 402

Glamour-making tendency and astralism, 112

Glands conditioning brain, 431-432

God is Fire, 82-88, 226

Goodwill —
and will-to-good, 573-574
energy, release, 578, 615
expansion, 50
fostering in masses, importance, 109, 110
human, focussed expression, production, 647
of Master, 645
secret purpose of planetary Logos, 645
to all forms in three worlds, 608 work, 254

Gospel story of Christ, symbolical meanings, 313-315

Great Bear —
energies, relation to energies of Pleiades, 405
relation to our solar system, 405, 422-423

Great Britain today, 428, 430, 624, 626-627, 631, 632

Great Invocation, use, 616

Great White Lodge vs. Black Lodge, 14

Group —
accepted, 49, 57, 58, 72
activity and initiation, significance, absorption, 261
antahkarana. *See* Antahkarana group.
aura, means of protection against potency of Master, 545
awareness, 17, 128, 365, 668
brought together, factors, 210
burning ground, 218
causal body, 218, 221
clear cold light, 73, 77
composition, 213-214, 224
consciousness —
awakening, 18
Cross concerned, 694

emotional, new, 579
transition to, 259
understanding, 249
unfoldment, 35
emphasis on in New Age, 137
endeavour, aim, 26
enterprise for service, 343-344
feeling apparatus, 218
finding, 58
forms, destruction, 306-307
functioning of initiate, 137
fusion and service, keynote of
newer meditation, 252
grasp of necessity for utilisation
of force of destruction, 210
identification with will or purpose of Monad, 32-33
identified with soul, 129
initiation —
basis, 17
definition, 36
fact, obviousness, 341-342
first steps toward, 17
four qualities needed, 209-215
Fourteen Rules, 19-319
inauguration in New Age, 111
key, 32
injunction to widen all rents
within veils, 191
invocative cry, response to, 77
leader and two assistants, 271
life —
aid to realisation, 103
evocation of response of Chohans, 136-147
expression on physical plane in
group formation, 218
fire at heart, spiritually destructive, 218
shift into Ashram on buddhic
levels, requirements, 219-
220
love —
basis, 32
evocation, 31-32
mind, organised and functioning
rhythmically, 218
need for patient endurance, 219
one's own, recognition, importance, 342, 343
onward moves in life, 124-132

personality, 97, 218, 219
point of united tension, suitable,
212
preparing for initiation, qualities needed, 215
preparation superseding old
methods, 239
purpose, 107-108, 599
qualities to be rooted out and destroyed, 210-212
recognition enabling passing into
Ashram, 119
relation, illumined, establishment, 225
rhythm, forward-moving establishment, 226
service, 91, 227-247
silence, cultivation, 214-215
soul, 218, 219, 221
sound, emitting, 226
sustenance and vitality, 129
synthesis, work, 276
tension needed, production, 226
terms, thinking in, automatic,
259
united action with full interior
unity, 217-218
vortex of force and field of service, simultaneous, 346
will. See Will, group.
Word, 219, 220-221, 222
work, 66-67, 68, 191
Groups —
affected by progressing initiatory
processes, 585-589
recognition by initiate, 57-58
seven greater, lesser, and planetary, 148-167
tested and failed, 208-209
under self-seeking leaders, 112
Guarantee of ultimate attainment,
312

H

Habits —
of thinking, eradication by substitution, 214
spiritual, offsetting all lower
physical tendencies, 126-127
Harmony through conflict, energy,
602-641

Head —
  centre of initiates, 165, 257
  heart and throat, entrance into
    being, 148
  light in. *See* Light in head.
  of initiate, three points of sensi-
    tivity, 257
  mechanism of disciple, dealing
    with, undesirability, 432
Healing, permissible or not, 164
Heart —
  as aspect of pure reason, 27-28
  doctrine, 457-458
  of the Sun, 536
Hell, descent into, 701-702
Hercules, work, 527
Hermaphrodite, Divine, 106
Hierarchical —
  consciousness, 466
  endeavour, result, 473
  intent, impression on mind of
    disciple, 549-555
  life, precipitation, premature,
    prevention, 112
  work in conjunction with Great
    Council, 146
  work, objectives, publicising,
    need for, 133-134
  workers, great need today, 281
Hierarchies, many, 440
Hierarchy —
  absorbed into Shamballa, 162
  activity, 307, 472
  approach to mankind, 89, 91,
    119
  as heart of God, manifestation,
    134
  attainment, 91
  awareness, 481
  changes due to development of
    man, 424
  characteristics, outstanding, 561
  conditioned by Aquarius, Taurus,
    and Pisces, 228-229
  consciousness, type, 127-128
  constitution, information regard-
    ing, given by D.K., 252
  crises of decision, 639
  differentiation of basic unity into
    49 Ashrams, 370

energy, direction into world, 690,
  691
entrance point, 117
evocation, 135-136
experiment of externalisation,
  111-112
expression of second aspect of
  first Ray, 647
externalisation. *See* Externalisation.
fact of existence to be emphasised, 300
impact of energies from cosmic
  astral, 357
implementation of Shamballa
  and Aquarian energy, 235
inspiration and stimulation of
  initiates, 585
interplay with Shamballa, 271
intuitive interpreter of Shamballa, 37
knowledge of, spread, 133
members —
  consciousness, 17, 363
  goal, 115
  increase in understanding, 238
  life, 363
  passing into higher work, 15-
    16
membership in, admission, 341
modern, creation, 381
moving nearer to fusion with
  humanity, 542
need to change technique cyclically, 235
new techniques and methods,
  245
personnel, 300, 367
planes, 119
problem in right timing, 717
rapport with, 543
reaching, rules, publicising, 133-
  134
readjustments, 15
relation to Shamballa, change,
  240
relationships, new, 18-19
reorganisation, interior, 383
return, result of first initiation of
  humanity, 333

retreating towards Shamballa, 119
ring-pass-not, 370
seven groups of Ashrams, 373
spiritual crisis, 334, 335
spiritual unfoldment, 333
task, 185, 307
teaching planned to precede and condition New Age, 255
technique, conveyance of inspiration, 230
three major Executives, 369
united, assistance to Christ, 647
work, 13, 230, 238-319
workers, two groups, 128
Hierophants at first three initiations, 56

Higher Evolution —
door, 283, 328, 334, 524
leading off cosmic physical plane, 328, 398-399
Path (or Way) —
after mastering illusion, 181
Christ upon, 291
factor of Antahkarana, 131, 279
initiations guarding, 352
leading to cosmic astral plane, 202
light upon, 138
monadic and logoic planes, 360
necessity for potency of Will, 718
preparation for, 177, 207, 225, 266, 390-391
requirement of abstract thought, 243
revelation of to initiate, 523, 644
seven ways into, 284
treading, benefit to Master, 363-364
See also Paths, Seven.
"The highest light controls", 518
Hilarion, Master, work, 586

History —
from angle of occultism, 559
totality, Aryan, 560
Hitler, use of Shamballa force, 35-36

Human —
affairs, turning-point, 621
being, electrical unit of power and light, 351
triple mechanism, aspects of electricity, 351
consciousness, 466
development along astral lines, 187
evolution, impetus, 548
thought, potency, results, 188-189
unfoldment, culminating point, 598

Humanity —
appeal, response to, 470
creative crisis, causes, 550-551
creativity, future, 552
early history, 380-381
effect of first Ray today, 646-653
emotional and psychic life, reorganisation, 578
entrance point, 117
facing second initiation, 674
free to settle its own destiny, 430
growth through presentation of moments of crisis, 393
heart centre, creation, 619
importance, 160
invocative cry, 76
masses, attainment of initiation, 648
One, world-wide recognition, 659
personnel of Hierarchy, 369
today —
concern with right human relations, 394, 499-500, 612-613, 614
condition of churches, 614
at entrance to Path of Discipleship, 498-499
effects of alignment, 472
fifth-Ray energy, 593-596
generating point of tension, 589
influence of Shamballa, 411, 471, 580
linking of personality with soul, 451, 499
need to link Triad, soul, and personality, 466

new truths and emergence of new actors, 77-78, 389-390
opportunity unparalleled, 473
unfoldment of consciousness, 119, 409, 412, 413, 448
undeveloped, symbol, 470
world disciple on verge of major awakening, 365
world disciple, recovery from test, 383

## I

"I AM movement", indictment, 16
"I am that I am", 104
"I am the light of the world", 539
"I and my Father are one", 455, 476
"I assert the fact", 515-516
"I, if I be lifted up", 165, 375, 697
"I see the Greatest Light", 516-517
Ideas —
  definition, 50
  divine, as intuitions, 717
  divine, transformation into ideals, 592
  impulsive energy, contact with illumined lower mind, 711
  recognition and receptivity to, need for, 446
  world of, work, 63
Identification —
  act, responsibility of Buddha of Activity, 269
  attainment, 44, 45
  definition, 61
  due to alignment, 62
  evolutionary, 372
  nature of, 282; 283
  superseding consciousness, 82
  transformation of consciousness into, 283
  with life aspect, 226
  with soul and Hierarchy, requirement, 45
Identity —
  preserved after mergence in whole, 455
  with others complete, 168
Ideologies —
  destruction, 306-307
  great conditioning, 596, 602, 637

new and better, emergence, 580
world, creation, 579-580
Illumination —
  due to first contact with Shamballa, 175-176
  of humanity, effect of fifth Ray energy, 595
  of mind, 592
Illusion —
  appearance, 188
  battle with, 600
  definition, 600
  Great, production, 183
  mastered under Law of Synthesis, 264
  to be mastered via mental plane, 180-181
Imagination —
  creative —
    of man, achievements, 244-245
    relation to astral life, 442-443
    use, 252, 443, 482, 487, 489, 491, 511, 512, 712
    value, uses, and purpose, discovery, 442
  relation to intuition, 54, 488
Immortality —
  basis, 449
  definitions, 730, 731
Impartation, climaxing point in attainment of point of tension, 263
Impersonality, pure, 44, 209
Impression on mind of disciple of hierarchical intent, 549-555
Impressions —
  received by mind, sources, 591
  three vibratory, awareness of, 543
Incarnation —
  definition, 337
  of very advanced souls since 1925, 122-123
  story, 201
Incarnations, long series, principle of intelligent synthesis, 216
Inclusiveness —
  key to understanding of consciousness, 537
  of moment that IS, 437
India, characteristics, 623-624

Indifference, divine, 210, 218, 219, 718

Individual disciple —
  duty, 638, 640
  results of 4th Ray activity, 637-638

Individualisation —
  act, work of Buddha of Activity, 268
  Initiation, Identification, 372

Ineffable Name, 53, 54, 55

Inflow and activity of new and higher energies, 14-18

Initiate —
  activity, conscious, controlling, rules for, 225-227
  awareness, 471
  beginning to form his own Ashram, 262, 586
  cause of evolutionary process, 61
  control, final, of substance, 469
  cooperation with Will of Shamballa, 319
  creation and destruction, 308
  definitions, 72, 366
  development, functioning on higher planes of solar system, 178
  fifth-degree. See Fifth-degree initiate.
  first-degree. See First-degree initiate.
  focus, 103-104
  fourth-degree. See Fourth-degree initiate.
  function in group, 137
  goal, 53
  head. See Head.
  knowledge regarding mayavic energies, 182
  major liability, 156
  master of own individual situation, 577
  movement, 471
  normal consciousness, 167
  second-degree. See Second-degree initiate.
  silence, meaning of term, 214-215
  stimulation from Shamballa, 651
  symbol, 470

synthetic activity and group consciousness, 249
task, 292, 293-294, 303
third-degree. See Third-degree initiate.
training. See Training, initiate.
true, indication, 359
use of pure will, 310-311
work between initiations, keynotes, 312
work, obligatory, 182
work within veils of maya, 182-185
would-be, attitude, basic, requirements, 33

Initiate-consciousness —
  process of recognition and registration, leading to, 125
  unfoldment in disciples, work with, 128

Initiates —
  above third degree, main field of unfoldment, 178
  dynamism, result in new quality, 120
  effects on humanity, 374
  expression of love-wisdom, 296
  higher, potency, stepping down, 373
  Rules. See Rules.
  work between initiations, keynotes, 312-318
  work on mental levels behind scenes, 230

Initiation —
  act, Buddha of Activity responsible for, 268-269
  Ascension. See Ascension initiation.
  ceremony, 530-532
  definitions —
    awareness of oneself as soul, 341
    crisis, climaxing event, 662
    culminating moment of achievement, 337, 662
    expanding series of inclusive recognitions, 341
    experiment with energy, 549
    fusion of lights progressively entered, 540

graded series of liberations, 685

growth in experience, 557

knowing, seeing, and grasping in greater light, 538

points of tension, 541, 557, 565

process of hard work becoming what he is, 685

process of light recognition and utilisation, 538

process of successive integrations, with expansions, 563

recognition in brain consciousness of divine awareness, 259

recognition of goals implemented from Shamballa, 207

sequence of directed energy impacts, 565, 724

success in experiments with energy, 337

understanding of Way, 557

disciples, many, due to avataric stimulation, 15

each, expression of sum total of all past achievement, 720

each, two tests, 47

effects on disciple, 539-540, 557-558

factors of major importance, 434

fifth. *See* Fifth initiation.

first. *See* First initiation.

fourth. *See* Fourth initiation.

group. *See* Group initiation.

keynote, major, 737

of Decision. *See* Decision initiation.

prerequisite, recognition of one's own group, 342, 343

processes, abstraction leading to resurrection, 164

readiness for, 539

requirements, 442, 662

Resurrection. *See* Resurrection initiation.

seeking before door, plane, 351

stages, three, 469

success in, 337

tests. *See* Tests of initiation.

third. *See* Third initiation; Transfiguration.

three aspects, 532

*Initiation, Human and Solar* —
date, 389

protection of book, 250

Initiations —
earlier, no longer exist, 412

first to ninth, names, 532

five, energy impulses of Rays, 567

guarding Way to Higher Evolution, 352

higher, 124, 155, 438, 439

major, possible only after transfiguration, 216

nine, characteristics, 340, 661-738

of Masters, 15

of Threshold, 41

seven and nine of our planetary life, 656-661

seven, effects on seven centres, 338-339

seven, revelation of seven Ray qualities, 338

Initiatory process —
activation, 534-535

between first and second initiations, 577-578

dual life, 431-443

effect on dual life of disciple, 535-536

energies causing, 534-535

goal, 79

meaning, 530-555

test, 433

Inspiration —
by Hierarchy, 585

by Masters through workers, 230

conveyance by Hierarchy, 230

from Spiritual Triad, 266

of first-Ray disciple, 508

Inspirations for future of mankind, 14

Integration —
Direction, Science, directive words for disciple, 691-692

major planetary, 273-274

of mind, emotional nature, and physical brain, 562-563

preceding conscious initiation, 560

Intelligence —
energy, technique, mastery, 394
evolutionary objective, 120
servant of will, 472
trained, required for distinction between intuition and psychism, 447

Interlude between initiations, 337, 577

Interpretations registered by brain infallibly correct, 436

Interpretive capacity, need for, 442

Introspection, life of, 548

Intuition —
allied with prevision, 131
assimilation of detail, 378
awakening, 229, 442
concern, 711
effect of occult meditation, 447
en rapport with mind, 447
energy, definition, 445, 711
evocation, 125, 132
in every man, 11
inflow, source of sustenance and vitality for group, 129
of Masters and higher initiates, 393
realm, energy projection into, 446-447
relation to imagination, 54
revelatory power, 131
unfoldment, plane, 463
with spiritual mind, synthesis, 445

Intuitional plane —
Ashrams on, 119
full consciousness, 463

Intuitive —
development, effects, 424
faculty, relation to aspiration, 443
knowledge, clothing in right thought-forms, 447
perception, infallible, 39
perception, production, 358-359
realisation, distinction from higher psychism, 447

understanding, registration, importance, 131-132
understanding superseding knowledge-wisdom, 468-469

Invocation —
and creative activity, results, 553
and evocation, 35, 383-384, 493-495, 519-530
by group able to bring forth response, 528
by humanity, results, 382, 383
Great, vii
mutual, effect, 470
of divinity, power, establishment, 226

Invocative —
agent, great, 443
and evocative initiates, 262
appeal, effects, 303-304
note of united evolution, effects, 398
tension, point, 493-494

Invocative-evocative activity, effects, 541-542

Invoking area of relationship for Sanat Kumara, 366, 379

Isolated unity, 60, 176

Israel today (April, 1947), 429-430

Italy, characteristics, 621, 625

J

Jesus, Master —
characteristic, outstanding, 220
crises of initiation, 83
crucifixion, 523-524, 697
five initiations, 599
fourth initiation, 192, 193, 290, 386, 524
life, 93
overshadowed Mahomet, 254
overshadowing, 192, 193, 198, 290, 524
probable assumption of part of Messiah under Christ, 706
Transfiguration initiation, 599

Jewel in the lotus —
anchorage of Monad, 491, 492

correspondence in Ashram, 378
fire, removal into Triad, 215-219

Jewish —
dispensation, 548
race, 534, 640

Jews —
creative art and scientific discovery, 243-244
forfeit of privilege, 705-706
today, 429-430, 634-637

Joy, happiness, and bliss, displacing sorrow, 234

## K

K.H. *See* Koot Hoomi, Master.
Kama-manasic impulse mastered, 261

Karma —
definition, 318
negated, 437
past, good, accumulation, effect on decision, 724
planetary, liberated from, 724
termination, scientific process, 100-101

"Kill out desire", 210

Kingdom —
seventh, 130
sixth, 129-130

Kingdoms —
four, unfoldment, perception of, 125
fourth and fifth, mergence, 134
subhuman, work with, 400

Know, injunction to initiate, 286-292, 312-315

Knowledge —
concrete, energy, functions, 589-592
conversion to wisdom, 349
occult, 7
of initiate contrasted with that of aspirant, 288-289
transmutation into Wisdom, 453, 468, 492, 540

Knowledge-force, concern, 453
Knowledge-wisdom, superseding, 468-469

Koot Hoomi, Master —
aid by Master D.K., V, 169
Ashrams, 169-170, 586
creation of body for His own use, 705
slated to post of World Teacher, 398

Krishna, Shri, achievements, 91, 527

## L

Labour —
and capital, problem in U.S.A., 633
movement initiated by one of Masters, 255

Law —
definition, 375
demand for change, 164-165
demand for right direction guiding entering forces, 165
of —
Analogy, 131, 217, 267, 268, 270, 489, 661
Attraction, 248, 264, 310, 375, 397, 399, 404, 417, 508
Cause and Effect, 442, 565, 620, 652, 724
Cleavages, 596, 602, 725
Correspondences, 180
Cycles, 238
Cyclic Compensation, 238
destruction, 76
Economy, 264, 417
Evolution, 262, 265, 417, 519, 587
Fixation, 725
Freedom, 417-418
God, establishment, 192, 193, 194
Inevitability, 439
Integration, 384
Karma, 85, 226, 437, 519, 607, 609, 728-729
Life or of Spirit, 157-158
Life of Sun, 520
Life or Synthesis, 163
Life Purpose of planetary Logos, 520

Magnetic Work, 404
Magnetisation, 248
Occult Continuity, 212
Rebirth, 226, 649
Sacrifice, 266, 268
Service, 439
Supplementary Seven, 151-167, 226
Vibration, 54

Law of Synthesis —
aspect or quality, magnetic action, 375
clue, 262
cosmic, 417
demonstrating synthesis underlying all life, 404
governing first divine aspect, 334, 508
indication of revelation, 258
monadic sphere of life, 310
or Law of Life, 163
reference to relationship of Spirit and matter, 264
understanding by group, 247, 248
working, 266

Laws —
and qualities related to second Ray, 375
of —
Nature, 156-157
that which radiates, 248
Soul, 157
Spirit, 263
universe, definition, 25
Laya Yoga, 557
Lemurian initiation, 345
Lenin, writings, interpretation, 680
Leo, informing life, 269
"Let the Forces of Light", use, 71
"Let the Lords of Liberation", use, 71
Liaison Officers between Christ and Avatar of Synthesis, 655
Liberation —
at fourth initiation, 132, 697, 700-701
at sixth initiation, 728-729
from three worlds, 56, 445, 466-468, 728-729

Libra —
energies entering our solar system, 404, 405, 424-425
informing Life, 267
periphery, Lives working on, 404
Life —
and light interchangeable terms, 143
aspect —
and its expression in life of initiates, work with, 128
first, 217
of planet relates initiate, 97
recognition process, 105
definition, 300
focus, 45, 468
impregnated dispersed through all forms, 414-415
interpretation by initiate, 469
is one and naught can ever take it, 124-132
liberation in destruction of causal body, 132
"more abundantly", 389, 732
of accepted disciple, stages, 542-543
ordered, regulation, results, 11
organisation, influence producing, 575
planetary, synthesis of ordered activity, 588
principle from cosmic mental plane centered in Shamballa, 414
Quality, Appearance, 120
significance known, 472
stream, unbroken, immutable, from centre to periphery, 449
thread, 453, 455, 458, 469, 475, 476, 477
thread. See also Sutratma.
transference, problem, 221
whole story, 124
Life-appearance, two points of living purpose, 280
Life-force decentralised by Sound at Shamballa, 289
Life-form, dualism of divine nature, 472

Life-tendency, definitely directed, importance, 447

Light —
and love, great revealers, 329
and substance, synonymous, 174
clear cold, 27, 31-32, 39
contacted and utilised, revelation, 298
expression in physical-plane life, 216
forces relating to, revelation, 648
from identification with spiritual will, 74
in head, 42, 73, 143, 671
inner mechanism, development, 170
let in rents in veils of maya, 181, 184, 189, 191-196
line between Monad and personality, establishment, 475
living, concentrated point, 732
living, strand of antahkarana, 119
of —
    Ashram, 73
    Atma, 73
    atom of matter, 118
    blended soul and personality, 74
    buddhi, 73
    egoic group, 74
    form, 112, 118
    Hierarchy, 73, 74
    life, available through initiation, 665
    of Logos, response to, 592
    Master, uses, 642-643
    mind, blending with light of soul, 665
    pure reason, 73-74
    soul, 73, 77, 112, 118, 144, 516, 577
    Spiritual Triad, 118, 209
    Spiritual Will, 73-74
point, after fourth initiation, 106
reflected by Spiritual Triad upon mental plane, 74
relation to revelation, 74

revelation —
    of nature and purpose of cosmic etheric, 729
    of nature of divine purpose, 729
    with destruction of illusion, glamour, and maya, 286
    symbol of world of meaning, 177
    theme underlying planetary purpose, 142-146
    upon astral plane, clearer, production in New Age, 238
Light-substance, planetary, 184
Lighted Way —
    along, evolutionary pushing forward, 519-520
    between personality and Spiritual Triad, 447
    leading to Nirvana, 516
Lights which carry out the Will of God, 136-147
Listening and knowledge, 288, 291-292
"Little ones" or "little child", 116
Lives, lesser, nourishment, 92
Livingness in form, sense of, 123
Logoi, seven planetary, expression, 106
Logoic plane of transfiguration, 276, 281, 463
Logos —
    light, response to, 592
    planetary —
        and essential Purpose, expressions, 311
        and solar Logos, interplay, 550
        centres, 733
        creation of world, 55
        creative activity, evocation, 241-242
        creative Agents, 587
        energy, direction into world, 690-691
        enunciation of sound, 83
        first contact with, 56
        goal, 644
        initiation, 238, 551-555, 661
        life-purpose, 142

living consciousness, theme, 737
name, 248, 263
plane, 206
purpose grasped, 645, 652
relation to Sanat Kumara, 205, 206
sacrifice, 564
space-time schedule, 111
supreme task, 407-408
vehicle of manifestation, 550
will, 567
solar, 106, 412, 654, 729
Lord of the World —
holding manifested world in state of fusion, 542
purpose, cooperation with, 118
will-purpose, 16
work, 94, 124, 165
*See also* Sanat Kumara.
Lords of —
Karma, 118, 429, 724
Liberation, 13, 71, 76-77, 335
the Rays, definition, 568
Yoga, 481
Lotus —
egoic, love petals, 362, 451, 492
solar, 6
Love —
and light, great revealers, 329
and mind, close relation, 593, 601
and pure reason, 27-28, 29
attractive energies of, manipulator, 338
circle, all things held within by synthesis, 716
definition, 45, 114
divine, progression down to focal point, 619-620
energy, 5, 328, 377
evolutionary objective, 120
expression in physical-plane life, 216
importance in solar system, 47
intelligent, 107
magnetic power, 119
nature in purpose of Shamballa, 311
nature of One in Whom We Live and Move, 311

of Cosmic Astral plane, 357
of Master, 645
opening of door to Higher Evolution, 328
pure, active in heart of initiates, 415
pure, quality, primary, of Sanat Kumara, 387
revelation on Earth, 728
sacrificial, 32
servant of Will, 472
spiritual, plane, Ashram and hierarchy on, 119
true divine from cosmic astral, 392
true, understood rightly, 468
Universal, plane, 358
Love-wisdom —
Ashram, 383-384
basis, 560-561
becoming dominant, 560-561
inflow, stupendous, future, 593
linking agent, 89
Ray of planet Earth, 590
Lunar lords, 8, 9-11, 100, 101

## M

M. *See* Morya, Master.
Macrocosm understood in light of microcosm, 107
Magic —
ceremonial —
energy, 567
realm, 574
Ray. *See* Ray seventh.
white, 574, 575, 584
Magical work, true, 10, 672
Magician —
black. *See* Black magician.
white, becoming, 673
Magnetic —
action allied to first Ray functioning, 375
energy of first aspect at heart of Ashrams, 378
potency, definition, 375
Magnetisation —
five meanings, 248
of initiate, 262
Magnetism, Shamballic, 376
Mahachohan, aid to Christ, 379

Mahomet overshadowed by Master Jesus, 254

Man —
development, mental and intuitive, effects, 424
monadically conscious, 455
responsibility, 76-77
today. *See* Humanity today.
trinity, becomes duality, means, 475
*See also* Humanity; Mankind; Masses.

Manasic awareness, 167

Manifestation —
cyclic panorama, basis, 14
secret, 53

Mankind —
situation today, causal factors, 13
spiritual history, alteration, 411
*See also* Humanity; Man.

Manu —
aid to Christ, 379
secret of life, working through, 241

Marx, writings, interpretation, 680

Masonic —
tradition, ritual, and Mysteries, 330-331
tradition, value, 51-52
work, 533-534

Masonry —
coming form in New Age, 533-534
connected with Path to Sirius, 418
organised under Sirian influence, 331, 418
reform, 418-419
revitalisation, 332

Masses —
energy, transmission to by initiate, 689
levelling, problem in U.S.S.R., 633

Master —
active on monadic plane, affected by Shamballa, 360-361
and disciple, flow of thought, 546
attainments, 81, 284

attention, evocation by disciple, 546, 547
attention, object, 440-441
awareness, 433, 440
comprehension, 177
consciousness, fusion with that of disciple, 542-549
consciousness, no suffering or pain, 723
contact with, stages, 545-547
cosmic dualism, 437
creation of body of manifestation, 51, 101, 455
crises confronting, 395-396
development, 360-361
distributor of triadal energy, 713
dual existence, 437-441
fifth-degree, training for Decision initiation, 413
focus, 103-104
form used, 101
free from limitations of time not of space, 437
freedom from consideration of time equation, 439
liberated, spiritual endeavour, 440
liberation from Ray limitations, 391, 392
light, uses, 642-643
occult decision in Ashram, 395
of ninth initiation, no need of energy centres, 699
potency, tremendous, protection from 545
preoccupation, primary, 362
relation between Monad and form unbroken, 50-51
relation to Ashram, 362
revelation —
followed by realisation and recognition, 713
of cosmic astral plane, 283
of goals of seven Paths, 424
seven Paths confronting, 371, 395-425
success in piercing planetary ring-pass-not, 284
task, 48-49
teaching in Ashram, 544-545

telepathic contact, instruments used, 546-547

vibration, consciousness of by disciple, 543

without personality, 101

Masters —
aid to Christ, 655
attitude to disciples, new, 251-252
conscious receptivity or sensitivity to cosmic astral, 398
drawn closer to humanity, 119
facing sixth initiation, decision, effects, 553-554, 555
fifth-Ray on Second Path, 401
groups and types, many, 439-440
initiations, 15
intuition of phases of divine intention, 712
invocation of higher Beings, 136
knowledge of, spread, 133
knowledge of what must be done, 238
limitations, 389
of sixth initiation, aid to Buddhas of Activity, 587
problem, 393
task, 660, 661
technique of permitting a fallacy to remain uncorrected, 125-126
training, 391, 393, 413, 420-421, 691
traits today, 424
will, 392-393, 713, 722
withdrawal, history, 381-382
work, 184, 230, 281-283, 691

Masters' Book of Rules, quotation, 190-191

Materialism —
renunciation, collective, 606
undermining by initiatory process, 665

Matter —
conditioned by previous solar system, 359
destructive energy, 87
eighteen states constituting personality, 100

spirit at lowest point of manifestation, 264

Maya —
control by, negation, 264
field, work of initiate, 182-183
nature of, 183
overcome, 181
realm, devas active, 179
realm, energies let loose within, 186-187
veils —
destruction, 190-191, 226
four, 199-200
nature of, 183, 189-190, 195
rents, light through, 191, 192, 193, 194, 196, 226
rules of work of Army of the Voice, 179
work within, rules, 181-207

Mayavirupa —
definition, 481
See also Body, created; Form, self-created.

Mechanisms of light and of contact, development, 170

Meditation —
creative, 73
fusion of minds of disciple and Master, 545-546
means of building antahkarana, 446, 447, 494
occult, effect on intuition, 447
processes, preparation for withdrawal, 77
work, prime intent, 446

Meditations, newer type, presentation, 252

Men of good will, duty, 640, 641

Mental —
and monadic planes, relation, 593
body non-existent, 481
cosmic plane —
influences, reaction of Shamballa to, 357
Paths, leading to, 399
planetary Logos on, 206
reaction to, 357, 392
stream of energy from, 414
third solar system, 377

White Lodge roots on, 202
work consciously on by
    Master, 405
development, effects, 188-189
levels, focus on, requirement,
    446
matter, work in, 446
plane —
    antahkarana building, 466-
        467, 469
    departments, 467
    orientation on, 441
    retention of impression by dis-
        ciple, 543
    substance, 590
    symbolism of light on, 74
principle, unfoldment, effects,
    579
substance, use in bridging, 467,
    475, 485
unit —
    and manasic permanent atom,
        50, 481
    use, 475

Mercury speed the group, let, 227-
    228

Merging of vertical way of life
    with horizontal way of service,
    113

Messiah, coming, 705-706

Mind —
    abstract —
        area of consciousness, 167
        description, 461
        functions, 50, 588, 598
        impact, offsetting, 590
        impression of purpose aspect
            of Plan, 549
    concrete, description, 460
    concrete lower, and higher, gap,
        bridging, 113
    control —
        achievement, 446
        development, 6
    disciplining, constant need for,
        447
    dual activity, 119-120
    endeavour to implement will
        nature of Monad, 278
    energies, invocation, 443

higher —
    and lower, link of antah-
        karana, 442
    and lower, response between,
        447
    expression of will, 311
    field of initiate's effort, 137
illuminator of lower planes, 592
light-bearer, 592
linking with physical-astral,
    energy anchored, 448
lower —
    analytical concrete controlled
        and superseded, 249
    and higher of accepted dis-
        ciple, 542
    fusing with higher mind, 216
of —
    fourth-degree initiate, 700
    God, nature and purposes, re-
        action to, 392
    planetary Logos, tune in, 529
principle, Custodian, 422
Son, description, 460-461
soul-illumined, control, 674
stuff, substance of antahkarana,
    464
three activities, 598
three aspects, 272, 460-461, 475
training to receive communica-
    tions, 432-433
transcendence, 107
transmitting agent of light of
    soul, 577
Universal —
    characteristic, major, 595
    creative agent, 593
    expressions, 599
    key, 591
use by disciple, 713

Monad —
    anchorage, 491
    and antahkarana left at fourth
        initiation, 101
    and form on physical plane re-
        maining, 480
    and physical-plane expression,
        rapport, 455
    awareness of, 599
    building of bridge, 43

creation of personality, 216
destruction by, 30
direct channel of communication with personality, 216
divine will of Christ, 39
energy, use by initiates, 65, 184
experience in three worlds of service, 472
expression, 28, 30
fire, destruction of causal body, 475
in Shamballa, 61
interpreting agent, 50
light, 30, 643
of initiate, 96
purpose, 31, 33
Ray, determination of use of pure will, 310-311
Ray, factor in evolution, 7
recognition, method, 105
reflected in Triad, work on lower planes, 216-217
relates initiate to Forces, 96
relation to soul, means, 470
relation, unbroken, to form used, 50-51
source of triadal life, 472
vibration to, 81
will. *See* Will of Monad.
Monad-Soul-Personality today, 473
Monadic —
and mental planes, relation, 593
consciousness —
and self-created form, 439
development, 108
leading to life expression and fifth initiation, 117
control in group, 256
control possessing soul-infused personality, 663
energy, pure, activity, 588
force, purificatory and destroyer aspects, 86
influence registered, 265
influence with full awareness, bringing in, 471
life —
functioning within, 266
impact upon substance, 280
sphere, ascension into, 495
living, law, 264

plane —
awareness on, 463
Chohan on, 284
expression on, 729
of transfiguration, 281
reception of love energy, 377
solution of mystery of brotherhood, 276
potency available, 310
process of emanation, beginning, 351
relation, destructive, 85
sense of essential duality, door into Shamballa, 141
signatures, 287
vibration unknown, 110
Morya, Master —
aid to by Master D.K., V
Ashrams, 170, 586
Head of esoteric schools, 373, 380
secret of life working through, 241
Moses, rent in veil of Maya, 192, 193
Mother Aspect, description, 464
Motive, superseding, 28
Music, effect of Mysteries, 332
Mysteries —
ancient, origins and contents, 330-331
ancient, restoration, 111, 135, 330, 331, 333
revealed by action of certain processes, 337
safeguarding, 112
Mysticism, cycle, 113

N

Name —
and form synonymous, 53
egoic, hidden, 263
sevenfold of planetary Logos, 263
Nations, modern —
effect of fourth Ray, 620-637
Rays, personality and soul, 623-632, 634
Near East today (April, 1947), 430

Need for collection of scattered information on initiation, 669

Negation —
secret and significance, 202
spiritual, 226

Nervous system, use by Sutratma, 451

Network —
of goodwill, 253
of light, 253

New —
civilisation, platform, 194
methods, approaches, and modes of work, 231
techniques, mastery by Masters, 235
world order, 574, 580, 596, 622

New Age —
clearer light on astral plane, production, 238
emergence, 639
enterprises, coming, Agents, 14
functioning on etheric plane, 191
inauguration, 241
people incarnating, 122-123, 390
preparation for by reform of Masonry, 418-419
quality, 19
religion, 521
techniques, embodiment, 26
training in synthesis, 120
work, making possible, 225
See also Aquarian Age.

New Group of World Servers —
accepted disciples learning to work, 230
ajna centre of Sanat Kumara, 368
aura, symbol in, 233
brought under Aquarian influence by disciples, 231
development of will-to-good, 110
dynamism, result, 120
emergence, 554
field of service for new disciple, 230
filling of ranks, 667
guidance, 88

illumined by Taurus, 229
information about, 253
inspiration by Masters, 230
linking with, 735
relating group and transforming station, 373
ruled by Taurus, 232
source of ideologies, 580
stream of will from Shamballa, 240
training of needed disciples, 230
transmitters of energy, 734
two future functions, 373-374
unity, 299
vanguard of Kingdom of God, 301
work, 191, 225, 239, 586

Nine —
forces, transmutation into divine energies, 456
number of initiation, 79, 81

1903, decision of group of Masters regarding cosmic evil, 722

1925 ushering in very advanced souls, 122-123

1952, decision affecting humanity, 721-722

1975 —
impact of will upon humanity, 716
teaching, revelatory, 255

Ninth initiation —
inspiration and expression, 535
nature of, 697-698
not related to earth life, 699
of Christ, 170
preparation for, 711-712
Rays governing, 656
Refusal initiation, 736-737
refusal of recognition of cosmic evil, 696
renunciation, 342
revelation concerning nature of Being, 728
through illumined revelation, 531-532

Nirmanakayas —
initiations taken, 735
work, 69

Nirvana —
definition, 472

leading to, 516
readiness for, 472
Nirvanic awareness, plane, 463
Noble Middle Path, 372
Note of form elemental, sounding, 8
Notes of soul and personality in unison, effect on Triad, 457
Number, significance, 81

## O

Obedience, seed, 291
Observer, attitude of disciple in Ashram, 99-100
Occult age, teaching, 113
Occultism, new schools, requirements, basic, 115
Occultist —
hallmark, 11
true, work, 174
O.M. —
conflict with A.U.M., 53-54
correct sounding, effects, 52-53, 56, 201, 202
definitions, 51, 263
dual, 53
hearing, 53, 55, 182, 202
lost word, recovery, 53, 54
meaning, 51-53, 182, 203-204, 513
no longer moved by, effects, 201
not productive of knowledge of initiate, 288
portrayal, symbolical, 54-55
related to vibration, 54
replacing A.U.M., 200
transmutation, 285
use, 51, 470, 514
useless, 514
Omnipresence of God, 39
Omniscience of divine Whole, 40-41
One —
functioning on all planes, 494
symbolised by Divine Hermaphrodite, 106
One About Whom Naught May Be Said, 339, 366-367
One in Whom we live and move . . ., 311, 535

Oneness —
and synthesis, demonstration, 301
associated with monadic consciousness, registration, 363
Opportunity —
confronting humanity, 584
for re-energising, 231
hitherto unparalleled in history, 473-474
Opposites, pairs, battleground, 674
Order out of chaos, 572-573
Organisation, Energy of, 85-86
Orientation —
focussed, attained at fourth initiation, 650-651
right, results, 469
shifting, expression in World War, 606
Originating activity, source in four planes, 358
"Our God is a consuming fire", 217
"Overshadowing cloud of knowable things", 712
Overshadowing Jesus, 192, 193, 198
"Overshadowing Triads", 129-130, 132
Overstimulation, effects, 545, 546

## P

Path —
of —
Absolute Sonship, 422-423
Discipleship, 114, 610, 693
Earth Service, 392, 396, 397-400, 426, 660
Higher Evolution. See Higher Evolution.
Liberation, 188
Magnetic Work, 401-405, 424-427
Return, 445, 476
Solar Logos, 421-422
Training for Planetary Logoi, 405-408, 427, 721
Ray, 419-421, 427
to Sirius, 413-419, 427
treading, requirements, 466-468

Paths, seven —
  choice, 360, 361, 390, 396, 400, 411-412, 654, 655
  concerns, 371, 426
  confronting Master, 395-427
  lists, 396, 399
Peace, world, attainment, 238, 626, 630
Perception —
  growing, of initiate, 433
  intellectual, definition, 27
Perfection of Master, 438
Personality —
  blended energies, projecting consciously across gap, 454
  bridging to Triad, 475
  centered in, 259
  cold light of, 77
  control, complete, demonstration, 597-598
  created by Monad, 216
  definition, 57
  development, sustaining factor, 216
  disappearance, 56
  effects of third initiation, 278
  effects of Transformation, 278
  eighteen states of matter, 100
  expressions, each composed of one of seven Ray energies, 563
  focus in, results, 343
  force, transmutation into egoic energy, 248
  integrated, 26, 37, 562-563
  knowledge, transmutation into wisdom, 468
  medium for expression of soul, 441
  of race today, effects, 473
  Ray, subordination to Ray of soul, 57
  relates initiate, 96-97
  relation to soul, production, 470
  rendering soul-infused, agents, 669
  soul-infused —
    effect of seventh Ray, 571, 573
    orientation, 441
    synthesis of Rays, 563

  ties of group members to be destroyed, 211
  work in building antahkarana, 467-468
Phenomenal —
  life of higher consciousness, sane registration, 436
  world, living in, 438
Philosophy, thoughtform area of consciousness, 594, 601
Physical —
  appetites, control by, freedom from, 126-127
  life, regulation, 669-671
  plane, changes, result of subjective causes, 12
    cosmic, 15
    dense, use in attack on veils of Maya, 190
    focussing of will-to-good and sense of universality on, 588
    work on, type of energy used, 183
  substance, dense, not a principle, 377
Physico-astral plane, source of energy of senses, 592
Pineal gland —
  and pituitary body, relationship, 575
  region of initiate, 257
  relation to brain, 431
Piscean —
  Age, characteristics, 109
  Age, end, changes resulting, 551
  cycle, characteristics, 676-677
  energy opposed to incoming energies, 234-235
Pisces, influence, 578-579
Pituitary body —
  of initiate, 257
  relation to brain, 431
Plan —
  concern, 307
  cooperation with, 246
  definition, 376
  divine creative, motivated, 469
  divine, nature of, publicising, need for, 134
  externalisation of Purpose, 703

hierarchical, guidance by, 599
hierarchical, light on, 645
implementing, 307, 376, 717
knowledge of given to humanity, 229
of creation, consummation, 4
precipitation onto physical plane, 712
purpose aspect, impression on mind of disciple, 549
reflective concentration upon, 294
what lies behind, realisation, 177
Plane and state of consciousness, synonymous, 435
Planetary —
body of light-substance, 184
centres, connecting cables, production, 474
centres, three, needed relationship, 257
life on seven subplanes of cosmic physical conditioned, 360
Planets —
esoteric, use in astrology, 253
seven, of solar system, energies, work with, 159
seven sacred, Logoi, divine will, 106
Pleiades, energies, relation to energies of Great Bear, 405
Point within circle, point of tension, liberation from three worlds, 56
Political field, work of Master M., 586
Politics, situation today, 613
Power, right use, demonstration after third initiation, 714
Powers, radiatory and magnetic, 337
Prana —
aspect of etheric energy, 352
higher correspondence, 376
Prayer, definition, 70
Prevision allied to intuition, 131
Principle of —
Cleavage, 600
Conflict, 604-614, 617-623, 637, 640

Decision, 608-609
economy, 264
freedom, 416-417
Harmony, 621, 639
liberated Being, 609
limitation, 564
privation, 600
Sharing, 612-613
Probationary Path—
goal, 113-114
no longer on, indications, 469
preparatory to acceptance into Ashram, 225
requirements, changes, 114
Programme planned by Hierarchy prior to Externalisation, 707-708
Project of Master, 643
Proof of—
having right to be initiated, 174
interrelation of units of divine life, 134
spiritual realities, necessity, 134
Prophecies regarding—
Aryan Race, 499, 592-593
Avatar's response to sound, 93-94
Christ and Master K.H., 398
Christianity, 296-297, 614
churches, 135
close of this century, 287
coming of Avatar, 257
creative art, 244, 572
culture and civilisation, 87, 135, 574
development of thinking principle in man, 648
dissipation of glamour, 238
disclosures of Mysteries, 331-332
education, 121-123, 133, 221, 324
externalisation, 382-383
fourth initiation of humanity, 614
humanity, 191, 237-238, 367, 369-370, 594-595, 597
incoming first Ray, results, 649-650
mankind, in Old Commentary, 332
Masonry, 332, 418-419, 533-534

Masters, 330
meanings of death, 101-102
mystery of electricity, 331
nature of Will, 101-102
New Age, 88, 109, 111, 120-121, 123, 133, 134, 191, 238, 287
New Group of World Servers, 120, 368
new world religion, 75, 594
principle of sharing. 613
psychology, 594-595
religion, 238
restoration of Mysteries, 330
revelations, 74-75, 257, 648
right human relations, 637
sex relationship, 572
Shamballa, 382, 660
sixth Root Race, 659
Solar Logos activity, 654
teaching by D.K., 255
work of Hierarchy, 238
Protection —
  at eighth initiation, 726-727
  of Christ by Masters, 655
Psychic unfoldment, future, basis in knowledge, 450
Psychics, errors, 436
Psychism, higher, forms, distinction from intuition, 447
Psychology —
  esoteric, era, inauguration, 628
  human, investigation, 594
  thoughtform area of consciousness, 594, 601
Pure reason, 27-28, 73, 537, 588, 599
Purification —
  energy, 84
  of second initiation, 675
Purity —
  at fourth initiation, 698
  physical, 125
  preceding third initiation, 688
Purpose —
  and plan, distinction, 85
  and Will, distinction, 69
  custodian, head centre, 714
  definition, 50
  divine, 124, 338, 567, 729
  externalising itself through Plan, 703

  manifestation by use of will, 714
  of Deity, mental proposition required, 270
  of God, implementing Plan, 307
  revelation during five initiations after fourth, 714-715
"Purpose itself am I", 517

## Q

Quality, development, 166

## R

R., Master —
  Ashrams, 169, 170, 586
  effect of Aquarian energy, 232
  supervision of development of forms, 170
Races —
  connection with three Buddhas of Activity, 272
  first three human, correspondence to first three initiations, 664
Radiant energy, application and control, 545
Radiation —
  of Hierarchy, 375
  of initiate, 261-262
  production, 375
Raincloud of knowable things, 229, 717
Rapport of disciple, 441
Ray —
  crisis points, 369
  energies, egoic, use, 502-503
  process of initiatory activity, fifth —
    energy, effects, 595, 601-602
    effect on humanity today, 593
    inflow during third initiation, 688
    influences, 597
    Masters on Second Path, 401
  first —
    activity, incoming, results, 649-650
    aspect, characteristics, 410-411, 502
    association with first aspect of divinity, 714

connections, 85, 642, 643-653
destroyer aspect working through mineral kingdom, 120
effect on humanity today, 646-653
inflow during fifth initiation, 688
Lord of, work, 269
quality, highest known divine, 645
related to Shamballa, 373
souls, choice of Ray Path, 420
three aspects, 191-192, 645
fourth —
    effects, 605, 637-638
    importance, 605
    out of full incarnation, effects, 244
impacts, effects via soul, 585
incarnation, results, 646
incoming, effects, 569
limitations, liberation from, 391, 392
Lords, evolutionary unfoldment, 419
Lords, seven, work and meditation, 733-734
monadic. *See* Monad, Ray.
Love-wisdom. *See* Love-wisdom Ray; Ray second.
of —
    Harmony, control by Love-wisdom, 614, 617-618
    Harmony in modern world, 620-637
    personality, subordination to Ray of soul, 57
    right human relations, 611
Path, training for, 420-421
qualities —
    demonstration, 7
    expression, 378
    of seven initiations, 338
    seven, brought into expression, 85
second —
    choice of Ray Path, 420-421
    control of fourth Ray, 604
    inflow during seventh initiation, 688-689

Lord of, 269
lowest aspect implemented by second aspect of first Ray, 647
transmission to planet at seventh initiation, 689
seventh —
    aspirants, characteristics, 502
    energy, use by initiate, 183
    functions, 384, 571-572, 672
    incoming, 551
sixth —
    characteristics, 676-677
    energy, effects, 581-584
    energy of idealism and devotion, 575-589
    governing astral plane, 578
    period, factories characteristic, 572
    power lessening, 551
third, Decision Initiation, 653-656
type, effect on work, 338
Rays —
    cyclic appearance, contribution to evolutionary process, 419
    minor, true nature, 567
    of Aspect, 558-559, 560, 641-656
    of Attribute, 310, 558-559, 560
    personality and soul, of modern nations, 623-632, 634
    second and fifth, relationship, 593
    seven —
        energies from planet to planet, 406
        relation to initiations, 557-566
        subrays of second, 387, 397
        teaching by Master D.K., 252
        three aspects contacted, 644-645
        three major, concern with group initiation, 345-346
*Rays and Initiations,* book —
    instructions, dates, 324
    purpose, 82, 161
    Ray approach, 423
Real Man, emancipation, 10
Realignment of lower sheath, 7

Realisation —
new state, recognition, 47
process, first stage, 470-471

Reason, door into Shamballa, 139-140

Rebirth, Wheel, 92

Recognition —
ideological, essential qualities, expression, 579
of group member by world or Master, reaction toward, 211-212

Reconstruction, need for, 255

Recording agent, 442

Redemption, planetary, science, key, 735-736

Refusal Initiation, ninth, 609, 656

Registrants of the Purpose, work, 69, 70

Religion —
definition, 520-521
effect of Mysteries, 332
New World, prophecies, 75, 254, 284, 318, 521, 594

Religions, three major world, intimately related, 254

Renunciation —
Ascension, Revelation, 718-719
Great, preparation for, 224
Initiation, fourth, 605, 607, 609, 614, 639

Renunciations, progressive, 341, 342

Repolarisation of entire lower man, 3-6

Reservoir of —
energy on inner and etheric side of life, 274
life, lesser lives return to, 96-104

Responsiveness to vision conveyed by ashramic group, 443

Resurrect, injunction to initiates, 286-287, 312-315, 317-319

Resurrection —
from cave of personal life, 495
initiation, 93, 163, 391, 567, 656
meaning, distorted and true, 317-318
on physical plane, 286

Reveal, injunction to initiates, 286-287, 297-305, 316

Revealers, great, 329

Revelation —
accorded to Master, key, 646
all of life, 452
at fifth initiation, significance, 643-644
concern, 298
continuity, 203
for which all men wait, 74-75
graded, and balanced sequence, 174
induced by Will, 714-718
inducing, part of energy, 708-714
initiation of, 391, 643-653
mechanism, possession, 337
new, in future, 114
of —
divine intention, right timing, 717
divine purpose after fourth initiation, 714-715
divine purpose at third initiation, 349
divinity, 469
nature of divine Purpose at fifth initiation, 567
Nirvana, 472
oneness of all life, 299
relation to light, 74
right interpretation, necessity for, 718
source, 331
underlying purpose, 241

Rhythm, unified, 148, 155, 161, 163

Right human relations —
attainment, factors, 88, 277, 394, 573-574, 584, 637, 641
cannot be stopped, 573
establishment by Christ, 578, 615, 619
establishment, concept of harmony, 621, 640
goal of all earth endeavour, 737-738

Ring-pass-not —
ashramic, 379
of Hierarchy, 370

Roman Catholic Church, sin, 622-623

Roosevelt, F. D., word "freedom", 687

Rule, occult meaning of term, 25-26

Rules —
application, forms, 26, 36-38
for disciples and initiates —
I, group significance, 27-48
II, 48-67
III, 67-88
IV, 88-110
V, 111-123
VI, 124-132
VII, 132-147
VIII, 147-167
IX, 167-178
X, 178-207
XI, 208-225
XII, 225-247
XIII, 247-285
XIV, 285-319
for group initiation, obedience to, results, 227
fourteen, for applicants, disciples and initiates, 19-24
lesser, in time and space, 124-132
of work within veils of Maya, 181
XIII and XIV concerning work of Hierarchy in Aquarian Age, 238-247

Russia —
sin, major, 595, 622-623, 679-680
today, 428, 429, 430, 630-631, 632, 633, 679

S

Sacrifice —
nature of, true, 129, 468, 492, 699-700
of fourth-degree initiate, 699-700
of planetary Logos, 564

Sanat Kumara —
Advisors, 267
Ashram, 238, 252
daily life implemented, 246-247
description, 367
head and heart centres linking, 273
heart centre, development, 381
initiation, 550-551, 690-691
initiatory process, 542
knowledge of nature of divine purpose, 714
Life Plan, 130
name, 248, 273
overshadowing, 392, 415
potency, 205-206
presence due to Will, 392
purposes, 241, 242, 362, 394, 660
quality, primary, 387
reason for evolutionary creative process, 717
relationships, 205, 206, 414, 422, 652
request for great Lives from other planets, 398
sounding of O in O.M., 207
success, 412, 413
transfer on three Crosses, 693
transfiguration, 260

Saturn, triangle related to, 269

Saul of Tarsus, rending of veil of Maya, 193-194

Saviour —
mark above aura of group as it toils in Pisces, 227-230, 233-235, 239
task completed, 476

Saviours, World, accomplishments, 526-528

Schools —
new esoteric, development of sense of synthesis, 121-123
of Enlightenment, emphasis on life aspect, 221
of the Mysteries, foundational courses, 262
preparatory, 123

Science —
effect of Mysteries, 332
of —
Antahkarana, 40, 450
comparison, 131
Impression, 371, 398, 407-408, 543

Invocation, 220
Invocation and Evocation, 67, 69-71, 76, 147, 470, 523, 524
Invocation and Evocation. *See also* Invocation and Evocation.
Magnetic Rapport, 471
occultism, 594
Service of Plan, 34
Social Evolution, 470
Sound, 67
Sound. *See also* Sound.
Tension, 520
Tension. *See also* Tension.
thoughtform area of consciousness, 594, 601
Scientific discoveries, work of Master Hilarion, 586
Searchlight of mind, turning in two directions, 446
Second —
  divine aspect, expression, instrument, 216
  initiation —
    antahkarana building, 483
    Baptism in Jordan, Ray, 575-589
    ceremony used, 531
    concern, 535
    demonstration, 588
    energy, 352
    indications, 663
    injunction to express, 315
    keynotes, 682-683
    preparatory to third initiation, 663, 687-688
    qualifications, 579
    realisation after, 315-316
    release from emotional control, 682
    requirements, 127, 678-679
    training for, use of Sirian energy, 415
    vision, 678
Second-degree initiate —
  appellation, 116
  goal, 677-678
  Word of Power received, 175
Secrecy, occult, shared in Ashram, 346

Secret of transforming planet to sacred status, 260
Self-consciousness, Cross of, 694
Self-forgetfulness, 127
Self-initiation, individual, 72-73
Self-interest, transition from to universal state of consciousness, 297
Selfishness, spiritual, 210, 343
Selflessness, cultivation, 549
Selves, no other, injunction to group, 171-173
Senses —
  five, activation of mind, 592
  plus common-sense, 433-434
  seven, use, 543-544
Sensitivity —
  development, 166, 727
  each initiation, 736-737
  higher, cultivation, 549
  involved in visualisation, 442
  preparatory, production of true perception, 723
  symbolic, 442
  to —
    contact, development, 543-544
    cosmic astral plane by Masters, 398
    higher impression and inner inspiration, 276
    to increasingly high impression, developing, 363
  unfoldment, reflective process, 362
Sentiency, development, use, mastery and negation, 283
Sentiment, elimination from group, 209-210
Separateness, termination, massed efforts, 580
Septenaries —
  interrelations, 371-372
  *See also* Seven.
Service —
  activities, direction and causation, 537
  antahkarana, building, 497
  Earth, Path, 392, 660
  extra-planetary, 398
  life, expression of initiation, 547

of group as indicated by Aquarius, 227-247
of Master in conditioning and control of Ashram, 362
of Plan, 34, 376, 380
of third-degree initiate, plane, 692

Seven —
Ashrams of Masters, appearance, 188
groups, greater, lesser, planetary, and supplementary, 148-167
lotuses functioning, 188
major energies, use by initiate, 185
numerical value, 80
planes, subplanes of cosmic physical, 166
Spirits before Throne of God, 206
supplementary centres of energy, 151-152, 154
supplementary. See also Law of Supplementary Seven.

Seventh initiation —
Chohan transfigured, 284
divorced from all considerations of form, 732
group awareness, development, registration, 365
inspiration, 535
nature of, 688-689
Ray energy, 656, 688-689
through illumined revelation, 531-532
true resurrection, 643
two groups of Beings attending, 733

Seventh Root Race, characteristics, 561
Seventh-degree initiates, Shamballa functioning, 735

Sex —
relationship, effect of seventh Ray, 571-572, 574
sublimation, 670-671

Shamballa —
accepted by, 56
and humanity, mediating place between, 373

approach to by group, 138
Being, state, attainment, 362
consciousness, 466
contact with, 35, 120
definition, 276
demands for preparing groups for initiation, 112, 113
direction of destruction, 308-309
dynamic "pull", 171
effects on humanity, 646-647
electric fire, evocation, 91-92
energy, 120, 130, 230, 232, 240-247, 311, 411, 412, 580
entrance point, 117, 163, 177
evocation of spirit of man, 76
force, 35, 37, 189, 471, 715
form taking in future, 382
functioning of seventh-degree initiates, 735
Great Council, 18
Great Lives in direct relation with humanity, 117-118
Hierarchy, and Humanity, closer relation, 89
impressions from, registration, 549
in cosmic etheric substance, 382
in direct relation with humanity, 28
influences from cosmic mental plane, 357
interplay with Hierarchy, 271
invocation, 35, 76
life, 132-147, 379
magnetism, 376
nature of, 204
numerical value, 79-81
origin of creative work, 275
originating source of Son of Man, 730
outpouring, 94
plans, reorganisation forced, 412
radiance behind world rebuilding, 144
reaching prematurely, danger, 110
reaction to cosmic mental plane, 392
relationships, 226, 306, 481
responsiveness to, 68
task, future, 660

teaching on by Master, D.K., 251

three doors, 139-142

three great energies focussed, 84-88

Way into, 30

Will impelling, 338

Workers, way to Central Spiritual Sun, 399-400

Sharing today, 612-613, 614

Shri Krishna, earlier incarnation of Christ, 254

Sign of the Cross, origin, 692

Silence —
  cultivation by group, required for initiation, 214-215, 220
  nature of, 214
  occult, shared in Ashram, 346

Sirian Lodge, true "Blue Lodge", 415-416

Sirius —
  buddhi from at heart of every atom, 415
  emanating source of Manas, 426
  energy, 415
  Great White Lodge, 130, 330-331, 415-416, 737
  influence, aspect in principle of freedom, 416
  Lives, 418, 737
  no evil, 351
  relation to Solar Logos, 413
  Source of Earth Life, 687
  star, organised activities, consummation, 202

666, number of the Beast, 79-80

Six, significance, 79

Sixth initiation —
  Chohan transcends spiritual Triad, 284
  Choice, basis, 392, 394, 412
  Decision, 718-729
  disappearance of illusion, 600
  door, indication conveyed, 356
  group dedication to Path of Earth Service, 660
  higher correspondence to second, 719-720
  in Gethsemane, 290
  liberation into monadic awareness, 361

of Christ, 548
  preparation for, 392, 394-395, 411-412, 415, 652-653
  preparatory to seventh, 722
  related to second aspect, 535
  through illumined revelation, 531-532
  wider field of experience, 439

Sixth Root Race, characteristics, 561, 597, 659

Sixth-Degree initiates —
  aid to Buddhas of Activity, 587
  final decision regarding human affairs, 721
  freedom from karma, 725
  liberation from His past, 728
  no longer under jurisdiction of Hierarchy, 722
  work, 587

Socialism, problem in Great Britain, 633

"Society of Illumined and Organised Minds", 130-131

Solar —
  Entities dealing with problem of evil, 737
  fire. See Fire, solar.
  Lord, rhythm, imposition upon lunar lords, 10-11
  system —
    previous, origin of black magicians, 350
    purpose, 728
    quality, revelation, 728
    third, 377, 660

Son —
  Aspect, description, 464
  of Mind, 216, 475
  work completed, 476

Soul —
  anchorage in body, points, 451-452
  and its mechanism of expression, unity, 451
  and personality fused, 432-433
  and personality, united effort to produce bridge, 454-455
  animating energies, 445
  aspect within solar system, work with, 406

assumption of dominant position, 674
attractive power, steady impact on humanity, 187
body. *See* Causal body.
by-passed, 216
consciousness, 561
contact, increasing, effects, 443
contribution to sumtotal of manifestation, 106
control of ajna centre, results, 671
crucifixion, 455
destruction of forms, 309, 310
emergence in glory, 56
energies animating, 445
energy, impressions on concrete mind, 592
finding by initiate, 58
focus of will in cycle of incarnations, 216
full expression, 475-476
group consciousness, 341
hold upon instruments of expression, intensification, effects, 57
human, imprisonment, 444
human, mystery, revelation, 645
imaginative quality, 443
in incarnation, becoming, 504
instruments in head, 431
interpretation and understanding, response to, 26
knowledge, superseding, 131
language, ability to speak, 10
light, 643
means of bridging between Triad and personality, 475
nature of, 111
of all things, 17
of initiate, 96, 690, 691
on its own plane an initiate, 259
overshadowing, absorption and use of magnetic power, 375
perception, plane, 463
personality agents, 598
reincarnation, process, 101
relates initiate, 96
relation to Monad, production, 470
relation to personality production, 470

release from glamour and enchantment, 52
spiritual pull towards Ashram, 375
storage of imparted knowledge, 392
synthesis of energy of Life, intuition and spiritual mind, 445
true nature, revelation, 628
union of three energies, 445
will and purpose aspect, petals, 349
Word, 57
work within all forms, 183-184
world of, entered, all forms used wisely, 128
Soul-infused personality. *See* Personality, soul-infused.
Soul-personality intention, expressions, 279
Souls, two, human and free, 444
Sound —
appreciation, 83
attractive, note, 464
A.U.M., and O.M., 200-202
basis of new esoteric science, 470
creation by, 55, 147
distinction from breath, 54
from Central Spiritual Sun, hearing, 54
of —
acceptance as group, 57
group, 220
Ineffable Name, 55
letter of name of planetary Logos, hearing, 263
Soul, 51, 54
spiritual hierarchies, 76
spiritual reality lost, 54
originating, 285
physical, negative in effect, 513-514
production by, 288-289
reaching out after by disciple, 54
related to vibration, 54
self-initiated, hearing, 56
soundless, hearing, 53
synthetic, note, 464

source of glamour and maya, 52
the, definition, 53
the, utterance, 201
Sounds —
many, resolving into Word, 137
of all beings, understanding, 10
Space —
an eternal Entity, 437
and substance, 105
and Time, 54-55
significance, 105-107
Speech, control, 214
Spirit —
and matter, 62, 85, 264, 605-606
aspect, qualities, 180
destroying power, 87
freeing by steadily developing forms, 419
on its own plane becoming dominant, 166
"Spirit mounted on shoulders of matter", 475-476
Spirit of Peace, invocation, 76-77
Spirit-matter —
of divine nature, 472
two points of living purpose, 280
Spiritual —
activity on physical plane, 34
contact, establishing, 118, 226
definition, 364-365
energy, electrical interplay, results, 737
sense, attentive, enabling impression and interpretation, 549
sensory perception, 737
Spirituality, definition, 204
St. Paul —
quotation, 73
See also Saul of Tarsus.
Star —
five-pointed, 90, 176
of One Initiator, 175, 176
six-pointed, 69, 270
Status, one's own, inquiry into, 669
Subconscious realm, relegation of normal human experience to, 138-139

Subhuman kingdoms, work with by initiate, 587
Subjective —
aspect in man, emergence into manifestation, 6
causes, emanation, 12
Substance —
concept of soul, 106
control, final, by initiate, 469
definition, 105-106
form-making capacity, 174
impact of monadic energy on, channel, 280
light responsive to Light of Soul, 77
mental, nature of, 590
mental, use to build bridge, 467, 475
"unprincipled", origin, 359
Suffering and Pain, essential requirements, 243
Sun —
Central Spiritual —
awareness of, 652
initial contact with, 728
relation of Master to, 395
route to, 356, 653
Seven Paths leading to, 356, 399-400
significance and attractive potency, 391
Sound from, hearing, 54
statement having reference to, 516
veiled by Spiritual Triad, 118
Heart of —
closer to, 727-728
energies from Libra entering our system, 404
initiate vantage point in, 652
relation of Hierarchy to, 395
revelation of quality of solar system, 728
unique relation to of our Earth, 728
Superconscious and consciousness, continuity between, 452
Sutratma —
anchored, 449-450
and antahkarana, distinction between, 449

blending with other two threads, 475
bridge between Monad, soul, and personality, 458
definition, 449
energy, use, early, 186
four aspects, 477
functions, 449
left after crucifixion, 455
nature, comprehension, 7
on Lemuria, 477, 479
use by Spiritual Triad, 457
used by Father or Will aspect, 464

Symbol in aura of New Group of World Servers, 233

Symbolic sensitivity, 442

Symbols —
between ourselves and reality, 178
for aspirant, disciple, and initiate, 470
use in initiations, 531

Syntheses in evolution, 58

Synthesis —
between Shamballa and Hierarchy, Will and Love, 290-291
coherent holding planet in one whole, 646
dictation of trend of evolutionary processes, 121
great, emergence, 163
group, work, 276
loving in action, 300
mass effect, 120
need for, 112-113
of —
active intelligence, active love, and active will, 407
chain of hierarchical Existences, unfoldment, 134
energy of Life itself, attainment, 445
lesser lights, 118
love, will, and intelligence, initiate perfecting, 257
Master, 438
ordered activity, planetary life, 588

relationships of Beings working on Earth, 13
Shamballa, Hierarchy, and Humanity, 394
two energies of Atma-Buddhi, 407
production, 11, 703, 716
real, following establishment of concept of unity, 300
revealed at fifth initiation, 645
sense of, 115, 121, 123, 130
spiritual, of united Ashrams, 441
unfolding, 395
unity, and fusion, distinction, 264-265
value, 120

Synthetic effort, synthetic understanding, and synthetic activity, 249

System of identification, 141

## T

Task —
ahead, immediate, for disciples, 498
of —
all great World Saviours, 526
Masters, 660, 661
planetary Logos, 660
Saviour or Mediator completed, 476
to discover group for affiliation, 344

Tasks of disciple and initiate, 303, 455-456

Taurus —
energy, effect on New Group of World Servers, 232-233
illumination and attainment of vision, 227-230, 232-233, 237

Teaching —
by Master, in Ashram, 544-545
on newer truths, 251-254
planned by Hierarchy, given out by Master D.K., 255
revelatory, to emerge after 1975, 255

Telepathic —
contact of disciple, instrument, 547

influence of Christ, 615
interplay of humanity, 597
interplay, part of dual life of
    disciples, 548
rapport, highest form on Earth,
    392-393
Telepathy —
    contacts between Master and
        disciple, 545-547
    medium of communication with
        Council Chamber, 405
Temperance in all things, 127
Temple of Solomon, 132, 279-280
Tension —
    definitions, 45, 48
    group, needed, production, 226
    invocative, point, 493-494
    newer, toward, 44, 45
    planetary, achievement, 17
    point —
        achievement, 725
        creation, 216-217, 537-538,
            540-542
        creative, 55
        finding, 49-50
        in life now reached, 623
        liberation from three worlds,
            56
        of Germany, 624
        of United States, 624
        stimulation, 726
        work from, 49, 51, 496
    points —
        from which sacred Word
            goes forth, 49, 55
        leading to control by will
            aspect, 56
        planetary, and crisis in lives
            of individuals, 589
        relation to initiation, 537-538,
            724
        seven, of involutionary arc,
            55
Test of —
    burning ground, 39, 47, 49
    clear cold light, 39, 47
Tests —
    leading to initiation, 7-8, 343
    of initiation, reason for, 339
Theologies man-made, repudia-
    tion, 301

Theosophical Society, useful work
    and false claims, 678-679
Thinking —
    abstractly, 304
    capacity of man, achievements,
        244-245
    human, reorientation, results,
        647
Third-degree initiate —
    ability to respond to will of
        Monad, 312
    base of spine centre, 367-368
    consciousness, 445
    divine attributes and capacities,
        118-119
    energy of Sirius felt, 415
    grasp of nature of life-energy or
        spirit, 157-158
    in Sirian Lodge, 416
    integration, 58
    knowledge of nature of will,
        714
    mind, 688
    monadic comprehension, 124
    occult perception, 118
    participation in Ashram, re-
        sultant movement releasing
        Master, 371
    Ray energy applied via Triad,
        585
    release from planes of unprin-
        cipled substance, 359
    revelation of three aspects, 316
    "rich young man", 116
    service, 472
    task, 691
    will, 34, 472
    work, 587-589
Third-degree initiates —
    monadic potency available, 310
    numbers, 473
    work, 230
Third initiation —
    antahkarana completed, 444,
        445
    changes, 543
    comprehension, 105
    concern, 535
    consummation of process of
        building relation, 455

control of personality, complete, demonstration, 597
control of soul-illumined mind, 674
demonstration, 588-589
direction of energies into world, 689-691
disappearance of lower pair of opposites, 471
discovery of Word of soul, 54
energy from Spiritual Triad, 349
energy increasingly monadic, stages, 588
energy of mind, 353
equipment of four truths, 139-140
Father aspect, 99
first major initiation, 41, 81, 265
fusion, 265
goal of human evolution, 497
grasp of meaning of fire, 82
group awareness, development, registration, 365
group consciousness, 117
hearing Sound, 54
implementation, 593
karma, 85
lines of force inter-related, 451
made possible, 598
magnetic pull of potency of will felt, 376
mantram appropriate, 175
monadic process, beginning, 351
nature of, 688
need of completion of antahkarana, 437
of humanity, 595, 596, 597
of individual, 597-598
personality tendencies obliterated, 110
planes involved, 351
preparation for, 473, 687, 688
preparatory efforts to serve, 614
process, initial steps, 595
pre-requisite, 385
process preceding, 598
Ray energy, 589-602, 688
relation to Shamballa, 79
requirements, 127, 688

result, 598-599
secret, 44-45
seeing star and hearing sound, 83
sensing of interplay between Shamballa and Hierarchy, 271
sound heard, 81-82
Transfiguration, Ray fifth, 589-602
transmutation of physical body, 598
will aspect in control, 56
work of Buddha of Activity, 268-269
world of Spiritual Triad, 286
Thought —
certain lines refused admission, 214
powers and uses, self-training in, 446
Thoughtform —
building, 275, 446
of —
goodwill, 275-276
initiate, 103
materialistic living split on mental plane, 647
Thoughtform-making energy, 590
Thoughtforms—
destruction, 306-307
dispelling, 8
right, clothing of intuitive knowledge, 447
Thread of consciousness occultly snapped, 710
Threads —
three, 450, 459, 469, 471-472, 476, 477-480
two, constituting Sutratma, 450
See also under names of individual threads.
"Three minds unite", 518
Time —
and Space, 54-55, 105-110
control, 11
definition, 382, 408
equation, consideration, freedom from, 439

factor in brain registration, 436-437
limitations ending, 437
overcoming, indication, 436
recognition, 600
regarded by Master, 439
sense, definition, 697
significance, 105, 107
Totalitarian systems, cause, 573
Touch and express, 292, 297
Training —
disciples, new methods, 17
disciples, technique, change, 239
initiates, specific rules, 148, 149
objective and exoteric, 239
Transfiguration —
agent, 598
definition, 278, 280
extending to entire planet, 285
following Transformation, 277-285
initiation, 42, 44, 56, 284-285, 687-692
initiation. See also Third initiation.
making possible major initiations, 216
of Christ, 193
of personality, 598
phases, 281, 284
planes used, 281
true, on logoic plane, 284
Transformation —
agent, 598
definitions, 278, 280, 283
higher correspondence, 31
of astral life and aspiration, 442-443
of emotional nature, success, 598
phases, 281, 283
planes involved, 281
Transition —
Initiation, eighth, 656
period today, 221
Transmutation —
achievement in world of forms by initiate, 262
agent, 598
completed, plane, 281, 598

definitions, 248, 278-279, 280, 670
disappearance, 277, 280, 281
higher correspondence, 31
of —
desire into aspiration, results, 246
energy, requirements, 5-6
knowledge, 453, 468, 492, 540
lower creativity, 669-671
nine forces into divine energies, 456
O.M. into originating SOUND, 285
process, 279, 468
Triad, Spiritual —
activities governing, 74, 264, 306-317
agent, 182, 442
and mind, bringing into close relationship, 442
area, 15
at fifth initiation, 511
attitude, 27
awakening of head centre, 457
bridging to personality, 61, 475, 591
channel to brain, 442, 695
consciousness focussed in, 261
dimming light of soul, 112, 115
emanation approaching lower aspect of bridge, 494, 495
energies, 132, 158, 349, 592, 595, 598-599, 602, 663, 709-712
evocation of, 501, 510
evocative power, 29
function as intermediary, 432
functioning in, 263, 266
fusion with soul-infused personality, 541
impression of mind of disciple, 542, 591
life, 43
light, 118, 209
magnetic response to lower man, evocation, 454, 457
perceiving by group in unison, 112
planes involved in work of Masters, 281-284

rapport with personality, process, 443

response to three demands, 61

shining, 112, 116, 123

source of sustenance and vitality for group, 129

stimulation, of fire of group, 218

work through abstract mind, 598

Triadal —
existence, realm of initiate, 149
impression, reaction to, 287
perception due to antahkarana, 119, 226

Triangle —
of —
ajna, throat, and base of spine, 270
Bramarandra, ajna, and alta major, 273-274
Buddhas of Activity, 273
Central Spiritual Sun, Venus, and Earth, 69
energies from Great Bear, Heart of Sun or Solar Logos, and seven sacred planets, 423
Gemini, Libra, and our solar system, 424-425
Hierarchy, world of souls, and human souls, 373
light within head, 273-274
One, Solar Logos, and Planetary Logos, 423
Sirius, Hierarchy, and Heart of Sun, 414
three glands in head, 431-432
thyroid and para-thyroid glands, 270
United States, Great Britain, and Russia, 632-633, 640
work, 253, 254, 273, 274-275, 402

Triangles —
function, understanding, importance, 271
six, 269-270

Trinity of Aspects, threads, 464

Triplicity resolved into duality, 216

Troubles, present world, causes, 234-235

Truths —
new, dimly sensed, 77-78
newer, transmitting by Master D.K., 251-254
24, significances, 79, 80

"Two merge with One", 518

2000 A.D., impact of Shamballa force upon humanity, 715-716

## U

Understanding with united breath and unified rhythm, 148, 161, 163

United action with full interior unity, 217-218

United Nations, 237, 430, 623, 636, 639, 681, 716

United States, characteristics, 428, 429, 430, 621, 624, 628-630, 631-632

Unity —
and oneness of Universal Mind, revelation, 595
attainment by initiate, 266
definition, 265-266
diversity in, required by group, 212-214
isolated, 416, 420
nature of, 299
of all things, fact in consciousness, 476
of New Group of World Servers, 299
world, essential etheric, 580

Universal consciousness passing into cosmic consciousness, 694

Universality, sense of, and will-to-good, focussing on physical plane, 588

Unprincipled substance, conditioned by previous solar system, 359

Unveiling of Self, process, 6

## V

Vegetarianism, practice, 84, 125
Vehicles, refining with perfection, 11
"Veil of the temple rent", 475, 491, 702
Venus —
  and Earth, planetary antahkarana relating, 406
  custodian of principle of mind, 422
  removal to for training, 405
Vibration —
  in unison, energy of aspirant and door of initiation, 351
  of Ashram, registration by disciple, 543
  of Master, consciousness of, 543
  of own soul, awareness of, 543
  sounds related to, 54
Vision —
  and revelation, distinction between, 241, 298
  apotheosis, future, 75
Visualisation —
  Art, development, 123
  effects, 123
  in meditation, emphasis, 252
  need for, 442
  pictorial and symbolic sensitivity, 442
  relation to vision of divine Plan, 442
  use in building antahkarana, 467, 488-490
Voice —
  from Shamballa, hearing, 60
  of Master, hearing, 60
  of Silence, 60
Vyasa, work, 526

## W

"Walk humbly with their God", 258
War —
  between Forces of Light and Black Lodge, 603
  World, 75-76, 85, 235-237, 499, 603-604, 646

Way —
  into Shamballa, 30
  of Higher Evolution. See Higher Evolution.
  protection from glamoured disciple, 155
  the Truth, and the Life, 139-140
"We stand where the One Initiator is invoked", 175
Wesak —
  activity of Lord Buddha, 90
  relationship set up, 68-69
Wheel of Life, 92-96, 105-110, 339
Wheels, lesser, revolution, 105-110
White Lodge, Great, 187, 189-190, 202, 415
Whole —
  Greater, integration into, 226
  Greater, manifestation in work, 47
  macrocosmic, perception by group, 112, 115
  understanding in Light of part, 107
Will —
  and love, linking, 252
  and purpose, distinction, 69
  aspect —
    control, beginning, 56
    developed in Ashram, 380
    domination of man, 28
    egoic, 32
    evocation, method, 105
    expression, 47, 109-110
    first, thought of death connected with, 101
    need for synthesis related to, 113
    responsiveness to, fuller, 18
    time related to, 107
  aspects, second and third, 216
  cause of Sanat Kumara's presence, 392
  colored by love, 472
  creativity needed, 475
  definition, 47
  demonstration increasing after third initiation, 714

demonstration through long cycle of incarnations, 216
developed in Ashrams, 373
divine, 33, 39, 91-92, 106, 108, 181
door into Shamballa, 140-141
dynamic —
    energising enabling Hierarchy to move forward, 376-377
    energy, impact on mind and brain, 712
    point focussed in soul using form, 107
    use, 60
energy, 164-165, 184, 232, 378, 380, 715
enlightened in place of occult obedience, 60
evocation, 35, 104-105, 107, 492-493
first divine aspect, 101
focus in Son of Mind, 216
focussed, 45, 101, 469
force, premature inflow, consequences, offsetting, 472
group, 28, 212, 223
implementation of purpose, 714
in inducing revelation, 714-718
in next solar system, 47
interpretations, 170-171
invocation, 35
life-giving energy added to energy of love, 231
nature, 377, 714
of —
    God, 146, 238-239, 371, 661
    Master completely merged in that of planetary Logos, 722
    Monad, 30, 31, 144, 278, 312
    personality, contact with higher will, 49-51
    planetary Logos, nature, 567
    Shamballa, 232, 338
    Spiritual Triad, contacted by personal will, 49-51
    third-degree initiate, 472
potency, use on Way of Higher Evolution, 718
principle of abstraction, actively present or not, 164
productiveness, 103, 703
pure, use by initiate, 310-312
qualities making possible manifestation of divine will, 120
ruler of time and organiser of space, 107
sacrificial, of soul, 32, 33
second aspect, destruction of causal body, 216
servants, 472
Spiritual, 28, 30, 31, 73, 129, 391, 463, 588
use at initiation, 689, 694
use in building bridge, 503, 504, 506, 507, 508, 512
vital concentrated, 164
See also Free will.
Will-to-abstract, cause of death, 164-165
Will-to-be, 104, 106
Will-to-good, 104, 106, 109, 110, 588, 599, 608, 619, 654, 655
Will-to-know, 106
Will-to-law, 194
Will-to-live —
    as spiritual being, 447
    in physical body, withdrawal, 164-165
Will-to-love, 194
Will-to-synthesis, 194, 655
Wisdom —
    definitions, 204, 591
    from knowledge, transmutation, 453, 468, 492, 540
    used, definition, 453
Wisdom-energy, expression, 453
Womb, symbol, meanings, 117
Word —
    from point of tension, 49, 57
    hearing, 59, 60
    lost, discovery, 53, 54
    made flesh, 55
    of —
        group, 219, 220-221, 222
        Power, communicated by Christ, 175
        Power, uses, 490-491, 493, 494
        Ray of soul, 263
        soul, 57
        soul. See also Sound of soul.

released from form, 52
Sacred, from points of tension, 55
sounding instructions, 56
the, living, 53
to carry-out task, finding, 219-222
use, 51
Words of Power, seven, use in building antahkarana, 501, 503, 504, 506, 510-518
Work —
of initiate, between initiations, keynotes, 312
of restoration forwarded, 229
World —
disciple, humanity, destiny, 429
of —
    Being, 103-104
    causes, 149, 158
    energies, life of occult student, 549-550
    essential truth, 303
    events, 177
    light, 149
    meaning, 103, 149, 177, 285-286, 287, 297, 303, 485, 511

mediation, 177, 178
purpose, 177, 178
reality, 303
seeming and illusion, 149
significances, 285, 286, 303
symbols, 286, 287, 303
phenomena, fundamental divine intent, perception of, 124
problems, clue, keynotes, 682
situation today, causal factors, 13

## Z

Zionism, aggression and use of force, 679-681
Zionist Movement, 429-430
Zodiac —
lesser, 25,000-year cycle, conclusion, 550
sun's evolutionary passage through, 534
Zodiacal —
influences, dual effect, 339
Wheel of Life, reversal of disciple on, 339